P9-DUB-667

The State of The Nation's Ecosystems
2008

Measuring the Lands,
Waters, and Living Resources
of the United States

THE H. JOHN HEINZ III CENTER FOR
SCIENCE, ECONOMICS AND THE ENVIRONMENT

THE
HEINZ
CENTER

ISLANDPRESS

About The Heinz Center

At the crossroads of science and environmental policy, The Heinz Center brings leaders together from business, government, academia, and environmental groups to brainstorm solutions that are both scientifically and economically sound. Founded in 1995 in honor of Senator H. John Heinz III, the Center's guiding philosophy is that only by working together can we solve today's environmental challenges and leave the world a better place for generations to come.

ISBN 13: 978-1-59726-441-9 (cloth)
ISBN 10: 1-59726-441-5

ISBN 13: 978-1-59726-471-6 (paper)
ISBN 10: 1-59726-471-7

ISSN 1945-7030

Design by Janin/Cliff Design, Alexandria, Virginia

Printed on recycled, acid-free paper

Manufactured in the United States of America

10 9 8 7 6 5 4 3 2 1

The H. John Heinz III Center for Science, Economics and the Environment
900 17th Street NW, Suite 700
Washington, DC 20006
Tel: (202) 737-6307   Fax: (202) 737-6410   e-mail: info@heinzctr.org
http://www.heinzctr.org/ecosystems

Contents

Contents

State of the Nation's Ecosystems Project Participants (2002–2008)*

Design Committee

The Design Committee provides strategic guidance and decision making for the State of the Nation's Ecosystems project. This role includes active decision making and monitoring, as well as oversight of project activities to assess their conformity with the project's strategic directions.

William C. Clark, *Chair,* Harvard University

Ann M. Bartuska, USDA Forest Service

Rosina Bierbaum, University of Michigan

Bradley Campbell, New Jersey Department of Environmental Protection

Norman L. Christensen, Duke University

Craig Cox, Soil and Water Conservation Society

Steve Daugherty, Pioneer Hi-Bred International, Inc.

John H. Dunnigan, National Oceanic and Atmospheric Administration

Paul Gilman, U.S. Environmental Protection Agency

Larry F. Greene, Sacramento Metropolitan Air Quality Management District

Charles G. Groat, University of Texas at Austin

Theodore Heintz, White House Council on Environmental Quality

Michael Hirshfield, Oceana

Sara Schreiner Kendall, Weyerhaeuser Corporation

John L. Knott, The Noisette Company

John Kostyack, National Wildlife Federation

P. Patrick Leahy, American Geological Institute (formerly U.S. Geological Survey)

Rebecca Lent, National Oceanic and Atmospheric Administration

Al Lucier, National Council for Air and Stream Improvement, Inc.

Suzanne Iudicello Martley, Independent Marine Conservation Writer

Steven Murawski, National Oceanic and Atmospheric Administration

Mark D. Myers, U.S. Geological Survey

Gordon Orians, University of Washington

Don Parrish, American Farm Bureau Federation

Duncan Patten, Montana State University

Peter W. Preuss, U.S. Environmental Protection Agency

Randolph S. Price, Consolidated Edison Company of New York, Inc.

Lynn Scarlett, U.S. Department of the Interior

Bruce Stein, NatureServe

Mark Stoler, General Electric

Greg Wandrey, Pioneer Hi-Bred International, Inc.

Bud Ward, Morris A. Ward, Inc.

Douglas P. Wheeler, Hogan and Hartson, LLP

John A. Wiens, PRBO Conservation Science (formerly The Nature Conservancy)

Terry Young, Environmental Defense Fund

Agency Liaisons

Rich Guldin, USDA Forest Service

Laura Nielsen, U.S. Environmental Protection Agency

Denice Shaw, U.S. Environmental Protection Agency

Design Committee Subcommittees

Indicator Refinement Subcommittee

Gordon Orians, *Chair,* University of Washington

Suzanne Iudicello Martley, *Vice Chair,* Independent Marine Conservation Writer

G. Thomas Bancroft, National Audubon Society (formerly The Wilderness Society)

Ann M. Bartuska, USDA Forest Service

Scott Dyer, Procter Gamble

Richard Guldin, USDA Forest Service

James A. LaGro, Jr., University of Wisconsin

Rebecca Lent, National Oceanic and Atmospheric Administration

Craig Loehle, National Council for Air and Stream Improvement, Inc.

Gail Mallard, U.S. Geological Survey

Thomas C. Malone, Ocean.US and University of Maryland Center for Environmental Science

---

* Many other people also contributed a great deal to the development of the 2002 report but are not listed here. To view a list of participants in the State of the Nation's Ecosystems Project for 1997–2002, please see the 2002 report or http://www.heinzctr.org/ecosystems/2002report/intro/participants_sr_adv.shtml.

Duncan Patten, Montana
State University

Terry Young, Environmental
Defense Fund

**Strategic Marketing
Subcommittee**

John L. Knott, *Chair*, The
Noisette Company

Craig Cox, Soil and Water
Conservation Society

Daniel S. Fogel, Wake
Forest University

Suzanne Iudicello Martley,
Independent Marine
Conservation Writer

Laura Nielsen, U.S. Environmental
Protection Agency

Randolph S. Price, Consolidated
Edison Co. of New York, Inc.

Bud Ward, Morris A. Ward, Inc.

Working Groups

The Working Groups are
responsible for revising or
selecting indicators for a specific
ecological topic, assessing
potential data sources, and
contributing to report contents.

**Air Quality
Working Group**

Larry F. Greene, *Chair*, Sacramento
Metropolitan Air Quality
Management District

William L. Chameides,
Environmental Defense Fund

Jeanette E. Clute, Ford
Motor Company

Mark Cohen, National Oceanic and
Atmospheric Administration

Kenneth A. Colburn, Symbiotic
Strategies, LLC

Charles T. Driscoll, Jr.,
Syracuse University

Joyce E. Epps, Pennsylvania
Department of
Environmental Protection

Howard J. Feldman, American
Petroleum Institute

Charles H. Goodman,
Southern Company

Timothy G. Hunt, American
Forest and Paper Association

Martha Keating, Clean
Air Task Force

Anne Rea (*Alternate*),
U.S. Environmental
Protection Agency

John Trajnowski (*Alternate*),
Ford Motor Company

Randall G. Waite, U.S.
Environmental
Protection Agency

**Biological Community
Conditions Working
Group**

Patrick Comer, NatureServe

Curtis H. Flather, USDA
Forest Service

Robert Goldstein, Electric
Power Research Institute

Root Gorelick, U.S. Environmental
Protection Agency

Dennis Grossman, Consultant
(formerly with NatureServe)

Charles P. Hawkins, Utah
State University

Brian J. Kernohan, Forest
Capital Partners, LLC

Craig Loehle, National Council
for Air and Stream
Improvement, Inc.

Ellen Natesan, San Francisco
Public Utilities Commission

Deborah Neher, University
of Vermont

Gordon Orians, University
of Washington

Duncan Patten, Montana
State University

Taylor Ricketts, World
Wildlife Fund

Michael Rosenzweig,
University of Arizona

John Stoddard, U.S. Environmental
Protection Agency

Terry Young, Environmental
Defense Fund

**Coastal Pattern
Working Group**

Susan Bell, University of
South Florida

Tundi Agardy, Sound Seas

Jimmy Johnston, U.S. Geological
Survey (*retired*)

Richard Lathrop, Rutgers
University

Thomas Minello, National
Oceanic and Atmospheric
Administration

Gerald Niemi, University of
Minnesota Duluth

Charles Simenstad, University
of Washington

Drew Talley, San Francisco Bay
National Estuarine Research
Reserve and University
of California Davis

Roman Zajac, University
of New Haven

**Ecosystem Services
Working Group**

Jill Baron, Colorado State
University and U.S.
Geological Survey

William C. Clark, Harvard
University

Christopher Field, Carnegie
Institution of Washington
and Stanford University

Geoffrey Heal, Columbia
Business School

Carolyn Kousky, Harvard
University

Jerry Melillo, The Marine
Biological Laboratory

Robert Naiman, University
of Washington

Gordon Orians, University
of Washington

Margaret A. Palmer, University
of Maryland

Alexander S. P. Pfaff,
Columbia University

Steven W. Running, University
of Montana

Osvaldo E. Sala, Brown University

José Sarukhán, Ciudad
Universitaria (Mexico)

George M. Woodwell, Woods Hole Research Center

Non-native Species Working Group

Ann M. Bartuska, *Chair,* USDA Forest Service

Jerome Beatty, USDA Forest Service

Faith Campbell, The Nature Conservancy

Gabriela Chavarria, Defenders of Wildlife

Chris Dionigi, National Invasive Species Council

Pam Fuller, U.S. Geological Survey

Nelroy E. Jackson, Monsanto (*retired*)

Terri Killeffer, Information International Associates, Inc. (formerly NatureServe)

Richard N. Mack, Washington State University

Gary C. Matlock, National Oceanic and Atmospheric Administration

Sarah Reichard, University of Washington

Peter M. Rice, University of Montana

Gregory Ruiz, Smithsonian Environmental Research Center

Thomas Stohlgren, U.S. Geological Survey

David Thomas, Illinois Natural History Survey

Landscape Pattern Working Group

Norman Christensen, *Chair,* Duke University

G. Thomas Bancroft, National Audubon Society (formerly The Wilderness Society)

Susan S. Bell, University of South Florida

Rick Brown, Defenders of Wildlife

Chris Frissell, Pacific Rivers Council

Sharon Haines (*deceased*), International Paper

Dan Heagerty, David Evans and Associates

K. Bruce Jones, U.S. Geological Survey

A. J. Jordan, Halderman Farm Management Service, Inc.

John Kupfer, University of South Carolina

James A. LaGro, Jr., University of Wisconsin–Madison

Kurt Riitters, USDA Forest Service

Gary J. Roloff, Michigan State University (formerly with Boise Cascade Corporation)

Ed Thompson, Jr., American Farmland Trust

Agency Liaison

John Gross, National Park Service

Stream Flows Working Group

Colin Apse, The Nature Conservancy

Leo Eisel, Brown and Caldwell

Glenn Hodgkins, U.S. Geological Survey

Harry Lins, U.S. Geological Survey

Duncan Patten, Montana State University

N. LeRoy Poff, Colorado State University

Richard Vogel, Tufts University

David Wolock, U.S. Geological Survey

External Reviewers

External reviews for the 2008 *State of the Nation's Ecosystems Report* were solicited from academia, environmental nonprofits, federal and state government agencies, and industry.

Sean Anderson, California State University Channel Islands

Martin Apple, Council of Scientific Society Presidents

Jennifer Bennett, Environmental Defense Fund

Richard Birdsey, USDA Forest Service

Steven Bradbury, Environmental Protection Agency

Steve Carpenter, University of Wisconsin–Madison

Virginia Dale, Oak Ridge National Laboratory

Hilda Diaz-Soltero, U.S. Department of Agriculture

Jenny Dowil, Pioneer Hi-Bred International, Inc.

Paul H. Dunn, USDA Forest Service

Marjorie Ernst, National Oceanic and Atmospheric Administration

Richard Forman, Harvard University

Susan J. Frankel, USDA Forest Service

Jeroen Gerritsen, TetraTech

Colleen Haney, Environmental Protection Agency

Susan Haseltine, U.S. Geological Survey

Jerry L. Hatfield, U.S. Department of Agriculture

Charles A. Hernick, Massachusetts Office of Coastal Zone Management

Sarah Hobbie, University of Minnesota

Simon Hook, NASA

Robert M. Hughes, Oregon State University and Environmental Protection Agency

Charles Hutchinson, Arizona State University

Chris James, Connecticut Department of Environmental Protection

James Karr, University of Washington

John Kartesz, Biota of North America Program (BONAP)

Joan Kenny, U.S. Geological Survey

Mimi Lam, University of British Colombia

Gunnar Lauenstein, National Oceanic and Atmospheric Administration

Norman LeBlanc, National Association of Clean Water Agencies

Steven Lohrenz, University of Southern Mississippi

Philip Lounibos, University of Florida

Sarah Lovell, University of Vermont

Meg Lowman, New College of Florida

Timothy Male, Environmental Defense Fund

Kimberli Miller, U.S. Geological Survey

Jeffrey Morisette, NASA Goddard Space Flight Center

Frank Neil, U.S. Environmental Protection Agency

Gerald C. Nelson, University of Illinois

Lee Norfleet, U.S. Department of Agriculture

Marilyn Barrett O'Leary, Louisiana State University

Wayne Padgett, USDA Forest Service

Charles Perry, USDA Forest Service

David Pimentel, Cornell University

Teague Prichard, Wisconsin Department of Natural Resources

William Puckett, U.S. Department of Agriculture

Dale Quattrochi, NASA

Jon Ranson, NASA

Jamie K. Reaser, Ecos Systems Institute

Jake Rice, Fisheries and Oceans Canada

Larry Riley, The State of Arizona Game and Fish Department

Paul L. Ringold, U.S. Environmental Protection Agency

Guy Robertson, USDA Forest Service

Vic Rudis, USDA Forest Service

Vicki Sandiford, U.S. Environmental Protection Agency

Duane L. Shroufe, The State of Arizona Game and Fish Department

Daniel Simberloff, University of Tennessee

Brad Smith, USDA Forest Service

Ethan T. Smith, Sustainable Water Resources Roundtable

Jonathan Smith, U.S. Geological Survey

William Stefanov, NASA

Deb Swackhamer, University of Minnesota

Michael Thompson, Iowa State University

Borys Tkacz, USDA Forest Service

Arnaud Trouvé, University of Maryland

Woody Turner, NASA

Paul Unger, U.S. Department of Agriculture (*retired*)

Dave Van Voorhees, National Oceanic and Atmospheric Administration

Jennifer Vollmer, BASF Corporation

Randy Westbrooks, U.S. Geological Survey

Dave Whitall, National Oceanic and Atmospheric Administration

Robert Wiedenmann, University of Arkansas

Dean Wilkinson, National Invasive Species Council

Chris Woodall, USDA Forest Service

Ecosystem Contact Groups

The Ecosystem Contact Groups are made up of individuals who participated in development of the 2002 State of the Nation's Ecosystems Report in the first phase of the project (before 2002). Between 2002 and 2008, these individuals were kept informed of progress on the project and provided advice, input, and recommendations, particularly on matters that might affect indicators in their areas of ecosystem expertise.

Coasts and Oceans

Walter Boynton, University of Maryland Center for Environmental Science

James Cloern, U.S. Geological Survey

Robert Bailey, Oregon Department of Land Conservation and Development

Brock Bernstein, Independent Consultant

David J. Detlor, National Oceanic and Atmospheric Administration

William S. Fisher, U.S. Environmental Protection Agency

Jim Good, Oregon State University

Robert Howarth, Cornell University

Dale Kiefer, University of Southern California

Patrick O'Brien, Chevron Energy Technology Company

John C. Ogden, Florida Institute of Oceanography

Andrew Robertson, The Earth Institute of Columbia University

Linda Sheehan, California Coastkeeper Alliance

J. Kevin Summers, U.S. Environmental Protection Agency

Mike Weber, Resources Legacy Foundation

Steve Weisberg, Southern California Coastal Water Research Program

Farmlands

Frank Casey, Defenders of Wildlife

Jerry L. Hatfield, U.S. Department of Agriculture

Ralph Heimlich, Agricultural Conservation Economics

James A. LaGro, Jr., University of Wisconsin

Daryl Lund, U.S. Department of Agriculture

Deborah Neher, University of Vermont

Thomas E. Nickson, Monsanto Company

Steven Peck, Brigham Young University

B. A. Stewart, West Texas
A&M University

Dennis Tierney, Syngenta
Crop Protection, Inc

Paul W. Unger, U.S. Department
of Agriculture

William G. Wilber, U.S.
Geological Survey

Fresh Waters

Robin Abell, World Wildlife Fund

Barbara Bedford, Cornell
University

Paul Bertram, U.S. Environmental
Protection Agency

Patrick Brezonik, University
of Minnesota

Scott Dyer, Procter and
Gamble, Inc.

Leo M. Eisel, Brown and Caldwell

Otto Gutenson, U.S. Environmental
Protection Agency

Patrick Havens, Dow
AgroSciences LLC

Jonathan Higgins, The
Nature Conservancy

Dave Lenat, Lenat
Consulting Services

Gail Mallard, U.S.
Geological Survey

Daniel Markowitz, Malcolm
Pirnie, Inc.

Larry Master, NatureServe (retired)

Judy L. Meyer, University of
Georgia and American Rivers

Robert Putz, Freshwater
Institute (retired)

Charles Spooner, U.S.
Environmental
Protection Agency

Ralph Stahl, DuPont Corporation

Ralph Tiner, U.S. Fish and
Wildlife Service

Bill Wilen, U.S. Fish and
Wildlife Service

Terry Young, Environmental
Defense Fund

Grasslands–Shrublands

Carl Bock, University of
Colorado at Boulder

Jane Bock, University of
Colorado at Boulder

Bob Budd, Wyoming Wildlife
and Natural Resource Trust

Len Carpenter, The Wildlife
Management Institute

Alison Hill, USDA Forest Service

Richard Mayberry, Bureau
of Land Management

John McLain, Resource
Concepts, Inc.

Bill Miller, Malpai
Borderlands Group

John E. Mitchell, USDA
Forest Service

Rachel Muir, U.S.
Geological Survey

James T. O'Rourke, Chadron
State College

J. Michael Scott, U.S.
Geological Survey

Michael L. Scott, U.S.
Geological Survey

Timothy Seastedt, University
of Colorado

Gregg Simonds, Open
Range Consulting

Phillip L. Sims, U.S. Department
of Agriculture

Thomas J. Stohlgren, U.S.
Geological Survey and
Colorado State University

John Tanaka, Society for
Range Management

Steven C. Torbit, National
Wildlife Federation

Johanna Wald, Natural Resources
Defense Council

Neil West, Utah State University

George Wuerthner, Freelance
Writer/Photographer/Ecologist

Urban–Suburban

William Alverson, Field Museum

Roger Bannerman, Wisconsin
Department of Natural
Resources

Margaret M. Carreiro,
University of Louisville

Caren Glotfelty, The Heinz
Endowments

Richard Hammerschlag, U.S.
Geological Survey

George R. Hess, North Carolina
State University

David Hulse, University of Oregon

Michael W. Klemens, Wildlife
Conservation Society

Michael Pawlukiewicz, The
Urban Land Institute

Richard Pouyat, USDA
Forest Service

Pete Sandrock, Sandrock
Consulting Services

Jeff Tryens, Oregon Progress
Board (retired)

Sara Vickerman, Defenders
of Wildlife

Jianguo Wu, Arizona State
University and Inner
Mongolia University

Wayne Zipperer, USDA
Forest Service

Workshop Groups

The Workshop Groups are
individual task groups convened
to inform the design or refinement
of specific indicators.

**Workshop on Carbon
Storage Reporting**
February 28, 2006

Linda S. Heath, USDA
Forest Service

Richard Houghton, Woods
Hole Research Center

Gary Kaster, Carbon
Projects Services

Stephen Ogle, Colorado
State University

R. Neil Sampson, The
Sampson Group

Gordon Smith, Ecofor LLC

Eric Sundquist, U.S.
Geological Survey

Merritt Turetsky, Michigan
State University

**Harmful Algal
Blooms Workshop**
May 5, 2005

Donald Scavia, *Chair*,
University of Michigan

Donald Anderson, Woods Hole
Oceanographic Institution

Wayne W. Carmichael, Wright
State University

Quay Dortch, National
Oceanic and Atmospheric
Administration

Joanne Jellett, Jellett
Biotek Consulting

Gregg W. Langlois, California
Department of Health Services

Jack Rensel, Rensel Associates
Aquatic Science Consultants

Patrick Rose, Save the
Manatee Club

Kevin Sellner, Chesapeake
Research Consortium, Inc.

Theodore Smayda, University
of Rhode Island

Vera Trainer, National Oceanic and
Atmospheric Administration

Landscape Pattern Indicators in the Coastal Zone Workshops (2)

*Workshop on Landscape Pattern
Indicators in the Coastal Zone*
September 2–3, 2004

Susan Bell, *Chair,* University
of South Florida

Virginia Burkett, U.S.
Geological Survey

Joshua Collins, San Francisco
Estuary Institute

John Dixon, California
Coastal Commission

Lesley Ewing, California
Coastal Commission

Rikki Grober-Dunsmore, U.S.
Geological Survey

Jimmy Johnston, U.S. Geological
Survey *(retired)*

Richard Lathrop, Rutgers
University

Thomas Minello, National
Oceanic and Atmospheric
Administration

Gerald Niemi, University of
Minnesota Duluth

Charles Roman, National Park
Service and University
of Rhode Island

Charles Simenstad, University
of Washington

Robert Stewart, U.S. Geological
Survey *(retired)*

Drew Talley, San Francisco Bay
National Estuarine Research
Reserve and University
of California Davis

Roman Zajac, University
of New Haven

Joy Zedler, University of
Wisconsin–Madison

*Second Workshop on
Landscape Pattern Indicators
for the Coastal Zone*
May 15–16, 2006

Susan Bell, *Chair,* University
of South Florida

Tundi Agardy, Sound Seas

William S. Fisher, U.S.
Environmental
Protection Agency

Jimmy Johnston, U.S. Geological
Survey *(retired)*

Richard Lathrop, Rutgers
University

Thomas Minello, National
Oceanic and Atmospheric
Administration

Matt Nicholson, U.S.
Environmental
Protection Agency

Gerald Niemi, University of
Minnesota Duluth

Charles Simenstad, University
of Washington

Eric Stein, Southern California
Coastal Water Research Project

Daniel O. Suman, University
of Miami

Drew Talley, San Francisco Bay
National Estuarine Research
Reserve and University
of California Davis

Roman Zajac, University
of New Haven

Non-native Species Workshops (4)

*I. Percent Plant Cover
Indicator Workshop*
November 16, 2004

Lars W. J. Anderson, U.S.
Department of Agriculture and
University of California Davis

Andrew Gray, USDA Forest Service

Drew Kerr, King County Noxious
Weed Control Program

Richard N. Mack, Washington
State University

Beth Schulz, USDA Forest Service

Greg Spyreas, University of Illinois
at Urbana–Champaign

Sarah Reichard, University
of Washington

*II. Ad Hoc Consultation on
Non-native Species Indicators:
Animal Pathogens*
October 13, 2004

Josh Dein, U.S. Geological Survey

Sylvia Fallon, Natural Resources
Defense Council

Grace S. McLaughlin, National
Wildlife Health Center

Scott Miller, Smithsonian
Institution National Museum
of Natural History

Marc Minton, Smithsonian
Environmental
Research Center

Greg Ruiz, Smithsonian
Environmental
Research Center

Lou Sileo, U.S. Geological
Survey *(retired)*

*III. Non-native Invertebrates
Indicator Workshop*
December 16, 2004

Jim Carlton, The Maritime
Studies Program of Williams
College and Mystic Seaport

Valerie Eviner, University
of California Davis

Peter Groffman, Cary Institute
of Ecosystem Studies

Andrew Liebhold, USDA
Forest Service

Gary Lovett, Cary Institute
of Ecosystem Studies

Anthony Ricciardi, McGill
University

David Strayer, Cary Institute
of Ecosystem Studies

Katalin Szlavecz, Johns
Hopkins University

Klement Tockner, Swiss Federal Institute for Environmental Science and Technology (EAWAG)

IV. Ad Hoc Meeting on the Non-native Vertebrate Indicator
December 9, 2004

Richard Engeman, U.S. Department of Agriculture

Mercedes S. Foster, U.S. Geological Survey / National Museum of Natural History

Pam Fuller, U.S. Geological Survey

Larry Master, NatureServe *(retired)*

Roy McDiarmid, U.S. Geological Survey / National Museum of Natural History

Charles Nilon, National Science Foundation

Plant Growth Index Workshop
August 22, 2006

David Skole, *Chair*, Michigan State University

Craig Daughtry, U.S. Department of Agriculture

Paul Doraiswamy, U.S. Department of Agriculture

Scott Goetz, Woods Hole Research Center

Alfredo Huete, University of Arizona

Ranga Myneni, Boston University

Rama Nemani, NASA Ames Research Center

Steve Prince, University of Maryland at College Park

Steve W. Running, University of Montana

Jay Samek, Michigan State University

John Townsend, Virginia Natural Heritage Program (formerly University of Maryland at College Park)

Stream Flows Workshops (3)

I. Workshop on the Core National Indicator for Change in Stream Flows
July 26, 2005

Colin Apse, The Nature Conservancy

Leo Eisel, Brown and Caldwell

Glenn Hodgkins, U.S. Geological Survey

Harry Lins, U.S. Geological Survey

Duncan Patten, Montana State University

LeRoy Poff, Colorado State University

Ken Potter, University of Wisconsin

Richard Vogel, Tufts University

Second Workshop to Develop a Core National Indicator for Change in Stream Flows
November 29, 2005

Leo Eisel, Brown and Caldwell

Glenn Hodgkins, U.S. Geological Survey

X. Jay Jian, U.S. Geological Survey

Harry Lins, U.S. Geological Survey

Duncan Patten, Montana State University

LeRoy Poff, Colorado State University

Richard Vogel, Tufts University

David Wolock, U.S. Geological Survey

Terry Young, Environmental Defense Fund

Third Workshop to Develop a Core National Indicator for Change in Stream Flows
April 7, 2006

Colin Apse, The Nature Conservancy

Leo Eisel, Brown and Caldwell

Glenn Hodgkins, U.S. Geological Survey

Harry Lins, U.S. Geological Survey

Duncan Patten, Montana State University

LeRoy Poff, Colorado State University

Richard Vogel, Tufts University

David Wolock, U.S. Geological Survey

Heinz Center Project Staff

Robin O'Malley, Program Director

Kent Cavender-Bares, Deputy Project Director

Anne S. Marsh, Research Associate

Christine Negra, Research Associate

Jonathan Mawdsley, Research Associate

David Bernard, Research Associate

Bonnie Keeler, Research Associate

Caroline Cremer Sweedo, Research Assistant

Claire Hayes, Executive Assistant

Former Project Staff

Laura Meyerson, Research Associate

Ian Carroll, Research Assistant

Holly Alyssa MacCormick, Research Assistant

Elissette Rivera, Research Assistant

Robert Friedman, Vice President

Jeannette Aspden, Editor

Kate Wing, Research Assistant

Heather Blough, Research Assistant

Heinz Center Staff

Thomas E. Lovejoy, President

David Bernard, Research Associate, Environmental Reporting Program

Karen Boler, Receptionist and Office Manager/ Meeting Planner

Kent Cavender-Bares, Deputy Project Director, Environmental Reporting Program

Robert W. Corell, Program Director, Global Change Program

Ariane de Bremond, Research Associate, Global Change Program

Claire Hayes, Executive Assistant, Environmental Reporting Program

Acknowledgments

The continued support of our many collaborators both past and present sustains this important work. We are grateful to the many institutions and hundreds of individuals who have contributed in a variety of ways to this effort over the past decade. Committee members and workshop participants, reviewers, advisors, and partners—your contributions are deeply appreciated, and, quite simply, this book would not exist without you.

We would like to express our sincere thanks to our corporate, foundation, and federal funders for their support. A list of all funders over the lifetime of the project can be found on page xvi.

So many institutions and people gave generously of their resources and time by providing data, serving on committees, reviewing draft materials, and offering other services. The names of the many people who took part in this project are listed on pages vi–xiii, and the institutions that provided data are listed on page xvi. But there are a number of groups that deserve special mention for their extraordinary efforts. The U.S. Geological Survey, the USDA Forest Service, and NatureServe provided large amounts of both data and general support for this project, and remain important partners. To the Non-native Species and Landscape Pattern Working Groups and to participants in the associated workshops, your heroic efforts to complete an evaluation of specific groups of indicators across multiple ecosystems were invaluable, and we hope that you will see the fruits of your work in this report and in future editions to come. We also thank those members of working groups and workshops that were tasked with revising or defining new indicators, on topics such as air quality, biological community condition, carbon storage, ecosystem services, harmful algal events, plant growth index, and stream flows. Your job was not easy, and we appreciate your expertise, insights, and open minds.

Special thanks to Jeannette Aspden and Yvonne Baskin for serving as editors of this report. Your careful work has helped us to create a coherent, engaging, and relevant story, and for that we are very grateful.

We are also grateful to Cynthia Cliff and James Durham of Janin/Cliff Design, Inc., for their endless patience and professional work. As usual, they went well above and beyond our expectations.

We also owe thanks to Greg Neuschafer, our Project Officer at the Office of Naval Research (ONR) for his tireless assistance, and to ONR for providing grant administration support for the past ten years.

Our thanks also go out to our Heinz Center colleagues, who supported our work in a thousand different and important ways.

We owe especially deep debts of gratitude to two individuals, who contributed mightily to both the 2002 and 2008 editions of *The State of the Nation's Ecosystems*. Professor Bill Clark of Harvard's Kennedy School of Government has served as Chair of the Design Committee from the very beginning of this project in 1997; he will be greatly missed as he relinquishes his position upon the publication of this report. He provided an enormous intellectual contribution, was a major force toward keeping us on track (when temptations to stray were mighty), and was masterful at shepherding a diverse and opinionated committee. We will miss you.

Kent Cavender-Bares, who was until recently the Deputy Project Director on the Heinz Center project team, has been a steady and insightful colleague and collaborator, a major financial supporter, and an articulate and creative thinker on how best to achieve the project's goals. Pages such as this one are replete with "this project could not exist without . . ." statements, but in this case it is true—his enormous effort and his contributions of scientific understanding, logic, perseverance, writing, reviewing, and editing have made this volume a reality. We are deeply in his debt.

Finally, we thank the members of The Heinz Center's Board of Trustees for their recognition and support of this effort over the last ten years and more.

Support for *The State of the Nation's Ecosystems 2008*

Funders

The State of the Nation's Ecosystems is supported by a balanced mix of public and private funds. Half of the project's current annual budget is provided by corporate and foundation sources. The remaining funds are provided by several federal agencies, whose participation was organized by the White House Council on Environmental Quality and the Office of Science and Technology Policy. Nonfederal funds account for approximately 45% of the project's overall budget since its inception in 1997. We are deeply grateful to the following entities for their financial support of the State of the Nation's Ecosystems project:

Bureau of Land Management
Melinda Blinken
Alison M. Byers
Chevron Corporation
Cleveland Foundation
    Special Fund No. 6
John Deere and Company
Foundation for Environmental
    Research
Electric Power Research Institute
Exxon Mobil Corporation
Federal Emergency
    Management Agency
Georgia-Pacific Corporation
Mark Gorenberg

Vira I. Heinz Endowment
Teresa and H. John Heinz
    III Charitable Fund
International Paper
Andrew W. Mellon Foundation
Richard King Mellon Foundation
Charles Stewart Mott Foundation
National Aeronautics and
    Space Administration
National Oceanic and Atmospheric
    Administration
National Science Foundation
Office of Naval Research
    (grant administration)

David and Lucile Packard
    Foundation
Pioneer Hi-Bred International, Inc.
Procter & Gamble
Royal Caribbean Cruise Lines, Inc.
Robert and Patricia Switzer
    Foundation
U.S. Department of Agriculture
U.S. Department of Defense
U.S. Department of Energy
U.S. Department of the Interior
U.S. Environmental
    Protection Agency

Data Sources for *The State of the Nation's Ecosystems 2008*

The data that underpin this project also derive from varied sources, both public and private, and we greatly appreciate the agencies and organizations that contributed data to the 2008 report:

Federal Agencies

Environmental Protection Agency
National Coastal Assessment
National Exposure Research Laboratory
Office of Air and Radiation
Office of Water: Wadeable Streams Assessment

National Aeronautics and Space Administration
Global Inventory Monitoring and Modeling Studies
Goddard Space Flight Center: Sea-viewing
    Wide Field-of-view Sensor
Physical Oceanography Distributed
    Active Archive Center

National Interagency Fire Center

U.S. Department of Agriculture
Economic Research Service
Farm Service Agency
Forest Service
    Forest Health Monitoring Program
    Forest Inventory and Analysis Program
    Southern Research Station
National Agricultural Statistics Service
Natural Resources Conservation Service:
    National Resources Inventory

Continued

U.S. Department of Commerce
Bureau of Economic Analysis
Census Bureau
National Oceanic and Atmospheric Administration
    National Environmental Satellite, Data,
        and Information Service: National
        Climatic Data Center; Advanced Very
        High Resolution Radiometer; National
        Oceanographic Data Center
    National Marine Fisheries Service: National
        Marine Mammal Laboratory
    National Ocean Service: Office of
        Response and Restoration; National
        Status & Trends Program
    Office of Oceanic and Atmospheric Research

U.S. Department of Energy
Oak Ridge National Laboratory

U.S. Department of the Interior
U.S. Fish and Wildlife Service
    National Wetlands Inventory
U.S. Geological Survey
    Biological Resources Discipline:
        Breeding Bird Survey
    Geography Discipline: Geographic
        Analysis and Monitoring Program;
        National Land Cover Dataset
    Water Resources Discipline: National Water
        Information System, National Water-Quality
        Assessment Program; National Stream Quality
        Accounting Network; Hydro-Climatic Data
        Network; National Hydrography Dataset

Nonfederal Organizations
Environmental Systems Research Institute, Inc.
Louisiana Universities Marine Consortium
Natural Resource Ecology Laboratory,
    Colorado State University
NatureServe
Scripps Institution of Oceanography CO_2 Program
Virginia Institute of Marine Science

Federal and Nonfederal Partnerships
Chesapeake Bay Program
National Atmospheric Deposition Program
National Snow and Ice Data Center
National Survey on Recreation and the Environment

Chapter 1:
The State of the Nation's Ecosystems 2008: Information Matters

Call it *the environment, the outdoors, nature, ecosystems.* Whatever the term, Americans care deeply about what is happening to their surroundings. Indeed, changes in or predictions about the state of our environment have become a staple of both local and national news. Much of the coverage focuses on events, especially the sensational or worrisome—a new invasive species, new fishing restrictions, new contaminants in our waters, or changes attributed to the warming climate. Increasingly, the media also spotlights serious debates in our society over how best to address environmental challenges. These include thorny questions such as how to allocate limited water supplies, manage fish and wildlife populations, accommodate and shape suburban and rural development, and maintain forest, farm, and many other land uses.

The outcomes of such debates have vital implications—not only for the condition of the nation's ecosystems, but for people and their pocketbooks as well. Non-native species impose billions of dollars in costs on landowners, farmers, ranchers, and others, and yet may generate profits for some sectors. Communities lose business when beaches are closed or mercury restrictions limit fish consumption, yet stricter regulations on sewage or industrial effluents imposes costs on cities and industries. Inadequate and disputed water supplies can restrict development and economic growth or threaten aquatic species. And attempts to sustain forestry, fishing, and farming communities frequently involve tradeoffs with other environmental values.

The core premise of this second *State of the Nation's Ecosystems* report is that American citizens should have access to high-quality, nonpartisan, science-based information on the state of our lands, waters, and living resources. As with the first edition of this series, issued in 2002, *The State of the Nation's Ecosystems 2008* was produced by The Heinz Center in partnership with hundreds of collaborators in businesses, academic institutions, environmental organizations, and federal, state, and local governments.

The State of the Nation's Ecosystems 2008 aims to provide information that will inform discussion, debate, and effective decision making on the key environmental matters facing the nation. Land use and other policy decisions, as well as a changing climate, are likely to drive significant change in the nation's ecosystems over the coming decades, and thus the need for such information is paramount. The availability of up-to-date, high-quality, scientifically credible information should allow the public and decision makers to focus on the most constructive ways to balance society's diverse goals, rather than arguing about the dimensions of the problems at hand. Decision makers need sound factual information to distinguish urgent and growing issues from ones that are under control, to anticipate new problems before they become unmanageable, and to track whether society's investments in solutions are paying the hoped-for dividends.

Better Information Is Needed

Americans demand reliable and up-to-date answers to such fundamental questions as: *How is the environment changing? Are the problems we face getting better or worse? What new challenges are arising? Are government or private programs dealing effectively with these challenges?* And Americans expect that our information-rich society can provide these answers. After a decade of working to deliver comprehensive information about trends in the nation's ecological condition, however, The

Heinz Center and its collaborators have identified key weaknesses in the nation's ability to collect and deliver environmental information.

It is not yet possible to provide answers to many of these basic questions. The nation's environmental monitoring and reporting enterprise—on which this report rests—is not matched to the problems, concerns, and decision-making needs of the 21st century. In too many cases, information on the state of our surroundings is isolated, overly technical, not comparable from one place to another, or simply unavailable.

Businesses recognize the value of information, and they spend significant amounts of money to gather the information they need to help manage their assets. As a nation, we have also recognized the value of information in some realms—witness the creation of a national system for providing timely, high quality, agenda-free information about the state of the economy, using indicators such as inflation, unemployment, and gross domestic product. Americans deserve similar information about changes in our environment. Attempting to manage our vast and valuable natural resources without this level of information is akin to driving a vehicle with the front and rear windshields largely obscured.

Citizens, governments, and businesses increasingly struggle with problems that span borders: endangered species that live in multiple states, water and air pollution that causes problems in regions far from their origins, invasive species that spread across state and agency boundaries, and national and global market processes that affect demand for the nation's forest and farm products. It is clear that the nation's needs are poorly served by isolated and fragmented information-gathering efforts and the resulting lack of well-coordinated solutions to such cross-boundary problems. An important lesson from the Heinz Center's work is that building integrated information-gathering capacity is a necessary step toward the development of integrated solutions to environmental problems.

The environmental monitoring systems in place today were developed incrementally, often in response to specific management needs or environmental concerns. Many of these monitoring programs provide the high-quality factual data that underpins this report.

Our work, however, has made it abundantly clear that significant improvements are required in the amount and the consistency of information collected and reported if the American public and decision makers are to have the kind of information they need and expect as they manage the nation's ecological resources. The Heinz Center's recommendations for addressing this crucial need appear in a separate publication, *Environmental Information: Road Map to the Future*.

Building a National Report on Ecosystem Condition and Use

Since 1997, federal agencies, foundations, and corporations have supported the Heinz Center's State of the Nation's Ecosystems initiative to identify and report on a modest number of key *indicators*— specific biological, chemical, or physical measurements that describe important trends in the condition and use of our lands, waters, and living resources—the nation's ecosystems. This novel initiative was originally commissioned in 1997 by the White House Office of Science and Technology Policy and has more recently been supported by its sister agency, the Council on Environmental Quality.

The diverse contributors to this project were asked to identify key aspects of our nation's coasts and oceans, fresh waters, forests, farmlands, grasslands and shrublands, and urban and suburban areas that should be tracked through time to provide a consistent and comprehensive view of trends in these types of ecosystems. The inclusion of participants with very different perspectives ensures that the report reflects a broad view of those aspects of ecosystems most valued by American society, and that the report's tone and language remain neutral and nonpartisan. [See Box 1.1 for a description of the project's design principles, Appendix A (p. 252) for an account of the report's development, and pages vi–xiii for a list of participants in the preparation of this 2008 report.]

BOX 1.1   Design Principles

Over the years, five main design principles have guided the development of the *State of the Nation's Ecosystems* reports:

- *Focus on condition and trends.* Describe important characteristics and trends for the nation's lands, waters, and living resources, rather than identifying the causes or cures for problems (or perceived problems). Thus, the reports document the ultimate **outcome** of all such activities—the resulting condition of the ecosystems and the goods and services they provide.

- *Be relevant to contemporary policy issues.* Present information that is relevant to and can be used by decision makers and opinion leaders. To this end, the indicators are designed to provide a "big picture" view that is succinct and strategic rather than exhaustive.

- *Select and report on an unbiased and balanced array of indicators.* Provide information that informs policy, but do not endorse particular positions or outcomes, and avoid, as far as possible, political bias, the use of inflammatory or "hot button" language, or reference to subjective benchmarks. The report's consultative development process balances value-driven choices about what features of ecosystems should be reported with scientific rigor.

- *Report only data that meet high standards for quality and coverage across the nation and through time.* The reports are based on the most current scientific knowledge and a rigorous peer-review process.

- *Update periodically and learn from experience.* The reports are dynamic "works in progress," not a limited-time effort. Periodic and ongoing updates are needed to supply users with the most recent data and to allow for incorporation of scientific advances and enhancements to the nation's monitoring and reporting infrastructure. Where available data fail to meet quality and coverage criteria, the relevant indicator is left blank and the data shortcomings that led to its omission are explained.

This is the second full *State of the Nation's Ecosystems* report to emerge from this intensive collaboration. The outcome clearly demonstrates that it *is* possible to identify indicators that describe key trends in a fashion that is both nonpartisan and faithful to the underlying science and also relevant and accessible to nonscientists.

Reporting on Ecosystems

The term "ecosystems" refers to the combination of living organisms and their nonliving environment. Ecosystems possess intrinsic value and provide fundamental life-support services for people and other organisms, including generating vital goods such as crops, timber, fish, and drinking water. Ecosystems also supply cultural, social, and recreational services, from treasured scenery to bathing beaches and places to hike, fish, or watch birds. More recently, society has begun to recognize the value of other ecosystem services, such as retention of flood waters, coastline stabilization, soil renewal, pollination of crops and trees, and carbon sequestration.

Ecosystems are dynamic and complex, varying in size, numbers and types of species, amount of solar energy they capture, and how they use and transport nutrients and energy through food webs and the physical environment. They are also inextricably interconnected—the constant movement of seeds, animals, nutrients, sediments, water, and other materials and energy means that what happens in one ecosystem can profoundly affect others. All ecosystems are affected by geographic influences such as regional climate and geology, by natural disturbances such as fire or hurricanes, and by how people use or alter them.

This report focuses on a modest number of key characteristics, describing their current status and, where possible, trends over the past few decades, both nationally and for the nation's major ecosystem types—coasts and oceans, farmlands, forests, fresh waters, grasslands and shrublands, and urban and suburban areas. The report's organization is intended to help readers review the overall trends through time for specific ecosystems or the nation as a whole; the main indicator chapters provide both individual indicators and summary text and tables on this basis. In addition, as can be seen in the table that follows this chapter (The Indicators at a Glance, p. 10), the four major categories of ecosystem characteristics and the specific groups of indicators (such as those dealing with non-native species or contaminants) enable readers to explore specific topics across ecosystems. Indicator descriptions and summary text highlight connections among ecological characteristics both within and between ecosystems.

Because the purpose of this report is to describe, not to evaluate, it does not contain assessments of whether changes are positive or negative, nor does it identify or speculate on the specific causes of observed trends (see Box 1.2). Such steps are a crucial element of understanding environmental change and determining appropriate responses. However, they involve either value judgments or making judgments about as-yet unsettled scientific questions. Much as the Bureau of Labor Statistics does not comment, when reporting changes in unemployment, on whether trends are good or bad or what caused them, we have chosen to provide a firm factual basis for further exploration and debate.

Box 1.2   Pointing Fingers: Drivers and Ecosystem Condition

This report does not focus on the effects of specific "drivers" or "stresses" on ecosystems (nor does it describe specific policies or actions). Rather, it reports on the outcomes of the full range of artificial (or "man-made") and natural factors and policies that ecosystems are subject to. Much as a doctor may check "vital signs" and, if irregular results are found, may order additional tests or may take immediate action, so decision makers may check the indicators of overall ecosystem condition in this report and then take further action or collect further data.

Specific indicators may be subject to multiple forces of change, or drivers. For example, indicators of the amount of **nitrogen in the nation's waters** are potentially affected by many such drivers. (Nitrogen is an important plant nutrient, but in excess it can cause water quality problems.) These include urbanization and livestock and cropping practices that can increase the amount of nitrogen in runoff or in sewage treatment discharges, fossil fuel combustion that can lead to nitrogen deposition on land or water, and reduction in wetlands and streamside vegetation, which often act as "biological filters" that absorb nitrogen from runoff.

Single drivers may also affect multiple ecosystem characteristics, and thus multiple indicators. For example, **climate change** has the potential to alter ecosystems in many ways, and examples of such changes have been reported in both the press and the scientific literature. Because climate plays an important role in shaping ecosystems, changes in climate may affect many different indicators, and this report contains multiple examples. Key aspects of predicted climate change include physical changes— increased sea surface temperature, altered precipitation patterns, and increased storm intensity. These changes are predicted by climate scientists to vary regionally rather than nationally. Resulting biological changes may include more active algae growth in coastal waters, leading to more frequent harmful algal blooms, increased area with depleted oxygen, and reduced recreational water quality. On land or in fresh waters, warmer temperatures may help the spread of non-native species or waterborne human diseases, accelerate or cause the decline of native species, and decrease urban air quality. Effects on farming and forestry may be beneficial or harmful, depending on regional patterns.

The State of the Nation's Ecosystems 2008

This 2008 report builds on the successful 2002 *State of the Nation's Ecosystems* report (www. heinzcenter.org/ecosystems) and contains many improvements and extensions. With important exceptions, the two volumes report on the same indicators, because the goal is to provide consistent reporting on key trends. Six new indicators were added to address key items not addressed in 2002, and fifty-seven indicators were modified or refined. These additions and refinements were undertaken in line with the report's initial goal of providing a consistent but continually refined set of indicators (see Appendix B for a description of this process).

The 2008 report is organized in the same way as the 2002 report. It describes four key categories of important ecosystem characteristics for the nation as a whole and for the nation's six principal ecosystem types (coasts and oceans, farmlands, forests, fresh waters, grasslands and shrublands, and urban and suburban landscapes; see also Box 1.3 and Figure 1.1). Chapter 2 presents a national perspective on trends across major ecosystems (the core national indicators), while Chapters 3 through 8 provide integrated views of conditions and trends in the nation's coasts and oceans, farmlands, forests, freshwaters, grasslands and shrublands, and urban and suburban landscapes. In all, 108 indicators are presented. Four appendixes and extensive technical notes complement and support these chapters, offering in-depth information on the design process used in this project, indicator refinement efforts, key data gaps, and descriptions of major national monitoring programs.

Box 1.3 What Does *The State of the Nation's Ecosystems 2008* Report?

This report aims to be comprehensive but not exhaustive—that is, to provide a "big picture" view. It describes large-scale patterns, conditions, and trends across the United States by describing a modest number of key ecological characteristics, rather than attempting to report every bit of monitoring information. We do so by reporting on "indicators"—specific, well-defined, and measurable variables that reflect key characteristics that can be tracked through time. Indicators include measurements of ecosystem components, ecological processes, and the goods and services generated by ecosystems.

The four major categories of ecological characteristics (and indicators) are

- **Ecosystem extent and pattern.** The area of ecosystems and how they are intermingled across the landscape—for example, the area of wetlands, the distance from farmlands to nearby housing, the extent of impervious surface in urban and suburban areas.
- **Chemical and physical characteristics.** Key ecosystem requirements such oxygen, carbon, and nutrients; contaminants in ecosystems; and key physical factors such as erosion and water flows—for example, the amount of nitrogen delivered by major rivers to the nation's coastal waters, the detection of contaminants and the degree of exceedance of relevant benchmarks, and soil erosion from farmlands.
- **Biological components.** The condition of plants, animals, and living habitats and the productivity of these systems—for example, the percentage of species in a region that are not native, the fraction of species at elevated risk of extinction, and the condition of plant and animal communities.
- **Goods and services.** Things people derive from the natural world, such as food, fiber, water, recreation, and less easily measured benefits, called "natural ecosystem services"—for example, pollination of plants and retention of floodwaters.

The table on page 10 lists all 108 indicators in this report, organized by ecosystem and characteristic.

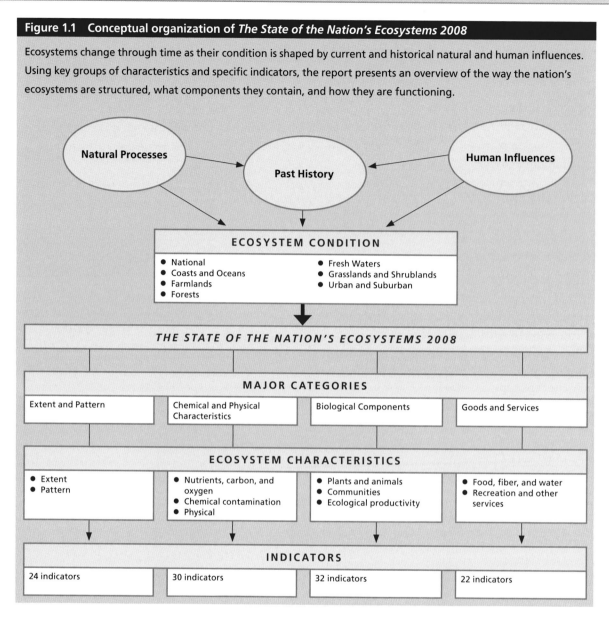

Figure 1.1 Conceptual organization of *The State of the Nation's Ecosystems 2008*

Ecosystems change through time as their condition is shaped by current and historical natural and human influences. Using key groups of characteristics and specific indicators, the report presents an overview of the way the nation's ecosystems are structured, what components they contain, and how they are functioning.

Natural Processes

Past History

Human Influences

ECOSYSTEM CONDITION
- National
- Coasts and Oceans
- Farmlands
- Forests
- Fresh Waters
- Grasslands and Shrublands
- Urban and Suburban

THE STATE OF THE NATION'S ECOSYSTEMS 2008

MAJOR CATEGORIES

Extent and Pattern	Chemical and Physical Characteristics	Biological Components	Goods and Services

ECOSYSTEM CHARACTERISTICS

• Extent • Pattern	• Nutrients, carbon, and oxygen • Chemical contamination • Physical	• Plants and animals • Communities • Ecological productivity	• Food, fiber, and water • Recreation and other services

INDICATORS

24 indicators	30 indicators	32 indicators	22 indicators

Another important feature continued in this second report is the highlighting of key indicators for which data are not available at the national level. The 2002 report first highlighted these "data gaps," and the Center issued a separate report in 2006—*Filling the Gaps: Priority Data Needs and Key Management Challenges for National Reporting on Ecosystem Condition*—recommending priorities for investment in environmental monitoring. In addition, a 2005 Government Accountability Office report (*Environmental Information: Federal Programs That Support Environmental Indicators*, GAO-05-376) highlighted potential future loss of information if existing programs are not adequately supported.

The State of the Nation's Ecosystems 2008 offers
- *New data.* The report updates all 68 indicators for which data are available and reports multiyear trends for 41 indicators (up from 31 in 2002).
- *New and improved indicators.* More than half the report's 108 indicators have been redesigned or refined to reflect the most recent data collection or analysis methods and provide the most relevant information on appropriate scales. In addition, several new indicators have been added to cover topics not adequately addressed in 2002 (landscape pattern, non-native species, carbon storage, air pollution in ecosystems, and changing stream flows)

- *Enhanced presentation.* The report includes more maps, improved summary tables for immediate scanning of trends and data coverage information, and additional explanatory text and technical notes.

Partners in Progress

Over the decade in which the *State of the Nation's Ecosystems* project has been in existence, many other important indicator or assessment efforts have been initiated. The Heinz Center views these projects as complementary rather than competitive, serving similar but distinct needs. For example, the Millennium Ecosystem Assessment was global in scope and included components such as projections and policy recommendations that are not included here. The U.S. Environmental Protection Agency (EPA) is now preparing its second *Report on the Environment* (ROE—see www.epa.gov/roe). While the first ROE had many similarities to the 2002 *State of the Nation's Ecosystems* report, the second one will focus more closely on EPA's legal and policy objectives and be tied directly to that agency's strategic planning process. There are also several "sustainable resource roundtables"—collaborative multisectoral efforts that originally grew out of the Montreal Process Criteria and Indicators for the Conservation and Sustainable Management of Temperate and Boreal Forests, an international group in which the United States has been an active participant. These roundtables, established for forests (http://www.sustainableforests.net/), rangelands (http://sustainablerangelands.warnercnr.colostate.edu/), fresh water (http://acwi.gov/swrr/), and minerals (http://www.unr.edu/mines/smr/), generally incorporate indicator development or reporting as key aspects of their work, but do so only for a subset of the topics in *The State of the Nation's Ecosystems 2008*. We see many similarities between the basic approaches of all these projects and look forward to continued collaboration, refinement, and harmonization of these important efforts.

The Work Continues

There was healthy skepticism in 1997 that it would be possible to pull together the many interest groups, scientists, and fragmented data sources needed to develop a broad, accurate picture of how the nation's ecosystems are changing. Ten years of work and the release of this second *State of the Nation's Ecosystems* report have put that debate to rest.

The *State of the Nation's Ecosystems 2008* is an important step in a longer journey toward continued periodic, science-based, and nonpartisan reporting on key aspects of ecosystem condition. The purpose is to inform the public policy dialog on environmental issues by providing basic answers to reasonable questions about changes in the nation's ecosystems. The process attends carefully to the values of multiple sectors of society, and the report remains scientifically credible yet accessible to nonspecialists. It is comprehensive rather than narrowly focused, providing the framework for comparisons across regions and programs, and has been revised since 2002 in a way that maintains as much continuity as possible.

Despite the successes so far, much remains to be done
- To increase the availability of key monitoring data
- To ensure that the indicators keep up with advancing scientific findings and policy needs
- To connect and reconcile these national indicators with those used by states, local governments, tribes, and federal agencies
- To create the institutional capacity to continue this monitoring and assessment effort routinely over the coming decades

Despite the high quality of existing programs and incremental improvements over the past decade, the problem of a fragmented national monitoring and reporting infrastructure remains acute. (As noted above, in *Environmental Information: Road Map to the Future*, The Heinz Center recommends a series of actions to address this problem.)

Other types of national infrastructure efforts, such as creation of the federal interstate highway system or the capacity for reporting national economic indicators, have required decades of patience, persistence, and a long-term perspective. The environmental problems faced by citizens, businesses, and governments across the United States are real and will not fade away. Indeed, over the next 50 to 100 years, the nation's ecosystems are expected to change at unprecedented rates, driven in part by a changing climate as well as by land use and other policy decisions. To cope successfully with the environmental challenges ahead, we must have timely, reliable, unbiased, scientifically rigorous feedback about changes and trends in the state of the nation's ecosystems—that is, a clear window on where we are and where we are heading. *The State of the Nation's Ecosystems 2008* is that window.

T

This table serves as an overall guide to *The State of the Nation's Ecosystems 2008*. It lists all indicators in the report and shows both the indicators used to describe a specific *ecosystem type* (in the columns) and the indicators used to describe specific *ecosystem characteristics* (in the rows). Indicators added or modified since the 2002 *State of the Nation's Ecosystems* report are also identified.

Core National Indicators   **Coasts and Oceans**   **Farmlands**

EXTENT AND PATTERN

	Core National Indicators	Coasts and Oceans	Farmlands	
Extent	• Ecosystem Extent*	• Coastal Living Habitats • Shoreline Types	• Total Cropland* • The Farmland Landscape*	
Pattern	• Pattern of "Natural" Landscapes†	• Pattern in Coastal Areas‡	• Proximity of Cropland to Residences† • Patches of "Natural" Land in the Farmland Landscape†	

CHEMICAL AND PHYSICAL CHARACTERISTICS

Nutrients, Carbon, and Oxygen	• Movement of Nitrogen* • Carbon Storage‡	• Areas with Depleted Oxygen*	• Nitrate in Farmland Streams and Groundwater* • Phosphorus in Farmland Streams* • Soil Organic Matter*	
Chemical Contamination	• Chemical Contamination*	• Contamination in Bottom Sediments*	• Pesticides in Farmland Streams and Groundwater*	
Physical	• Change In Stream Flows‡	• Coastal Erosion • Sea Surface Temperature*	• Potential Soil Erosion • Soil Salinity • Stream Habitat Quality†	

BIOLOGICAL COMPONENTS

Plants and Animals	• At-Risk Native Species* • Established Non-native Species‡	• At-Risk Native Marine Species • Established Non-native Species in Major Estuaries* • Unusual Marine Mortalities	• Status of Animal Species in Farmland Areas • Established Non-native Plant Cover in the Farmland Landscape†	
Communities	• Native Species Composition*	• Harmful Algal Events* • Condition of Bottom-Dwelling Animals	• Soil Biological Condition	
Ecological Productivity	• Plant Growth Index*	• Chlorophyll Concentrations*		

GOODS AND SERVICES

Food, Fiber, and Water	• Production of Food and Fiber and Water Withdrawals	• Commercial Fish and Shellfish Landings • Status of Commercially Important Fish Stocks* • Selected Contaminants in Fish and Shellfish	• Major Crop Yields • Agricultural Inputs and Outputs* • Monetary Value of Agricultural Production	
Recreation and Other Services	• Outdoor Recreation • Natural Ecosystem Services*	• Recreational Water Quality	• Recreation in Farmland Areas	

Indicator refined since the 2002 State of the Nation's Ecosystems Report (original metric or metrics retained)
†Indicator redesigned since the 2002 State of the Nation's Ecosystems Report
‡New indicator since the 2002 State of the Nation's Ecosystems Report

Forests   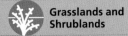 **Fresh Waters**    **Grasslands and Shrublands**   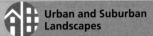 **Urban and Suburban Landscapes**

Forests	Fresh Waters	Grasslands and Shrublands	Urban and Suburban Landscapes
• Forest Area and Ownership* • Forest Types* • Forest Management Categories*	• Extent of Freshwater Ecosystems* • Altered Freshwater Ecosystems*	• Area of Grasslands and Shrublands* • Land Use in Grasslands and Shrublands	• Area and Composition of the Urban and Suburban Landscape* • Total Impervious Area
• Pattern of Forest Landscapes†	• In-Stream Connectivity‡	• Pattern of Grassland and Shrubland Landscapes†	• Streambank Vegetation • Housing Density Changes in Low-Density Suburban and Rural Areas† • "Natural" Lands in the Urban and Suburban Landscape†
• Nitrate in Forest Streams* • Carbon Storage*	• Phosphorus in Lakes, Reservoirs and Large Rivers*	• Nitrate in Grassland and Shrubland Groundwater • Carbon Storage	• Nitrate in Urban and Suburban Streams* • Phosphorus in Urban and Suburban Streams*
	• Freshwater Acidity‡		• Urban and Suburban Air Quality* • Chemical Contamination*
	• Water Clarity • Stream Habitat Quality†	• Number and Duration of Dry Periods in Grassland and Shrubland Streams and Rivers* • Depth to Shallow Groundwater	• Urban Heat Island
• At-Risk Native Forest Species* • Established Non-native Plant Cover in Forests	• At-Risk Native Freshwater Species* • Established Non-native Freshwater Species* • Animal Deaths and Deformities	• At-Risk Native Grassland and Shrubland Species* • Established Non-native Grassland and Shrubland Plant Cover* • Population Trends in Invasive and Non-invasive Birds	• Species Status • Disruptive Species
• Forest Age* • Forest Disturbance: Fire, Insects, and Disease* • Fire Frequency • Forest Community Types with Significantly Reduced Area	• Status of Freshwater Animal Communities* • At-Risk Freshwater Plant Communities*	• Fire Frequency • Riparian Condition	• Status of Animal Communities in Urban and Suburban Streams
• Timber Harvest* • Timber Growth and Harvest*	• Water Withdrawals • Groundwater Levels • Waterborne Human Disease Outbreaks	• Cattle Grazing	
• Recreation in Forests	• Freshwater Recreational Activities	• Recreation on Grasslands and Shrublands	• Publicly Accessible Open Space per Resident • Natural Ecosystem Services*

Contents page

Chapter 2:
The Nation's Ecosystems: Core Indicators

America's ecosystems are vast and immensely varied, stretching from Alaska to Florida, from Hawaii to the Sea Islands of Georgia. Arctic tundra, rain forest, desert, and prairie; farms, grasslands, forests, beaches, wetlands, cities, towns, and suburbs—the rich mosaic of the nation's ecosystems is made up of all these, and more. Besides their intrinsic value, ecosystems provide us with goods and services, and not just the obvious ones, like crops and timber and drinking water and outdoor recreation, but the less quantifiable but no less vital ones, like water purification, flood control, and erosion protection.

The Core National Indicators
Extent and Pattern
● Ecosystem Extent
● Pattern of "Natural" Landscapes
Chemical and Physical Characteristics
● The Movement of Nitrogen
● Carbon Storage
● Chemical Contamination
● Change in Stream Flows
Biological Components
● At-Risk Native Species
● Established Non-native Species
● Native Species Composition
● Plant Growth Index
Goods and Services
● Production of Food and Fiber and Water Withdrawals
● Outdoor Recreation
● Natural Ecosystem Services

The small set of *core national indicators* in this chapter describes the condition and use of our nation's ecosystems—coasts and oceans, farmlands, forests, fresh waters, grasslands and shrublands, and urban and suburban landscapes—as a whole. These thirteen indicators, which are complemented by related indicators in the six ecosystem-level chapters that follow, report on the most important aspects of overall ecosystem condition. They also highlight key factors important to understanding the overall functioning of our ecosystems, their interaction with each other, and their capacity to provide benefits important to society. They make it possible to understand data on a national level, identify tradeoffs involved in land use and other environmental management decisions, and provide a core factual basis for the many programmatic and policy decisions required at the federal level. Local and regional data collection efforts are not always comparable across states or regions. National indicators can promote consistency among monitoring programs by serving as a uniform starting point.

In the sections that follow, we present information from both the core national indicators and several related indicators in the ecosystem-specific chapters (Chapters 3–8). The indicators fall into the four categories of ecosystem condition and use outlined in Chapter 1: the extent of the nation's ecosystems and their pattern on the landscape, their chemical and physical characteristics, the condition of species and biological communities, and the many human benefits (goods and services) derived from ecosystems. We highlight information currently available as well as information that we need to know, but do not because the required data monitoring and analysis programs are not in place. (See Appendix D for definitions of the regions used throughout this report.)

Extent and Pattern
Two of the most basic characteristics of an ecosystem are how large an area it covers (extent) and whether it is composed of continuous stretches of land or is intermingled in patches with other ecosystems or land uses (pattern).

National ecosystem extent data may reveal changes that cannot be seen at a local level, such as whether the nation is gaining or losing forest or farmland. As land is converted from one ecosystem type to another, the pattern of ecosystems in the landscape often changes along with their extent—suburban developments may be built in areas that were formerly forest or grasslands, or abandoned farms may become forest again. Changes in both extent and pattern have consequences for ecosystem processes and also for the quantity and nature of goods and services the ecosystem can provide. Suburban development changes habitat quality and thus the community of species an ecosystem can sustain—many songbirds require large unbroken expanses of forest, away from humans, while pigeons and starlings prosper in urban environments.

Ecosystems are not isolated entities: they constantly exchange materials, such as sediment in runoff, energy (exported as food for people or animals), and species across their boundaries. Changes in the area and configuration of ecosystems can have far-reaching effects on water quality, soil stability, and aesthetics, and decisions involving land use change always involve tradeoffs. For example, conversion of forests to suburban development use may provide attractive housing opportunities and boost the local economy and tax base, but it may also reduce wildlife habitat or local timber stocks, diminish recreational opportunities, and increase the runoff of nutrients and other contaminants into area streams and wells.

Extent and pattern indicators provide insight into trends that are of growing interest to the American public. The amount of land available for farming and forests, for example, is currently of interest because farmlands could be used to produce biofuel feedstocks and forests store carbon in their plants and soils, possibly offering a way to slow climate change. Suburban development, too, is often a source of policy conflict, as it may be seen as a way of providing affordable housing for middle-class Americans or as mere "sprawl," threatening the landscape and values that local people hold dear. The indicators of extent and pattern may provide those on both sides of such disputes with the data they need to make informed decisions.

Data in this report show that
- In the lower 48 states, there are
  - 5 million acres of coastal wetlands on the Gulf and Atlantic Coast
  - 400 million acres of croplands
  - 621 million acres of forests
  - 96 million acres of freshwater wetlands
  - 6 million acres of freshwater ponds
  - 694 million acres of grasslands and shrublands
  - 45 million acres of urban and suburban landscapes
- In the past half century, the area of coastal and freshwater wetlands has declined, while the area of ponds has increased. The area of developed land (a proxy for the area of urban and suburban landscapes) has also increased significantly.
- The nation's forests and croplands have not changed significantly in area since the 1950s, although croplands have shown a significant decline in recent decades.
  - The area of forests has increased in the North while decreasing in the South and the Pacific Coast (see p. 132).
  - The area of cropland has declined nationwide since 1982. However, cropland acreage in the two river basins with the greatest agricultural acreage—the Missouri and the Souris–Red Rainy/Upper Mississippi—has remained relatively stable (see p. 102).
- Twenty-three percent of the land cover in the lower 48 states is considered "core natural" land (parcels of land surrounded by at least 240 acres of other "natural" lands). "Natural" land cover includes forests, grasslands and shrublands, wetlands, lakes, and coastal waters.
  - The Rocky Mountain region has the highest percentage of its landscape in "core natural" land, as well as the highest percentage in "core natural" patches of 1000 square miles or larger.
  - The Midwest region has the lowest percentage of "core natural" land area; the Midwest and Northeast/Mid-Atlantic regions have the lowest percentage of this core natural area in very large patches.

Data are not adequate for national reporting on
- The area of wetlands along the Pacific Coast
- The area of seagrasses, submerged vegetation, shellfish beds, and coral reefs along the entire coast
- The area of lakes
- Trends in conversion between "natural" lands (forests, grasslands, shrublands, and wetlands), cropland, and developed lands
- Changes in the area of important ecosystem subtypes such as wetlands and of rare community types such as Everglades Wet Prairie and West Gulf Coastal Plain Beech–Magnolia Forest

Besides the two extent and pattern indicators described in this chapter, 22 other indicators focus on extent and pattern at an ecosystem level (see The Indicators at a Glance, pp. 10–11).

Chemical and Physical Characteristics

Chemical and physical indicators report on key chemical building blocks of ecosystems, contaminants that may harm people or affect plants and animals, and physical features that influence the way ecosystems work and the benefits humans derive from them. The core national indicators in this category measure the movement of nitrogen, the storage of carbon, levels of chemical contaminants, and changes in stream flow.

Chemical and physical indicators allow us to ask critical questions about the underlying factors that shape the way ecosystems work: Are essential elements and compounds available? Are some present in excess? Have chemical or physical conditions changed, possibly affecting what species (if any) can live in an area? The answers can be important to fishermen, coastal managers, and environmental advocates who seek to track the quantities of nitrogen in rivers, which have been linked to the development of low- or no-oxygen areas ("dead zones") in coastal waters. Food security is a pressing concern, and these indicators can provide information about underlying trends in the fertility and future productive capacity of our nation's farmland ecosystems. Those interested in reducing atmospheric carbon dioxide and methane concentrations will be able to use the indicators to track trends in the amount of carbon (as soil organic matter, standing timber, and so on) stored in U.S. forests, grasslands, and croplands when additional data become available. The indicators can be used now to understand patterns of chemical contamination.

Nitrogen

Nitrogen is a vital nutrient for plants and animals; it can also move easily from one landscape or ecosystem type to another and, in excess, can alter the makeup and functioning of those systems. As excess nitrogen runs off the land or is released into the atmosphere, it can change the composition of forests, acidify lakes, contaminate groundwater wells, and trigger the growth of algae in coastal waters.

Carbon

Carbon, like nitrogen, is essential to life. In the form of organic matter, carbon is a key element of productive ecosystems, and, when stored in ecological reservoirs such as soils and plant materials, carbon can offset emissions of carbon dioxide and methane to the atmosphere, where they contribute to the greenhouse effect. Carbon storage—be it in agricultural soils, prairie grasses, forest trees, wood products, wetlands, or ocean sediments—is an important factor in efforts to reduce future climate change.

Chemical Contamination

Modern society produces a host of useful compounds—pesticides, fertilizers, drugs—many of which are now found as contaminants in air, water, stream and coastal sediment, soil, and human and animal tissues. These chemical contaminants, as well as elevated levels of naturally occurring metals and nutrients, can affect the biological functioning of ecosystems and affect the availability of the goods and services they provide. Contaminants can affect the safety of the food we eat, the waters we drink or swim in, and even the land we live on. The indicators track the extent of contamination and its potential impact on human heath and aquatic life and further illustrate the ability of some compounds to move between ecosystems.

Water

Like carbon and nitrogen, water is a critical component of ecosystems. The presence or absence of water, the amount available, and the timing of its availability help shape ecosystems physically (such as through erosion) and also influence what species, including human beings, can live in an area. Land use in a watershed affects the amount and variability of flow in streams, which in turn influences such human uses as energy generation and municipal and industrial water supplies.

Data in this report show that

Nitrogen

- Nitrogen moves from land and air to fresh waters, and for more than half of our nation's land area measured, this occurs at a rate greater than 600 pounds per square mile per year.
- Three of our largest river systems—the Mississippi, the Columbia, and the Susquehanna— together discharge approximately 1 million tons of nitrogen per year to coastal waters, with more than 90% of that nitrogen carried by the Mississippi. While nitrate discharge from the Mississippi has doubled since the 1950s, there has been no clear upward or downward trend in discharge from the Mississippi since 1983, or from the Susquehanna or Columbia since the mid-1970s.
  - Nitrate concentrations in farmland streams are higher than in streams draining forested watersheds and watersheds dominated by urban and suburban development (see p. 107, p. 140, and p. 238).
  - Streams and groundwater with nitrate concentrations exceeding the federal drinking water standard for nitrate (10 ppm) were found only in farmland areas (including about 20% of groundwater wells and 13% of stream sites sampled) (see p. 107).
  - Since 1985 the percentage of monitoring sites that receive high levels of nitrogen deposition in precipitation (4–6 pounds per acre annually) has increased slightly, from 27% to 31% of sites (see p. 176).

Carbon

- In recent decades the amount of carbon stored in the nation's forests (excluding soils), croplands, and private grasslands and shrublands (excluding roots and above-ground plant matter) increased. Forests, excluding soils, gained the most—about 150 million metric tons per year (1995–2005)—while cropland soils added 16.5 million metric tons per year (1990–1999) and private grassland–shrubland soils added about 1.6 million tons per year (1990–1999).
  - For forest trees, the Northern region stored the most carbon in the lower 48 states, while the Intermountain West stored the least (see p. 142).
- Atmospheric carbon dioxide concentrations have increased by 36% over preindustrial levels; atmospheric methane concentrations have increased by 160% over preindustrial levels.

Chemical Contamination

- At least one contaminant was detected in about 75% of the groundwater wells tested, virtually all the streams and streambed sediments tested, about 80% of the estuarine sediments tested, about 80% of the freshwater fish tested, and nearly all of the saltwater fish tested.
- Half or more of the stream water, stream sediment, estuarine sediment, and freshwater fish tissue samples had at least one contaminant at concentrations above benchmarks set to protect aquatic life.
  - About 57% of farmland streams had at least one pesticide at concentrations exceeding benchmarks for the protection of aquatic life, and about 16% had at least one pesticide at levels exceeding benchmarks for protection of human health (see p. 111).
  - About 83% of urban and suburban streams had contaminant levels exceeding benchmarks for the protection of aquatic life; 7% of these streams had contaminant levels exceeding benchmarks for protection of human health (see p. 243).
- One-third of the groundwater wells, one-third of the saltwater fish samples, and 20% of streams tested had one or more contaminants at concentrations exceeding benchmarks set to protect human health.
- In 2005, daytime ozone levels were higher than 0.06 parts per million for more than 30 hours during the growing season in 4% of the land area of the United States.
  - In 2005, high ozone levels were recorded at 30% of urban and suburban monitoring stations on four or more days; 61% had high levels on at least one day (see p. 241).
- Some 28% of urban sites nationwide measured fine particulate matter at concentrations of 15 micrograms per cubic meter or above (comparable to EPA's national annual standard).

Stream Flows

- Since the early 1960s, a higher proportion of streams have had increased low flows, reduced high flows, and less variability in their flow (in all cases, comparisons are made to a 1941–1960 baseline period).
  - The percentage of grassland–shrubland streams with zero-flow periods has declined since 1963, and the proportion of streams with zero-flow periods substantially shorter than during the 1941–1960 baseline period has increased (see p. 208).

Data are not adequate for national reporting on

- The atmospheric deposition of nitrogen to coastal waters
- The carbon stored in forest soils, the soils of public grasslands and shrublands, grassland–shrubland biomass, wetlands (including peatlands), water and sediment in aquatic systems, and urban and suburban areas
- Contaminants in plant tissues and in animals other than fish
- The number of contaminants in freshwater fish that exceed benchmarks to protect human health
- The number of contaminants in saltwater fish that exceed benchmarks to protect aquatic life
- Combined urban and rural measurements of fine particulate matter in air

Besides the chemical and physical characteristics indicators described in this chapter, 27 other indicators focus on chemical and physical characteristics at an ecosystem level (see The Indicators at a Glance, pp. 10–11).

Biological Components

While extent and pattern indicators provide a broad view of the size and shape of ecosystems, biological components indicators provide information on a smaller scale, focusing on the organisms that make these ecosystems their home. Each ecosystem has many plant and animal *communities*—for example, the unique plant and animal assemblage that might inhabit a spring in an arid grassland landscape, or an old-growth forest. Each of these communities is made up of many *species* of plants, animals, and microorganisms. These living components interact with their physical and chemical surroundings, influencing the overall structure of the ecosystem as well as key processes such as nutrient cycling and exacerbating or moderating natural disturbances such as fire, floods, and insect damage. To capture the condition of biological components at multiple scales, specific indicators focus on plants and animals, communities, and ecosystem productivity (a measure of biological activity at the largest scale, describing the ecosystem's ability to capture and use the sun's energy).

Biological components indicators offer insight into important policy issues. Non-native species are of concern across the country, and understanding the scope of this problem and the degree to which control efforts are succeeding is important for policymakers and managers alike. Likewise, recent projections of climate change suggest that suitable habitat for many native species and communities will undergo significant geographic shifts. The at-risk species indicators and community composition indicators can help provide a "big–picture" view of the ability of species and communities to adapt to such shifts.

At-Risk Native Species and Established Non-native Species

Since all species contribute to an ecosystem's appearance and functioning, the presence or absence of particular species can be ecologically significant. The loss of native species changes the composition of biological communities and may affect the ability of the ecosystem to function or respond to stress (for example, corals and redwoods define the very character of their ecosystems, and some microbes take up vital elements from air or soil and make them available to other species). Established non-native species may act as predators or parasites of native species, cause diseases, compete for food or habitat,

or alter habitat; on the other hand, they may provide ecosystem services such as soil stabilization or forage for grazing animals.

Native Species Composition

This indicator looks at the condition of the living community as a whole, comparing the native species composition of an area with the composition of the "least disturbed" communities in a similar area in order to identify places that have lost or gained species. Such changes often result from disturbance and may signal a loss of resiliency—the ability of a community to return to its original state after a disturbance or stress.

Plant Growth Index

Photosynthesis—the ability of plants to use energy from the sun to turn carbon dioxide in the air plus water and nutrients into plant matter—sustains nearly all life. Changes in plant growth can thus signal changes in ecosystem functioning, increases or decreases in yields of products such as wood and food crops, and possibly changes in the numbers and types of species that live in the region.

Data in this report show that

- One-third of native plant and animal species (excluding marine species) are at risk of extinction. Among the native vertebrate animal species at risk, 28% have declining populations, 23% have stable populations, and 1% have increasing populations. Population trends among the remaining at-risk vertebrate species (48%) are unknown.
  - The percentage of at-risk native animals is higher in fresh waters (37%) than in forests (19%) or grasslands and shrublands (18%). In all three ecosystem types, a large majority of at-risk vertebrate animal species with known population trends have populations that are either stable or declining, and 3% or fewer have populations that are increasing (see p. 180, p. 144, and p. 211).
- From 1982 to 2003, the plant growth index remained similar to the long-term average across much of the United States. Overall, cropland and grassland areas showed slight increases in the proportion of area with increases in plant growth, while forest and shrubland areas showed no clear up or down trend.
  - Chlorophyll concentrations in coastal waters (out to 200 miles from the shoreline) have increased in the Pacific Northwest, Southern California, and North Atlantic regions. Chlorophyll concentrations have decreased in Hawaii. (The amount of chlorophyll in coastal waters is an indicator of marine primary productivity; see p. 86.)

Data are not adequate for national reporting on

- The status and population trends of native marine plant and animal species
- Population trends of at-risk native invertebrate animals and at-risk native plants
- The number of new non-native species that become established over time
- The area with different numbers of established non-native species
- The area with different proportions of established non-native species, as a percentage of total species
- The plant growth index in fresh waters, estuaries, and open ocean waters

Further indicator development is needed to report on

- Native species composition

Besides the biological components indicators described in this chapter, 28 other indicators focus on biological components at an ecosystem level (see The Indicators at a Glance, pp. 10–11).

Goods and Services

Society derives enormous benefits from natural systems. Commodities such as fish, timber and other forest products, crops and livestock, and water are easiest to quantify and involve the direct appropriation of a valued ecosystem component for human use. Recreational uses, like bird-watching or hiking, and less tangible benefits such as enjoyment of prized scenery or spiritual renewal are also highly valued but more difficult to quantify. Also difficult to measure are services such as flood control, soil renewal, and water purification performed by intact ecosystems. The core national indicators attempt to capture changes in these and other ecosystem goods and services. They do not, however, attempt to place a dollar value on these services, focusing rather on the actual changes in services, leaving the translation to monetary value for others. Because the overall condition of our nation's ecosystems affects the goods and services they can provide, indicators in this section are closely related to indicators of extent and pattern, chemical and physical characteristics, and biological components.

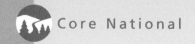

Three core national indicators characterize the use of our nation's ecosystems: Production of Food and Fiber and Water Withdrawals, Outdoor Recreation, and Natural Ecosystem Services. These indicators do not provide information about the degree to which current consumption of goods and service can be sustained over time. Nonetheless, they represent important benchmarks. In combination with ecosystem-level indicators, these core national indicators provide a crucial view of the nation's ability to manage our ecosystems to produce the goods and services we desire.

Production of Food and Fiber and Water Withdrawals

The United States relies heavily on domestic resources to meet its food, fiber, and water needs. We build homes with timber from U.S. forests; savor fruits and vegetables from local farms and from

large-scale farming operations; eat meat from livestock grazed on our grasslands and shrublands and fed grain from our croplands; and divert water from our rivers, lakes, and aquifers to drink, irrigate our crops, and run our factories and hydroelectric plants. Changes in the quantities of these extracted goods can affect both the economy and human well-being. America's desire to safeguard and sustain production of such goods is embodied both in legislation, such as the Magnuson–Stevens Fishery Conservation and Management Act and the Farm Bill, and in government and private programs at the federal, state, regional, and national level. As our population grows, the demand for products from our nation's ecosystems is almost certain to grow as well. Use of new technologies and management approaches may lead to increases in productivity, but productivity may also be compromised by changing ecosystem conditions, including those driven by climate change and land use decisions.

Outdoor Recreation

As the popularity of our national parks and other recreational areas attests, the U.S. public enjoys outdoor recreation. Our ecosystems offer a diversity of settings in which to engage in a wide range of activities—everything from whitewater rafting in the Rockies, deep-sea fishing off Florida, biking across the vast Midwest plains, or hunting in the Maine woods, to dog sledding in Alaska and surfing in Hawaii. The core national indicator on outdoor recreation integrates the enjoyment, health benefits, and even educational benefits we receive from a variety of ecosystem types.

Natural Ecosystem Services

Other services we receive from our nation's ecosystems are less familiar but no less important. They include such critical processes as purification of air and water, regulation of climate and floodwaters, erosion and pest control, pollination, seed dispersal, and renewal of soil fertility. Changes in these natural ecosystem services can affect not only the condition of our environment, but also our ability to obtain more tangible goods and services from the nation's ecosystems on a sustainable basis. At present, the scientific community is wrestling with how best to describe the extent and value of these services at any location, and to detect and evaluate changes. Our indicators reflect this need for continued development.

Data in this report show that

- Nationally, production of agricultural goods, harvest of forest products, and withdrawals of fresh water have all increased. However, only the production of agricultural products has grown at a rate exceeding population growth.
  - Yields per acre of five major crops—wheat, soybeans, corn, cotton, and hay—have increased since 1950, with corn yields alone increasing nearly fourfold (see p. 119).
  - Less labor, energy, and land and fewer durable goods are used to produce agricultural products today than in 1948. However, more pesticides are being used per unit output (see p. 120).
  - Timber harvest has increased in the Northern and Southern regions, where growth exceeds harvest (see p. 155).
- Nationally, marine fisheries landings have shown no clear upward or downward trend since 1978; however, landings have increased on the Pacific Coast (because of an expanding U.S. fleet in Alaska—see p. 87) and decreased in the Northeast/Mid-Atlantic and Southeast.
- Americans over the age of 16 participate in outdoor recreational activities 58 billion times per year, and almost half (45%) of total recreation occurs in forests (see p. 157). Walking is the most popular activity (23 billion times per year) followed by nature viewing (15 billion times per year), and all other land-based activities (15 billion times per year). Americans participate in water-based activities approximately 5 billion times a year.

Data are not adequate for national reporting on

- Participation in running and jogging
- The distinction between freshwater and saltwater recreational activities
- Recreational participation of residents under the age of 16

Further indicator development is needed to report on

- Natural ecosystem services

Besides the goods and services indicators described in this chapter, 19 other indicators focus on goods and services at an ecosystem level (see The Indicators at a Glance, pp. 10–11).

Status and trends for all core national indicators are summarized in the following table and described in detail in the remainder of the chapter. The table on page 10 (The Indicators at a Glance) lists all the ecosystem-specific indicators and shows their connection with the core national indicators. See Appendix D (p. 266) for regions and related definitions used in this chapter.

Indicators	What Do the Most Recent Data Show?		How Have Data Values Changed over Time?

EXTENT AND PATTERN

Ecosystem Extent, p. 28	**Coasts and Oceans:** 4.6 million acres of wetlands on the Atlantic and Gulf coasts (2004 data).		Since the mid-1950s, wetland acreage on the Atlantic and Gulf Coasts has declined.
	Coasts and Oceans: Data are not adequate for reporting on the area of wetlands along the Pacific Coast and the area of seagrass/submerged vegetation, shellfish beds and coral reefs along all portions of the coast.		
	Farmlands: 400 million acres of cropland (23% of the lower 48 states) (2003 data).		Since 1949, there has been no clear trend in cropland acreage.
	Forests: 621 million acres of forest in the lower 48 states (36% of lower 48 states); 742 million acres, including Alaska (2006 data).		Since the 1950s, there has been no clear trend in forest area nationwide.
	Fresh Waters: 96 million acres of wetlands (not including ponds; 6% of lower 48 states) (2004 data).		Since 1955, wetland area has declined.
	Fresh Waters: 6.2 million acres of ponds (2004 data).		Since 1955, pond acreage has increased.
	Fresh Waters: Data are not adequate for national reporting on the area of lakes.		
	Grasslands and Shrublands: almost 700 million acres (about 40% of the lower 48 states) (2001 data).		Data are not adequate for national reporting on changes in grassland–shrubland area.
	Urban and Suburban Landscapes: 45 million acres (2.6% of the lower 48 states) (2001 data).		Since 1945 land characterized by development has increased (2002 Census Bureau data).
	Data are not adequate for national reporting on the amount of land area converted between broad categories ("natural" lands, cropland, developed land).		
	Data are not adequate to report on changes in area of critical ecosystem subtypes.		
Pattern of "Natural" Landscapes, p. 33	Twenty-three percent of total land cover in the lower 48 states is in a "core natural" landscape pattern (natural lands surrounded by 240 acres of other "natural" lands).		Data are not adequate for national reporting on changes in the composition of land surrounding "natural" lands.

CHEMICAL AND PHYSICAL CHARACTERISTICS

Movement of Nitrogen, p. 36	Most of the watersheds with the most nitrogen delivered to streams and rivers are within the Mississippi River basin, which includes more than 40% of the land area of the lower 48 states.		The area of land area delivering low nitrogen yields (600 pounds N per square mile per year or less) was greater in 2001–2005, than in 1996–2000.
	The Mississippi, Columbia, and Susquehanna Rivers combined discharge approximately one million tons of nitrogen (in the form of nitrate) into coastal waters, the vast majority from the Mississippi (2002 data).		Since 1955, N discharge (in the form of nitrate) from the Mississippi River has increased.
			Since 1983, N discharge (in the form of nitrate) from the Mississippi has fluctuated, with discharges lower than 1983 in all years but 1993.
			There has been no significant change in N discharge (in the form of nitrate) from the Columbia and Susquehanna Rivers since the mid-1970s.
	Data are not adequate for national reporting on the deposition of nitrogen on coastal waters.		

Indicators	What Do the Most Recent Data Show?	How Have Data Values Changed over Time?

CHEMICAL AND PHYSICAL CHARACTERISTICS (CONTINUED)

Carbon Storage, p. 38

Forests: Forests (excluding soils) gained nearly 150 million metric tons of carbon per year from 1995 to 2005. About twice as many forest acres are gaining carbon (62%) as are losing carbon (32%) (1995–2005 data).

Data are not adequate for national reporting on changes in carbon stored by forests or changes in carbon stored per unit of land area for more than one time reference (1995–2005).

Data are not adequate for national reporting on the carbon stored in forest soils.

Croplands: Cropland soils gained an average of 16.5 million tons of carbon per year during the 1990s. Almost half of cropland acres (45%) are gaining soil carbon, 13% are losing soil carbon, and 42% have only minimal change (1990–1999 data).

 Cropland soils stored 5 million more tons of carbon per year during the 1990s than during the 1980s. More cropland acres gained soil carbon in the 1990s (45%) than in the 1980s (35%); more cropland acres lost soil carbon in the 1990s (13%) than in the 1980s (9%).

Grasslands and Shrublands: Soils on private grasslands and shrublands gained 1.6 million tons of carbon per year during the 1990s. 9% of private grass/shrub acres are gaining soil carbon, 6% are losing soil carbon, and 85% have only minimal change (1990–1999 data).

 Grassland–shrubland soils on private lands stored 1.6 million more tons of carbon per year during the 1990s than during the 1980s.

Grasslands/Shrublands: Data are not adequate for national reporting on carbon storage in soils of public grasslands and shrublands and above- or below-ground biomass in all grasslands and shrublands.

Fresh Waters: Data are not adequate for national reporting on carbon storage in freshwater systems.

Coasts and Oceans: Data are not adequate for national reporting on carbon storage in ocean waters and sediments.

Urban and Suburban Landscapes: Data are not adequate for national reporting on carbon storage in urban and suburban areas.

Atmosphere: Carbon dioxide has increased by over 36% (2006 index value of 1.36) and methane has increased by over 160% (2005 index value of 2.61), relative to average preindustrial concentrations.

 Since 1950, carbon dioxide and methane concentrations have increased by about 20% and 55%, respectively.

Chemical Contamination, p. 42

Water, Sediments, and Fish: At least one contaminant was detected in about 74% of groundwater wells tested (1993–2001 data); 99% of streams, 97% of stream sediments and 82% of freshwater fish tested (1992–2001 data); 78% of estuary sediments and all saltwater fish tested (1998–2002 data).

Data are not adequate for national reporting on changes in contaminants *detected* in water, sediments, and fish.

Data are not adequate for national reporting on contaminants in plant tissues and animals other than fish.

Benchmark values are not available to determine the number of contaminants exceeding aquatic life benchmarks in saltwater fish.

At least one contaminant exceeded aquatic life benchmarks in 54% of streams, 94% of streambed sediments, and 77% of freshwater fish tested (1992–2001 data); 59% of estuary sediments tested (1998–2002 data).

Data are not adequate for national reporting on changes in contaminants exceeding benchmarks to protect aquatic life in water, sediment, and fish.

Benchmark values are not available to determine the number of contaminants exceeding human health benchmarks in freshwater fish

 = significant decrease    =significant increase   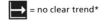 = no clear trend*    = insufficient data for trend analysis

= Data not available for adequate reporting.

* may be due to little numerical change in the data or large numerical fluctuations in data resulting in no single trend

Continued

Indicators	What Do the Most Recent Data Show?	How Have Data Values Changed over Time?

CHEMICAL AND PHYSICAL CHARACTERISTICS (CONTINUED)

Chemical Contamination (cont.), p. 42	**At least one contaminant exceeded human health benchmarks** in 33% of groundwater wells tested (1993–2001 data); 20% of streams tested (1992–2001 data); 33% of saltwater fish tested (1998–2002 data).	Data are not adequate for national reporting on changes in contaminants exceeding benchmarks to protect human health in water, sediment, and fish.
	Outdoor Air: Ozone index (SUM06) values were below 10 (relatively low total exposure) for 34% of the area of the lower 48 states; for 4% of the U.S., index values were above 30 (relatively high total exposure) (2005 data).	Since 1994 there has been no significant change in ground-level ozone index values.
	28% of urban sites had fine particulate matter concentrations of 15 micrograms per cubic meter or above (2005 data).	Since 2000, the percentage of sites with fine particulate matter concentrations above 20 micrograms per cubic meter dropped from 2.9% to 0.3%.
	Data are not adequate for reporting nationally on combined urban and rural measurements of fine particulate matter concentrations	
Change in Stream Flows, p. 47	A larger proportion of streams showed decreases in high flow than increases in high flow compared to the baseline period of 1941–1960 (2002–2006 data).	Since 1961–1965, the percentage of streams that have lower (>30%) high flows than the baseline period has increased.
	A larger proportion of streams showed increases in low flow than decreases in low flow compared to a baseline period of 1941–1960 (2002–2006 data).	Since 1961–1965, the percentage of streams that have higher (>30%) low flows than the baseline period has increased.
	A larger proportion of streams show decreases in the variability of flow than increases in the variability of flow compared to a baseline period of 1940–1960 (2002–2006 data).	Since 1961–1965, the percentage of streams that have lower (>30%) variability in flow than the baseline period has increased.
		Since 1961–1965, the percentage of streams that have higher (>30%) variability in flow than the baseline period has decreased.

BIOLOGICAL COMPONENTS

At-Risk Native Species, p. 50	About one-third of terrestrial and freshwater plant and animal species are considered to be at-risk of extinction (2006 data).	Data are not adequate for national reporting on changes in the number of at-risk species.
	28% of at-risk native vertebrate animal species have declining populations, 23% have stable populations, and 1% have increasing populations (2006 data).	Data are not adequate for national reporting on changes in population trends in at-risk vertebrate animals.
	Data are not adequate for national reporting on population trends in at-risk native invertebrate animals and at-risk native plants.	
	Data are not adequate for national reporting on the status or population trends of native marine plant and animal species.	
Established Non-native Species, p. 52	Data are not adequate for national reporting on the number of new non-native species that become established over time; the area with different numbers of established non-native species; and the area with different proportions of established non-native species, as a percentage of total species.	
Native Species Composition, p. 53	Indicator Development Needed	

Indicators	What Do the Most Recent Data Show?	How Have Data Values Changed over Time?

BIOLOGICAL COMPONENTS (CONTINUED)

Plant Growth Index, p. 54	For all ecosystem types, most of the area had index values similar to the long-term average (2003 data).	Since 1982, the area of grasslands with higher than average plant growth index values has increased.
		Since 1982, the area of croplands with higher than average plant growth index values has increased.
		Since 1982, there has been no significant change in the area of shrublands with plant growth index values above or below the long-term average.
		Since 1982, there has been no significant change in the area of forests with plant growth index values above or below the long-term average.

Data are not adequate for reporting on the plant growth index value in fresh waters, estuaries and open ocean waters.

GOODS AND SERVICES

Production of Food and Fiber and Water Withdrawals, p. 56	Since 1996, at a national level, harvest of forest products, freshwater withdrawals, and marine fish landings have not kept pace with U.S. population growth. Only the production of agricultural products has grown at a rate exceeding U.S. population growth.	Since 1950, agricultural production has increased.
		Since 1978, there has been no clear up or down trend in marine fish landings.
		Since 1952, the harvest of forest products has increased.
		Since 1960, total freshwater withdrawals have increased.
Outdoor Recreation, p. 58	U.S. adults participate in outdoor recreational activities 58 billion times per year (2003–2005 data).	Since 1994–1995 total participation in outdoor recreational activities has grown, however more years of data are needed to determine whether or not this increase is significant.

Data are not adequate for national reporting on running and jogging, on the distinction between freshwater and saltwater activities, or on youth participation in recreational activities.

| Natural Ecosystem Services, p. 60 | Indicator Development Needed | |

 = significant decrease   =significant increase   = no clear trend*   = insufficient data for trend analysis

= Data not available for adequate reporting.

* may be due to little numerical change in the data or large numerical fluctuations in data resulting in no single trend

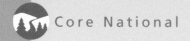
EXTENT AND PATTERN	CHEMICAL AND PHYSICAL	BIOLOGICAL COMPONENTS	GOODS AND SERVICES
Extent	Nutrients, Carbon, and Oxygen	Plants and Animals	Food, Fiber, and Water
Pattern	Chemical Contamination	Communities	Recreation and Other Services
	Physical	Ecological Productivity	

Ecosystem Extent

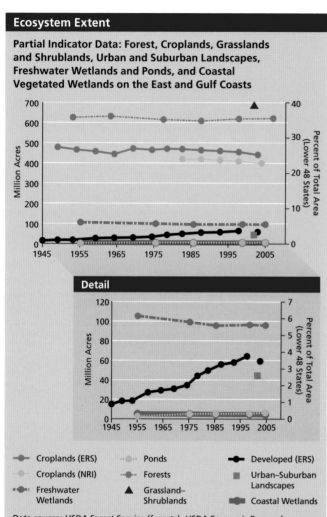

Ecosystem Extent

Partial Indicator Data: Forest, Croplands, Grasslands and Shrublands, Urban and Suburban Landscapes, Freshwater Wetlands and Ponds, and Coastal Vegetated Wetlands on the East and Gulf Coasts

Detail

- Croplands (ERS)
- Croplands (NRI)
- Freshwater Wetlands
- Ponds
- Forests
- Grassland–Shrublands
- Developed (ERS)
- Urban–Suburban Landscapes
- Coastal Wetlands

Data source: USDA Forest Service (forests), USDA Economic Research Service (croplands, developed), Multi-Resolution Land Characterization (MRLC) Consortium and ESRI (road map used in analysis of urban–suburban landscapes); analysis by the U.S. Environmental Protection Agency and the U.S. Forest Service (grasslands and shrublands, urban and suburban landscapes), and the U.S. Fish and Wildlife Service National Wetlands Inventory (freshwater wetlands and ponds). Coverage: lower 48 states. Note: Data presented here are from multiple sources; they do not add up to 100% of the U.S. land area.

Why Is the Area of Different Ecosystem Types Important? The nationwide extent of a particular ecosystem type, like forests or farmlands, both describes a basic characteristic of the overall landscape and relates to the total quantity of goods and services produced by that ecosystem type. Changes in extent are a result of conversions between ecosystem types, such as from grasslands to forests or from forests to farmlands. The extent of different ecosystem types may change because of shifts in climate, land use, or natural patterns of succession. This indicator does not report on the composition or habitat quality of ecosystems (see Pattern of "Natural" Landscapes, p. 33). In addition to its intrinsic value, extent can be used to estimate other properties of ecosystems, such as the percentage of forest subject to different types of management.

What Does This Indicator Report?

- The area of the six major ecosystem types addressed in this report (coasts and oceans, farmlands, forests, fresh waters, grassland and shrublands, and urban and suburban landscapes—see definitions, p. 31); for farmlands, the area of croplands is reported (see also The Farmland Landscape, p. 103).

- When data become available, the amount of land area converted between broad categories: "natural" lands (forest, grasslands, shrublands, and wetlands), croplands, and developed lands.

- The change in area of both important ecosystem subtypes, such as wetlands, and—when data become available—rare community types, such as Everglades Wet Prairie and West Gulf Coastal Plain Beech–Magnolia Forest.

Ecosystem Extent *(continued)*

U.S. Land Cover and Ocean Depth

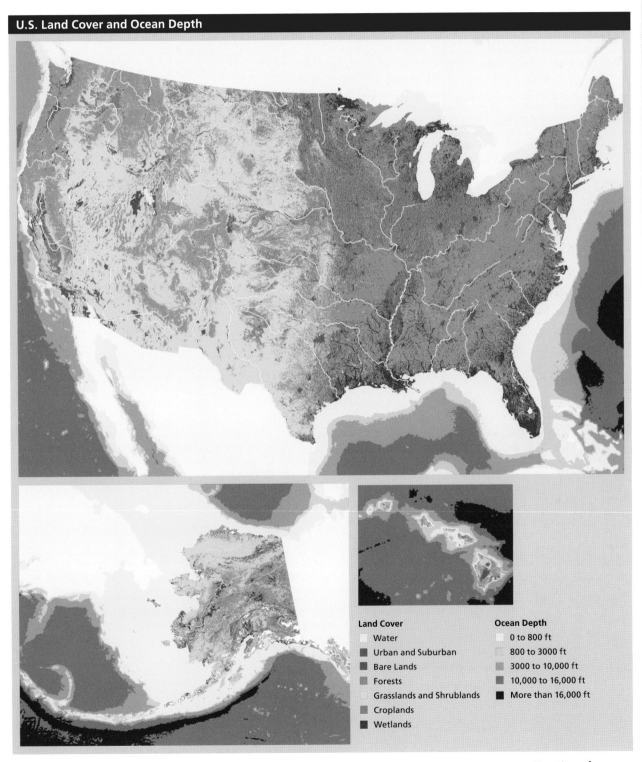

Land Cover
- Water
- Urban and Suburban
- Bare Lands
- Forests
- Grasslands and Shrublands
- Croplands
- Wetlands

Ocean Depth
- 0 to 800 ft
- 800 to 3000 ft
- 3000 to 10,000 ft
- 10,000 to 16,000 ft
- More than 16,000 ft

Continued

EXTENT AND PATTERN	CHEMICAL AND PHYSICAL	BIOLOGICAL COMPONENTS	GOODS AND SERVICES
Extent	Nutrients, Carbon, and Oxygen	Plants and Animals	Food, Fiber, and Water
Pattern	Chemical Contamination	Communities	Recreation and Other Services
	Physical	Ecological Productivity	

Ecosystem Extent *(continued)*

Ecosystem Extent

Data Gap

Data are not adequate for national reporting on

- **The area of wetlands along the Pacific Coast and the area of seagrass/submerged vegetation, shellfish beds and coral reefs along the entire coast**
- **The area of lakes**
- **The amount of land area converted between broad categories ("natural" lands, cropland, developed land)**
- **The area of rare ecosystem subtypes**

What Do the Data Show?

Coasts and Oceans

- Since the mid-1950s, the acreage of coastal vegetated wetlands on the Atlantic and Gulf coasts has declined by about 9%. In 2004, coastal wetlands covered about 4.6 million acres.

Croplands

- Cropland area, while fluctuating somewhat historically, has decreased significantly since 1982. Current estimates from two USDA sources [National Resources Inventory (NRI) and Economic Research Service (ERS)] that utilize different methodologies vary in their estimates of current cropland extent. The NRI estimate of about 400 million acres, or about 23% of the land area of the lower 48 states (2003 data), is the most consistent with the description of croplands used in this report (see Total Cropland, p. 102).

Forests

- Since 1953, total forest area has not changed significantly. In 2006, forests covered 36% of the land area of the lower 48 states, or about 621 million acres. When Alaskan forests are included, total forest area increases to about three-quarters of a billion acres (see Forest Area and Ownership, p. 132).

Fresh Waters

- The area of freshwater wetlands has decreased by 9% since 1955. In 2004, there were 96 million acres of wetlands (not including ponds—see below) in the lower 48 states, or about 6% of total land area.
- The area of ponds (both man-made and naturally occurring) has increased steadily since 1955, reaching 6.2 million acres in 2004, an increase of about three-quarters of a million acres since 1998.

Grasslands and Shrublands

- Grasslands and shrublands occupied about 40% of the land area of the lower 48 states in 2001, or nearly 700 million acres. Note that pastures, included in the Area of Grasslands and Shrublands (p. 202), are excluded here because the cropland area estimates (see above) include the area of many pastures.

Urban and Suburban Landscapes

- The area characterized by development ("urban and suburban landscapes") in 2001 is estimated, using satellite-derived data on land cover, at about 45 million acres, or 2.6% of the area of the lower 48 states.
- Using a very different and less restrictive Census-based definition, ERS reports an increase in "developed" land from 15 million acres in 1945 to almost 60 million acres in 2002. See the technical note for information on classification changes in the Census definition of developed land that causes a discontinuity in the ERS developed land trend. (Also see Area and Composition of Urban and Suburban Landscapes, p. 230.)

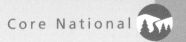
EXTENT AND PATTERN	CHEMICAL AND PHYSICAL	BIOLOGICAL COMPONENTS	GOODS AND SERVICES
Extent	Nutrients, Carbon, and Oxygen	Plants and Animals	Food, Fiber, and Water
Pattern	Chemical Contamination	Communities	Recreation and Other Services
	Physical	Ecological Productivity	

Ecosystem Extent *(continued)*

Some Definitions

- **Ecosystems** are interdependent webs of organisms and the physically defined environments they exist in. Ecosystems may range in scale from the size of a pond or smaller, to a broad region such as the Gulf of Maine. For this report, the nation's lands and waters are divided into six broad ecosystem types (coasts and oceans, farmlands, forests, fresh waters, grasslands and shrublands, and urban and suburban landscapes) based on dominant vegetation or physical and chemical characteristics.
- **Coasts and oceans** include all waters in the U.S. Economic Exclusion Zone (EEZ), which extends 200 miles from the coastline (an area of over 3 million square miles. This indicator focuses on the area covered by coastal wetlands, coral reefs, and shellfish and seagrass beds (see Coastal Living Habitats, p. 72). Note that the map shows ocean depth to distinguish shallow coastal waters from the deep ocean; the area of the EEZ changes only when territory is acquired or international law changes.
- **Farmlands** are represented in this indicator by the total area of cropland, including pasture and acreage in set-aside programs such as the Conservation Reserve Program (this land is not permanently taken out of production). Elsewhere in this report we report on the "farmland landscape," which includes both croplands and intermingled and adjacent forests, grasslands and shrublands, wetlands, and developed areas (see p. 103).
- **Forests** are lands—at least one acre in size—that have more than 10% tree cover.
- **Freshwater ecosystems** include wetlands, ponds, lakes, reservoirs, streams, and rivers (the length of small, medium, and large streams and rivers is reported in Extent of Freshwater Ecosystems, p. 170). Wetlands occur in many ecosystem types, so their area is often also counted as part of the area of forests, grassland and shrublands, farmlands, and urban and suburban areas
- **Grasslands and shrublands** include lands ranging from coastal meadows in the Southeast to tundra in Alaska. Those in the West are often called rangelands because of their historic association with cattle grazing.
- **Urban and suburban landscapes** are defined in this report as land that is surrounded by sufficient amounts of developed land based on satellite imagery. Parcels of land were classified as urban–suburban landscapes if a square area (270 acres) surrounding the parcel was composed of at least 60% developed land cover. Because this definition is based on actual land cover, rather than on an indirect estimate of developed land area based on population density, the satellite-based definition of urban and suburban landscapes appears to be more appropriate for this report and is used as the basis for the urban and suburban indicators (see Area and Composition of Urban and Suburban Landscapes, p. 230). Because multiple time points of land cover data are not available, the area of "developed" land estimated by ERS, which is based upon the Census Bureau definition of urban areas, is included.
- **"Natural" lands** include forests, grasslands, shrublands, wetlands, other fresh waters, and coastal waters. In general, the term "natural" lands is applied to those lands that are not highly managed. However, a range of management conditions may be included in the "natural" category because classification of "natural" lands relies primarily on satellite-based *land cover* maps, not on *land use*. For example, forests with similar land cover patterns are considered equally "natural," regardless of their management regimes.

Why Can't This Entire Indicator Be Reported at This Time? Data for coral reefs and seagrasses and other "submerged aquatic vegetation" are available for many areas, but these data have not been synthesized to produce national estimates. Data on coastal vegetated wetlands are available only for the East (Maine to Florida) and Gulf coasts (see Coastal Living Habitats, p. 72). Data are not adequate for national reporting on the area of lakes.

Forthcoming data will provide estimates for the conversion of land between cropland, "natural," and developed land. However, the land cover maps from the two available time points (1992 and 2001) cannot now be compared.

Data necessary to report on the area of rare community types may become available soon (see technical note), although consistent estimates over time will be needed to enable reporting on trends.

Continued

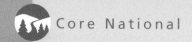
EXTENT AND PATTERN	CHEMICAL AND PHYSICAL	BIOLOGICAL COMPONENTS	GOODS AND SERVICES
Extent	Nutrients, Carbon, and Oxygen	Plants and Animals	Food, Fiber, and Water
Pattern	Chemical Contamination	Communities	Recreation and Other Services
	Physical	Ecological Productivity	

Ecosystem Extent *(continued)*

What Is Not Shown by This Indicator? Currently, this indicator reports only land cover, not land use. As a result, the indicator does not distinguish between, for example, more "natural" grasslands and heavily grazed rangeland, or a multiaged forest and a tree farm or plantation. The addition of land use information will greatly improve our understanding of ecosystem extent, because land use is a key factor in understanding ecological functioning. For example, a tree plantation that is optimized to produce wood fiber may lack the diversity of a more "natural" forest; indicators in the forest chapter are designed to provide information on how well forests are functioning ecologically, even though only limited land use data are available (At-Risk Native Forest Species, p. 144; Forest Community Types with Significantly Reduced Area, p. 153).

The definition of "urban and suburban landscapes" used here is appropriate for this ecosystem-focused report but may not be appropriate in other contexts. Even though a relatively small percentage of the country is covered by homes, buildings, and roads, considerably more land is directly influenced by this development. The "developed" category in this indicator excludes development in outlying, rural areas (often termed "exurban"). Other indicators in this report address development beyond "urban and suburban landscapes" (see Housing Density Change in Low-Density Suburban and Rural Areas, p. 234; Proximity of Croplands to Residences, p. 105).

Understanding the Data Before European settlement, the area of the lower 48 states was split nearly evenly between forest and grassland–shrubland ecosystems. Wetlands, many of which are integral parts of these ecosystems, occupied more than twice their current area (note that, because of data limitations, the large land area of Alaska is not currently included in the graphics or this discussion).

People have converted hundreds of millions of acres of these lands for agriculture, settlement, and other purposes, creating new types of ecosystems—notably farmlands and urban–suburban landscapes. Land conversions continue today and will affect trends in ecosystem extent as well as future data on the transition of land area between ecosystem types.

Not all land conversions are permanent, but not all are equally reversible. Abandoned farmlands in New England often return to forest cover, but in other situations, soil loss through erosion or depletion of fertility may cause regrowth to take centuries or may ultimately lead to a very different type of "natural" land cover.

This indicator also describes the area of rare ecosystem types, because loss of these may reduce the habitat for specially adapted species, increasing the likelihood of their extinction.

The technical note for this indicator is on page 276.

EXTENT AND PATTERN	CHEMICAL AND PHYSICAL	BIOLOGICAL COMPONENTS	GOODS AND SERVICES
Extent	Nutrients, Carbon, and Oxygen	Plants and Animals	Food, Fiber, and Water
Pattern	Chemical Contamination	Communities	Recreation and Other Services
	Physical	Ecological Productivity	

Pattern of "Natural" Landscapes

Why Are Patterns of "Natural" Landscapes Important? Changes in the broad patterns that describe the structure of ecosystems can affect many aspects of the functioning of these ecosystems. Some species can tolerate only large, unbroken habitats that are well buffered from substantial human presence; others easily adapt to modified surroundings. Development, including roads, or agricultural land in a region or watershed is often associated with increases in nutrients, contaminants, siltation, and physical changes to streams and other water bodies. Alterations to landscape pattern can have chemical and physical effects on its surroundings, such as increases in temperature and drier soils at the boundary between "natural" and developed lands. In addition, many people enjoy the aesthetic qualities of landscapes, such as those characterized by rocky cliffs along coastlines, meadows with meandering streams, or farm fields interspersed with woodlots.

What Does This Indicator Report?
"Natural" lands (forest, grassland, shrubland, wetlands, lakes, and coastal waters; see definition on p. 35) are placed into one of several categories, depending on the composition of their surroundings. Satellite imagery is used to create a land cover map that is then broken up into more than 8 billion ~1/4-acre-square parcels (or pixels) based on cover type. Specifically, this indicator reports

- The composition of the 240 acres surrounding each "natural" parcel, reported in terms of the relative proportions of three land cover types: "natural," cropland, or development
- The size and abundance of patches made up of "core natural" parcels (those having 100% "natural" surroundings)

Continued

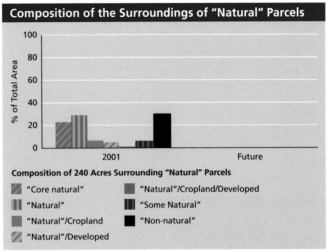

Composition of the Surroundings of "Natural" Parcels

Composition of 240 Acres Surrounding "Natural" Parcels

- "Core natural"
- "Natural"
- "Natural"/Cropland
- "Natural"/Developed
- "Natural"/Cropland/Developed
- "Some Natural"
- "Non-natural"

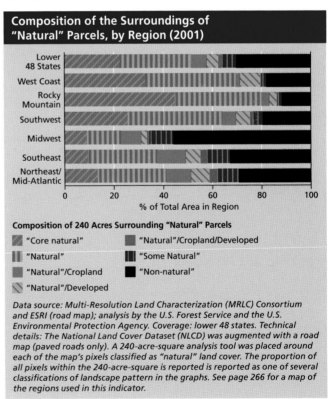

Composition of the Surroundings of "Natural" Parcels, by Region (2001)

Composition of 240 Acres Surrounding "Natural" Parcels

- "Core natural"
- "Natural"
- "Natural"/Cropland
- "Natural"/Developed
- "Natural"/Cropland/Developed
- "Some Natural"
- "Non-natural"

Data source: Multi-Resolution Land Characterization (MRLC) Consortium and ESRI (road map); analysis by the U.S. Forest Service and the U.S. Environmental Protection Agency. Coverage: lower 48 states. Technical details: The National Land Cover Dataset (NLCD) was augmented with a road map (paved roads only). A 240-acre-square analysis tool was placed around each of the map's pixels classified as "natural" land cover. The proportion of all pixels within the 240-acre-square is reported as one of several classifications of landscape pattern in the graphs. See page 266 for a map of the regions used in this indicator.

Pattern of "Natural" Landscapes (continued)

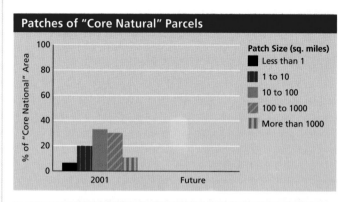

Patches of "Core Natural" Parcels

Patch Size (sq. miles)
- Less than 1
- 1 to 10
- 10 to 100
- 100 to 1000
- More than 1000

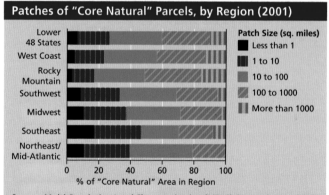

Patches of "Core Natural" Parcels, by Region (2001)

Patch Size (sq. miles)
- Less than 1
- 1 to 10
- 10 to 100
- 100 to 1000
- More than 1000

Source: Multi-Resolution Land Characterization (MRLC) Consortium and ESRI (road map); analysis by the U.S. Forest Service and the U.S. Environmental Protection Agency. Coverage: lower 48 states. Technical details: See above; in addition, those pixels with 100% "natural" surroundings were formed into patches of touching pixels, the size of which are reported in the graphs. Note: Current technical limitations required that patches be "cut" by state boundaries, meaning that these data represent minimum patch sizes. We do not know how this analysis limitation affected the data.

What Do the Data Show? Based on 2001 land cover data for the lower 48 states:

- Twenty-three percent of the total area was "core natural," based on the composition of its surroundings (see definitions). The percentage of "core national" lands was higher in Western regions; overall, "core national" ranged from a high of 45% in the Rocky Mountain region to a low of 9% in the Midwest region.

- Thirty percent of the total area had a "natural" landscape pattern dominated by "natural" lands with some croplands and/or developed lands mixed in. Regional patterns were similar to that for "core natural."

- About 7% of the total area had a "natural"/ cropland landscape pattern that includes some cropland and minimal amounts of developed lands. This pattern was evident in 8–12% of the East and Midwest regions, while less than 2% of lands in the West Coast region had this landscape pattern.

- About 5% of the total area had a "natural"/ development pattern. For most regions, 5–8% of land area had this pattern. The Rocky Mountain and Midwest regions had only 2–3% of their area with this pattern.

- Very little of the total area (about 1%) had a "natural"/cropland/developed landscape pattern.

- "Core natural" parcels were most often (one-third of the time) found in patches of 10–100 square miles; 11% of "core natural" parcels were in patches of at least 1000 square miles.

- The Rocky Mountain region had the highest proportion (16%) of "core natural" in patches larger than 1000 square miles and the lowest proportion (about 50%) in patches smaller than 100 square miles.

- The Northeast/Mid-Atlantic region had the highest proportion (about 80%) of "core natural" in patches smaller than 100 square miles and no patches larger than 1000 square miles.

What Is Not Shown by This Indicator? The patterns described here are based on *land cover* and not on *land use*. As in the previous indicator, Ecosystem Extent (p. 28), the underlying data do not permit a distinction between a more natural forest and an intensively managed tree farm, or a more natural prairie and a heavily grazed rangeland. This and other indicators would be greatly enhanced in the future if the underlying data could be enriched with information on land use. Also, because only a single time point of data can be shown at this time (land cover data from 1992 could not be compared to these more recent data when these analyses were performed), it is not possible to characterize potential changes in patterns.

EXTENT AND PATTERN	CHEMICAL AND PHYSICAL	BIOLOGICAL COMPONENTS	GOODS AND SERVICES
Extent	Nutrients, Carbon, and Oxygen	Plants and Animals	Food, Fiber, and Water
Pattern	Chemical Contamination	Communities	Recreation and Other Services
	Physical	Ecological Productivity	

Pattern of "Natural" Landscapes *(continued)*

Understanding the Data About 68% of the land area of the lower 48 states is "natural" land cover. This indicator describes the pattern of the landscape surrounding small parcels of this "natural" land cover. The regions reported here differ in area, meaning that a similar proportion of a particular pattern type within two regions may represent very different acreages, so landscape patterns should be evaluated together with data on the extent of the various land cover types involved.

Note that this report includes a related indicator for coastal areas (see p. 74)

The technical note for this indicator is on page 277.

Some Definitions

- **"Natural" Land Cover** includes forests, grasslands, shrublands, wetlands, other fresh waters, and coastal waters. In general, the term "natural" lands is applied to those lands that are not highly managed. However, a range of management conditions may be included in the "natural" category because classification of "natural" lands relies primarily on satellite-based land cover maps, not on land use. For example, forests with similar land cover patterns are considered equally "natural," regardless of their management regimes.
- **"Core Natural"** is a landscape pattern attributed to a single small parcel (~1/4 acre) of "natural" land cover whose surrounding 240 acres is composed solely of other "natural" parcels.
- **"Natural" Landscape Pattern** is attributed to a small parcel of "natural" land cover whose surrounding 240 acres has more than 80% other "natural" parcels with a mix of cropland and development, but with neither of these exceeding 10%.
- **"Natural"/Cropland** is a landscape pattern attributed to a small parcel of "natural" land cover whose surrounding 240 acres has more than 80% other "natural" parcels with more than 10% cropland but less than 10% development mixed in.
- **"Natural"/Developed** is a landscape pattern attributed to a small parcel of "natural" land whose surrounding 240 acres has more than 80% other "natural" parcels with more than 10% development but less than 10% cropland mixed in.
- **"Natural"/Cropland/Developed** is a landscape pattern attributed to a small parcel of "natural" land whose surrounding 240 acres has more than 60% other "natural" parcels with more than 10% development and more than 10% cropland mixed in.
- **"Some Natural"** is a landscape pattern attributed to a small parcel of "natural" land whose surrounding 240 acres has at 60% or less other "natural" parcels, with the remainder made up of development and/or cropland.
- **"Non-natural"** is simply a small parcel whose land cover is either cropland or development—its surroundings are not evaluated.

EXTENT AND PATTERN	CHEMICAL AND PHYSICAL	BIOLOGICAL COMPONENTS	GOODS AND SERVICES
Extent	Nutrients, Carbon, and Oxygen	Plants and Animals	Food, Fiber, and Water
Pattern	Chemical Contamination	Communities	Recreation and Other Services
	Physical	Ecological Productivity	

The Movement of Nitrogen

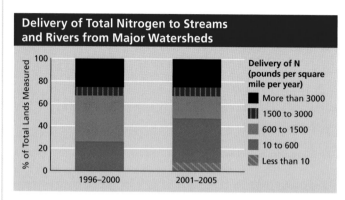

Delivery of Total Nitrogen to Streams and Rivers from Major Watersheds

Delivery of N (pounds per square mile per year)

- More than 3000
- 1500 to 3000
- 600 to 1500
- 10 to 600
- Less than 10

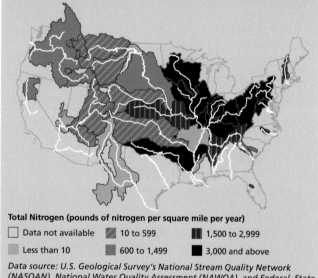

Delivery of Total Nitrogen to Streams and Rivers from Major Watersheds (2001–2005)

Total Nitrogen (pounds of nitrogen per square mile per year)

- Data not available
- Less than 10
- 10 to 599
- 600 to 1,499
- 1,500 to 2,999
- 3,000 and above

Data source: U.S. Geological Survey's National Stream Quality Network (NASQAN), National Water Quality Assessment (NAWQA), and Federal–State Cooperative Program. Coverage: areas of the lower 48 states with major river basins and available data. Technical details: The delivery of nitrogen to streams and rivers is averaged across the area of the watershed and reported as pounds of nitrogen per square mile.

Why Is the Movement of Nitrogen to Coastal Waters Important? Nitrogen is an important plant nutrient and is essential to all life. Nitrogen is an abundant component of the earth's atmosphere, but it is unavailable to most life in gaseous form. In order to be used by plants and other organisms, nitrogen gas must be "fixed," or converted to a "reactive" form, that plants can use, such as nitrate. Nitrogen is fixed and accumulates in ecosystems through natural processes, such as the growth of nitrogen-fixing plants like clover and soybeans. However, human activity has greatly increased the amount of reactive nitrogen added to ecosystems. The largest human-caused input of nitrogen to ecosystems comes from the conversion of atmospheric nitrogen gas into fertilizers. Additional reactive nitrogen gas is produced by the combustion of fossil fuels. Reactive nitrogen from all these sources can ultimately enter streams and rivers. Excess nitrogen transported to coastal waters by rivers can lead to low oxygen conditions, threaten fish and animal life, and degrade coastal water quality.

What Does This Indicator Report?

- For major watersheds, the amount of nitrogen that enters rivers and streams through discharges, runoff, and other sources
- For several major rivers, the input of nitrate to coastal waters (nitrate is often the most abundant form of nitrogen that is readily usable by aquatic plants and algae)
- When data become available, atmospheric deposition of nitrogen on coastal waters

What Do The Data Show?

- Most of the watersheds with the most nitrogen delivered to streams and rivers are within the Mississippi River basin, which covers more than 40% of the land area of the lower 48 states.
- For 21% of the land area measured, the amount of nitrogen moving from the land to streams dropped from more than 600 pounds per square mile per year in 1996–2000 to less than 600 pounds per square mile per year in 2001–2005. More years of data will be needed in order to establish whether this is a downward trend or simply variability between years.
- The Mississippi, Susquehanna, and Columbia combined discharged approximately 1 million tons of nitrogen in the form of nitrate to coastal waters in 2002; the Mississippi alone accounted for more than 90% of the total.

EXTENT AND PATTERN	CHEMICAL AND PHYSICAL	BIOLOGICAL COMPONENTS	GOODS AND SERVICES
Extent	Nutrients, Carbon, and Oxygen	Plants and Animals	Food, Fiber, and Water
Pattern	Chemical Contamination	Communities	Recreation and Other Services
	Physical	Ecological Productivity	

The Movement of Nitrogen *(continued)*

- Between 1955 and 2004 the discharge of nitrate from the Mississippi doubled; since 1983, there has not been a significant trend in discharge, although additional years of data may reveal a statistically significant downward trend in discharge.
- There has been no clear upward or downward trend in nitrate input to the coast from the Susquehanna and Columbia rivers since records were first taken in the mid-1970s.

Why Can't This Entire Indicator Be Reported at This Time? A complete picture of nitrogen loading to coastal waters would account for all sources, including nitrogen deposited from the atmosphere to land and water surfaces. The data presented here include atmospheric nitrogen that enters coastal waters after being deposited on terrestrial and freshwater systems, but atmospheric nitrogen that is deposited directly onto coastal water surfaces is not included. Direct atmospheric deposition may represent an important source of nitrogen in coastal systems, but data are not available for reporting on the nation's coastal waters.

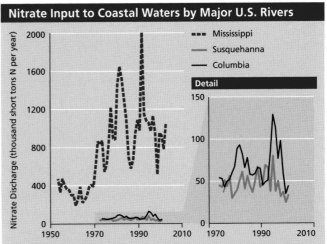

Nitrate Input to Coastal Waters by Major U.S. Rivers

- - - Mississippi
— Susquehanna
— Columbia

Data Source: U.S. Geological Survey's National Stream Quality Network (NASQAN), National Water Quality Assessment (NAWQA), and Federal–State Cooperative Program. Coverage: major rivers with available data. Note that the 2002 Report included data for the St. Lawrence River, but monitoring of the St. Lawrence has since been discontinued.

Movement of Nitrogen

Data Gap

Data are not adequate for national reporting on atmospheric deposition of nitrogen on coastal waters.

Understanding the Data Nitrogen transported from the land to waterways, and ultimately to the ocean, can stimulate plant growth in coastal waters. Excessive growth of algae can lead to hypoxic areas in coastal waters (hypoxia is a term for very low oxygen conditions in which most fish and other marine animals cannot survive). For more information on hypoxia in coastal waters, see Areas with Depleted Oxygen, p. 75.

A variety of human activities increase the availability of nitrogen on land and the subsequent movement of nitrogen from streams and rivers into coastal waters. Humans "fix" nonreactive nitrogen gas in the production of fertilizer. Direct discharge into streams and rivers occurs from sewage systems (due to both normal treatment plant discharges and "overflows" that occur during storms in those systems that are combined with storm drains) and industrial discharges, such as those that contain nitrogen-rich corrosion inhibitors. Indirect, or nonpoint, sources of nitrogen include runoff from fertilized cropland and lawns, failing septic systems, and malfunctioning facilities for storing animal manure. Years with higher than usual rainfall in a river basin will likely lead to higher than usual amounts of nitrogen being delivered to streams and rivers and ultimately coastal waters.

Atmospheric deposition is also a significant source of nitrogen in some ecosystems. Exhaust from engines and other combustion sources adds reactive forms of nitrogen to the air, where they contribute to the formation of smog and increased ground-level ozone. Nitrogen is also lost to the air as ammonia and nitrogen oxides from agricultural fields. Nitrogen in the air is transported and redeposited as ammonia gas, or combined with snow, rain, or dust and deposited either on land or directly in coastal waters.

Other indicators report on the amount of nitrate in streams or groundwater in farmlands (p. 107), forests (p. 140), grasslands and shrublands (p. 205), and urban and suburban areas (p. 238).

The technical note for this indicator is on page 277.

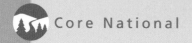
Core National

EXTENT AND PATTERN	CHEMICAL AND PHYSICAL	BIOLOGICAL COMPONENTS	GOODS AND SERVICES
Extent	Nutrients, Carbon, and Oxygen	Plants and Animals	Food, Fiber, and Water
Pattern	Chemical Contamination	Communities	Recreation and Other Services
	Physical	Ecological Productivity	

Carbon Storage

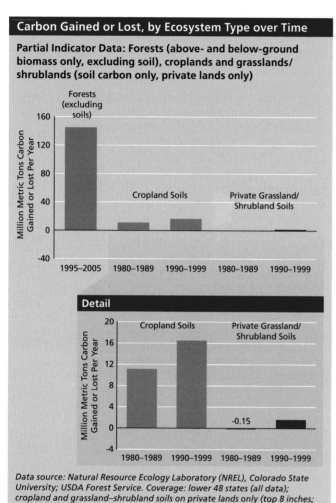

Carbon Gained or Lost, by Ecosystem Type over Time

Partial Indicator Data: Forests (above- and below-ground biomass only, excluding soil), croplands and grasslands/shrublands (soil carbon only, private lands only)

Data source: Natural Resource Ecology Laboratory (NREL), Colorado State University; USDA Forest Service. Coverage: lower 48 states (all data); cropland and grassland–shrubland soils on private lands only (top 8 inches; NREL data); above-ground forest carbon, both live and dead (Forest Service). See technical note for additional details. Unit conversion: 1 metric ton = 1.10 U.S. tons.

Why Is Carbon Storage by Ecosystems Important? The quantity of carbon stored in terrestrial and aquatic ecosystems influences their productive capacity and, hence, their ability to provide services such as soil fertility, water storage, and resistance to soil erosion. In the atmosphere, carbon dioxide and methane gases contribute to the greenhouse effect, while carbon stored in plants, soils, sediments, and the ocean does not. For this reason, carbon storage by ecosystems has become a focus in domestic and international negotiations as one of several strategies for the mitigation of climate change.

What Does This Indicator Report?
- The overall amount of carbon gained or lost over time by major ecosystem types
- The change in the amount of carbon stored per unit area of land or water (carbon density), by major ecosystem type
- Recent trends in the concentrations of major carbon-containing gases—carbon dioxide and methane—in the atmosphere compared to average preindustrial concentrations

Forests

What Do the Data Show about Forests?
- Overall, above- and below-ground biomass in the nation's forests (not including soils) gained nearly 150 million metric tons of carbon per year from 1995 to 2005, with about twice as many forest acres (about 60%) gaining carbon as losing carbon (about 30%) in above- and below-ground biomass.

- From 1995 to 2005, 62% of forest lands had annual increases in carbon density (in above- and below-ground biomass, not including soils) of more than 0.04 metric tons of carbon per acre; 6% of forest lands gained more than 0.8 metric tons of carbon per acre annually.

- More than 0.04 metric tons of carbon were lost per acre each year on 32% of forest acres, and 3% of forest acres had carbon losses greater than 0.8 metric tons per year.

- The remaining 6% of forest lands experienced minimal annual change (less than 0.04 metric tons per acre) in carbon density.

What Does This Indicator Not Show about Forests? Data for forest soils are not adequate for national reporting. Estimating forest soil carbon presents challenges because the amount of carbon varies with soil type (especially texture and drainage attributes), within soil type (regionally), and even by soil depth. Uncertainty in measurements of soil carbon hinders researchers' ability to estimate total changes in forest carbon storage. Understanding carbon

EXTENT AND PATTERN	CHEMICAL AND PHYSICAL	BIOLOGICAL COMPONENTS	GOODS AND SERVICES
Extent	Nutrients, Carbon, and Oxygen	Plants and Animals	Food, Fiber, and Water
Pattern	Chemical Contamination	Communities	Recreation and Other Services
	Physical	Ecological Productivity	

Carbon Storage *(continued)*

storage in soils is especially important because this is a large and dynamic pool that can rapidly lose carbon directly to the atmosphere when trees are removed from the land during logging operations or are otherwise disturbed, for example by wildfire or insect damage. Climate factors such as temperature and precipitation also affect carbon storage in soils.

Note that forest data reported here do not include carbon stored in wood products (such as structures and furniture) or carbon emissions related to the transportation and processing of wood products or burned biowaste. Estimates of carbon storage in forests of Alaska and Hawaii are not reported, because the survey from which data for this indicator were derived has not yet been expanded to these areas on a consistent basis.

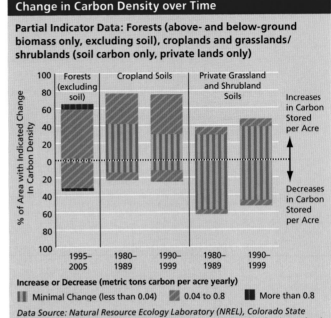

Change in Carbon Density over Time

Partial Indicator Data: Forests (above- and below-ground biomass only, excluding soil), croplands and grasslands/shrublands (soil carbon only, private lands only)

Increase or Decrease (metric tons carbon per acre yearly)

Minimal Change (less than 0.04)   0.04 to 0.8   More than 0.8

Data Source: Natural Resource Ecology Laboratory (NREL), Colorado State University; USDA Forest Service. Coverage: lower 48 states (all data); cropland and grassland–shrubland soils on private lands only (top 8 inches; NREL data); above-ground forest carbon, both live and dead (Forest Service). See technical note for additional details. Unit conversion: 1 metric ton = 1.10 U.S. tons.

Croplands

What Do the Data Show about Croplands?

- Overall, soils on the nation's croplands gained 11.1 million metric tons of carbon per year during the 1980s and 16.5 million metric tons of carbon per year during the 1990s. Some croplands gained carbon (35% in the 1980s and 45% in the 1990s), while others lost carbon (9% in the 1980s and 13% in the 1990s). The remainder had minimal change in carbon stocks.

- There were annual increases in carbon density of more than 0.04 metric tons of soil carbon per acre on 35% of croplands in the 1980s and on 45% of croplands in the 1990s. Additional years of data will be required to determine if this is part of a larger trend over time.

- More than 0.04 metric tons of soil carbon were lost per acre each year on 9% of croplands in the 1980s and on 13% of croplands in the 1990s.

What Does This Indicator Not Show about Croplands? These data are restricted to private croplands, but there are relatively few public croplands. Above-ground plant matter that is typically harvested each year is not included in this indicator component, although the soil carbon estimate does include a factor to account for the practice of returning crop residues to the soils through practices that reduce or eliminate plowing each year (low- or no-till) and other soil conservation measures. The data presented here are limited to the top 8 inches of soil and do not include roots.

Grasslands and Shrublands

What Do the Data Show about Private Grassland and Shrubland Soils?

- Overall, soils on the nation's private grasslands and shrublands lost 150 thousand metric tons of carbon per year in the 1980s and gained 1.6 million metric tons per year during the 1990s. Some private grasslands and shrublands gained carbon (about 9% in both the 1980s and 1990s), while others lost carbon (5% in the 1980s and 6% in the 1990s).

Continued

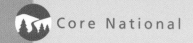
Carbon Storage *(continued)*

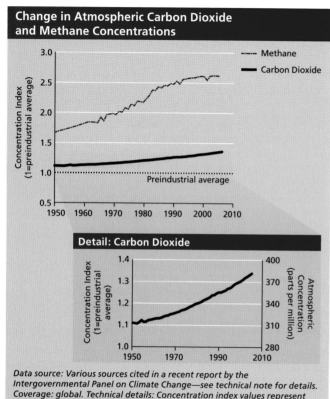

Change in Atmospheric Carbon Dioxide and Methane Concentrations

Data source: Various sources cited in a recent report by the Intergovernmental Panel on Climate Change—see technical note for details. Coverage: global. Technical details: Concentration index values represent annual measures from recent decades divided by a long-term preindustrial (AD 1000–1750) average concentration.

Carbon Storage

Data Gap

Data are not adequate for national reporting on the carbon stored in
- Forest soils
- Soils of public grasslands and shrublands
- Above- or below-ground biomass in all grasslands and shrublands
- Wetlands (including peatlands)
- Water and sediment in aquatic systems
- Urban and suburban areas

- In both the 1980s and 1990s, 0.04 metric tons of soil carbon or more were gained per acre each year on almost 9% of private grasslands and shrublands; about 85% of private grasslands and shrublands experienced minimal change in carbon density during this time period.

- There were annual decreases in carbon density of 0.04 metric tons of soil carbon or more per acre on 5% of private grasslands and shrublands in the 1980s and on 6% of private grasslands and shrublands in the 1990s.

What Does This Indicator Not Show about Grasslands and Shrublands? This indicator reports on private grasslands and shrublands, which account for approximately 60% of total grassland and shrubland area in the lower 48 states. Thus, the estimates shown here present an incomplete picture of carbon storage on the nation's grasslands and shrublands. Furthermore, the soil carbon estimates presented here are limited to the top eight inches of soil and do not include roots. Future estimates should include above- and below-ground plant matter as well; some estimates report that 5–30% of carbon grasslands and shrublands is contained in live plant matter.

What Do the Data Show about Carbon in the Atmosphere?

- In 2006, the global atmospheric concentration of carbon dioxide (381 parts per million) was 36% higher—an index value of 1.36—than the average concentration during preindustrial times (concentrations ranged from 274 to 284 parts per million from AD 1000 to 1750). Carbon dioxide concentrations have increased by 20% since the 1950s (see inset graph), when they were 11% above preindustrial concentrations.

- In 2005, the global atmospheric concentration of methane (1805 parts per billion) was 160% higher—an index value of 2.61—than the average preindustrial concentration (concentrations ranged from 644 to 723 parts per billion from AD 1000 to 1750). Methane concentrations have increased 55% since the 1950s, when they were 66% higher than preindustrial concentrations.

Why Can't This Entire Indicator Be Reported? When all data become available, this indicator will present a full picture of how much, and where, carbon is gained or lost by U.S. ecosystems. At this time, the data gaps mean that the "net" gain or loss of carbon cannot be adequately represented. No national-

EXTENT AND PATTERN	CHEMICAL AND PHYSICAL	BIOLOGICAL COMPONENTS	GOODS AND SERVICES
Extent	Nutrients, Carbon, and Oxygen	Plants and Animals	Food, Fiber, and Water
Pattern	Chemical Contamination	Communities	Recreation and Other Services
	Physical	Ecological Productivity	

Carbon Storage *(continued)*

scale carbon storage data are currently being collected on forest soils, public grasslands and shrublands, wetlands of all types (including peatlands, and coastal and freshwater wetlands), ocean waters and sediments, freshwater systems, or urban and suburban areas. Data for wetlands and peatlands, which are rich accumulations of partially decayed plant matter, are of particular interest for this indicator. Wetlands and peatlands are rich in stored carbon and are found in areas sensitive to rapid system changes, with the potential to store or release (to the atmosphere) a great deal of carbon.

Understanding the Data Carbon is an essential component of all organisms, and large quantities are stored above ground (in plants, live or dead trees, and organic debris), below ground (in soil organic matter, decaying plant material, and roots), in fresh waters and the oceans (dissolved, in organisms, in particles, and in sediments), and in the atmosphere. Carbon accumulates in ecosystems (through photosynthesis), where it contributes to a wide range of ecological services such as soil fertility, water storage, food and fiber production, and food and habitat for organisms. Where soils are rich in carbon, agriculture may require less irrigation and fertilizer application and watersheds may have less runoff, higher water quality and better recharge of groundwater.

Carbon is released primarily as carbon dioxide and methane to the atmosphere, where these gases trap solar energy. Although its atmospheric concentration is substantially lower, the heat-trapping capacity of methane is 20 times that of carbon dioxide, which has been central to climate change mitigation policy.

Concentrations of these gases were considerably lower during the time that most biological organisms and ecological communities evolved. Higher carbon dioxide levels are reportedly already leading to acidification of ocean waters and shell dissolution in marine organisms and may lead to increases in photosynthesis rates for some plants, although ecosystem-level responses will most likely be complex. Net increases in carbon storage by terrestrial and aquatic ecosystems remove carbon from the atmosphere and can help to offset current industrial and other carbon emissions, or counteract past emissions. U.S. carbon emissions from residential, commercial, industrial and transportation energy use were 1624 million metric tons in 2005.

Ecosystem types have characteristic carbon storage patterns. For example, forests, unlike grasslands, store a lot of carbon in above-ground biomass. There is also considerable variability in carbon levels within ecosystem types. For example, soil carbon stored in croplands can vary dramatically, depending on climate, native soil type, and management activities. Over time, carbon density (amount stored per acre) in ecosystems can change in response to land management practices, temperature and moisture conditions, and disturbances such as wildfires or pest outbreaks. The amount of carbon stored in major ecosystem types can change in response to changes in total area of different ecosystem types (see Ecosystem Extent, p. 28). For example, individual wetlands may increase in carbon density as plant residues accumulate in their low-oxygen sediments, while conversion of wetland areas to other ecosystem types, such as cropland or suburban areas, could result in a decrease in total carbon stored by wetlands nationally.

The increase in forest carbon storage (in above- and below-ground plant matter) from 1995 to 2005 is likely due to forest management practices that increase biomass on existing forest lands, and the regrowth of trees of previously cleared forest areas, since the area of forests nationally has not changed significantly in recent years (see Forest Area and Ownership, p. 132). Increases in soil organic carbon on croplands may be due to changing farming practices, such as tillage practices designed to maintain or increase soil organic matter (conservation tillage) or cropping sequences designed to help control pests by exposing the ground surface during the summer (bare summer fallow).

See related indicators: farmlands, p. 110; forests, p. 142; and grassland and shrublands, p. 207.

The technical note for this indicator is on page 278.

EXTENT AND PATTERN	CHEMICAL AND PHYSICAL	BIOLOGICAL COMPONENTS	GOODS AND SERVICES
Extent	Nutrients, Carbon, and Oxygen	Plants and Animals	Food, Fiber, and Water
Pattern	**Chemical Contamination**	Communities	Recreation and Other Services
	Physical	Ecological Productivity	

Chemical Contamination

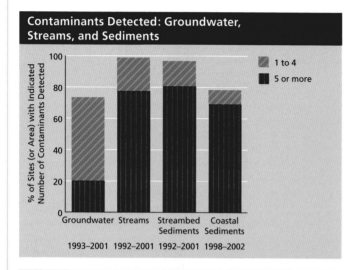

Contaminants Detected: Groundwater, Streams, and Sediments

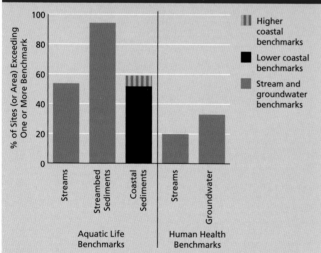

Detected Contaminants Exceeding at Least 1 Benchmark: Groundwater, Streams, and Sediments

Data source: U.S. Geological Survey National Water Quality Assessment (NAWQA) Program, U.S. Environmental Protection Agency National Coastal Assessment Program (NCA). Coverage: 51 major river basins and 54 major aquifers across the nation (NAWQA data); all coastal states (in Alaska, south-central region only) and Puerto Rico (NCA data). Technical details: 85 contaminants sampled at 186 stream sites (1992–2001); 104 contaminants sampled at 957 streambed sites (1992–2001); 194 contaminants sampled in 2282 groundwater wells (1993–2002); 81 contaminants sampled in 2146 coastal sediment sites (1998–2002) reported as "% of area." The upper graph excludes detections of naturally occurring compounds (nitrate, ammonia, metals, radionuclides). The lower graph excludes contaminants for which relevant benchmarks have not been set. See NAWQA and NCA program descriptions (p. 272 and 269) for further details. Note: In the 2002 Report, data for an earlier time period were reported, but these data are not comparable to the data presented here because of changes in the number of sites sampled and revised benchmarks.

Why Are Contaminants Found in Ecosystems Important? Synthetic chemicals, heavy metals—when present above natural background levels—and other contaminants in ecosystems can, in sufficient quantities, harm people, wildlife, and plants.

Groundwater, Streams, and Sediments
What Does This Indicator Component Report?
- How often key types of contaminants are detected
- How often contaminant levels exceed benchmarks set to protect aquatic life or human health

What Do the Data Show?
Groundwater
- About three-quarters of groundwater wells tested had one or more contaminants at detectable levels; 20% had five or more.
- About one-third had contaminants at levels that exceeded human health benchmarks.

Streams
- Virtually all streams tested had one or more contaminants at detectable levels; 77% had five or more.
- About half of all streams had one or more contaminants at levels exceeding aquatic life benchmarks; one-fifth had at least one contaminant at levels exceeding human health benchmarks.

Streambed sediments
- Nearly all streambed sediments tested had at least one contaminant at detectable levels; 80% had five or more.
- Ninety-four percent of all sites tested had one or more contaminants at concentrations exceeding aquatic life benchmarks.

EXTENT AND PATTERN	CHEMICAL AND PHYSICAL	BIOLOGICAL COMPONENTS	GOODS AND SERVICES
Extent	Nutrients, Carbon, and Oxygen	Plants and Animals	Food, Fiber, and Water
Pattern	Chemical Contamination	Communities	Recreation and Other Services
	Physical	Ecological Productivity	

Chemical Contamination *(continued)*

Coastal sediments
- About 80% of estuary sediments tested had one or more contaminants at detectable levels.
- About half of estuary sediments had one or more contaminants above lower aquatic life benchmarks; an additional 7% had contaminant levels exceeding the higher benchmarks.

What Is Not Shown by This Indicator Component?
Many of the monitored contaminants ("analytes") have no established benchmarks. Aquatic life benchmarks are not available for 26% of stream analytes, 49% of stream sediment analytes, and 26% of coastal sediment analytes. Human health benchmarks are not available for 13% of stream analytes and 24% of groundwater analytes. Potential effects on reproductive, nervous, and immune systems, as well as on particularly sensitive people, are poorly understood. Limited knowledge about the effects of mixtures of contaminants and very high seasonal concentrations increases the importance of information about how commonly contaminants are detected. Data for water and sediments have been gathered for only one time period and do not allow detection of trends in chemical contamination.

Plant and Animal Tissues

What Does This Indicator Component Report?
- How often key types of contaminants are detected
- How often these contaminants exceed benchmarks set to protect fish-eating wildlife or human health, and which contaminants are most commonly found to exceed these benchmarks

What Do the Data Show?
Freshwater fish
- About 80% of fish tested had at least one contaminant at detectable levels; more than 40% had at least 5 contaminants.
- One third of fish tested had one or more contaminants at levels that exceeded lower wildlife benchmarks; an additional 43% exceeded the higher benchmarks.
- Of the 26 tested chemicals that have established wildlife benchmarks (mercury was not tested for), PCBs and DDT were most commonly found above these levels.

Continued

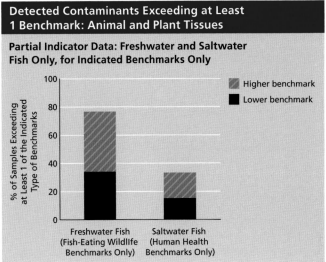

Contaminants Detected: Animal and Plant Tissues

Partial Indicator Data: Freshwater and Saltwater Fish Only

y-axis: % of Samples with Indicated Number of Contaminants Detected

Legend: ▨ 1 to 4   ■ 5 or more

x-axis: 1992–2001 Freshwater Fish | 1998–2002 Saltwater Fish

Detected Contaminants Exceeding at Least 1 Benchmark: Animal and Plant Tissues

Partial Indicator Data: Freshwater and Saltwater Fish Only, for Indicated Benchmarks Only

y-axis: % of Samples Exceeding at Least 1 of the Indicated Type of Benchmarks

Legend: ▨ Higher benchmark   ■ Lower benchmark

x-axis: Freshwater Fish (Fish-Eating Wildlife Benchmarks Only) | Saltwater Fish (Human Health Benchmarks Only)

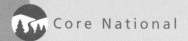
Chemical Contamination *(continued)*

Specific Contaminants Exceeding at Least 1 Benchmark: Animal and Plant Tissues

Partial Indicator Data: Freshwater and Saltwater Fish Only, for Indicated Benchmarks Only

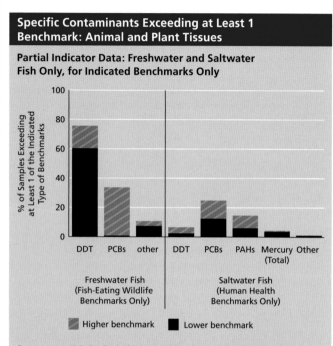

Data source: U.S. Geological Survey National Water Quality Assessment (NAWQA) Program, U.S. Environmental Protection Agency National Coastal Assessment Program (NCA). Coverage: 51 major river basins across the nation (NAWQA data); all coastal states (in Alaska, south-central region only) and Puerto Rico (NCA data). Technical details: 28 contaminants sampled in freshwater fish at 700 stream sampling sites (1992–2001); 81 contaminants sampled in saltwater fish and shellfish at 1277 estuarine sampling sites (1998–2002). The two lower graphs exclude contaminants for which relevant benchmarks have not been set. See NAWQA and NCA program descriptions (pp. 272 and 269) for further details. Note: In the 2002 Report, data for 1990–1997 were reported, but those data are not comparable to the data presented here because of changes in the number of sites sampled and revised benchmarks.

Chemical Contamination—Plant and Animal Tissues

Data Gap

- Data are not adequate for national reporting on contaminants in plant tissues and animals other than fish or on mercury and other metals in freshwater fish.
- Benchmark values are not available to determine the number of contaminants exceeding aquatic life benchmarks in saltwater fish or the number of contaminants exceeding human health benchmarks in freshwater fish.

What Do the Data Show?

Ground-level ozone

- Between 1994 and 2005, there has been no clear trend up or down in the index of ground-level ozone exposure.
- For most years since 1994, index values have been below 10 (relatively low total exposure) for approximately 30% of the area of the lower 48 states; for just over 10% of the U.S., index values have been 30 or higher (relatively high total exposure).

Saltwater fish

- Nearly all saltwater fish tested had at least five contaminants at detectable levels.
- About 15% of fish tested had one or more contaminants at levels that exceeded lower human health benchmarks; an additional 18% exceeded higher benchmarks.
- Of 68 tested chemicals with established human health benchmarks, total DDT, PCBs, PAHs, and mercury were most commonly found above these levels.

What Is Not Shown by This Indicator Component? There are no national-scale monitoring programs in place for contamination of plants or animals, other than fish. Aquatic life benchmarks are not available for 7% of freshwater fish analytes (none are available for saltwater fish). Human health benchmarks are not available for 16% of saltwater fish (none are available for freshwater fish). As a result, data shown here offer an incomplete picture of potential threats to aquatic life and human health. Note that data on fish from the Great Lakes have not been included, in part because of differences in methodologies and statistical coverage. Data from that region indicate that all fish tested had five or more detected contaminants, and the majority of sport fish fillets had PCB concentrations that exceeded human health benchmarks for unlimited consumption and all whole fish exceeded PCB concentrations to protect fish-consuming wildlife.

Outdoor Air

What Does This Indicator Component Report?

- How often ground-level ozone exceeds typical background concentrations
- The amount of fine particulate matter present in outdoor air

Chemical Contamination *(continued)*

Fine particulate matter

- In 2005, 28% of sites had fine particle concentrations of 15 micrograms per cubic meter or above, which is comparable to the concentration that would trigger a violation of the annual national air quality standard.

- Between 2000 and 2005, there was a significant decrease in the small percentage of sites with concentrations of 20 micrograms per cubic meter or above (from 2.9% to 0.3%); there was no significant change in other concentration ranges.

What Is Not Shown by This Indicator Component?
The data presented here report ambient fine particle concentrations in urban areas only and have not been integrated with fine particulate matter data gathered in rural areas.

Understanding the Data Exposure of people, animals, and plants to contaminants in streams, sediments, groundwater, and air can affect human health and ecological functioning. Through absorption or digestion, plants and animals can incorporate contaminants into their tissues, causing possible harm to themselves or to organisms that consume them. Contaminants in the environment have a variety of sources, including vehicles, consumer products, power plants, agriculture, and industry.

Many naturally occurring chemicals, such as metals and nitrogen compounds, are essential nutrients for all organisms. Often, however, human activities cause elevated concentrations of such naturally occurring chemicals, leading to ecological and human health problems. A host of other chemicals have been manufactured for specific uses. In most cases, their potential impact on ecosystems or people is poorly understood. Furthermore, many synthetic chemicals, such as PCBs, persist in the environment long after their use has been discontinued. The contaminants reported in this indicator are those monitored by federal agency programs, which may, from time to time, expand their monitoring to include additional contaminants.

Continued

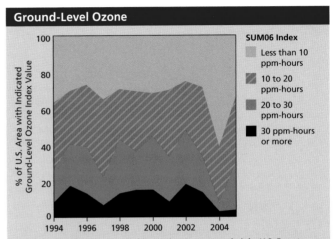

Ground-Level Ozone

SUM06 Index
- Less than 10 ppm-hours
- 10 to 20 ppm-hours
- 20 to 30 ppm-hours
- 30 ppm-hours or more

Data source: U.S. Environmental Protection Agency, analysis by U.S. Forest Service. Coverage: lower 48 states. Technical details: The index reported here is known in the technical literature as 12-hour SUM06, the total hourly average ozone concentrations above 0.06 ppm during the daytime in June, July, and August. SUM06 is cumulative for the year and is measured in ppm-hours.

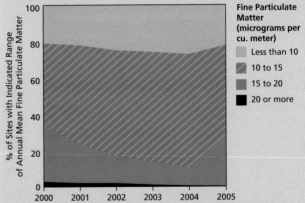

Fine Particulate Matter in Outdoor Air

Partial Indicator Data: Fine Particulate Matter in Urban Areas

Fine Particulate Matter (micrograms per cu. meter)
- Less than 10
- 10 to 15
- 15 to 20
- 20 or more

Data source: U.S. Environmental Protection Agency. Coverage: lower 48 states. Technical details: These are PM2.5 data, a term that is used to designate airborne particles or droplets that are 2.5 microns or less in width; there are about 25,000 microns in an inch. Note that these data can be compared to the national air quality standard for fine particulate matter, which is 15 micrograms per cubic meter, although deciding whether a site is in attainment involves a more complex analysis.

Chemical Contamination—Outdoor Air

Data Gap

Data are not adequate for reporting nationally on combined urban and rural measurements of fine particulate matter concentrations.

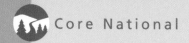
Core National

EXTENT AND PATTERN	CHEMICAL AND PHYSICAL	BIOLOGICAL COMPONENTS	GOODS AND SERVICES
Extent	Nutrients, Carbon, and Oxygen	Plants and Animals	Food, Fiber, and Water
Pattern	**Chemical Contamination**	Communities	Recreation and Other Services
	Physical	Ecological Productivity	

Chemical Contamination *(continued)*

Characterizing the effect of contaminants in the environment is an extremely complex issue. The number of contaminants found in water, sediments, and living tissues provides basic information on how widespread these compounds are in the environment. However, the presence of chemical contamination does not necessarily mean that the levels are high enough to cause problems. Comparison to benchmarks, when they exist, can help assess the significance of contamination, although this is not a true risk assessment, which would include many other factors, such as actual exposure of humans or other organisms to contaminants at specific concentration levels. Benchmarks for the protection of aquatic life are often numerically lower than related benchmarks for human health. Aquatic animals spend much or all of their life in water and may be more sensitive to specific contaminants.

Acute and chronic exposure of plants to elevated ozone levels has been linked to such effects as leaf damage, plant stress, and reduced rates of photosynthesis, although effects vary for different plant species. Elevated concentrations of fine particulate matter reduce visibility and are also associated with human (and presumably wildlife) health effects. Deposition of particulate matter can injure leaf surfaces and reduce sunlight transmission for photosynthesis. Particulate deposition on soil can affect nutrient cycling by altering soil biological activity and pH.

See also the coastal (p. 77), farmland (p. 111), and urban and suburban (p. 241 and 243) contamination indicators.

The technical note for this indicator is on page 280.

Change in Stream Flows

Why Are Changes in Stream Flow Important? The amount of water carried by a stream during periods of high and low flow—and how this amount changes over time—plays a critical role in determining which plants and animals can inhabit the stream and adjacent riparian areas. For example, low flows define the smallest area the stream or river will occupy and thus the minimum amount of fish habitat that will be available year-round; high flows shape the river channel, clear silt and debris, and influence which species will occur in the stream and the floodplain. Changes in the volume of water can also affect estuary and coastal areas by changing the salinity of water entering the oceans and the overall extent of brackish waters. Changes in the variability of flow can influence plants and animals that rely on specific flow volumes at different times in their life cycle in order to survive and reproduce.

What Does This Indicator Report?
- The percentage of stream sampling sites with changes in high and low flow rates compared to a 1941–1960 baseline period
- The percentage of sampling sites with changes in the variability of stream flow rates compared to a 1941–1960 baseline period

Change in flow was measured at "reference" sites—sites that have seen little change in land use and have not been substantially affected by dams and diversions during the measurement period (1941 onward)—as well as at "nonreference sites"—sites that may or may not have undergone such change. We report on changes in flow at both site types to allow readers to separate changes in flow that might be attributed to climate or other natural factors, such as change in the age structure of the community, from changes that might be due to new confounding anthropogenic influences on flow.

Continued

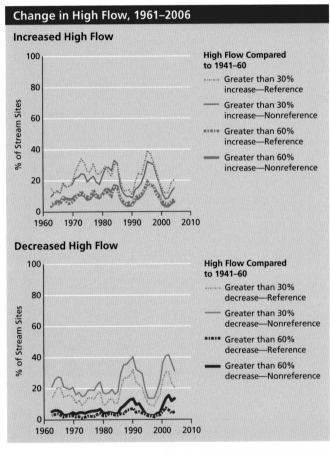

Change in High Flow, 1961–2006

Increased High Flow

% of Stream Sites

High Flow Compared to 1941–60
- Greater than 30% increase—Reference
- Greater than 30% increase—Nonreference
- Greater than 60% increase—Reference
- Greater than 60% increase—Nonreference

Decreased High Flow

% of Stream Sites

High Flow Compared to 1941–60
- Greater than 30% decrease—Reference
- Greater than 30% decrease—Nonreference
- Greater than 60% decrease—Reference
- Greater than 60% decrease—Nonreference

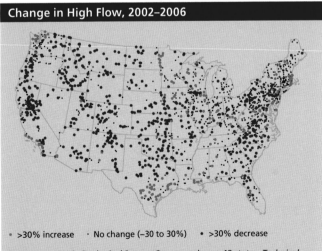

Change in High Flow, 2002–2006

- >30% increase   · No change (−30 to 30%)   · >30% decrease

Data source: U.S. Geological Survey. Coverage: lower 48 states. Technical details: The value for a given year is based on a 5-year rolling median, compared to that site's flow parameter from a 1941–1960 baseline period; thus data for 2004 in the graphs above actually represent the 5-year rolling median for 2002–2006. Maps include reference and nonreference streams. Increases or decreases of less than 30% are not considered substantial.

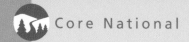
Core National

EXTENT AND PATTERN	CHEMICAL AND PHYSICAL	BIOLOGICAL COMPONENTS	GOODS AND SERVICES
Extent	Nutrients, Carbon, and Oxygen	Plants and Animals	Food, Fiber, and Water
Pattern	Chemical Contamination	Communities	Recreation and Other Services
	Physical	Ecological Productivity	

Change in Stream Flows *(continued)*

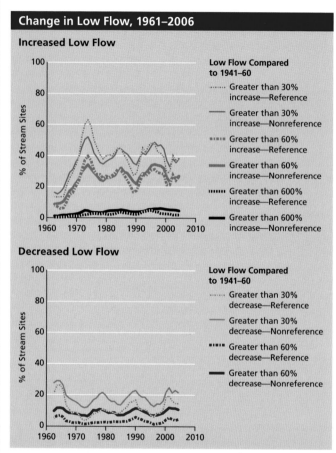

Change in Low Flow, 1961–2006

Increased Low Flow

% of Stream Sites

Low Flow Compared to 1941–60
- ·········· Greater than 30% increase—Reference
- ——— Greater than 30% increase—Nonreference
- ▪▪▪▪▪ Greater than 60% increase—Reference
- ▬▬▬ Greater than 60% increase—Nonreference
- ▪▪▪▪▪▪ Greater than 600% increase—Reference
- ▬▬▬ Greater than 600% increase—Nonreference

Decreased Low Flow

% of Stream Sites

Low Flow Compared to 1941–60
- ·········· Greater than 30% decrease—Reference
- ——— Greater than 30% decrease—Nonreference
- ▪▪▪▪▪ Greater than 60% decrease—Reference
- ▬▬▬ Greater than 60% decrease—Nonreference

Change in Low Flow, 2002–2006

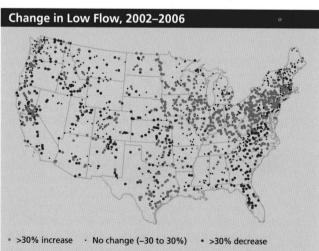

- ● >30% increase · No change (−30 to 30%) ● >30% decrease

Data source: U.S. Geological Survey. Coverage: lower 48 states. Technical details: The value for a given year is based on a 5-year rolling median, compared to that site's flow parameter from a 1941–1960 baseline period; thus data for 2004 in the graphs above actually represent the 5-year rolling median for 2002–2006. Maps include reference and nonreference streams. Increases or decreases of less than 30% are not considered substantial.

What Do the Data Show?

High Flows

- High flow rates have increased and decreased in a roughly an equal number of streams across the nation compared to the 1941–1960 baseline period. However, the proportion of streams with decreases in high flow has increased significantly since 1961–1965. Decreases in high flow were more common in nonreference streams than in reference streams.
- Between 2002 and 2006, some coastal areas and portions of the Northeast had proportionally more streams with large increases in high-flow volume than other areas of the country (see map).
- Similar year-to-year patterns are seen in the reference and nonreference stream data.

Low Flows

- Since the late 1960s, more streams have had an increase than a decrease in low flow compared to the baseline period.
- The proportion of streams showing increases in low flow of more than 30%, 60%, and 600% (compared to the baseline period) has increased since 1961–1965.
- For the most recent time period (2002–2006), twice as many streams had increases in low flow of more than 30% as had decreases in low flow of more than 30%, compared to the baseline period; increased low flows were common in the Northeast and in some Midwestern states (see map).
- Fewer reference streams showed large decreases in low flow than nonreference streams.
- Similar year-to-year patterns are seen in the reference and nonreference stream data.

Variability of Flow

- Since the late 1960s, more streams have had a decrease, rather than an increase, in the variability of their flow, compared to the 1941–1960 baseline period.
- Since the early 1960s, an increasing proportion of streams have had a reduction in the variability of their flow, compared to the 1941–1960 baseline period; a decreasing proportion of streams have had an increase in the variability of their flow during the same time period.

Change in Stream Flows *(continued)*

- There is no clear geographic pattern to the increases and decreases in flow variability for the most recent period (2002–2006) (see map).
- Decreases in variability of greater than 30% compared to the baseline period are more common in nonreference streams than reference streams.
- Similar year-to-year patterns are seen in the reference and nonreference stream data.

What Is Not Shown by This Indicator?

For watersheds that receive significant snowfall, when and how rapidly the accumulated snow pack melts has a direct impact on stream flow. For example, a shift in the timing of snow melt to earlier in the season can result in a more gradual melting of the snow pack and less overall variability in stream flow. For this reason, there is great interest in expanding this indicator to capture the timing of high flows. However, a measure is needed of the timing of high flows that takes into account regional phenomena, such as melting snow and hurricanes.

Understanding the Data

Climate can play a key role in altering high and low flows as well as the variability of flow. Its effect is likely seen in the similar year-to-year changes of both reference and nonreference streams, such as those changes seen in high and low flows in the 1990s.

Dams affect stream flow rates and the variability of flow by storing water in upstream reservoirs and regulating the release of water downstream. Watershed development and agricultural activities can change stream flows by diverting or withdrawing water from the stream for drinking, irrigation, or industrial use and by pumping groundwater from adjacent aquifers. Land cover can likewise affect streams, by influencing the amount of precipitation that reaches streams (rather than being stored in soil, absorbed by plants, or evaporating) and the rate at which water reaches streams. In some cases, the interaction of several management activities, such as paving areas and building dams, may counterbalance the effect on stream flows of any single management activity.

The technical note for this indicator is on page 282.

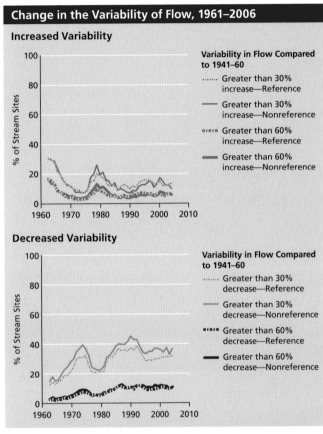

Change in the Variability of Flow, 1961–2006

Increased Variability

% of Stream Sites

Variability in Flow Compared to 1941–60
- ······ Greater than 30% increase—Reference
- —— Greater than 30% increase—Nonreference
- ▪▪▪▪ Greater than 60% increase—Reference
- ▬▬▬ Greater than 60% increase—Nonreference

Decreased Variability

% of Stream Sites

Variability in Flow Compared to 1941–60
- ······ Greater than 30% decrease—Reference
- —— Greater than 30% decrease—Nonreference
- ▪▪▪▪ Greater than 60% decrease—Reference
- ▬▬▬ Greater than 60% decrease—Nonreference

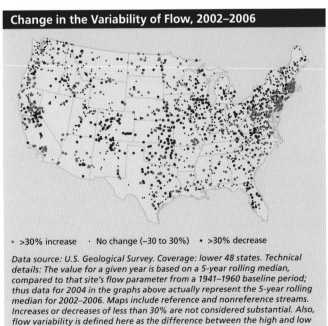

Change in the Variability of Flow, 2002–2006

- · >30% increase   · No change (–30 to 30%)   · >30% decrease

Data source: U.S. Geological Survey. Coverage: lower 48 states. Technical details: The value for a given year is based on a 5-year rolling median, compared to that site's flow parameter from a 1941–1960 baseline period; thus data for 2004 in the graphs above actually represent the 5-year rolling median for 2002–2006. Maps include reference and nonreference streams. Increases or decreases of less than 30% are not considered substantial. Also, flow variability is defined here as the difference between the high and low flows divided by the median flow in a year.

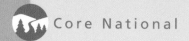
At-Risk Native Species

At-Risk Native Species, by Risk Category (2006)

Partial Indicator Data: Native Terrestrial and Freshwater Plant and Animal Species

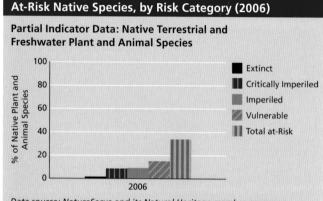

Legend:
- Extinct
- Critically Imperiled
- Imperiled
- Vulnerable
- Total at-Risk

Data source: NatureServe and its Natural Heritage member programs. Coverage: all 50 states. Technical details: The degree of risk for any particular species varies considerably, from those species that are relatively secure, to those that are in imminent danger of extinction. The data cover many of the best-known groups of terrestrial and freshwater native plants and animals, totaling about 22,600 native species. Species are assessed based on such factors as the number and condition of individuals and populations, population trends, the area occupied by the species, and known threats. In all cases, a wide variety of factors contribute to overall ratings.

At-Risk Native Species, by State (2006)

Partial Indicator Data: Native Terrestrial and Freshwater Plant and Animal Species

Percent At-Risk Species
- Less than 3%
- 3 to 6%
- 6 to 9%
- 9 to 12%
- 12 to 15%
- More than 15%

Data source: NatureServe and its Natural Heritage member programs. Coverage: all 50 states. Note that state data are not available for the following: the Giant Silkworm, Royal Moths, Sphinx Moths and Grasshopper. These taxa are included in the graph above but are not included in this map.

Why Are Native Species Important?

Native species are valued for a variety of reasons: they provide products, including food, fiber, and genetic materials, which may have various medicinal, industrial, and agricultural uses; they serve as key elements of ecosystems, which provide valuable goods and services; and many people value them for their intrinsic worth or beauty.

What Does This Indicator Report?

- The relative risk of extinction for more than 22,600 native plants, mammals, birds, reptiles, insects, freshwater and anadromous fish, and freshwater shellfish—presented as 3 categories: vulnerable, imperiled, and critically imperiled (see definitions)
- The percentage of native species that are extinct
- Population trends for those native species classified as at risk of becoming extinct

What Do the Data Show?

- As of 2006, about 17% of native animal and plant species in the U.S. were ranked as "imperiled" or "critically imperiled," and another 2% of native plants and animals may already be extinct—that is, they have not been observed despite intensive searches. When "vulnerable" species were included, about one-third of native plant and animal species were considered to be at risk.
- Hawaii had a much higher percentage of at-risk native plants and animals than any other state (81%), followed by California (29%), Nevada (16%), and Alabama (15%); the Midwest and Northeast/Mid-Atlantic had the lowest percentages.
- For at-risk native vertebrate animal species for which population trends were known in 2006 (about half of the total), a larger proportion have declining populations (28%) than have stable (23%) or increasing (1%) populations.

At-Risk Native Species *(continued)*

Why Can't This Entire Indicator Be Reported? Even though status data were reported for this indicator in the 2002 edition of this report, change in rank status is not presented here because the vast majority of changes in risk rankings result from new or better information, rather than actual changes in species' status (see the discussion in the program description for NatureServe, p. 275). That said, since the 2002 edition of this report, the condition of 21 species has declined enough to lead to their reclassification into higher risk categories, while the condition of only two species has increased enough for them to be reclassified into a lower risk category.

Identifying the predominant reason for a species' decline, such as natural rarity, disease, overharvesting, or human alteration of available habitat, is a key data need for the future. Population trend data are not available for at-risk invertebrates and plants because data are unavailable for the majority of species; available data provide an incomplete picture of these groups as a whole.

Data are not available on at-risk species in U.S. coastal waters. Some data are available on marine species, but these data do not cover a broad cross-section of species (see At-Risk Native Marine Species, p. 80).

Discussion A recent study indicates that there are at least 200,000 plant and animal species known to live in the United States, but little is known about the status and distribution of most of them. There are perhaps 2–3 times as many plant and animal species that have yet to be named in the United States, and most likely many more microbial species, for which much remains to be learned about their status and distribution. This indicator summarizes the status of more than 22,600 plant and animal species, providing a powerful snapshot of the condition of U.S. plant and animal species.

Increased risk levels for a particular species may be due to historical or recent population declines, or they may reflect natural rarity; biologists often consider very rare species to be at risk even in the absence of recent declines or current threats. Data on population trends complement the risk category data by showing how species of most conservation concern are faring over time. The ability to track changes in the condition of species over time will be further enhanced when it is possible to report the population trends of a larger number of species.

See also the indicators for at-risk native marine (p. 80), forest (p. 144), freshwater (p. 180), and grassland and shrubland species (p. 211), as well as for species in farmland areas (p. 116) and the urban and suburban landscape (p. 246).

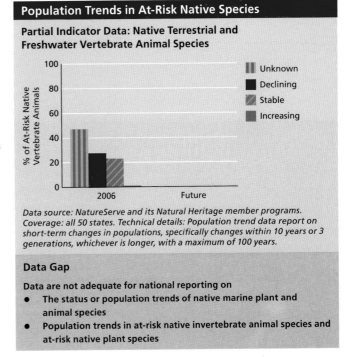

Population Trends in At-Risk Native Species

Partial Indicator Data: Native Terrestrial and Freshwater Vertebrate Animal Species

Data source: NatureServe and its Natural Heritage member programs. Coverage: all 50 states. Technical details: Population trend data report on short-term changes in populations, specifically changes within 10 years or 3 generations, whichever is longer, with a maximum of 100 years.

Data Gap

Data are not adequate for national reporting on
- The status or population trends of native marine plant and animal species
- Population trends in at-risk native invertebrate animal species and at-risk native plant species

Some Definitions

- "Critically imperiled" species often are found in five or fewer places, may have experienced very steep declines, or show other evidence of very high risk.
- "Imperiled" species often are found in 20 or fewer places, may have experienced steep declines, or display other risk factors.
- "Vulnerable" species often are found in fewer than 80 places, may have recently experienced widespread decline, or show other signs of moderate risk.
- The remaining plant and animal species are regarded as "secure" or "apparently secure."

The technical note for this indicator is on page 283.

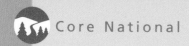
Established Non-native Species

Established Non-native Species

Data Gap

Data are not adequate for national reporting on
- **The number of new non-native species that become established over time**
- **The area with different numbers of established non-native species**
- **The area with different proportions of established non-native species, as a percentage of total species**

Why Is Understanding the Prevalence of Non-native Species Important? Non-native species may act as predators or parasites of native species, cause diseases, compete for food or habitat, and alter essential habitat. They also may threaten human health and economic well-being. Non-native species can provide benefits, such as soil stabilization on eroding slopes, forage for grazing animals, food for people, and barriers to prevent the spread of wildfires. Established non-native species survive and reproduce without human intervention. Non-native species are also called "nonindigenous," "exotic," or "introduced." Those that spread aggressively are termed "invasive."

What Will This Indicator Report? For plants, animals, and plant and animal pathogens across all ecosystem types:
- The number of new non-native species that become established over time, by decade
- The area with different numbers of established non-native species (note that for any given time period, a species would only be included if it is surviving and reproducing during that time period; those species that were formerly—but are no longer—established would not be counted)
- The area with different proportions of established non-native species, as a percentage of total species

Why Can't This Indicator Be Reported at This Time? Data on the number of new non-native species established over time are not available on a national scale. Also, with the exception of fish species (see Established Non-native Freshwater Species, p. 182), current data on the number of established non-native species are not available. National-level standardized data collection efforts for non-native species are currently limited. Therefore, although many datasets for non-native species exist at the county, state, or regional levels, metrics and collection methods (including scale) vary considerably, making data aggregation difficult or even impossible.

Information describing whether or not a non-native species becomes established in a particular area does not by itself provide a complete picture of the impact it may have on ecosystem function. Ideally, this indicator would report on the actual impact non-native species have on the various ecosystem types. A good example of such data would be the area of forest damaged by pests and pathogens (see Forest Disturbance: Fire, Insects, Disease, p. 149; but note that those data cannot currently be split between native and non-native pests). A partial "impact" indicator would be measures of non-native plant cover (see pages 146 and 213). The amount of non-native plant cover is more telling than simply the number or proportion of non-native species, yet is not as informative as, for example, the amount of native vegetation displaced by the non-native plants. Continued research and monitoring is necessary to enable the eventual expansion of this indicator's scope to measure impacts of non-native species. Until then, the more modest design presented here—when data become available—will provide a valuable picture of the numbers and types of non-native species that are becoming established and spreading throughout the nation's ecosystems.

When data become available, a portion of this indicator will report on non-native plant and animal pathogens. The effects of animal pathogens on livestock in both farmlands and grasslands–shrublands, on fish in the nation's freshwater and marine systems, and on wildlife everywhere are among the most important consequences of the introduction of non-native species.

See the related indicators for coasts and oceans (p. 81), farmlands (p. 117), forests (p. 146 and p. 149), fresh waters (p. 182), grasslands and shrublands (p. 213 and p. 214), and urban and suburban landscapes (p. 247).

The technical note for this indicator is on page 283.

Native Species Composition

Why Is Native Species Composition Important? The number, abundance, and type of native species provide an important measure of the condition of biological communities. Individual species help determine a community's structure, biomass and ecological function.

> **Native Species Composition**
>
> **Indicator Development Needed**

What Will This Indicator Report? When defined, this indicator will most likely compare the observed species composition for an area with the expected species composition had the area been relatively unaffected by disturbance, management, and physical alteration. The indicator will likely report the ratio of observed to expected species composition for both animals and plants and will focus exclusively on native species (for non-native species, see Established Non-native Species, p. 52). In order to provide more detailed information on the condition of the community, the indicator may report separately on trees, shrubs, and herbaceous plant species and on specific taxonomic groups of animals for which data are more extensive.

Why Can't This Indicator Be Reported at This Time? More than a dozen experts helped The Heinz Center develop this indicator, which focuses on the condition of biological communities, but no final design emerged. A promising candidate metric for this indicator requires further testing before the indicator is formally proposed. Data are available to compare existing to expected species composition for certain taxa, such as freshwater bottom-dwelling animals (see p. 185); however, there are no such data for most plants and animals across the country. In addition, the appropriate methods for computing the metric using data on both plants and animals have yet to be fully tested.

The technical note for this indicator is on page 284.

Plant Growth Index

Why Is This Index of Plant Growth Important? Plants use energy from the sun to turn carbon dioxide, plus water and nutrients, into plant matter. This process, photosynthesis, drives and sustains virtually all life on earth. Changes in the amount of energy captured by plants over large areas, as reported in this indicator, may signal significant changes in ecosystem functioning. These changes could lead to increases or decreases in yield of products such as crops (p. 119) or wood (p. 154), changes in carbon storage (p. 38), and changes in the number and types of species that live in a region (p. 53).

What Does This Indicator Report?

- For several ecosystem types, the percentage of area with yearly increases or decreases in plant growth, as estimated using an index calculated from satellite data
- For these same ecosystem types combined, whether or not there is an overall trend (1982–2003) in this index of plant growth

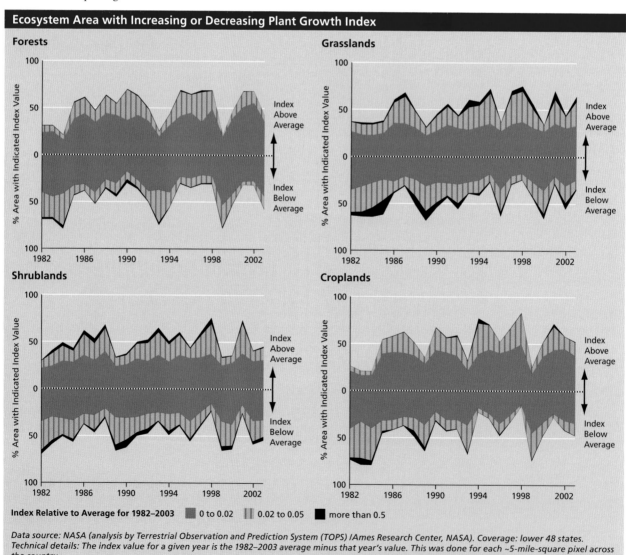

Ecosystem Area with Increasing or Decreasing Plant Growth Index

Index Relative to Average for 1982–2003 ▨ 0 to 0.02 ▥ 0.02 to 0.05 ■ more than 0.5

Data source: NASA (analysis by Terrestrial Observation and Prediction System (TOPS) /Ames Research Center, NASA). Coverage: lower 48 states. Technical details: The index value for a given year is the 1982–2003 average minus that year's value. This was done for each ~5-mile-square pixel across the country.

EXTENT AND PATTERN	CHEMICAL AND PHYSICAL	BIOLOGICAL COMPONENTS	GOODS AND SERVICES
Extent	Nutrients, Carbon, and Oxygen	Plants and Animals	Food, Fiber, and Water
Pattern	Chemical Contamination	Communities	Recreation and Other Services
	Physical	**Ecological Productivity**	

Plant Growth Index *(continued)*

What Do the Data Show?

- There was a slight but significant increase in the proportion of grassland and cropland areas with increases in plant growth index over the 1982–2003 period. Forests and shrublands showed no clear upward or downward trend in the area of land with different levels of the plant growth index over the 1982–2003 period.

- Each ecosystem type shown had years for which there was noticeably more or less area with a given index value.

- There were similar short-term changes across ecosystems; in 1999, for example, all ecosystems had more area with lower index values.

- The Southeast had a trend of increasing index values from 1982 to 2003, while other areas, such as California and parts of the Northeast, had decreasing trends (see map).

Why Can't This Entire Indicator Be Reported at This Time?

Data on plant growth in the open ocean are not adequate for national reporting (see related indicator Chlorophyll Concentrations, p. 86). Data for estuaries and fresh waters, including the Great Lakes, are unavailable.

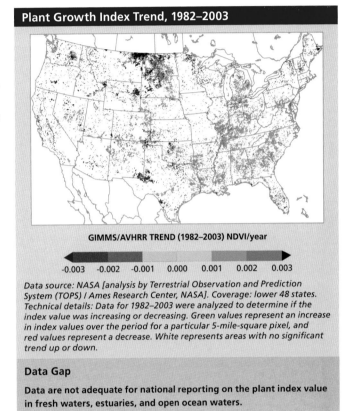

Plant Growth Index Trend, 1982–2003

GIMMS/AVHRR TREND (1982–2003) NDVI/year

-0.003 -0.002 -0.001 0.000 0.001 0.002 0.003

Data source: NASA [analysis by Terrestrial Observation and Prediction System (TOPS) / Ames Research Center, NASA]. Coverage: lower 48 states. Technical details: Data for 1982–2003 were analyzed to determine if the index value was increasing or decreasing. Green values represent an increase in index values over the period for a particular 5-mile-square pixel, and red values represent a decrease. White represents areas with no significant trend up or down.

Data Gap

Data are not adequate for national reporting on the plant index value in fresh waters, estuaries, and open ocean waters.

Understanding the Data The index shown here provides an estimate of the potential for plant growth by estimating the amount of light absorbed by plants, which is a key factor in estimating rates of photosynthesis. There are more direct estimates of how much plants are actually growing, such as net primary productivity (NPP), but continued validation of the models used to estimate NPP with actual measurements made at field sites is needed.

Thus, although we cannot directly estimate the magnitude of changes in plant growth over time, the data suggest that there are trends of interest, both increasing and decreasing, for several broad areas across the country and several ecosystem types. Such broad trends will likely be linked to the capacity of ecosystems to provide various goods and services, as well as to support a variety of other species.

Changes in climate (including temperature and the timing and amount of precipitation), as well as such factors as ground-level ozone, increased atmospheric deposition of nitrogen, and increased levels of carbon dioxide, might cause or contribute to changes in plant growth. Changes in land use can affect plant growth. Management changes, such as the cultivation of different crops or tree species or the use of fertilizers, also typically lead to changes in plant growth.

The technical note for this indicator is on page 285.

Production of Food and Fiber and Water Withdrawals

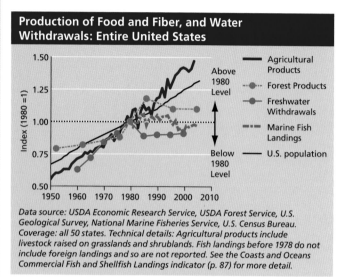

Production of Food and Fiber, and Water Withdrawals: Entire United States

Index (1980 =1)

Agricultural Products
Forest Products
Freshwater Withdrawals
Marine Fish Landings
U.S. population

Above 1980 Level
Below 1980 Level

Data source: USDA Economic Research Service, USDA Forest Service, U.S. Geological Survey, National Marine Fisheries Service, U.S. Census Bureau. Coverage: all 50 states. Technical details: Agricultural products include livestock raised on grasslands and shrublands. Fish landings before 1978 do not include foreign landings and so are not reported. See the Coasts and Oceans Commercial Fish and Shellfish Landings indicator (p. 87) for more detail.

Why Are the Quantities of Food and Fiber Produced by Ecosystems and the Amount of Water Withdrawn from Rivers and Groundwater Important? Products from U.S. ecosystems meet many of the nation's food, fiber, and water needs. Changes in the quantities of these goods over time may be a result of underlying changes in the condition of our nation's ecosystems, reflect shifts in resource demand and supply, or be a result of changes in how goods are obtained from ecosystems.

What Does This Indicator Report?
This indicator reports the production of food and fiber and the withdrawals of fresh water, using an index with 1980 arbitrarily set as the base year. Values above 1.0 indicate that production or withdrawals were greater than in 1980; values below 1.0 indicate that production or withdrawals were lower than in 1980.

What Do the Data Show?
- Nationally, only the production of agricultural products has grown at a rate exceeding population growth.
  - Since 1978, data show no clear trend in marine fish landings, which are down 3% since 1980 (based on 2005 data).
  - The harvest of forest products increased by 40% from 1952 to 2005.
  - Total withdrawals of fresh water have increased since 1960, with a slight decline in the mid-1980s.
- Regionally, the production of food and fiber and water withdrawals match the national patterns, with a few notable exceptions:
  - From 1960 to 2000, water withdrawals increased in the Southeast, Midwest, and Southwest regions. Withdrawals in the Northeast/Mid-Atlantic, Pacific Coast, and Rocky Mountain regions have shown no significant up or down change since 1960. In all regions except the Midwest, regional population is increasing at a higher rate than growth in water withdrawals.
  - Since the late 1970s, marine fish landings increased on the Pacific Coast (because of an expanding U.S. fleet in Alaska—see fish landings indicator, p. 87) and decreased in the Northeast/Mid-Atlantic and Southeast.

What Is Not Shown by This Indicator? This indicator does not show whether or not goods and services are obtained in a sustainable manner. Other indicators in this report are designed to describe the capacity of ecosystems to continue producing food and fiber—a first step in understanding sustainable resource production (Timber Growth and Harvest, p. 155; and Status of Commercially Important Fish Stocks, p. 88). Finally, reasons for the observed changes in the production of food and fiber or withdrawals of water are not analyzed in this report, nor are the ways that increases in one use may affect availability of goods for other uses—for example, an increase in agricultural productivity in one region may increase the demand for fresh water.

Understanding the Data This indicator reports the amounts of food and fiber produced and water withdrawn in different years. For example, the highest production for agricultural products since 1950 was in 2004, when it was about 47% greater than the 1980 value. The index also allows comparison of the rate

Production of Food and Fiber and Water Withdrawals *(continued)*

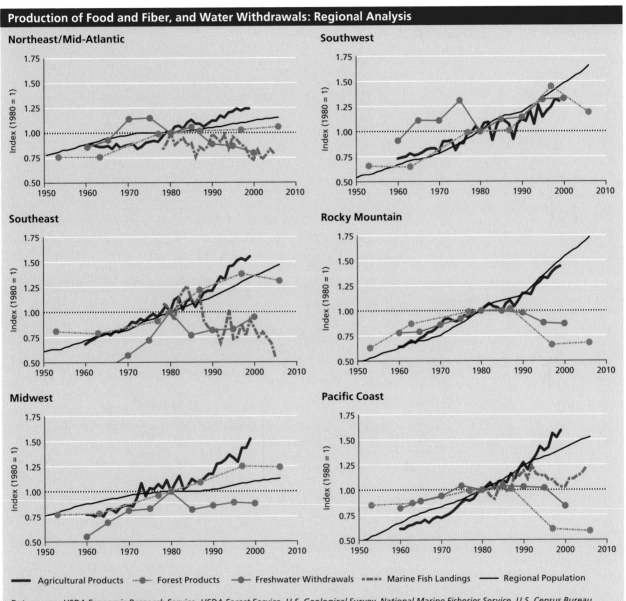

Production of Food and Fiber, and Water Withdrawals: Regional Analysis

Legend: Agricultural Products ●●● Forest Products ●━● Freshwater Withdrawals ━━━ Marine Fish Landings ━━━ Regional Population

Data source: USDA Economic Research Service, USDA Forest Service, U.S. Geological Survey, National Marine Fisheries Service, U.S. Census Bureau. Coverage: all 50 states. Technical details: Agricultural products include livestock raised on grasslands and shrublands. Note: The freshwater withdrawal values for the Southeast region in 1960 and 1965 cannot be seen on the above graph: the index value for 1960 is 0.3, and the value for 1965 is 0.44.

of growth or decline in production of different goods over time and among different regions. Agricultural production, for instance, has increased steadily in all regions over the time period shown, but the production of other resources has been much more variable over time and among different regions. This indicator also compares trends in production and population growth: only agricultural products have increased more than population growth.

This indicator addresses only tangible goods derived from ecosystems (there are other intangible services that cannot currently be quantified—see Natural Ecosystem Services, p. 60).

The technical note for this indicator is on page 285.

Core National

EXTENT AND PATTERN	CHEMICAL AND PHYSICAL	BIOLOGICAL COMPONENTS	GOODS AND SERVICES
Extent	Nutrients, Carbon, and Oxygen	Plants and Animals	Food, Fiber, and Water
Pattern	Chemical Contamination	Communities	Recreation and Other Services
	Physical	Ecological Productivity	

Outdoor Recreation

Participation in Outdoor Recreation Activities

Partial Indicator Data: Listed Activities

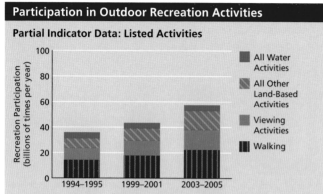

Data source: USDA Forest Service. Coverage: all 50 states. Note: For the "Other Land-Based Activities" figure, data on participation in biking activities are not available for all time periods (see graph below). Technical details: Note that these data do not track the amount of time spent on a particular outdoor activity; rather, they measure the number of different activities an individual engages in during a 24-hour day. Thus, the data do not distinguish between several activities on the same day or on separate days in a given year.

Breakdown of "Other Land-Based Activities"

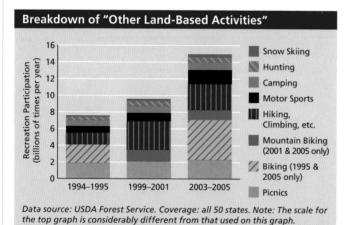

Data source: USDA Forest Service. Coverage: all 50 states. Note: The scale for the top graph is considerably different from that used on this graph.

Breakdown of Water-Based Activities

Partial Indicator Data: Listed Activities

Data source: USDA Forest Service. Coverage: all 50 states. Note: The scale for the first graph is considerably different from that used on this graph.

Why Is It Important To Track Participation in Outdoor Recreational Activities? Millions of Americans participate in outdoor recreation each year. Participation in outdoor recreation has associated economic, health, and educational values. Recreation is a benefit that is derived from ecosystems, in much the same way as we derive products such as food, fiber, and water.

What Does This Indicator Report? The average number of times per year U.S. adults took part in a variety of outdoor recreational activities. When data become available, recreational activity of children would also be reported.

What Do the Data Show?
- In 2003–2005, U.S. adults participated in recreation activities 58 billion times per year.
- The most popular outdoor activity was walking, followed by viewing activities (sightseeing, bird-watching, and wildlife viewing).
- The most frequently participated in land-based activities were biking, hiking, and picnicking.
- Adults in the United States participated in water activities just under 5 billion times per year, with swimming and fishing being about equally popular.
- In general, participation in outdoor recreation appears to be increasing over the three time periods shown—more time points will be needed to determine if observed increases are statistically significant trends.

What Is Not Shown by This Indicator? The surveys used to track recreation reported in this indicator currently only survey individuals over the age of 16 and therefore are not representative of the entire U.S. population. A youth survey is planned for future Forest Service national recreation surveys. Recent surveys by the U.S. Fish and Wildlife Service report significant declines in the recruitment and retention of youth participants in fishing, hunting, and wildlife-associated recreation.

Core National

EXTENT AND PATTERN	CHEMICAL AND PHYSICAL	BIOLOGICAL COMPONENTS	GOODS AND SERVICES
Extent	Nutrients, Carbon, and Oxygen	Plants and Animals	Food, Fiber, and Water
Pattern	Chemical Contamination	Communities	Recreation and Other Services
	Physical	Ecological Productivity	

Outdoor Recreation *(continued)*

Understanding the Data People derive many different benefits from ecosystems; some, such as the benefits gained from participating in outdoor activities—enjoyment, stress relief, and improved cardiovascular heath (through activities involving physical exertion)—are inherently challenging to quantify.

> **Outdoor Recreation**
>
> **Data Gap**
>
> Data are not adequate for national reporting on
> - Running and jogging
> - The distinction between freshwater and saltwater activities
> - Recreation participation for residents under the age of 16

This indicator reports the results of national telephone surveys conducted by the U.S. Forest Service to track participation in various outdoor activities. The surveys report the number of times residents participated in various activities—not how long they spent—so an hour-long walk and a day at the beach count the same (as noted above, each day in a multiday trip is counted as a separate event). Therefore, the fact that people participated more frequently in some activities (such as walking) does not necessarily mean that they spent more time on this than on another activity.

The technical note for this indicator is on page 286.

Core National

EXTENT AND PATTERN	CHEMICAL AND PHYSICAL	BIOLOGICAL COMPONENTS	GOODS AND SERVICES
Extent	Nutrients, Carbon, and Oxygen	Plants and Animals	Food, Fiber, and Water
Pattern	Chemical Contamination	Communities	Recreation and Other Services
	Physical	Ecological Productivity	

Natural Ecosystem Services

Natural Ecosystem Services

Indicator Development Needed

Why Are Natural Ecosystem Services Important? In addition to the familiar goods we derive from ecosystems—timber, crops, and medicines, for example—people benefit enormously from other services that ecosystems provide. These services include such vital processes as purification of air and water, detoxification and recycling of wastes, regulation of climate through storage of carbon dioxide, regeneration of soil fertility, and maintenance of the earth's startling variety of plants and animals, which we use to sustain ourselves but which we also enjoy for their own sake. Natural ecosystem processes reduce the severity of floods, promote pollination of crops and natural vegetation, facilitate dispersal of seeds, control agricultural pests, and protect coasts and hillsides from erosion.

What Will This Indicator Report? Key services provided by "natural" ecosystems—forests, grasslands and shrublands, fresh waters, and coasts and oceans.

Why Can't This Indicator Be Reported at This Time? It is straightforward to quantify the goods or products that ecosystems provide—such as fish, wood products, and food—and place a monetary value upon them (key ecosystem products are described in Production of Food and Fiber and Water Withdrawals, p. 56). Some services, such as recreation, are also fairly easily quantified (see the national, farmlands, forest, freshwater, and grasslands and shrublands recreation indicators—pages 58, 122, 157, 191, and 219, respectively).

Many of the services provided by natural ecosystems are less tangible and more difficult to quantify. Furthermore, the appropriate scale for quantifying these services varies. For example, crop pollination could be quantified on the scale of a field, whereas water purification by a forested watershed should be quantified for the entire watershed. It will be challenging to use a single standardized approach to aggregate multiple ecosystem services. Successful aggregate indicators will most likely need to weight the relative contributions of various services. Because management decisions are likely to necessitate trade-offs among services, as well as between the present and future supply of a service, these aspects should also be taken into account. For example, converting a forest to agriculture increases food production but likely decreases natural ecosystem services such as biodiversity, water purification, and climate regulation.

Significant progress has been made in the past 5 years in refining approaches to ecosystem services, and this continues to be an area of active research among ecologists and ecological economists. For example, the path-breaking Millennium Assessment (www.maweb.org) grouped ecosystem services into four general types: provisioning, regulating, cultural, and supporting services. Even though an integrated technological framework to measure most natural ecosystem services does not yet exist at the national scale, such an approach is feasible—especially if variables are measured consistently and comparably across the entire country.

Discussion Ecosystem services are often unrecognized, or at best taken for granted—until conversion or loss of the ecosystem results in loss of the services. For example, wetlands and floodplains can play a vital role in minimizing flood peaks, but this is often not recognized until downstream flooding increases following upstream conversion and filling. Or a steep hillside, formerly stabilized by trees and shrubs, slides downward, taking with it the houses that replaced the trees. Indeed, one of the greatest environmental, social, and economic disasters in the nation's history—the Dust Bowl—occurred when the intangible services provided by the natural grassland ecosystem were lost as a result of widespread conversion of land to agriculture.

EXTENT AND PATTERN	CHEMICAL AND PHYSICAL	BIOLOGICAL COMPONENTS	GOODS AND SERVICES
Extent	Nutrients, Carbon, and Oxygen	Plants and Animals	Food, Fiber, and Water
Pattern	Chemical Contamination	Communities	**Recreation and Other Services**
	Physical	Ecological Productivity	

Natural Ecosystem Services *(continued)*

Land can also revert from agricultural use to a more natural condition (this occurs less often for urban lands). For example, demographic and economic changes in New England have replaced farmlands with forest ecosystems, and the Conservation Reserve Program (which removes environmentally sensitive farmlands from production) implicitly acknowledges that the ecosystem services provided by these lands can outweigh the value of their agricultural production.

We report indirectly on some ecosystem services by reporting on changes in the extent of major ecosystem types. For example, a major change in forest area is likely to lead to a change in the availability of wood products as well as of services such as water purification. Since many ecosystem services are lost or exchanged for other, different services when natural ecosystems are converted to farmland or urban–suburban use, or when wetlands are filled, tracking changes in ecosystem extent is the first step toward characterizing changes in ecosystem services. In addition to changes in ecosystem extent, changes in the condition of an ecosystem—short of outright conversion to another land use—can alter the amount and type of services the system provides.

There is no technical note for this indicator.

Contents   page

Chapter 3:
Indicators of the Condition and Use of Coasts and Oceans

The coastal and ocean ecosystems of the United States begin at the shoreline, where sand beaches, rocky headlands, and the mouths of estuaries, streams, and rivers interact with rising and falling tides, and extend into the open ocean. The U.S. coastline ranges from arctic to tropical waters, and includes the rocky coast of Maine and the mangrove swamps of Florida, the glacial fjords of Alaska and the black lava cliffs of Hawaii, the seagrass beds of Chesapeake Bay, and the pebble beaches of California. Offshore, fish, shellfish, seabirds, and marine mammals live and feed among kelp beds and coral reefs and in the open ocean.

This vast realm is shaped by the robust interaction of land, sea, and air, as well as the interplay of fresh and salt water. Coastal marine and estuarine waters receive inputs of energy and materials from the land, atmosphere, and ocean basins that can cause changes in ecological conditions. This chapter, however, focuses not on sources of external inputs but on the condition and use of coastal and ocean ecosystems themselves.

More than half the U.S. population lives within 50 miles of the coast, and the shoreline hosts a large portion of the nation's economic and recreational activities. Millions of people visit the shore to swim, surf, sunbathe, fish, and relax. Coastal real estate is in demand in many parts of the nation, and there is pressure to convert these lands to residential, commercial, and industrial uses. U.S. ports bustle with fishing fleets, cruise ships, tankers, and cargo vessels en route around the globe. In addition, the nation relies on coastal and ocean ecosystems to supply an array of other goods and services: sheltering the land from storms and waves, processing and filtering nutrients and contaminants washed off the land, and providing habitat for a rich mosaic of species, from commercially important fish and shellfish to migrating cranes and whales.

Changes in coastal and ocean conditions can alter the mix of goods and services people derive from the system, and a wide array of policies, programs, and public and private investments compete either to effect or avert such changes. Coastal dwellers react to the natural dynamism of wind, waves, and storms by building jetties and seawalls, restoring beaches, or adopting zoning laws (requiring, for example, building standards sufficient to protect structures against storms of particular sizes); the sea's living bounty is allocated among competing parties, whether states and countries or recreational and commercial fishers; and major regulatory and investment programs are designed to reduce the input of nutrients and other chemicals that affect water quality and ultimately the living communities that inhabit coastal waters.

The following sections and the table on page 70 describe the four categories of ecosystem condition and use outlined in Chapter 1 and summarize the most recent data and trends for coasts and oceans. Individual indicators focus on critical dimensions and components of coastal and ocean ecosystems at a variety of scales, ecological processes necessary for the functioning of coastal and ocean ecosystems, living elements of coasts and oceans, and the benefits people derive from these ecosystems.

Extent and Pattern

The indicators in this section focus on key aspects of coastal extent and pattern because the nature of the coastline tells us much about the condition of coastal habitats as well as its capacity to provide services to people. Although natural forces constantly alter the character of the shoreline, the most rapid and extensive changes are now driven by human activities such as filling wetlands for building sites, dredging marinas, and installing levees and seawalls. The unprecedented death toll and economic devastation caused by hurricanes Katrina and Rita along the Gulf coast in 2005 spotlighted the condition of the U.S. coastline, particularly the combined effects of coastal armoring, human development, loss of the storm-buffering capacity of wetlands and broad sandy beaches, and coastal erosion and subsidence (see also Chemical and Physical Characteristics, below). Human activities as well as natural processes can also affect the coastal habitats required by many species for feeding and breeding. Some of the most economically and ecologically vital coastal habitats are those that are either composed of living organisms (seagrass meadows, kelp beds, mangrove forests, and other vegetated wetlands) or are built by organisms (coral reefs and shellfish beds). Three-quarters of commercially valuable fish and shellfish depend on these habitats during critical life stages.

Decisions that affect the extent and pattern of various components of our coastal lands and waters are often subject to multiple jurisdictions, including local land use and zoning regulations; statewide controls on coastal access and use such as those enacted in California and other states; federal responsibilities under laws ranging from the Clean Water Act's Section 404 wetlands program to navigational safety programs, the Endangered Species Act, and the Migratory Bird Treaty; and international treaty obligations.

Data in this chapter show that
- From the mid-1950s to 2004, vegetated wetland acreage on the Atlantic and Gulf coasts declined by 9%.
- In linear terms, vegetated wetlands account for the largest proportion of the mapped U.S. shoreline (43%). The remainder is beach, steep or rocky shorelines, and sand or mud flats; roughly 6% of the shoreline is "armored" or developed.

Data are not adequate for national reporting on
- The extent of wetland loss along the Pacific coast or in Hawaii and Alaska
- The area of seagrasses, shellfish beds, or coral reefs

Further indicator development is needed to report on
- Patterns in coastal areas

Chemical and Physical Characteristics

Water quality is often measured as the concentration of dissolved chemicals such as nutrients, as well as pesticides and other contaminants (see Core National indicators on Movement of Nitrogen and on Chemical Contaminants, pp. 36 and 42). Nutrients are delivered to coastal waters by rivers and streams, sewage outfalls, and atmospheric deposition, and also by the upwelling of deep, nutrient-rich waters, which are brought to the surface by ocean currents. Chemical contaminants can be introduced directly to coastal waters by human activities, or they can be delivered from the land to the ocean by streams and rivers or atmospheric deposition. This section describes two key aspects of marine ecosystems that can be affected by such inputs: oxygen depletion in coastal waters and contamination in ocean and estuarine sediments.

Excess inputs of plant nutrients (primarily nitrogen and phosphorus) can spur algal growth and decomposition, a process that depletes dissolved oxygen in estuarine and marine waters. Oxygen-depleted areas (hypoxic zones) kill some fish and other animals directly, damage habitats such as seagrass and kelp beds, and disrupt migration patterns. The nation's largest oxygen-depleted zone recurs each summer in the northern Gulf of Mexico, suffocating less mobile species such as clams and lobsters and even some more mobile species that fail to escape. Fish, shrimp, and most other mobile sea life are driven away from thousands of square miles of one of the nation's premier fishing grounds. Contaminants such as pesticides, heavy metals, and organic pollutants can accumulate in marine sediments where they are absorbed by small organisms at the base of the food chain, often starting a process called biomagnification, in which these chemicals increase in concentration in fish and other larger animals as they move up the food chain.

Coastal erosion and changes in ocean water temperature are two physical indicators that affect the goods and services we derive from coastal and ocean ecosystems. Erosion can damage coastal properties and structures directly, reduce the extent and recreational value of beaches, and render the land more vulnerable to storm damage. Predicted sea level rise (driven by the expansion of warming ocean waters and inputs from melting ice sheets) will likely exacerbate such effects. Changes in ocean water temperature can affect the distribution of marine life, contribute to coral reef bleaching, and alter the frequency and severity of algal blooms. Warmer surface waters have also been linked to an increase in the intensity of hurricanes.

Reducing inputs of nutrients and chemical contaminants to the nation's coastal waters is a major policy goal at many levels of government. Since most fresh waters eventually reach the coast, water quality regulations, programs, and policies across the nation can affect coastal water quality either directly or indirectly. These regulations include not only restrictions on discharges of nutrients such as nitrogen, but also policies that impact agricultural practices, energy and resource use, and even land-use change. Finally, dealing with coastal erosion costs billions of dollars every year in the United States, and the cost is likely to increase as sea level rise accelerates.

Data in this chapter show that
- The midsummer extent of the depleted oxygen zone in the Gulf of Mexico has more than doubled over the past 22 years, from about 3800 square miles in 1985 to about 7900 square miles in 2007. There is no clear trend in the extent of depleted oxygen in the Chesapeake Bay estuary. From 1985 to 2006, between 10% and 25% of the Bay experienced depleted oxygen conditions in midsummer.
- In 1998–2002, bottom sediments in about half of the estuarine area in the United States contained one or more contaminants at levels exceeding benchmarks that indicate "possible or probable adverse effects" on aquatic life.
- From 1985 to 2006, sea surface temperature increased significantly in the Gulf of Mexico, Gulf of Alaska, and South Atlantic.

Data are not adequate for national reporting on
- The percentage of U.S. coastline that is managed in an effort to control erosion or on the extent of shoreline erosion and the opposite process, accretion

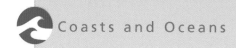

Biological Components

Coastal waters nurture some of the most diverse plant and animal communities on earth, from microscopic algae and nematode worms to oysters and anchovies, albacore and whales. Indicators in this section shed light on the status of native marine species as well as on trends in overall marine productivity, the spread of non-native species, and other factors that affect the fate of biological communities in coastal waters. Changes in population trends of native marine species can indicate changes in the physical or chemical conditions of marine ecosystems or signal shifts in habitat extent and pattern. Populations of non-native species, which can act as predators or parasites of native species, cause diseases, damage human infrastructure, compete with native species for food or habitat, and alter essential habitat, may also fluctuate in abundance in response to changes in ecosystems. Major mortalities ("die-offs") of marine species, harmful algal events (such as *Pfisteria* "blooms" off the Mid-Atlantic coast, "red tides" off Florida, or toxic *Pseudonitzschia* outbreaks off California) and changes in the condition of bottom-dwelling animal communities or overall algal production (monitored by chlorophyll levels) also provide information on the status of marine biological systems. For example, greater algal production (and thus higher chlorophyll levels) tends to support larger fish populations, yet excessive algal growth can degrade water quality and lead to oxygen depletion. In many cases, the immediate causes of changes in these indicators are not clear and most probably involve multiple factors.

Marine life provides people with a broad range of benefits, from fish and other seafood to recreational fishing and whale watching. Loss of influential or keystone marine species can lead to changes in vital habitats such as kelp beds and coral reefs. Harmful algal events can close swimming beaches and render shellfish inedible. Changes in coastal productivity, as measured by chlorophyll concentration, can signal alterations in coastal food webs or changes in the inputs of nutrients to coastal waters. And non-native (or exotic) species such as zebra mussels—which blanket some Great Lakes beaches with their tiny razor-sharp shells—can alter people's enjoyment of the shoreline as well as damage water intake pipes and other human infrastructure.

Broad federal efforts to manage marine species range from restrictions on fishing seasons and catch limits, designed to maintain sustainable harvests of commercially valuable species, to application of the Endangered Species Act and the Marine Mammal Protection Act, designed to prevent extinction. Non-native species have been the subject of federal legislation, multiple federal task forces, and a wide range of federal, state, and private efforts. Events such as marine mammal die-offs, algal blooms, or degradation in animal communities often generate significant public attention and may lead to demands for increased vigilance and cleanup efforts.

Data in this chapter show that

- Between 1990 and 2006, the number of whales, dolphins, porpoises, seals, sea lions, sea otters, and manatees dying each year in unusual marine mortality events fluctuated widely, from zero to several hundred animals.
- The seafloor community in more than a third of the estuary area in Puerto Rico, the Mid-Atlantic, and the Gulf of Mexico was classified as "degraded." In the North Atlantic, South Atlantic, and Pacific coast, less than 10% of the estuary area was classified as "degraded" (1999–2002).
- From 1997 to 2006, chlorophyll concentrations in the Pacific Northwest, Southern California, and North Atlantic regions increased and chlorophyll concentrations in Hawaii decreased. Other U.S. coastal regions showed no significant trends in chlorophyll concentrations.

Data are not adequate for national reporting on
- Native marine species at risk of extinction
- Unusual mortalities among sea turtles, seabirds, fish, and shellfish
- The condition of bottom-dwelling animal communities in open ocean waters nationally and in the estuaries of Hawaii and Alaska

Further indicator development is needed to report on
- Harmful algal events
- Established non-native species in major estuaries

Goods and Services

Two important human uses of the nation's coastal and ocean waters, both socially and economically, are fishing and recreation. The amount of fish caught is a direct measure of the value of the fishery for food and other commercial uses. Other key indicators of the current and future value of fisheries include whether commercially important fish populations are increasing or decreasing and the condition of the fish— that is, whether the fish contain chemicals at concentrations that exceed advisable limits for human consumption. A key indicator of the status of recreational use of the shoreline—and an important public health concern—involves the frequency and degree of sewage contamination of coastal waters. Swimming in waste-polluted waters can cause a range of ailments, from sore throats and diarrhea to life-threatening meningitis and encephalitis. Beach closures, in turn, can affect the tourism economy and coastal property values.

Management and governance of the nation's fisheries is often highly contentious. Fisheries in federal waters are managed regionally, with states managing their own waters and participating in federal regional councils that oversee fisheries management policies. States also generally set standards for contamination levels in fish. Monitoring of sewage contamination in coastal bathing waters and decision making on beach closures, however, are handled locally and are based on a wide array of standards.

Data in this chapter show that
- Total fish and shellfish landed in U.S. waters increased nearly 90% from 1950 to 2005. However, since 1978, landings have declined for all regions except Alaska, where landings have increased.
- Among commercially important fish stocks with known population trends, the percentage with increasing population trends has grown over the past two decades in all regions except for Alaska and the Pacific coast, where fewer stocks show increasing trends.
- Since the late 1980s the percentage of coastal sites with mussels and oysters containing high PCB concentrations (above 400 ppb) and the percentage of sites with high DDT concentrations (above 90 ppb) have declined.

Data are not adequate for national reporting on
- The population trends of nearly 80% of all U.S. fish stocks
- The concentration of DDT, PCBs, and mercury in fish in U.S. waters
- The frequency of beach closures triggered by bacterial indicators of sewage contamination, and the mileage of U.S. beaches affected

Status and trends for all coasts and oceans indicators are summarized in the table that follows; the indicators themselves take up the remainder of the chapter. Each indicator page offers a graphic representation of the available data, defines the indicator and explains why it is important, and describes either the available data or the gaps in the data.

Indicators	What Do the Most Recent Data Show?	Have Data Values Changed over Time?
EXTENT AND PATTERN		
Coastal Living Habitats, p. 72	There are 4.6 million acres of vegetated wetlands on the Atlantic and Gulf Coasts (2004 data).	Since the 1950s, wetland acreage on the Atlantic and Gulf coasts has decreased by 9%.
	Data are not adequate for national reporting on the area of vegetated wetlands along the Pacific coast, Hawaii, or Alaska. Data are also not adequate for national reporting on the area of seagrasses/submerged vegetation, shellfish beds and coral reefs nationwide.	
Shoreline Types, p. 73	The U.S. shoreline is 43% vegetated wetland, 21% beach, 13% mud and sand flats, 17% steep or rocky shoreline, and 6% armored shoreline (2006 data).	Data are not adequate for reporting on changes in the length of different shoreline types over time.
Pattern in Coastal Areas, p. 74	Indicator Development Needed	
CHEMICAL AND PHYSICAL CHARACTERISTICS		
Areas with Depleted Oxygen, p. 75	Thirteen percent of Chesapeake Bay and nearly 8000 square miles of the Gulf of Mexico had depleted levels of dissolved oxygen in midsummer (2006 and 2007 data).	Since 1985, the size of the zone of depleted oxygen in the Gulf of Mexico has increased.
		Since 1985, there is no clear trend in the percentage area of the Chesapeake Bay with depleted oxygen.
	Data are not adequate for national reporting on depleted oxygen conditions in coastal and estuarine waters outside the Chesapeake Bay and Gulf of Mexico.	
Contamination in Bottom Sediments, p. 77	Over half of estuarine sediments tested had concentrations of one or more contaminants above lower benchmarks, and 7% have concentrations above higher benchmarks (1998–2002 data).	Data are not adequate for reporting on changes over time in contaminants in estuarine sediments.
	Data are not adequate for national reporting on the amount of contamination in bottom sediments in ocean waters within 25 miles of the coast.	
Coastal Erosion, p. 78	Data are not adequate for national reporting on the percentage of U.S. coastline that is managed in an attempt to control erosion, or that is eroding, accreting, or stable.	
Sea Surface Temperature, p. 79	In 2006, the sea surface temperature (SST) index for six of the nine regions studied was above the long-term average.	Since 1985, SST has increased in the Gulf of Alaska, Gulf of Mexico, and South Atlantic.
		Since 1985, there is no clear trend in SST in the North and Mid- Atlantic, Bering Sea, Pacific Northwest, Southern California, and Hawaii.
BIOLOGICAL COMPONENTS		
At-Risk Native Marine Species, p. 80	Data are not adequate for national reporting on the percentage of native marine species at various levels of risk of extinction and the population trends of at-risk species.	
Established Non-native Species in Major Estuaries, p. 81	Indicator Development Needed	
Unusual Marine Mortalities, p. 82	In 2006, there were 131 whales, dolphins and porpoises and 81 seals, sea lions and sea otters involved in unusual marine mortality events.	Since 1990, the number of individuals involved in unusual marine mortality events has fluctuated widely.
	Data are not adequate for national reporting on the number of unusual marine mortalities in sea turtles, seabirds, fish, and shellfish.	

Indicators	What Do the Most Recent Data Show?	Have Data Values Changed over Time?

BIOLOGICAL COMPONENTS (CONTINUED)

Harmful Algal Events, p. 83	Indicator Development Needed	
Condition of Bottom-Dwelling Animals, p. 84	30–90% of the bottom areas of estuaries have communities in undegraded condition; 5–45% of the bottom areas of estuaries have communities in degraded condition (1999–2002 data).	**[?]** Between 1990–1997 and 1999–2002, the area with degraded bottom-dwelling changed from 23% to 44% in the Gulf of Mexico 17% to 4% in the South Atlantic 23% to 36% in the Mid-Atlantic
	Data are not adequate for national reporting on the condition of bottom-dwelling communities in U.S. oceans or in estuaries in Alaska and Hawaii.	
Chlorophyll Concentrations, p. 86	In 2006, chlorophyll concentrations in all regions except Hawaii and the Gulf of Mexico were higher than the 10-year average.	**[↗]** Since 1997, chlorophyll concentrations have increased in the Pacific Northwest, Southern California, and North Atlantic regions.
		[↘] Since 1997, chlorophyll concentrations have decreased in Hawaii.
		[→] Since 1997, there is no clear trend in chlorophyll concentrations in the Bering Sea, Gulf of Alaska, Mid- and South Atlantic, or Gulf of Mexico.
	Data are not adequate for national reporting on chlorophyll concentrations in estuaries.	

GOODS AND SERVICES

Commercial Fish and Shellfish Landings, p. 87	In 2005, 4.6 million tons of fish and shellfish were landed in U.S. waters.	**[↗]** Since 1978, fish and shellfish landings have increased in Alaska (with and without foreign landings).
		[↘] Since 1978, fish and shellfish landings have decreased in the Atlantic, Gulf of Mexico, West Coast, and Hawaii.
Status of Commercially Important Fish Stocks, p. 88	For stocks with known status: about 16% of stocks are decreasing and about 35% stocks are increasing (1996–2005 data).	**[↗]** Since the mid-1980s, the percentage of stocks with increasing trends has grown in all regions except Alaska and the Pacific Coast.
	Data are not adequate for reporting on stocks without known population trends.	
Selected Contaminants in Fish and Shellfish, p. 90	About half of sampled U.S. coastal waters have mussels and oysters with mercury concentrations above 0.10 ppm. About 60% of sites have shellfish with DDT concentrations of at least 10 ppb, and 22% of sites have shellfish with PCB concentrations greater than 200 ppb (2003–2004 data).	**[↘]** Since 1987–1988, the percentage of sites with higher PCB (>400 ppb), mercury (>0.05 ppm), and DDT (>90 ppb) concentrations in mussels and oysters has decreased.
	Data are not adequate for national reporting on contaminants in fish.	
Recreational Water Quality, p. 92	Data are not adequate for national reporting on the percentage of beach-mile-days affected by various levels of *Enterococcus*.	

 = significant decrease    =significant increase    = no clear trend*   = insufficient data for trend analysis

= Data not available for adequate reporting.

* may be due to little numerical change in the data or large numerical fluctuations in data resulting in no single trend

EXTENT AND PATTERN	CHEMICAL AND PHYSICAL	BIOLOGICAL COMPONENTS	GOODS AND SERVICES
Extent	Nutrients, Carbon, and Oxygen	Plants and Animals	Food, Fiber, and Water
Pattern	Chemical Contamination	Communities	Recreation and Other Services
	Physical	Ecological Productivity	

Coastal Living Habitats (Coral Reefs, Vegetated Wetlands, Seagrasses, and Shellfish Beds)

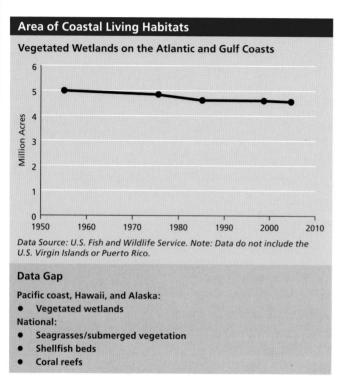

Area of Coastal Living Habitats

Vegetated Wetlands on the Atlantic and Gulf Coasts

Data Source: U.S. Fish and Wildlife Service. Note: Data do not include the U.S. Virgin Islands or Puerto Rico.

Data Gap

Pacific coast, Hawaii, and Alaska:
- **Vegetated wetlands**

National:
- **Seagrasses/submerged vegetation**
- **Shellfish beds**
- **Coral reefs**

Why Is the Area of Coastal Living Habitats Important? Coastal living habitats—those habitats that are composed of living organisms (such as seagrasses, mangrove forests, and coastal wetlands) or are built by them (such as coral reefs or shellfish beds)—are some of the most biologically productive ecosystems. Loss of these habitats can lead to the decline of coastal species. The habitats described here are critical for many species of crabs, fish, and seabirds, as well as for smaller animals that provide food for these larger creatures. When these habitats decline in area, organisms that depend on them are lost or displaced. Vegetated wetlands also help buffer shorelines against erosion and storm events, and they filter out plant nutrients, such as nitrogen and phosphorus, that would otherwise be transported to coastal waters.

What Does This Indicator Report?
- The area of vegetated wetlands
- The area of seagrasses/submerged vegetation, shellfish beds, and coral reefs

What Do the Data Show? From the mid-1950s to 2004, more than 400,000 acres of vegetated wetlands on the Atlantic and Gulf coasts were lost, a decline of about 9%.

Why Can't This Entire Indicator Be Reported at This Time? Data for coral reefs and for seagrasses and other submerged aquatic vegetation are available for many areas, but these data have not been synthesized to produce national estimates. The National Oceanic and Atmospheric Administration's Ocean Service is working to map, assess, inventory, and monitor all U.S. coral reef ecosystems, but data are not yet available for most of the nation's coastal habitats. Data on the area of shellfish beds are available, but changes in the area covered by monitoring programs may obscure changes in the area of shellfish beds. Data on vegetated wetlands are available only for the Atlantic (Maine to Florida) and Gulf coasts.

Understanding the Data Coastal living habitats are an essential component of coastal food webs, and in some cases (such as shellfish beds) they continue to provide habitat even after the animals that built them are no longer living. These areas can also act as buffers that help protect inland areas by absorbing energy from wind and waves. The current extent of coastal wetlands is, by some estimates, less than half the presettlement area. Researchers believe that, over the long term, the most significant conversion of coastal wetlands has occurred in California—an area for which we lack contemporary data—and along the Atlantic coast near major population centers. Coastal wetlands are also vulnerable to loss during storms—the U.S. Geological Survey has reported that some 140,000 acres of coastal land, much of which is thought to have been wetlands, was lost during the 2005 hurricane season, which included storms Katrina and Rita. These may be temporary losses, so further years of data collection and analysis will be needed to determine the full effect of these hurricanes.

The technical note for this indicator is on page 287.

EXTENT AND PATTERN	CHEMICAL AND PHYSICAL	BIOLOGICAL COMPONENTS	GOODS AND SERVICES
Extent	Nutrients, Carbon, and Oxygen	Plants and Animals	Food, Fiber, and Water
Pattern	Chemical Contamination	Communities	Recreation and Other Services
	Physical	Ecological Productivity	

Shoreline Types

Why Is the Composition of Different Shoreline Types Important? Whether a shoreline is, for example, beach, mudflat, wetland, steep cliffs, or armored for erosion control determines both the way people and other organisms use that shoreline and its ecological function.

What Does This Indicator Report?
The percentage of U.S. shoreline—including oceanfront areas and the shoreline of estuaries, bays, and tidally influenced rivers—that is described as steep sand, rock, or clay; mud or sand flat; beach; vegetated wetlands (marshes, mangrove, and swamps); or armored with bulkheads and riprap. For the purposes of this indicator, shoreline is defined as the intertidal zone, the area between low and high tides. A length of shoreline may contain more than one type—for example, mudflats bordered by salt marsh, or beach backed by rocky cliffs.

What Do the Data Show?
- About 43% of mapped U.S. shoreline is classified as wetland, and 21% as beach.
- Steep or rocky shorelines and mud and sand flats together make up about 30% of the total shoreline length. Armored shorelines account for about 6% of the total.
- Vegetated wetlands are the most common shoreline type in five regions—North, Mid-, and South-Atlantic; Gulf of Mexico, and the Bering Sea. In Southern California, beaches are the most common shoreline type, while in Hawaii and the Gulf of Alaska steep sand, rock, or clay shorelines are most common.

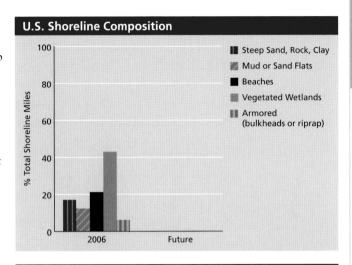

U.S. Shoreline Composition

Legend:
- Steep Sand, Rock, Clay
- Mud or Sand Flats
- Beaches
- Vegetated Wetlands
- Armored (bulkheads or riprap)

y-axis: % Total Shoreline Miles (0–100)
x-axis: 2006, Future

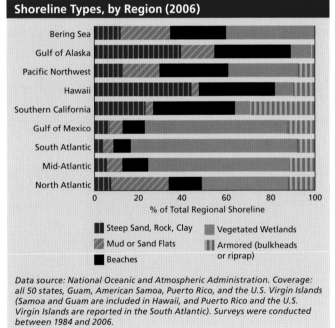

Shoreline Types, by Region (2006)

Regions (top to bottom): Bering Sea, Gulf of Alaska, Pacific Northwest, Hawaii, Southern California, Gulf of Mexico, South Atlantic, Mid-Atlantic, North Atlantic

x-axis: % of Total Regional Shoreline (0–100)

Legend:
- Steep Sand, Rock, Clay
- Mud or Sand Flats
- Beaches
- Vegetated Wetlands
- Armored (bulkheads or riprap)

Data source: National Oceanic and Atmospheric Administration. Coverage: all 50 states, Guam, American Samoa, Puerto Rico, and the U.S. Virgin Islands (Samoa and Guam are included in Hawaii, and Puerto Rico and the U.S. Virgin Islands are reported in the South Atlantic). Surveys were conducted between 1984 and 2006.

Understanding the Data "Armored" includes built structures like docks, piers, and ports in addition to retaining walls, riprap, bulkheads, and other shoreline stabilization structures. Armoring stabilizes beach or shoreline in an attempt to reduce erosion and property loss from storms and coastal flooding (see Coastal Erosion, p. 78). Bulkheads and other erosion control structures can isolate coastal wetlands from tidal influence, dramatically altering their hydrology. Armoring can also prevent the inland migration of coastal habitats as sea level rises. In addition, these structures may provide only temporary erosion control and may ultimately result in complete loss of the beach.

The technical note for this indicator is on page 287.

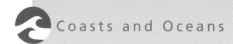

EXTENT AND PATTERN	CHEMICAL AND PHYSICAL	BIOLOGICAL COMPONENTS	GOODS AND SERVICES
Extent	Nutrients, Carbon, and Oxygen	Plants and Animals	Food, Fiber, and Water
Pattern	Chemical Contamination	Communities	Recreation and Other Services
	Physical	Ecological Productivity	

Pattern in Coastal Areas

Pattern in Coastal Areas

Indicator Development Needed

Why Are Patterns in Coastal Areas Important? The interplay between various types of coastal habitats (such as wetlands and open waters), as well as between these habitat types and human development in the coastal zone (such as built structures and dredged areas) provide a general description of the structural pattern of coastal areas. The structural pattern of these areas can be linked to how well they function ecologically and to the amount and type of ecosystem services humans receive from them.

What Will This Indicator Report? This indicator is likely to describe the intermingling of "natural" and "non-natural" landscape (or seascape) features in coastal areas.

Why Can't This Indicator Be Reported at This Time? The study of pattern in coastal areas is relatively new, and there is no agreement on how to characterize coastal pattern using a single indicator.

Discussion One of the objectives of a coastal pattern indicator is to distinguish coastline with "non-natural" features, such as houses, bulkheads, or trawl zones, from "natural" habitats (see the core national indicator Pattern of "Natural" Landscapes, p. 33). Another important aspect to measure is the degree to which habitat and hydrologic connections between upland and coastal areas are maintained. For example, the flow of water and sediments from the land to the ocean may be impeded by structures such as roads or causeways. Habitat connectivity of ecologically important habitats like marshes and wetlands could be characterized using a measure of habitat edge length relative to habitat area although such data would need to be tracked along with marsh area because the ratio can increase, even though total marsh area is declining.

A future pattern indicator might be paired with a new indicator describing the use of coastal areas (equivalent to a "land use" indicator—see pages 136 and 203, for example) that would report the extent of protected areas, as well as various human uses, such as trawling for bottom fish and shellfish. In addition, it would be ideal if the current extent indicator (Coastal Living Habitats, p. 72) reported the area of rare habitat types (this should eventually be captured to some degree in the core national extent indicator—see p. 28).

There is no technical note for this indicator.

EXTENT AND PATTERN	CHEMICAL AND PHYSICAL	BIOLOGICAL COMPONENTS	GOODS AND SERVICES
Extent	Nutrients, Carbon, and Oxygen	Plants and Animals	Food, Fiber, and Water
Pattern	Chemical Contamination	Communities	Recreation and Other Services
	Physical	Ecological Productivity	

Areas with Depleted Oxygen

Why Are Oxygen Levels in Estuaries and Coastal Waters Important?

Very low (hypoxic) oxygen levels in coastal and estuarine waters can cause stress or death to fish, shellfish, and marine mammals. Prolonged periods of low oxygen levels can affect recreational and commercial fisheries and harm coastal plant and animal communities.

What Does This Indicator Report?

- The area of U.S. estuarine and coastal waters with hypoxic, or depleted, oxygen conditions (below 2 ppm) for at least one month out of the year. Although data are not adequate for full reporting nationally, data are available for coastal areas that receive riverine input from two major rivers, the Susquehanna (Chesapeake Bay) and the Mississippi River (Gulf of Mexico).

- Eventually, the area of coastal and estuarine waters with anoxic (no oxygen present), hypoxic (less than 2 ppm), low (2 to 4 ppm), and adequate (more than 4 ppm) dissolved oxygen.

What Do the Data Show?

- The size of the July hypoxic zone in the Gulf of Mexico has more than doubled over the past 22 years, from about 3800 square miles in 1985 to about 7900 square miles in 2007.

- From 1985 to 2006, between 10% and 25% of the area of the Chesapeake Bay experienced hypoxic conditions in July. There is no clear trend in the extent of hypoxia in the Chesapeake Bay during this period.

Why Can't This Entire Indicator Be Reported at This Time?

Dissolved oxygen levels are monitored in many U.S. estuaries and coastal areas by state-level programs and research groups (see technical note for links to regional dissolved oxygen reporting programs). However, long-term consistent datasets on dissolved oxygen levels are not available for regions outside the northern Gulf of Mexico and Chesapeake Bay. Dissolved oxygen levels are highly variable at different times of the year, at different locations in an estuary or coastal region, and by depth, making it difficult to record consistent and comparable long-term data.

Continued

Extent of Hypoxia (Dissolved Oxygen less than 2 ppm) in July

Partial Indicator: Gulf of Mexico

Size of the hypoxic zone in July (square miles)

Partial Indicator: Chesapeake Bay

Percent of estuary area that is hypoxic in July

Data source: Gulf of Mexico hypoxia studies of N.N. Rabalais and R.E. Turner and the Chesapeake Bay Program. Coverage: Northern Gulf of Mexico and Chesapeake Bay only. Note: The Gulf of Mexico data are plotted as absolute area (not percent area). Data for the Gulf of Mexico and Chesapeake Bay data are from July only, the month during which hypoxic conditions are considered to be most prevalent.

EXTENT AND PATTERN	CHEMICAL AND PHYSICAL	BIOLOGICAL COMPONENTS	GOODS AND SERVICES
Extent	Nutrients, Carbon, and Oxygen	Plants and Animals	Food, Fiber, and Water
Pattern	Chemical Contamination	Communities	Recreation and Other Services
	Physical	Ecological Productivity	

Areas with Depleted Oxygen *(continued)*

Areas with Depleted Oxygen

Data Gap

Data are not adequate for national reporting on

- **Estuarine and coastal waters outside the Gulf of Mexico and Chesapeake Bay**
- **The area of coastal and estuarine waters with anoxic (no oxygen present), hypoxic (less than 2 ppm), low (2 to 4 ppm), and adequate (more than 4 ppm) dissolved oxygen**

Understanding the Data Although low-oxygen conditions can occur naturally, excess nutrients delivered to coasts (see Movement of Nitrogen, p. 36) are thought to play a role in prolonged hypoxic conditions. Nutrients stimulate algal and zooplankton growth (see Chlorophyll Concentration, p. 86; Harmful Algal Events, p. 83). When these algae and zooplankton die, they sink into deeper waters and are decomposed by bacteria, which consume oxygen in the process. As a result, oxygen levels in deep waters can decline to the point of being harmful to bottom-dwelling organisms. In estuaries and coastal regions, hypoxic zones persist in deep waters because of natural formation of water layers (stratification) that prevent low-oxygen deep water from mixing with oxygen-rich surface water.

Some marine and estuarine species are able to tolerate lower levels of dissolved oxygen better than others, but many species are adversely affected once dissolved oxygen levels fall below 2 to 4 ppm. These conditions can result in reduced survival and growth rates, loss of species diversity (species may abandon oxygen-poor waters, or they may die out), habitat loss, mass mortalities (see Unusual Marine Mortalities, p. 82), and areas of unsuitable habitat that migratory species, such as striped bass and salmon, must avoid.

The technical note for this indicator is on page 288.

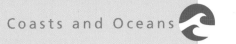

EXTENT AND PATTERN	CHEMICAL AND PHYSICAL	BIOLOGICAL COMPONENTS	GOODS AND SERVICES
Extent	Nutrients, Carbon, and Oxygen	Plants and Animals	Food, Fiber, and Water
Pattern	**Chemical Contamination**	Communities	Recreation and Other Services
	Physical	Ecological Productivity	

Contamination in Bottom Sediments

Why Are Changes in Contaminants Found in Sediments Important?

Sediments in estuaries and oceans can function as "storehouses" of contaminants that can be resuspended, taken up by marine organisms, and passed through the food chain.

What Does This Indicator Report?

How often contaminants in estuary and ocean sediments exceed benchmarks set to protect aquatic life.

What Do the Data Show?

- In 1998–2002, over half of estuary sediments tested had concentrations of one or more contaminants above lower benchmarks (designed to predict "possible adverse effects" on aquatic life); 7% had concentrations above higher benchmarks (designed to predict "probable adverse effects").

Why Can't This Entire Indicator Be Reported at This Time?
No program exists to provide nationally consistent data on sediment contamination in ocean waters along the coast. Data for estuaries in Alaska are available only for the south-central region. Also, benchmarks are not available for 26% of contaminants tested in coastal sediments.

Understanding the Data
Polluted sediments can be a starting point for contamination throughout the food chain, potentially damaging marine life

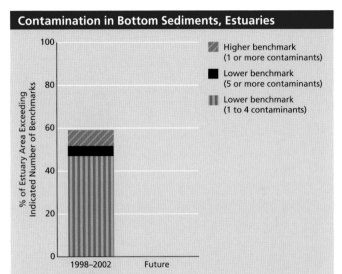

Contamination in Bottom Sediments, Estuaries

y-axis: % of Estuary Area Exceeding Indicated Number of Benchmarks

Legend:
- Higher benchmark (1 or more contaminants)
- Lower benchmark (5 or more contaminants)
- Lower benchmark (1 to 4 contaminants)

x-axis: 1998–2002, Future

Data source: U.S. Environmental Protection Agency National Coastal Assessment (NCA). Coverage: Estuaries off all 50 states and Puerto Rico (for Alaska, south-central region only). (Note that in 2002, we reported data for 1990–1997, but these are not comparable to 1998–2002 data because they did not include North Atlantic and Pacific Coast estuaries.) Technical details: The graph reports exceedances of lower benchmarks (Effects Range-Low, ERL) and higher benchmarks (Effects Range-Median, ERM) benchmarks for 9 trace metals (including mercury) and 51 organic compounds (including total DDT and PCBs). The lower benchmarks identify concentrations below which adverse effects rarely occur and above which adverse effects are considered possible. The higher benchmarks identify concentrations above which adverse effects are considered probable.

Data Gap

Alaskan estuaries beyond the south-central region

Contamination in Bottom Sediments, Ocean

Data Gap

Data are not adequate for national reporting.

and affecting human health (see Selected Contaminants in Fish and Shellfish, p. 90). Pollutants from industrial discharges, burning of fossil fuels, and runoff from farms and urban and suburban areas are carried to coastal waters by rivers, rainfall, and wind, where they accumulate on the bottom. If pollutants are released to the water column, small organisms incorporate these contaminants into their bodies, and when they are eaten by other organisms, the contaminants may become more concentrated in animal tissues as they move up the food chain (bioaccumulation). Areas with contaminated sediments may also be unsafe for swimming and other recreation.

The technical note for this indicator is on page 289.

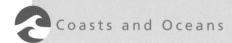
EXTENT AND PATTERN	CHEMICAL AND PHYSICAL	BIOLOGICAL COMPONENTS	GOODS AND SERVICES
Extent	Nutrients, Carbon, and Oxygen	Plants and Animals	Food, Fiber, and Water
Pattern	Chemical Contamination	Communities	Recreation and Other Services
	Physical	Ecological Productivity	

Coastal Erosion

Coastal Erosion

Data Gap

Data are not adequate for national reporting on
- Percentage of U.S. coastline managed to control erosion
- For unmanaged areas, percentage of coastline that is eroding, accreting, or stable

Why Is Erosion along the Coastline Important? Coastal erosion costs hundreds of millions of dollars a year, including damage caused by storms and flooding, losses of property value, costs of erosion prevention, and expenses to dredge channels and harbors. Additionally, erosion can result in habitat loss or alteration, redistribute nutrients and sediments, and affect coastal recreational activities.

What Will This Indicator Report?
- The percentage of U.S. coastline that is managed in an attempt to control erosion
- For unmanaged areas, the fraction of coastline that is eroding, accreting (gaining land area), or stable

Why Can't This Indicator Be Reported at This Time? Assessments of shoreline stability are now conducted as short-term or single-purpose projects that are neither regional nor national in scope. Local assessments often use different methods, which makes it difficult to combine results into an accurate national picture. Priority should be given to using the large amount of existing local data, which will require assessment of coverage, quality, and comparability. Also, standard methods and definitions should be developed for nationwide use, ensuring the compatibility of data collected in the future.

Scientists and coastal managers will need to agree on numerical definitions of "eroding" or "accreting" (this is likely to be in the range of one-half to several feet horizontally per year). There will also need to be agreement on whether a formerly managed area along the coast should always be considered as managed. For example, if an area received additions of sand through a management scheme called "beach nourishment," would it still be appropriate ten years later to classify this area as actively managed?

Discussion Poorly designed or poorly sited development can lead to erosion, while measures to control erosion in one place may exacerbate coastal erosion in others, and may have significant environmental impacts of their own. Erosion can change the extent and condition of coastal living habitats (see p. 72) and impact fish and shellfish communities. Accretion may also create problems, as when inlets fill in, interfering with coastal navigation. Many experts predict that warmer global temperatures associated with climate change will contribute to rising sea levels, resulting in increased coastal erosion worldwide.

Management methods to control erosion or mitigate its effects include beach nourishment and construction of bulkheads or other "armoring" (see Shoreline Types, p. 73).

The technical note for this indicator is on page 289.

EXTENT AND PATTERN	CHEMICAL AND PHYSICAL	BIOLOGICAL COMPONENTS	GOODS AND SERVICES
Extent	Nutrients, Carbon, and Oxygen	Plants and Animals	Food, Fiber, and Water
Pattern	Chemical Contamination	Communities	Recreation and Other Services
	Physical	Ecological Productivity	

Sea Surface Temperature

Why Is Sea Surface Temperature Important? Water temperature directly affects the species of plants (such as algae, seagrasses, marsh plants, and mangroves) and animals (microscopic animals, larger invertebrates, fish, birds, and mammals) that live in a particular region. In addition, increases in sea surface temperature (SST) are thought to be associated with the degradation of coral reefs (bleaching) and may increase the frequency or extent of blooms of harmful algae (see Harmful Algal Events, p. 83). Increases in SST due to global climate warming could lead to changes in the location and increases in the intensity of storms. Shifts in SST may also drive shifts in ocean currents, such as the Gulf Stream, with implications for regional climate.

What Does This Indicator Report? Whether SST is above or below average. Using an index, the indicator tracks how much regional average temperatures in any given year deviate from the average for the 20-year period, for waters within the U.S. Economic Exclusion Zone (nominally 200 miles from the coast).

What Do the Data Show?
- SST varies noticeably from year to year, with no observable trend for the North and Mid-Atlantic, Southern California, Bering Sea, Pacific Northwest, or Hawaii.
- From 1985 to 2006, SST increased significantly in three regions: Gulf of Alaska, Gulf of Mexico, and South Atlantic.

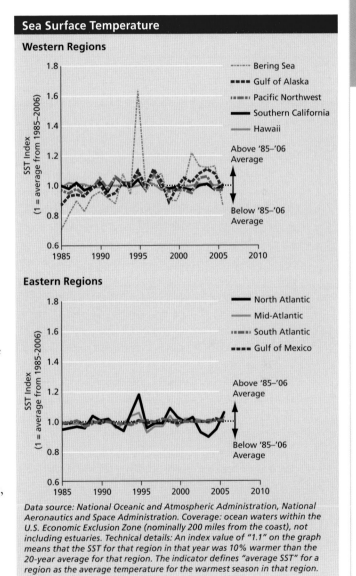

Sea Surface Temperature

Data source: National Oceanic and Atmospheric Administration, National Aeronautics and Space Administration. Coverage: ocean waters within the U.S. Economic Exclusion Zone (nominally 200 miles from the coast), not including estuaries. Technical details: An index value of "1.1" on the graph means that the SST for that region in that year was 10% warmer than the 20-year average for that region. The indicator defines "average SST" for a region as the average temperature for the warmest season in that region.

What Is Not Shown by This Indicator? The temperature estimates shown here are for surface waters only, but recent research has demonstrated that deep ocean temperature trends (to a depth of 700 meters) match surface temperature trends. This is important because very slight changes in temperature in deeper waters can have great significance in terms of the amount of heat stored by the vast quantities of water contained in the world's oceans.

Understanding the Data SST among regions is influenced by different factors. Changes in sea ice extent and ocean circulation patterns can increase or decrease SST. Changes in precipitation regimes on land can also affect runoff and thus SST. The SST spike in the Bering Sea in 1995 was likely related to reduced sea ice coverage.

The technical note for this indicator is on page 290.

EXTENT AND PATTERN	CHEMICAL AND PHYSICAL	BIOLOGICAL COMPONENTS	GOODS AND SERVICES
Extent	Nutrients, Carbon, and Oxygen	Plants and Animals	Food, Fiber, and Water
Pattern	Chemical Contamination	Communities	Recreation and Other Services
	Physical	Ecological Productivity	

At-Risk Native Marine Species

At-Risk Native Marine Species

Data Gap

Data are not adequate for national reporting on the percentage of native marine species at various levels of risk of extinction and on the population trends of at-risk species.

Why Are Native Marine Species Important? Species are valued for a variety of reasons: they provide products, including food, fiber, and genetic materials, which provide potential for a variety of medicinal, industrial and agricultural products; they are key elements of ecosystems, which themselves provide valuable goods and services; and many people value them for their intrinsic worth or beauty.

What Will This Indicator Report?

- The relative risk of extinction of native marine species (plants and animals), presented in several categories, such as vulnerable, imperiled, critically imperiled, and extinct
- The percentage of all native marine species that are at risk, by major ocean region
- Population trends of at-risk native marine species (declining, stable, increasing)

Why Can't This Indicator Be Reported at This Time? Data are available on the status and trends of only a few marine species, mostly those of commercial interest (see p. 88) and those that are listed for protection under the Endangered Species Act and the Marine Mammal Protection Act. However, these programs do not address the status of a broad cross-section of marine species, as is needed for this indicator.

NatureServe and its member Natural Heritage programs (see www.natureserve.org) report on the status of about 22,600 U.S. species [see the forest (p. 144), freshwater (p. 180), grasslands and shrublands (p. 211), and core national (p. 50) at-risk species indicators]. These programs provide a useful framework for reporting on marine species, but so far their datasets contain information on only a relatively small number of marine species. The Ocean Biogeographic Information System's SEAMAP (http://seamap.env.duke.edu/) provides an extensive spatially referenced database on marine mammal, seabird, and sea turtle observations but at present has limited information on species status.

There is no technical note for this indicator. See p. 275 for information on NatureServe's Natural Heritage monitoring program.

EXTENT AND PATTERN	CHEMICAL AND PHYSICAL	BIOLOGICAL COMPONENTS	GOODS AND SERVICES
Extent	Nutrients, Carbon, and Oxygen	Plants and Animals	Food, Fiber, and Water
Pattern	Chemical Contamination	Communities	Recreation and Other Services
	Physical	Ecological Productivity	

Established Non-native Species in Major Estuaries

Why Is Understanding the Prevalence of Non-native Species Important?

Non-native species often spread aggressively and crowd out species native to a region; they may act as predators

---
Established Non-native Species in Major Estuaries

Indicator Development Needed
---

or parasites of native species, cause diseases, compete for food or habitat, and alter habitat structure. These species—whose spread has been promoted by increased travel and trade—may also pose threats to human health (e.g., exotic diseases and harmful algae) and economic well-being, such as loss of shellfish production. Non-native species are also called "nonindigenous," "exotic," "alien," or "introduced" species. Particularly aggressive species are termed "invasive."

What Will This Indicator Report?
The proportion of all species within major estuaries in the United States that are established non-native species, including plants, vertebrates, invertebrates and plant and animal pathogens affecting native species. Established non-native species are those that are known to be surviving and reproducing.

Why Can't This Indicator Be Reported at This Time?
The percentage of species that are established non-native species is not equivalent to habitat occupancy or resource use, but it does suggest the impact that non-native species may have on an estuary. Further development is needed to decide whether this would provide sufficient information to be a useful indicator, or if other dimensions, such as habitat occupancy, would need to be measured.

Suitable data are unlikely to be available immediately to report on this indicator nationally. Including estuarine species from all four taxonomic groups (plants, vertebrates, invertebrates, and plant and animal pathogens affecting native species) is recommended. Data necessary to report on the proportion of species that are established non-natives in any particular ecosystem would be a subset of the data reported in the core national indicator (p. 52). The discussion in the core national indicator describes the limited data availability for the pattern and distribution of plants, vertebrates, invertebrates, and pathogens.

Non-native species groups that are not well documented, including pathogens, invertebrates, and fishes, are major components of all ecosystems, but their significance in estuarine habitats, where waterborne diseases and the status of fisheries are directly relevant to economic and recreational values, is broadly recognized. The lack of data on these taxa and the current inability to parse available data (such as NatureServe's) on non-native species by habitat usage prevent implementation of this indicator at a national level.

Discussion
U.S. estuaries are now home to many non-native species. Some non-native species, such as the Chinese mitten crab and the invasive sea squirt, may be accidentally introduced through the ballast water of international ships. Other species, such as lionfish along the southeast coast and Caulerpa seaweed in California, are introduced when they are accidentally or sometimes intentionally released from home aquariums. Big, busy ports can be trouble spots—the San Francisco Bay area is well known for its high population of non-native species: more than 230 non-native species are known to exist there, accounting for some 90% of the bay's aquatic species.

The technical note for this indicator is on page 290.

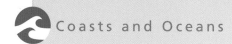
EXTENT AND PATTERN	CHEMICAL AND PHYSICAL	BIOLOGICAL COMPONENTS	GOODS AND SERVICES
Extent	Nutrients, Carbon, and Oxygen	Plants and Animals	Food, Fiber, and Water
Pattern	Chemical Contamination	Communities	Recreation and Other Services
	Physical	Ecological Productivity	

Unusual Marine Mortalities

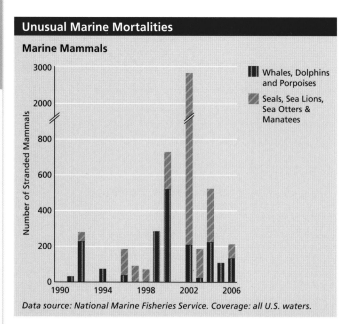

Unusual Marine Mortalities

Marine Mammals

Number of Stranded Mammals

Whales, Dolphins and Porpoises

Seals, Sea Lions, Sea Otters & Manatees

Data source: National Marine Fisheries Service. Coverage: all U.S. waters.

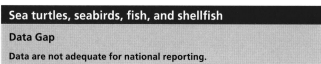

Sea turtles, seabirds, fish, and shellfish

Data Gap

Data are not adequate for national reporting.

Why Are Unusual Marine Mortalities Important? Events in which marine mammals, birds, fish, and turtles die unexpectedly in high numbers or under unusual circumstances may threaten sensitive marine populations and may indicate that stresses such as toxins, pollution, or changing weather patterns are affecting marine ecosystems.

What Does This Indicator Report?
- The number of marine mammals involved in events classified as Unusual Mortality Events (UME), in two groups (whales, dolphins, and porpoises; seals, sea lions, sea otters, and manatees)
- The number of sea turtles involved in UMEs
- The number of seabirds, fish, or shellfish involved in UMEs

Why Can't This Entire Indicator Be Reported at This Time? National data on turtle, seabird, fish, and shellfish mortality events are not available. Further work is required to define the criteria for UMEs for seabirds, fish, and shellfish.

What Do the Data Show?
- The number of unusual marine mortalities for the two groups of marine mammals reported here varies over time from zero to several hundred marine mammals, with no clear trend.
- In 2002, nearly 2800 marine mammals were involved in events classified as UMEs. The majority of these mortalities were believed to be caused by infectious disease or biotoxins (produced by algae).

Understanding the Data Unusual mortality events are tracked and classified by NOAA's National Marine Fisheries Service. In classifying an event as a UME several criteria are considered, including the number of animals involved, the age and sex of the animals, the location and timing of the event, any abnormal pathological or behavioral findings, and the status of the affected species (threatened, endangered, declining). Factors that may contribute to unusual mortalities include infectious diseases, biotoxins produced by algae (see Harmful Algal Events, p. 83), malnutrition, and uncommon weather patterns.

This indicator reports only unusual events. Mortalities caused by old age, recreational boat strikes, or entanglement in fishing nets (bycatch) are not reported. By restricting reporting in this way, the indicator focuses on events that may indicate changes in the state of the overall marine ecosystem.

The technical note for this indicator is on page 291.

EXTENT AND PATTERN	CHEMICAL AND PHYSICAL	BIOLOGICAL COMPONENTS	GOODS AND SERVICES
Extent	Nutrients, Carbon, and Oxygen	Plants and Animals	Food, Fiber, and Water
Pattern	Chemical Contamination	Communities	Recreation and Other Services
	Physical	Ecological Productivity	

Harmful Algal Events

Why Are Harmful Algal Events Important? Harmful algal events can cause mass mortalities of aquatic organisms (see Unusual Marine Mortalities, p. 82) and may be a public health risk. They

> **Established Non-native Species in Major Estuaries**
>
> **Indicator Development Needed**

can cause economic damage through medical costs and declines in tourism, shellfish bed closures, reductions in the market value of seafood, and increases in the cost of monitoring and mitigation. Harmful algal events are defined as an increased abundance of algae species that can cause direct damage to animal tissues (for example, by clogging fish gills) or illness among people or animals by producing toxins. Events may also be defined by the actual occurrence of algae-caused illnesses.

What Will the Indicator Report? Ideally, the number of harmful algal events of low, medium, and high intensity for estuaries and waters within 200 miles of shore.

Why Can't This Indicator Be Reported at This Time? There are no nationwide monitoring or reporting programs for harmful algal events, nor are there generally accepted definitions of low, medium, and high intensity.

Discussion Microscopic algae, also called phytoplankton, are directly or indirectly the source of food for virtually all aquatic animals, including commercial and sport fish. Most species are not toxic, and most algal blooms do not involve species that produce toxins harmful to people or animals; however, even nontoxic blooms may reduce oxygen concentrations (see Areas with Depleted Oxygen, p. 75) and light penetration in coastal waters, which can harm coastal organisms and habitat.

The intensity of harmful algal events is difficult to quantify on a national scale because events involve numerous species and toxins, are sporadic, and vary in their extent and duration. Event intensity may best be captured by an index that would combine several metrics—for example, concentrations of toxins in fish and shellfish, fish and marine mammal mortalities that can be attributed directly to harmful algal events, and chlorophyll concentrations or cell numbers, measured in such a way as to capture algal blooms. Such an index has yet to be developed on a national scale. Further, it may be appropriate to report, in addition, the concentration of algal toxins in the Selected Contaminants in Fish and Shellfish indicator (p. 90)

There are indications that harmful algal events may be occurring more frequently, both in the United States and worldwide. The causes are not fully known, but changes in sea surface temperature (see p. 79), nutrient inputs (see the national nitrogen indicator, p. 36), some aquaculture practices, ballast water discharge, and overfishing are believed to play a role.

The Great Lakes are similar to the oceans in many ways. The expectation is that harmful algal events in the Great Lakes would be included in this indicator, perhaps as a separate region.

The technical note for this indicator is on page 291.

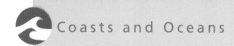

Condition of Bottom-Dwelling Animals

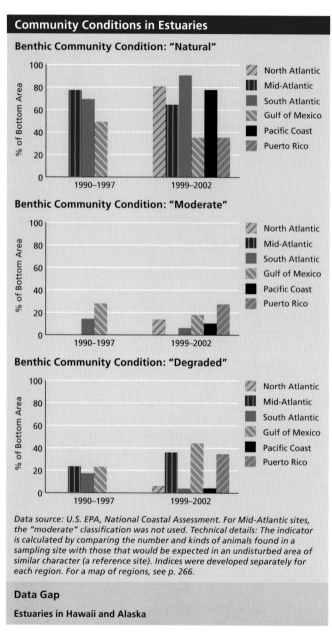

Data source: U.S. EPA, National Coastal Assessment. For Mid-Atlantic sites, the "moderate" classification was not used. Technical details: The indicator is calculated by comparing the number and kinds of animals found in a sampling site with those that would be expected in an undisturbed area of similar character (a reference site). Indices were developed separately for each region. For a map of regions, see p. 266.

Data Gap

Estuaries in Hawaii and Alaska

Community Conditions in Ocean Waters Title

Data Gap

Data are not adequate for national reporting on ocean areas within 25 miles of the coast.

Why Are Bottom-Dwelling Animals Important? The condition of worms, clams, snails, and shrimplike animals in bottom sediments ("benthic communities") reflects the influence of contaminants, oxygen levels, physical changes in habitat (such as from trawl fishing), and shifts in temperature or salinity. Benthic animals are influenced by the productivity of the water column and are a key part of the food chain, supporting both fish and invertebrates.

What Does this Indicator Report? The area in which benthic communities are in "natural," "moderate," and "degraded" condition.

Why Can't This Entire Indicator Be Reported at This Time? Data are not available from Hawaii and Alaska. Only limited data are available for ocean waters out to 25 miles.

What Do the Data Show?
* In 1999–2002, from 60% to 90% of the estuary area on the Atlantic and Pacific coasts was "natural." About a third of the estuary area in the Gulf of Mexico and in Puerto Rico had benthic communities in "natural" condition.
* In 1999–2002, over a third of the estuary area in the Mid-Atlantic, the Gulf of Mexico, and Puerto Rico had benthic communities in "degraded" condition; in other regions, less than 10% had benthic communities in degraded condition. In all regions but Puerto Rico, less than 20% of estuarine area had benthic communities in moderate condition. There was no moderate classification for the Mid-Atlantic region.
* Between 1990–1997 and 1999–2002, benthic communities became more degraded in the Gulf of Mexico and Mid-Atlantic and less degraded in the South Atlantic. Additional data are required to determine if these changes are part of larger trends or are simply fluctuations.

EXTENT AND PATTERN	CHEMICAL AND PHYSICAL	BIOLOGICAL COMPONENTS	GOODS AND SERVICES
Extent	Nutrients, Carbon, and Oxygen	Plants and Animals	Food, Fiber, and Water
Pattern	Chemical Contamination	Communities	Recreation and Other Services
	Physical	Ecological Productivity	

Condition of Bottom-Dwelling Animals *(continued)*

Understanding the Data Benthic organisms are good indicators of community condition because contaminants accumulate in bottom sediments and hypoxia (lack of oxygen) is most severe there. Also, they can live several years, so their response often reflects exposure to these stresses over time. Because benthic organisms are fairly immobile, their condition strongly reflects conditions at the site where they were collected [see Areas with Depleted Oxygen (p. 75) and Contaminants in Bottom Sediments (p. 77).

Some Definitions

"Natural" communities: benthic animals found at a site are similar in number and type of species to those expected in an undisturbed site in that region.

"Moderate" communities have fewer species, more pollution-tolerant species, and fewer pollution-sensitive species than "natural" communities.

"Degraded" communities show greater alteration in species number and type than "moderate" communities.

The technical note for this indicator is on page 292.

EXTENT AND PATTERN	CHEMICAL AND PHYSICAL	BIOLOGICAL COMPONENTS	GOODS AND SERVICES
Extent	Nutrients, Carbon, and Oxygen	Plants and Animals	Food, Fiber, and Water
Pattern	Chemical Contamination	Communities	Recreation and Other Services
	Physical	Ecological Productivity	

Chlorophyll Concentrations

Ocean Waters

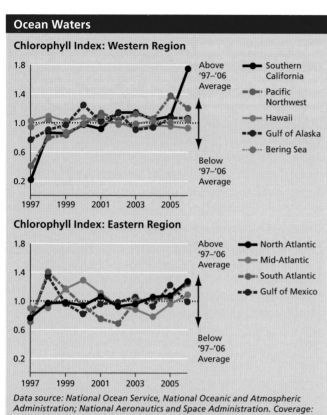

Chlorophyll Index: Western Region

Southern California
Pacific Northwest
Hawaii
Gulf of Alaska
Bering Sea

Chlorophyll Index: Eastern Region

North Atlantic
Mid-Atlantic
South Atlantic
Gulf of Mexico

Data source: National Ocean Service, National Oceanic and Atmospheric Administration; National Aeronautics and Space Administration. Coverage: all U.S. waters, including Alaska and Hawaii, within 25 miles of the coast. Technical details: Chlorophyll estimates are made using satellite data. An index value of "1.1" on the graph means that the average chlorophyll for that region in that year was 10% higher than the 10-year average for that region. The indicator defines "average chlorophyll" for a region as the average chlorophyll for the season with the highest average chlorophyll in that region. For a map of regions, see page 266.

Estuaries

Data Gap

Data are not adequate for national reporting.

Why Is Chlorophyll Concentration Important? Chlorophyll concentration is a measure of the abundance of algae, also called phytoplankton. These tiny organisms account for most of the photosynthesis in the ocean and are the direct or indirect source of food for most marine animals. Although more phytoplankton (as estimated by changes in chlorophyll) tend to support larger fish populations, excessive growth often leads to degraded water quality—for example, decreases in water clarity, bothersome odors, oxygen depletion, and fish kills—and may be linked to harmful algal events.

What Does This Indicator Report?

- Whether chlorophyll is above or below average. Using an index, the indicator tracks how much regional average chlorophyll values in any given year deviate from the average for the 10-year period, for waters within 25 miles from the coast.
- When data become available, the percentage of estuary area with chlorophyll in several ranges.

What Do the Data Show?

- Chlorophyll concentrations in the ocean are highly variable regionally and among years.
- Chlorophyll concentrations increased in the Pacific Northwest, Southern California, and North Atlantic regions (1997–2006).
- Chlorophyll concentrations decreased in Hawaii (1997–2006). Additional years of data are needed to determine if there are upward or downward trends in the other regions.

Why Can't This Entire Indicator Be Reported at This Time? Most estuaries are not sampled frequently enough or thoroughly enough to produce comparable data on seasonal chlorophyll levels as a percentage of estuarine area.

Understanding the Data Chlorophyll concentrations vary seasonally, which is why data are presented for the season with the highest values for a given year. A number of factors contribute to variation in chlorophyll concentrations. For example, increased nutrient inputs (especially nitrogen—see the Movement of Nitrogen, p. 36) can produce excessive algae growth in coastal waters, which can lead to reduced levels of dissolved oxygen (see Areas with Depleted Oxygen, p. 75). Declines in the abundance of filter-feeding organisms like oysters, clams, and mussels can also contribute to increased chlorophyll concentrations.

The technical note for this indicator is on page 293.

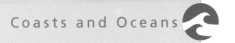

EXTENT AND PATTERN	CHEMICAL AND PHYSICAL	BIOLOGICAL COMPONENTS	GOODS AND SERVICES
Extent	Nutrients, Carbon, and Oxygen	Plants and Animals	**Food, Fiber, and Water**
Pattern	Chemical Contamination	Communities	Recreation and Other Services
	Physical	Ecological Productivity	

Commercial Fish and Shellfish Landings

Why Is the Amount of Fish and Shellfish Taken from U.S. Ocean Waters Important? The amount of fish and shellfish caught for food, meal, and oil is a measure of society's use of the coasts and oceans for these products.

What Does This Indicator Report? The weight of fish, shellfish, and other products taken from U.S. waters.

What Do the Data Show?
- In 2005, 4.6 million tons of fish and shellfish were landed in U.S. waters, an increase of almost 90% since 1950.
- Since 1990, Alaskan waters have provided the bulk of U.S. commercial landings.
- Alaska is the only region where landings have increased since 1978. Landings have decreased from 1978 to 2005 in the West Coast and Hawaii, the Gulf of Mexico, and the North, Mid-, and South Atlantic.

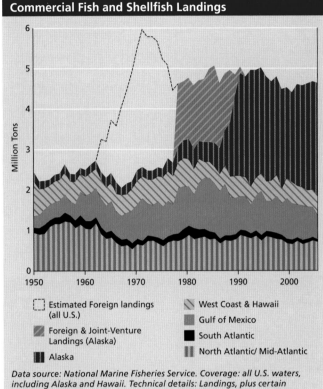

Commercial Fish and Shellfish Landings

Data source: National Marine Fisheries Service. Coverage: all U.S. waters, including Alaska and Hawaii. Technical details: Landings, plus certain aquaculture harvests, are shown for five regions that cover all waters out to the 200-mile EEZ limit. For a map of regions, see p. 266.

Understanding the Data In the late 1970s, the United States established a Fishery Conservation Zone (FCZ) that extended 200 miles from the coast, covering hundreds of thousands of square miles of formerly international waters (this zone is now known as the Exclusive Economic Zone, or EEZ). Foreign fishing in these waters was eliminated immediately, except in Alaska, where it was phased out, ending completely in 1991. The total foreign catch in the FCZ is uncertain, as indicated by the dotted line on the graph, and pre-1963 estimates are not available.

This indicator does not provide information on the condition of fish stocks (see Status of Commercially Important Fish Stocks, p. 88). Furthermore, these aggregate landing figures do not reveal that, over the years, fishing efforts have repeatedly shifted from species that have been depleted or overfished to others that have been relatively unexploited. The data also report only fish and shellfish brought to dock and therefore do not include bycatch (unwanted fish that are caught and then discarded).

Of total landings (for 2004–2005), 80% is for human consumption, 15% is for meal, oil, and other industrial purposes, and the remainder is used for bait and animal feed. In 2005, 88% of the landings were fish, 11% shellfish, and 1% other species, including sea urchins and worms.

The technical note for this indicator is on page 294.

EXTENT AND PATTERN	CHEMICAL AND PHYSICAL	BIOLOGICAL COMPONENTS	GOODS AND SERVICES
Extent	Nutrients, Carbon, and Oxygen	Plants and Animals	**Food, Fiber, and Water**
Pattern	Chemical Contamination	Communities	Recreation and Other Services
	Physical	Ecological Productivity	

Status of Commercially Important Fish Stocks

Status of Commercially Important Fish Stocks

Percentage of Known Stocks Increasing

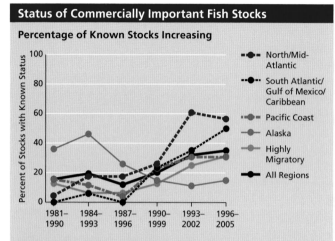

Percentage of Known Stocks Decreasing

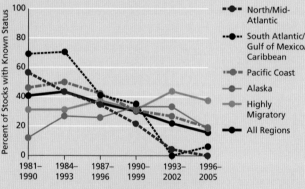

Percentage of Stocks with Known Population Trends (1996–2005)

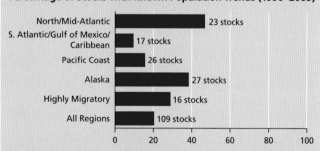

Data source: NOAA National Marine Fisheries Service. Coverage: Nearshore stocks (generally in state waters within 3 miles of shore) are excluded. Technical details: In the top two figures, only stocks whose population increased or decreased by at least 25% are reported. Trends are based on the estimated weight, or "biomass," of the entire stock. Highly migratory species are reported separately because they inhabit more than one ocean region. Nearshore and anadromous species are not included in this dataset. The West Pacific EEZ is an important fishery, but data for the West Pacific are unavailable. The "highly migratory" category includes stocks that inhabit West Pacific waters during at least part of their life cycle. For a map of regions, see p. 266.

Data Gap

Stocks without known population trends

Why Is the Status of Commercial Fish Stocks Important?

Fish harvests are an important benefit provided by marine ecosystems (see Commercial Fish and Shellfish Landings, p. 87). Landings of a given stock cannot be maintained indefinitely if that stock's population declines. If declines persist, stocks can become too small to fish, with attendant economic and social consequences. Reductions in fish stocks can also indicate significant changes in the marine ecosystem.

What Does This Indicator Report?

This indicator tracks the percentage of commercially important fish stocks with known trends that are increasing or decreasing in size.

What Do the Data Show?

- From 1996 to 2005, with the exception of Alaskan and migratory stocks, a greater percentage of known stocks have increasing population trends than decreasing trends.
- Since the 1980s, the percentage of known stocks with increasing trends has grown for all regions (including highly migratory stocks) except Alaska and the Pacific Coast. The percentage of stocks decreasing has declined in all regions except Alaska and highly migratory stocks.
- Thirty-nine percent of stocks in Alaska and 47% of stocks in the North/Mid-Atlantic region have known trends.

What Is Not Shown by This Indicator?

A large number of stocks do not have known population trends, and this varies by region. Thus, the data shown here do not provide a complete picture of the condition of commercially important fish stocks (data are for 109 stocks, or about 21% of all commercial fish stocks, which account for a large proportion of the total fish caught). Further, this indicator does not consider the commercial importance of stocks that are increasing or decreasing, nor does it consider how the number of different types of stocks in a region might be changing over time. Finally, this

EXTENT AND PATTERN	CHEMICAL AND PHYSICAL	BIOLOGICAL COMPONENTS	GOODS AND SERVICES
Extent	Nutrients, Carbon, and Oxygen	Plants and Animals	**Food, Fiber, and Water**
Pattern	Chemical Contamination	Communities	Recreation and Other Services
	Physical	Ecological Productivity	

Status of Commercially Important Fish Stocks *(continued)*

indicator reports only stocks with known trends since the 1980s, excluding stocks whose populations declined before monitoring began.

Understanding the Data An increasing number of stocks with positive population growth trends may signal an increased ability of a stock to support commercial fishing, or it may reflect the recovery of an overfished stock. This latter case is likely in the North and Mid-Atlantic, where strict catch restrictions have been imposed in response to severe stock declines.

The technical note for this indicator is on page 294.

EXTENT AND PATTERN	CHEMICAL AND PHYSICAL	BIOLOGICAL COMPONENTS	GOODS AND SERVICES
Extent	Nutrients, Carbon, and Oxygen	Plants and Animals	**Food, Fiber, and Water**
Pattern	Chemical Contamination	Communities	Recreation and Other Services
	Physical	Ecological Productivity	

Selected Contaminants in Fish and Shellfish

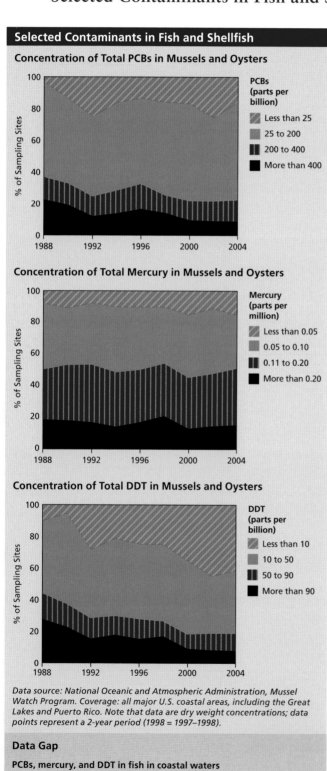

Selected Contaminants in Fish and Shellfish

Concentration of Total PCBs in Mussels and Oysters

PCBs (parts per billion)
- Less than 25
- 25 to 200
- 200 to 400
- More than 400

Concentration of Total Mercury in Mussels and Oysters

Mercury (parts per million)
- Less than 0.05
- 0.05 to 0.10
- 0.11 to 0.20
- More than 0.20

Concentration of Total DDT in Mussels and Oysters

DDT (parts per billion)
- Less than 10
- 10 to 50
- 50 to 90
- More than 90

Data source: National Oceanic and Atmospheric Administration, Mussel Watch Program. Coverage: all major U.S. coastal areas, including the Great Lakes and Puerto Rico. Note that data are dry weight concentrations; data points represent a 2-year period (1998 = 1997–1998).

Data Gap

PCBs, mercury, and DDT in fish in coastal waters

Why Are Contaminants in Seafood Important? Consumption of seafood with high concentrations of PCBs, mercury, or DDT can be harmful to people.

What Does This Indicator Report? For U.S. coastal waters, the percentage of sampling sites with concentrations of total PCBs, mercury and DDT in

- Mussels and oysters
- Saltwater fish (edible tissues), when data become available

What Do the Data Show?

- Since 1987–1988, sites with levels of PCBs in mussels and oysters above 400 ppb have declined from 23% to 9%, and sites with less than 25 ppb have increased from 3% to 16%.
- About half the sites have mercury concentrations in mussels and oysters above 0.10 ppm, and sites with levels of mercury less than 0.05 ppm have increased from 8% to 15% since 1987–1988.
- Sites with DDT in mussels and oysters above 50 ppb have declined from 44% to 19%, and sites with DDT below 10 ppb have increased from 10% to 41% since 1987–1988.

What Is Not Shown By This Indicator? Concentrations are shown for dried mussel and oyster tissues. FDA benchmarks for determining contamination in seafood are for wet weight concentrations. Thus, contamination levels cannot be directly compared to available benchmarks.

Why Can't This Entire Indicator Be Reported? Although a variety of federal and state monitoring programs gather data on PCBs, mercury, and DDT concentrations in saltwater fish, these programs do not provide a basis for national reporting on these contaminants in edible tissues.

EXTENT AND PATTERN	CHEMICAL AND PHYSICAL	BIOLOGICAL COMPONENTS	GOODS AND SERVICES
Extent	Nutrients, Carbon, and Oxygen	Plants and Animals	Food, Fiber, and Water
Pattern	Chemical Contamination	Communities	Recreation and Other Services
	Physical	Ecological Productivity	

Selected Contaminants in Fish and Shellfish *(continued)*

Understanding the Data Many coastal environments are contaminated with synthetic toxic substances like DDT and PCBs, and mercury is ubiquitous in the marine environment. Bottom-dwelling organisms can ingest and store these contaminants; these organisms are eaten by fish that are in turn eaten by larger fish, and contaminants can become more and more concentrated in tissues of the progressively larger fish in a process called bioaccumulation. Even though the manufacture, distribution, and use of PCBs and DDT has been banned in the United States since the 1970s, deposits in watersheds and sediments (see Contamination in Bottom Sediments, p. 77) as well as leakage from landfills and electrical transformers continue to provide an active source of contamination. Mercury can come from industrial releases, abandoned mines, the burning of fossil fuels for electric power generation, and the weathering of rock.

The technical note for this indicator is on page 296.

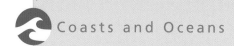

EXTENT AND PATTERN	CHEMICAL AND PHYSICAL	BIOLOGICAL COMPONENTS	GOODS AND SERVICES
Extent	Nutrients, Carbon, and Oxygen	Plants and Animals	Food, Fiber, and Water
Pattern	Chemical Contamination	Communities	**Recreation and Other Services**
	Physical	Ecological Productivity	

Recreational Water Quality

Recreational Water Quality

Data Gap

Data are not adequate for national reporting on the percentage of beach-mile-days affected by *Enterococcus*.

Why Is Reporting on Recreational Water Quality Important? Coasts and oceans offer recreational opportunities for millions of U.S. residents. Water pollution can limit the areas suitable for water recreation and can make people sick. Swimming in sewage-contaminated waters can cause minor ailments, like sore throats and diarrhea, as well as more serious, even fatal, illnesses like severe gastroenteritis, meningitis, and encephalitis.

What Will This Indicator Report? This indicator will report the percentage of "beach-mile-days" affected by various levels of *Enterococcus*, a bacterium that indicates contamination with human or animal waste. A beach-mile-day is one mile of beach affected for one day—100 miles of beach affected for one day would count the same as 1 mile affected for 100 days.

Why Can't This Indicator Be Reported at This Time? Although information is collected on coastal recreational water quality nationally, the data are compiled by many individual jurisdictions employing different methods and standards. As a result, only the total number of beach closings can be reported nationally, with no information on the area affected or the degree of contamination.

Recent federal legislation provides increased incentives to monitor coastal water quality using nationally consistent methods, so data for this indicator should be available in the future. There are other aspects of water quality, such as the presence of contaminated sediments (see Contamination in Bottom Sediments, p. 77) that are not addressed by this indicator.

Discussion Recreational water quality can be affected by a variety of sources, including contamination from sources such as sewage treatment plant malfunctions, overflow of combined sewer systems during rainstorms, discharges from boats, leaking septic systems, and runoff containing animal waste. Stormwater runoff is the most commonly cited cause of degraded beach water quality, although the exact source of many contaminants that end up closing beaches is unknown. Beach monitoring is typically conducted by city or county health departments which frequently use different methods, and many areas choose not to monitor beach water quality at all. This indicator will report the most commonly used indicator organism, *Enterococcus*, which is also recommended by EPA, but some beach monitoring relies upon other organisms.

Beach-based activities, like sunbathing, surfing, and swimming, are popular (see the core national Outdoor Recreation indicator, p. 58), add billions of dollars to the economy, and contribute to the value of coastal properties.

The technical note for this indicator is on page 297.

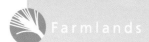
Farmlands

Contents	page

INDICATORS

Chapter 4:
Indicators of the Condition and Use of Farmlands

Farmlands are a rich part of the American landscape and a treasured reminder of the nation's rural heritage. They vary from seemingly endless fields of corn, soybeans, and wheat across the nation's heartland to laser-flat lettuce and strawberry fields in California's Central Valley, rolling vineyards in Oregon, sprawling cattle ranches across the intermountain west, picturesque dairy farms in the Northeast, and vast sugarcane fields in Florida and Puerto Rico.

Farmlands are heavily modified by humans and managed for the resources they provide: food, fiber, fuels, and economic benefits for rural communities, agribusiness, and the U.S. economy as a whole. However, these working landscapes also provide habitat for wildlife and add beauty, variety, and increasingly prized "open space" to the countryside.

Farmland ecosystems—"farmland landscapes" in this report—include both lands used for producing crops and livestock (croplands) and associated hedgerows, streams, ponds, wetlands, prairies, woodlots, and even houses, along with lands withdrawn from production under government programs. Thus, the farmland landscape encompasses features described in other ecosystem chapters in this report, ranging from patches of forest and grassland to low-density development.

Establishing and maintaining fertile farmlands and a thriving farm economy have always been major goals of our nation's politics and policies. Initially, society's primary goal was to ensure farming's stability and the nation's food security in a changing economic milieu, and global trends clearly continue to shape many farmland decisions. More recently, environmental concerns such as soil erosion, nutrient and pesticide runoff, habitat conservation, suburbanization and the construction of homes in predominantly agricultural areas, and issues related to conserving strong rural communities have gained prominence in farm policy discussions.

The following sections and the table on page 100 describe the four categories of ecosystem condition and use outlined in Chapter 1 and summarize the most current data and trends for farmland landscapes. Individual indicators focus on critical dimensions and components of farmland ecosystems at a variety of scales, on ecological processes necessary for the functioning of farmland ecosystems, on living elements of farmed landscapes, and on the benefits people derive from these ecosystems.

Extent and Pattern

Land is an indispensable agricultural resource, and its quantity, distribution, and pattern directly affect the goods and services farmlands provide. Changes in total cropland acreage over time are influenced by the demand for specific crops, the efficiency of agricultural production, and the ability of the land to support agriculture. The regional distribution of croplands—and shifts in that distribution over time—indicates which areas of the United States are the most valuable in terms of crop production and also most susceptible to environmental change due to farming. Additionally, changes in the extent of croplands affect the distribution of other ecosystem types and interact with other economic and ecological indicators that are sensitive to land prices, agricultural management practices, and land use change.

The degree to which farmlands are intermingled with other natural and developed lands across the landscape has a major influence on their use for producing crops and livestock. For example, suburban encroachment and increased housing density in farmland areas may lead to declines in production as

new residents object to long-standing farming practices such as aerial pesticide spraying, burning of stubble, or field application of manure. Also, rising property values and taxes can encourage farmers to sell even high-quality farmland for development. On the other hand, patches of forests and wetlands intermingled with crop fields and pastures can provide important benefits to farmers in the form of windbreaks and necessary habitat for pollinators of agricultural crops.

The size of intermingled "natural" parcels is also likely to be linked to the capacity of the farmland landscape to provide other noncrop ecological services. Remnant wooded areas along streams, for example, not only provide wildlife corridors but also filter nutrient runoff, control erosion, and enhance groundwater recharge.

Data in this chapter show that

- Cropland area has declined since 1982 in most major river basins and now covers some 400 million acres, or about one-quarter of the total land area of the lower 48 states (2003 data).
- The nation's farmland landscape is covered primarily by croplands (51% of land area), with forest (18%), grassland and shrubland (16%), wetlands (5%), developed land (8%), and water (4%) accounting for the remaining noncultivated areas.
- Noncropland components of farmland landscapes in the Northeast/Mid-Atlantic region have the highest percentage of forest (70%); the Rocky Mountain region has the highest percentage of grassland and shrubland (78%); and the West Coast region, the highest percentage of development (24%).
- Patches of "natural" lands in the farmland landscape range in size from less than ½ square mile to more than 1000 square miles. Most patches (about 60%) range from 1 to 100 square miles. About 16% of "natural" patches are smaller than ½ square mile. The Midwest has the greatest percentage of "natural" area in small patches (2001 data).

Data are not adequate for national reporting on

- The proximity of croplands to residences

Chemical and Physical Conditions

Croplands are highly controlled systems in which vegetation, soil, and water are managed and chemicals such as fertilizers and pesticides are commonly added. Indicators of the chemical and physical condition of agricultural soil and water provide key information for understanding not only the current and future productive potential of farmlands but also their effect on other ecosystems. Soil organic matter is a key determinant of soil productivity; the loss of soil through erosion has both on- and off-farm impacts; and soil salinity—the buildup of salt—can negatively affect cropland productivity. Additionally, the water quality of farmland streams, in terms of their pesticide and nutrient concentrations, indicates not only the loss of these inputs from croplands, but also the potential for farmland practices to affect other ecosystems downstream.

Phosphorus and nitrogen fertilizers and other chemicals such as pesticides are applied across many croplands in an effort to maximize crop yields and minimize losses due to pests and disease. Phosphorus and nitrogen are key plant nutrients, but in excess they can stimulate algal growth in streams, lakes, and coastal areas (see Areas with Depleted Oxygen, p. 75; Phosphorus in Lakes, Reservoirs, and Large Rivers, p. 174; and Movement of Nitrogen, p. 36). In sufficient amounts, nitrogen in the form of nitrate in drinking water supplies can also create human health problems. Some pesticides that leak from farmed soils into streams and groundwater can affect wildlife and human health long after the pesticides have been removed from active use because some of these compounds break down slowly in the environment.

Management of environmental quality on and around farmlands involves many considerations. Policies and practices that encourage efficient fertilizer and pesticide application allow farmers to minimize runoff and ensure that on-farm costs do not exceed the yield benefits of chemical treatments perceived by farmers. Practices that favor low inputs of chemicals, including organic farming and the use of genetically engineered crops and organisms, may reduce chemical losses from farms but also have the potential to create other environmental consequences. Legal constraints, such as the Clean Water Act and state regulatory programs, are intended to limit chemical and fertilizer runoff. Regulations can also affect individual farm activities such as plowing practices and the maintenance of buffers along streams. Many entities play a role in farmland ecosystem management and conservation, including federal and state agencies that regulate air and water quality and local entities such as soil and water conservation districts, and extension services.

Data in this chapter show that

- Streams and groundwater wells in areas dominated by agriculture had higher concentrations of nitrate than streams and groundwater in forested or urban areas. About 20% of the groundwater wells and 13% of stream sites sampled in farmland areas had nitrate concentrations that exceeded the federal drinking water standard (10 ppm).

- Phosphorus concentrations in farmland streams are similar to those found in urban-suburban streams but higher than in forested streams. Eighty-five percent of sampled farmland stream sites had concentrations of phosphorus of at least 0.1 part per million (ppm), the EPA-recommended goal for preventing excess algal growth in streams not draining directly into a lake or impoundment.

- One or more pesticides were detected in all streams and more than 60% of groundwater wells monitored in farmland areas. Pesticide levels exceeded aquatic life benchmarks in about 57% of streams and exceeded human health benchmarks in 16% of streams and fewer than 1% of groundwater wells.

- The percentage of croplands most susceptible to wind and water erosion has declined by nearly one-third since the early 1980s. Western U.S. croplands are most susceptible to wind erosion; croplands most prone to water erosion are found in the East.

Data are not adequate for national reporting on

- Total carbon storage and the percent soil organic matter of cropland soils
- The percentage of cropland with varying levels of salinity
- Habitat quality, including the condition of sediments, in-stream fish habitat, and riffles and pools, in farmland streams

Biological Components

Besides providing people with food, fuel, and fiber, farmed landscapes are home to many species of native and non-native plants and animals. The abundance, diversity, and distribution of organisms in farmland ecosystems can have economic and ecological consequences. For example, some non-native plants species established in farmland ecosystems can alter overall farmland biodiversity, impact crop yields, or change the suitability of habitat for different species of wildlife.

The question of how to measure and monitor biological conditions on farmlands is complex. The suite of species in any given area reflects the former landscape (whether the farm was created from forest or prairie, for example), as well as new migrant and introduced species (native and non-native) that thrive in cropland landscapes. Measurement of the coverage of noncropland areas by invasive or otherwise undesirable non-native plant species, which can reduce habitat quality for native wildlife, is complicated by the fragmented nature of "natural" patches within the broader farmland landscape.

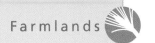

Finally, the condition of soil organisms is an important indicator of the degree of soil disturbance, but these communities are difficult to measure, and there is no national monitoring system for soil organisms in croplands.

Data are not adequate for national reporting on
- The condition of the communities of soil organisms in cropland soils
- The extent of established non-native plant cover in noncropland areas of the farmland landscape

Further indicator development is needed to report on
- The status of animal species in farmland areas

Goods and Services

Farmlands are created and maintained primarily to generate agricultural products, so crop yields, monetary returns, and details about the cost of production (such as the balance of inputs and outputs) offer important insights into the value of the services that farmland ecosystems provide to society. Recreational activities such as hunting, fishing, and wildlife watching are also potentially valuable farmland "products."

The United States invests heavily in managing its agricultural sector. This investment includes a variety of programs that support prices, encourage exports, carry out research, and educate or otherwise assist producers. The effects of these programs and policies are reflected in the indicators included in this chapter. The relative yields and monetary value of different crops have changed over time in response to shifting demand as well as to farm subsidies and incentives, and they are likely to continue to change.

Data in this chapter show that
- Output from U.S. agriculture has increased steadily over time. Since 1948, total output has increased by about 170%.
- Yields per acre of five major crops—wheat, corn, soybeans, cotton, and hay—have increased since 1950, with corn yields alone increasing nearly fourfold.
- Per unit of output, inputs in the form of labor, energy, durable goods, and land declined since 1948. Land showed the greatest decrease in inputs per output, a decline of more than 70%.
- Conversely, inputs of pesticides and fertilizers per unit output increased from 1948 to 2004. Fertilizer inputs increased by 46% and pesticide inputs doubled.
- The monetary value of agricultural goods produced has increased since the 1950s. Farmers received 8% more for their goods during 2004–2005 (about $239–247 billion) than the average for the previous 20 years.

Data are not adequate for national reporting on
- The number of recreation days spent on the farmlands

Status and trends for all farmland indicators are summarized in the following table and described in detail in the remainder of the chapter. Regions and related definitions used throughout this chapter are described in Appendix D.

Indicators	What Do the Most Recent Data Show?	Have Data Values Changed over Time?
EXTENT AND PATTERN		
Total Cropland, p. 102	Cropland covers about 400 million acres, or about a quarter of the land area of the lower 48 states (2003 data).	Cropland area has fluctuated since 1948 (ERS data)
		There has been a decrease in cropland area since 1982 (NRI and ERS data).
The Farmland Landscape, p. 103	The nation's farmland landscape is covered primarily by croplands (51% of land area), with the remaining noncultivated areas composed of forest (18%), grassland and shrubland (16%), wetlands (5%), developed land (8%), and water (4%).	Data are not adequate for national reporting on changes in the percentage of cropland in the farmland landscape.
	The proportion of various non-cropland components of the farmland landscape vary greatly by region (2001 data).	Data are not adequate for national reporting on changes in non-cropland components of the farmland landscape.
Proximity of Croplands to Residences, p. 105	Data are not adequate for national reporting on the proportion of cropland found within several distance ranges of a house.	
Patches of "Natural" Lands in the Farmland Landscape, p.106	16% of "natural" patches in the farmland landscape are less than ½ sq. mile; 60% are in patches ranging from 1 to 100 sq. miles (2001 data).	Data are not adequate for national reporting on changes in the size of "natural" patches in the farmland landscape.
CHEMICAL AND PHYSICAL CHARACTERISTICS		
Nitrate in Farmland Streams and Groundwater, p. 107	40% of streams and 42% of groundwater wells have nitrate concentrations of less than 2 ppm; 13% of streams and 20% of groundwater wells have nitrate concentrations greater than 10 ppm (1992–2003 data).	Data are not adequate for national reporting on changes in nitrate concentrations in farmland streams and groundwater.
Phosphorus in Farmland Streams, p. 109	85% of streams have phosphorus concentrations of at least 0.1 ppm; 13% have phosphorus concentrations of at least 0.5 ppm (1992–2001 data).	Data are not adequate for national reporting on changes in phosphorus concentrations in farmland streams.
Soil Organic Matter, p. 110	Data are not adequate for national reporting on the percentage of organic matter and the amount of organic carbon stored in cropland soils.	
Pesticides in Farmland Streams and Groundwater, p. 111	One or more pesticides detected in all streams and >60% of groundwater wells. Pesticide levels exceeded aquatic life benchmarks in ~57% of streams; human health benchmarks were exceeded in 16% of streams and <1% of groundwater wells (1992–2003 data).	Data are not adequate for national reporting on changes in pesticides in farmland streams and groundwater wells.
Potential Soil Erosion, p. 112	About 64% of cropland is considered least prone to wind erosion, 19% moderately prone, and 16% most prone (2003 data).	From 1982 to 2003, the proportion of U.S. farmland most prone to wind erosion decreased.
	About 41% of cropland is considered least prone to water erosion, 28% moderately prone, and 21% most prone (2003 data).	From 1982 to 2003, the proportion of U.S. farmland most prone to water erosion decreased.
Soil Salinity, p. 114	Data are not adequate for national reporting on the percentage of cropland soils with different salt levels.	
Stream Habitat Quality, p. 115	Data are not adequate for national reporting on the condition of sediments, in-stream fish habitat, and riffles and pools in farmland streams.	

Indicators	What Do the Most Recent Data Show?	Have Data Values Changed over Time?

BIOLOGICAL COMPONENTS

Status of Animal Species in Farmland Areas, p. 116	Indicator Development Needed	
Established Non-native Plant Cover in the Farmland Landscape, p. 117	Data are not adequate for national reporting on the extent of established non-native plant cover in the noncropland portion of the farmland landscape.	
Soil Biological Condition, p. 118	Data are not adequate for national reporting on the condition of communities of soil organisms in cropland soils.	

GOODS AND SERVICES

Major Crop Yields, p. 119	With some year-to-year variation, per acre yields of corn, soybeans, wheat, and cotton have continued a long-term increase since 1950. Yields of hay have not changed for at least the past 25 years.	Wheat, corn, soybean, hay, and cotton yields have increased since 1950.
Agricultural Inputs and Outputs, p. 120	In recent years, per unit of output, the inputs of energy, labor, durable goods, and land have continued a decline documented since 1948. Inputs of pesticides per unit of output have continued to increase since 1948, although fertilizer inputs per unit of output have not changed since 1975.	Since 1948, there has been a decrease in the amount of energy, labor, durable goods, and land used per unit output.
		Since 1948, there has been an increase in the amount of pesticides and fertilizers used per unit output.
	Total outputs are about 170% higher than in 1948 (2004 data).	Total outputs from U.S. agriculture have increased since 1948.
Monetary Value of Agricultural Production, p. 121	Farmers receive about $239 billion for agricultural products, such as meat, cotton, eggs, fruits, and vegetables (2005 data).	Since 1950, the money received by farmers for their goods has increased.
Recreation in Farmland Areas, p. 122	Data are not adequate for national reporting on the number of recreation days spent on farmlands.	

 = significant decrease  =significant increase 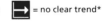 = no clear trend*  = insufficient data for trend analysis

= Data not available for adequate reporting.

* may be due to little numerical change in the data or large numerical fluctuations in data resulting in no single trend

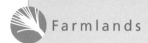

EXTENT AND PATTERN	CHEMICAL AND PHYSICAL	BIOLOGICAL COMPONENTS	GOODS AND SERVICES
Extent	Nutrients, Carbon, and Oxygen	Plants and Animals	Food, Fiber, and Water
Pattern	Chemical Contamination	Communities	Recreation and Other Services
	Physical	Ecological Productivity	

Total Cropland

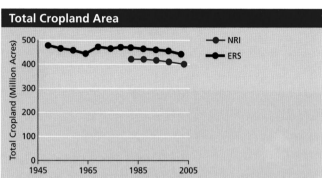

Total Cropland Area

Data source: USDA Natural Resources Conservation Service, National Resources Inventory (NRI) program. USDA Economic Research Service (ERS). Coverage: lower 48 states. Technical details: NRI data appear to be a better predictor of current cropland acreage, while the ERS data provide a good historic trend.

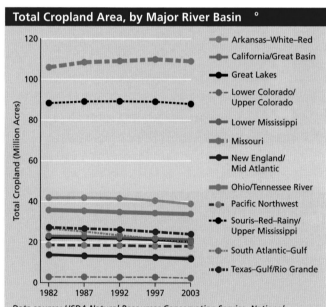

Total Cropland Area, by Major River Basin °

- Arkansas–White–Red
- California/Great Basin
- Great Lakes
- Lower Colorado/Upper Colorado
- Lower Mississippi
- Missouri
- New England/Mid Atlantic
- Ohio/Tennessee River
- Pacific Northwest
- Souris–Red–Rainy/Upper Mississippi
- South Atlantic–Gulf
- Texas–Gulf/Rio Grande

Data source: USDA Natural Resources Conservation Service, National Resources Inventory (NRI) program. Coverage: lower 48 states. Note: see p. 267 for map of river basins.

Why Is Total Cropland Area Important? Agriculture is a major component of the U.S. economy. The amount of land used for agriculture and the distribution of cropland across the nation has broad economic, societal, and ecological effects. The expansion or contraction of cropland area affects adjacent land uses and is reflected in changes in the extent of other ecosystem types.

What Does This Indicator Report? The amount of land used for crops, including cultivated lands and noncultivated lands. Also included in total cropland estimates are lands enrolled in long-term set-aside programs, such as the Conservation Reserve Program (CRP), and permanent haylands or pasturelands in rotation with crops.

What Do the Data Show?
- Cropland covered about 400 million acres in 2003, according to the USDA's National Resources Inventory (NRI).
- Based on long-term estimates from the USDA's Economic Research Service (ERS), cropland area fluctuated from 1948 to 2002. Since 1982, cropland area has declined significantly.
- All major river basins, except the Missouri and the Souris–Red–Rainy/Upper Mississippi river basins, exhibited significant declines in cropland area since NRI data collection began in 1982; cropland area showed no significant change in either the Missouri or the Souris–Red–Rainy/Upper Mississippi river basin.

Understanding the Data Cropland may be used for crops one year, be left idle for one or many years, and then returned to production. Changes in government programs or crop prices may cause land to be left idle for short periods or to be used for different crops. For example, farmers are currently returning CRP land to corn production and converting from cotton and soybean production to corn production in order to enter the lucrative biofuels market. In contrast, fairly permanent long-term changes in cropland acreage may result from conversion to other uses, such as development. The current indicator design recognizes that CRP lands remain in the nation's inventory of available lands, but it does not pinpoint changes in the area of land enrolled in this program (see Land Use in Grasslands and Shrublands, p. 203).

The technical note for this indicator is on page 297.

EXTENT AND PATTERN	CHEMICAL AND PHYSICAL	BIOLOGICAL COMPONENTS	GOODS AND SERVICES
Extent	Nutrients, Carbon, and Oxygen	Plants and Animals	Food, Fiber, and Water
Pattern	Chemical Contamination	Communities	Recreation and Other Services
	Physical	Ecological Productivity	

The Farmland Landscape

Why Is the Composition of Landscapes Dominated by Cropland Important? Croplands define the farmland landscape, but they are intermingled with patches of forest, wetlands, ponds, and development in the form of houses, roads, and other built structures. The noncropland elements of the farmland landscape (other than development) provide wildlife habitat, serve as streamside buffers and windbreaks, and lend a distinctive visual character to the landscape.

What Does This Indicator Report?

- The percentage of the farmland landscape that is cropland—land that is actively used for crop production, pasture, or haylands
- The composition of the noncropland area in the farmland landscape that is forest, wetland, grassland and shrubland, water, or development

What Do the Data Show?

- For 2001, the Midwest and West Coast had the highest percentages (about 60%) of cropland in their farmland landscapes; the Northeast/Mid-Atlantic and Southeast had the lowest percentage of cropland (34% and 38%, respectively).
- The Northeast/Mid-Atlantic had the highest percentage (70%) of forest in the noncropland portion of the farmland landscape; the Rocky Mountain region had the lowest percentage (4%).
- The Rocky Mountain region had the highest percentage (78%) of grassland/shrubland in the noncropland portion of the farmland landscape; the Northeast/Mid-Atlantic had the lowest percentage (3%).
- The Southeast had the highest percentage (17%) of wetlands in the noncropland portion of the farmland landscape; all other regions had less than 10%.
- The West Coast had the highest percentage (24%) of development in the noncropland portion of the farmland landscape; the other regions had between 10% and 20%.
- Water accounted for less than 5% of the noncropland portion of the farmland landscape for all regions.

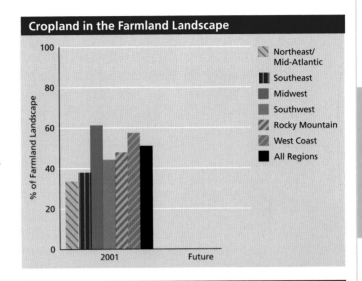

Cropland in the Farmland Landscape

Legend: Northeast/Mid-Atlantic, Southeast, Midwest, Southwest, Rocky Mountain, West Coast, All Regions

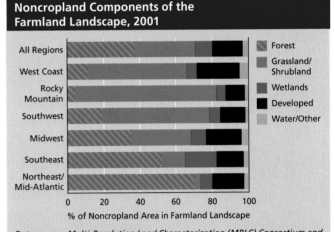

Noncropland Components of the Farmland Landscape, 2001

Legend: Forest, Grassland/Shrubland, Wetlands, Developed, Water/Other

Data source: Multi-Resolution Land Characterization (MRLC) Consortium and ESRI (road map); analysis by U.S. Environmental Protection Agency and the U.S. Forest Service. Coverage: lower 48 states. Technical details: the National Land Cover Dataset (NLCD) was augmented with a road map (paved roads only). A protocol was used to create patches of pixels across the country that are characterized by their proximity to cropland (see technical note). The land cover within these polygons is reported in the graphs. Note that identifying wetlands on croplands is difficult; wetlands data should be interpreted cautiously. Also, pasture and haylands are intermediate in character between "natural" grasslands and cultivated croplands; for this indicator, they are counted as croplands. Note further that the analytic approach used here differs substantially from that used in the 2002 edition.

Continued

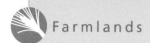

EXTENT AND PATTERN	CHEMICAL AND PHYSICAL	BIOLOGICAL COMPONENTS	GOODS AND SERVICES
Extent	Nutrients, Carbon, and Oxygen	Plants and Animals	Food, Fiber, and Water
Pattern	Chemical Contamination	Communities	Recreation and Other Services
	Physical	Ecological Productivity	

The Farmland Landscape *(continued)*

Understanding the Data This indicator describes the degree to which croplands dominate the landscape and the degree to which other land cover types are intermingled. However, because this indicator relies on land cover data, it does not describe the quality of noncropland habitat, nor does it provide information on the degree of management in place on these lands.

This indicator should, over time, be sensitive to the expansion of urban and suburban land use into farmland areas as well as to the conversion of forest, grassland, or other land cover to cropland. However, the data reported here do not measure very low density "exurban" development (denser than scattered rural settlements, but less dense than "suburban"—see Proximity of Cropland to Residences, p. 105).

The technical note for this indicator is on page 298.

EXTENT AND PATTERN	CHEMICAL AND PHYSICAL	BIOLOGICAL COMPONENTS	GOODS AND SERVICES
Extent	Nutrients, Carbon, and Oxygen	Plants and Animals	Food, Fiber, and Water
Pattern	Chemical Contamination	Communities	Recreation and Other Services
	Physical	Ecological Productivity	

Proximity of Cropland to Residences

Why Is the Distance between Cropland and Residences Important?
Society is dependent on food and fiber produced on our nation's croplands. As metropolitan areas expand and as people choose to settle in less-developed areas,

> **Proximity of Cropland to Residences**
>
> **Data Gap**
>
> Data are not adequate for national reporting on the proportion of cropland found within several distance ranges of a house.

more homes are located near or adjacent to croplands. There are advantages and disadvantages to having residents in close proximity to cropland, but a particular concern is that diminishing distances between croplands and residences may lead to the permanent removal of high-quality farmland from production.

What Will This Indicator Report? This indicator will describe the proportion of cropland at varying distances from dwellings. Specifically, the proportion of cropland found within several distance ranges (less than 100 feet, 100 to 300 feet, and so on) of a house will be reported.

Why Can't This Entire Indicator Be Reported at This Time? This analysis will require detailed data on household locations in areas with significant agricultural operations. Such data are available for only a few areas across the country, although as more property data become available in electronic format, coverage is expected to increase. Currently available land cover data provide information on residential development, but the resolution of such data is coarser than would be necessary to distinguish individual homes in the farmland landscape.

Discussion Rather than simply reporting the number of homes within a given area, this indicator will provide information on the spatial pattern of residences in relation to cropland. For example, the indicator will distinguish between the effects of a number of houses clumped together and the effects of the same number spread out more evenly across an agricultural landscape—more cropland will be nearer to a residence in the latter case.

Housing and other development in farmland areas may compromise the economic viability of farming by, for example, increasing land values to a point that encourages farmers to sell. Beyond basic issues such as fertility and availability of water, the food and fiber production capacity of agricultural land is a function of the ability to use farming practices without causing harm or annoying residential neighbors from noise, dust, or chemical overspray, for example. Complaints from neighbors can lead to the elimination of agriculture in an area, or to its restriction to smaller parcels (note that some types of agriculture, such as vegetable farms, may be able to flourish in such a fragmented farmland landscape because of the proximity of customers).

This indicator, by quantifying one key pattern of farmland landscapes, focuses on the collective ability of farmers to continue farming. Of course, farming may affect nonfarm residents, both nearby and not, in other ways—see, for example, Pesticides in Farmland Streams and Groundwater (p. 111), the indicators for nitrogen and phosphorus in farmland streams and groundwater (p. 107 and 109), and Recreation in Farmland Areas (p. 122).

The technical note for this indicator is on page 298.

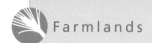

EXTENT AND PATTERN	CHEMICAL AND PHYSICAL	BIOLOGICAL COMPONENTS	GOODS AND SERVICES
Extent	Nutrients, Carbon, and Oxygen	Plants and Animals	Food, Fiber, and Water
Pattern	Chemical Contamination	Communities	Recreation and Other Services
	Physical	Ecological Productivity	

Patches of "Natural" Land in the Farmland Landscape

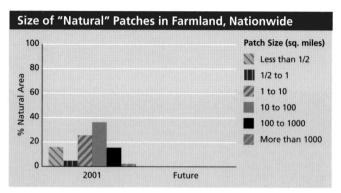

Size of "Natural" Patches in Farmland, Nationwide

Patch Size (sq. miles)
- Less than 1/2
- 1/2 to 1
- 1 to 10
- 10 to 100
- 100 to 1000
- More than 1000

Size of "Natural" Patches in Farmland, by Region (2001)

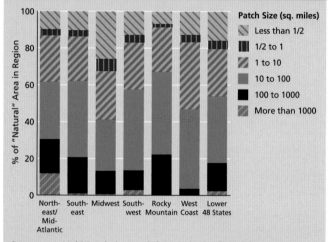

Patch Size (sq. miles)
- Less than 1/2
- 1/2 to 1
- 1 to 10
- 10 to 100
- 100 to 1000
- More than 1000

Data source: Multi-Resolution Land Characterization (MRLC) Consortium and ESRI (road map); analysis by the U.S. Environmental Protection Agency and the U.S. Forest Service. Coverage: lower 48 states. Technical details: all "natural" pixels within the farmland landscape (p. 35) were formed into patches of touching pixels, the size of which is reported in the graphs. Note: current technical limitations required that patches be "cut" by state boundaries, meaning that these data should be considered to represent minimum patch sizes. We do not know how this analysis limitation affected the data.

Why Are Patches of "Natural" Land Important? Patches of "natural" land (forests, grasslands, shrublands, and wetlands) help control erosion and movement of sediments, facilitate groundwater recharge, provide critical habitat for wildlife, and support other important ecological processes, such as carbon storage.

What Does This Indicator Report?
The size of "natural" patches in the farmland landscape, nationally and regionally

What Do the Data Show?
- In 2001, 16% of the "natural" patches in the farmland landscape were less than ½ square mile (320 acres). About 60% of patches ranged from 1 to 100 square miles; there were few patches of ½ to 1 square mile and even fewer larger than 1000 square miles.
- The Northeast/Mid-Atlantic had the highest proportion of "natural" area (30%) in patches larger than 100 acres, and several very large patches accounted for 12% of the total "natural" area in the region; the West Coast had the lowest proportion of "natural" area (4%) in patches larger than 100 acres.
- The Midwest had proportionally more "natural" area (33%) and the Rocky Mountain region had proportionally less (9%) in patches smaller than 1 acre than the other regions.

Understanding the Data In landscapes dominated by agriculture, the size of these often small and isolated remnants of "natural" lands, along with restored conservation areas, such as Conservation Reserve Program (CRP) lands, directly influences the amount and type of ecosystem services provided—beyond crop production. Note that the size of "natural" patches may be strongly influenced by ownership and land use history—for example, in some regions, property lines have historically been marked by fencerows and trees or other vegetation.

Further conversion of land to cropland can fragment the existing "natural" lands. In general, the smaller the patches of "natural" habitat, the lower the quality of habitat for native plant and animal species (although this is not necessarily true for wetlands); smaller patches also provide less solitude and fewer recreational opportunities for people. Smaller patches of habitat may favor common, human-tolerant native and non-native species like squirrels, white-tailed deer, starlings, and sparrows over less common species that require larger areas, such as some birds (pileated woodpeckers, broad-winged hawks, and many warblers), mammals (bears, mountain lions, wolves, coyotes, mink, otters, and weasels), and amphibians and reptiles.

The technical note for this indicator is on page 299.

EXTENT AND PATTERN	CHEMICAL AND PHYSICAL	BIOLOGICAL COMPONENTS	GOODS AND SERVICES
Extent	Nutrients, Carbon, and Oxygen	Plants and Animals	Food, Fiber, and Water
Pattern	Chemical Contamination	Communities	Recreation and Other Services
	Physical	Ecological Productivity	

Nitrate in Farmland Streams and Groundwater

Why Is Nitrate in Streams and Groundwater Important? Elevated nitrate in drinking water is a serious health threat to infants; untreated water from household groundwater wells poses a particular risk (municipal water supply systems typically take steps to remove nitrate), and such wells are common in farming areas. High levels of nitrate in streams indicate that farmlands receive more nitrogen than can be stored in soils or taken up by plants. Excess nitrogen in streams that ultimately empty into coastal waters can lead to algal blooms, decreasing recreational and aesthetic values and depleting oxygen needed by fish and other animals (see Movement of Nitrogen, p. 36, and Areas with Depleted Oxygen, p. 75).

What Does This Indicator Report?

- For streams and groundwater wells in areas that are primarily farmland, average nitrate concentrations
- A comparison of nitrate concentrations in streams and groundwater in farmlands, forests, and urban–suburban landscapes

What Do the Data Show?

- Forty percent of stream sites and 42% of groundwater wells sampled in farmlands had concentrations of nitrate below 2 parts per million (ppm).
- Twenty percent of the groundwater wells and about 13% of stream sites sampled in farmland areas had concentrations that exceeded the federal drinking water standard (10 ppm).
- Groundwater samples from areas dominated by agricultural use have higher concentrations of nitrate than urban or forested areas, with forested lands having the lowest concentrations. Farmland and urban areas both had sites that exceeded the 10 ppm federal drinking water standard.

Continued

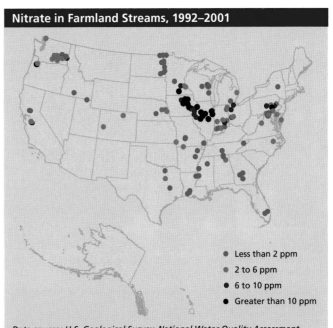

Nitrate in Farmland Streams, 1992–2001

- ● Less than 2 ppm
- ● 2 to 6 ppm
- ● 6 to 10 ppm
- ● Greater than 10 ppm

Data source: U.S. Geological Survey, National Water Quality Assessment. Coverage: all 50 states. Technical details: Each sampling site was sampled intensively for approximately 2 years during 1992–2001; 51 major river basins were sampled. Within each river basin, streams were sampled where the surrounding land was dominated by agriculture or pasture. Values are parts per million nitrate-nitrogen (ppm); see technical note.

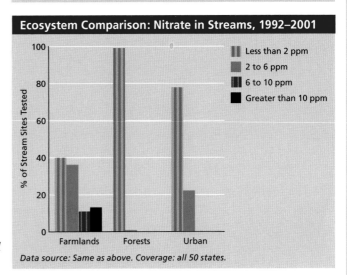

Ecosystem Comparison: Nitrate in Streams, 1992–2001

- Less than 2 ppm
- 2 to 6 ppm
- 6 to 10 ppm
- Greater than 10 ppm

Data source: Same as above. Coverage: all 50 states.

Nitrate in Farmland Streams and Groundwater *(continued)*

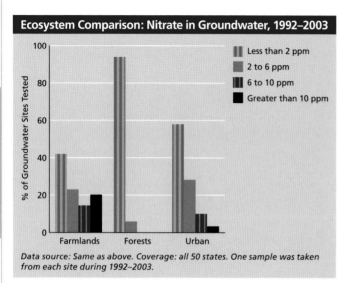

Ecosystem Comparison: Nitrate in Groundwater, 1992–2003

Legend:
- Less than 2 ppm
- 2 to 6 ppm
- 6 to 10 ppm
- Greater than 10 ppm

Y-axis: % of Groundwater Sites Tested

X-axis: Farmlands, Forests, Urban

Data source: Same as above. Coverage: all 50 states. One sample was taken from each site during 1992–2003.

Understanding the Data Nitrate is a naturally occurring form of nitrogen; it is an important plant nutrient. In farmland ecosystems, however, the largest inputs of nitrogen are from non-natural sources, primarily fertilizer additions and runoff from manure associated with animal feeding operations. If more fertilizer is applied than can be used by plants or stored in the soil, nitrates seep into groundwater or drain into streams.

The technical note for this indicator is on page 299.

EXTENT AND PATTERN	CHEMICAL AND PHYSICAL	BIOLOGICAL COMPONENTS	GOODS AND SERVICES
Extent	Nutrients, Carbon, and Oxygen	Plants and Animals	Food, Fiber, and Water
Pattern	Chemical Contamination	Communities	Recreation and Other Services
	Physical	Ecological Productivity	

Phosphorus in Farmland Streams

Why Is Phosphorus in Farmland Streams Important? Phosphorus is an essential nutrient for all life forms; it occurs naturally in soils and aquatic systems. Phosphorus applied as fertilizer on farm fields can end up in streams and rivers, which may then transport it to lakes and coastal waters. At high concentrations in freshwater ecosystems, excess phosphorus can cause algal blooms, which decrease recreational and aesthetic values and can deplete oxygen needed by fish and other animals.

What Does This Indicator Report?

- For streams draining watersheds that are primarily farmland, the percentage of streams with average annual phosphorus concentrations in each of four ranges
- The concentration of phosphorus in farmland streams, compared to concentrations measured in forest and urban and suburban streams

What Do the Data Show?

- Eighty-five percent of sampled farmland stream sites had concentrations of phosphorus that were at least 0.1 part per million (ppm), and about 13% of farmland stream sites had phosphorus concentrations of at least 0.5 ppm.
- Phosphorus concentrations in farmland streams are similar to concentrations in streams in urban and suburban areas (p. 240) and are higher than concentrations in streams draining forested watersheds.

Understanding the Data Sources of phosphorus in farmlands streams include chemical fertilizers and runoff from manure associated with animal-raising operations. If more fertilizer is applied than can be used by plants or stored in the soil, phosphorus drains into adjacent streams.

Background concentrations of total phosphorus can vary regionally because of differences in geology, but a recent U.S. Environmental Protection Agency (EPA) report indicates that they are typically low (0.01–0.16 ppm). The EPA has recommended 0.1 ppm as a goal for preventing excess algae growth in streams not draining directly into a lake or other impoundment. There is no federal drinking water standard for phosphorus.

The technical note for this indicator is on page 300.

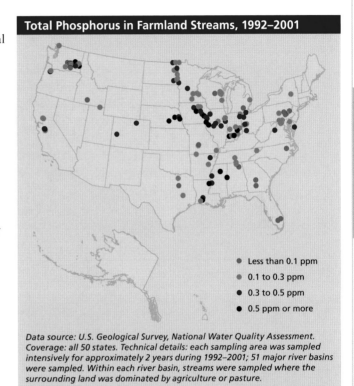

Total Phosphorus in Farmland Streams, 1992–2001

- Less than 0.1 ppm
- 0.1 to 0.3 ppm
- 0.3 to 0.5 ppm
- 0.5 ppm or more

Data source: U.S. Geological Survey, National Water Quality Assessment. Coverage: all 50 states. Technical details: each sampling area was sampled intensively for approximately 2 years during 1992–2001; 51 major river basins were sampled. Within each river basin, streams were sampled where the surrounding land was dominated by agriculture or pasture.

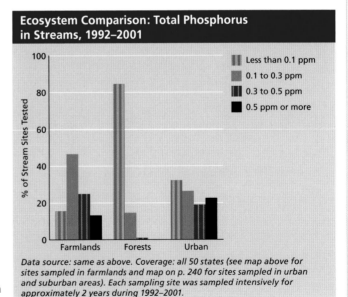

Ecosystem Comparison: Total Phosphorus in Streams, 1992–2001

- Less than 0.1 ppm
- 0.1 to 0.3 ppm
- 0.3 to 0.5 ppm
- 0.5 ppm or more

Data source: same as above. Coverage: all 50 states (see map above for sites sampled in farmlands and map on p. 240 for sites sampled in urban and suburban areas). Each sampling site was sampled intensively for approximately 2 years during 1992–2001.

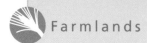
EXTENT AND PATTERN	CHEMICAL AND PHYSICAL	BIOLOGICAL COMPONENTS	GOODS AND SERVICES
Extent	**Nutrients, Carbon, and Oxygen**	Plants and Animals	Food, Fiber, and Water
Pattern	Chemical Contamination	Communities	Recreation and Other Services
	Physical	Ecological Productivity	

Soil Organic Matter

Soil Organic Matter
Data Gap
Data are not adequate for national reporting on the percentage of organic matter and the amount of organic carbon stored in the top 12 inches of cropland soils.

Why Is Soil Organic Matter Important? Organic matter helps soil hold water and store nutrients, functions that are crucial for crop production and other ecosystem services, such as protection against erosion and support of a healthy and diverse set of microscopic organisms. Soils store large quantities of carbon in the form of organic matter, and tracking the change in the amount of carbon stored by ecosystems is of growing importance in international negotiations on greenhouse gas emissions (see Carbon Storage, p. 38).

What Will This Indicator Report? When data are available, the percentage of organic matter and the amount of organic carbon stored in the top 12 inches of cropland soils (nationally and regionally).

Why Can't This Indicator Be Reported at This Time? Soil Survey reports produced by the USDA Natural Resources Conservation Service provide baseline estimates of the amount of organic matter in soils across the United States, but there is no mechanism for systematic monitoring of changes in these amounts at a national scale.

Discussion Soil Organic Matter, Potential Soil Erosion (p. 112), Soil Salinity (p. 114), and Soil Biological Condition (p. 118) are key indicators of soil quality, reflecting the influence of changing crop and soil management practices, as well as moisture and temperature conditions.

Soil organic matter is usually measured as the percentage of organic matter (by dry weight) in surface soil, where human activities have the most influence on soil condition. Large regional differences exist in soil organic matter content because of climate and other factors, but changes in this indicator nationally and within regions will provide important information on the effects of cropland management and climate.

The amount of organic matter in soil varies considerably across locations and regions, and the amount of carbon in soil organic matter varies with soil type (especially texture and drainage attributes), and even within soil type (regionally). The percentage of organic matter (by dry weight) in surface soil, where human activities have most influence on soil condition, is commonly measured directly or estimated based on organic carbon content and other soil properties. Changes in soil organic matter and soil organic carbon, at regional and national scales, will reflect the effects of factors such as cropland management, climate, soil nitrogen content, and vegetation type.

The technical note for this indicator is on page 300.

EXTENT AND PATTERN	CHEMICAL AND PHYSICAL	BIOLOGICAL COMPONENTS	GOODS AND SERVICES
Extent	Nutrients, Carbon, and Oxygen	Plants and Animals	Food, Fiber, and Water
Pattern	Chemical Contamination	Communities	Recreation and Other Services
	Physical	Ecological Productivity	

Pesticides in Farmland Streams and Groundwater

Why Are Changes in Pesticides in Farmland Streams and Groundwater Important? In farmland ecosystems, pesticides and their breakdown products can, in sufficient quantities, harm people as well as wildlife and plants.

What Does This Indicator Report? For water in farmland streams and groundwater wells, how often pesticides are detected, and how often they exceed benchmarks set to protect human health or aquatic life.

What Do the Data Show?

- All streams tested had one or more pesticides at detectable levels, and 86% had five or more.
- More than 60% of tested groundwater wells had one or more pesticides at detectable levels; about 10% had five or more.
- About 57% of streams had one or more pesticides at levels exceeding benchmarks for the protection of aquatic life, and, of these, 12% had four or more.
- About 16% of streams had at least one pesticide at levels exceeding benchmarks for the protection of human health.
- Fewer than 1% of groundwater wells had pesticide concentrations that exceeded benchmarks for the protection of human health.

What Is Not Shown by This Indicator? Some pesticides have no established benchmarks. Of the 83 tested pesticide compounds, 73 have established human health benchmarks and 62 have aquatic life benchmarks.

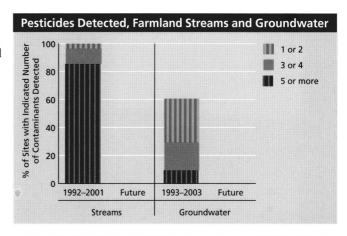

Pesticides Detected, Farmland Streams and Groundwater

Legend: 1 or 2; 3 or 4; 5 or more

Y-axis: % of Sites with Indicated Number of Contaminants Detected

Streams: 1992–2001, Future | Groundwater: 1993–2003, Future

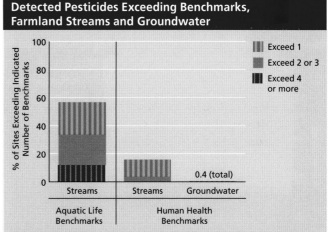

Detected Pesticides Exceeding Benchmarks, Farmland Streams and Groundwater

Legend: Exceed 1; Exceed 2 or 3; Exceed 4 or more

Y-axis: % of Sites Exceeding Indicated Number of Benchmarks

Aquatic Life Benchmarks: Streams | Human Health Benchmarks: Streams, Groundwater (0.4 total)

Data source: U.S. Geological Survey National Water Quality Assessment (NAWQA) Program. Coverage: watersheds characterized by agricultural land use based on sampling at 83 stream sites and in 1412 wells within 51 major river basins across the nation. Technical details: each site was sampled intensively for 83 pesticides and pesticide breakdown products. The lower graph excludes tested pesticides for which relevant benchmarks have not been set. Note: in the 2002 Report, data for 1992–1998 were reported, but those data are not comparable to the 1992–2001 data presented here because of changes in the number of sites sampled and revised benchmarks.

Understanding the Data Of the wide variety of pesticides that have been manufactured and used in agriculture and other applications, some persist or are transformed in the environment. Exposure of people and other organisms to pesticides in streams and groundwater can affect ecological functioning and human health. The number of detections provides basic information on how widespread pesticides are in the environment. Comparison to benchmarks can help to assess whether levels are high enough to cause problems, although a true risk assessment would include many other factors, such as actual exposures. Human health benchmarks apply to both streams and groundwater as potential sources of drinking water. Aquatic life benchmarks are not applied to groundwater and are often numerically lower than human health benchmarks because aquatic animals spend much or all of their life in streams and may be more sensitive to specific contaminants.

The technical note for this indicator is on page 301.

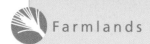
EXTENT AND PATTERN	CHEMICAL AND PHYSICAL	BIOLOGICAL COMPONENTS	GOODS AND SERVICES
Extent	Nutrients, Carbon, and Oxygen	Plants and Animals	Food, Fiber, and Water
Pattern	Chemical Contamination	Communities	Recreation and Other Services
	Physical	Ecological Productivity	

Potential Soil Erosion

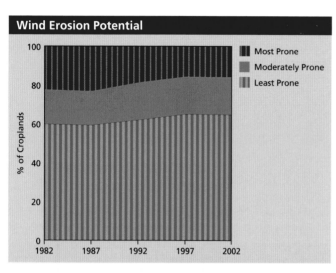

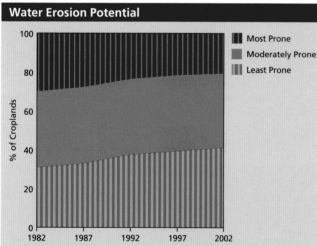

Data source: USDA Natural Resources Conservation Service. Coverage: lower 48 states; data cover cropland and Conservation Reserve Program lands, but not pasture. Technical details: data are based on an index that combines information on soil characteristics, topography, and management activities such as tillage practices and whether crop residue is left on the field or not.

Why Is Soil Erosion Important?

Agricultural soil erosion reduces soil quality and degrades water quality. Even relatively small shifts in soil—for example, from the top of a slope to the bottom—can cause changes in soil structure that can reduce fertility and make normal cropping practices difficult. When soil moves further, eventually ending up in streams and lakes, it causes water quality problems, in part because eroded sediments often carry both fertilizers and pesticides. Even without such pollution, sedimentation alone imposes significant costs on reservoirs and water treatment facilities, navigation, and other water and waterway users. It would take thousands of years to replace farmland soils through natural weathering, but incorporation of crop residues and other management practices can lead to measurable gains in topsoil over decades.

What Does This Indicator Report?

- The percentage of U.S. croplands, including lands in the Conservation Reserve Program, according to their potential for erosion by wind or water
- Locations where croplands are most prone to wind and water erosion

What Do the Data Show?

- From 1982 to 2003, the proportion of U.S. croplands with the greatest potential for wind erosion decreased nearly a third, to about 16% of U.S. croplands (64 million acres).
- The proportion with the greatest potential for water erosion decreased by nearly a third, to about 21% of U.S. croplands (83 million acres).
- Although both water and wind erosion occur throughout the United States, the potential for water erosion is greater in the eastern half of the nation, while the potential for wind erosion is greater in the West.

EXTENT AND PATTERN	CHEMICAL AND PHYSICAL	BIOLOGICAL COMPONENTS	GOODS AND SERVICES
Extent	Nutrients, Carbon, and Oxygen	Plants and Animals	Food, Fiber, and Water
Pattern	Chemical Contamination	Communities	Recreation and Other Services
	Physical	Ecological Productivity	

Potential Soil Erosion *(continued)*

Understanding the Data Reductions in erosion and the potential for erosion can result from changes in management practices. Common practices used to reduce soil erosion are no-till or minimum tillage, creation of terraces and field windbreaks, and contour farming. In addition, removal of highly erosion-prone lands from cultivation (for example, enrollment in the Conservation Reserve Program) lowers erosion potential.

Potential erosion was chosen as an indicator because of the difficulty of measuring actual erosion and its effects on a landscape national, regional, or even landscape scale. Potential Soil Erosion, Soil Organic Matter (p. 110), Soil Salinity (p. 114), and Soil Biological Condition (p. 118) are all key indicators of soil quality.

The technical note for this indicator is on page 301.

Croplands Most Prone to Wind Erosion, 2003

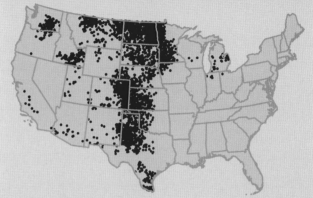

● Each dot represents approximately 20,000 acres of cropland that is most prone to wind erosion.

Data source: USDA Natural Resources Conservation Service; 2003 Annual National Resources Inventory, August 2006. Coverage: lower 48 states; data cover cropland and Conservation Reserve Program land, but not pasture. Note that the dots in these maps may not be used to determine site-specific information. Acres are aggregated by state and 8-digit hydrologic unit. The dots are placed randomly within these boundaries.

Croplands Most Prone to Water Erosion, 2003

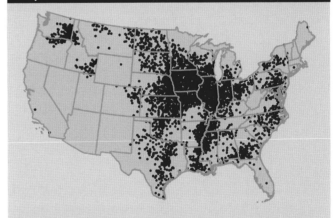

● Each dot represents approximately 20,000 acres of cropland that is most prone to water erosion.

Data source: USDA Natural Resources Conservation Service; 2003 Annual National Resources Inventory, August 2006. Coverage: lower 48 states; data cover cropland and Conservation Reserve Program land, but not pasture. Note that the dots in these maps may not be used to determine site-specific information. Acres are aggregated by state and 8-digit hydrologic unit. The dots are placed randomly within these boundaries.

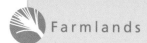
Farmlands

EXTENT AND PATTERN	CHEMICAL AND PHYSICAL	BIOLOGICAL COMPONENTS	GOODS AND SERVICES
Extent	Nutrients, Carbon, and Oxygen	Plants and Animals	Food, Fiber, and Water
Pattern	Chemical Contamination	Communities	Recreation and Other Services
	Physical	Ecological Productivity	

Soil Salinity

Soil Salinity

Data Gap

Data are not adequate for national reporting on the percentage of cropland soils with different salt levels.

Why Is Soil Salinity Important? Excess salt has the same effect on plants as drought: too much salt in soil reduces the ability of plants to take up water, which interferes with their growth and reduces their vitality. Excess salt in soils can also enter groundwater and surface water. Highly saline water is hazardous to freshwater fish, and waterfowl accustomed to fresh water avoid it. Some salts, like those containing sodium, can change the physical condition of the soil, reducing infiltration, increasing runoff and erosion, and impairing biological activity.

What Will This Indicator Report?

- The percentage of cropland with different levels of salt content, measured in decisiemens (dS) per meter (less than 2 dS/m, 2–4 dS/m, greater than 4 dS/m).
- The percentage of land in each major cropland region with elevated salt levels, for example over 4 dS/m.

Why Can't This Indicator Be Reported at This Time? Salinity measurements are often included in routine soil tests conducted by farmers, government agencies, and researchers. National data are available on the salinity in U.S. soils, but the data are not cropland-specific and are not updated regularly, so trends cannot be monitored over time.

Discussion Soil salinity, along with Soil Organic Matter (p. 110), Potential Soil Erosion (p. 112), and Soil Biological Condition (p. 118), is a key indicator of soil quality. Soil salinization is often the result of irrigated agriculture, and it is generally a problem in arid areas. Water used for irrigation contains small amounts of salt, and when water evaporates from the soil surface or from the leaves of plants, it leaves salt behind in the soil. In arid areas, these salts can accumulate and cause problems. In areas with greater rainfall, salts are drained from the soil by the larger volumes of water flowing through the soil and tend not to accumulate to high levels.

Although much less widespread, salinization can occur in the absence of irrigation. Some areas have naturally high salt content in their soil, and saline seeps can occur when water moves through the soil, picking up salts, and then emerges at a seep or spring.

The technical note for this indicator is on page 302.

EXTENT AND PATTERN	CHEMICAL AND PHYSICAL	BIOLOGICAL COMPONENTS	GOODS AND SERVICES
Extent	Nutrients, Carbon, and Oxygen	Plants and Animals	Food, Fiber, and Water
Pattern	Chemical Contamination	Communities	Recreation and Other Services
	Physical	Ecological Productivity	

Stream Habitat Quality

Why Is Stream Habitat Quality Important? Streams that have a natural and diverse array of underwater and bank habitats can support a diverse array of native species. These stream qualities are often indicative of relatively undisturbed flow patterns (see Change in Stream Flows, p. 47) and

> **Stream Habitat Quality**
>
> **Data Gap**
>
> **Data are not adequate for national reporting on the condition of sediments, in-stream fish habitat, and riffles and pools in farmland streams.**

of streams that have vegetation along their banks—physical features that help maintain the conditions necessary to support a healthy biological community over the long term.

What Will This Indicator Report? The percentage of farmland stream-miles that have streambed sediments, in-stream fish habitat features (the presence of boulders, logs, undercut banks, roots), and riffles and pools in one of four condition categories—natural, moderate, degraded, and unknown.

The indicator would compare the specific stream habitat features in any given farmland stream segment against the habitat features that would be found in a relatively undisturbed stream in the same region. "Natural" habitat features would be found at sites that are similar in type to the range of features expected in the least disturbed sites in that region. "Degraded" habitat features would be more degraded than 95% of least disturbed sites in the region, reflecting one or more negative influences. "Moderate" habitat features would be more degraded than 75% of least-disturbed sites in the region. A companion freshwater indicator (p. 179) reports on all streams, not just on those in farmlands.

Why Can't This Indicator Be Reported at This Time? While there are data on streambed sediments and in-stream habitat features on a national scale (see p. 179), these data cannot currently be used to report specifically on farmland streams. In addition, there are currently no national data on the condition of riffles and pools in streams, let alone in farmland streams.

Discussion Like their counterparts on land, stream-dwelling animals and plants require specific habitat conditions in order to survive and reproduce. Because each species has its own particular habitat requirements, a variety of habitats along a stream are needed to maintain the stream's natural complement of plants and animals.

There is no technical note for this indicator. The technical note for the freshwater indicator Stream Habitat Quality, which reports on wadeable streams in multiple ecosystems, including farmlands, is on page 319.

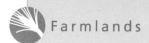

EXTENT AND PATTERN	CHEMICAL AND PHYSICAL	BIOLOGICAL COMPONENTS	GOODS AND SERVICES
Extent	Nutrients, Carbon, and Oxygen	Plants and Animals	Food, Fiber, and Water
Pattern	Chemical Contamination	Communities	Recreation and Other Services
	Physical	Ecological Productivity	

Status of Animal Species in Farmland Areas

Status of Animal Species in Farmlands Areas
Indicator Development Needed

Why Is the Status of Animal Species in Farmland Areas Important?
Farmlands—including both croplands and the patches of natural lands that are intermingled with them—are home to many kinds of wildlife. Some of these species would have been found in the forests, grasslands, or shrublands from which the farmlands were created. Such species may have fewer habitat opportunities in farmland areas, but they may take advantage of remaining patches of habitat and stay in the area, but at lower population levels. However, many species favor the kinds of conditions found in areas with extensive farmlands, and these species are often more common than they were before conversion to agriculture.

What Will This Indicator Report? Broadly, the status of wildlife in farmland areas.

Why Can't This Indicator Be Reported at This Time? An indicator is needed that would account for both types of species found on farmlands—those that favor the preagricultural landscape and those that favor landscapes dominated by agriculture. This approach must necessarily differ from that taken in reporting on marine, forest, grassland and shrubland, and freshwater species, because it is not possible to define a set of "farmland" species in the same way that one can identify species that have evolved to depend on these other ecosystem types.

The technical note for this indicator is on page 303.

EXTENT AND PATTERN	CHEMICAL AND PHYSICAL	BIOLOGICAL COMPONENTS	GOODS AND SERVICES
Extent	Nutrients, Carbon, and Oxygen	Plants and Animals	Food, Fiber, and Water
Pattern	Chemical Contamination	Communities	Recreation and Other Services
	Physical	Ecological Productivity	

Established Non-native Plant Cover in the Farmland Landscape

Why Is It Important to Understand How Much Land Non-native Plants Cover? Where croplands dominate the landscape, wildlife rely more heavily on the remaining areas for their habitat needs. Since vegetation dominated by non-native species often has much lower value as wildlife habitat, a high proportion of non-native plant species in

> **Established Non-native Plant Cover in the Farmland Landscape**
>
> **Data Gap**
>
> Data are not adequate for national reporting on the extent of established non-native plant cover in the noncropland portion of the farmland landscape.

the remaining noncropland areas may affect wildlife populations. For example, when lands in the Conservation Reserve Program, which provides payments to farmers who retire lands important for conservation, are converted from non-native grasses to native prairie grass, some bird populations typically found in mid-elevation "uplands," such as the upland sandpiper, may increase significantly.

What Will This Indicator Report? The amount of noncropland area with different proportions of established non-native species plant cover relative to total plant cover within the farmland landscape.

Why Can't This Indicator Be Reported at This Time? No national-level datasets on non-native plant cover were identified from state or federal agencies or from the private sector. The farmland landscape (p. 103) consists of multiple ecosystem types. Therefore, the challenges associated with collecting comparable data on plant cover across ecosystem types must be resolved before this indicator can be reported.

The monitoring conducted by the Illinois Natural History Survey (INHS-CTAP) provides an example, at the state level, of trends in percentage cover by non-native plants in three ecosystem types, but no comparable data exist for the nation as a whole. Data resolution would need to be sufficient to account for non-native plant cover in small patches of habitat interspersed within a mosaic of cropland.

Discussion The farmland landscape contains patches of woods, grasslands, and shrublands and is interwoven by streams; all these components serve as important habitat for native species. The remaining native vegetation on noncropland farmland is a relatively scarce but important resource for native insects, birds, and other wildlife that do not use croplands as habitat, because non-native plant cover can further limit opportunities for these native wildlife species.

There is no technical note for this indicator.

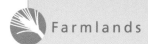

EXTENT AND PATTERN	CHEMICAL AND PHYSICAL	BIOLOGICAL COMPONENTS	GOODS AND SERVICES
Extent	Nutrients, Carbon, and Oxygen	Plants and Animals	Food, Fiber, and Water
Pattern	Chemical Contamination	**Communities**	Recreation and Other Services
	Physical	Ecological Productivity	

Soil Biological Condition

Soil Biological Condition

Data Gap

Data are not adequate for national reporting on the condition of communities of soil organisms in cropland soils.

Why Is the Biological Condition of Soils Important? The number and type of different species of soil organisms, including many microscopic animals, is a key indicator of the degree of disturbance in agricultural soils.

What Will This Indicator Report? The percentage of croplands in three different ranges on the Nematode Maturity Index (NMI), an index that measures the types of roundworms, or nematodes, in the soil. Croplands with low index values (indicating disturbed soils) would be mapped to show the regional distribution of soil disturbance.

Why Can't This Indicator Be Reported at This Time? Nematodes have been shown to be good indicators of soil disturbance, a key aspect of soil quality. This is true in part because they are present in almost all soils, where they affect decomposition and nutrient cycling, and are an important part of the soil food web. The Nematode Maturity Index is a promising indicator for measuring soil disturbance in cropland soils, but it has not yet been adopted by a nationwide monitoring program. NMI has been applied successfully in two statewide surveys (North Carolina and Nebraska) carried out in cooperation with the National Agricultural Statistics Service. Large-scale implementation of the indicator described here could be done through an existing national monitoring program, or through state-based monitoring using consistent methods that would allow the resulting information to be aggregated at the national level.

Discussion Monitoring communities of soil organisms is one way to track soil disturbance, including the influence of changing crop and soil management practices. Soil biological condition, taken together with Soil Organic Matter (p. 110), Potential Soil Erosion (p. 112), and Soil Salinity (p. 114), can be used to characterize soil quality.

This indicator depends on the identification of various types of nematodes, each of which has a different tolerance for soil disturbance. Calculation of the NMI is based on the proportion of nematodes with different levels of tolerance for disturbance. Low NMI values (less than 2.5) are often found in soils subjected to intensive agricultural production methods, like monoculture and the use of high levels of nitrogen fertilizer and pesticides. Midrange values (from 2.5 to 3.5) suggest a more diverse soil community and often reflect such practices as crop mixtures and rotations and no-till farming. High NMI values (greater than 3.5) are rarely found on cultivated lands.

The technical note for this indicator is on page 303.

EXTENT AND PATTERN	CHEMICAL AND PHYSICAL	BIOLOGICAL COMPONENTS	GOODS AND SERVICES
Extent	Nutrients, Carbon, and Oxygen	Plants and Animals	**Food, Fiber, and Water**
Pattern	Chemical Contamination	Communities	Recreation and Other Services
	Physical	Ecological Productivity	

Major Crop Yields

Why Is Information on Major Crop Yields Important? Five crops—corn, soybeans, wheat, cotton, and hay—account for about 90% of harvested acreage in the United States and more than half the monetary value of all crops (see Monetary Value of Agricultural Production, p. 121). The increase in amount of crops grown per acre has allowed U.S. agriculture to produce more food and fiber without corresponding increases in farm acreage. In fact, the total acreage used for crop production has declined slightly over the past half-century (see Total Cropland, p. 102), and a significant increase in the acreage devoted to agriculture is generally considered unlikely.

What Does This Indicator Report? This indicator reports the per acre yield of corn, soybeans, wheat, hay, and cotton, converted to an index with 1975 as the base year.

What Do the Data Show?

- Yields of these five crops have increased since 1950. Per acre yields of corn, wheat and cotton more than doubled, with corn yields increasing nearly fourfold. Soybean and hay yields nearly doubled.

- Four crops—corn, soybeans, wheat, and cotton—had their highest reported crop yields between 2003 and 2006. Hay yields during this period were the second highest reported for the 56-year dataset (hay yields peaked in 1995).

- Data from recent decades (post-1990) show a continuation of the overall trend of increasing yields for corn, soybeans, and cotton.

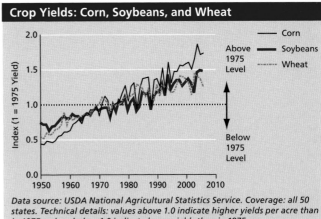

Crop Yields: Corn, Soybeans, and Wheat

Data source: USDA National Agricultural Statistics Service. Coverage: all 50 states. Technical details: values above 1.0 indicate higher yields per acre than in 1975; values below 1.0 indicate lower yields than in 1975.

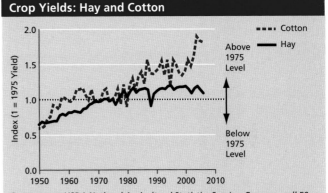

Crop Yields: Hay and Cotton

Data source: USDA National Agricultural Statistics Service. Coverage: all 50 state. Technical details: values above 1.0 indicate higher yields per acre than in 1975; values below 1.0 indicate lower yields than in 1975.

Understanding the Data A combination of factors may produce increases in crop yields, including improvements in breeding, advances in biotechnology, changes in cultivation practices, and increased use of a variety of inputs, including pesticides and fertilizers. More intensive use of farmland is thought to play an important role in improving yields, but it may also have negative effects, such as increased concentrations of nitrogen, phosphorus, or pesticides in streams, lakes, and coastal waters (see Nitrate in Farmland Streams and Groundwater, p. 107; Phosphorus in Farmland Streams, p. 109; Pesticides in Farmland Streams and Groundwater, p. 111; and the core national indicator Movement of Nitrogen, p. 36).

The technical note for this indicator is on page 304.

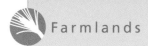

EXTENT AND PATTERN	CHEMICAL AND PHYSICAL	BIOLOGICAL COMPONENTS	GOODS AND SERVICES
Extent	Nutrients, Carbon, and Oxygen	Plants and Animals	**Food, Fiber, and Water**
Pattern	Chemical Contamination	Communities	Recreation and Other Services
	Physical	Ecological Productivity	

Agricultural Inputs and Outputs

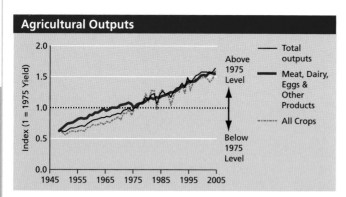

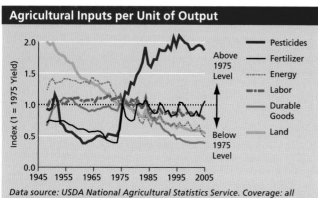

Data source: USDA National Agricultural Statistics Service. Coverage: all 50 states. Technical details: for any input, the index value for a given year describes whether more or less of that input was used to produce a unit of output in that year than in 1975. For example, for both graphs, a value of 1.5 corresponds to a value that is 50% greater than the value in 1975.

Why Are Agricultural Inputs and Outputs Important? Agricultural production requires inputs in the form of energy, land, labor, goods, and chemicals. Inputs can have both environmental and economic costs. Therefore, input trends—compared to output trends—are an important measure of the efficiency and health of the agricultural enterprise and the associated environmental impacts of farming.

What Does This Indicator Report?
- Total agricultural outputs over time, compared to the output in 1975
- The amount of inputs used to produce one unit of output, compared to the value in 1975

What Do the Data Show?
- Output from U.S. agriculture has increased steadily over time. Since 1948, total output increased by about 170%.
- In recent years, per unit of output, the inputs of energy, labor, durable goods, and land have continued a decline documented since 1948. The greatest decrease in inputs per output since 1948 was in land, which declined by over 70%, followed by declines in durable goods (42%), energy (60%), and labor (19%).
- Conversely, inputs of pesticides and fertilizers per unit output increased from 1948 to 2004. Fertilizer inputs increased by 46%, and pesticide inputs doubled. However, while pesticide inputs per unit of output have continued to increase since 1975, fertilizer inputs per unit of output have not changed since 1975.

Understanding the Data This indicator aggregates agricultural inputs and outputs. For example, all fertilizers used on U.S. farms were divided by all agricultural outputs—even if different amounts of fertilizer were used to produce each commodity. A decreasing input index may be the result of more efficient input use by farmers, such as less fertilizer per ton of corn due to targeted application, or of a series of technological advances (for example, less labor required because of increased mechanization, biotechnology, or more effective pesticides).

As technology and farming practices have changed, the qualities of inputs have also changed considerably. For example, a smaller quantity of pesticide used today may achieve the same results as a larger quantity in the past because of improvements in farming practices and pesticide quality. To facilitate comparisons of different inputs and outputs over time, this indicator takes into account both the changing character of inputs and the changing market values for agricultural outputs (see technical note for more details).

The indicator focuses on a few major, quantifiable, inputs. This means that some factors, such as changes in plant breeding (including the introduction of genetically engineered crops), are not included at all, and some inputs, such as water, are included only indirectly (in this case, through the energy costs associated with irrigation).

The technical note for this indicator is on page 304.

EXTENT AND PATTERN	CHEMICAL AND PHYSICAL	BIOLOGICAL COMPONENTS	GOODS AND SERVICES
Extent	Nutrients, Carbon, and Oxygen	Plants and Animals	**Food, Fiber, and Water**
Pattern	Chemical Contamination	Communities	Recreation and Other Services
	Physical	Ecological Productivity	

Monetary Value of Agricultural Production

Why Is the Value of Agricultural Production Important? The value of agricultural goods is a function of the amount of goods produced and the price paid to farmers for those goods. Measuring the variation in the monetary value of agricultural production among regions shows where farming is a greater or lesser component of the local economy and highlights differences in the value of agricultural crops among regions.

What Does This Indicator Report? The dollar value of the annual output of major crops and livestock, both nationally over time and by location for the most recent year available.

What Do the Data Show?

- Since 1950, the total money received by farmers (in constant 2005 dollars) for their goods has increased—with a low of about $166 billion in 1957 and a high of about $305 billion in 1973.
- The increase in total monetary value is driven by significant increases in the value of fruits, vegetables, and other crops and food/feed grains. The value of meat, dairy, eggs, and cotton and oilseed has not changed significantly over the time period measured.
- Farmers received 6% more for their goods in 2005 ($239 billion) than the average for the previous 20 years.
- Agricultural sales per square mile are highest in California (2004 data).

Understanding the Data Advances over the past 55 years have enabled farmers to produce more goods per acre of land (see Major Crop Yields, p. 119) and to increase total physical outputs, while requiring, in general, fewer inputs, with the exception of pesticides (see Agricultural Inputs and Outputs, p. 120). The monetary value of many agricultural products has increased over time, but at a much lower rate than the increase in outputs per input. The values reported here are gross revenues—the value of the harvest from croplands dairy and livestock production, and other agricultural products. They do not report on the profitability of farming in the United States. This indicator also reports the money received by farmers, not the retail price of farm products. Finally, these data do not include agricultural income support or other government payments.

The technical note for this indicator is on page 304.

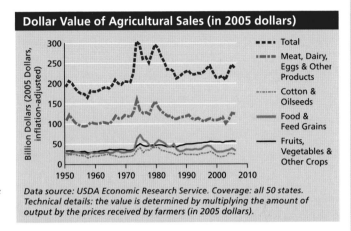

Dollar Value of Agricultural Sales (in 2005 dollars)

Data source: USDA Economic Research Service. Coverage: all 50 states. Technical details: the value is determined by multiplying the amount of output by the prices received by farmers (in 2005 dollars).

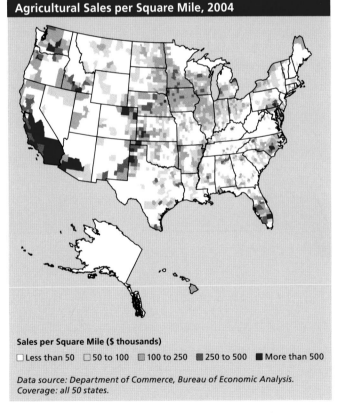

Agricultural Sales per Square Mile, 2004

Sales per Square Mile ($ thousands)
☐ Less than 50 ☐ 50 to 100 ▨ 100 to 250 ▨ 250 to 500 ■ More than 500

Data source: Department of Commerce, Bureau of Economic Analysis. Coverage: all 50 states.

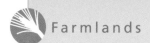

EXTENT AND PATTERN	CHEMICAL AND PHYSICAL	BIOLOGICAL COMPONENTS	GOODS AND SERVICES
Extent	Nutrients, Carbon, and Oxygen	Plants and Animals	Food, Fiber, and Water
Pattern	Chemical Contamination	Communities	**Recreation and Other Services**
	Physical	Ecological Productivity	

Recreation in Farmland Areas

Recreation in Farmland Areas

Data Gap

Data are not adequate for national reporting on the number of recreation days spent on farmlands.

Why Is Measuring Recreation in Farmland Areas Important? The farmland landscape supports a variety of recreational activities, including hunting, fishing, bird-watching, biking, and wine-tasting. Farmers and landowners living in farmland areas may supplement their income by charging for recreational access to their land for hunting or fishing. Revenue from recreation provides incentives for landowners to protect wildlife and their habitat, improve stream habitat quality, and invest in the overall scenic character of their land. Income from recreation is an important contributor to the local economy of many small agricultural communities.

What Will This Indicator Report? This indicator will report the number of days spent fishing, hunting, viewing wildlife, or engaged in other recreational activities on farmland.

Why Can't This Indicator Be Reported at This Time? There are no national datasets that document recreation on farmlands. The National Survey of Fishing, Hunting, and Wildlife-Associated Recreation (http://wsfrprograms.fws.gov/Subpages/NationalSurvey/NatSurveyIndex.htm) and the National Survey on Recreation and the Environment (www.srs.fs.usda.gov/trends/Nsre/nsre2.html) both provide reliable data on recreation participation, but neither survey identifies activities that take place on farmlands. The Census of Agriculture (http://www.agcensus.usda.gov/) provides information on a wide range of farm-related subjects, but it does not cover recreational activities. Adequate reporting would require modification of existing surveys to elicit information either on the location of recreational activities or on the amount of recreation on farms. (See the core national indicator on Outdoor Recreation, p. 38; and Recreation in Forests, p. 157.)

There is no technical note for this indicator.

Contents
	page

Chapter 5:
Indicators of the Condition and Use of Forests

America's forests range from the majestic redwood groves of California to the cypress swamps of Florida, from the gnarled pinyon pine and juniper stands of the arid Southwest to the maple, oak, and hickory woodlands that set New England ablaze with color each fall. People treasure trees, whether they shade our boulevards and backyards, grow wild across our public lands, or stand in croplike rows on private timber plantations.

Forests provide the nation not only with valuable goods such as timber and other wood products, but also with a wide array of services: clean water supplies and watersheds less prone to erosion, habitat for wildlife, opportunities for hunting, hiking, camping, and the unquantifiable pleasure of solitude.

Forests often overlap or intermingle with other ecosystem types in the landscape. Forested wetlands are common in the Southeast, for example, while mosaics of forest and grasslands or shrublands are widespread in the Intermountain West. In the East, mixed farm and woodlot landscapes are common. Across the nation, suburban expansion is increasingly pushing subdivisions up to the forest edge. Agency definitions of "forest" differ, especially on the matter of how large and how densely wooded an area needs to be to be considered a forest. This report generally uses the USDA Forest Service definition, which requires that a forest must cover at least one acre and have more than 10 percent forest cover.

Society has differing and strongly held views of the way forests should be used, protected, and managed. Congress, the courts, and agency planners, as well as advocacy and interest groups, all seek to influence choices between timber harvest and recreation or wilderness, watershed, and habitat protections on public lands. Management of private forests has also become a matter of public debate as recognition grows of the many ecological goods and services the public derives from these lands. Reconciling landowners' rights and needs with their obligation to maintain the capacity of forest ecosystems to generate benefits to society remains a complex issue.

The following sections and the table on page 130 describe the four categories of ecosystem condition and use outlined in Chapter 1 and also summarize the most current data and trends for forest ecosystems. Individual indicators focus on the extent and pattern of forest ecosystems, chemical and physical processes and conditions necessary for the functioning of forest ecosystems, biological communities in forests, and the human benefits derived from forest ecosystems.

Extent and Pattern

Knowing the overall extent of forest ecosystems and specific type of forest—whether red maple, red pine, or redwood—provides fundamental information about the nature of the land and the uses to which it may be put. Trends in the nation's overall forest acreage are driven by conversion of forest to other uses and regeneration of forest from, for example, abandoned farmland. Increases or decreases in the extent of specific forest types can be driven by natural forest succession, human activities, or changes in climate. (This section addresses trends in broad forest types as defined by their dominant species, such as oak-hickory and aspen–birch. The Biological Components section of this chapter includes an indicator focused on specific forest types that have had major decreases in area.) Different forest types, in turn, generate different benefits—habitat for a different community of animals and understory plants, timber for different uses, and varying recreational opportunities.

The way forests are managed—as wilderness or timber plantation, for example—and the degree to which forests remain as large tracts of "core" habitat or are intermingled with houses and farmlands also strongly influence the recreational opportunities, wildlife habitat, and other goods and services they provide. Public and private forest owners have different goals and assumptions, which are reflected in management priorities and practices. There is intense public interest in preserving the ecological values of forests, but debates on the issue vary greatly between regions, often influenced by the proportion of public to private lands and the extent of protected lands in a region.

Data in this chapter show that
- Since 1953, total forest area in the U.S. has changed by less than 1%. Regionally, forested land in the South and on the Pacific Coast has declined significantly, while forests in the North have increased (2006 data).
- Most forests in the North and South are privately owned. In contrast, most forested land in the Interior West, Pacific Coast, and Alaska is publicly owned.
- The composition of U.S. forests is changing. Since 1963, certain forest types, such as ponderosa pine and elm–ash–cottonwood, have declined in area, while other forest types, such as fir–spruce and maple–beech–birch, have increased.
- Since 1953, both reserved (protected) forest land and planted timberland have increased as a percentage of total forest area, while the proportion of natural and semi-natural timberland has decreased.
- Most (82%) of the forest patches classified as "core forest" (forest patches surrounded by at least 90% "natural" cover) are less than 100 square miles in size (based on 2001 data). Forests with the greatest proportion of large patches of "core forest" (larger than 100 square miles) are primarily located in the western United States.

Data are not adequate for national reporting on
- Forest management in private reserve lands and some public reserve lands.

Chemical and Physical Characteristics

Forests use and store resources in the form of energy, nutrients, and water and also export resources to other ecosystems. As forests grow, carbon and nutrients accumulate in and are recycled between forest trees and soils. How forests process the inputs and outputs of key elements such as nitrogen and carbon provides important insight into their condition and functioning. For example, relatively undisturbed forests generally release very little nitrate into streams. Increased inputs (from nitrogen deposition, for example; see Freshwater Acidity p. 176) or other stresses such as timber harvesting, fire, or pest outbreaks can result in higher releases, sometimes acidifying forest soils as well as leading to higher stream nitrate levels. Because elevated nitrate in streams can cause health problems for people who use well water for drinking and can also fuel algal growth in lakes and coastal waters, trends in nitrate levels provide information important to understanding both the condition of the forests themselves and the effects they may be having downstream.

Forests are important components of the global carbon cycle—they have the capacity to store vast amounts of carbon in living and dead plant biomass, forest floor litter, and underground roots and soil. In this way, forests provide an important "carbon sequestration" service that not only translates into harvestable wood products but may also play a role as our nation develops its carbon and climate

policies. Individual forest areas may gain or lose carbon depending on management practices, inputs of nutrients or chemicals from other systems, forest age, or other factors (see the national Carbon Storage indicator, p. 38; Forest Age, p. 147; and Forest Management Categories, p. 136).

Data in this chapter show that

- Ninety-seven percent of all forest stream sites sampled have nitrate concentrations below 1 part per million (ppm), well below the federal drinking water standard of 10 ppm (data from 1992–2001). On average, forest streams have lower nitrate concentrations than streams draining urban/suburban areas and farmlands.
- From 1953 to 2005, the amount of carbon stored in live trees in forests increased by 43%.
- Since 1990, the amount of carbon stored in other forest pools, including downed dead and standing dead trees, understory vegetation, and forest floor litter, increased by 4–8%.

Data are not adequate for national reporting on

- Carbon stored in forest soils, which comprises a substantial proportion of total carbon in forests

Biological Components

Key indicators of the biological condition of forests include the status of individual species (especially native species that are highly adapted to forests), trends in the extent of specific forest community types, and the age structure of forests. A diversity of community types and forest age groupings are needed to support the full diversity of native species. Other influences on the status and diversity of forest ecosystems include the level of invasion by non-native species and the degree of disturbance by factors such as fire, insects, and disease. Some non-native plant species, such as kudzu and salt cedar, can outcompete or otherwise displace native species. Non-native pests and pathogens such as the gypsy moth and chestnut blight, by damaging or killing trees, continue to play a significant role in reshaping the nation's forests. Although fire, insect damage, and disease are natural components of many forest types, when these disturbances occur at high intensities or frequencies they can lead to significant changes in forest ecosystem condition and structure.

Extensive public and private efforts are focused on management of the biological composition of our forests. Federal and state laws require that the needs of rare or declining species be addressed, a task that is often accomplished by ensuring the maintenance of specific community types (and their proximity

to one another) and forest age profiles. In turn, this may require the use of management tools such as controlled burns or restrictions on harvest or recreational activities. Introduction of non-native plants, insects, and diseases as well as changes in climate can complicate efforts to maintain forests for a variety of societal uses and can have direct impacts on forest species as well.

Data in this chapter show that

- Nineteen percent of native forest animals are considered to be "at risk." Among at-risk vertebrate forest species, 27% are declining in population size and only 1% are increasing. However, population trends for nearly half (46%) of at-risk vertebrate forest animals remain unknown.
- Hawaii has the largest percentage of at-risk native forest species (76%).
- Nationwide, more than half of U.S. timberland is less than 60 years old (2006 data), while 12% is more than 100 years old. Alaska had the largest percentage of forests more than 200 years old, and the South had the largest percentage of forests less than 20 years old (2006 data).
- Nationally, the acreage of forest and grasslands and shrublands disturbed by fire increased from 1979 to 2006. The area of large patches of forest killed by insects has increased since 1997.

Data are not adequate for national reporting on

- The percentage of at-risk native plant species in forests
- Population trends for at-risk native plants and invertebrate animals in forests
- The area covered by established non-native plant cover in forests
- The age structure of forests other than timberlands (a USDA Forest Service designation for areas with trees that grow fast enough to support timber harvests and on which harvest is not prohibited by law)
- Disease in forests
- The area occupied by forest types that have declined significantly in extent since presettlement times

Further indicator development is needed to report on

- The frequency with which forests burn

Goods and Services

People rely on forests for a number of products and services, including construction materials, furniture, paper products, recreation, solitude, and scenery. Harvest and other management activities provide employment and generate economic benefits while supplying society's demand for products. U.S. timber harvests are affected by many environmental, social, and economic factors, including the cost and availability of foreign timber. The use of forested land for recreational activities reflects the public's demand for this service, the scenic quality of forested lands, their ability to support game and nongame wildlife, and the availability of infrastructure such as trails, picnic facilities, and water access.

Managing the competing demands for goods and services on public forest lands can be a contentious matter and involves deeply held values and cultural traditions as well as economic considerations such as international trade. Determining appropriate harvest levels, conservation targets, and management practices is complicated by the involvement of multiple levels of government, both private and public landowners, and uncertainty about the effects of changing climate and economic conditions.

Data in this chapter show that

- Nationally, timber harvest increased from 1952 to 2005. The harvest of sawlogs increased by 11% and pulpwood and composites harvests increased by 182%.
- In 2005, one-third of total timber harvest was used to produce sawlogs. The rest was logging residues (29%), pulpwood and composites (23%), fuelwood, veneer wood, and other products.
- Despite increased timber harvests, timber growth still exceeds harvest on both public and private timberlands nationally (2005 data).
- The greatest increase in timber growth occurred on private timberlands, which account for 90% of the national timber harvest and make up the largest percentage of total forested land in the North and the South.
- Recent surveys found increased participation for most outdoor recreational activities in forests from the 1999–2001 to 2003–2005 survey periods.

Data are not adequate for national reporting on

- Youth participation in forest recreation activities

Status and trends for all forest indicators are summarized in the following table and described in detail in the remainder of the chapter. Regions and related definitions used throughout this chapter are described in Appendix D.

Indicators	What Do the Most Recent Data Show?		Have Data Values Changed over Time?
EXTENT AND PATTERN			
Forest Area and Ownership, p. 132	There are nearly 750 million acres of forest in the U.S.; 44% is publicly owned and 56% is privately owned (2006 data).	→	Since 1953, forest area has not changed significantly.
Forest Types, p. 134	Forest types showing no significant change in area account for 56% of U.S. forest acreage. 30% of U.S. forest is covered by types that are increasing in size and 14% is covered by types that are decreasing in size (2006 data).	↗	Since 1963, 7 forest types have increased in area.
		↘	Since 1963, 9 forest types have decreased in area.
Forest Management Categories, p. 136	Nationwide, 8% of forests are planted timberland, 21% are in forest reserves or too remote to harvest; 61% are natural or seminatural timberland, and 10% ("other forests") are subject to a wide variety of both management practices and restrictions on use; there are wide regional variations (2006 data).	↘	Since 1953, the proportion of natural/semi-natural timberland has decreased nationally, with the largest decline in Alaska and the South.
		↗	Since 1953, the proportion of both planted timberland and reserved forest has increased nationally.
	Data are not adequate for national reporting on private reserved lands and some public reserved lands.		
Pattern of Forest Landscapes, p. 138	51% of "core forest" patches in the forest landscape are less than 10 square miles; 31% are 10–100 square miles; just over 2% are more than 1000 square miles (2001 data).		Data are not adequate for national reporting on changes in the size of "core forest" patches in the forest landscape.
CHEMICAL AND PHYSICAL CHARACTERISTICS			
Nitrate in Forest Streams, p. 140	97% of forest streams have nitrate concentrations below 1 ppm; 33% have nitrate concentrations of less than 0.1 ppm (1992–2001 data).		Data are not adequate for national reporting on changes in nitrate concentrations in streams.
Carbon Storage, p. 142	25 billion metric tons of carbon is stored in forests in the lower 48 states (excluding soils). 69% is found in live trees, 18% in the forest floor, and the remainder in dead trees/wood and the understory (2005 data).	↗	Since 1953, the amount of carbon stored in live trees has increased.
		↗	Since 1990, the amount of carbon stored in forest floor, down dead wood, understory, and standing dead trees (as well as live trees) has increased.
	Data are not adequate for national reporting on the amount of carbon in forest soils.		
BIOLOGICAL COMPONENTS			
At-Risk Native Forest Species, p. 144	19% of native forest animals are "at risk" (2006 data).		Data are not adequate for national reporting on changes in at-risk species.
	Data are not adequate for national reporting on the percentage of at-risk native forest plants at different levels of risk of extinction.		
	27% of at-risk native vertebrate animal species in forests have declining populations, 26% have stable populations, and 1% have increasing populations (2006 data).		Data are not adequate for national reporting changes in population trends in at-risk native vertebrate animals in forests.
	Data are not adequate for national reporting on population trends in at-risk native plants and invertebrate animals.		

Indicators	What Do the Most Recent Data Show?	Have Data Values Changed over Time?

BIOLOGICAL COMPONENTS (CONTINUED)

Indicators	What Do the Most Recent Data Show?	Have Data Values Changed over Time?
Established Non-native Plant Cover in Forests, p. 146	Data are not adequate for national reporting on the proportion of established non-native plant cover in forests.	
Forest Age, p. 147	Over half of U.S. timberland is less than 60 years old; 12% is more than 100 years old; less than 1% is of uneven age (2006 data)	Since 1987, the age of timberlands in the North and South has increased.
		Since 1987, the proportion of uneven-aged timberlands has decreased.
	Data are not adequate for national reporting on the age of forests that are not timberlands.	
Forest Disturbance: Fire, Insects, and Disease, p. 149	In 2006, fire affected almost 10 million acres of forest, grasslands, and shrublands; insect damage (defoliation and tree mortality) affected an additional 13 million acres of forest.	Since 1916, the acreage of forests and grasslands/shrublands disturbed by fire has decreased.
		Since 1979, the acreage of forests and grasslands/shrublands disturbed by fire has increased.
		Since 1997, the number of acres of tree mortality due to insect damage has increased.
	Data are not adequate for national reporting on disease in forests.	
Fire Frequency, p. 151	Indicator Development Needed	
Forest Community Types with Significantly Reduced Area, p. 153	Data are not adequate for national reporting on the area occupied by forest types that have significantly declined in area since presettlement times and on whether these forest types are increasing, remaining stable, or decreasing in area.	

GOODS AND SERVICES

Indicators	What Do the Most Recent Data Show?	Have Data Values Changed over Time?
Timber Harvest, p. 154	21.2 billion cubic feet were harvested in 2005. Thirty-four percent of this harvest was sawlogs, 29% logging residues, 23% pulpwood/composites, and the remainder fuelwood, veneer logs, and other products.	Since 1952, the harvest of fuelwood and veneer logs has not changed significantly.
		Since 1952, the harvest of pulpwood and composites, logging residues, and sawlogs has increased.
		Since 1952, the harvest of other forest products has declined.
Timber Growth and Harvest, p. 155	Nationwide, growth exceeds harvest on timberlands; private lands account for 92% of total harvest (2005 data).	Since 1952, timber growth on both public and private lands nationally has increased.
Recreation in Forests, p. 157	Americans participate in recreation in forests about 26 billion times per year. The most popular forest recreational activities are viewing activities, walking, and picnicking (2003–2005 data).	The public participated in recreation in forests 5.5 billion more times in 2003–2005 than in 1999–2001.
	Data are not adequate for national reporting on youth participation in forest recreation activities.	

 = significant decrease   =significant increase   = no clear trend*   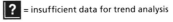 = insufficient data for trend analysis

= Data not available for adequate reporting.

* may be due to little numerical change in the data or large numerical fluctuations in data resulting in no single trend

EXTENT AND PATTERN	CHEMICAL AND PHYSICAL	BIOLOGICAL COMPONENTS	GOODS AND SERVICES
Extent	Nutrients, Carbon, and Oxygen	Plants and Animals	Food, Fiber, and Water
Pattern	Chemical Contamination	Communities	Recreation and Other Services
	Physical	Ecological Productivity	

Forest Area and Ownership

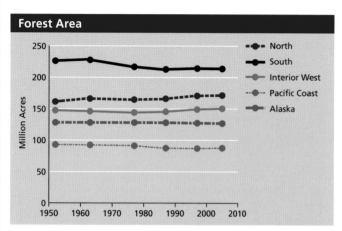

Forest Area

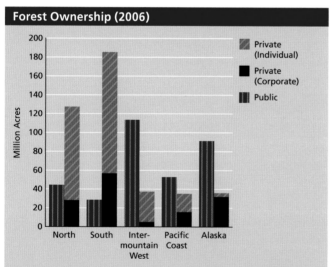

Forest Ownership (2006)

Data source: USDA Forest Service. Coverage: all 50 states; see p. 267 for description of regions. Technical details: Forests across the country have historically been sampled periodically and reported every 10 years or so. Thus, data reported for a given year, such as 1987, may reflect a range of sample years for any given region. See the technical note for more details.

Why Is the Area and Ownership of Forests Important? Knowing how much land is forested and who owns that land is vital to making informed decisions about forests. Gains and losses in forest area directly affect the public's continued enjoyment of the goods and services that forests provide—recreation, lumber, watershed protection, wildlife habitat, and many other things. Public and private land owners often have different goals and are subject to different regulations. These differences may be reflected in management priorities and practices that affect forest condition.

What Does This Indicator Report?
- The total area of forest land by region
- The ownership of forest land by private corporations or individuals (including family trusts and tribes) or public entities

What Do the Data Show?
- In 2006, there were nearly 750 million acres of forest in the United States (North, 171 million acres; South, 214 million acres; Interior West, 151 million acres; Pacific Coast, 88 million acres; Alaska, 127 million acres).
- Since 1953, forest area for the nation as a whole has not changed significantly (less than 1%). Regionally, however, forest lands in the South and Pacific Coast have decreased significantly in area since 1953, while forests in the North have increased.
- Three hundred and thirty million acres (44 %) of U.S. forests are publicly owned and 420 million

acres (56 %) are privately owned. There are striking regional differences in forest ownership. The North has nearly three times as much private land as public. Similarly, in the South, the "wood basket" of the nation, 87% (185 million acres) is privately owned (57 million acres is owned by private corporations such as timber holding companies and forest product firms, and the remaining 128 million acres is held by individuals, including family trusts and tribes). In contrast, most of the forest land in the western United States is held as public land—in particular, 60% (53 million acres) in the Pacific Coast and 72% (91 million acres) in Alaska are publicly owned.

EXTENT AND PATTERN	CHEMICAL AND PHYSICAL	BIOLOGICAL COMPONENTS	GOODS AND SERVICES
Extent	Nutrients, Carbon, and Oxygen	Plants and Animals	Food, Fiber, and Water
Pattern	Chemical Contamination	Communities	Recreation and Other Services
	Physical	Ecological Productivity	

Forest Area and Ownership *(continued)*

Understanding the Data Forests today cover about a third of the total land area of the United States, down from about 1 billion acres at the time of European settlement. Most forest clearing occurred in the East for agriculture, predominantly between 1850 and 1900.

In recent years, private land ownership patterns have changed in the United States. Many corporations that rely on a constant supply of timber, such as those in the pulp and paper industry, have divested themselves of their substantial holdings of forest lands. In many cases, these lands have been purchased by timber investment management organizations and real estate investment trusts.

See also Forest Management Categories (p. 136).

The technical note for this indicator is on page 305.

EXTENT AND PATTERN	CHEMICAL AND PHYSICAL	BIOLOGICAL COMPONENTS	GOODS AND SERVICES
Extent	Nutrients, Carbon, and Oxygen	Plants and Animals	Food, Fiber, and Water
Pattern	Chemical Contamination	Communities	Recreation and Other Services
	Physical	Ecological Productivity	

Forest Types

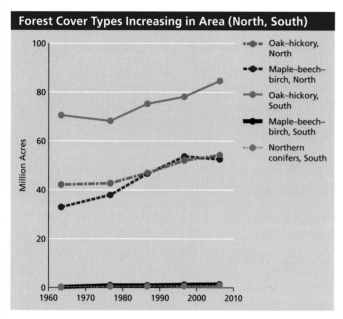

Forest Cover Types Increasing in Area (North, South)

Legend:
- Oak–hickory, North
- Maple–beech–birch, North
- Oak–hickory, South
- Maple–beech–birch, South
- Northern conifers, South

Y-axis: Million Acres (0 to 100)
X-axis: 1960 to 2010

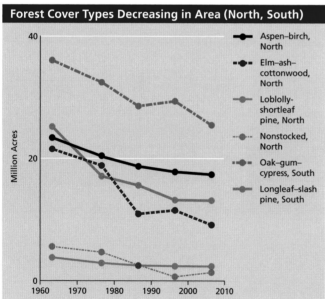

Forest Cover Types Decreasing in Area (North, South)

Legend:
- Aspen–birch, North
- Elm–ash–cottonwood, North
- Loblolly–shortleaf pine, North
- Nonstocked, North
- Oak–gum–cypress, South
- Longleaf–slash pine, South

Y-axis: Million Acres (0 to 40)
X-axis: 1960 to 2010

Why Is the Area of Different Forest Types Important? Forest type not only determines the plant and animal communities that live in a particular forest, but also influences the way people use forests for recreation and the products that forests yield.

What Does This Indicator Report?
The acreage of a variety of forest "cover types" that have changed significantly in area since the 1960s. Cover types are based on the dominant species of trees (for example, oak–hickory forests are dominated by oaks and hickories but include other kinds of trees as well).

What Do the Data Show?
- In 2006, forest types decreasing in area accounted for 105 million acres (14% of total U.S. forest area) and those increasing in area accounted for 226 million acres (30% of forest area), leaving 419 million acres (56% of forest area) covered by types that were neither increasing or decreasing in area.
- From 1963 to 2006, the North and South saw significant increases in oak–hickory forest (26 million acres) and maple–beech–birch forest (21 million acres) and a smaller increase in northern conifer forest (0.6 million acres, South only).
- Over the same period in the North and South, there were significant declines in six regional forest types. The largest declines were in elm–ash–cottonwood cover in the North (12 million acres) and longleaf–slash pine cover in the South (12 million acres), which declined by 58% and 48%, respectively.
- In the West, significant increases were seen in the cover of fir–spruce forests (9 million acres, Interior West), and "other softwood" forests (9 million acres, Pacific Coast). The largest declines were seen in ponderosa pine, which declined by nearly 12 million acres in the Pacific Coast and 5 million acres in the Interior West.

EXTENT AND PATTERN	CHEMICAL AND PHYSICAL	BIOLOGICAL COMPONENTS	GOODS AND SERVICES
Extent	Nutrients, Carbon, and Oxygen	Plants and Animals	Food, Fiber, and Water
Pattern	Chemical Contamination	Communities	Recreation and Other Services
	Physical	Ecological Productivity	

Forest Types *(continued)*

Understanding the Data Forest type may change as a result of direct human intervention (fire suppression, planting and harvesting, development, and grazing), natural succession, or ecosystem processes (see Forest Disturbance, p. 149). Increases in some forest types may be a result of maturation of second- and third-growth forests. This likely explains the increase in oak–hickory and maple–beech–birch forests in the eastern United States since 1963. Decreases in ponderosa pine may be caused by a combination of increased severity of fires, insect and disease infestations, and changes in grazing and logging practices. Shifts in temperature and precipitation patterns may also affect the area of different forest types. Although forest area has remained fairly constant on a national scale (see Forest Area and Ownership, p. 132), changes in forest composition and age (see Forest Age, p. 147) have consequences for wildlife habitat, ecosystem function, timber harvest, and carbon storage, among other things.

The technical note for this indicator is on page 306.

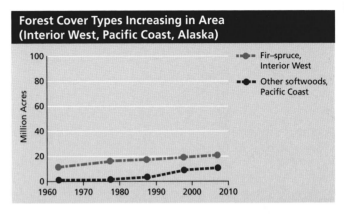

Forest Cover Types Increasing in Area (Interior West, Pacific Coast, Alaska)

- Fir–spruce, Interior West
- Other softwoods, Pacific Coast

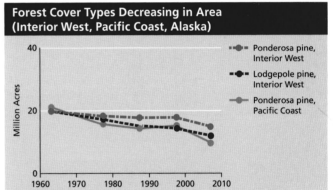

Forest Cover Types Decreasing in Area (Interior West, Pacific Coast, Alaska)

- Ponderosa pine, Interior West
- Lodgepole pine, Interior West
- Ponderosa pine, Pacific Coast

Data source: USDA Forest Service. Coverage: all 50 states; see p. 267 for description of regions. Technical details: Forest types not changing significantly in area from 1963 to 2006 (and thus not represented in the graphs above) include: North: northern conifers, oak–pine, oak–gum–cypress; South: loblolly–shortleaf pine, oak–pine, elm–ash–cottonwood, aspen–birch, and nonstocked; Interior West: Douglas–fir, hemlock–Sitka spruce; pinyon–juniper, other softwoods, western hardwoods, and nonstocked; Pacific Coast (including Hawaii): Douglas–fir, fir–spruce, hemlock–Sitka spruce, lodgepole pine, pinyon–juniper, western hardwoods, and nonstocked; Alaska: fir–spruce, hemlock–Sitka spruce, lodgepole pine, other softwoods, western hardwoods, and nonstocked. Forest types showing no significant change in area account for nearly 420 million acres or about 56% of the total forest acreage. There are no forest types in Alaska that are significantly increasing or decreasing in area. Because there is no consistent ground-based survey in Alaska, forest types are assigned via aerial survey, so most of these data represent softwood tree species in Alaska that could not be further identified. See technical note for more detail.

EXTENT AND PATTERN	CHEMICAL AND PHYSICAL	BIOLOGICAL COMPONENTS	GOODS AND SERVICES
Extent	Nutrients, Carbon, and Oxygen	Plants and Animals	Food, Fiber, and Water
Pattern	Chemical Contamination	Communities	Recreation and Other Services
	Physical	Ecological Productivity	

Forest Management Categories

Why Is the Proportion of Forest Area in Different Management Categories Important? How a forest is managed influences the goods and services that it provides. Heavily managed areas produce fiber and other wood products, while the value of reserved areas may lie in the solitude they offer, the rare plants and animals they shelter, or the watersheds they protect.

What Does This Indicator Report? The percentage of forest area in several different management categories. These range from "reserved lands" (forests in national parks, wilderness areas, and other similar areas) to "planted timberlands" (intensively managed forests that are replanted after harvest).

What Do the Data Show?

- In 2006, 8% of forests nationally was planted timberland; 10% was in forest reserves; 11% was in interior Alaska, which is currently considered as being too remote to harvest; 61% was natural or semi-natural timberland; and 10% ("other forests") were subject to a wide variety of both management practices and restrictions on use.

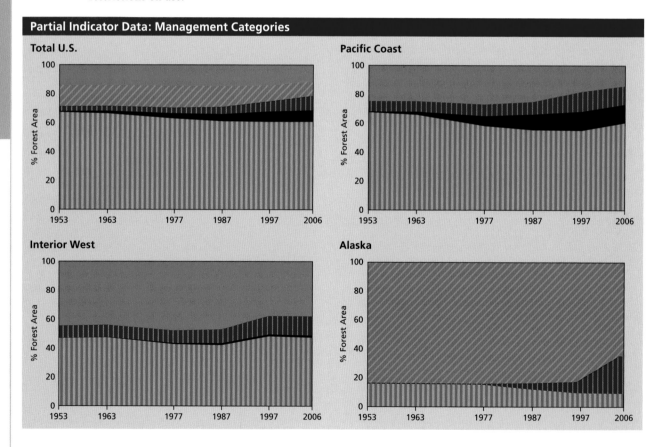

Partial Indicator Data: Management Categories

EXTENT AND PATTERN	CHEMICAL AND PHYSICAL	BIOLOGICAL COMPONENTS	GOODS AND SERVICES
Extent	Nutrients, Carbon, and Oxygen	Plants and Animals	Food, Fiber, and Water
Pattern	Chemical Contamination	Communities	Recreation and Other Services
	Physical	Ecological Productivity	

Forest Management Categories *(continued)*

- From 1953 to 2006, both reserved forest land and planted timberland increased nationally as a percentage of total forest area. In 2006, planted timberland ranged from 0% (Alaska) to 20% (South) of the total forest area in a region; reserved forest land (see figure legend for definition) ranged from 2% (South) to 26% (Alaska) of the total forest area in a region.
- Between 1953 and 2006, the proportion of natural/seminatural timberland declined nationally, with the largest declines in the South and Alaska.

Understanding the Data Changes in the relative proportion of forest management types may be due to changing forest policy, industry practices, or conservation status. The large changes in reserved forest land and natural/seminatural timberland in Alaska may be the result of changes in classification of lands, rather than in their management or legal status (see technical note for detailed data on reclassification of Alaska forest land).

The technical note for this indicator is on page 306.

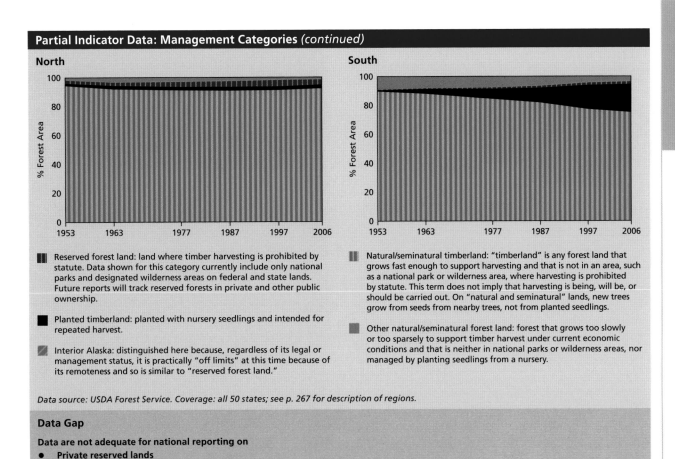

Partial Indicator Data: Management Categories *(continued)*

North — % Forest Area, 1953–2006

South — % Forest Area, 1953–2006

Reserved forest land: land where timber harvesting is prohibited by statute. Data shown for this category currently include only national parks and designated wilderness areas on federal and state lands. Future reports will track reserved forests in private and other public ownership.

Planted timberland: planted with nursery seedlings and intended for repeated harvest.

Interior Alaska: distinguished here because, regardless of its legal or management status, it is practically "off limits" at this time because of its remoteness and so is similar to "reserved forest land."

Natural/seminatural timberland: "timberland" is any forest land that grows fast enough to support harvesting and that is not in an area, such as a national park or wilderness area, where harvesting is prohibited by statute. This term does not imply that harvesting is being, will be, or should be carried out. On "natural and seminatural" lands, new trees grow from seeds from nearby trees, not from planted seedlings.

Other natural/seminatural forest land: forest that grows too slowly or too sparsely to support timber harvest under current economic conditions and that is neither in national parks or wilderness areas, nor managed by planting seedlings from a nursery.

Data source: USDA Forest Service. Coverage: all 50 states; see p. 267 for description of regions.

Data Gap

Data are not adequate for national reporting on
- **Private reserved lands**
- **Some public reserved lands (those not in national parks or federally designated wilderness areas)**

EXTENT AND PATTERN	CHEMICAL AND PHYSICAL	BIOLOGICAL COMPONENTS	GOODS AND SERVICES
Extent	Nutrients, Carbon, and Oxygen	Plants and Animals	Food, Fiber, and Water
Pattern	Chemical Contamination	Communities	Recreation and Other Services
	Physical	Ecological Productivity	

Pattern of Forest Landscapes

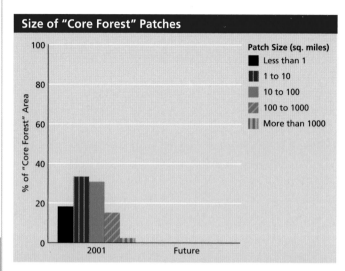

Size of "Core Forest" Patches

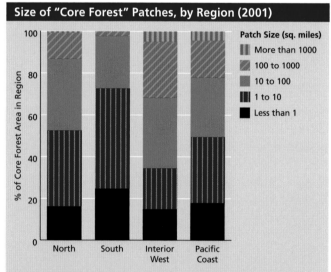

Size of "Core Forest" Patches, by Region (2001)

Data source: Multi-Resolution Land Characterization (MRLC) Consortium and ESRI (road map); analysis by the U.S. Forest Service and the U.S. Environmental Protection Agency. Coverage: lower 48 states. Technical details: the National Land Cover Dataset (NLCD) was augmented with a road map (paved roads only). A 240-acre-square analysis tool was placed around each pixel of the map with forest cover. Those pixels with at least 90% natural surroundings were formed into patches of touching pixels, the size of which is reported in the graphs. Note: current technical limitations required that patches be "cut" by state boundaries, meaning that, in some cases, these data represent minimum patch sizes. We are uncertain what impact this analysis limitation had on the data.

Why Is the Pattern of Forest Landscapes Important? The structural pattern of forest landscapes can influence the function of forest ecosystems and the types of plant and animal communities they support. For example, a landscape with small forest patches provides very different habitat from a landscape with large expanses of forest.

What Does This Indicator Report? The size of patches of "core forest," nationally and regionally. ["Core forest" is defined as small parcels (~1/4 acre), or pixels, of forest—defined by land cover data— surrounded by a specific amount (in this case, 90%) of forest and other "natural" land cover (grasslands, shrublands, wetlands, other fresh waters, and coastal waters).]

What Do the Data Show?

- For 2001, about the same amount of "core forest" was in patches ranging from 1 to 10 square miles (33%) as was in the 10–100 square mile category (31%). Eighteen percent of "core forest" was in patches of less than 1 square mile, about 15% was found in 100–1000 square mile patches, and just over 2% was found in the largest patches, of more than 1000 square miles.

- The Interior West region had the highest percentage of "core forest" in large patches (nearly 30% in patches 100 to 1000 square miles in size and 5% found in patches larger than 1000 square miles); the Pacific Coast had the next highest percentage of "core forest" in large patches.

- The South had the highest percentage of "core forest" in smaller patches (nearly three-quarters found in patches 10 square miles or less); the North and Pacific Coast regions each had about 50%, and the Interior West had about one-third of "core forest" in patches of 10 square miles or less.

EXTENT AND PATTERN	CHEMICAL AND PHYSICAL	BIOLOGICAL COMPONENTS	GOODS AND SERVICES
Extent	Nutrients, Carbon, and Oxygen	Plants and Animals	Food, Fiber, and Water
Pattern	Chemical Contamination	Communities	Recreation and Other Services
	Physical	Ecological Productivity	

Pattern of Forest Landscapes *(continued)*

Understanding the Data In 2001, 70% of total forest area in the lower 48 states met the definition of "core forest" (data not shown) and was found in the various patch sizes shown above. "Core forest" land cover has a minimum buffer of about 1500 feet of "natural" land cover, including other forest, surrounding it. Thus, larger patches of "core forest" have more contiguous forest and other "natural" land that is buffered from "non-natural" land cover types, such as croplands, roads, and development. It is important to note that this indicator considers all forest types equally, meaning that there is no distinction made between, for example, stands of old growth forest and plantations. For a discussion of the importance of augmenting the underlying data with land use information and other issues, see the core national indicator, Pattern of "Natural" Landscapes (p. 33), specifically the "What Is Not Shown by This Indicator" section.

There is not currently a comprehensive understanding of how landscape pattern (or structure) affects the functioning of forest ecosystems, and the size of "core forest" patches does not explicitly describe how well these ecosystems function. Rather, the proportion of total "core forest" that is found in patches of different sizes describes the degree to which forest land cover is mixed with "non-natural" land cover types. Species differ in their responses to structural aspects of landscapes. Some species, such as lynx, require large tracts of unbroken forest, while other species, like deer, can adapt to heterogeneous landscapes with small patches of forest. Thus, for the foreseeable future, a change in landscape pattern will need to be interpreted differently for different species and groups of species.

The technical note for this indicator is on page 307.

Nitrate in Forest Streams

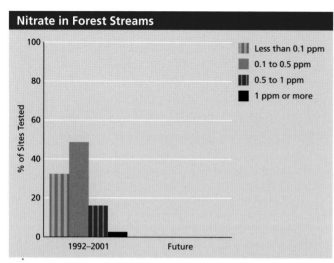

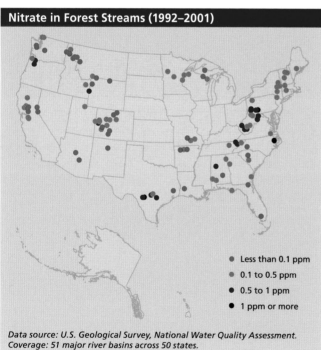

Data source: U.S. Geological Survey, National Water Quality Assessment.
Coverage: 51 major river basins across 50 states.

Why Is Nitrate in Streams Important?

At high concentrations, nitrate can cause water quality problems and contribute to low-oxygen conditions downstream in coastal areas (see Areas with Depleted Oxygen, p. 75). High levels of nitrate in forest streams can indicate that forest ecosystems are no longer able to store additional nitrogen. As excess nitrate "leaks" from soils into streams, it can carry other important plant nutrients with it, acidifying forest soils. Under such nitrogen-saturated conditions, forests may show decreased growth and increased susceptibility to disturbance and disease.

What Does this Indicator Report?

- For streams draining watersheds that are primarily forested, the percentage of sites with different nitrate concentrations
- The nitrate concentration in forest streams, compared with the nitrate concentration in farmland and urban and suburban streams

What Do the Data Show?

- Almost all forest streams (97%) had nitrate concentrations below 1 part per million (ppm), and 33% had concentrations of less than 0.1 ppm.
- Virtually all forest streams sampled had nitrate concentrations below 2 ppm, while about 80% of urban and suburban streams sampled and 40% of farmland streams sampled had nitrate concentrations below 2 ppm.

EXTENT AND PATTERN	CHEMICAL AND PHYSICAL	BIOLOGICAL COMPONENTS	GOODS AND SERVICES
Extent	Nutrients, Carbon, and Oxygen	Plants and Animals	Food, Fiber, and Water
Pattern	Chemical Contamination	Communities	Recreation and Other Services
	Physical	Ecological Productivity	

Nitrate in Forest Streams *(continued)*

Discussion Nitrate is a naturally occurring form of nitrogen and an important plant nutrient. Nitrate accumulates in ecosystems when inert, or "nonreactive," nitrogen in the atmosphere is "fixed" by microorganisms or lightning. Additional nitrogen in a plant-available or "reactive" form enters ecosystems through the use of synthetic fertilizers and fossil fuel combustion. Reactive nitrogen in the atmosphere can be transported and deposited in forest ecosystems as gas, dust or precipitation (see Freshwater Acidity, p. 176). Elevated levels of nitrate in forest streams may be a result of such nitrogen deposition or may indicate that forest ecosystems are under stress and can no longer retain nitrogen. In less-managed ecosystems (including many forested watersheds), most nitrate is used and reused by plants within an ecosystem, so there is relatively little "leakage" into either surface runoff or groundwater, and stream concentrations are very low. A decrease in area of forested wetlands may increase nitrate runoff to streams, as wetlands have the capacity to convert nitrate into a gaseous, nonreactive form. Elevated concentrations of nitrate in streams can pose problems when downstream rivers are used as a source of municipal drinking water (the federal drinking water standard for nitrate is 10 ppm). See also the core national indicator Movement of Nitrogen (p. 36) and related indicators for farmlands (p. 107) and urban and suburban areas (p. 238).

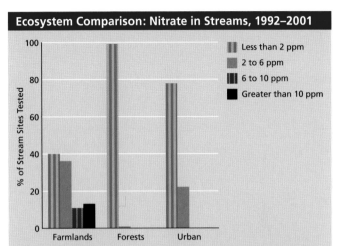

Ecosystem Comparison: Nitrate in Streams, 1992–2001

Legend:
- Less than 2 ppm
- 2 to 6 ppm
- 6 to 10 ppm
- Greater than 10 ppm

Data source: U.S. Geological Survey, National Water Quality Assessment. Coverage: 51 major river basins across 50 states. Technical Details: Data are from sites with upstream land cover that was primarily forested (generally less than or equal to 25% agricultural and less than 5% urban, and where the total area of forested land was greater than that of grassland or shrubland). Ecosystem comparison data are from sites with upstream land cover that was primarily farmlands and urban–suburban. Each site was sampled intensively for approximately 2 years during 1992–2001. Nitrate refers to the concentration of nitrate-nitrogen (see technical note).

The technical note for this indicator is on page 307.

EXTENT AND PATTERN	CHEMICAL AND PHYSICAL	BIOLOGICAL COMPONENTS	GOODS AND SERVICES
Extent	Nutrients, Carbon, and Oxygen	Plants and Animals	Food, Fiber, and Water
Pattern	Chemical Contamination	Communities	Recreation and Other Services
	Physical	Ecological Productivity	

Carbon Storage

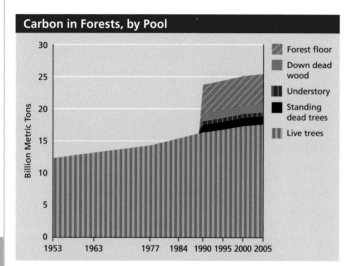

Carbon in Forests, by Pool

Legend: Forest floor, Down dead wood, Understory, Standing dead trees, Live trees

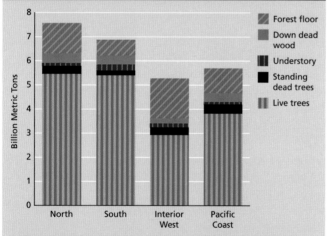

Carbon Stored in Forests, by Geographic Region, 2005

Legend: Forest floor, Down dead wood, Understory, Standing dead trees, Live trees

Data source: USDA Forest Service. Coverage: all forests in lower 48 states; see p. 267 for description of regions. Technical details: forests across the country have historically been sampled periodically and reported on a roughly 10-year basis, so data reported for a given year, such as 2005, may reflect a range of sample years for any given region. Note that estimates for forest floor, down dead wood, understory, and standing dead trees before 1990 are not available. See the technical note for more details.

Data Gap

Data are not adequate for national reporting on
- **The amount of carbon in forest soils**
- **Carbon storage in Alaska and Hawaii**

Why Is Carbon Storage in Forests Important? Forests contain large quantities of carbon—in trees and other vegetation, in organic debris, and in soil. The amount of carbon in these pools affects to some degree the amount and quality of the wood that is available to be harvested, as well as the capacity of ecosystems to provide services such as soil fertility, water storage, and food and habitat for organisms. Forests assimilate carbon dioxide, a potent greenhouse gas, from the atmosphere and store the carbon in the form of plant biomass. The total amount of carbon stored depends on a variety of factors, including prior forest conditions and age of the forest (see the core national Carbon Storage indicator, p. 38).

What Does This Indicator Report?
- Trends in the amount of carbon stored in forests, including standing and downed trees and forest floor litter
- Eventually, the amount of carbon in forest soils

What Do the Data Show?
- In 2005, U.S. forests in the lower 48 states stored just over 25 billion metric tons of carbon (soil carbon excluded): 17.6 billion metric tons (69%) is found in live trees, 4.6 billion metric tons (18%) in the forest floor, nearly 1.3 billion metric tons (about 5%) for both standing dead trees and down dead wood, and just over half a billion metric tons (nearly 3%) in the understory.
- Since 1953, the amount of carbon stored in live trees—the largest carbon pool in forests reported here—has increased by 43%.
- Since 1990, the amount of carbon stored in other forest carbon pools (down dead and standing dead trees, forest floor litter, and understory vegetation) has increased by 4% to 8%.
- Forests in the North store the most forest carbon in the lower 48 states (7.6 billion metric tons).
- Forests in the Interior West store the least live tree carbon of the four regions reported here (2.9 billion metric tons), but the most forest floor litter carbon (1.7 billion metric tons).

Forests

EXTENT AND PATTERN	CHEMICAL AND PHYSICAL	BIOLOGICAL COMPONENTS	GOODS AND SERVICES
Extent	**Nutrients, Carbon, and Oxygen**	Plants and Animals	Food, Fiber, and Water
Pattern	Chemical Contamination	Communities	Recreation and Other Services
	Physical	Ecological Productivity	

Carbon Storage *(continued)*

Why Can't This Entire Indicator Be Reported at This Time? Although estimates of carbon stored in forest soils can be calculated, the Forest Service continues to test and further develop its estimation methods. Uncertainty about the amount of carbon stored in soils hinders researchers' ability to estimate total forest carbon, as soil carbon is potentially a large component of total forest carbon storage. Estimates of carbon storage in forests of Alaska and Hawaii are not reported, since the underlying survey on which the estimates are calculated has not yet been expanded to these areas on a consistent basis. In 1995, the Forest Service estimated 16 billion metric tons of carbon in Alaskan forests, most of it in the soil (12 billion metric tons).

Understanding the Data The amount of carbon stored by forests changes as new additions of carbon, such as through tree growth, are offset by losses, such as through logging. Overall, carbon storage varies greatly among regions and different forest types and is influenced by climate, management practices, and disturbances such as disease, fire, and land use change. See the core national Carbon Storage indicator (p. 38) for a discussion of the various influences on carbon storage.

The technical note for this indicator is on page 308.

EXTENT AND PATTERN	CHEMICAL AND PHYSICAL	BIOLOGICAL COMPONENTS	GOODS AND SERVICES
Extent	Nutrients, Carbon, and Oxygen	Plants and Animals	Food, Fiber, and Water
Pattern	Chemical Contamination	Communities	Recreation and Other Services
	Physical	Ecological Productivity	

At-Risk Native Forest Species

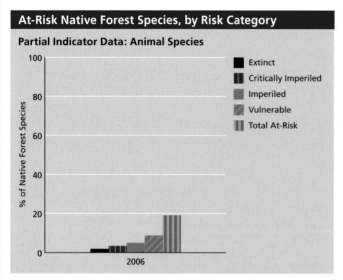

At-Risk Native Forest Species, by Risk Category

Partial Indicator Data: Animal Species

Legend:
- Extinct
- Critically Imperiled
- Imperiled
- Vulnerable
- Total At-Risk

Y-axis: % of Native Forest Species (0 to 100)

X-axis: 2006

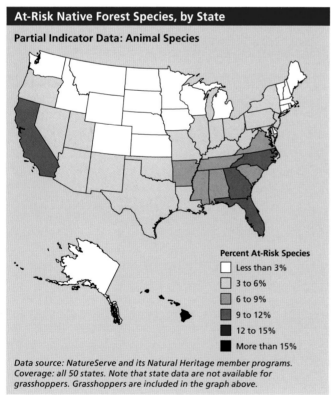

At-Risk Native Forest Species, by State

Partial Indicator Data: Animal Species

Percent At-Risk Species
- Less than 3%
- 3 to 6%
- 6 to 9%
- 9 to 12%
- 12 to 15%
- More than 15%

Data source: NatureServe and its Natural Heritage member programs. Coverage: all 50 states. Note that state data are not available for grasshoppers. Grasshoppers are included in the graph above.

Why Are Native Species Important?

Native species are valued for a variety of reasons: they provide products, including food, fiber, and genetic materials, which may have various medicinal, industrial, and agricultural uses; they are key elements of ecosystems, which themselves provide valuable goods and services; and many people value them for their intrinsic worth or beauty.

What Does This Indicator Report?

- The relative risk of extinction of native forest species (plants and animals that live in forests during at least part of their lives and depend on forest habitats for survival), presented as four categories: vulnerable, imperiled, critically imperiled, and extinct (see definitions)
- The percentage of native forest species that are at risk in each state
- Population trends of at-risk native forest species (declining, stable, increasing)

What Do the Data Show?

- Nineteen percent of native forest animals are considered to be at risk. This group includes 3% that are critically imperiled, 5% that are imperiled, 9% that are vulnerable, and 2% that may already be extinct.
- Hawaii has a much larger percentage of at-risk native forest animal species (76%) than any other state.
- A similar percentage of at-risk native vertebrate forest animals have declining populations (27%) and stable populations (26%); relatively few have increasing populations (1%). Population trend data are unknown for many at-risk native vertebrate forest animals (46%).

EXTENT AND PATTERN	CHEMICAL AND PHYSICAL	BIOLOGICAL COMPONENTS	GOODS AND SERVICES
Extent	Nutrients, Carbon, and Oxygen	**Plants and Animals**	Food, Fiber, and Water
Pattern	Chemical Contamination	Communities	Recreation and Other Services
	Physical	Ecological Productivity	

At-Risk Native Forest Species *(continued)*

Why Can't This Entire Indicator Be Reported? This indicator reports on over 1700 species of mammals, birds, reptiles, amphibians, grasshoppers, butterflies, and skippers. Data on other groups have not been included either because too little is known to assign risk categories or, as with most plants, because determinations of which species are associated with forests, grasslands, or other habitats have not been completed. Population trend data are known for too few at-risk invertebrate forest animal species (15%) to report on the group as a whole.

While status data were reported for this indicator in the 2002 edition of this report, changes in rank status can occur for a variety of reasons, including changes in the actual status of species, improved knowledge of the species' condition, or changes in taxonomy. Consequently, 2000 status data are not presented here (see discussion in Program Note for NatureServe data, p. 275).

Understanding the Data Interpreting data on the status of species is complicated because some species are naturally rare. Thus, the rankings are influenced by differences among regions and species groups in the number of naturally rare species, as well as by different types and levels of human activities that can cause species declines. Data on population trends complement the risk category data by showing how species of most conservation concern are faring over time. The ability to track changes in the condition of species over time will be further enhanced when it is possible to report on the population trends of a larger percentage of species.

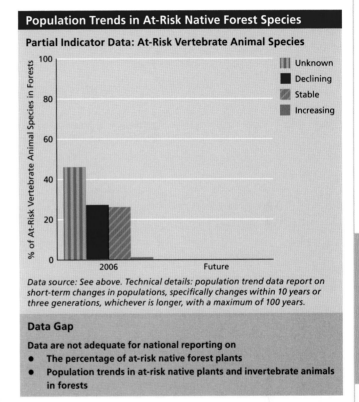

Population Trends in At-Risk Native Forest Species

Partial Indicator Data: At-Risk Vertebrate Animal Species

Data source: See above. Technical details: population trend data report on short-term changes in populations, specifically changes within 10 years or three generations, whichever is longer, with a maximum of 100 years.

Data Gap

Data are not adequate for national reporting on
- The percentage of at-risk native forest plants
- Population trends in at-risk native plants and invertebrate animals in forests

Some Definitions

- "Critically imperiled" species often are found in five or fewer places, may have experienced very steep declines, or show other evidence of very high risk.
- "Imperiled" species often are found in 20 or fewer places, may have experienced steep declines, or display other risk factors.
- "Vulnerable" species often are found in fewer than 80 places, may have recently experienced widespread decline, or show other signs of moderate risk.
- The remaining plant and animal species are regarded as "secure" or "apparently secure."

See also the core national At-Risk Native Species indicator (p. 50) and the indicators for at-risk native coastal, freshwater, and grassland and shrubland species (pp. 80, 180, and 211), as well as the indicators for animal species in farmlands (p. 116) and species status in urban and suburban areas (p. 246).

The technical note for this indicator is on page 308.

EXTENT AND PATTERN	CHEMICAL AND PHYSICAL	BIOLOGICAL COMPONENTS	GOODS AND SERVICES
Extent	Nutrients, Carbon, and Oxygen	**Plants and Animals**	Food, Fiber, and Water
Pattern	Chemical Contamination	Communities	Recreation and Other Services
	Physical	Ecological Productivity	

Established Non-native Plant Cover in Forests

Established Non-native Plant Cover in Forests

Data Gap

Data are not adequate for national reporting.

Why Is the Amount of Non-native Plant Cover Important? In forest ecosystems the structure and composition of plant communities provides critical resources for animals, influences ecosystem functioning, and determines the goods and services forests provide. Established non-native species can change the structure and composition of forest vegetation. The percentage cover occupied by established non-native plants reflects the extent to which forest ecosystems are influenced by non-natives. In general, forests with greater coverage by non-native species are subject to more ecological disruption, which may in turn have economic consequences.

What Will This Indicator Report? The amount of forest area with different proportions of established non-native plant cover relative to total plant cover.

Why Can't This Indicator Be Reported at This Time? At this time, the necessary data are not being collected at the national scale. Some data are available at the state level (for example, the Critical Trends Assessment Program of the Illinois Natural History Survey). At the national scale, the USDA Forest Service is currently the only agency or organization known to be developing the necessary protocols to monitor vegetation structure. It is critical that, as protocols for percentage cover by non-native plants are developed, those agencies and organizations responsible for data collection take into consideration the need to standardize protocols and aggregate data across ecosystem types (see technical note).

Discussion Within the United States, species are generally considered to be non-native if their natural range does not include North America, although there is growing recognition that species that are native to one part of the United States may cause problems if they spread to other areas. Non-native species may spread aggressively and crowd out native species by shading native plants or by consuming large quantities of water.

Well-known non-native plant species in the eastern United States include kudzu, melaleuca, and ailanthus, while western species include medusahead and salt cedar. Some non-native plants were introduced accidentally; others were originally planted for landscaping, like Norway maple and multiflora rose, or for purposes such as erosion control, like kudzu and Russian olive.

The technical note for this indicator is on page 309.

EXTENT AND PATTERN	CHEMICAL AND PHYSICAL	BIOLOGICAL COMPONENTS	GOODS AND SERVICES
Extent	Nutrients, Carbon, and Oxygen	Plants and Animals	Food, Fiber, and Water
Pattern	Chemical Contamination	**Communities**	Recreation and Other Services
	Physical	Ecological Productivity	

Forest Age

Why Is the Age of Forests Important? Forests of different ages often provide different goods, services, and values. For example, woodpeckers and species that need trunk cavities for nesting find suitable habitat in the dead trees of older forests. Younger forests, with their rapid growth and smaller trees, provide habitat for species such as the Kirtland's warbler, which can only live in pine forests recently regrown after fire. The age of forests can also affect rates of nutrient cycling and carbon storage. For example, young, rapidly growing forests have greater demands for nitrogen and store carbon at a faster rate than older, slower-growing stands.

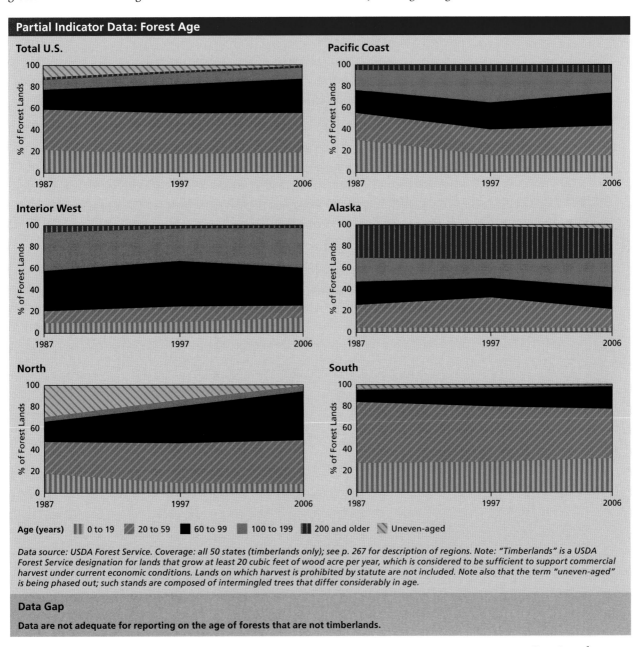

Partial Indicator Data: Forest Age

Total U.S. / Pacific Coast / Interior West / Alaska / North / South

Age (years) ▮ 0 to 19 ▨ 20 to 59 ■ 60 to 99 ▮ 100 to 199 ▮ 200 and older ◣ Uneven-aged

Data source: USDA Forest Service. Coverage: all 50 states (timberlands only); see p. 267 for description of regions. Note: "Timberlands" is a USDA Forest Service designation for lands that grow at least 20 cubic feet of wood acre per year, which is considered to be sufficient to support commercial harvest under current economic conditions. Lands on which harvest is prohibited by statute are not included. Note also that the term "uneven-aged" is being phased out; such stands are composed of intermingled trees that differ considerably in age.

Data Gap

Data are not adequate for reporting on the age of forests that are not timberlands.

Continued

Forest Age *(continued)*

What Does This Indicator Report? The percentage of forest lands in various age classes.

What Do the Data Show?

- In 2006, over half of U.S. timberland was less than 60 years old; 12% was more than 100 years old, and less than 1 percent was of uneven age.
- In 2006, Alaska had the largest percentage of forests more than 200 years old, while the South had the largest percentage of forests less than 20 years old.
- From 1987 to 2006 only the uneven-aged class decreased nationally as a percentage of timberland area, due to decreases in the North and South.
- Between 1987 and 2006, the age structure shifted to slightly older trees in the North and South. Both the North and the South experienced increases in the 60–99-year age class; the South also had an increase in the 200+ year age class and a decrease in the 20–59-year age class.

Why Can't This Entire Indicator Be Reported at This Time? Data on the age class of forest trees are not available for national parks and wilderness areas and other forest land not classified as timberlands. Forests in these wilderness areas and national parks, which are most common in the West, contain many old stands (see Forest Management Categories, p. 136).

Understanding the Data Forest age structure reflects historic and current management as well as natural factors. The high percentage of younger forests in the North and South reflects the reforestation of former agricultural land, the management of many private landholdings for commercial harvesting, and the fact that very old stands are much less common in the eastern United States. High percentages of younger forests in these regions probably contribute to the significant amount of carbon stored in them (see Carbon Storage, p. 142). Age structure and tree type (see Forest Types, p. 134) influence the types of wildlife found in forests, may be related to how well ecosystems function, and are important factors for managing timber harvest. It is important to note that declines in age class do not necessarily mean that a large forest area has been harvested or has died off. The loss of a few old trees in a given stand may cause the average age to drop significantly. In addition, older stands are more prone to losing the oldest trees. The apparent decline in uneven-aged stands is due to the phasing out of this category in the Forest Service inventory.

The technical note for this indicator is on page 309.

Forests

EXTENT AND PATTERN	CHEMICAL AND PHYSICAL	BIOLOGICAL COMPONENTS	GOODS AND SERVICES
Extent	Nutrients, Carbon, and Oxygen	Plants and Animals	Food, Fiber, and Water
Pattern	Chemical Contamination	Communities	Recreation and Other Services
	Physical	Ecological Productivity	

Forest Disturbance: Fire, Insects, and Disease

Why Are Forest Disturbances Important? Fires, insects, and diseases are part of a natural cycle of disturbance and regrowth in forests. However, human interventions or changes in ecosystem condition, both within and surrounding forests, can increase the frequency and severity of disturbances. For example, fire suppression over large areas and long periods of time may foster the conditions necessary for catastrophic fires, and introduced pests like gypsy moths and Dutch elm disease can devastate large areas of forest.

What Does This Indicator Report?
- The acreage of forests affected each year by forest fires (both wild and prescribed), insects, and diseases
- When data become available, acres affected by non-native and native insects and by disease, reported separately

What Do the Data Show?
- In 2006, fires burned on 9.8 million acres of forests and grasslands/shrublands, 8.4 million acres of forest was defoliated by insects, and an additional 4.7 million acres of trees were killed in large patches by insects ("continuous mortality").
- Since 1916, there has been a significant decline in the number of forest and grassland/shrubland acres burned due to wildfires. In recent years this trend has reversed, with a slight but significant increase in the area disturbed by fire (1979–2006).
- Between 1979 and 1996, insect damage in forests declined; since 1997, continuous mortality has been observed in an increasing number of acres of forest. In the 1980s, gypsy moth and spruce budworm accounted for much of the damage reported.
- During recent years, 2001 stood out as having the most acres affected by insect damage. Three insect species accounted for over 90% of the damage, totaling more than 30 million acres (see technical note). Although not shown here, most of that damage occurred in the eastern United States.

Continued

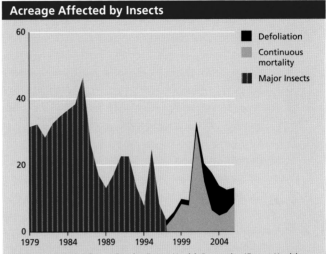

Acreage Affected by Insects

Legend: Defoliation; Continuous mortality; Major Insects

Data source: USDA Forest Service Forest Health Protection/Forest Health Monitoring Program. Coverage: all 50 states. Note that data from 1979–1996 represent damage caused by five major insect pests. See technical note for details and list of insects reported.

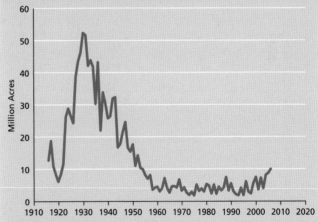

Wildfire Acreage (Forests and Grasslands/Shrublands)

Data source: USDA Forest Service, National Forest System (1916–1959) and the National Interagency Fire Center (1960–2006). Coverage: all 50 states. Note that these data include all wildland fires (forests, grasslands and shrublands).

Data Gap

Data are not adequate for national reporting on
- Diseases
- Native and non-native insect and/or disease species independently

Forest Disturbance: Fire, Insects, and Disease *(continued)*

Why Can't This Entire Indicator Be Reported? Data on the acreage affected by forest diseases are only collected by the Forest Service on an as-needed basis to monitor specific disease outbreaks. Aerial survey data can allow for reliable assessment of damage caused by native vs. non-native species, but they are not reported here because not all data have been checked against ground-based observations, and damage cannot necessarily be attributed to any one organism. Often the damage is categorized by general damage classes, which can be difficult to compare from year to year if tracking a particular pest. It is also not yet possible to report on acreage affected by forest fires (as distinct from other wildfires), on the acreage subject to different levels of fire intensity, and on the acreage of prescribed fire (fires set intentionally as a management tool).

Understanding the Data The decline in fire disturbance over the past 100 years is largely due to fire suppression policies and practices. Climatic variability, however, also affects the degree of fire disturbance. For example, periods of drought often lead to more acres of wildfires. This has likely been an important factor in recent years, as well as in the 1930s. Much of the variation in insect data over the past 25 years results from population cycles for gypsy moth and southern pine beetle, and more recently for the forest tent caterpillar and mountain pine beetle. The Forest Health Monitoring (FHM) Program's insect and disease detection surveys since 1997 do not depict low-level or subtle damaging levels of insects or diseases (scattered mortality). This subtle damage will eventually contribute to annual tree mortality, which is reported by the FHM insect and disease detection surveys.

Wildfires, insect and disease infestations, changing climate, increasing non-native plant cover (see p. 146), and other factors, can all have interactive effects. For example, insect activity in forests can affect the extent and severity of fires, and fires can predispose trees to subsequent insect attack (see also Fire Frequency, p. 151).

The technical note for this indicator is on page 310.

EXTENT AND PATTERN	CHEMICAL AND PHYSICAL	BIOLOGICAL COMPONENTS	GOODS AND SERVICES
Extent	Nutrients, Carbon, and Oxygen	Plants and Animals	Food, Fiber, and Water
Pattern	Chemical Contamination	**Communities**	Recreation and Other Services
	Physical	Ecological Productivity	

Fire Frequency

Why Is Fire Frequency Important?

As a natural disturbance, fire plays an important role in the structure and function of forest ecosystems. As fire frequency increases, fire-adapted species thrive

Fire Frequency

Indicator Development Needed

and other, less fire-tolerant species decline. Fire frequency can also alter the age class of tree stands, change nutrient availability in the soil, and affect wildlife habitat. The frequency of fires influences the degree of canopy openness, the types of tree and understory species that are present in forests, and the susceptibility of forested areas to experience destructive high-intensity fires.

What Will This Indicator Report?

When fully designed, this indicator will compare current fire frequencies to historic estimates. Simply defining what is meant by "fire frequency" is complex. For example, it may not be useful to report the interval between a less-intense ground fire and a very intense fire that burned tree crowns. The timing of fire will need to be taken into account, because fires in different seasons will have different ecological effects. In addition, a fire that covers a small area may have a very different impact on ecosystem functioning at a regional scale compared to a fire covering a broad area. Furthermore, relatively small differences in topography between two sites can lead to very different fire susceptibilities—both currently and historically. For all these reasons, the developed indicator will likely need to be evaluated over areas small enough to be able to capture local variability so that the values can be summarized regionally and nationally. Finally, because people actively suppress or have otherwise deliberately altered natural fire cycles, the indicator will need to distinguish areas with active fire management from those lacking such management.

Why Can't This Indicator Be Reported at This Time?

As described above, comparing current and historic fire frequencies will require that several parameters, both current and historic, be estimated over relatively small areas—the appropriate scale will need to be determined and will most likely vary geographically. For a given area, the recurrence pattern of fires is known as the area's "fire regime." Historic fire regimes can be estimated from tree ring scars, but a complete indicator would need to link historic vegetation types to particular fire regimes (the vegetation type's "characteristic fire regimes"). Doing so is complicated because characteristic fire regimes vary considerably within a forest type and topographically, such as between ridges and valleys. Additionally, gradual changes in climate can lead to biased estimates of characteristic fire regimes; these estimates need to be adjusted to reflect how changes in climate may have influenced the frequency and intensity of fires. The interagency LANDFIRE program is expected to be a substantial resource for estimating historic fire regimes.

It is more straightforward to estimate current fire frequency, although this is not without complications. For example, documenting a fire regime with fires occurring every 50 or 100 years will require a database that does not currently exist. A useful starting point will be to estimate how recently an area has been burned, which will be part of the interagency Monitoring Trends in Burn Severity (MTBS) program.

Discussion

For the past 10,000 years (since the last Ice Age), most forests in the lower 48 states burned regularly, with fires started by lightning or by American Indians, who used fire to manage forests and grasslands. There is increasing interest in forest management practices that incorporate fire and other disturbances in ways that mimic historic patterns.

Continued

 Forests

Fire Frequency *(continued)*

Whether a forest ecosystem was maintained by fires ignited by lightning or by people, active suppression of fires dramatically changes composition, structure, and how forests function ecologically. In suppressed areas, there are often more trees per acre and a higher frequency of certain species whose spread was formerly controlled by fire. In the East, for example, red maple has increased in eastern oak and pine forests, and in the West white fir and incense cedar are now more common in ponderosa pine and giant sequoia forests. In some forests, like ponderosa pine, the denser forests produced by fire suppression are subject to hotter fires, which kill more trees when they do occur. In other areas, such as eastern oak forests, fire suppression favors trees like maples, birches, and beech, with a corresponding decrease in both flammability and the number of oaks.

See also the grasslands and shrublands Fire Frequency indicator (p. 216).

The technical note for this indicator is on page 311.

EXTENT AND PATTERN	CHEMICAL AND PHYSICAL	BIOLOGICAL COMPONENTS	GOODS AND SERVICES
Extent	Nutrients, Carbon, and Oxygen	Plants and Animals	Food, Fiber, and Water
Pattern	Chemical Contamination	**Communities**	Recreation and Other Services
	Physical	Ecological Productivity	

Forest Community Types with Significantly Reduced Area

Why Is a Reduction in the Area of Forest Community Types Important?

Forest community types, such as Virginia pine–oak, American beech–southern magnolia, Douglas fir, and longleaf pine–oak, are found in particular climates, landscapes, and soil types. They are characterized

Forest Community Types with Significantly Reduced Area

Data are not adequate for reporting on the area occupied by forest types that have significantly declined in area since presettlement times and on whether these forest types have increased, remained stable, or decreased in area.

by plant and animal species that depend on the habitat provided by that forest type. When the area occupied by a forest community declines, populations of those animals and plants that are highly dependent upon that community type may also decrease.

What Will This Indicator Report?

● The total area occupied by much-reduced forest community types—those that have been reduced by 70% or more in area since European settlement (1600–1800)

● Whether these significantly reduced community types have increased, remained stable, or decreased in area

Why Can't This Indicator Be Reported at This Time?
Data on historic and current area of many forest types are not available. Methods are being developed to obtain estimates of current area from existing USDA Forest Service inventory data. Estimates of both historic and current extent may be derived from ongoing national mapping efforts (LANDFIRE and USGS Gap Analysis Program).

The technical note for this indicator is on page 311.

EXTENT AND PATTERN	CHEMICAL AND PHYSICAL	BIOLOGICAL COMPONENTS	GOODS AND SERVICES
Extent	Nutrients, Carbon, and Oxygen	Plants and Animals	**Food, Fiber, and Water**
Pattern	Chemical Contamination	Communities	Recreation and Other Services
	Physical	Ecological Productivity	

Timber Harvest

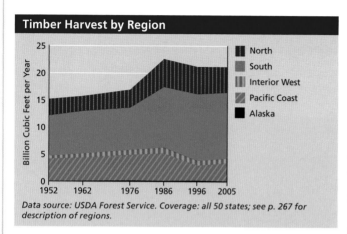

Timber Harvest by Region

Data source: USDA Forest Service. Coverage: all 50 states; see p. 267 for description of regions.

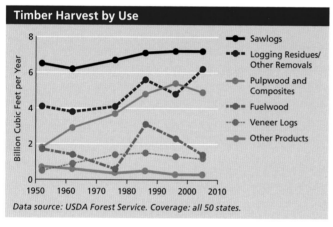

Timber Harvest by Use

Data source: USDA Forest Service. Coverage: all 50 states.

Why Is the Amount of Timber Harvested Important? The production of wood products provides employment, generates economic benefits, and meets society's needs for wood, paper, and other products. Demand for these products drives harvesting and other forest management activities.

What Does This Indicator Report?
This indicator reports trends in timber harvest volume, by region and by primary product category (sawlogs, pulpwood, and so on); unlike Timber Growth and Harvest (p. 155), this indicator includes all harvest material, such as rotten trees or trees that do not meet specific size standards (not just "growing stock," which is defined on p. 313) and also includes lands other than those classified as timberlands.

What Do the Data Show?
- In 2005, 21.2 billion cubic feet of timber were harvested from U.S. forests: 7.2 billion cubic feet (34%) sawlogs, 6.2 billion cubic feet (29%) logging residues, 4.9 billion cubic feet (23%) pulpwood, and the remainder in fuelwood, veneer logs, and other products.
- Nationally, timber harvest increased from 1952 to 2005, with significant increases in the production of sawlogs (11% increase), logging residues (52% increase) and pulpwood and composites (182% increase); significant declines were seen only in the production of other products (64% decline). Much of the national increase can be attributed to increased timber production in the South and North (see Timber Growth and Harvest, p. 155).
- In 2005, 57% of U.S. timber was harvested in the South, 23% was harvested in the North, 16% was harvested in the Pacific Coast region, and the remainder harvested in Alaska and the Interior West.
- Regional harvests in the North and South have increased significantly since 1952; however, the volume of wood harvested in other regions has not changed significantly over time.

Understanding the Data Patterns of forest harvest both by region and by product category describe the demand for the variety of products that are obtained from forested areas. Both economic and social changes in our society can influence regional patterns of forest harvest, as well as the types of products that are in demand at a given time. For example, a decline in U.S. paper and paperboard production from 1999 to 2001 was linked to the strength of the U.S. dollar (which both reduced the price of competing imported goods and reduced demand for U.S. products abroad) and to an overall slowing of the U.S. economy, which decreased domestic demand for paper and paperboard, which is made from pulpwood.

See Timber Growth and Harvest (p. 155) for a discussion of harvest trends on public and private timberlands.

The technical note for this indicator is on page 312.

EXTENT AND PATTERN	CHEMICAL AND PHYSICAL	BIOLOGICAL COMPONENTS	GOODS AND SERVICES
Extent	Nutrients, Carbon, and Oxygen	Plants and Animals	Food, Fiber, and Water
Pattern	Chemical Contamination	Communities	Recreation and Other Services
	Physical	Ecological Productivity	

Timber Growth and Harvest

Why Is It Important to Compare Timber Growth and Harvest? The comparison between growth and harvest in the nation's forests indicates whether harvests are less than, are balanced by, or exceed growth.

What Does This Indicator Report? The volume of new wood grown and the volume of wood harvested each year on public and private timberlands—those lands classified as capable of supporting commercial harvests. The indicator is restricted to "growing stock," which excludes some commercially undesirable trees and tree parts (see technical note).

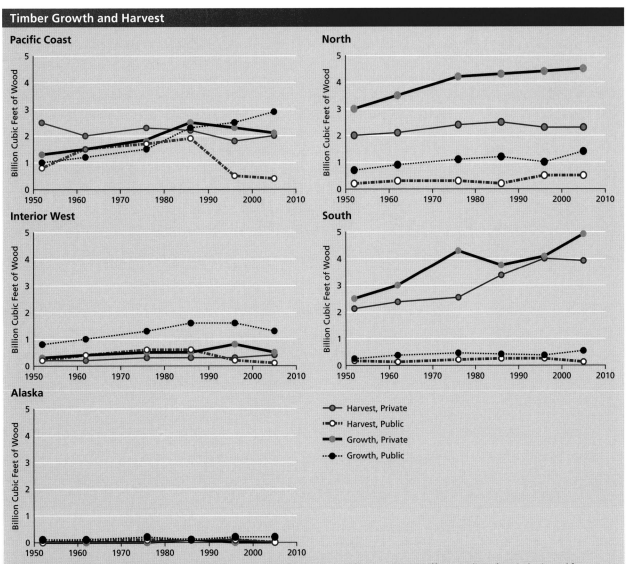

Timber Growth and Harvest

Legend:
- Harvest, Private
- Harvest, Public
- Growth, Private
- Growth, Public

Data source: USDA Forest Service. Coverage: all 50 states; see p. 267 for description of regions. Notes: Different scaling of vertical axis used for the South graph. "Timberlands" is a USDA Forest Service designation for lands that grow at least 20 cubic feet of wood per acre per year, which is considered to be sufficient to support commercial harvest under current economic conditions. Lands on which harvest is prohibited by statute are not included as timberlands.

Continued

The State of the Nation's Ecosystems 2008: The Indicators   155

 Forests

EXTENT AND PATTERN	CHEMICAL AND PHYSICAL	BIOLOGICAL COMPONENTS	GOODS AND SERVICES
Extent	Nutrients, Carbon, and Oxygen	Plants and Animals	**Food, Fiber, and Water**
Pattern	Chemical Contamination	Communities	Recreation and Other Services
	Physical	Ecological Productivity	

Timber Growth and Harvest *(continued)*

What Do the Data Show?
- In 2005, growth in the nation's forests exceeded harvest by 10.4 billion cubic feet.
- Growth exceeded harvest on public and private timberlands in the North and South and on public timberlands in the Interior West and Pacific Coast regions.
- Since 1952, timber growth on public and private lands has increased significantly in all regions except the Interior West and on private lands in Alaska. The largest regional increase in growth—5.8 billion cubic feet—has occurred on private lands in the South.
- In 2005, private lands accounted for over 90% of total national harvest, a figure that has not increased significantly since the 1950s.

Understanding the Data Whether owned by public or private entities, timberlands are managed to provide timber products, as well as a variety of benefits including ecosystem services (see p. 60), wildlife habitat, recreational opportunities (see p. 157), in order to meet a variety of societal goals. While timber harvest on public lands is governed by federal provisions, private owners may set their own management goals, using federal standards as a guide or not as they feel appropriate. Each land owner may have a different understanding of what levels of timber harvests can be sustained, with the forest still providing the full range of ecosystem services, both now and in the future. See also Timber Harvest (p. 154), which includes all harvested material (not just growing stock, as in this indicator) and also includes harvest on lands other than those classified as timberlands.

The technical note for this indicator is on page 312.

EXTENT AND PATTERN	CHEMICAL AND PHYSICAL	BIOLOGICAL COMPONENTS	GOODS AND SERVICES
Extent	Nutrients, Carbon, and Oxygen	Plants and Animals	Food, Fiber, and Water
Pattern	Chemical Contamination	Communities	**Recreation and Other Services**
	Physical	Ecological Productivity	

Recreation in Forests

Why Is Measuring Recreation in Forests Important? Forested lands support a variety of popular recreational activities such as wildlife viewing, picnicking, hiking, and hunting. Recreation is a benefit that is derived from forest ecosystems, in much the same way as we derive products such as timber from forests.

What Does This Indicator Report? This indicator reports the number of times per year U.S. residents 16 years of age or older participate in a variety of outdoor recreational activities in a forest setting. When data are available, this indicator will also report on youth participation in forest recreation.

What Do the Data Show?

- In 2003–2005, Americans 16 years old and older engaged in recreational activities in forest settings approximately 26 billion times per year, 27% more than in 1999–2001.
- With the exception of mountain biking, recent data (2003–2005) show increased participation for all outdoor recreational activities reported in this indicator, compared to 1999–2001. More years of data are required to determine if these increases are part of a long-term upward trend in recreation participation.
- The three most popular recreational activities in forests are viewing activities, walking, and picnicking.

Understanding the Data Data are collected from telephone surveys, and no attempt is made to check the accuracy of respondents' self-reported participation in activities in a "forest setting." In addition, data do not include information on how long people participated in various activities, but rather the number of times they participated; each day in a multiday trip is counted as a separate event.

This report includes other indicators of recreational activity. See Outdoor Recreation (p. 58), Recreation in Farmland Areas (p. 122), Freshwater Recreation Activities (p. 191), and Recreation on Grasslands and Shrublands (p. 219).

The technical note for this indicator is on page 313.

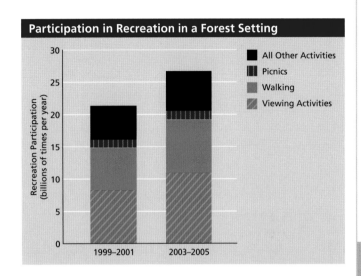

Participation in Recreation in a Forest Setting

Legend: All Other Activities, Picnics, Walking, Viewing Activities

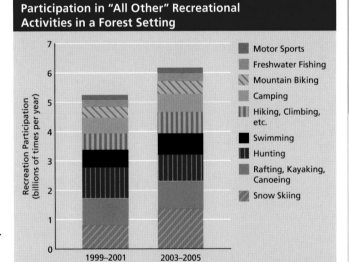

Participation in "All Other" Recreational Activities in a Forest Setting

Legend: Motor Sports, Freshwater Fishing, Mountain Biking, Camping, Hiking, Climbing, etc., Swimming, Hunting, Rafting, Kayaking, Canoeing, Snow Skiing

Data source: USDA Forest Service. Coverage: all 50 states. Technical details: note that these data do not track the amount of time spent on a particular outdoor activity; rather, they measure the number of different activities an individual engages in during a 24-hour day. Thus, the data do not distinguish between doing several activities during the same day or on separate days in a given year. Note that the scale for the top graph is considerably different from that used on the bottom graph.

Data Gap

Data are not adequate for national reporting on recreation participation for residents under the age of 16.

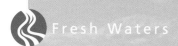

Contents

	page

INDICATORS

Chapter 6:
Indicators of the Condition and Use of Fresh Waters

The freshwater resources of the United States are extensive and occur in an astounding variety of forms: from seasonal streams to the mighty Mississippi River, which captures water from 40% of the U.S. land mass; from ephemeral prairie potholes and farm ponds to the Great Lakes; and from shallow rain-fed groundwater to deep regional "fossil" aquifers. Fresh waters also include marshes, forested wetlands, and riparian areas—the habitat adjacent to streams and rivers. Although some freshwater ecosystems may appear isolated, many are connected to other aquatic systems through groundwater, runoff, and streams or rivers. Fresh waters also link different terrestrial, or land-based, ecosystem types, flowing through forests, grasslands, farmlands, suburbs, and cities on their way downstream to the oceans. In this way, fresh waters serve as a terrestrial "circulatory system," accumulating nutrients, carbon, and chemicals from a variety of landscapes, moving them through other ecosystems, and eventually discharging them into coastal waters. In addition, freshwater systems provide habitat for aquatic plants and animals, many of which are adapted to very specific conditions, such as seasonal changes in water flows.

The uses of fresh water are as diverse as aquatic systems themselves. Water is extracted and used for drinking, other household uses, industrial processes, and irrigation. Rivers and lakes themselves serve as receiving waters for treated waste, as major transportation corridors, as sources of hydroelectric power, as scenic vistas, and as vacation playgrounds for fishing, swimming, and boating.

The wide array of benefits generated by freshwater ecosystems opens up opportunity for conflict as well. Use, extraction, or degradation of water in one place almost invariably means higher costs or reduced opportunities elsewhere. Water is the subject of an extraordinary array of laws, regulations, and policies—and disputes. There are federal laws concerning disposal of wastes in waterways, dredging for navigation, filling of wetlands, conservation of endangered aquatic species, and shared use of interstate and international water resources. State and local laws address many of these same issues, often using different strategies. Court challenges over issues such as wetlands regulation and allocation of limited water resources are common. In recent years, decisions partitioning scarce water supplies between endangered species and irrigators have even prompted civil disobedience.

This chapter provides a broad overview of the condition of the nation's fresh waters. Because fresh waters form an important component of most other ecosystems, the data in this chapter are complemented by indicators in the core national, forests, farmlands, grasslands and shrublands, and urban and suburban landscapes chapters that describe the chemical, physical, and biological conditions and human uses of freshwater resources specific to these ecosystems. These related indicators are listed below at the end of each section.

Extent and Pattern

The indicators in this section focus both on 'how much' of the resource we have—that is, how many miles of streams and rivers and how many acres of wetlands, ponds, lakes, and reservoirs—and on how these areas have been altered. Freshwater systems can be altered in many ways—for example, by damming or channelizing rivers and streams, excavating or impounding wetlands, or converting the edge of a lake or river to a different land use, such as vacation homes or crops. Such alterations can change the nature of a freshwater system as well as the range of services it generates. Converting a free-flowing stream to a reservoir, for example, may provide warm water fisheries, flood control, and power

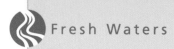

production, but it can also eliminate the cold water fishery, migratory fish passage, and whitewater recreation formerly supplied by the free-flowing stream. In other cases, as with wetland draining or filling, both the system itself and the goods and services it provided—flood control, filtration of runoff, habitat and nursery grounds for fish—may be lost.

Choosing which benefits to enhance and which to sacrifice—flood control or migratory fish habitat, water filtration or private development, for example—can be contentious and often involve complex disagreements over public goods versus private use. Competing demands for use and alteration of freshwater ecosystems manifest themselves in such issues as the scope and nature of wetlands regulation, the allocation of water for irrigation versus maintenance of endangered fish populations, and the replacement or strengthening of levees after flooding.

Data in this chapter show that
- Since the 1950s, freshwater wetland area has declined by 9%. The rate of wetland loss has slowed considerably since 1985 (2004 data).
- Over the same period, the area of ponds (usually less than 20 acres each and often constructed) more than doubled.
- About 80% of the riparian habitats near streams and rivers are forested or covered with other natural vegetation. The remaining 20% is considered "altered"—bordered by agricultural lands or urban development (2001 data).

Data are not adequate for national reporting on
- The area of lakes and reservoirs and the miles of streams and rivers of different sizes
- Alterations to lakeshores or wetlands, or streams and rivers that have been leveed, channelized, or impounded
- The extent of connectivity in streams—that is, the length of free-flowing streams as measured by the distance downstream to the nearest dam or diversion

Other indicators in the report that describe the extent and pattern of fresh waters:
- Stream Bank Vegetation (Urban and Suburban Landscapes, p. 233)

Chemical and Physical Characteristics

Freshwater ecosystems are integrally connected to land-based ecosystems through the movement of ground and surface waters and inputs from rain, snow, and surface runoff and are frequently connected to one another. Indicators of freshwater chemical and physical conditions are therefore valuable in understanding both the quality and quantity of goods and services provided by fresh waters, as well as the condition of surrounding terrestrial ecosystems. The chemical condition of fresh waters can be measured by levels of certain dissolved and suspended chemicals, and the indicators of chemical conditions found both in this section and throughout the report focus on the most important nutrients and contaminants that affect water quality (biological indicators of water quality are described in the next section). Phosphorus and nitrogen are key plant nutrients that, at high concentrations, can stimulate excess algal growth, which in turn can reduce water clarity and decrease the dissolved oxygen available to fish and other aquatic animals. Usually, additions of phosphorus create these effects in fresh waters (especially in lakes and slow-moving rivers), whereas added nitrogen tends to cause these effects primarily in estuaries and coastal waters. Additions of sulfur and nitrogen from the atmosphere can acidify sensitive lakes and streams, altering the types of species that can live in their waters and, at extreme levels, sterilizing these ecosystems.

The amount of water that flows in a stream at a particular season affects its ability to serve as habitat for fish and other animals and to supply water for human uses. Simply measuring the number of cubic feet of water passing a given point every second captures most of the difference between the Mississippi River and an Oregon trout stream. Low flows define the smallest amount of permanent fish habitat in a freshwater system, while high flows shape the river channel and clear silt and debris. Variability in flow also affects animals and plants, which often depend on particular flow volumes during different times of their life cycle.

The federal Clean Water Act and Clean Air Act, as well as related state laws and regulations, are designed to protect water quality. The Clean Water Act does this by regulating discharges into waterways from point and nonpoint pollution sources. The Clean Air Act affects freshwater systems by regulating airborne emissions that contribute to acidification and eutrophication. In addition, federal and state regulations and incentives encourage "best practices" in agriculture and forestry to reduce sediment and nutrient runoff. Allocation of water for human uses, and thus the amount and timing of water flows remaining in streams, has traditionally been left to state law; however, it is increasingly common for federal agencies to get involved when the needs of fish and wildlife become an issue.

Data in this chapter show that

- About half of all large river sites tested had phosphorus concentrations at or above 100 ppb.
- From 1985 to 2005, the percentage of sites that received higher levels of atmospheric nitrogen deposition increased slightly; the percentage of sites receiving higher levels of sulfate deposition decreased.
- The majority of wadeable streams exhibit no evidence of acidification (2000–2004 data). Fewer than 1% of streams were found to be sensitive to acidification (typically during rainfall events), and just over 2% of streams were considered already acidic.
- Approximately half of wadeable stream-miles in the lower 48 states have sediments and in-stream fish habitat features in a "natural" or undegraded state. About 25% of stream-miles have "degraded" sediments, and about 20% have "degraded" in-stream fish habitat features.

Data are not adequate for national reporting on

- Phosphorus concentrations in lakes and reservoirs
- The amount of dry deposition of nitrogen and sulfate or deposition of organic nitrogen
- The acid sensitivity of lakes and ponds
- Water clarity in lakes and reservoirs
- The condition of pools and riffles in streams

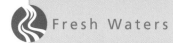

Other indicators in the report that describe chemical and physical characteristics of fresh waters:

- Movement of Nitrogen (Core National, p. 36)
- Chemical Contamination (Core National, p. 42)
- Change in Stream Flows (Core National, p. 47)
- Nitrate in Farmland Streams and Groundwater (Farmlands, p. 107)
- Phosphorus in Farmland Streams (Farmlands, p. 109)
- Pesticides in Farmland Streams and Groundwater (Farmlands p. 111)
- Stream Habitat Quality (Farmlands, p. 115)
- Nitrate in Forest Streams (Forests, p. 140)
- Nitrate in Grassland and Shrubland Groundwater (Grasslands and Shrublands, p. 206)
- Number and Duration of Dry Periods in Grassland and Shrubland Streams and Rivers (Grasslands and Shrublands, p. 208)
- Depth to Shallow Groundwater (Grasslands and Shrublands, p. 210)
- Nitrate in Urban and Suburban Streams (Urban and Suburban Landscapes, p. 238)
- Phosphorus in Urban and Suburban Streams (Urban and Suburban Landscapes, p. 240)
- Chemical Contamination (Urban and Suburban Landscapes, p. 243)

Biological Components

People value freshwater species for their recreational potential, as food, as a source of unique genetic material, and for their intrinsic worth or aesthetic beauty. Aquatic plants and animals and the communities they create (including wetlands and riparian areas) also generate other vital services such as removal of nutrients from runoff, storage of carbon, and habitat for aquatic species. Population declines or extinctions of animal species, similar reductions in plant communities, and changes in the composition of fish or bottom-dwelling animal assemblages can signal potential loss of these benefits. Likewise, introductions and spread of non-native species can signal substantial changes in ecosystems. These introductions can be either accidental (zebra mussels, hydrilla) or intentional (European brown trout), but in either case, non-native species may increase some benefits derived from freshwater ecosystems (trout fishing) while decreasing others (lower water clarity, less habitat for native species). These new inhabitants can prey on, parasitize, or spread diseases among native species, damage human infrastructure, compete with native species for food or habitat, and alter essential habitat. Finally, large die-offs among fish, birds, and other freshwater animals may also signal problems such as chemical contamination or an animal disease outbreak.

Management of aquatic animals ranges from activities under the Endangered Species Act aimed at preventing extinctions to restrictions on fishing seasons and catch limits designed to keep popular species widely available. Unique aquatic and wetland plant communities may also become rare and face elimination, but wetlands regulations generally do not distinguish between rare and common communities or mandate protections for the former. In recent years, regulatory programs have increasingly begun to use measures of biological integrity in managing aquatic systems, consistent with the Clean Water Act's intent to "restore and maintain the chemical, physical, and biological integrity of the Nation's waters." Non-native species have been the subject of federal legislation, multiple federal task forces, and a wide range of federal, state, and private efforts. These efforts range from legislation requiring proper management of ballast water for ships entering the Great Lakes to an initiative by the Aquatic Nuisance Species Task Force to prevent the westward spread of zebra mussels and other non-native species by inspecting and cleaning trailered boats.

Data in this chapter show that

- Thirty-seven percent of native freshwater animal species that depend on streams, lakes, wetlands, or riparian areas are considered to be at risk. Of these, almost 4% may already be extinct. A larger proportion of at-risk native freshwater vertebrate animals have declining populations than stable or increasing populations.
- About 58% of freshwater watersheds contain more than 10 established non-native fish species (2007). Only two watersheds nationwide have no reported established non-native fishes.
- Bottom-dwelling animal communities in 28% of wadeable streams in the lower 48 states are considered in "natural" condition; 42% of streams had communities in "degraded" condition; and 25% had communities in "moderate" condition (2000 to 2004 data).
- About 62% of the freshwater plant communities in wetland and riparian areas are considered to be at risk. About 10% of these are critically imperiled, 22% are imperiled, and 30% are vulnerable.

Data are not adequate to report nationally on

- Population trends in at-risk native freshwater vascular plants and invertebrate animals
- The number of new non-native species established each decade in fresh waters, including plants, animals, pathogens, and parasites
- The number of established non-native freshwater and riparian plants, vertebrates (other than fish), invertebrates, parasites, and plant and animal pathogens
- The proportion of total species that are established non-native freshwater and riparian plants, vertebrates, invertebrates, parasites, and plant and animal pathogens
- Die-offs of fish, waterfowl, amphibians, or mammals
- Amphibian deformities
- The condition of fish communities in streams, lakes, and rivers and the condition of bottom-dwelling communities in lakes and rivers

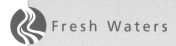
Other indicators in the report that describe biological components of fresh waters:
- Native Species Composition (Core National, p. 53)
- Riparian Condition (Grasslands and Shrublands, p. 217)
- Status of Animal Communities in Urban and Suburban Streams (Urban and Suburban Landscapes, p. 248)

Goods and Services

People withdraw water from freshwater ecosystems for many purposes, including domestic, industrial, and agricultural uses. How much water is used and how it is allocated among various users is an important gauge of this key ecosystem benefit. Likewise, the balance between groundwater use and recharge is an important indicator of the sustainability of our groundwater withdrawals. The time people spend fishing, swimming, bird-watching, boating, and pursuing similar recreational pastimes provides another important indicator of how our society uses and values aquatic ecosystems. Finally, the number of disease outbreaks that can be attributed to contaminated fresh water is a direct measure of the suitability of the nation's waters for drinking, recreation, or other human contact.

Competition among various human uses of freshwater systems, and between human use and in-stream retention of water for ecological purposes, is a major focus of water policy. All states have laws and regulations governing the allocation of water to competing uses, and federal laws govern interstate allocations. Increasingly, market-based instruments are being devised to mediate water transfers between competing users. Additionally, despite significant expenditures for water pollution control, waterborne disease remains a concern among public health officials and the public.

Data in this chapter show that

- From 1960 to 2000, total freshwater withdrawals increased by 46%. This increase was driven by increases in both surface water (37% increase) and groundwater (81% increase) withdrawals.

Data are not adequate for national reporting on

- Changes in groundwater levels
- The number of waterborne disease outbreaks
- Participation in freshwater recreational activities

Other indicators in the report that describe goods and services provided by fresh waters:

- Production of Food and Fiber, and Water Withdrawals (Core National, p. 56)
- Outdoor Recreation (Core National, p. 58)
- Recreation in Forests (Forests, p. 157)

Status and trends of all freshwaters indicators are summarized in the following table and described in detail in the remainder of the chapter. Regions and related definitions used throughout this chapter are described in Appendix D.

Indicators	What Do the Most Recent Data Show?	Have Data Values Changed over Time?

EXTENT AND PATTERN

Extent of Freshwater Ecosystems, p. 170	There are 95.8 million acres of wetlands (2004 data).	Since 1955 wetland area has declined.
	There are 6.2 million acres of ponds (2004 data).	Since 1955 pond area has increased.
	Data are not adequate for national reporting on the area of lakes and reservoirs and the length of streams and rivers.	
	54% of riparian areas are grassland, shrubland or wetland, 26% are forested, and 20% are in urban or agricultural areas (2001 data).	Data are not adequate for national reporting on changes in riparian area land cover.
Altered Freshwater Ecosystems, p. 172	20% of riparian areas are considered "altered" (2001 data).	Data are not adequate for national reporting on changes in "altered" riparian areas.
	Data are not adequate for national reporting on the percentage of lakes, wetlands, rivers, streams, and ponds that have been "altered" by development or agriculture.	
In-Stream Connectivity, p. 173	Data are not adequate for national reporting on the distance downstream from the stream "pour point" to the nearest dam or diversion.	

CHEMICAL AND PHYSICAL CHARACTERISTICS

Phosphorus in Lakes, Reservoirs, and Large Rivers, p. 174	About 50% of river sites have phosphorus (P) concentrations of 100 ppb or more; 26% of sites have P concentrations below 50 ppb (2001–2005 data).	The percentage of sites with P concentrations greater than 20 ppb increased from 91% 1996–2000 to 99% in 2001–2005.
	Data are not adequate for national reporting on phosphorus concentrations in lakes and reservoirs.	
Freshwater Acidity, p. 176	Nitrogen deposition: 1% of sites receive more than 6 lb per acre; 31% of sites receive 4–6 lb per acre; 39% of sites receive 2–4 lb per acre (2005 data).	Between 1985 and 2005, there was an increase in the percentage of sites that received more than 2 lb of atmospheric nitrogen deposition per acre.
	Sulfate deposition: 2% of sites receive more than 20 lb per acre; 45% of sites receive 10–20 lb per acre; 20% of sites receive 5–10 lb per acre (2005 data).	Between 1985 and 2005, there was a decrease in the percentage of sites that received more than 20 lb of sulfate per acre.
	93% of wadeable streams do not show signs of acidification; just over 2% are considered already acidic (2000–2004 data).	Data are not adequate for national reporting on changes in the sensitivity of wadeable streams to acid inputs.
	Data are not adequate for national reporting on the amount of dry deposition of nitrogen and sulfate and the amount of deposition of organic nitrogen.	
	Data are not adequate for national reporting on the acid sensitivity of lakes and ponds.	
Water Clarity, p. 178	Data are not adequate for national reporting on the water clarity of lakes and reservoirs.	
Stream Habitat Quality, p. 179	Quality of sediments (% wadeable stream length): 50% of streams are "natural"; 20% of streams are "moderate"; 25% of streams are "degraded" (2000–2004 data).	Data are not adequate for national reporting on changes in sediment condition.
	Quality of fish habitat features (% of wadeable stream length): 52% of streams are "natural"; 25% of streams are moderate; 20% of streams are degraded (2000–2004 data).	Data are not adequate for national reporting on changes in fish habitat features.
	Data are not adequate for national reporting on the condition of riffles and pools.	

Indicators	What Do the Most Recent Data Show?	Have Data Values Changed over Time?

BIOLOGICAL COMPONENTS

At-Risk Native Freshwater Species, p. 180	37% of native freshwater animal species are at risk: 13% are critically imperiled, 9% are imperiled, 11% are vulnerable, and 4% may be extinct (2006 data).	Data are not adequate for national reporting on changes in at-risk species.
	Data are not adequate for national reporting on the percentage of at-risk native plants and invertebrates in fresh waters.	
	29% of at-risk native vertebrate animals in freshwaters have declining populations; 24% have stable populations and 1% have increasing populations (2006 data).	Data are not adequate for national reporting on changes in the population trends of at-risk vertebrate animals in fresh waters.
	Data are not adequate for national reporting on population tends in at-risk freshwater plants and vertebrate animals.	
Established Non-native Freshwater Species, p. 182	Data are not adequate for national reporting on the number of new non-native species that become established each decade.	
	58% of watersheds have more than 10 established non-native fish species. Only 2 watersheds have no established non-native species.	Between 2002 and 2007, the percentage of watersheds with more than 10 established non-native fish increased from 56% to 58%.
	Data are not adequate for national reporting on the number of established non-native freshwater and riparian plants, vertebrates (other than fish), invertebrates, parasites, and plant and animal pathogens. Data are also not adequate for national reporting on the proportion of total species that are established non-native freshwater and riparian plants, vertebrates, invertebrates, parasites, and plant and animal pathogens.	
Animal Deaths and Deformities, p. 184	Data are not adequate for national reporting on unusual mortality events for waterfowl, mammals, fish, and amphibians and on amphibian deformities.	
Status of Freshwater Animal Communities: Fish and Bottom-Dwelling Animals, p. 185	Condition of bottom-dwelling animals (% of wadeable stream length): 28% of streams are "natural"; 25% of streams are "moderate"; 42% of streams are "degraded" (2000–2004 data).	Data are not adequate for national reporting on changes in the condition of bottom-dwelling animals.
	Data are not adequate for national reporting on the condition of fish communities in streams, rivers, and lakes or on the condition of bottom-dwelling communities in lakes and rivers.	
At-Risk Freshwater Plant Communities, p. 187	62% of freshwater plant communities are at risk: 10% are critically imperiled, 22% are imperiled, and 30% are vulnerable (2006 data).	Data are not adequate for national reporting on changes in at-risk plant communities.

GOODS AND SERVICES

Water Withdrawals, p. 188	The United States uses 345 billion gallons of water per day (24% groundwater, 76% surface water). Withdrawals for irrigation and thermoelectric use are greatest, followed by municipal, industrial, and rural uses (2000 data).	Total freshwater withdrawals have increased since 1960.
		Industrial water use has decreased since 1960.
Groundwater Levels, p. 189	Data are not adequate for national reporting on changes in groundwater levels.	
Waterborne Human Disease Outbreaks, p. 190	Data are not adequate for national reporting on the number of outbreaks due to waterborne disease from either drinking water or recreational contact.	
Freshwater Recreational Activities, p. 191	Data are not adequate for national reporting on the amount of recreation that takes place in the nation's fresh waters.	

 = significant decrease    =significant increase   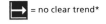 = no clear trend*   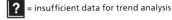 = insufficient data for trend analysis

= Data not available for adequate reporting.

* may be due to little numerical change in the data or large numerical fluctuations in data resulting in no single trend

EXTENT AND PATTERN	CHEMICAL AND PHYSICAL	BIOLOGICAL COMPONENTS	GOODS AND SERVICES
Extent	Nutrients, Carbon, and Oxygen	Plants and Animals	Food, Fiber, and Water
Pattern	Chemical Contamination	Communities	Recreation and Other Services
	Physical	Ecological Productivity	

Extent of Freshwater Ecosystems

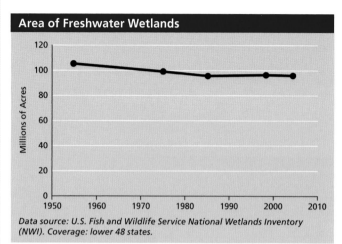

Area of Freshwater Wetlands

Data source: U.S. Fish and Wildlife Service National Wetlands Inventory (NWI). Coverage: lower 48 states.

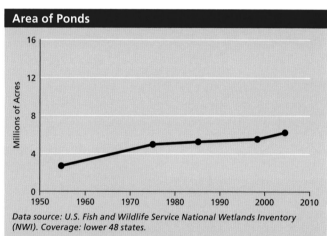

Area of Ponds

Data source: U.S. Fish and Wildlife Service National Wetlands Inventory (NWI). Coverage: lower 48 states.

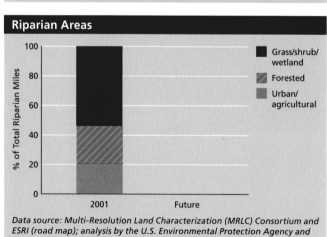

Riparian Areas

Grass/shrub/wetland
Forested
Urban/agricultural

Data source: Multi-Resolution Land Characterization (MRLC) Consortium and ESRI (road map); analysis by the U.S. Environmental Protection Agency and the U.S. Forest Service. Coverage: lower 48 states.

Why Is the Extent of Freshwater Ecosystems Important? America's fresh waters provide critical fish and wildlife habitat and are an important component of most other ecosystems. They also provide people with many goods and services, including drinking water; water for industrial use, livestock, and irrigation; and opportunities for recreation. In addition, wetlands and vegetated riparian areas help filter runoff and reduce flooding, and rivers and lakes receive and process a variety of discharged wastes.

What Does This Indicator Report?
- The area of wetlands (not including ponds) and, when data become available, the area of lakes, reservoirs, and ponds
- When data become available, the length of small, medium, and large streams and rivers
- The type of land cover—forest; grasslands, shrublands, or wetlands; and urban–suburban or agricultural land—on shorelines and adjacent areas ("riparian" areas) for streams and rivers

What Do the Data Show?
- In 2004, there were 96 million acres of freshwater wetlands and 6 million acres of ponds.
- From 1955 to 2004, the area of freshwater wetlands declined by 9%. The rate of wetland loss has slowed in recent years. About half of all presettlement wetland acreage in the lower 48 states has been converted to agriculture, development, or other land uses.
- The area of ponds (usually less than 20 acres) has increased by over 100% since the mid-1950s. This probably reflects the construction of small ponds, but the data do not distinguish natural from constructed ponds.
- Most of the riparian area along streams and rivers is forested or covered with other "natural" vegetation (grasslands, shrublands, or wetlands). The remaining 20% of riparian miles are agricultural or developed lands.

Extent of Freshwater Ecosystems *(continued)*

Why Can't This Entire Indicator Be Reported at This Time? In the 2002 edition of this report, the area of lakes was included, based on data from the National Wetlands Inventory. U.S. Fish and Wildlife Service staff recommended not using

> **Extent of Freshwater Ecosystems**
>
> **Data Gap**
>
> Data are not adequate for national reporting on the area of lakes and reservoirs and the length of streams and rivers.

these data because of concerns that they do not provide an accurate estimate of lake area. In addition, several methods are used to classify streams—by discharge, by drainage area, or by the number of tributaries. No single method has been agreed upon for general use, so there are no national datasets for reporting on stream size. The EPA's National Hydrology Dataset Plus provides a potential data source, but there are concerns that the smallest streams—those that are thought to be most frequently shortened or eliminated by culverting and related activities—are not characterized equally well across the country.

The technical note for this indicator is on page 314.

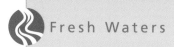
EXTENT AND PATTERN	CHEMICAL AND PHYSICAL	BIOLOGICAL COMPONENTS	GOODS AND SERVICES
Extent	Nutrients, Carbon, and Oxygen	Plants and Animals	Food, Fiber, and Water
Pattern	Chemical Contamination	Communities	Recreation and Other Services
	Physical	Ecological Productivity	

Altered Freshwater Ecosystems

Altered Freshwater Ecosystems

Partial Indicator Data: Altered Riparian Areas (streams and rivers)

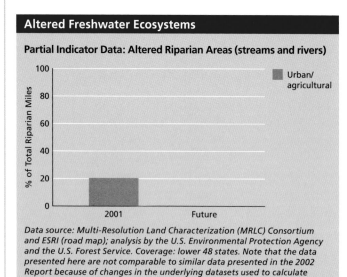

Data source: Multi-Resolution Land Characterization (MRLC) Consortium and ESRI (road map); analysis by the U.S. Environmental Protection Agency and the U.S. Forest Service. Coverage: lower 48 states. Note that the data presented here are not comparable to similar data presented in the 2002 Report because of changes in the underlying datasets used to calculate this indicator.

Altered Freshwater Ecosystems

Data Gap

Data are not adequate for national reporting on the percentage of lakes, wetlands, rivers, streams, and ponds that have been altered.

Why Is the Area of Altered Freshwater Ecosystems Important?
Physically altering a body of fresh water can affect the plants and animals that depend on it, as well as the goods and services people receive from it. Such alterations are usually intended to achieve some benefit: improved navigation, flood control and recreation (by creating reservoirs), erosion control to protect property, more land for farming or development, or supply of municipal, industrial, and irrigation water. However, these alterations can reduce fish and wildlife habitat, disrupt patterns and timing of water flows, serve as barriers to animal movement, and reduce or eliminate the natural filtering of sediment and pollutants.

What Does This Indicator Report?
The percentage of riparian zone miles (the area at the edge of streams and rivers) that have agricultural or urban–suburban land cover within 100 feet of the water's edge. Eventually, this indicator will include

- Stream and river miles that have been leveed, channelized, or impounded behind a dam
- Ponds and lake shoreline-miles that have agricultural or urban–suburban land cover within 100 feet of the water's edge (reservoirs and constructed lakes are excluded)
- Wetland acres that have been excavated, impounded, diked, partially drained, or farmed

What Do the Data Show?
- About 20% of the riparian area along stream and rivers is considered "altered" (land cover is dominated by croplands, pasture, or urban development).

Why Can't This Entire Indicator Be Reported at This Time?
Data on the degree to which streams and rivers are channelized, leveed, or impounded behind dams are not available, nor are data on the extent of wetland alteration. In addition, available data on lake and pond shoreline alteration do not distinguish between natural and constructed bodies of water.

This indicator describes a few key types of alterations. As monitoring and reporting techniques improve, reporting on other alterations may be possible. Stream Habitat Quality (pp. 115 and 179) and Change in Stream Flows (p. 47) also report on stream condition.

The technical note for this indicator is on page 315.

EXTENT AND PATTERN	CHEMICAL AND PHYSICAL	BIOLOGICAL COMPONENTS	GOODS AND SERVICES
Extent	Nutrients, Carbon, and Oxygen	Plants and Animals	Food, Fiber, and Water
Pattern	Chemical Contamination	Communities	Recreation and Other Services
	Physical	Ecological Productivity	

In-Stream Connectivity

Why Is In-Stream Connectivity Important? The downstream transport of water, energy, nutrients, and sediments is affected by the presence of dams and diversions. These features provide numerous benefits to people, such as flood control, irrigation, recreation, and power generation, yet they also alter freshwater habitats and can limit or block the movement of organisms such as spawning fish.

What Will This Indicator Report? For large river basins across the country, the proportion of watersheds with different levels of in-stream connectivity, measured as the distance downstream from the "pour point" (where the stream leaves the watershed) to the nearest dam or diversion, such as a pumping station (see illustration). This indicator will also report the proportion of watersheds that contain streams with unobstructed flow to their natural endpoint, typically the ocean or a large lake.

Why Can't This Indicator Be Reported At This Time? The required analysis depends on merging data on stream networks, the location of dams and diversions, and the delineation of watersheds on a fine scale. The Heinz Center completed this for selected geographic areas as a test of this indicator, but considerable effort was required by technical experts and achieving such a merged dataset for the whole nation would require a substantial investment of resources. It is anticipated that work under way at USGS on the National Hydrography Dataset will meet this data need in the coming years. An additional challenge in reporting this indicator will be evaluating what percentage of dams are omitted because they are too small to be registered in the national database on dams. Further, comprehensive data on diversions are not currently available.

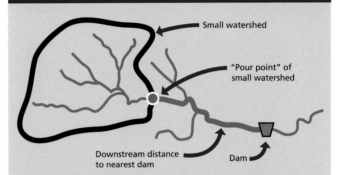

In-Stream Connectivity: Distance from Small Watershed Downstream to Nearest Dam (or Diversion)

Small watershed

"Pour point" of small watershed

Downstream distance to nearest dam

Dam

Technical details: Watersheds are areas, often bordered by physical features such as ridges, within which water drains into a single stream, river, or river system. Watersheds are generally hierarchical, meaning that one can describe many smaller watersheds within one large watershed, or basin. For the purposes of this indicator, the smallest watersheds for which data can reasonably be assembled should be used. Measurements will be made from the point in the watershed where the stream or river exits ("pour point"), either into a receiving body, such as a lake, or until a dam or diversion is reached (see the heavy blue line in drawing). Watersheds that have a dam or diversion within them will be given a value of zero. See technical note for further details.

In-Stream Connectivity

Data Gap

Data are not adequate for national reporting on the distance downstream from the "pour point" to the nearest dam or diversion.

Discussion The presence of a dam or diversion disrupts the connectivity of a stream or river, affecting aquatic species and sediment flow. Migratory fish, such as salmon, are greatly affected by changes in in-stream connectivity. Fish ladders are used to help adult migratory fish navigate past dams, although this indicator would not distinguish between dams with and without fish ladders. This indicator will also not report on natural barriers to connectivity such as beaver dams or fallen trees. Natural barriers tend to affect some species or life stages at certain times or flow conditions, but not others. This indicator focuses on loss of connectivity over and above any natural discontinuities in aquatic systems.

Finally, other important phenomena can affect the connectivity of freshwater systems, such as zones of low oxygen, fragmented riparian areas, and seasonal periods of reduced or zero stream flow. For example, low-oxygen waters can block the movement of fish along a stream, fragmented riparian areas can affect the movement of other aquatic species, and stream segments that dry up periodically can isolate species in pools or otherwise disrupt the movement of species.

The technical note for this indicator is on page 315.

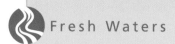
Phosphorus in Lakes, Reservoirs, and Large Rivers

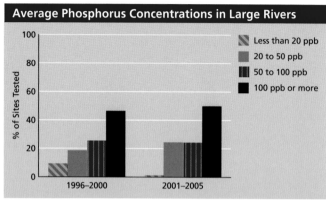

Average Phosphorus Concentrations in Large Rivers

Legend: Less than 20 ppb; 20 to 50 ppb; 50 to 100 ppb; 100 ppb or more

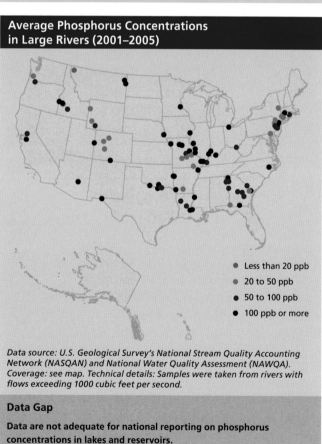

Average Phosphorus Concentrations in Large Rivers (2001–2005)

Legend: Less than 20 ppb; 20 to 50 ppb; 50 to 100 ppb; 100 ppb or more

Data source: U.S. Geological Survey's National Stream Quality Accounting Network (NASQAN) and National Water Quality Assessment (NAWQA). Coverage: see map. Technical details: Samples were taken from rivers with flows exceeding 1000 cubic feet per second.

Data Gap

Data are not adequate for national reporting on phosphorus concentrations in lakes and reservoirs.

Why Is Phosphorus in Lakes, Reservoirs, and Large Rivers Important? Increased phosphorus concentrations are associated with increased growth of algae in lakes, reservoirs, and large rivers. Algae sustain the growth of most other aquatic life forms; when overabundant, however, they can contribute to reductions in dissolved oxygen, cause fish kills, and cause shifts in the number and type of fish and other aquatic animals. Algal blooms can also diminish aesthetic and recreational values.

What Does This Indicator Report? The percentage of lakes, reservoirs, and large river sites with average concentrations of phosphorus in four ranges: below 20 parts per billion (ppb), from 20 to 50 ppb, from 50 to 100 ppb, and 100 ppb or more. Note that indicators reporting on phosphorus in other chapters use parts per million (ppm)—a concentration of 1 ppb means that there is one thousand times less phosphorus than if the concentration were 1 ppm.

What Do the Data Show?

- In 2001–2005, about 50% of all river sites tested had phosphorus concentration levels of 100 ppb or higher. Twenty-six percent of the tested sites had concentrations below 50 ppb.
- The percentage of river sites with concentrations greater than 20 ppb increased from 91% in 1996–2000 to 99% in 2001–2005; more data are required to determine if this increase represents a trend over time.
- In 2001–2005, regional trends in phosphorus concentrations were not apparent.

Phosphorus in Lakes, Reservoirs, and Large Rivers *(continued)*

Why Can't This Entire Indicator Be Reported at This Time? There are currently no datasets that provide representative phosphorus values for the nation's lakes and reservoirs. EPA's data storage and retieval archive (STORET) might serve as a source of data, but considerable research would be required to determine whether the samples reported there are representative of overall conditions.

Understanding the Data This indicator will become easier to interpret when more trend data become available because it will become easier to differentiate sites that have naturally higher or lower concentrations from those that have become higher or lower over time. Lakes and reservoirs with phosphorus concentrations of less than 20 ppb are generally free of negative effects; higher concentrations are accompanied by increasing effects. The U.S. Environmental Protection Agency's (EPA) recommended goal for preventing excess algal growth in streams that do not flow directly into lakes or other impoundments is 100 ppb. There is no federal drinking water standard for phosphorus.

This report also includes indicators for total phosphorus concentrations in farmland streams (p. 109) and urban and suburban streams (p. 240).

The technical note for this indicator is on page 316.

EXTENT AND PATTERN	CHEMICAL AND PHYSICAL	BIOLOGICAL COMPONENTS	GOODS AND SERVICES
Extent	Nutrients, Carbon, and Oxygen	Plants and Animals	Food, Fiber, and Water
Pattern	Chemical Contamination	Communities	Recreation and Other Services
	Physical	Ecological Productivity	

Freshwater Acidity

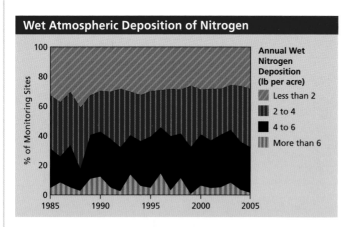

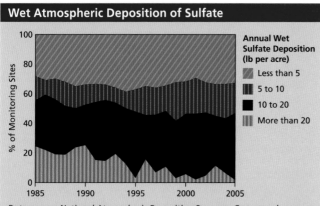

Data source: National Atmospheric Deposition Program. Coverage: lower 48 states. Technical Details: Atmospheric deposition occurs during rain and snow events (wet) and at other times (dry). Data are for total wet inorganic nitrogen and sulfate.

Why Are Changes in Freshwater Acidity Important? Nitrogen and sulfate compounds deposited from the atmosphere can acidify soils and surface waters, especially in areas that are naturally sensitive to acidification or that have received significant acidic deposition over time. Acidification can have direct effects on plants and sensitive freshwater species like trout and salmon, and indirect effects on the availability of heavy metals such as aluminum, which is toxic to many fish and other organisms.

What Does This Indicator Report?

- The amount of nitrogen and sulfate deposited from the atmosphere to watersheds each year
- The percentage of stream miles and area of lakes and ponds with different levels of acid-neutralizing capacity, a measure of sensitivity to acidification

What Do the Data Show?

- Since 1985, the percentage of monitoring sites that received between 4 and 6 pounds of wet (from precipitation) atmospheric nitrogen deposition annually per acre increased slightly (from 27% to 31% of sites); fewer monitoring sites received less than 2 pounds per acre (from 33% to 28% of sites), indicating that some areas are receiving increased levels of wet, inorganic nitrogen deposition.
- Since 1985, the percentage of monitoring sites that received more than 20 pounds of wet atmospheric sulfate deposition annually per acre has decreased (from 24% to 2% of sites), indicating that some areas are receiving decreased levels of sulfate deposition; the percentage of monitoring sites receiving between 5 and 20 pounds of sulfate has increased (from 47% to 65% of sites).
- During 2000–2004, the vast majority of wadeable streams did not exhibit evidence of acidification. Less than 1% of streams were described as being sensitive to acidification (typically during rainfall events), and just over 2% of streams were considered already acidic. The Eastern Highlands (for definition of regions, see p. 268) had a somewhat greater percentage of acidic streams than the national average, and the West had the lowest percentage.

Why Can't This Entire Indicator Be Reported? Data are not gathered at a national scale for dry deposition of atmospheric nitrogen and sulfate, which can account for 20–80% of total deposition, or for organic nitrogen. Data for acid-neutralizing capacity in lakes and ponds are not available but will be gathered in future assessments by the U.S. Environmental Protection Agency.

EXTENT AND PATTERN	CHEMICAL AND PHYSICAL	BIOLOGICAL COMPONENTS	GOODS AND SERVICES
Extent	Nutrients, Carbon, and Oxygen	Plants and Animals	Food, Fiber, and Water
Pattern	**Chemical Contamination**	Communities	Recreation and Other Services
	Physical	Ecological Productivity	

Freshwater Acidity *(continued)*

Understanding the Data Nitrogen and sulfur compounds are released into the air from fossil fuel combustion, agricultural production, and other activities. In the atmosphere, these compounds react with water and other chemicals to form ammonium and nitric or sulfuric acids and can be carried short or long distances by the prevailing winds. Dissolved in rain, snow, and fog or as solid and gaseous particles, these acidifying compounds are deposited in watersheds (on soil surfaces and vegetation) and are transported to streams and lakes by surface runoff or groundwater flow. Increased acidity in soils can damage vegetation, especially at higher elevations. Acidified surface waters can become unsuitable for fish and other organisms that cannot tolerate acidity or are affected by toxic metals liberated under these conditions. In some areas, freshwater acidification is accelerated by drainage waters from mines and mine tailings that become strongly acidic from oxidation of sulfur-rich minerals. Both types of acidification can cause toxic metals to become dissolved in water.

The technical note for this indicator is on page 317.

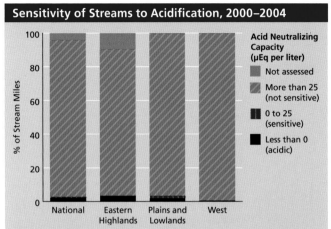

Sensitivity of Streams to Acidification, 2000–2004

Acid Neutralizing Capacity (µEq per liter)
- Not assessed
- More than 25 (not sensitive)
- 0 to 25 (sensitive)
- Less than 0 (acidic)

Data source: U.S. EPA, Wadeable Streams Assessment. Coverage: lower 48 states (for definition of regions, see p. 268). Technical details: Acid-neutralizing capacity (ANC) measures the number of charged molecules in the water (in microequivalents, µEq, per liter) at base flow conditions—typical stream flow rather than very high or very low flow. Note that ANC values less than 0 indicate that a stream is acidic and cannot buffer further acidic inputs.

Data Gap

- Data are not adequate for national reporting on the amount of dry deposition of nitrogen and sulfate and on the amount of deposition of organic nitrogen.
- Data are not adequate for national reporting on the acid sensitivity of lakes and ponds.

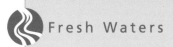

EXTENT AND PATTERN	CHEMICAL AND PHYSICAL	BIOLOGICAL COMPONENTS	GOODS AND SERVICES
Extent	Nutrients, Carbon, and Oxygen	Plants and Animals	Food, Fiber, and Water
Pattern	Chemical Contamination	Communities	Recreation and Other Services
	Physical	Ecological Productivity	

Water Clarity

Water Clarity

Data Gap

Data are not adequate for national reporting on the water clarity of lakes and reservoirs.

Why Is Water Clarity Important?
People like clearer water to swim in, to drink, and for aesthetic reasons. Aquatic plants need light to grow, and fish and other animals need light to feed and reproduce. Lakes and reservoirs can become cloudy when streams and runoff carry silt, clay, and organic materials into them. Runoff may also add phosphorus and other nutrients to lake or reservoir water; these added nutrients can fuel the process of eutrophication and algae growth (see Phosphorus in Lakes, Reservoirs, and Large Rivers, p. 174), which also reduces water clarity and can lead to low-oxygen conditions.

What Will This Indicator Report? The percentage of lake and reservoir area with low-, medium-, and high-clarity water (ponds are not included because of their shallow depth).

Why Can't This Indicator Be Reported at This Time? Although considerable amounts of water clarity data are available from various sources (see technical note), some areas are heavily sampled, while in other areas few or no lakes are tested. Thus, the available data do not provide representative coverage at a national level.

It is important to track water clarity over time, because lakes and reservoirs in different regions have different degrees of natural clarity. By tracking clarity over time, it will be possible to identify areas with declining or improving clarity and to distinguish these from naturally cloudy or clear areas.

The technical note for this indicator is on page 318.

EXTENT AND PATTERN	CHEMICAL AND PHYSICAL	BIOLOGICAL COMPONENTS	GOODS AND SERVICES
Extent	Nutrients, Carbon, and Oxygen	Plants and Animals	Food, Fiber, and Water
Pattern	Chemical Contamination	Communities	Recreation and Other Services
	Physical	Ecological Productivity	

Stream Habitat Quality

Why Is Stream Habitat Quality Important?
Streams that have a natural and diverse array of underwater and bank habitats are capable of supporting a diverse array of native species. These streams are also more likely to have relatively undisturbed flow patterns and to have vegetation along their banks—physical features that help support a healthy biological community over the long term.

What Does This Indicator Report?
- The percentage of stream-miles that have streambed sediments in "natural," "moderate," or "degraded" condition
- The percentage of stream-miles that have in-stream fish habitat features (for example, presence of boulders, large wood, undercut banks, roots) in "natural," "moderate," or "degraded" condition
- When data are available, the percentage of stream-miles that have riffles and pools in "natural," "moderate," or "degraded" condition

What Do the Data Show?
- About half of stream-miles in the lower 48 states have "natural" streambed sediments, and about 25% have "degraded" sediments. Sediments are in "moderate" condition for 20% of stream miles.
- Over half of stream-miles in the lower 48 states have "natural" in-stream fish habitat; this habitat is "degraded" along 20% of streams and in "moderate" condition along 25% of streams.

Why Can't This Indicator Be Fully Reported at This Time?
At this time there are no national data on the presence, let alone the condition, of riffles and pools in streams.

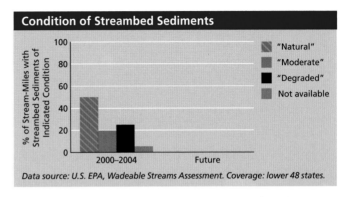

Condition of Streambed Sediments

Legend: "Natural", "Moderate", "Degraded", Not available

Data source: U.S. EPA, Wadeable Streams Assessment. Coverage: lower 48 states.

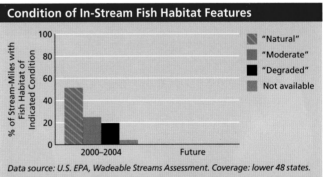

Condition of In-Stream Fish Habitat Features

Legend: "Natural", "Moderate", "Degraded", Not available

Data source: U.S. EPA, Wadeable Streams Assessment. Coverage: lower 48 states.

Data Gap

Data are not adequate for national reporting on the condition of riffles and pools.

Some Definitions
- "Natural": habitat features found at a site are similar in type to the range of features expected in the least disturbed sites in that region.
- "Moderate": habitat features are more degraded than 75% of least disturbed sites in the region.
- "Degraded": habitat features are more degraded than 95% of least disturbed sites in the region, reflecting one or more negative influences.

Discussion Stream-dwelling animals and plants require specific habitat conditions to survive and reproduce. Because each species has its own particular habitat requirements, a variety of habitats along a stream is needed to maintain the stream's natural complement of plants and animals. A companion indicator reports on farmland Stream Habitat Quality, p. 115.

Sediments in "degraded" streams are less stable than those found in "natural" streams. Decreased stability of sediments can result from a change in stream flows (see Change in Stream Flows, p. 47) or an increase in erosion of sediment from lands surrounding the stream (see Potential Soil Erosion, p. 112). Human use of streams and the riparian area can lead to a loss of in-stream habitat when habitat features such as vegetation, woody debris, and boulders are disturbed or removed.

The technical note for this indicator is on page 319.

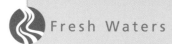

EXTENT AND PATTERN	CHEMICAL AND PHYSICAL	BIOLOGICAL COMPONENTS	GOODS AND SERVICES
Extent	Nutrients, Carbon, and Oxygen	Plants and Animals	Food, Fiber, and Water
Pattern	Chemical Contamination	Communities	Recreation and Other Services
	Physical	Ecological Productivity	

At-Risk Native Freshwater Species

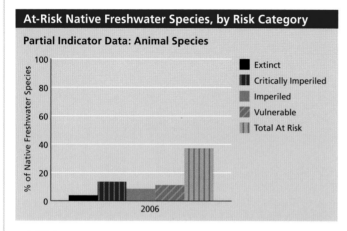

At-Risk Native Freshwater Species, by Risk Category

Partial Indicator Data: Animal Species

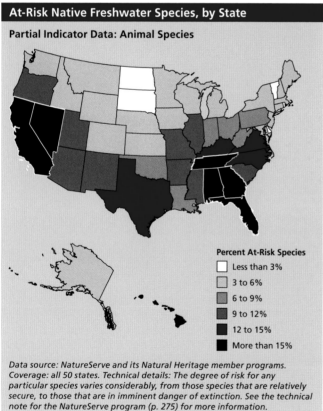

At-Risk Native Freshwater Species, by State

Partial Indicator Data: Animal Species

Percent At-Risk Species
- Less than 3%
- 3 to 6%
- 6 to 9%
- 9 to 12%
- 12 to 15%
- More than 15%

Data source: NatureServe and its Natural Heritage member programs. Coverage: all 50 states. Technical details: The degree of risk for any particular species varies considerably, from those species that are relatively secure, to those that are in imminent danger of extinction. See the technical note for the NatureServe program (p. 275) for more information.

Why Are Native Freshwater Species Important? Species are valued for a variety of reasons: they provide products, including food, fiber, and, genetic materials, which may have various medicinal, industrial, and agricultural uses; they are key elements of ecosystems, which themselves provide valuable goods and services; and many people value them for their intrinsic worth or beauty.

What Does This Indicator Report?
- The relative risk of extinction of native freshwater species (plants and animals that live in freshwater, wetland, or riparian habitats during at least part of their life cycle and depend on these habitats for survival), presented as four categories; vulnerable, imperiled, critically imperiled, and extinct (see definitions)
- The percentage of native freshwater species that are at risk in each state
- Population trends of at-risk native freshwater species (declining, stable, increasing)

What Do the Data Show?
- Thirty-seven percent of native freshwater animal species are considered to be at risk. This group includes 13% that are critically imperiled, 9% that are imperiled, 11% that are vulnerable, and almost 4% percent that may already be extinct.
- Hawaii, California, Nevada, and several southeastern states have a higher percentage of at-risk native freshwater animal species than other states (54% of all native freshwater species in Hawaii are at risk of extinction).
- A larger proportion of at-risk native vertebrate freshwater animals have declining populations (29%) than stable (24%) or increasing (1%) populations. Population trend data are unknown for many at-risk vertebrate freshwater animals (46%).

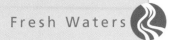
EXTENT AND PATTERN	CHEMICAL AND PHYSICAL	BIOLOGICAL COMPONENTS	GOODS AND SERVICES
Extent	Nutrients, Carbon, and Oxygen	Plants and Animals	Food, Fiber, and Water
Pattern	Chemical Contamination	Communities	Recreation and Other Services
	Physical	Ecological Productivity	

At-Risk Native Freshwater Species *(continued)*

Why Can't This Entire Indicator Be Reported? This indicator reports on 4100 species of fish; aquatic mammals; aquatic birds; reptiles and amphibians; mussels; snails; crayfishes; fairy, clam, and tadpole shrimp; butterflies and skippers, and dragonflies and damselflies. Data on freshwater plants are not included because additional analyses are required to categorize correctly the habitats of all North American plants. Population trend data are known for only 32% of at-risk native invertebrate freshwater animal species, so it is impossible to report on the group as a whole.

While status data were reported for this indicator in the 2002 edition of this report, changes in rank status can occur for a variety of reasons, including changes in the actual status of species, improved knowledge of the species' condition, or changes in taxonomy. Consequently, previous status data are not presented here (see discussion in the program description for NatureServe data, p. 275).

Understanding the Data Interpreting figures on species status is complicated because some species are naturally rare. Thus, the rankings are influenced by differences among regions and species groups in the number of naturally rare species, as well as by different types and levels of human activities that can cause species declines. Data on population trends complement the risk category data by showing how species of most conservation concern are faring over time. The ability to track changes in the condition of species over time will be further enhanced when it is possible to report on the population trends of a larger percentage of species.

See also the national At-Risk Native Species indicator (p. 50) and the indicators for at-risk coastal, forest, and grassland and shrubland species (pp. 50, 144, and 211), as well as those for species in farmlands (p. 116) and urban and suburban areas (p. 246).

The technical note for this indicator is on page 319.

Population Trends in At-Risk Native Freshwater Species

Partial Indicator Data: At-Risk Native Vertebrate Animal Species

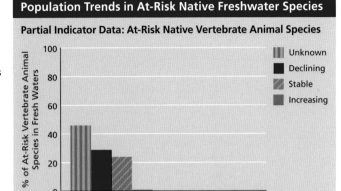

Data source: NatureServe and its Natural Heritage member programs. Coverage: all 50 states. Technical details: Population trend data report on short-term changes in populations, specifically changes within 10 years or three generations, whichever is longer, with a maximum of 100 years.

Data Gap

Data are not adequate for national reporting on population trends in at-risk native vascular plants and invertebrate animals in fresh waters.

Some Definitions

- "Critically imperiled" species often are found in five or fewer places, may have experienced very steep declines, or show other evidence of very high risk.
- "Imperiled" species often are found in 20 or fewer places, may have experienced steep declines, or display other risk factors.
- "Vulnerable" species often are found in fewer than 80 places, may have recently experienced widespread decline, or show other signs of moderate risk.
- The remaining plant and animal species are regarded as "secure" or "apparently secure."

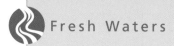
EXTENT AND PATTERN	CHEMICAL AND PHYSICAL	BIOLOGICAL COMPONENTS	GOODS AND SERVICES
Extent	Nutrients, Carbon, and Oxygen	Plants and Animals	Food, Fiber, and Water
Pattern	Chemical Contamination	Communities	Recreation and Other Services
	Physical	Ecological Productivity	

Established Non-native Freshwater Species

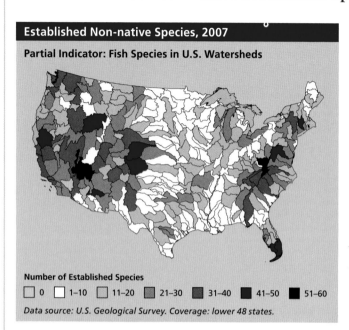

Established Non-native Species, 2007

Partial Indicator: Fish Species in U.S. Watersheds

Number of Established Species

☐ 0   ☐ 1–10   ☐ 11–20   ▨ 21–30   ▨ 31–40   ■ 41–50   ■ 51–60

Data source: U.S. Geological Survey. Coverage: lower 48 states.

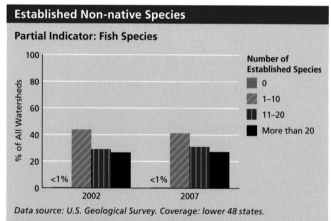

Established Non-native Species

Partial Indicator: Fish Species

Number of Established Species
■ 0
▨ 1–10
▥ 11–20
■ More than 20

% of All Watersheds

<1%   2002   <1%   2007

Data source: U.S. Geological Survey. Coverage: lower 48 states.

Data Gap

- Data are not adequate for national reporting on the number of new non-native species that become established each decade, including plants, animals, pathogens, and parasites.
- Data are not adequate for national reporting on the number of established non-native freshwater and riparian plants, vertebrates (other than fish), invertebrates, parasites, and plant and animal pathogens.
- Data are not adequate for national reporting on the proportion of total species that are established non-native freshwater and riparian plants, vertebrates, invertebrates, parasites, and plant and animal pathogens.

Why Is Understanding the Prevalence of Non-Native Species Important?

Non-native species are also called nonindigenous, exotic, or introduced; those that spread aggressively are termed invasive. They may act as predators or parasites of native species, cause diseases, compete for food or habitat, and alter essential habitat. They also may threaten human health and economic well-being. Non-native species may also provide benefits, such as stabilizing sloping riparian areas prone to erosion and providing fish protein for human consumption. Established non-native species are those that are known to be surviving and reproducing.

What Does This Indicator Report?

- Watersheds with different numbers of freshwater fish species that are established non-natives
- When data become available, the number of new non-native species that become established over time, by decade
- When data become available, watersheds with different numbers of other established non-native freshwater and riparian species, including plants, vertebrates other than fish, invertebrates, parasites, and plant and animal pathogens
- When data become available, the proportion of all freshwater species that are established non-native species, by watershed

What Do the Data Show?

- Fifty-eight percent of watersheds have more than 10 established non-native fish species. Only two watersheds in the lower 48 states are unaffected by non-native fish species.
- Watersheds in the central United States generally have the fewest established non-native fish species.
- From 2002 to 2007, there were small changes in the percentage of watersheds in the three abundance ranges, with an apparent shift toward more watersheds having higher numbers of established non-native fish species. More data are required to determine if this increase is part of a larger trend over time.

Established Non-native Freshwater Species *(continued)*

Why Can't This Entire Indicator Be Reported at This Time? Data are not currently available to report on many species groups. Data necessary to report on the proportion of species that are established non-natives in any particular ecosystem would be a subset of the data reported in the national Established Non-native Species indicator (p. 52). The discussion in the core national indicator describes the limited data availability for the pattern and distribution of non-native plants, vertebrates, invertebrates and pathogens.

Understanding the Data Watersheds with a higher proportion of non-native species are likely to experience greater ecological and economic disruption. In addition, non-native species may become established more easily in watersheds with other types of disturbance (such as degraded water quality, altered temperatures, and alterations to habitat or flows). In general, care should be taken to avoid overinterpreting changes between two time points. This is especially important for the data presented here, because determining whether or not a non-native species is actually "established" can take time, and preliminary judgments are occasionally reversed in light of emerging information.

Some non-natives do provide positive benefits, as intended. For example, brown trout are native to Europe, and rainbow trout to western North America; both are popular and widely stocked game fish throughout the nation. Fishing is an important recreational pastime (see Freshwater Recreational Activities, p. 191, and Outdoor Recreation, p. 58). Other non-native species that have been introduced intentionally for good purposes can have negative consequences: several species of Asian carp, originally introduced to combat algae populations in catfish farms, have spread into much of the Mississippi River Basin and are threatening native fish populations there.

Unintentional non-native species introductions can have negative consequences as well—for example, the zebra mussel was likely introduced to the Great Lakes region in ballast water from overseas vessels and has damaged power plants, water treatment facilities, and other structures and has significantly changed freshwater ecosystems in the region.

The nation's fresh waters host some of the highest profile non-native invasive species and pathogens, including Eurasian water milfoil, Asian (Burmese) pythons, Northern Snakehead fish, and viral hemorrhagic septicemia.

The technical note for this indicator is on page 320.

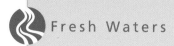
EXTENT AND PATTERN	CHEMICAL AND PHYSICAL	BIOLOGICAL COMPONENTS	GOODS AND SERVICES
Extent	Nutrients, Carbon, and Oxygen	Plants and Animals	Food, Fiber, and Water
Pattern	Chemical Contamination	Communities	Recreation and Other Services
	Physical	Ecological Productivity	

Animal Deaths and Deformities

Animal Deaths and Deformities

Data Gap

Data are not adequate for national reporting on unusual mortality events for waterfowl, mammals, fish, and amphibians and on amphibian deformities.

Why Is Tracking Animal Deaths and Deformities Important? When large numbers of fish, birds, and other freshwater animals die suddenly, or when amphibian deformities are reported, considerable public concern is generated. People may perceive a danger to their own health, or they may be concerned about disruptions to the ecosystem, loss of recreational opportunities and tourism income, and fish and game that cannot be eaten or sold.

What Will This Indicator Report? Unusual mortality events for waterfowl, mammals, fish, and amphibians (defined as the death of multiple animals in a concentrated area over a relatively short period of time). Definitions of what qualifies as an unusual mortality event will vary by species and will most likely be based on the following criteria: number of individuals, location of death, duration of die-off, species status, cause of death, and credibility of reporting. When data are available, this indicator will also report on deformity events for amphibians.

Why Can't This Indicator Be Reported at This Time? The U.S. Geological Survey (USGS) Wildlife Health Center collects mortality information on waterfowl, mammals and amphibians. These USGS data were presented in the 2002 edition of this report but they are not included in this edition because of concerns that they are not comparable across years because of changes in the factors influencing the reporting of animal deaths (see technical note for more details). Currently, there is no national reporting mechanism for fish die-offs. (For information on mortality events in coastal waters, see Unusual Marine Mortalities, p. 82.) There are some regional databases on amphibian deformities, but the data are not adequate to report on deformities at a national level.

Discussion The monitoring agencies that collect data on animal deaths and deformities can collect data only on *reported* mortality and deformity events and therefore cannot capture all incidences. Waterfowl die-offs can be caused by infectious diseases, nutritional problems resulting from too little or poor quality feed, toxins, trauma, environmental/habitat problems, weather extremes, or a combination of factors.

The technical note for this indicator is on page 321.

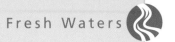

EXTENT AND PATTERN	CHEMICAL AND PHYSICAL	BIOLOGICAL COMPONENTS	GOODS AND SERVICES
Extent	Nutrients, Carbon, and Oxygen	Plants and Animals	Food, Fiber, and Water
Pattern	Chemical Contamination	**Communities**	Recreation and Other Services
	Physical	Ecological Productivity	

Status of Freshwater Animal Communities: Fish and Bottom-Dwelling Animals

Why Are Freshwater Animal Communities Important? Undisturbed lakes and streams in a particular region have a relatively predictable set of fish and bottom-dwelling animals, which occur in predictable proportions of species. Alterations to the stream or lake can change the composition and condition of these biological communities—the biological integrity—from this undisturbed or "reference" condition. Ecosystems that have natural animal communities are more likely to withstand natural and man-made stresses and to provide a range of ecosystem services (see Natural Ecosystem Services, p. 60).

What Does This Indicator Report? The percentage of freshwater streams, lakes, and rivers in which the suite of fish and bottom-dwelling (or benthic) animals (including insects, worms, mollusks, and crustaceans) are in "natural," "moderate," and "degraded" condition.

What Do the Data Show?

- Bottom-dwelling animals are in "natural" condition in 28% of wadeable streams in the lower 48 states; 42% of streams had bottom-dwelling animal communities in "degraded" condition; and 25% of wadeable streams had bottom-dwelling animals in "moderate" condition (2000–2004 data).

- Streams in the West had a higher proportion of stream miles with "natural" bottom-dwelling communities than streams in the Eastern Highlands and the Plains and Lowlands (for definition of regions, see p. 268). The Eastern Highlands had a larger proportion of "degraded" streams (52%) than any other region.

Continued

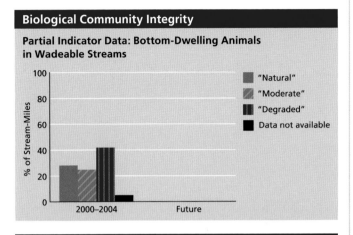

Biological Community Integrity

Partial Indicator Data: Bottom-Dwelling Animals in Wadeable Streams

Legend: "Natural", "Moderate", "Degraded", Data not available

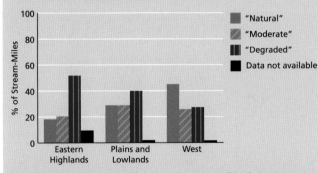

Biological Community Integrity, by Region, 2000–2004

Partial Indicator Data: Bottom-Dwelling Animals in Wadeable Streams

Legend: "Natural", "Moderate", "Degraded", Data not available

Regions: Eastern Highlands, Plains and Lowlands, West

Data source: U.S. EPA, Wadeable Streams Assessment (2006). Coverage: lower 48 states. Technical detail: Tests of biological integrity assess the number of different species, the number and condition of individuals, and food chain interactions.

Data Gap

- Data are not adequate for national reporting on the condition of fish communities in streams, lakes, and rivers of the United States.
- Data are not adequate for national reporting on the condition of bottom-dwelling communities in lakes and rivers.

Some Definitions

- "Natural" communities: fish and benthic animals found at the site are similar to those expected in the least disturbed sites in that region.
- "Moderate" communities: fish and benthic animals are more degraded than 75% of those found at least disturbed sites in the region.
- "Degraded" communities: fish and benthic animals are more degraded than 95% of those found at least disturbed sites in the region, reflecting one or more negative influences.

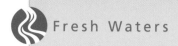
EXTENT AND PATTERN	CHEMICAL AND PHYSICAL	BIOLOGICAL COMPONENTS	GOODS AND SERVICES
Extent	Nutrients, Carbon, and Oxygen	Plants and Animals	Food, Fiber, and Water
Pattern	Chemical Contamination	**Communities**	Recreation and Other Services
	Physical	Ecological Productivity	

Status of Freshwater Animal Communities:
Fish and Bottom-Dwelling Animals *(continued)*

Why Can't This Entire Indicator Be Reported? The tests of biological integrity (whether or not the biological communities are in "natural" condition) now in use have been developed primarily for streams and wadeable rivers; methods for major rivers are not as well developed on a national scale. U.S. EPA is currently assessing the bottom-dwelling animal communities in lakes, but data collection is not complete. To date, national assessments of lake and wadeable stream communities based on deviation from regional standards have not focused on fish.

Understanding the Data The condition of animal communities is measured as the degree to which the communities resemble what one might find in a relatively undisturbed stream in the same region. Alterations that affect biological integrity include decreased water quality, introduction of non-native species, changes in the amount or timing of water flows, and modification of the lake or stream bed or shoreline. Some lakes and streams are so modified that, for example, both the number of species and the number of individuals are very low when compared with undisturbed areas, and many of the individuals that remain are diseased or otherwise damaged.

The technical note for this indicator is on page 322.

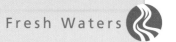
EXTENT AND PATTERN	CHEMICAL AND PHYSICAL	BIOLOGICAL COMPONENTS	GOODS AND SERVICES
Extent	Nutrients, Carbon, and Oxygen	Plants and Animals	Food, Fiber, and Water
Pattern	Chemical Contamination	**Communities**	Recreation and Other Services
	Physical	Ecological Productivity	

At-Risk Freshwater Plant Communities

Why Is the Status of Freshwater Plant Communities Important?

Different plant communities (groups of plants that tend to occur in similar environmental conditions) support distinct species combinations, such as the Bald Cypress–Sweetgum–Sycamore–Common Pawpaw forest community type, and may provide unique ecosystem services (see Natural Ecosystem Services. p. 60). Areas with a higher variety, or diversity, of community types generally provide a wider range of potential habitat that supports a wider range of species. Furthermore, some plant communities may provide essential habitat for specific rare plant and animal species.

What Does This Indicator Report?

- The relative risk of elimination of wetland and riparian communities, presented as three categories: vulnerable, imperiled, and critically imperiled
- The percentage of at-risk freshwater plant communities in each state

What Do the Data Show?

- Sixty-two percent of the wetland and riparian communities ranked here are considered to be at risk: about 10% are critically imperiled, 22% are imperiled, and about 30% are vulnerable (2006 data).
- The percentage of at-risk freshwater communities is particularly high in the Southeast. In all states but West Virginia, Maine, New Hampshire, Rhode Island, and Vermont, more than 20% of wetland and riparian communities are at risk.

Understanding the Data Interpreting these figures is complicated because some of these wetland and riparian community types have never been widely distributed, while others once covered much larger areas and have been reduced in area by conversion to other uses. Because the data do not distinguish between naturally rare community types and those that are declining, this indicator will be much more informative when trend data become available. At present, the at-risk plant communities reported here generally occupy small areas and thus probably represent less than 60% of total wetland and riparian area acreage.

The technical note for this indicator is on page 322.

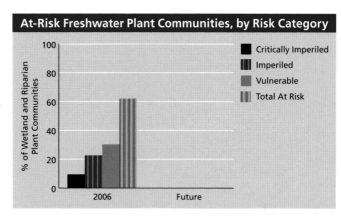

At-Risk Freshwater Plant Communities, by Risk Category

Legend: Critically Imperiled, Imperiled, Vulnerable, Total At Risk

Y-axis: % of Wetland and Riparian Plant Communities

X-axis: 2006, Future

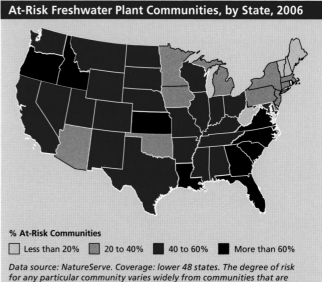

At-Risk Freshwater Plant Communities, by State, 2006

% At-Risk Communities
Less than 20% | 20 to 40% | 40 to 60% | More than 60%

Data source: NatureServe. Coverage: lower 48 states. The degree of risk for any particular community varies widely from communities that are relatively secure to those that are in imminent danger of elimination. The data covers more than 2500 wetland and riparian plant communities. Each plant community is assessed based on such factors as the remaining number and condition of occurrences of the community, the remaining acreage, and the severity of threats to the community type. In all cases, a wide variety of factors contribute to overall ratings.

Some Definitions

- **"Critically Imperiled"**: at very high risk of elimination because of extreme rarity (often 5 or fewer occurrences), very steep declines, or other factors
- **"Imperiled"**: at high risk of elimination because of very restricted range, very few occurrences (often 20 or fewer), steep declines, or other factors
- **"Vulnerable"**: at moderate risk of elimination because of a restricted range, relatively few occurrences (often 80 or fewer), recent and widespread declines, or other factors

EXTENT AND PATTERN	CHEMICAL AND PHYSICAL	BIOLOGICAL COMPONENTS	GOODS AND SERVICES
Extent	Nutrients, Carbon, and Oxygen	Plants and Animals	**Food, Fiber, and Water**
Pattern	Chemical Contamination	Communities	Recreation and Other Services
	Physical	Ecological Productivity	

Water Withdrawals

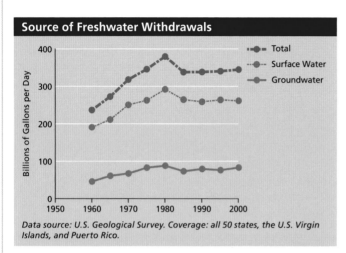

Source of Freshwater Withdrawals

Data source: U.S. Geological Survey. Coverage: all 50 states, the U.S. Virgin Islands, and Puerto Rico.

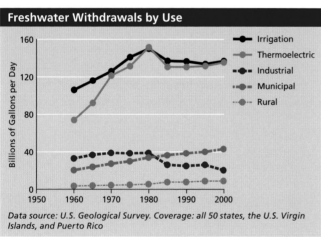

Freshwater Withdrawals by Use

Data source: U.S. Geological Survey. Coverage: all 50 states, the U.S. Virgin Islands, and Puerto Rico

Why Are the Amount and Use of Freshwater Withdrawals Important?

People rely on fresh water obtained from surface water (lakes, streams, rivers) and groundwater (aquifers) for drinking, irrigation, commercial, and industrial uses. Accurate information about the nation's water withdrawals—the amount of fresh water used—and what it is being used for will help planners and managers assess the efficacy of water management policies, regulations, and conservation activities and project future demand, enabling them to make better decisions about the nation's water resources.

What Does This Indicator Report?

The total amount of surface fresh water and groundwater withdrawn for use in the municipal, rural, industrial, thermoelectric, and irrigation sectors (see the technical note for a description of these categories).

What Do the Data Show?

- From 1960 to 2000, total freshwater withdrawals increased by 46%. The increase in total withdrawals was driven by increases in both surface water (37% increase) and groundwater (81% increase) withdrawals.
- Municipal, rural, and thermoelectric water uses increased from 1960 to 2000. Over the same period, industrial withdrawals declined.
- Irrigation withdrawals increased until 1980 but leveled off in recent years.

Understanding the Data Trends in water withdrawals are influenced by a number of factors, including climate, changes in the energy and food production sectors, and U.S. population growth (see Production of Food and Fiber and Water Withdrawals, p. 56).

The degree to which withdrawals represent consumptive use varies by category of use. For example, most of the water withdrawn for thermoelectric use is returned to the river for use downstream for irrigation, municipal water supply, and so on. However, the quality of water returned to the environment after being used may be lower than when it was initially withdrawn. Finally, withdrawal rates that exceed natural rates of freshwater recharge can have negative impacts on river-dwelling organisms and freshwater habitats and can ultimately threaten the sustainability of the resource. This indicator does not address either the quality of returned water or the relationship between rates of water withdrawal and recharge.

The technical note for this indicator is on page 323.

188   The State of the Nation's Ecosystems 2008: The Indicators

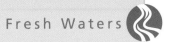

EXTENT AND PATTERN	CHEMICAL AND PHYSICAL	BIOLOGICAL COMPONENTS	GOODS AND SERVICES
Extent	Nutrients, Carbon, and Oxygen	Plants and Animals	Food, Fiber, and Water
Pattern	Chemical Contamination	Communities	Recreation and Other Services
	Physical	Ecological Productivity	

Groundwater Levels

Why Are Changes in Groundwater Levels Important? Groundwater provides about 40% of the nation's municipal water supply and is the source of much of the water used for irrigation. For most people in rural America, groundwater from their own wells is their only source of water. Groundwater is a major contributor to flow in many streams and rivers, and it has a strong influence on river and wetland habitats for plants and animals living near springs and seeps.

> **Groundwater Levels**
>
> **Data Gap**
>
> **Data are not adequate for national reporting on changes in groundwater levels.**

What Will This Indicator Report? The percentage of the area of the nation's major regional aquifers in which water levels are increasing, decreasing, or stable (this would be reported as the fraction of the aquifer area that declined, increased, or remained stable in comparison to a previous period, and it would be reported every 5 years).

Why Can't This Indicator Be Reported at This Time? Data on groundwater levels are collected by federal, regional, state, and local agencies. All states have some coverage, but there are areas of the country for which very little information is available. The data that do exist have not been aggregated to provide systematic measurements of water levels in a significant portion of the nation's major aquifers. Furthermore, there will be challenges in determining a useful way to summarize data regionally and nationally, given the variability in aquifer types and associated hydrology.

The first step in producing national coverage would be to locate and assess the quality and consistency of existing data. It would then be necessary to aggregate those data and determine where there is sufficient geographic coverage of the major aquifers and adequate characterization of conditions in those aquifers. In areas where data coverage is inadequate, additional measurements would be necessary.

Discussion Changes in water levels reflect changes in the amount of groundwater pumped from or returned to major aquifers; changes may also reflect climate variability or climate change. The indicator reports on changes in the quantity of groundwater: it does not address the quality of that water or its suitability for use. See Depth to Shallow Groundwater (p. 210).

The technical note for this indicator is on page 324.

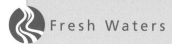
EXTENT AND PATTERN	CHEMICAL AND PHYSICAL	BIOLOGICAL COMPONENTS	GOODS AND SERVICES
Extent	Nutrients, Carbon, and Oxygen	Plants and Animals	Food, Fiber, and Water
Pattern	Chemical Contamination	Communities	Recreation and Other Services
	Physical	Ecological Productivity	

Waterborne Human Disease Outbreaks

Waterborne Human Disease Outbreaks

Data Gap

Data are not adequate for national reporting on the number of outbreaks due to waterborne disease from either drinking water or recreational contact.

Why Is Reporting on Waterborne Human Disease Outbreaks Important? Ensuring that water is fit to drink and swim in without fear of disease is a basic societal objective. The number of disease outbreaks—defined as at least two people getting sick—that can be attributed to contaminated water is a measure of both freshwater ecosystem condition and the effectiveness of water quality management (see Recreational Water Quality, p. 92, for information on contamination that can lead to waterborne diseases in coastal waters).

What Will this Indicator Report? The number of disease outbreaks attributed to
- Drinking water that is untreated, or where treatment has failed to remove disease-causing organisms
- Swimming or other recreational contact from lakes, streams, or rivers

Why Can't This Indicator Be Reported at This Time? The Centers for Disease Control and Prevention (CDC) report on the number of waterborne human disease outbreaks nationally. However, CDC data appear to be heavily influenced by reporting effort, and therefore do not adequately represent waterborne human disease outbreaks nationally. The CDC and the U.S. Environmental Protection Agency are working to improve the structure of national waterborne disease reporting programs. In the future, this indicator may report the number of individuals affected rather than the number of outbreaks.

The technical note for this indicator is on page 325.

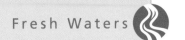

Freshwater Recreational Activities

Why Is It Important To Track Participation in Freshwater Recreational Activities? Recreation in and around water, from birdwatching and fishing to sailing and swimming, is a valuable benefit provided

> **Freshwater Recreational Activities**
> **Data Gap**
> Data are not adequate for national reporting on the amount of recreation that takes place in the nation's fresh waters.

by ecosystems. Information on trends in participation documents the demand for recreation opportunities, the ability of ecosystems to support recreational activities, and the potential for recreation to affect other ecosystem characteristics and services.

What Will This Indicator Report? This indicator will show the number of days that U.S. residents, 16 years of age and older, took part in a variety of freshwater recreational activities. A "recreation day" for this measure is any day during which a person was engaged in the activity, whether for only a few minutes or for many hours.

Why Can't This Indicator Be Reported at This Time? Data are available for the recreational activities shown in the national Outdoor Recreation indicator (p. 58), but, with the exception of freshwater fishing, these national data do not distinguish activities that took place in fresh water from activities that took place in saltwater. According to the national data, in the 2003–2005 survey period U.S. residents participated in freshwater fishing activities 1.4 billion times per year and in nonfishing water activities (boating, swimming, water skiing in fresh water and saltwater) 3.1 billion times per year. Future editions of the *National Survey on Recreation and the Environment* will separate freshwater recreational activities from other types of recreation.

There is no technical note for this indicator. The program description for the *National Survey on Recreation and the Environment* is found in the technical note on page 286.

Contents | page

Chapter 7:
Indicators of the Condition and Use of Grasslands and Shrublands

Grasslands and shrublands represent the largest single ecosystem type in the United States, covering more than one-third of the land area of the lower 48 states and several hundred million acres in Alaska. Although they are primarily located in drier regions, grasslands and shrublands occur in wetter climates when other physical or chemical conditions limit the growth of trees. The grassland and shrubland ecosystem type includes Midwestern tall grass prairies, high sagebrush steppes in the Intermountain West, California's coastal prairies, pastures and haylands (also considered part of the farmland ecosystem), deserts, mountain meadows, and Alaskan tundra and scrub. Many grasslands and shrublands are also referred to as "rangelands," even if they are not used for livestock grazing. Grasslands and shrublands loom large in our cultural lore, evoking images of buffalo hunters and cowboys, sodbusters and homesteaders pushing west in wagon trains to tame the frontier and fulfill the nation's "Manifest Destiny" to extend its domain to the Pacific. Although some of these landscapes may seem barren and unproductive, grasslands and shrublands provide us with food and fiber, huntable and watchable wildlife, clean fresh water, open space and views, wilderness experiences, and inspiration.

Public policy regarding grasslands and shrublands has evolved considerably over the nation's history, from the Louisiana Purchase and a century of incentives for homesteading and exploitation to more recent policies emphasizing conservation, multiple use, and prairie restoration. Although grasslands and shrublands are vast, they can also be fragile. What seemed a nearly infinite frontier in the 19th century is now experiencing rapid population growth and increased demand for resources, setting the stage for conflicts among various users, managers, and public constituencies.

Management of public lands clearly presents different sets of choices and involves much greater oversight by government agencies and the public than does management of private grasslands and shrublands. Rights and desires of private landowners are key considerations for private land management, but public land managers must consider society's needs and interests when weighing competing uses. However, because of the extensive intermingling of public and private grasslands and shrublands and the tradition of leasing large areas of public lands for grazing, these two spheres are more intertwined than is often the case, for example, in forest management.

The following sections and the table on page 200 describe the four categories of ecosystem condition and use outlined in Chapter 1 and also summarize the most current data and trends for grassland and shrubland ecosystems. Individual indicators focus on the extent and nature of these ecosystems, ecological processes and conditions necessary for their functioning, biological communities, and the human benefits derived from grasslands and shrublands.

Extent and Pattern

As with all ecosystems, knowing the basic extent of grasslands and shrublands is important in assessing the condition of the system and the benefits it provides. Conversion of grasslands or shrublands to forests or cropland, for example, signals a change in the goods and services these lands can be expected to produce. However, transitions *within* grasslands and shrublands—for example, from prairie to sage and cactus shrubland—or in the *use* of these lands—from grazing to intensive motorized recreation— are equally important indicators of the status of these lands. The degree to which these lands are intermingled with other lands, especially with subdivisions or agricultural lands, can affect their value as wildlife habitat and their ability to provide services such as filtration of nutrient runoff.

Although outright conversion of grasslands and shrublands to other landscape types is an important issue, conflicts more often arise over their use—particularly the location of suburban developments and oil, gas, and other mining activities, off-road vehicle use, or the intensity of livestock grazing.

Data in this chapter show that

- There are more than one billion acres of grasslands and shrublands in the lower 48 states and Alaska. Approximately half of that is shrubland, one-quarter grassland, and the remainder pasture and haylands as well as tundra.
- Between 1994 and 2006, there was no clear up or down trend in the acreage of grasslands and shrublands enrolled in the Conservation Reserve Program (CRP). In 2006, 31 million acres of grasslands and shrublands were set aside in the CRP.
- In 2001, 22% of "core shrubland" and 13% of "core grassland" (core grasslands or shrublands are surrounded by other "natural" land cover rather than crops or human development) were in patches larger than 100 square miles.
- Patches of "core grassland" are smaller in the Northeast/Mid-Atlantic and Southeast regions than in the Midwest and the Rocky Mountain region. Large patches of "core shrubland" are most common in the West Coast, Southwest, and Rocky Mountain regions.

Data are not available for national reporting on

- The acreage used for livestock grazing; oil, gas, and mineral development; rural residences; "protected areas"; and high-intensity recreation

Chemical and Physical Characteristics

Like other ecosystems, grasslands and shrublands both receive and export nutrients, energy, and water. The status of key elements such as nitrogen and carbon provides important insight into the condition and functioning of these ecosystems. Since grasslands and shrublands are often found in water-scarce regions, understanding the location and timing of water availability is crucial to assessing their overall condition and the benefits they can supply.

Nitrate, a naturally occurring plant nutrient, is generally found at low levels in grassland and shrubland groundwater. Elevated levels of nitrate in groundwater may result from any of several alterations to these systems: increased human inputs of nitrogen, such as from fertilizers, animal wastes, or atmospheric deposition; changes in vegetation driven by fire suppression, grazing, or land conversion; or drought, climate change, or other factors that stress plants in the ecosystem. Excess nitrate in drinking water poses a health threat to young children as well as signaling changes in the grasslands and shrublands themselves.

Grasslands and shrublands typically store more than two-thirds of their carbon below ground in roots and soils, and the amount of carbon stored can be affected by changes in fire frequency, grazing intensity, plant cover, and land use. Carbon stored in soil organic matter serves as an indicator of soil fertility, enhances water storage in soil, reduces erosion, and can retain nitrate, thus preventing it from entering streams and groundwater. Increases in the amount of carbon stored in grassland and shrubland soils can also offset emissions of carbon dioxide that drive global warming.

Water is an important resource in all ecosystems and is especially scarce in the arid grasslands and shrublands of the Intermountain West. Streams and shallow groundwater are often highly connected, with groundwater serving as the main source of water for streams as well as for springs, seeps, wetlands, and prairie potholes.

Changes in groundwater levels and in the frequency and duration of dry periods in streams can exert powerful effects on fish, wildlife, and plants, as well as on people who depend on these aquatic systems for drinking water, irrigation, or other uses. Such changes can be caused by a number of factors, from natural variations in weather to longer-term climate change, increased water use, or changes in vegetation or land use.

Data in this chapter show that
- Since 1963, the percentage of streams with dry periods decreased in all grassland and shrubland ecoregions in the lower 48 states except Desert/Shrub.
- Also since 1963, the percentage of streams experiencing substantially shorter dry periods has increased compared to the 1941–1960 baseline period.

Data are not adequate for national reporting on
- Nitrate concentrations in groundwater in areas that are primarily grassland or shrubland
- The total amount of carbon stored in grasslands and shrublands
- Depth to shallow groundwater in grasslands and shrublands

Biological Components

Grasslands and shrublands support species that are adapted to the specific conditions found there. For the nation's central grasslands, that includes such iconic American animals as bison, pronghorn antelope, prairie dogs, and sage grouse. Key indicators of the status of grasslands and shrublands

include the condition of their native species and biological communities—particularly scarce or valuable habitats such as riparian areas (the lands immediately adjacent to a stream)—and the status of major processes that shape these ecosystems. The number of grassland- and shrubland-adapted species that are rare or in decline provides information both on the species themselves, which are valued by many people in their own right, and also on how well these lands are able to support a range of native species.

Non-native plants and animals can alter ecosystems by changing their fire susceptibility, reducing or increasing soil erosion, enhancing or diminishing the quality of feed for livestock or wildlife grazing, or displacing native species. Periodic wildfire is a vital feature of many grasslands and shrublands. Fire shapes and maintains these ecosystems by favoring fire-adapted plants and preventing encroachment by trees, large shrubs, and less fire-tolerant species. Fire patterns can be modified by fire suppression, grazing that reduces burnable grass, or invasion by certain non-native plants such as cheatgrass that provide increased fuel. Finally, riparian areas are particularly important habitats for many species, and their status can serve as an indicator of changes that have occurred throughout a watershed.

Maintaining rare or declining species, avoiding or reducing the negative effects of non-native species, and ensuring the integrity of riparian areas are major considerations in management of both public and private grasslands and shrublands. Controlled use of fire is becoming a more common management tool. The extensive intermingling of public and private lands can complicate large-scale management strategies, but it can also foster increased collaboration among landowners, public land managers, and other stakeholders.

Data in this chapter show that

- Eighteen percent of native grassland and shrubland animals are considered to be at risk. This group includes 3.5% that are critically imperiled, 6% that are imperiled, 8% that are vulnerable, and just under 1% that may already be extinct.
- For at-risk native vertebrate grassland and shrubland animals, 31% have declining populations, 29% have stable populations, and only 3% have increasing populations. Population trends for the remaining species (37%) are unknown.
- In 2001–2005, about 70% of invasive and 80% of non-invasive bird species had increasing populations.
- Since 1966–1970, the percentage of invasive and non-invasive bird species that have increasing populations shows no clear upward or downward trend.

Data are not adequate for national reporting on

- The proportion of grassland and shrubland area covered by established non-native plants

Further indicator development is needed to report on

- Changes in the frequency of grassland and shrubland fires
- The condition of riparian areas along grassland and shrubland streams.

Goods and Services

People use grasslands and shrublands for a wide variety of activities (see Land Use in Grasslands and Shrublands, p. 203). Two of the most important uses are livestock grazing and recreation, both of which rely on the ecological character of the land to achieve desired benefits. Many cattle and other livestock are grazed on open lands before being moved to feedlots (although some grazing also occurs in forested areas). This use of "rangelands" is a deep-seated, but at times contentious, aspect of the nation's public lands legacy. Grasslands and shrublands also support recreational activities such as fishing, hunting, off-road vehicle use, snowmobiling, and nature study. These recreational activities serve as a source of jobs and income for the people who own these lands or who provide guides, equipment, or other services.

Data in this chapter show that

- Since 1994, the number of cattle grazing on public and private grasslands and shrublands has declined by 9%. In 2007, 80 million cattle grazed on U.S. grasslands and shrublands.

Data are not adequate for national reporting on

- The amount of recreational activity taking place on grasslands and shrublands

Status and trends of all grassland and shrubland indicators are summarized in the following table and described in detail in the remainder of the chapter. Regions and related definitions used throughout this chapter are described in Appendix D.

Indicators	What Do the Most Recent Data Show?	Have Data Values Changed over Time?

EXTENT AND PATTERN

Area of Grasslands and Shrublands, p. 202	There are 830 million acres of grasslands and shrublands in the lower 48 states (2001 data, includes pasture) and 205 million acres of grasslands and shrublands in Alaska (1991 data).	Data are not adequate for national reporting on changes in the area of grasslands and shrublands.
Land Use in Grasslands and Shrublands, p. 203	There are 31 million acres of grasslands and shrublands enrolled in the Conservation Reserve Program (2006 data).	➡ Between 1994 and 2006 there was no clear upward or downward trend in acreage of grasslands and shrublands enrolled in the Conservation Reserve Program.
	Data are not adequate for national reporting on the area dedicated to livestock raising, oil/gas/ mining, rural residences, "protected areas," and high-intensity recreation.	
Pattern of Grassland and Shrubland Landscapes, p. 204	22% of "core shrubland" is in patches larger than 100 sq. miles; 13% of "core grassland" is in patches larger than 100 sq. miles (2001 data).	Data are not adequate for national reporting on changes in the size of "core shrubland" or "core grassland" patches.

CHEMICAL AND PHYSICAL CHARACTERISTICS

Nitrate in Grassland and Shrubland Groundwater, p. 206	Data are not adequate for national reporting on nitrate concentrations in groundwater in areas that are primarily grassland or shrubland.	
Carbon Storage, p. 207	Data are not adequate for national reporting on the total amount of carbon stored in soils and plants in grasslands and shrublands.	
Number and Duration of Dry Periods in Grassland and Shrubland Streams and Rivers, p. 208	19% of grassland and shrubland streams have periods of zero flow (2002–2006 data).	↘ Since 1963, the percentage of streams with zero-flow periods has decreased in all grassland and shrubland ecoregions except Desert/Shrub.
	15% of grassland and shrubland streams have substantially (greater than 14 days) longer periods of zero-flow compared to 1941–1960 baseline period (2002–2006 data).	➡ Since 1963, the percentage of streams with zero-flow periods substantially longer than the baseline period has shown no clear upward or downward trend.
	26% of grassland and shrubland streams had substantially shorter periods of zero-flow compared to the 1941–1960 baseline period (2002–2006 data).	↗ Since 1963, the percentage of streams with a substantially shorter period of zero-flow has increased compared to the baseline period.
Depth to Shallow Groundwater, p. 210	Data are not adequate for national reporting on the depth to shallow groundwater.	

Indicators	What Do the Most Recent Data Show?	Have Data Values Changed over Time?
BIOLOGICAL COMPONENTS		
At-Risk Native Grassland and Shrubland Animal Species, p. 211	18% of native grassland animal species are at risk (2006 data).	Data are not adequate for national reporting on changes in at-risk native species.
	Data are not adequate for national reporting on the percentage of at-risk native grassland and shrubland plants.	
	31% of at-risk native vertebrate animal species in grassland and shrublands have declining populations; 29% have stable populations and 3% have increasing populations (2006 data).	Data are not adequate for national reporting on changes in the population trends in at-risk native vertebrate animals in grasslands and shrublands.
	Data are not adequate for national reporting on population trends in at-risk native invertebrate animals and plants in grasslands and shrublands.	
Established Non-native Grassland and Shrubland Plant Cover, p. 213	Data are not adequate for national reporting on the proportion of established non-native plant cover on grasslands and shrublands.	
Population Trends in Invasive and Non-invasive Birds, p. 214	About 70% of invasive and 80% of non-invasive bird species have increasing populations (2001–2005 data).	➡ Since 1966–1970 there has been no clear upward or downward trend in the percentage of invasive bird species with increasing population trends.
		➡ Since 1966–1970 there has been no clear upward or downward trend in the percentage of non-invasive bird species with increasing population trends.
Fire Frequency, p. 216	Indicator Development Needed	
Riparian Condition, p. 217	Indicator Development Needed	
GOODS AND SERVICES		
Cattle Grazing, p. 218	Approximately 80 million cattle graze on grasslands and shrublands (2007 data).	⬈ Since 1994 the number of cattle grazing on grasslands and shrublands has declined.
Recreation on Grasslands and Shrublands, p. 219	Data are not adequate for national reporting on participation in recreational activities in grassland and shrubland areas.	

⬐ = significant decrease   ⬈ =significant increase   ➡ = no clear trend*   ❓ = insufficient data for trend analysis

◼ = Data not available for adequate reporting.

* may be due to little numerical change in the data or large numerical fluctuations in data resulting in no single trend

EXTENT AND PATTERN	CHEMICAL AND PHYSICAL	BIOLOGICAL COMPONENTS	GOODS AND SERVICES
Extent	Nutrients, Carbon, and Oxygen	Plants and Animals	Food, Fiber, and Water
Pattern	Chemical Contamination	Communities	Recreation and Other Services
	Physical	Ecological Productivity	

Area of Grasslands and Shrublands

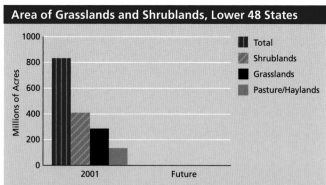

Area of Grasslands and Shrublands, Lower 48 States

Data source: Multi-Resolution Land Characterization (MRLC) Consortium and ESRI (road map); analysis by the U.S. Forest Service and the U.S. Environmental Protection Agency. Coverage: lower 48 states. Note: the data presented here are not comparable to the 1992 data presented in the 2002 edition of this report because of technical differences between the underlying datasets—please see technical note for further details.

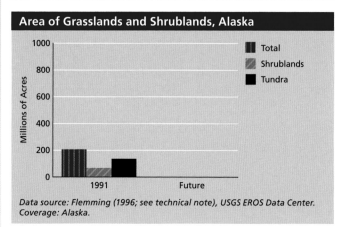

Area of Grasslands and Shrublands, Alaska

Data source: Flemming (1996; see technical note), USGS EROS Data Center. Coverage: Alaska.

Why Is the Area of Grasslands and Shrublands Important? Grasslands and shrublands cover more area than any other ecosystem type in the United States. Besides providing a basic description of these landscapes, changes in the extent of grassland and shrubland ecosystems over time indicate potential changes in the goods and services derived from them.

What Does This Indicator Report? The total acreage of U.S. grasslands and shrublands (including pasture and tundra).

What Do the Data Show?

- There were 830 million acres of grasslands and shrublands in the lower 48 states (2001 data) and 205 million acres of grasslands and shrublands in Alaska (1991 data), for a total of just over 1 billion acres.
- In the lower 48 states, there were 410 million acres of shrubland, 285 million acres of grassland, and 135 million acres of pasture and haylands. In Alaska, tundra occupied about 135 million acres and other shrublands about 70 million acres.

Understanding the Data The grasslands and shrublands reported here include arid grasslands and shrublands, coastal and mountain meadows, hot and cold deserts, and tundra. Also included are pastures and haylands, which share important characteristics with less managed grasslands. Pastures and haylands are also included in farmlands (see Ecosystem Extent, p. 28, and Total Cropland, p. 102). Note that the satellite-based data used in this indicator estimate land cover, not land use, so many acres of grasslands or shrublands that are actually used as pastures (also called rangeland) may not be reflected in these data.

Researchers estimate that there were between 900 million and 1 billion acres of grasslands and shrublands in the lower 48 states before European settlement, so up to 170 million acres of grasslands and shrublands have been converted to other uses since presettlement times. This may be an underestimate of the decline in area of relatively unmanaged "natural" grasslands and shrublands because pastures may be managed in such a way that little of their original character remains. Also, many Eastern pastures were formerly forests, so changes in pasture area over time could be due to a conversion from forest to agriculture. Particular subtypes, like tallgrass prairies, have experienced large historical declines. Researchers estimate that tallgrass prairies now cover no more than 5% of their presettlement acreage. No consistent, nationwide data are available on recent changes in acreage of grasslands and shrublands. The U.S. Department of Agriculture reports that from 1982 to 2003 the area of nonfederal rangelands, which represent only a portion of the grasslands and shrublands included in the data presented above, declined by about 10 million acres, with most of the drop occurring between 1982 and 1992.

The technical note for this indicator is on page 325.

EXTENT AND PATTERN	CHEMICAL AND PHYSICAL	BIOLOGICAL COMPONENTS	GOODS AND SERVICES
Extent	Nutrients, Carbon, and Oxygen	Plants and Animals	Food, Fiber, and Water
Pattern	Chemical Contamination	Communities	Recreation and Other Services
	Physical	Ecological Productivity	

Land Use in Grasslands and Shrublands

Why Is the Area of Different Land Uses Important? Grasslands and shrublands are used for livestock raising, rural residences, resource extraction, habitat conservation, and recreation, among other uses. The area devoted to different land uses can affect landscape pattern, wildlife habitat, and the goods and services provided to people.

What Does This Indicator Report? The acreage of grassland and shrubland enrolled in the Conservation Reserve Program (CRP) and, when data become available, the acreage in the following land use categories: livestock raising, oil/gas/mining, rural residences, "protected areas," and high-intensity recreation, such as motorized vehicle use (off-road vehicles, all-terrain vehicles).

What Do the Data Show?
- Since 1994, grassland and shrubland CRP acreage has not changed significantly. Grassland and shrubland CRP acreage fluctuated from a high of 33 million acres in 1994 and 1995 to a low of 26 million acres in 1999 and has ranged between 29 and 31 million since 2001.
- As of 2006, about 31 million acres of grasslands and shrublands were enrolled in the CRP.

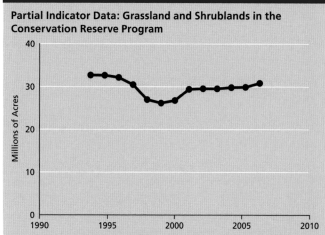

Grassland and Shrubland Land Use

Partial Indicator Data: Grassland and Shrublands in the Conservation Reserve Program

Data source: USDA Farm Service Agency. Coverage: All 50 states and Puerto Rico. Technical details: The CRP provides for 10-year lease payments to farmers to remove lands from production; this indicator includes only acreage on which grass, shrubs, or similar cover (not trees) are established.

Data Gap

Data are not adequate for national reporting on the area dedicated to livestock raising, oil/gas/mining, rural residences, "protected areas," and high-intensity recreation.

Why Can't This Entire Indicator Be Reported at This Time? With the exception of CRP lands, consistent reporting is not available for the amount of land in the categories included in this indicator. For example, there are data on the number of livestock raised (see Cattle Grazing, p. 218), but no data on the acreage used for this purpose. In addition, consistent definitions need to be developed for the land use categories that lack data. Further indicator development is needed to determine what level of recreational use qualifies an area as "high-intensity," what housing density, over how large an area, qualifies an area as "rural residences," and whether federal, state, and private lands are to be considered "protected areas."

Understanding the Data The area of grasslands and shrublands enrolled in the Conservation Reserve Program accounts for less than 4% of the total grassland shrubland landscape (see Area of Grasslands and Shrublands, p. 202). In the future, data on the land area used for different purposes, such as livestock raising or recreational activities, will quantify the land use requirements of different activities. Future data on the amount of grassland and shrubland area that has been developed for rural residences or that has been removed from set-aside programs such as the Conservation Reserve Program would indicate long-term shifts in land use. Shifts in landscape composition (for example, the amount of shrubland versus tundra) in the grassland and shrubland ecosystem will also affect use of these areas (see Area of Grasslands and Shrublands, p. 202).

The technical note for this indicator is on page 326.

EXTENT AND PATTERN	CHEMICAL AND PHYSICAL	BIOLOGICAL COMPONENTS	GOODS AND SERVICES
Extent	Nutrients, Carbon, and Oxygen	Plants and Animals	Food, Fiber, and Water
Pattern	Chemical Contamination	Communities	Recreation and Other Services
	Physical	Ecological Productivity	

Pattern of Grassland and Shrubland Landscapes

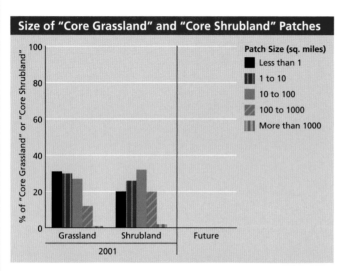

Size of "Core Grassland" and "Core Shrubland" Patches

Patch Size (sq. miles)
- Less than 1
- 1 to 10
- 10 to 100
- 100 to 1000
- More than 1000

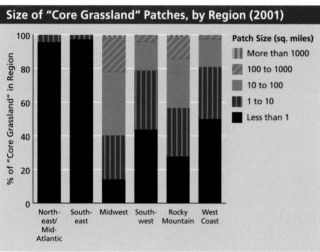

Size of "Core Grassland" Patches, by Region (2001)

Patch Size (sq. miles)
- More than 1000
- 100 to 1000
- 10 to 100
- 1 to 10
- Less than 1

Why is the Pattern of Grassland and Shrubland Landscapes Important?

Grasslands and shrublands are naturally intermingled with forest or other grasslands or shrublands. Each region has a characteristic mix of ecosystem types, and these intermingled patches provide the diversity of habitats needed by the different organisms native to a region. Activities such as fire suppression, grazing, agriculture, and residential, commercial, and industrial development can change landscape pattern in ways that affect the provision of ecosystem goods and services.

What Does This Indicator Report?

The size of "core grassland" and "core shrubland" patches (see definitions below), nationally and regionally.

What Do the Data Show?

- In 2001, more "core shrubland" (22%) than "core grassland" (13%), was in patches larger than 100 square miles.
- The Northeast/Mid-Atlantic and Southeast regions had relatively few patches of "core grassland" or "core shrubland" larger than 10 square miles. In the Midwest, there were few patches of "core shrubland" larger than 10 square miles, but about 60% of "core grassland" patches were above this size.
- The Midwest, followed by the Rocky Mountain region, had the most large patches of "core grassland," with 22% and 14% in patches larger than 100 square miles, respectively.
- The West Coast, Southwest, and Rocky Mountain regions had more large patches of "core shrubland," with 25%, 23%, and 22% in patches larger than 100 square miles, respectively.

EXTENT AND PATTERN	CHEMICAL AND PHYSICAL	BIOLOGICAL COMPONENTS	GOODS AND SERVICES
Extent	Nutrients, Carbon, and Oxygen	Plants and Animals	Food, Fiber, and Water
Pattern	Chemical Contamination	Communities	Recreation and Other Services
	Physical	Ecological Productivity	

Pattern of Grassland and Shrubland Landscapes *(continued)*

Understanding the Data In 2001, 66% of total grassland area and 87% of total shrubland area in the lower 48 states met the definition of "core grassland" or "core shrubland," respectively (data not shown), and was found in the various patch sizes shown above. The degree to which croplands and development are interspersed with grasslands and shrublands has a direct impact on the structural pattern of these landscapes. The expansion of agriculture or development, for example, can lead to these "natural" lands being broken into smaller, more isolated landscape units.

This indicator describes the structure of grassland and shrubland landscapes. The relationship between ecological functioning and structural patterns of landscapes, while not fully understood, undoubtedly varies by species, and this continues to be an active research focus of many landscape ecologists. Thus, the data presented here provide general information about the extent to which cropland and development are interspersed with grasslands and shrublands.

See also Pattern of Forest Landscapes, p. 138.

The technical note for this indicator is on page 327.

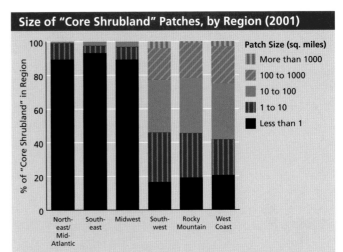

Size of "Core Shrubland" Patches, by Region (2001)

Patch Size (sq. miles)
- More than 1000
- 100 to 1000
- 10 to 100
- 1 to 10
- Less than 1

(Y-axis: % of "Core Shrubland" in Region; X-axis: Northeast/Mid-Atlantic, Southeast, Midwest, Southwest, Rocky Mountain, West Coast)

Data source: Multi-Resolution Land Characterization (MRLC) Consortium and ESRI (road map); analysis by the U.S. Forest Service and the U.S. Environmental Protection Agency. Coverage: lower 48 states. Technical details: The National Land Cover Dataset (NLCD) was augmented with a road map (paved roads only). A 240-acre-square analysis tool was placed around each pixel of the map with grassland or shrubland land cover. Those pixels with at least 90% natural surroundings were formed into patches of touching pixels, the size of which are reported in the graphs. Note: current technical limitations required that patches be "cut" by state boundaries, meaning that these data should be considered to represent minimum patch sizes. It is not clear what effect this analysis limitation had on the data.

Definition

Like "core forest" (see p. 138), "core grassland" is defined as small parcels (~1/4 acre) of grassland surrounded by a specific amount (in this case at least 90%) of grassland and other natural land cover (shrublands, forest, wetlands, other fresh waters, and coastal waters). "Core shrubland" is defined similarly. The criteria used to define both can be adjusted to provide further insight into the ecological implication of the patterns of grassland–shrubland landscapes.

EXTENT AND PATTERN	CHEMICAL AND PHYSICAL	BIOLOGICAL COMPONENTS	GOODS AND SERVICES
Extent	Nutrients, Carbon, and Oxygen	Plants and Animals	Food, Fiber, and Water
Pattern	Chemical Contamination	Communities	Recreation and Other Services
	Physical	Ecological Productivity	

Nitrate in Grassland and Shrubland Groundwater

Nitrate in Grassland and Shrubland Groundwater

Data Gap

Data are not adequate for national reporting on nitrate concentrations in groundwater in areas that are primarily grassland or shrubland.

Why Is Nitrate in Grassland and Shrubland Groundwater Important? Elevated nitrate in drinking water is a health threat to infants and is of particular concern for people using household groundwater wells; municipal water supply systems typically take steps to remove nitrate. Elevated amounts of nitrate in groundwater are often a sign that inputs from human sources have increased or that plants in the system are under stress.

What Will This Indicator Report? The percentage of groundwater sites with average nitrate concentrations in one of four ranges, in areas that are primarily grassland or shrubland.

Why Can't This Indicator Be Reported at This Time? Data on nitrate concentrations in grassland and shrubland groundwater are available in fragmentary form, collected by many different agencies and institutions using different methods, but they have not been aggregated to enable national reporting. The U.S. Geological Survey's National Water Quality Assessment, which provides consistent water quality data, may provide sufficient data in the future to allow reporting on a national level. First, however, studies must be undertaken to determine if currently sampled wells represent the range of grasslands and shrublands across the United States.

Discussion Nitrate, a naturally occurring form of nitrogen, is an important plant nutrient; it is often the most abundant of the forms of nitrogen that are usable by plants. Most nitrogen is used and reused by plants within an ecosystem. Thus, in less-disturbed grassland or shrubland ecosystems, little nitrogen leaks into either surface runoff or groundwater. Elevated amounts in those waters might come from fertilizer use, from disposal of animal waste, from atmospheric deposition (from rain and snowfall, for example—see also Freshwater Acidity, p. 176), or from changes in vegetation associated with fire suppression or overgrazing.

See also Movement of Nitrogen (p. 36) and the farmlands, forests, and urban and suburban nitrate indicators (pp. 107, 140, and 238).

The technical note for this indicator is on page 327.

EXTENT AND PATTERN	CHEMICAL AND PHYSICAL	BIOLOGICAL COMPONENTS	GOODS AND SERVICES
Extent	Nutrients, Carbon, and Oxygen	Plants and Animals	Food, Fiber, and Water
Pattern	Chemical Contamination	Communities	Recreation and Other Services
	Physical	Ecological Productivity	

Carbon Storage

Why Is Carbon Storage in Grasslands and Shrublands Important? Grasslands and shrublands contain large quantities of carbon. Although a significant amount is found in plants—up to a third of the total is found in above-ground biomass

> **Carbon Storage**
>
> **Data Gap**
>
> **Data are not adequate for national reporting on the total amount of carbon stored in soil and plants in grasslands and shrublands.**

and extensive root systems—most of the carbon in these systems is found in the soil. Carbon in soil—in the form of organic matter, or partially decayed plant and animal matter—helps the soil hold water and supply nutrients to plants; it also protects against erosion and helps support a thriving and diverse set of microscopic plants and animals. Increased carbon storage in these systems can offset emissions of carbon dioxide and methane gases to the atmosphere, where they contribute to the greenhouse effect (see Carbon Storage, p. 38).

What Will This Indicator Report? The total amount of carbon stored in soil and plants in grasslands and shrublands.

Why Can't This Indicator Be Reported at This Time? Estimates of the change in carbon stocks in grasslands and shrublands (for soils on private lands only) are available (see Carbon Storage, p. 38). At this time, there is no system of regular monitoring and reporting on total stocks of carbon in either aboveground or belowground pools in grassland and shrubland systems. In the near future, modeled estimates of total carbon stocks may be available for soils in private grasslands and shrublands. See also farmlands Soil Organic Matter, p. 110.

Discussion In general, the amount of carbon stored in grasslands and shrublands changes very slowly (tundra soils, however, have the potential to change quite rapidly, especially if they are subjected to drying and/or warming). Carbon storage may be affected by changes in fire frequency or grazing intensity, by the introduction of non-native species, by encroachment of woody plants, or by conversion of these lands to other uses (like agriculture). In grasslands (including alpine and arctic tundra), more than two-thirds of all carbon is stored below ground in soils and plant roots. By some recent estimates, grassland and shrubland soils in the United States store about half as much carbon as is thought to be stored in forests (all pools, including soil), but contain more than twice as much soil carbon as cropland soils. It is important to note that these figures are only estimates, in some cases with large margins of error (see technical note for more information).

The technical note for this indicator is on page 327.

EXTENT AND PATTERN	CHEMICAL AND PHYSICAL	BIOLOGICAL COMPONENTS	GOODS AND SERVICES
Extent	Nutrients, Carbon, and Oxygen	Plants and Animals	Food, Fiber, and Water
Pattern	Chemical Contamination	Communities	Recreation and Other Services
	Physical	Ecological Productivity	

Number and Duration of Dry Periods in Grassland and Shrubland Streams and Rivers

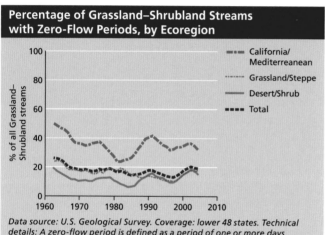

Percentage of Grassland–Shrubland Streams with Zero-Flow Periods, by Ecoregion

Data source: U.S. Geological Survey. Coverage: lower 48 states. Technical details: A zero-flow period is defined as a period of one or more days without flow. Data for each year are based on a 5-year rolling average.

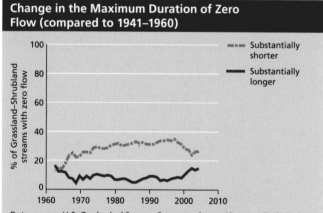

Change in the Maximum Duration of Zero Flow (compared to 1941–1960)

Data source: U.S. Geological Survey. Coverage: lower 48 states. Technical details: A zero-flow period is defined as a period of one or more days without flow. Data for each year are based on a 5-year rolling average. "Substantially longer" means the zero-flow period is more than 14 days longer; "substantially shorter" means the zero-flow period is more than 14 days shorter.

Why Are the Number and Duration of Dry Periods in Rivers and Streams Important?

Changes in stream flow can affect plants and animals accustomed to particular levels of flow. Zero-flow periods may lead to a loss of fish and aquatic animals (although some will survive short periods of zero flow in pools). Depending on the length of the zero-flow period, streamside vegetation and the wildlife habitat it provides may gradually be lost. In other cases, the absence of a zero-flow period (as in regulated flow below a dam) may also affect the animals and plants living in and around streams and rivers.

What Does This Indicator Report?

- The percentage of grassland–shrubland streams and rivers that have had a zero-flow period (at least one day of zero-flow) in a given year
- For streams with zero flow, the percentage that had a substantial change in the duration of the longest zero-flow period in a year (averaged over a rolling 5-year period), compared to a 1941–1960 baseline period

What Do The Data Show?

- Between 2002 and 2006, 19% of grassland and shrubland streams had zero-flow periods.
- Since 1963, the percentage of streams with zero-flow periods has decreased in all grassland and shrubland ecoregions except the Desert/Shrub ecoregion (see map, p. 268).
- The California/Mediterranean ecoregion has had a consistently higher percentage of streams with zero flow than Desert/Shrub or Grassland/Steppe ecoregions, although the difference between ecoregions was less pronounced during the early 1980s.
- Since the mid-1960s, more streams have had zero-flow periods that were substantially shorter than the 1941–1960 baseline than have had zero-flow periods that were substantially longer than the baseline.
- Since 1963, the percentage of streams with substantially shorter zero-flow periods has increased.

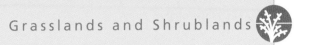

Number and Duration of Dry Periods in Grassland and Shrubland Streams and Rivers *(continued)*

Understanding the Data Stream flow is the lifeblood for a large number of ecologically important plant and animal species, as well as a major source of water for agricultural, municipal, and other uses. Some zero-flow periods occur naturally. Others occur because of increased water use for domestic, irrigation, or other purposes. Still others occur because of changes in land use, such as for animal grazing or development, or because of a change in vegetation that modifies the flow of surface water and the recharge of groundwater, such as the expansion of deep-rooted vegetation like pinyon–juniper that can draw down surface aquifers. Zero-flow periods may also be due to changing weather patterns or longer-term changes in regional climate, such as the longer periods of drought in the mid-1970s, while return of year-round flows may coincide with wet periods, such as the early 1980s. See Change in Stream Flows (p. 47).

The technical note for this indicator is on page 328.

EXTENT AND PATTERN	CHEMICAL AND PHYSICAL	BIOLOGICAL COMPONENTS	GOODS AND SERVICES
Extent	Nutrients, Carbon, and Oxygen	Plants and Animals	Food, Fiber, and Water
Pattern	Chemical Contamination	Communities	Recreation and Other Services
	Physical	Ecological Productivity	

Depth to Shallow Groundwater

Depth to Shallow Groundwater

Data Gap

Data are not adequate for national reporting on the depth to shallow groundwater.

Why Is the Depth to Shallow Groundwater Important? When shallow groundwater levels drop, wetland and streamside (or riparian) plant communities can experience dry conditions, springs and streams can dry up, and lake levels can drop. In many arid regions, such as grasslands and shrublands, shallow groundwater reserves are used to support agriculture and livestock. Changes in the depth to shallow groundwater can affect the access of ranchers and residents to this important freshwater resource.

What Will This Indicator Report? The percentage of grassland and shrubland areas where the depth to shallow groundwater aquifers falls within several ranges (less than 5 feet, 5 to 10 feet, 10 to 20 feet and more than 20 feet).

Why Can't This Indicator Be Reported at This Time? The depth to deep local or regional aquifers, which can be hundreds of feet below the surface, is often measured in monitoring and withdrawal wells across the country (see Groundwater Levels, p. 189). In contrast, there are limited data on shallow aquifers. A few states have mapped shallow aquifer levels, but these data have not been integrated at the national level.

Integration of data on shallow groundwater from different studies, complemented by expanded monitoring, is needed to support reporting for this indicator. Because shallow groundwater depth is particularly important for the maintenance of riparian and wetland communities, measuring shallow groundwater depth along rivers and streams should be a higher priority than measuring it in other areas.

Discussion Shallow groundwater aquifers are generally the primary water source for springs, seeps, wetlands, potholes, and riparian areas, all of which provide habitat for specialized microbes, plants, and animals. Shallow groundwater aquifers can be recharged directly from streams and rivers or from the percolation of rainwater or melted snow through soil. Recharge is reduced when the ground is compacted and less water can percolate through the soil. Recharge can also be reduced when streams are channelized, stream systems downcut (when the river bed drops in elevation), or streams are covered completely (by development, for example). Groundwater pumping can cause aquifer levels to drop, as can expansion of deep-rooted vegetation, such as pinyon–juniper and western juniper woodlands. Changes in climate and precipitation regimes can also affect flows to streams, wetlands, and springs.

See Groundwater Levels (p. 189) for information on deeper regional aquifers.

The technical note for this indicator is on page 329.

EXTENT AND PATTERN	CHEMICAL AND PHYSICAL	BIOLOGICAL COMPONENTS	GOODS AND SERVICES
Extent	Nutrients, Carbon, and Oxygen	Plants and Animals	Food, Fiber, and Water
Pattern	Chemical Contamination	Communities	Recreation and Other Services
	Physical	Ecological Productivity	

At-Risk Native Grassland and Shrubland Species

Why Are Native Grassland and Shrubland Species Important? Species are valued for a variety of reasons: they provide valuable products, including food, fiber, and genetic materials, which may have various medicinal, industrial, and agricultural uses. Native species are key elements of ecosystems, which themselves provide valuable goods and services, and many people value native species for their intrinsic worth.

What Does This Indicator Report?
- The relative risk of extinction of native grassland and shrubland species (plants and animals that live in these habitats during at least part of their life cycle and depend on them for survival), presented as four categories; vulnerable, imperiled, critically imperiled, and extinct (see definitions)
- The percentage of native grassland and shrubland species that are at risk in each state
- Population trends of at-risk native grassland and shrubland species (declining, stable, increasing)

What Do the Data Show?
- Eighteen percent of native grassland and shrubland animals are considered at risk. This group includes 3.5% that are critically imperiled, 6% that are imperiled, 8% that are vulnerable, and just under 1% that may already be extinct.
- Hawaii has a much higher percentage of at-risk native grassland and shrubland species than any other state (37%).
- A similar percentage of at-risk native vertebrate grassland and shrubland animals have declining populations (31%) and stable populations (29%); 3% have increasing populations. Population trend data are unknown for many at-risk native vertebrate grassland and shrubland animals (37%).

Why Can't This Entire Indicator Be Reported? This indicator reports on 1900 species of mammals, birds, reptiles, amphibians, grasshoppers, and butterflies and skippers. Data on other groups have not been included either because too little is known to assign to risk categories or, as with most plants, because determinations of which species are associated with forests, grasslands, or other habitats have not been completed. Population trend data are known for too few at-risk native invertebrate grassland and shrubland animal species (11%) to report on the group as a whole.

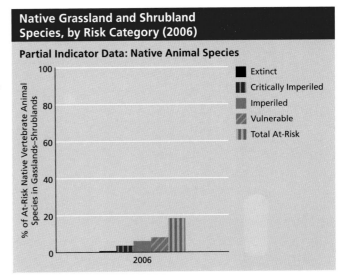

Native Grassland and Shrubland Species, by Risk Category (2006)

Partial Indicator Data: Native Animal Species

% of At-Risk Native Vertebrate Animal Species in Gasslands-Shrublands

Legend:
- Extinct
- Critically Imperiled
- Imperiled
- Vulnerable
- Total At-Risk

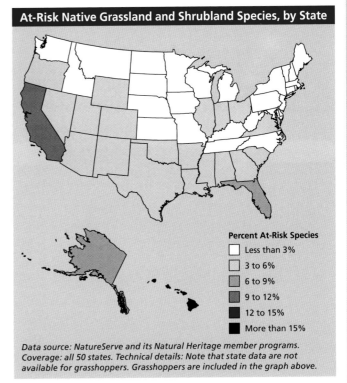

At-Risk Native Grassland and Shrubland Species, by State

Percent At-Risk Species
- Less than 3%
- 3 to 6%
- 6 to 9%
- 9 to 12%
- 12 to 15%
- More than 15%

Data source: NatureServe and its Natural Heritage member programs. Coverage: all 50 states. Technical details: Note that state data are not available for grasshoppers. Grasshoppers are included in the graph above.

Continued

Grasslands and Shrublands

EXTENT AND PATTERN	CHEMICAL AND PHYSICAL	BIOLOGICAL COMPONENTS	GOODS AND SERVICES
Extent	Nutrients, Carbon, and Oxygen	Plants and Animals	Food, Fiber, and Water
Pattern	Chemical Contamination	Communities	Recreation and Other Services
	Physical	Ecological Productivity	

At-Risk Native Grassland and Shrubland Species *(continued)*

Population Trends in At-Risk Native Grassland–Shrubland Species

Partial Indicator Data: At-Risk Native Vertebrate Animal Species

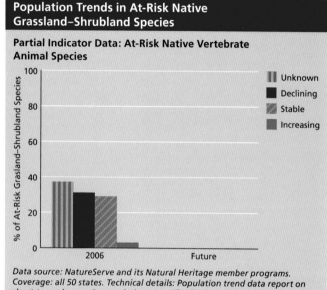

Data source: NatureServe and its Natural Heritage member programs. Coverage: all 50 states. Technical details: Population trend data report on short-term changes in populations, specifically changes within 10 years or 3 generations, whichever is longer, with a maximum of 100 years.

Data Gap

Data are not adequate for national reporting on the percentage of at-risk native grassland and shrubland plants. Data are not adequate for national reporting on population trends in at-risk native invertebrate animals and plants in grasslands and shrublands.

Some Definitions

- **"Critically imperiled"** species often are found in five or fewer places, may have experienced very steep declines, or show other evidence of very high risk.
- **"Imperiled"** species often are found in 20 or fewer places, may have experienced steep declines, or display other risk factors.
- **"Vulnerable"** species often are found in fewer than 80 places, may have recently experienced widespread decline, or show other signs of moderate risk.
- The remaining plant and animal species are regarded as **"secure"** or **"apparently secure."**

While status data were reported for this indicator in the 2002 edition of this report, changes in rank status can occur for a variety of reasons, including changes in the actual status of species, improved knowledge of the species condition, or changes in taxonomy. Consequently, 2002 status data are not presented here (see discussion in the program descriptions for NatureServe data, p. 275).

Understanding the Data Interpreting these figures is complicated because some species are naturally rare. Thus, the rankings are influenced by differences in the number of naturally rare species among regions and species groups as well as by different types and levels of human activities that can cause species declines. Data on population trends complement the risk category data by showing how species of most conservation concern are faring over time. The ability to track changes in the condition of species over time will be further enhanced when it is possible to report on the population trends of more species.

See also At-Risk Native Species (p. 50) and the coastal (p. 80), forest (p. 144), and freshwater (p. 180) native species indicators, as well as the indicators for species in farmland (p. 116) and urban–suburban landscapes (p. 246).

The technical note for this indicator is on page 329.

EXTENT AND PATTERN	CHEMICAL AND PHYSICAL	BIOLOGICAL COMPONENTS	GOODS AND SERVICES
Extent	Nutrients, Carbon, and Oxygen	Plants and Animals	Food, Fiber, and Water
Pattern	Chemical Contamination	Communities	Recreation and Other Services
	Physical	Ecological Productivity	

Established Non-native Grassland and Shrubland Plant Cover

Why Is the Area Covered by Non-native Plants on Grasslands and Shrublands Important? Plants that are not native to an area may be highly invasive, crowding out native plants, making areas more susceptible to

> **Established Non-native Grassland and Shrubland Plant Cover**
>
> **Data Gap**
>
> **Data are not adequate for national reporting on the proportion of established non-native plant cover on grasslands and shrublands.**

catastrophic fire, and radically changing the way an ecosystem functions. On the other hand, some non-natives help stabilize eroding soils, serve as part of a grazing system, and act as a barrier to fire. Non-native species such as crested wheatgrass have been intentionally seeded for these purposes in the past. Overuse of non-native species for these purposes may reduce natural ecosystem function.

What Will This Indicator Report? The amount of grassland and shrubland area with various proportions of plant cover for established non-native species relative to total plant cover. Established non-native species are those that are known to be surviving and reproducing.

Why Can't This Indicator Be Reported at This Time? Data are not currently available to report on this indicator. Although the challenges presented by rapidly spreading non-native grasses and other herbaceous plants, such as cheatgrass and smooth brome, are important management issues for grasslands and shrublands in the United States, national data on percentage cover are not currently available (see technical note for Established Non-native Plant Cover in Forests, p. 146). As non-native plants cover more of the landscape, they make it increasingly difficult to manage native grassland–shrubland resources and to conserve natural ecosystems and associated ecosystem services.

The monitoring conducted by the Illinois Natural History Survey (INHS-CTAP) provides an example, at the state level, of trends in percentage cover by non-native plants. No comparable data exist for the nation as a whole.

Discussion Some of the most troublesome non-native plants in grassland and shrubland ecosystems—such as cheatgrass—are much more likely than native plants to increase fire frequency. Exacerbating the problem, cheatgrass easily colonizes recently burned land, further increasing an area's flammability. Both cheatgrass and the common Mediterranean grass now dominate the Mojave Desert area—these grasses, along with a growing human population, are being blamed for an increase in fires. Some non-native plant species are categorized as "noxious weeds" (onionweed, for example); these species are recognized by the federal government as a significant threat to the health and value of U.S. agricultural, aquatic, or other natural resources.

Anecdotal information suggests that nearly all grassland and shrubland areas in the western United States have non-native species, such as the yellow star thistle, European wild oats, tamarisk, African lovegrass, purple loosestrife, and Russian olive. As non-native plants cover more of the landscape, they make it increasingly difficult to manage native grassland–shrubland resources and to conserve natural ecosystems and associated ecosystem services.

See also the national indicator on Established Non-native Species (p. 52) and the indicators on non-native plant cover in farmlands (p. 117) and forests (p. 146).

There is no technical note for this indicator.

EXTENT AND PATTERN	CHEMICAL AND PHYSICAL	BIOLOGICAL COMPONENTS	GOODS AND SERVICES
Extent	Nutrients, Carbon, and Oxygen	Plants and Animals	Food, Fiber, and Water
Pattern	Chemical Contamination	Communities	Recreation and Other Services
	Physical	Ecological Productivity	

Population Trends in Invasive and Non-invasive Birds

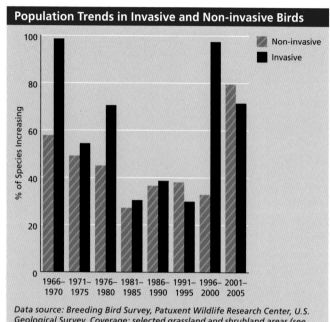

Population Trends in Invasive and Non-invasive Birds

% of Species Increasing

Non-invasive
Invasive

1966–1970, 1971–1975, 1976–1980, 1981–1985, 1986–1990, 1991–1995, 1996–2000, 2001–2005

Data source: Breeding Bird Survey, Patuxent Wildlife Research Center, U.S. Geological Survey. Coverage: selected grassland and shrubland areas (see the technical note). Technical details: A new method of determining the percentage of increasing species was applied to all years of data since the 2002 edition of this report; see technical note.

Why Is It Important to Compare Population Trends in Invasive and Non-invasive Birds? Birds respond quickly to environmental change. Because they are highly mobile (they can fly to a new location), birds may simply leave grassland and shrubland areas that no longer meet their habitat needs. When non-invasive bird populations, which are native to an area, increase while populations of invasive birds decrease, or vice versa, this may be indicative of ecosystem changes that have implications for the stability of other plant and animal populations living there, as well as for the provision of ecosystem services.

What Does This Indicator Report? A comparison between the percentage of selected invasive and non-invasive bird species with increasing populations in grassland and shrubland ecosystems. Because some native species can be invasive, only those that are considered to be non-invasive are included (see definition).

What Do the Data Show?

• About 70% of invasive and 80% of non-invasive bird species had increasing populations for the most recent period (2001–2005).

• Since 1966–1970, there has been no clear upward or downward trend in the percentage of invasive or non-invasive bird species that have increasing populations.

Understanding the Data This indicator focuses on increasing populations and does not present information about decreasing or stable populations, or changes within individual species. Therefore, while the data do not reveal a clear trend in increasing bird populations, there may be other changes occurring that are not captured by this indicator. Of course, many factors can cause short-term fluctuations in bird populations, but comparing these species groups across 5-year intervals may reveal information about changing ecosystem conditions.

The invasive species reported here are believed to be most abundant in areas that have experienced conversion to agriculture, habitat fragmentation due to suburban and rural development, and the spread of exotic vegetation (see Established Non-native Plant Cover, p. 213). Non-invasive bird species, which are native to an area, generally require relatively intact native grasslands and shrublands that have not been fragmented or overrun by non-native plants.

Population Trends in Invasive and Non-invasive Birds *(continued)*

Fluctuation is normal among bird populations. Because this indicator reports on combined categories rather than individual species, it may appear that there is no overall change in the total bird population, even though changes in species abundance are occurring. Populations of invasive birds that consistently increase compared to non-invasive birds would be interpreted as a sign that conditions favoring invasives—agricultural conversion, landscape fragmentation due to suburban and rural development, and the spread of exotic vegetation—are increasing. A higher percentage of non-invasive birds with increasing populations could indicate that conditions have not changed, that these birds are adapting to changing conditions, or that habitat areas have been restored to a condition more favorable for these birds.

The technical note for this indicator is on page 330.

> **Definition**
>
> Invasive species spread aggressively and can disrupt established native bird populations. While many invasive species are non-natives, they can also be native species that, because of a change in conditions, are able to spread aggressively.

Grasslands and Shrublands

EXTENT AND PATTERN	CHEMICAL AND PHYSICAL	BIOLOGICAL COMPONENTS	GOODS AND SERVICES
Extent	Nutrients, Carbon, and Oxygen	Plants and Animals	Food, Fiber, and Water
Pattern	Chemical Contamination	**Communities**	Recreation and Other Services
	Physical	Ecological Productivity	

Fire Frequency

Fire Frequency

Indicator Development Needed

Why Is Fire Frequency Important?
Fire is a major factor in the creation and maintenance of grassland and shrubland ecosystems. Periodic fire helps determine the makeup of grasslands and shrublands by allowing certain "fire-adapted" species to thrive, while removing other, less fire-tolerant, plants.

What Will This Indicator Report? The ultimate goal will be to document how current fire frequencies compare to historic estimates to gain an understanding of whether grasslands and shrublands burn as frequently and as intensely as they did before the advent of substantial human influence. This is an extremely complex topic, and further work is needed to define this indicator (and forest Fire Frequency, p. 151). For example, it is not enough to know simply the time between fires, because fires can vary in intensity, in seasonality, and in the amount of land that they cover, all of which have important ecological consequences. Furthermore, relatively small differences in topography between two sites can lead to very different fire susceptibilities—both currently and historically. For all these reasons, the developed index will likely need to be evaluated over areas sufficiently small to be able to capture local variability adequately.

Why Can't This Indicator Be Reported at This Time? To evaluate current fire frequencies, it will be necessary to estimate how frequently fires occurred historically and how intense these fires were—properties that define an area's "characteristic fire regime." It is perhaps even more challenging to estimate historic fire regimes for grasslands and shrublands than for forests because the vegetation is sparse and compiling a historical record based on physical evidence such as tree ring scars is sometimes impossible. Therefore, a better approach may be to link historic vegetation types to particular fire regimes. This is complicated by the fact that characteristic fire regimes can vary considerably geographically, with historical averages ranging from every 2 years in eastern grasslands to about every 80 years in Intermountain shrub areas. A further complication is that gradual changes in climate can lead to unrealistic estimates of characteristic fire regimes; these estimates need to be adjusted to reflect how changes in climate would have influenced the frequency and intensity of fires. The interagency LANDFIRE program will establish a national database of parameters relevant to this indicator.

It should be more straightforward to estimate how frequently fires are experienced now, although this is also not without complications. For example, documenting a fire regime with fires occurring every 50 or 100 years will require a substantial contemporary database that does not currently exist. A useful starting point will be to estimate how recently an area has been burned, which will be part of the interagency Monitoring Trends in Burn Severity (MTBS) program.

Further, we actively suppress or have otherwise deliberately altered natural fire cycles, and it would seem appropriate to design an indicator that distinguishes areas with active fire management from those lacking such management.

Discussion Since the last Ice Age (about 10,000 years ago), most grasslands and shrublands in the lower 48 states have burned regularly, with fires started by lightning or by American Indians for agricultural and other reasons. Active fire suppression or suppression due to the reduction in available fuel resulting from heavy grazing can increase tree and shrub density, decrease the extent of certain "soil-forming" grasses, and enhance the spread of species formerly controlled by fire. For example, a decrease in fire frequency in some sites in the Great Basin is resulting in conversion from mountain big sagebrush and Idaho fescue to western juniper and pinyon–juniper. In addition, some non-native species, such as cheatgrass, increase the frequency and intensity of fires (see Established Non-native Grassland and Shrubland Plant Cover, p. 213). Since native plants and animals did not evolve under these conditions, these new fire regimes can give non-native species an additional advantage.

The technical note for this indicator is on page 311 (forest Fire Frequency).

EXTENT AND PATTERN	CHEMICAL AND PHYSICAL	BIOLOGICAL COMPONENTS	GOODS AND SERVICES
Extent	Nutrients, Carbon, and Oxygen	Plants and Animals	Food, Fiber, and Water
Pattern	Chemical Contamination	**Communities**	Recreation and Other Services
	Physical	Ecological Productivity	

Riparian Condition

Why Is Riparian Condition Important? Riparian areas, the vegetated areas along streams and rivers, provide habitat for a variety of wildlife. Riparian areas also provide important services,

Riparian Condition

Indicator Development Needed

such as trapping sediment, modifying stream flows, and increasing groundwater recharge. Changes in riparian condition can enhance or degrade these functions.

What Will This Indicator Report? This indicator will describe the condition of riparian areas. Condition will be rated using an index that combines factors such as water flows, streambed physical condition, riparian vegetation composition and structure, and use by riparian species.

Why Can't This Indicator Be Reported at This Time? There is no single and generally accepted measure of riparian condition. In order to provide an overall index of condition, researchers have proposed metrics that take hydrology (e.g., relationship to natural flow patterns), geomorphology (e.g., stream sediment transport), and biology (e.g., canopy cover) into account.

Discussion The condition of riparian areas can indicate changes throughout a watershed. For example, shifts in vegetation or increased suburban development in a watershed can change the amount and timing of stream flows (see Change in Stream Flows, p. 47, and Number and Duration of Dry Periods in Grassland and Shrubland Streams and Rivers, p. 208), which affect both the streambed and the riparian zone. The regulation of water flow by dams, bank stabilization, diversion of water for irrigation and other uses, changes in land use in the watershed (such as increases in agriculture or grazing), and changes in vegetation (including the establishment of non-native species) or fire frequency can also affect riparian condition.

See related riparian condition indicators in the farmlands (p. 115), fresh waters (p. 179), and urban–suburban (p. 233) chapters.

The technical note for this indicator is on page 331.

EXTENT AND PATTERN	CHEMICAL AND PHYSICAL	BIOLOGICAL COMPONENTS	GOODS AND SERVICES
Extent	Nutrients, Carbon, and Oxygen	Plants and Animals	**Food, Fiber, and Water**
Pattern	Chemical Contamination	Communities	Recreation and Other Services
	Physical	Ecological Productivity	

Cattle Grazing

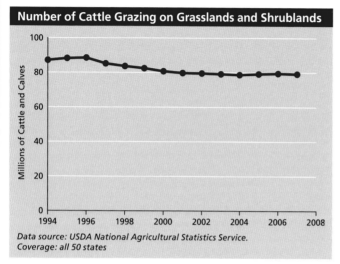

Number of Cattle Grazing on Grasslands and Shrublands

Millions of Cattle and Calves

Data source: USDA National Agricultural Statistics Service.
Coverage: all 50 states

Why Is the Number of Cattle Grazing on Grasslands and Shrublands Important? Cattle grazed on grasslands and shrublands provide agricultural goods and jobs for people working in the livestock industry. Livestock production remains an important part of community identity in many parts of the country. The number of cattle grazed over time is an indicator of both the ability of these ecosystems to support livestock and the demand for livestock production.

What Does This Indicator Report? This indicator reports the number of cattle grazing on grasslands and shrublands (including pastures but not feedlots) during July of each year.

What Do the Data Show?
- In 2007, approximately 80 million cattle grazed on grasslands and shrublands.
- The number of cattle grazing on grasslands and shrublands has declined by 9% since 1994.

Understanding the Data Because many cattle receive feed supplements during the winter months when adequate grazing land is scarce, July inventories of cattle are the most representative of overall grazing on grasslands and shrublands. A recent report estimated that, in 2006, 88% of beef cattle grazed on grasslands and shrublands during the summer months. The remaining animals may have been on feedlots or grazing in forests. In the future, this indicator may track the distribution of cattle on public and private grasslands and shrublands, which can change over time for a variety of economic and policy reasons.

The total number of grazing cattle and calves is subject to seasonal and year-to-year fluctuations. Roughly 10-year fluctuations in cattle inventory have been observed since the 1880s, mainly due to shifts in supply and demand. Cattle numbers based on January inventories (not shown here) suggest that cattle production peaked in 1975 and that national herd size has declined by about one-quarter since then (see technical note).

The grassland and shrubland ecosystem provides two of the most essential resources for livestock production: land (for animal-raising operations and grazing) and forage. Estimates of grazing cattle numbers are reported as an indicator of overall use of grasslands and shrublands for raising livestock. Besides directly affecting the amount of goods and services provided by these lands, changes in the number of grazing cattle may affect other ecosystem indicators, including changes in plant and animal populations, fire frequency, carbon storage, and riparian condition.

The technical note for this indicator is on page 331.

EXTENT AND PATTERN	CHEMICAL AND PHYSICAL	BIOLOGICAL COMPONENTS	GOODS AND SERVICES
Extent	Nutrients, Carbon, and Oxygen	Plants and Animals	Food, Fiber, and Water
Pattern	Chemical Contamination	Communities	**Recreation and Other Services**
	Physical	Ecological Productivity	

Recreation on Grasslands and Shrublands

Why Is Measuring Recreation on Grasslands and Shrublands Important? Grasslands and shrublands provide benefits to society through recreation in much the same way that they support the production of cattle. Not all

> **Recreation on Grasslands and Shrublands**
>
> **Data Gap**
>
> **Data are not adequate for national reporting on participation in recreational activities in grassland and shrubland areas.**

land uses are compatible; monitoring trends in participation in recreational activities can indicate whether certain activities are likely to conflict with others. For example, an increase in off-road vehicle use may suggest fewer opportunities for activities that focus on the enjoyment of solitude.

What Will This Indicator Report? This indicator will report the number of days per year that people engage in a variety of recreational activities on the nation's grasslands and shrublands. Activities will include hunting; off-road vehicle driving, motorsports, mountain biking, and snowmobiling; bird-watching and nature study; and hiking and camping. (Other categories may be added when data become available.)

Why Can't This Indicator Be Reported at This Time? There are no national datasets that document the type and amount of recreation on grasslands and shrublands. The National Survey of Fishing, Hunting, and Wildlife-Associated Recreation (http://wsfrprograms.fws.gov/Subpages/NationalSurvey/National_Survey.htm) and the National Survey on Recreation and the Environment (www.srs.fs.fed.us/trends/nsre.html) both report on national trends in recreation participation, but neither survey identifies whether these activities take place on grasslands or shrublands, or on farmlands.

Adequate reporting would require modification of existing surveys to elicit information on the location of recreational activities (see Recreation in Forests, p. 157; and Freshwater Recreational Activities, p. 191).

Discussion Recreational activities may also affect the ecological condition of grasslands and shrublands. For example, intensive off-road vehicle use may damage sensitive habitat and cause increased soil erosion. Some types of recreational activities can facilitate the spread of invasive species. Still, recreation is an important benefit humans derive from ecosystems, and most types of recreation are not harmful to the natural environment. Recreation can raise funds for natural areas and increase awareness and appreciation for ecosystems.

There is no technical note for this indicator.

Contents

	page

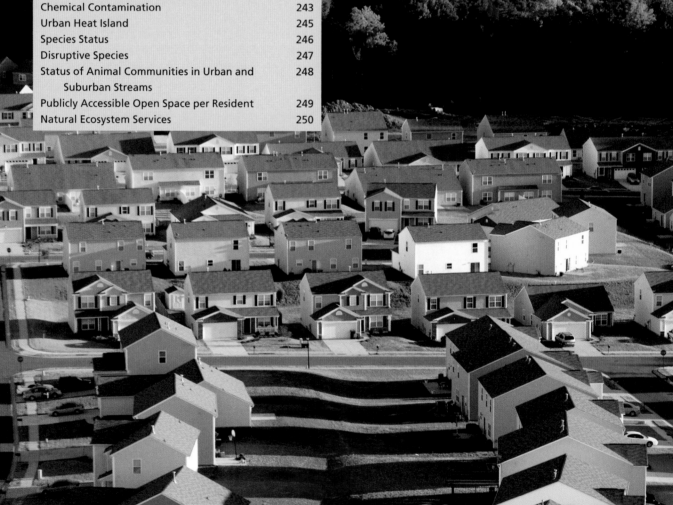

Chapter 8:
Indicators of the Conditions and Use of Urban and Suburban Landscapes

Urban and suburban areas occupy little more than 2% of the national landscape and yet house nearly 80% of the U.S. population. In this report, we define "urban and suburban landscapes" as those areas characterized by development such as major cities, suburbs, and other densely populated areas. People often do not think of these developed areas as ecosystems, but the houses, offices, factories, roads, and sidewalks, as well as the plants and animals that inhabit urban and suburban areas, both influence and are affected by many of the same processes as other ecosystems described in this report.

Cities and suburbs provide not only the infrastructure needed to support a growing U.S. population, but also many of the same goods and services provided by other ecosystems. For example, urban forests, city parks, and open spaces provide opportunities for recreation or quiet contemplation. In addition, trees, lawns, and gardens produce many other benefits, from the cooling shade supplied by trees (and reflected in lower air conditioning bills) to reduced runoff and protection for fish provided by vegetated corridors along urban streams.

Historically, people have preferred to settle near natural resources such as fertile farmland and navigable waterways. Advancements in technology, however, now allow people to settle in areas once considered too inhospitable because of inadequate water or extreme temperatures. Rapid influxes of residents to the "sunbelt," mountain resort communities, and coastal regions have catalyzed construction booms and new demands for public services in these areas, as well as important transformations of the biophysical landscape.

The mix of built and open spaces and the large-scale patterns of suburban expansion or urban infill that characterize our cities and suburbs are consequences of both public and private decisions. Public policies that shape development are defined largely by local and state laws, with little or no national coordination. Government responsibilities are often shared by many independent, and sometimes overlapping, jurisdictions, which has made regionwide management a long-standing challenge. Even acquiring information about the condition of urban and suburban areas is difficult because few state and national programs recognize these areas as distinct for reporting purposes. In some cases, where air or water quality or wildlife habitat has been seriously degraded, federal laws, such as the Clean Air Act, the Clean Water Act, and the Endangered Species Act, may restrict local or regional development.

Public attitudes about both the pace and the nature of development, and the degree to which public policies should constrain private decisions, directly affect the conversion of land and the character of resulting development. Historically, those interested in the ecological aspects of cities and suburbs focused on parks, recreation, wastewater treatment, and air quality concerns. Recently, topics such as how to integrate green infrastructure into planning, concerns over runoff that cannot be tied to a specific source, and development philosophies such as "slow growth" or "smart growth" have been brought into the debate.

The following sections and the table on page 228 describe the four categories of ecosystem condition and use outlined in Chapter 1 and also summarize the most current data and trends for urban and suburban landscapes. Individual indicators focus on the extent and nature of these ecosystems, ecological processes and conditions necessary for the functioning of urban and suburban landscapes, biological communities in urban and suburban areas, and the human benefits derived from urban and suburban ecosystems.

Extent and Pattern

Conversion of land from rural to urban or suburban is generally permanent, and this conversion profoundly changes the nature of the benefits and services the land provides. Not all cities and suburbs are the same, however, and differences in how development takes place can affect the quality of life for residents and workers as well as the quality of the habitat for plants and animals and the ecological services the land can provide. Key differences that shape these impacts include not only the total amount of land developed, but also the nature of that development.

The way in which developed and undeveloped land is intermingled in a landscape is a crucial characteristic at several scales. For any area that is developed, the proportion of land covered by impervious surfaces—roads, parking lots, driveways, sidewalks, rooftops, and the like—and the amount of vegetation remaining along stream banks greatly influence the ecological effects of development. For example, rainfall runs off nonporous surfaces quickly, reducing groundwater recharge, increasing flooding, and causing significant changes to stream habitat. Where streamside vegetation is abundant, it reduces the effects of runoff, serves as wildlife habitat, and keeps streams cool—an important service to fish and other stream life.

At a larger scale, the degree to which new development is located in densely developed areas or in sparsely settled areas, and the overall amount, size, and shape of remaining undeveloped lands, can affect quality of life for residents and have important ecological consequences as well. These issues often arise in contentious debates over where and how development should occur and revolve around factors such as the cost of providing water, sewer, schools, and transportation services to new homes in relatively rural areas; the effects on local wildlife habitat and open space; and the desire of many people to live in suburban or rural settings.

Data in this chapter show that

- In 2001, urban and suburban landscapes covered about 45 million acres (2% of the land area) in the lower 48 states.

- Undeveloped lands such as forests and grasslands within urban and suburban landscapes range from 9% of the urban and suburban landscape in the Midwest to 15% in the Rocky Mountain region.

- In 2001, nearly 60% of urban and suburban landscapes in the nation had more than 30% impervious surface cover, a level at which adverse impacts on stream ecosystems have been observed. Only 3% of urban and suburban landscapes had less than 10% impervious surface cover, a level at which the potential for impacts to streams is reduced.

- Between 1990 and 2000, about 3 million housing units were built in sparsely settled suburban and rural areas with preexisting housing densities of 1–10 acres per unit; about 1.4 million housing units were built in areas with preexisting densities of 10–160 acres per unit; and 45,000 housing units were built in areas with preexisting densities of 160 acres or more per unit.

- Ninety percent of "natural" patches (forest, grassland, wetlands, and the like) in urban–suburban landscapes of the lower 48 states are less than 100 acres, including virtually all remaining "natural" land patches in the Northeast/Mid-Atlantic, Southeast, and Midwest regions. Only 2% of "natural" lands exist in patches larger than 1000 acres, with the largest proportion in the Rocky Mountain region (2001 data).

Further indicator development is needed to report on

- Urban and suburban stream bank vegetation

Chemical and Physical Characteristics

The complex mix of residential, commercial, and industrial activities in cities and suburbs has important effects on the quality of indoor and outdoor air, soil and water, human health, and local, regional, and global climate patterns. These effects are reported here in three principal indicators—the quantities of nitrogen and phosphorus released in streams; the amount of harmful or potentially harmful compounds in air, water, and soil; and the difference between the temperatures in urban areas and those in nearby rural areas. Nitrogen and phosphorus are released into freshwater ecosystems by a wide range of urban and suburban sources, including sewage treatment plants, domestic animal wastes, and lawn fertilizers. Control of nutrient releases by reducing runoff (often called "non-point-source" pollution) or by increasing the efficiency of wastewater treatment is often complex and costly. Contamination of air, water, and soil are not unique to cities and suburbs, but the concentration of people and activities often means increased

concentration of contaminants and nutrients as well. Addressing these conditions is not only costly and difficult but can also raise questions of regional or national jurisdiction (as with regional ozone transport) and issues of accountability for past practices (cleanup liability for "brownfields" sites, for example). The warmer local temperatures generated by large expanses of asphalt, concrete, and other constructed materials can threaten human health, stress plants and animals, and increase energy use. This "urban heat island" effect can be countered by a variety of techniques ("green roofs" and use of certain construction materials, for example); however, such changes can be expensive, and new solutions take time to develop and implement.

Data in this chapter show that

- Sixty-one percent of the stream sites in areas dominated by cities and suburbs had concentrations of nitrate below 1 part per million (ppm), 32% had concentrations below 0.5 ppm, and 2% had concentrations of less than 0.1 ppm. (The federal drinking water standard for nitrate is 10 ppm.)
- Nitrate concentrations in streams in urban and suburban areas are lower than those in agricultural areas but higher than in forested watersheds.
- Sixty-eight percent of stream sites in urban and suburban areas had concentrations of phosphorus that were at least 0.1 ppm, and 23% of urban streams sites had concentrations of at least 0.5 ppm. (The EPA recommends 0.1 ppm as a goal for preventing excess algal growth in streams.)
- Streams in urban and suburban areas had average phosphorus concentrations similar to streams draining farmland watersheds and higher average concentrations than streams draining forested watersheds.

- In 2005, high ozone levels were recorded at 61% of urban and suburban monitoring stations on at least one day; 30% had high levels on 4 or more days during the year.
- From 1990 to 2005, the percentage of monitors recording high ozone levels 25 or more days per year declined to about 1%. The four monitors that still record high levels are in Southern and Central California.
- Eighty-three percent of streams in urban and suburban areas had contaminants at levels exceeding guidelines for the protection of aquatic life; about 7% had contaminant levels exceeding benchmarks for the protection of human health (1992–2001 data).

Data are not adequate for national reporting on

- The detection of toxic air contaminants and how often they exceed benchmarks for human health
- Chemical contamination in soils in urban and suburban areas and benchmark exceedances for some contaminants in streams that lack established benchmarks

Further indicator development is needed to report on

- The urban heat island effect: the degree to which temperatures in urban and suburban areas exceed those in less developed areas nearby

Biological Components

Species differ in their response to urban and suburban development, and cities and suburbs differ in their capacity to accommodate those plants and animals that were common in the area before cities arose. How thoroughly an area is developed, and whether habitat areas and corridors for wildlife are maintained (as indicated by indicators of extent and pattern, above) influence whether some species decline, disappear, or dominate the local area.

Urban and suburban development produces biological winners and losers. Plant and animal species and communities differ in how well they tolerate development, and the impact of cities and suburbs depends on their configuration and makeup (see indicators of extent and pattern, above). Conversion of rural land to urban or suburban development often spurs population declines or local extinctions of native plants and animals. In streams neighboring development, pollution can bring observable changes in aquatic communities, including both fish and smaller bottom-dwelling animals that are key to freshwater food webs.

Conversely, some species, such as deer, pigeons, and raccoons, may thrive in the altered habitat of cities and suburbs, sometimes causing problems for people, property, or other wildlife. For example, deer are so numerous in some suburban areas that damage to gardens, car–deer collisions, and increased incidence of Lyme disease have become serious political, safety, and health issues. Non-native species such as Scotch broom can also become invasive in urban and suburban areas and can cause problems such as clogging of drainage ditches.

Data are not adequate for national reporting on

- The degree to which "original" plants and animals—those that once inhabited areas that are now urbanized—are now locally absent or at risk of being lost
- The number and type of "disruptive species" such as white-tailed deer and Scotch broom in metropolitan areas
- The condition of fish and bottom-dwelling communities in urban and suburban streams

Goods and Services

Cities and suburbs are designed primarily as places for commerce and residence. However, people also benefit from the natural and semi-natural lands and waterways that remain. Open space—land that is dominated by "natural" surfaces such as grasslands or woodlands, along with lakes, rivers, beaches, and wetlands—is valued by many urban dwellers for recreation and general "quality of life." This "green infrastructure" of urban and suburban areas also provides tangible and intangible benefits such as reduced storm water runoff, cooler streets and buildings, and lower urban noise levels. Provision of adequate open space for public use—a common planning goal—is challenging in situations where land values are high, a factor that usually characterizes growth areas. The wide variety of valuable services provided by undeveloped lands in urban and suburban areas is often not recognized until these lands have been developed, functioning ecosystems have been altered, quality of life has been degraded, and perhaps millions or even billions of dollars are required to replace lost ecological services through technology.

Data are not adequate for national reporting on
- The amount of accessible public open space available per metropolitan resident

Further indicator development is needed to report on
- Natural ecosystem services provided by urban and suburban areas

Status and trends of all urban and suburban indicators are summarized in the following table and described in detail in the remainder of the chapter. Regions and related definitions used throughout this chapter are described in Appendix D.

Indicators	What Do the Most Recent Data Show?	Have Data Values Changed over Time?
EXTENT AND PATTERN		
Area and Composition of the Urban and Suburban Landscape, p. 230	Urban and suburban landscapes cover about 2% of the land area of the lower 48 states, or 45 million acres (2001 data).	Data are not adequate for national reporting on changes in the area and composition of urban and suburban landscapes (see p. 30).
Total Impervious Area, p. 232	In 2001, nearly 60% of urban–suburban landscapes nationally had greater than 30% impervious surface cover. Only 3% of urban and suburban landscapes had less than 10% impervious surface cover.	Data are not adequate for national reporting on changes in the percent impervious area in the urban and suburban landscape.
Stream Bank Vegetation, p. 233	Indicator Development Needed	
Housing Density Changes in Low-Density Suburban and Rural Areas, p. 234	Between 1990 and 2000, about 3 million housing units were built in areas with preexisting housing densities of 1–10 acres per unit; about 1.4 million houses were built in areas with preexisting densities of 10–160 acres per unit; 45 thousand houses were built in areas with preexisting densities of more than 160 acres per unit.	Data are not adequate for national reporting on changes in the number of housing units built in various density categories.
"Natural" Lands in the Urban and Suburban Landscape, p. 236	Ninety percent of "natural" patches in the urban and suburban landscape are less than 100 acres; about 2% of "natural" patches are in patches larger than 1000 acres (2001 data).	Data are not adequate for national reporting on changes in the area of "natural" patches.
CHEMICAL AND PHYSICAL CHARACTERISTICS		
Nitrate in Urban and Suburban Streams, p. 238	Sixty-one percent of urban and suburban stream sites have nitrate concentrations below 1 part per million (ppm); 32% had concentrations below 0.5 ppm, and 2% have concentrations of less than 0.1 ppm (1992–2001 data).	Data are not adequate for national reporting on changes in nitrate concentrations in urban and suburban streams.
Phosphorus in Urban and Suburban Streams, p. 240	Sixty-eight percent of sites have phosphorus concentrations of at least 0.1 ppm; 23% of sites have phosphorus concentrations of at least 0.5 ppm (1992–2001 data).	Data are not adequate for national reporting on changes in phosphorus concentrations in urban and suburban streams.
Urban and Suburban Air Quality, p. 241	Sixty-one percent of sites have high ozone levels (above 0.08 ppm) at least once a year; 30% of sites have high ozone levels 4 or more times a year (2005 data).	Between 1990 and 2005, the percentage of sites with high ozone concentrations for at least one day per year and for at least 25 days per year decreased.
	Data are not adequate for national reporting on the detection of toxic contaminants and how often they exceed benchmarks for human health.	
Chemical Contamination, p. 243	Eighty-three percent of streams have contaminants at levels exceeding guidelines for the protection of aquatic life; about 7% have contaminant levels exceeding benchmarks for the protection of human health (1992–2001 data).	Data are not adequate for national reporting on changes in contaminants in urban and suburban streams.
	Data are not adequate for national reporting on contaminants in urban and suburban soils. Benchmarks for the protection of aquatic life and human health have not been established for some monitored contaminants	
Urban Heat Island, p. 245	Indicator Development Needed	

Indicators	What Do the Most Recent Data Show?	Have Data Values Changed over Time?

BIOLOGICAL COMPONENTS

Species Status, p. 246	Data are not adequate for national reporting on the degree to which "original" plant and animal species are absent or at risk of being lost.	
Disruptive Species, p. 247	Data are not adequate for national reporting on the number and type of disruptive species found in metropolitan areas.	
Status of Animal Communities in Urban and Suburban Streams, p. 248	Data are not adequate for national reporting on the condition of fish and bottom-dwelling communities in urban and suburban streams.	

GOODS AND SERVICES

Publicly Accessible Open Space per Resident, p. 249	Data are not adequate for national reporting on the amount of open space accessible to the public in metropolitan areas.	
Natural Ecosystem Services, p. 250	Indicator Development Needed	

 = significant decrease   =significant increase   = no clear trend*   = insufficient data for trend analysis

▨ = Data not available for adequate reporting.

* may be due to little numerical change in the data or large numerical fluctuations in data resulting in no single trend

EXTENT AND PATTERN	CHEMICAL AND PHYSICAL	BIOLOGICAL COMPONENTS	GOODS AND SERVICES
Extent	Nutrients, Carbon, and Oxygen	Plants and Animals	Food, Fiber, and Water
Pattern	Chemical Contamination	Communities	Recreation and Other Services
	Physical	Ecological Productivity	

Area and Composition of the Urban and Suburban Landscape

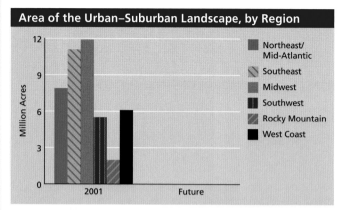

Area of the Urban–Suburban Landscape, by Region

Legend: Northeast/Mid-Atlantic, Southeast, Midwest, Southwest, Rocky Mountain, West Coast

y-axis: Million Acres
x-axis: 2001, Future

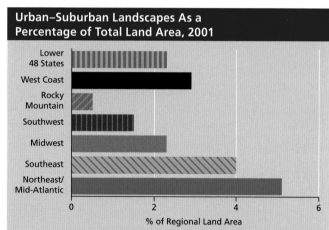

Urban–Suburban Landscapes As a Percentage of Total Land Area, 2001

Regions (top to bottom): Lower 48 States, West Coast, Rocky Mountain, Southwest, Midwest, Southeast, Northeast/Mid-Atlantic

x-axis: % of Regional Land Area (0, 2, 4, 6)

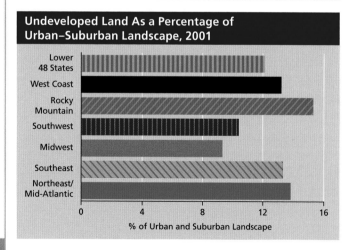

Undeveloped Land As a Percentage of Urban–Suburban Landscape, 2001

Regions (top to bottom): Lower 48 States, West Coast, Rocky Mountain, Southwest, Midwest, Southeast, Northeast/Mid-Atlantic

x-axis: % of Urban and Suburban Landscape (0, 4, 8, 12, 16)

Why Is the Area and Composition of the Urban and Suburban Landscape Important? Nearly 80% of Americans live on land that is urban or suburban in character ("urban and suburban landscape"). The various land cover types in these landscapes provide a coarse view of the intensity of development, which is related to the amount and type of open space available to a region's residents [see Publicly Accessible Open Space per Resident (p. 249), Total Impervious Area (p. 232), and the services provided by "natural" systems in urban and suburban areas (see Natural Ecosystem Services, p. 250)].

What Does This Indicator Report?
- The area of the urban and suburban landscape, both in acres and as a percentage of all land area
- The percentage of the urban and suburban landscape in a region that is undeveloped land
- The composition of undeveloped lands within the urban and suburban landscape, by region

What Do the Data Show?
- In 2001, urban and suburban landscapes covered about 45 million acres in the lower 48 states (2% of the land area of the lower 48 states).
- Most urban and suburban land is in the Southeast and Midwest; the Rocky Mountain region had the least urban and suburban land.
- Urban and suburban areas cover 0.5–5% of the landscape, with the Northeast/Mid-Atlantic region having the greatest percentage of urban and suburban cover and the Rocky Mountain region having the lowest percentage of urban and suburban cover.

Area and Composition of the Urban and Suburban Landscape *(continued)*

- Undeveloped lands covered from 9% of the urban and suburban landscape in the Midwest to 15% in the Rocky Mountain region. Within these undeveloped lands

  ○ Forests made up the largest fraction of undeveloped lands in the Northeast/Mid-Atlantic, Southeast, and Midwest.

  ○ In the Southwest, grasslands and shrublands made up the largest fraction of undeveloped urban and suburban land.

  ○ The Rocky Mountains and the West Coast had a higher percentage of barren land cover in the undeveloped portions of the urban and suburban landscape than other regions.

Understanding the Data This report defines urban and suburban landscapes based on land cover data (see definition). Of the nearly 60 million acres of developed land cover across the lower 48 states, about two-thirds is found within urban and suburban landscapes, as reported in this indicator. The urban–suburban landscape includes areas of substantial development (cities, suburbs, and outlying areas), as well as intermingled undeveloped lands that may be covered by croplands, forests, or other natural land covers. Increases in all development are generally permanent and may affect the use and character of surrounding lands (see Housing Density Changes in Low-Density Suburban and Rural Areas, p. 234). Undeveloped lands in the urban and suburban landscape can provide a range of recreational and other benefits to residents in these areas (see Publicly Accessible Open Space per Resident, p. 249).

The technical note for this indicator is on page 332.

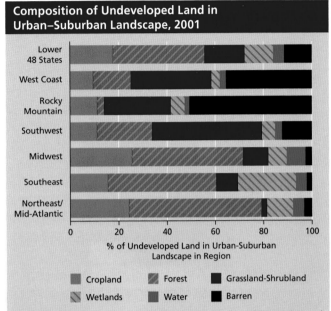

Composition of Undeveloped Land in Urban–Suburban Landscape, 2001

% of Undeveloped Land in Urban-Suburban Landscape in Region

Legend: Cropland, Forest, Grassland-Shrubland, Wetlands, Water, Barren

Data source: Multi-Resolution Land Characterization (MRLC) Consortium and ESRI (road map); analysis by the U.S. Environmental Protection Agency and the U.S. Forest Service. Coverage: lower 48 states (see p. 266 for definition of regions). Note: "Barren" includes areas of bedrock, desert pavement, sand dunes, strip mines, and gravel pits.

Definition

Urban and suburban landscapes are defined in this report as land that is surrounded by sufficient amounts of developed land. Satellite imagery is used to create a land cover map that is then broken up into more than 8 billion ~1/4 acre square parcels (or pixels) based on cover type. Parcels of land were classified as urban–suburban landscapes if a square area (240 acres) surrounding the parcel was composed of at least 60% developed land cover. In order to exclude very small areas of development from the final urban–suburban landscape, polygons of touching parcels meeting this density requirement had to exceed 270 acres to be included.

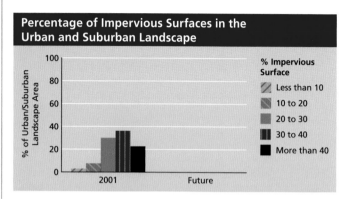

Urban and Suburban

EXTENT AND PATTERN	CHEMICAL AND PHYSICAL	BIOLOGICAL COMPONENTS	GOODS AND SERVICES
Extent	Nutrients, Carbon, and Oxygen	Plants and Animals	Food, Fiber, and Water
Pattern	Chemical Contamination	Communities	Recreation and Other Services
	Physical	Ecological Productivity	

Total Impervious Area

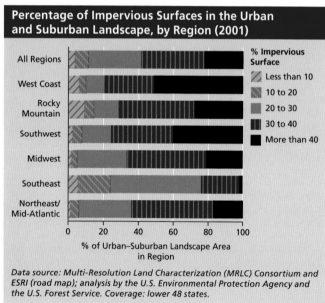

Percentage of Impervious Surfaces in the Urban and Suburban Landscape

% of Urban/Suburban Landscape Area

% Impervious Surface
- Less than 10
- 10 to 20
- 20 to 30
- 30 to 40
- More than 40

2001   Future

Percentage of Impervious Surfaces in the Urban and Suburban Landscape, by Region (2001)

All Regions
West Coast
Rocky Mountain
Southwest
Midwest
Southeast
Northeast/Mid-Atlantic

% Impervious Surface
- Less than 10
- 10 to 20
- 20 to 30
- 30 to 40
- More than 40

0   20   40   60   80   100
% of Urban–Suburban Landscape Area in Region

Data source: Multi-Resolution Land Characterization (MRLC) Consortium and ESRI (road map); analysis by the U.S. Environmental Protection Agency and the U.S. Forest Service. Coverage: lower 48 states.

Why Is the Extent of Impervious Surfaces Important? The extent of impervious surfaces is a direct measure of the degree of urbanization, and it strongly affects water quality and replenishment of groundwater. It is also most likely linked to the extent and intensity of the urban heat island effect (see Urban Heat Island, p. 245). Areas with more impervious, or nonporous, surfaces generate more runoff, which can not only contaminate and warm stream waters, but also degrade stream channels and banks. These changes have major effects on the fish and wildlife that inhabit streams. In general, the negative effects on streams increase as the percentage of impervious surface in a watershed increases.

What Does This Indicator Report? The percentage of the urban and suburban landscape covered by artificial impervious surfaces—roads, parking lots, driveways, rooftops, and the like. Urban–suburban landscapes include different land cover types, ranging from houses and office buildings to interspersed "natural" areas (see definition, p. 35).

What Do the Data Show?
- In 2001, nearly 60% of the urban–suburban landscape nationally had more than 30% impervious surface cover. Only 3% of the urban and suburban landscape had less than 10% impervious surface cover.
- There was considerable regional variation in the proportion of impervious cover within the urban–suburban landscape:
  - About a quarter of the urban–suburban landscape in the Southeast had more than 30% impervious cover; 65–80% of the urban–suburban landscape in all other regions had more than 30% impervious cover.
  - The urban–suburban landscape in the Rocky Mountain region had the most area (more than 9%) with less than 10% impervious surfaces. The urban–suburban landscape in the Southeast and West Coast had from 5–6% of their area covered by less than 10% impervious surfaces; the remaining regions had very little (1–2%) of their urban–suburban landscape's area covered by less than 10% impervious surfaces .

Understanding the Data Impervious surface cover is just one factor among many that affect the condition of urban–suburban landscapes and the ecosystem services they provide. Recent studies suggest that impervious surface cover of 10% or more in a watershed can produce negative effects on stream ecosystems; as impervious cover exceeds values approaching 30%, these effects become more pronounced. Also, the methods used may not capture all impervious surfaces, especially smaller ones such as sidewalks. New techniques and materials such as green roofs, permeable pavements, and rain gardens filter and manage runoff.

The technical note for this indicator is on page 333.

EXTENT AND PATTERN	CHEMICAL AND PHYSICAL	BIOLOGICAL COMPONENTS	GOODS AND SERVICES
Extent	Nutrients, Carbon, and Oxygen	Plants and Animals	Food, Fiber, and Water
Pattern	Chemical Contamination	Communities	Recreation and Other Services
	Physical	Ecological Productivity	

Stream Bank Vegetation

Why Is Stream Bank Vegetation Important? The amount of vegetation along a stream bank affects water quality, stream flow, and the kinds of fish and other animals that live in and along

Stream Bank Vegetation
Indicator Development Needed

streams. Vegetation along the stream bank shades the stream, making it cooler in summer, and serves as habitat for animals. Trees drop leaves and branches into the stream, providing food and habitat structure. Riparian plants also trap sediments and pollutants, improving water quality and reducing risk of contamination.

What Will This Indicator Report? Although not fully defined, this indicator will report on the percentage of miles of stream (stream-miles) in urban and suburban areas that are lined with trees, shrubs, and other plants.

Why Can't This Indicator Be Reported at This Time? Further indicator development is needed to standardize the approach for defining and measuring streamside vegetation. The criteria for what is considered "vegetated" need to be defined, specifically the minimum width of plant cover along banks and whether and to what degree "unnatural" plant cover such as lawns or crops should be counted as "vegetated." When suitable definitions are established, data sources for stream bank vegetation will be evaluated. Potential data sources include satellite-based imagery, some of which has the necessary resolution to describe narrow strips of vegetation, and locally generated information, which can be quite detailed, although it may be incompatible from location to location and expensive to obtain.

There is no technical note for this indicator.

⫴⫴ Urban and Suburban

EXTENT AND PATTERN	CHEMICAL AND PHYSICAL	BIOLOGICAL COMPONENTS	GOODS AND SERVICES
Extent	Nutrients, Carbon, and Oxygen	Plants and Animals	Food, Fiber, and Water
Pattern	Chemical Contamination	Communities	Recreation and Other Services
	Physical	Ecological Productivity	

Housing Density Changes in Low-Density Suburban and Rural Areas

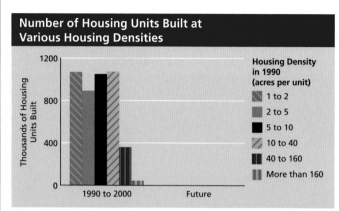

Number of Housing Units Built at Various Housing Densities

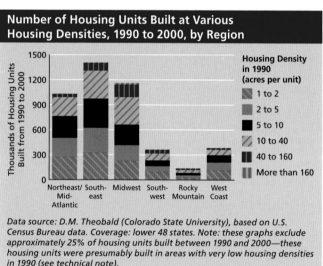

Number of Housing Units Built at Various Housing Densities, 1990 to 2000, by Region

Data source: D.M. Theobald (Colorado State University), based on U.S. Census Bureau data. Coverage: lower 48 states. Note: these graphs exclude approximately 25% of housing units built between 1990 and 2000—these housing units were presumably built in areas with very low housing densities in 1990 (see technical note).

Why Are Changes in Housing Density Important? Housing development is needed to keep pace with a growing population. However, development can result in the loss of "natural" lands, as well as lands that have historically been managed as croplands. New development in areas of low housing densities, such as suburban and rural areas, generally has more ecological consequences than the addition of new housing in areas that already support high housing densities.

What Does This Indicator Report? The number of new housing units (house, apartment, trailer, or other separate living quarters) added to suburban and rural areas, as a function of the preexisting housing density in an area.

What Do the Data Show?

- Nationally, between 1990 and 2000
  - Just over 1 million housing units were built on land with preexisting housing densities of one housing unit per 1–2 acres—the highest preexisting housing density reported here.
  - Just under 2 million housing units were built on land with a preexisting density of 2–10 acres per unit.
  - About 1.1 million housing units were built on land with a preexisting density of 10–40 acres per unit.
    - About 360,000 housing units were built on land with a preexisting density of 40–160 acres per unit.
    - Forty-five thousand housing units were built on very sparsely settled lands (one house on 160 acres or more).
- More housing units were built over this time period in the East and Midwest than in the western regions.
- The greatest number of housing units added at lower preexisting housing densities (one house on 40 acres or more) was in the Midwest.

Understanding the Data Development often leads to more development, with more land being converted to expand transportation networks, build schools, and accommodate businesses, which in turn may create a demand for still more housing. This is especially true in lower-density suburbs, areas further removed but still practically connected to metropolitan areas, and other areas experiencing rapid population growth—sometimes called "exurban" areas. As housing density increases in these lower-density areas, a point is reached (generally above one housing unit per one-half acre) where centralized utilities, such as sewage systems, become economical.

Housing Density Changes in Low-Density Suburban and Rural Areas *(continued)*

The ecological effects of development extend well beyond actual construction sites and are to some extent dependent on the density of development. Development can, for example, deforest and fragment habitat, interfere with the movement of animals, and reduce stream quality. See related indicators on the pattern of "natural lands" (core national, p. 33; forest, p. 138; grasslands and shrublands, p. 204; and urban and suburban, p. 236).

The terms "suburban," "exurban," and "rural" do not have universally accepted definitions in terms of housing density. The housing densities reported here do not include densely settled urban and suburban areas that have densities of more than one house per acre, which is appropriate given that the focus of this indicator is on development patterns in areas that have low housing densities.

The technical note for this indicator is on page 333.

AB Urban and Suburban

EXTENT AND PATTERN	CHEMICAL AND PHYSICAL	BIOLOGICAL COMPONENTS	GOODS AND SERVICES
Extent	Nutrients, Carbon, and Oxygen	Plants and Animals	Food, Fiber, and Water
Pattern	Chemical Contamination	Communities	Recreation and Other Services
	Physical	Ecological Productivity	

"Natural" Lands in the Urban and Suburban Landscape

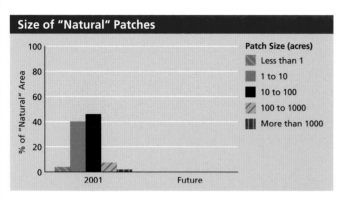

Size of "Natural" Patches

Patch Size (acres)
- Less than 1
- 1 to 10
- 10 to 100
- 100 to 1000
- More than 1000

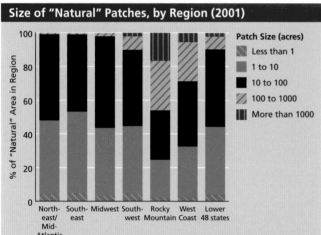

Size of "Natural" Patches, by Region (2001)

Patch Size (acres)
- Less than 1
- 1 to 10
- 10 to 100
- 100 to 1000
- More than 1000

Data source: Multi-Resolution Land Characterization (MRLC) Consortium and ESRI (road map); analysis by the U.S. Environmental Protection Agency and the U.S. Forest Service. Coverage: lower 48 states. Technical details: All "natural" pixels within the urban–suburban landscape (p. 35) were formed into patches of touching pixels, the size of which is reported in the graphs. Note: Current technical limitations required that patches be "cut" by state boundaries, meaning that these data should be considered to represent minimum patch sizes—in other words, some patches of "natural" lands that spanned a state boundary were split into two smaller patches. We do not know how this analysis limitation affected the data.

Why Are Patches of "Natural" Land Important? Many landscapes are characterized by human development, yet include significant amounts of "natural" lands (forest, grassland, shrubland, and wetlands). These "natural" lands help control erosion and movement of sediments, facilitate groundwater recharge, provide critical habitat for wildlife, and serve other important ecological functions such as filtering out contaminants from runoff. Further conversion of land to development in these areas can fragment the existing "natural" lands, creating new kinds of habitats that may disadvantage some native species and encourage non-native species. Across urban and suburban landscapes, "natural" lands can provide recreational opportunities and natural ecosystem services (p. 250), as well as some degree of solitude.

What Does This Indicator Report? The size of patches of "natural" lands in the urban–suburban landscape, nationally and regionally.

What Do the Data Show?
- In 2001, 90% of "natural" patches in urban–suburban landscapes of the lower 48 states were between 1 and 100 acres; about 2% of "natural" lands were in patches larger than 1000 acres.
- The Rocky Mountain region had the most "natural" land in large patches in its urban and suburban landscapes—nearly 50% in patches of 100 acres or more; the West Coast also had a substantial proportion (nearly 30%) of patches 100 acres or larger.

- The size distribution of "natural" patches in urban and suburban landscapes in the Southwest matched the distribution for the lower 48 states.
- In the Northeast/Mid-Atlantic, Southeast, and Midwest regions, virtually all "natural" land occurs in patches of 100 acres or less.

Understanding the Data Small patches have little or no "interior" habitat—that is, habitat that is insulated from outside influences—typically human activities—by a buffer zone. Since some species thrive only in interior habitat—where there is a relatively large and contiguous area of forest, grassland, or other "natural" cover [see the national Pattern of Natural Landscapes indicator (p. 33) and the forest (p. 138), and grassland–shrubland (p. 204) pattern indicators], small areas may not provide habitat for these species. Note that this is not necessarily

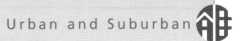
"Natural" Lands in the Urban and Suburban Landscape *(continued)*

true for wetlands, as even small wetlands can provide essential habitat. The shape of "natural" patches, which is not addressed by this indicator, can also affect the amount of interior habitat available and thus the quality of a patch's habitat. Large but narrow strips tend to have lower habitat value because little or no area is buffered from human activities, but these same strips of land may function quite well for erosion and sediment control.

Urban planners often attempt to maintain areas of open space (see Publicly Accessible Open Space per Resident, p. 249) in siting new development. In some cases, recent activities in urban and suburban landscapes may have less impact on the size of "natural" patches than past ownership and land use practices. For example, historic zoning policies may have left some blocks of "natural" lands untouched by development. In other cases, long-time property owners may have prevented lands from being subdivided and developed.

The technical note for this indicator is on page 334.

EXTENT AND PATTERN	CHEMICAL AND PHYSICAL	BIOLOGICAL COMPONENTS	GOODS AND SERVICES
Extent	Nutrients, Carbon, and Oxygen	Plants and Animals	Food, Fiber, and Water
Pattern	Chemical Contamination	Communities	Recreation and Other Services
	Physical	Ecological Productivity	

Nitrate in Urban and Suburban Streams

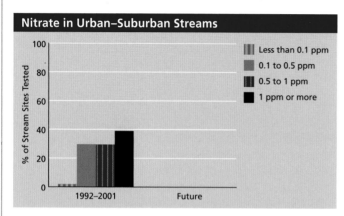

Nitrate in Urban–Suburban Streams

Legend:
- Less than 0.1 ppm
- 0.1 to 0.5 ppm
- 0.5 to 1 ppm
- 1 ppm or more

Y-axis: % of Stream Sites Tested
X-axis: 1992–2001, Future

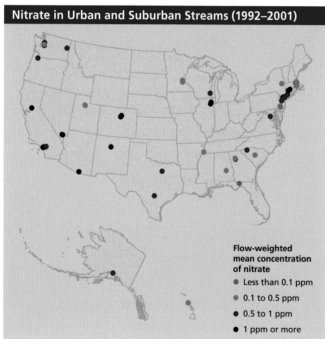

Nitrate in Urban and Suburban Streams (1992–2001)

Flow-weighted mean concentration of nitrate
- Less than 0.1 ppm
- 0.1 to 0.5 ppm
- 0.5 to 1 ppm
- 1 ppm or more

Why Is Nitrate in Urban and Suburban Streams Important? Nitrate in drinking water is a health threat for infants, and it must be removed at significant cost by municipalities that rely on river water. Excess nitrogen in streams that ultimately empty into coastal waters can lead to algal blooms, decreasing recreational and aesthetic values and depleting oxygen needed by fish and other animals (see Movement of Nitrogen, p. 36, and Areas with Depleted Oxygen, p. 75).

What Does This Indicator Report?
- The percentage of streams with average nitrate concentrations in one of four ranges, for streams draining watersheds that are primarily urban and suburban
- The nitrate concentration in urban and suburban streams in comparison with the nitrate concentration in farmland and urban and suburban streams

What Do the Data Show?
- Sixty-one percent of the stream sites in areas dominated by urban and suburban land use had concentrations of nitrate of less than 1 part per million (ppm), 32% had concentrations of less than 0.5 ppm, and 2% had concentrations of less than 0.1 ppm.
- Concentrations in streams in areas dominated by urban land use are lower than those in agricultural areas but higher than those in forests (see Nitrate in Forest Streams, p. 140; and Nitrate in Farmland Streams and Groundwater, p. 107).

Nitrate in Urban and Suburban Streams *(continued)*

Understanding the Data Nitrate is a naturally occurring form of nitrogen and an important plant nutrient. Plant-available or "reactive" forms of nitrogen can enter ecosystems through the use of synthetic fertilizers and fossil fuel combustion. Reactive nitrogen in the atmosphere can be transported by air currents and deposited in urban and suburban ecosystems in dust or precipitation (see Freshwater Stream Acidity, p. 176). Elevated amounts of nitrate in urban and suburban streams may also result from an inability of plants to absorb the nitrogen available for plant growth in the watershed. Nitrogen sources include effluent from sewage treatment plants, animal wastes, and fertilizers used on lawns, gardens, golf courses, and agricultural fields. The federal drinking water standard for nitrate is 10 ppm.

See also the national indicator Movement of Nitrogen (p. 36) and related indicators for farmlands (p. 107) and forests (p. 140).

The technical note for this indicator is on page 334.

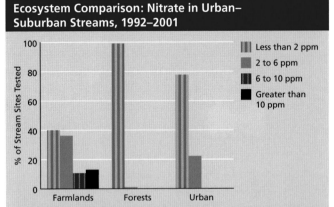

Ecosystem Comparison: Nitrate in Urban–Suburban Streams, 1992–2001

Legend:
- Less than 2 ppm
- 2 to 6 ppm
- 6 to 10 ppm
- Greater than 10 ppm

Data source: U.S. Geological Survey, National Water Quality Assessment. Coverage: 51 major river basins across 50 states. Technical details: Data are from sites that are primarily urban and suburban (upstream land cover is generally more than 25% urban and less than 25% agricultural). Ecosystem comparison data are from sites with upstream land cover that was primarily farmland or forest. Each sampling area was sampled intensively for approximately 2 years during 1992–2001. Nitrate refers to the concentration of nitrate-nitrogen (see technical note).

EXTENT AND PATTERN	CHEMICAL AND PHYSICAL	BIOLOGICAL COMPONENTS	GOODS AND SERVICES
Extent	**Nutrients, Carbon, and Oxygen**	Plants and Animals	Food, Fiber, and Water
Pattern	Chemical Contamination	Communities	Recreation and Other Services
	Physical	Ecological Productivity	

Phosphorus in Urban and Suburban Streams

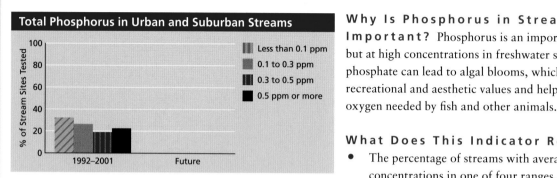

Total Phosphorus in Urban and Suburban Streams

% of Stream Sites Tested

Legend:
- Less than 0.1 ppm
- 0.1 to 0.3 ppm
- 0.3 to 0.5 ppm
- 0.5 ppm or more

1992–2001 / Future

Phosphorus in Urban and Suburban Streams (1992–2001)

Flow-weighted mean concentration of total phosphorus
- Less than 0.1 ppm
- 0.1 to 0.3 ppm
- 0.3 to 0.5 ppm
- 0.5 ppm or more

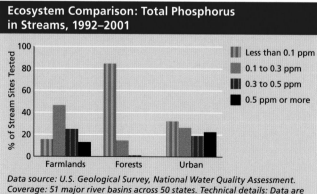

Ecosystem Comparison: Total Phosphorus in Streams, 1992–2001

% of Stream Sites Tested

Legend:
- Less than 0.1 ppm
- 0.1 to 0.3 ppm
- 0.3 to 0.5 ppm
- 0.5 ppm or more

Farmlands / Forests / Urban

Data source: U.S. Geological Survey, National Water Quality Assessment. Coverage: 51 major river basins across 50 states. Technical details: Data are from sites that are primarily urban and suburban (upstream land cover is generally more than 25% urban and less than 25% agricultural). Ecosystem comparison data are from sites with upstream land cover that was primarily farmland or forest. Each sampling area was sampled intensively for approximately 2 years during 1992–2001.

Why Is Phosphorus in Streams Important? Phosphorus is an important nutrient, but at high concentrations in freshwater systems, phosphate can lead to algal blooms, which can decrease recreational and aesthetic values and help deplete oxygen needed by fish and other animals.

What Does This Indicator Report?
- The percentage of streams with average phosphorus concentrations in one of four ranges, for streams draining watersheds that are primarily urban and suburban
- The phosphorus concentration in urban and suburban streams in comparison to the phosphorus concentration in farmland and forest streams

What Do the Data Show?
- Sixty-eight percent of stream sites in urban areas had concentrations of phosphorus that were at least 0.1 part per million (ppm), and 23% of urban stream sites had concentrations of at least 0.5 ppm.
- Streams in urban areas had similar average phosphorus concentrations to streams draining farmland watersheds and higher concentrations than streams draining forested watersheds.

Understanding the Data Phosphorus is an essential nutrient for all life forms and occurs naturally in soils and aquatic systems; phosphate is the most biologically active form of phosphorus. The EPA has recommended 0.1 ppm as a goal for preventing excess algal growth in streams not draining directly into a lake or other impoundment. There is no federal drinking-water standard for phosphorus.

Sources of phosphorus in urban streams include effluent from sewage treatment plants, animal wastes, some detergents, and fertilizers used on lawns, gardens, golf courses, and agricultural fields. Planting trees, widening forested or wetland buffers along streams, and minimizing the use of lawn fertilizers and phosphate-based detergents can lower phosphorus inputs to urban and suburban streams.

The technical note for this indicator is on page 335.

EXTENT AND PATTERN	CHEMICAL AND PHYSICAL	BIOLOGICAL COMPONENTS	GOODS AND SERVICES
Extent	Nutrients, Carbon, and Oxygen	Plants and Animals	Food, Fiber, and Water
Pattern	Chemical Contamination	Communities	Recreation and Other Services
	Physical	Ecological Productivity	

Urban and Suburban Air Quality

Why Are Changes in Air Pollutants Important? At elevated concentrations, ground-level ozone can cause respiratory problems for people and can harm vegetation, animals and the built environment. Exposure to toxic air contaminants is associated with a variety of adverse health effects including cancer and other serious illnesses.

What Does This Indicator Report?
For outdoor air in urban and suburban areas:

- How often air monitoring stations measure "high" (above 0.08 ppm) ozone concentrations
- When data become available, how often toxic air contaminants are detected and how often they exceed benchmarks for the protection of human health

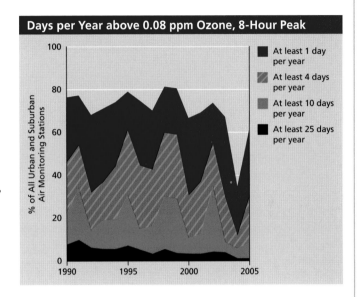

Days per Year above 0.08 ppm Ozone, 8-Hour Peak

Legend:
- At least 1 day per year
- At least 4 days per year
- At least 10 days per year
- At least 25 days per year

Y-axis: % of All Urban and Suburban Air Monitoring Stations

What Do the Data Show?

- In 2005, high ozone levels were recorded at 30% of urban and suburban monitoring stations on 4 or more days; 61% had high levels on at least one day.
- The percentage of ozone monitors recording high levels 25 or more days per year has declined from about 8% in 1990 to about 1% in 2005. The four monitors that still record high levels are in Southern and Central California.
- The percentage of ozone monitors recording high levels at least one day per year have also significantly declined since 1990.

Why Can't This Entire Indicator Be Reported? To understand how often toxic contaminants are detected in ambient air or exceed human health benchmarks, more robust monitoring and estimation methods for ambient concentrations are needed. Further scientific work is also needed to understand "natural" background levels for some toxic air contaminants.

Understanding the Data Ground-level ozone is one of the most pervasive air quality problems in the United States. Children and adults who are active outdoors, and people with respiratory diseases, are most likely to be harmed. Ozone can inflame lungs, make people more susceptible to respiratory infection, and aggravate respiratory diseases such as asthma; repeated exposure may lead to permanent lung damage. High concentrations can harm trees, other plants, wildlife, and pets, and can damage painted surfaces, plastics, and rubber materials. In contrast, ozone in the upper atmosphere absorbs harmful ultraviolet radiation.

Continued

AB Urban and Suburban

EXTENT AND PATTERN	CHEMICAL AND PHYSICAL	BIOLOGICAL COMPONENTS	GOODS AND SERVICES
Extent	Nutrients, Carbon, and Oxygen	Plants and Animals	Food, Fiber, and Water
Pattern	Chemical Contamination	Communities	Recreation and Other Services
	Physical	Ecological Productivity	

Urban and Suburban Air Quality *(continued)*

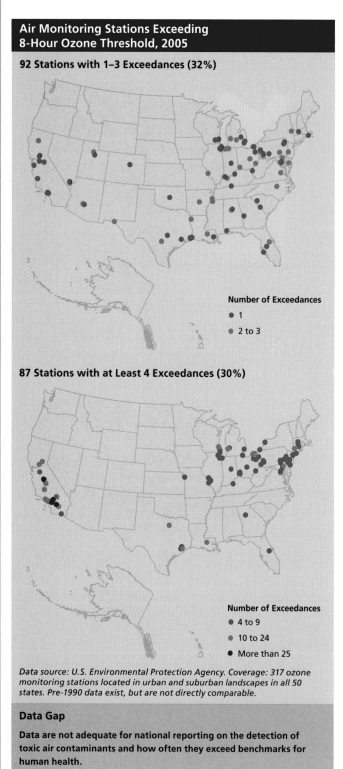

Air Monitoring Stations Exceeding 8-Hour Ozone Threshold, 2005

92 Stations with 1–3 Exceedances (32%)

Number of Exceedances
- 1
- 2 to 3

87 Stations with at Least 4 Exceedances (30%)

Number of Exceedances
- 4 to 9
- 10 to 24
- More than 25

Data source: U.S. Environmental Protection Agency. Coverage: 317 ozone monitoring stations located in urban and suburban landscapes in all 50 states. Pre-1990 data exist, but are not directly comparable.

Data Gap

Data are not adequate for national reporting on the detection of toxic air contaminants and how often they exceed benchmarks for human health.

When pollutants from vehicles, paints and solvents, unburned fuel, and industrial sources "bake" in hot, sunny, stagnant weather, ground-level ozone forms. Fluctuations in ozone concentrations are generally believed to result from a combination of year-to-year variability in weather conditions and changes in emissions of ozone-forming compounds. Exposure to toxic air contaminants—a broad range of synthetic and naturally occurring chemicals—is associated with cancer and other adverse human health effects; however, actual risk depends only in part on toxic air contaminant concentrations, which can vary considerably from place to place.

The technical note for this indicator is on page 335.

EXTENT AND PATTERN	CHEMICAL AND PHYSICAL	BIOLOGICAL COMPONENTS	GOODS AND SERVICES
Extent	Nutrients, Carbon, and Oxygen	Plants and Animals	Food, Fiber, and Water
Pattern	**Chemical Contamination**	Communities	Recreation and Other Services
	Physical	Ecological Productivity	

Chemical Contamination

Why Are Contaminants Found in Urban and Suburban Areas Important? In sufficient quantities, contaminants in urban and suburban ecosystems can harm people as well as wildlife and plants.

What Does This Indicator Report? For urban and suburban stream water and soils, how often contaminants are detected, and how often they exceed benchmarks set to protect human health or other organisms.

What Do the Data Show?
- Virtually all streams tested had at least one contaminant at detectable levels, and about three-quarters had five or more.
- Eighty-three percent of streams had contaminants at levels exceeding benchmarks for the protection of aquatic life, and 20% had four or more.
- About 7% had contaminant levels exceeding benchmarks for the protection of human health.

Why Can't This Entire Indicator Be Reported at This Time? Data are not currently available to report in a consistent manner on chemical contamination in urban and suburban soils. Also, the necessary benchmarks do not exist for all monitored contaminants. Of the 85 tested contaminants, 73 have established benchmarks for the protection of human health and 62 have established benchmarks for the protection of aquatic life.

Understanding the Data Exposure of plants, animals, and people to contaminants in streams and soils can affect ecological functioning and human health. A wide variety of pesticides have been manufactured and used in agriculture, landscaping, and other applications. Some of these pesticides persist or are transformed in the environment and can pose a threat to living things. At high concentrations, nitrate and ammonia can be directly toxic to fish and can create health problems for people.

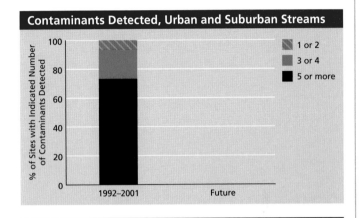

Contaminants Detected, Urban and Suburban Streams

% of Sites with Indicated Number of Contaminants Detected

Legend: 1 or 2; 3 or 4; 5 or more

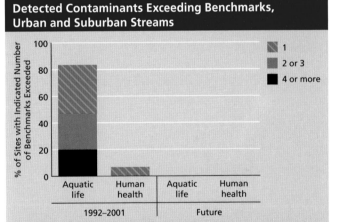

Detected Contaminants Exceeding Benchmarks, Urban and Suburban Streams

% of Sites with Indicated Number of Benchmarks Exceeded

Legend: 1; 2 or 3; 4 or more

Data source: U.S. Geological Survey National Water Quality Assessment (NAWQA) Program. Coverage: watersheds characterized by urban and suburban land use based on sampling at 30 stream sites within 51 major river basins across the nation. Technical details: Each site was sampled intensively for 85 contaminants for approximately 2 years during 1992–2001. The upper graph includes pesticides and their breakdown products (the chemicals into which they transform over time in the environment), but excludes naturally occurring ammonia and nitrate. The lower graph excludes tested pesticides for which relevant benchmarks have not been set. Note: In the 2002 Report, data for 1992–1998 were reported, but these data are not comparable to the 1992–2001 data presented here because of changes in the number of sites sampled and revised benchmarks.

Data Gap

Data are not adequate for national reporting on contaminants in urban and suburban soils. Benchmarks for the protection of aquatic life and human health have not been established for some monitored contaminants.

Continued

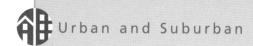
Urban and Suburban

EXTENT AND PATTERN	CHEMICAL AND PHYSICAL	BIOLOGICAL COMPONENTS	GOODS AND SERVICES
Extent	Nutrients, Carbon, and Oxygen	Plants and Animals	Food, Fiber, and Water
Pattern	Chemical Contamination	Communities	Recreation and Other Services
	Physical	Ecological Productivity	

Chemical Contamination *(continued)*

The number of contaminants found in water and soils provides basic information on how widespread these compounds are in the environment. However, the presence of chemical contamination does not necessarily mean that the levels are high enough to cause problems. Comparison with benchmarks, when they exist, can help assess the significance of contamination, although this does not represent a true risk assessment, which would include many other factors, such as actual exposures. Benchmarks for the protection of aquatic life are often set at lower contaminant concentrations than similar benchmarks for human health. Aquatic animals spend much or all of their lives in water and may be more sensitive to specific contaminants.

See also the national (p. 42), coastal (p. 77), and farmland (p. 111) contaminants indicators.

The technical note for this indicator is on page 336.

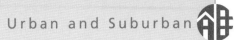

Urban Heat Island

Why Is the Urban Heat Island Effect Important? Hot weather is responsible for greater loss of human life in the United States each year than hurricanes, lightning, tornadoes, floods,

> **Urban Heat Island**
>
> **Indicator Development Needed**

and earthquakes combined. Building density and type, amount of road surface, and energy use, as well as local topography and regional weather patterns, all modify a city's climate. The urban heat island effect is most pronounced at night, when buildings and other constructed surfaces radiate heat accumulated during the day. Beyond posing a threat to human health (through heat stroke, for example) and raising air conditioning costs, the heat island effect can cause physiological stress in animals, change the community of plants and animals that live in the area, and even lead to changes in the distribution of pathogens. Elevated temperatures also accelerate the formation of ground-level ozone (see Urban and Suburban Air Quality, p. 241) and other air pollutants that adversely affect human health.

What Will This Indicator Report? The difference between temperatures in urban areas and those in adjacent rural areas.

Why Can't This Indicator Be Reported at This Time? There is a lack of agreement on how to monitor and measure the heat island effect. One proposed indicator is the percentage of U.S. metropolitan areas where the average annual difference between urban and rural air temperatures is small (less than 7°F), moderate (7° to less than 13°F), or large (more than 13°F). National Weather Service data could be used to determine current and historic heat island effects in many locations. To develop this indicator, appropriate pairs of urban and rural sites would need to be identified and monitored.

The technical note for this indicator is on page 337.

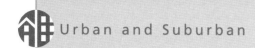

EXTENT AND PATTERN	CHEMICAL AND PHYSICAL	BIOLOGICAL COMPONENTS	GOODS AND SERVICES
Extent	Nutrients, Carbon, and Oxygen	Plants and Animals	Food, Fiber, and Water
Pattern	Chemical Contamination	Communities	Recreation and Other Services
	Physical	Ecological Productivity	

Species Status

Species Status in Metropolitan Areas

Data Gap

Data are not adequate for national reporting on the degree to which "original" plant and animal species are absent or at risk of being lost.

Why Is the Status of Species in Metropolitan Areas Important?

Species differ in their ability to cope with urban and suburban development; some species thrive in urban environments, while others cannot adapt to the changes in habitat, disturbance, food, and predation. Cities and suburbs also differ in their capacity to accommodate those species common in the area before European settlement ("original species"). The extent of development, degree of urban tree cover, and the presence of "natural" areas and corridors maintained for wildlife all influence species status in urban and suburban landscapes. Efforts to improve or restore habitat can increase the likelihood that original species will return to urban and suburban landscapes.

What Will This Indicator Report? The fraction of major metropolitan areas, where it is likely that effective monitoring programs can be established, with different percentages of original plant and animal species that are either absent entirely or are at risk of being lost from the particular metropolitan area.

Why Can't This Indicator Be Reported at This Time? The historical data necessary to establish lists of original species are incomplete, and current information on the status of these species, especially within cities and their suburbs, is not systematically collected and reported. The spatial and temporal coverage, quality, and format of the data that are available are extremely variable.

Discussion It is difficult to distinguish between species that are at risk of being lost from metropolitan areas and those that have already been lost, so both are included. Presettlement species abundance would likely be used as a benchmark to track changes in abundance, not because the full suite of original species would necessarily be a reasonable conservation goal in any given metropolitan area, but rather because presettlement abundance is a baseline from which to measure change.

This indicator will not report on all urban and suburban areas as defined in this report (see Area and Composition of the Urban and Suburban Landscape, p. 230). Smaller cities and towns lack the information, expertise, and financial resources to obtain the type of data needed to calculate this indicator, so only data for larger metropolitan areas will be reported. For example, reporting for this indicator may be based on data from a suite of cities (and their suburbs) whose population exceeds 100,000 or that cover at least 50 square miles.

The technical note for this indicator is on page 337.

Urban and Suburban

EXTENT AND PATTERN	CHEMICAL AND PHYSICAL	BIOLOGICAL COMPONENTS	GOODS AND SERVICES
Extent	Nutrients, Carbon, and Oxygen	Plants and Animals	Food, Fiber, and Water
Pattern	Chemical Contamination	Communities	Recreation and Other Services
	Physical	Ecological Productivity	

Disruptive Species

Why Are Disruptive Species Important? Some species of plants and animals are so abundant in urban and suburban areas that they disrupt other species and cause problems for people. In the Northeast, for example, white-tailed deer are major suburban pests. They damage native vegetation in natural areas, destroy crops and gardens, and are involved in numerous automobile accidents. In and around Portland, Oregon, Scotch broom, native to the British Isles, is spreading rapidly, often growing in dense, nearly impenetrable clumps that make maintenance of roads, ditches, canals, and power and telephone lines difficult and costly. Minneapolis, among other cities in the Midwest, is taking action against disruptive woody plants like buckthorn, Tartarian honeysuckle, and mulberry, which are taking over the city's woods and wetlands.

> **Disruptive Species**
>
> **Data Gap**
>
> Data are not adequate for national reporting on the number and type of disruptive species found in metropolitan areas.

What Will This Indicator Report? The number and type of "disruptive" species found in metropolitan areas. Disruptive species are those that have negative effects on natural areas and native species or cause damage to people and property. Specifically, the indicator will report the number of larger metropolitan areas with 5 or fewer, from 6 to 10, from 11 to 20, and more than 20 disruptive plant and animal species. It would also report the number of disruptive native and non-native plant and animal species, by region.

Why Can't This Indicator Be Reported at This Time? Regional lists of disruptive species do not exist. Creating them requires definition of thresholds that distinguish truly disruptive species from those that cause fewer problems, as well as consistent policies for including species based on their potential to cause damage, as shown by experience elsewhere. In addition, monitoring and reporting programs need to be put in place to track the occurrence of disruptive species. Many knowledgeable individuals and institutions could participate, but no entity currently has the mandate to coordinate such an activity.

Discussion Disruptive species may be native, or they may have been introduced from other regions or other countries. The altered landscape in urban and suburban areas encourages the growth of these species, which tolerate and even thrive around built-up areas. At the same time, populations of more sensitive species shrink, reducing competition and further encouraging the spread of disruptive species.

There is no technical note for this indicator.

Status of Animal Communities in Urban and Suburban Streams

Status of Animal Communities in Urban and Suburban Streams

Data Gap

Data are not adequate for national reporting on the condition of fish and bottom-dwelling animal communities in urban and suburban streams.

Some Definitions

- **"Natural":** fish and benthic animals found at the site are similar to those expected in the least disturbed sites in that region.
- **"Moderate":** fish and benthic animals are more degraded than 75% of those found at least disturbed sites in the region.
- **"Degraded":** fish and benthic animals are more degraded than those found at 95% of least disturbed sites in the region, reflecting one or more negative influences.

Why Are Animal Communities in Urban and Suburban Streams Important? "Natural" streams in a particular region have a relatively predictable set of fish and bottom-dwelling animals, which occur in predictable proportions of species. Alterations to the streams can change the composition and condition of these biological communities—the biological integrity—from this relatively undisturbed or "reference" condition. Ecosystems that have "natural" animal communities are more likely to withstand natural and man-made stresses and to provide a range of ecosystem services (see Natural Ecosystem Services, p. 250).

What Will This Indicator Report? The percentage of urban and suburban stream sites in which the suite of fish and bottom-dwelling (or benthic) animals (including insects, worms, mollusks, and crustaceans) are in "natural," "moderate," or "degraded" condition.

Why Can't This Indicator Be Reported at This Time? Tests of biological integrity now in use compare streams with an appropriate reference from within the same region, but there are no data on fish and bottom-dwelling communities specific to urban and suburban streams.

Discussion The condition of animal communities is measured as the degree to which the communities resemble what one might find in a relatively undisturbed stream in the same region. The composition and condition of these biological communities may be altered, often as a result of development in the stream's watershed. Sources of degradation include contaminated runoff from streets, driveways, lawns, golf courses, and the like, increased stream temperature caused by runoff that is warmed as it flows over paved surfaces, and channelizing or other modifications of the streambed. Some streams are so modified that both the number of species and the number of individuals are low when compared to undisturbed areas, and many of the species that remain are diseased or otherwise damaged.

A similar indicator reports on fish and bottom-dwelling animals in streams with a range of land cover types (see Status of Freshwater Animal Communities, p. 185)

The technical note for this indicator is on page 322 (Status of Freshwater Animal Communities).

Urban and Suburban

EXTENT AND PATTERN	CHEMICAL AND PHYSICAL	BIOLOGICAL COMPONENTS	GOODS AND SERVICES
Extent	Nutrients, Carbon, and Oxygen	Plants and Animals	Food, Fiber, and Water
Pattern	Chemical Contamination	Communities	**Recreation and Other Services**
	Physical	Ecological Productivity	

Publicly Accessible Open Space per Resident

Why Is the Amount of Publicly Accessible Open Space Important?

Americans enjoy outdoor recreation, and urban and suburban residents place a high value on access to public spaces where they can picnic, play ball, swim, hike, fish,

> **Publicly Accessible Open Space per Resident**
> **Data Gap**
> Data are not adequate for national reporting on the amount of open space accessible to the public in metropolitan areas.

walk their dogs, enjoy nature, and engage in any of a myriad of other outdoor activities. The amount of such open space per resident often determines how intensely such places will be used.

What Will This Indicator Report?
The amount of open space—land that is dominated by "natural" surfaces, like grass or woods, along with lakes, rivers, beaches, and wetlands—that is accessible to the general public in large metropolitan areas. Specifically, the indicator would report the percentage of metropolitan areas with different amounts of open space per resident.

Why Can't This Indicator Be Reported at This Time?
There are no consistent or comprehensive surveys of the amount of publicly accessible open space in cities and suburban areas. A combination of satellite remote sensing and local tax and land records would be required for reporting on this indicator.

Discussion
This indicator focuses on public areas that are natural or relatively undeveloped. In practice, this means that areas dominated by grass, woods, dirt, or other unpaved surfaces would be counted, while predominately paved areas would not (paved walkways in a park that is primarily grass would not "disqualify" the area). In addition, areas counted in this indicator are those that are accessible to the general public, even if fees (such as for a county-run golf course) are charged. Thus, a public golf course and even some cemeteries would qualify, but a farm or a country club would not. Note that a change in population without a change in amount of open space would change the value of this indicator. Area and Composition of the Urban and Suburban Landscape (p. 230) provides a context for this indicator because it reports the overall percentage of undeveloped lands in the urban and suburban landscape; however, it does not distinguish between publicly accessible and inaccessible lands.

The technical note for this indicator is on page 338.

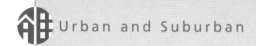

EXTENT AND PATTERN	CHEMICAL AND PHYSICAL	BIOLOGICAL COMPONENTS	GOODS AND SERVICES
Extent	Nutrients, Carbon, and Oxygen	Plants and Animals	Food, Fiber, and Water
Pattern	Chemical Contamination	Communities	**Recreation and Other Services**
	Physical	Ecological Productivity	

Natural Ecosystem Services

Natural Ecosystem Services

Indicator Development Needed

Why Are Natural Ecosystem Services Important in Urban and Suburban Landscapes? In urban and suburban landscapes, the loss of ecosystem services is often not recognized until a functioning ecosystem has already been altered, and millions or even billions of dollars are needed for technological fixes. Urban and suburban landscapes are defined by the built environment, but the remaining "natural" components—trees, meadows, streams, wetlands, and the like—provide valuable services to the residents of these developed areas. These ecosystem services are the benefits, both tangible and intangible, that these natural elements provide. For example, forested areas reduce stormwater runoff compared to paved areas, and trees cool streets and buildings, reducing energy consumption; trees also reduce urban noise levels. Natural areas, including forests, grasslands and shrublands, beaches, lakes, streams, and wetlands, also provide recreational opportunities, increase property values and community amenities, and are aesthetically pleasing.

What Will This Indicator Report? The ecosystem services provided to urban and suburban residents, recognizing that some of these benefits will be derived from lands or waters outside urban and suburban landscapes.

Why Can't This Indicator Be Reported at This Time? Scientists are uncertain how to measure ecosystem services in urban, and other, ecosystems. One possibility is to use tree canopy as a surrogate measure because of its influences on air quality, water flow, property values, microclimates, and aesthetics. Scientists are working to quantify the relationship, which is likely to be stronger in some areas than in others, between the amount of tree canopy and the levels of services provided. Other components of the urban and suburban ecosystem, such as wetlands, streams, and grasslands, also provide important services, and these should be incorporated as well.

Discussion Suburban development in the Catskill Mountains, the primary source of water for New York City, has jeopardized water quality, potentially requiring a filtration system costing billions of dollars to construct and millions of dollars a year to operate, in order to provide the same water quality as before development. In another example, the nonprofit organization American Forests found that trees in the Denver/Front Range area provide the equivalent of a $44 million stormwater management system.

Considerable scientific effort needs to be invested in understanding the relationship between various ecosystem components and the kinds of services they provide. Recently, the National Science Foundation's Long Term Ecological Research Network established research sites in Baltimore, Maryland, and Phoenix, Arizona, to study the ecology of cities (see http://lternet.edu/). These sites seek to understand the nature and functioning of urban and suburban ecosystems and how people influence and are influenced by them. Through such detailed studies and the accompanying long-term observation of changes in urban and suburban areas, it will be possible to quantify ecosystem services and understand how urbanization alters these services.

There is no technical note for this indicator.

Appendixes and Technical Notes

Appendix A:
State of the Nation's Ecosystems Project: History and Design Process

Project Origins

Each year, hundreds of millions of dollars are spent gathering data on our nation's forests, agricultural lands, grasslands and deserts, lakes, rivers, oceans, estuaries, coastal ecosystems, and urban–suburban environments. Our existing environmental monitoring programs have been developed over many years by a disparate collection of government agencies, nonprofit organizations, and research institutions. Many of these programs are poorly integrated and their data collection activities are driven primarily by agency-specific regulatory or management mandates. Recognizing the need to ensure the most efficient use of federal resources and help answer more synoptic questions, the White House Office of Science and Technology Policy (OSTP) convened an interagency effort in the mid-1990s to examine the existing monitoring programs and to provide a framework for their coherent operation. They concluded that a comprehensive report, drawing upon and integrating the best available information from all sources, was needed to provide high-level information for environmental policymaking. Subsequently, OSTP invited The Heinz Center to develop a reporting system that would synthesize current knowledge about environmental conditions and trends across the nation. An overview of major project activities during the past decade is provided in Table A-1.

Table A–1 Project Timeline	
Year	Activity
1997	Heinz Center initiates project, with support from OSTP, foundations, businesses, and multiple federal government agencies.
1997	The project's Design Committee and staff develop an overall framework for indicator selection and measurement. The framework clusters the nation's ecosystems into six major types and identifies three categories of fundamental ecological phenomena that should be included in a sound ecosystem indicator set. This framework was later elaborated to the four-category one used in this report (see 1999–2002, below and Chapter 1).
1997–1999	Working groups develop indicators for farmlands, forests, and coasts and oceans. The basic process used for designing and refining indicators and preparing materials for release involves six steps (discussed in more detail below).
1999	Publication of prototype report, *Designing a Report on the State of the Nation's Ecosystems: Selected Indicators for Croplands, Forests, and Coasts & Oceans*.
1999–2002	Working groups develop indicators for the remaining ecosystems—freshwaters, grasslands and shrublands, and urban and suburban systems—and update and refine indicators for the other three ecosystems. The original three-category framework is expanded by dividing "ecosystem condition" into a "chemical and physical characteristics" category and a "biological components" category. In addition, the first set of "core national" indicators is developed.
2002	Publication of first full national report, *The State of the Nation's Ecosystems: Measuring the Lands, Waters, and Living Resources of the United States*.
2002–2007	Indicator refinement—the Design Committee and working groups refine the existing set of indicators. Considerable effort is devoted to developing and refining the core national indicators and cross-cutting indicators that span ecosystems, such as non-native species, ecosystem services, landscape patterns, and stream flows.
2003, 2005	Web updates for selected indicators.
2006	Publication of *Filling the Gaps: Priority Data Needs and Key Management Challenges for National Reporting on Ecosystem Condition*, a report on data gaps in the first report.
2008	Publication of second full national report, *The State of the Nation's Ecosystems 2008*.

Project Organization and Design Principles

From the outset, the State of the Nation's Ecosystems project has followed a collaborative model that attempts to engage representatives from each of the major sectors involved in American public discourse: business and industry, environmental organizations, government and academia. Each sector has an important role in solving environmental problems, and each has a stake in ensuring that the information provided by the *State of the Nation's Ecosystems* reports is scientifically credible, politically neutral, and otherwise unbiased.

The organizational structure chosen for the State of the Nation's Ecosystems project has remained relatively constant over the years, with a Design Committee that provides overall leadership and strategic guidance, complemented by a suite of subcommittees and technical working groups tasked with addressing specific ecosystem-specific or technical issues (see pp. vi–xii for a detailed listing of project groups and participants).

Over the years, the Design Committee developed definitions and principles to help guide the project. The term "ecosystems" was selected to reflect the project's focus on lands, waters, and living resources, rather than "environment," a term that typically encompasses broader issues such as human health concerns, energy use, resource extraction, and waste management. The Design Committee chose to concentrate on "ecosystem types," rather than individual ecosystems. For example, a Southeastern pine wood and an Oregon Douglas fir stand are both "forest ecosystems." This use recognizes that, in many ways, forests are fundamentally alike and that many laws, policies, and practices apply to forested ecosystems and not, for example, to farmlands. This approach is also directly relevant for policymaking because many of the nation's natural resource management, monitoring, and regulatory activities are organized around similar distinctions.

Five design principles were developed by the Design Committee:

- *Focus on condition and trends.* The reports are about the "state" of and trends in the condition of living and nonliving components and processes that make up the nation's "ecological systems." The focus of the reports is not on causes of environmental problems or actions to protect and manage the environment but instead on the ultimate *outcome* of all such activities—the resulting condition of the ecosystems and the goods and services they provide to society.

- *Be relevant to contemporary policy issues.* The reports aim to present information that can be used by decision makers and opinion leaders to inform major decisions about the nation's ecosystems, while also providing a "big picture" view that is succinct and strategic, rather than exhaustive.

- *Select and report on an unbiased and balanced array of indicators.* Indicators are selected on the basis of what is needed to fairly characterize the state of the nation's ecosystems, rather than because data happen to be available. As far as possible, the intent is to develop indicators that avoid political bias, value-laden language, implications, or references to subjective benchmarks.

- *Report only data that meet the highest standards for quality and coverage across the nation and through time.* Reports are based on the most current scientific data and knowledge and must pass a rigorous peer-review process. Where available data fail to fulfill quality and coverage criteria, the relevant indicator is left blank and the data shortcomings that led to its omission are explained.

- *Update periodically and learn from experience.* The report series is a dynamic "work in progress," not a limited-time effort. Periodic and ongoing updates are needed to supply users with the most recent data; they also provide an opportunity to incorporate scientific advances and enhancements to the nation's monitoring and reporting infrastructure (see Appendix B for a review of research needs identified as crucial to future refinement of the current indicator set). In addition to reporting what is known about the state of the nation's ecosystems at any given time, the reports also identify "data gaps" and institutional challenges for continued and improved reporting (see Appendix C for a summary of remaining data gaps).

Steps in Indicator Development and Refinement

The basic process used for designing and refining indicators and preparing materials for release involved six steps (although in practice these were not always so neatly separated).

1. *Identification of key issues/ecological features.* Indicator working groups and the Design Committee came to consensus on the most important attributes or ecological features that needed to be measured at each level of analysis (core national and within each ecosystem). In some cases this process was more straightforward than in others.

2. *Development of specific metric(s).* Technical groups with representatives from all four sectors reviewed the suite of available measures for their ecosystem or topical area and identified those that were appropriate for national reporting. Steps in developing specific metrics include: reaching a consensus on the subject matter to be covered, delineating the rationale for choosing that subject matter, identifying the units of measure, identifying methods of aggregating data at a national level, and examining the feasibility of populating the indicator with data. During this step, technical groups focused on choosing or designing the most important measurable indicator, *regardless of whether currently available data are available for reporting of that indicator.* Indicators that could not be adequately defined but the working group were listed as "needing further development."

3. *Acquisition and analysis of data.* To help guide evaluation and selection of data, the project's staff and the Design Committee developed a set of clear criteria:

   ○ *Data quality*: Data must provide a reasonably accurate representation of actual conditions and must not include substantial known sources of bias or distortion. Quality was assessed using the expert knowledge of project participants, supplemented by information provided by managers of certain datasets; the project also commissioned some analyses of specific datasets.

   ○ *Data coverage*: A dataset must also provide enough information on the resource or issue in question. This criterion was met by datasets with complete geographic coverage (such as those based on satellite measurements) and those based on representative samples from which reasonably accurate estimates of overall conditions could be made. In practice, this led to selection of datasets that covered most states or a significant fraction of the ecosystem in question. Obviously, there are large amounts of high-quality data that do not meet this criterion. For example, states and research institutions collect many potentially relevant data, but unless they are aggregated and reviewed to determine whether the collection methods are compatible, in practical terms the data are not available for routine national reporting and so are not included in this report.

   ○ *Ongoing data collection*: Data must be from ongoing programs, with a reasonable chance that measurements will be repeated at regular intervals in the future. Although all monitoring and reporting programs are subject to changes in funding and priorities, established programs are clearly different from one-time studies. One-time efforts often break new ground scientifically and may serve as baselines against which to compare future conditions. However, unless and until they are performed regularly, they do not advance the goal of periodic national reporting.

   By applying these criteria, a number of high-quality, nationally representative datasets with good prospects for future continuity were identified. Inevitably, however, adequate datasets did not exist for all indicators. In cases where the data needed for reporting were currently lacking but the indicator was judged to be informative, the indicator was included in the report, along with a notation of the data gap using the standard phrase "data not adequate for national reporting." Appendix C provides a synopsis of changes in data availability since 2002, along with a summary of remaining data gaps and priorities for future work.

   In refining existing indicators, The Heinz Center follows the same basic principles in order to maintain scientific rigor and a balanced four-sector approach. Refinement efforts are typically led by technical groups or the data provider and are overseen by the project's Indicator Refinement Subcommittee and/or Design Committee.

In the 2008 report, there is greater emphasis on the use of statistical analyses to assess data trends over time. The Pearson product-moment correlation coefficient was calculated and only in those cases where the "Pearson's r" was statistically significant ($p = 0.05$) was the trend labeled as "increasing" or "decreasing." In order to capture real trends, rather than variability in the data, statistical analyses were performed for the entire dataset. Exceptions were only made where a noticeable multiyear shift was clearly evident. All data were carefully checked for transcription errors.

Historically, the State of the Nation's Ecosystems project has generally preferred data generated through field monitoring programs, rather than produced through computer models. For the 2008 report there was a shift toward determining the quality, relevance, and credibility of any given dataset, rather than being constrained by the type of data source. This was done in recognition that some level of statistical manipulation is present in even the most 'monitoring-based' datasets, and in response to recommendations to include specific modeled datasets for indicators where full-fledged monitoring programs may be impractical (e.g., soil carbon).

4. *Preparation of draft materials.* Staff, in consultation with the Design Committee and various working groups, prepared draft descriptions of indicators and graphical presentations of available data, along with accompanying technical notes describing methods of data analysis.

5. *External peer review.* The Center distributed over 400 copies of the draft report to current and past committee members, data providers and people who had contributed technical input during the indicator design process, people and organizations who had expressed interest in the project or who had participated in related activities, multiple individuals within most federal agencies, and people specifically recommended by participants as potential reviewers. In addition, more than a dozen people served as "targeted reviewers." These individuals were asked to focus their comments on particular chapters within the draft report to ensure a careful review of each chapter, ideally from multiple people distributed across the four sectors. Finally, over 300 people were notified by e-mail that a review draft was available for download from the project Web site.

For the 2008 report, reviews were received from 79 reviewers, although the actual number of reviewers is probably higher, since many agencies sent a combined comment file reflecting contributions by multiple individuals. Roughly half the comments came from government scientists, another quarter from the academic community, and the remainder roughly equally from the nonprofit and private sectors.

Center staff sorted all comments into several categories. Minor editorial comments were dealt with during the revision of text and graphics. For more substantial comments, staff determined if a response was possible within the scope of the current document; if not, the comment was flagged for reconsideration during future phases of the project. For major comments that required immediate attention, staff developed preliminary responses to reviewer comments. These preliminary responses were then revised and endorsed by one of the project's oversight groups, typically the Indicator Refinement Subcommittee or the Design Committee. In addition, in cases where a technical group was involved in crafting the material that was reviewed, that group was drawn into the process of approving responses to reviewer comments, although the appropriate oversight group had the final say in approving responses.

6. *Development of final report.* The final version of the report incorporates modifications recommended by external peer review and sanctioned by the project's oversight committees.

Appendix B:
Indicator Development Since 2002 and Future Research Needs

2008 Indicators: An Improved Suite

From its inception, the State of the Nation's Ecosystems project was designed to adapt to changes in science, technology, and availability of monitoring data. Our intent in the 2002 report was to provide the best suite of indicators possible at the time to measure the condition and use of ecosystems, rather than a "final" set. We did so knowing that refinement of understanding and advances in monitoring would motivate refinement of the indicators over time. This work will help ensure that the indicators we present here accurately capture essential ecosystem attributes with carefully designed indicator metrics that use appropriate spatial/temporal scales, rely on the most current understanding of ecosystem structure and function, and report the best available data.

The Heinz Center has worked in collaboration with the project's Design Committee, Indicator Refinement Subcommittee, and working groups (see pp. vi–xii) and with data providers to provide a new and improved suite of indicators. These committees and other participants are to be commended and thanked—their contributions were invaluable.

This report contains 108 indicators, including six new indicators not included in the 2002 report* (Table B.1) and 57 indicators that were included in the 2002 report but that have been redesigned (Table B.2) or refined (Table B.3). Redesign refers to a major conceptual change in the indicator with new metrics; refinement encompasses inclusion of new metric components, changes in the computation of the exiting metric, changes in the presentation of the data and further technical development of an indicator that that remains undefined.

Table B.1 New Indicators in 2008 Report	
INDICATOR	**GROUPS/WORKSHOPS INVOLVED WITH INDICATOR DEVELOPMENT**
Core National	
Carbon Storage	Workshop on Carbon Storage Reporting
Change in Stream Flows	Stream Flows Working Group
Established Non-native Species	Non-native Species Working Group
Coasts and Oceans	
Pattern in Coastal Areas	Coastal Patterns Working Group
Fresh Waters	
In-Stream Connectivity	Landscape Pattern Working Group
Freshwater Acidity	Air Quality Working Group

The project's Design Committee identified several priorities for indicator refinement: the need to complete and strengthen the set of core national indicators, to improve the degree of consistency in how similar (or the same) ecological phenomena are reported in different ecosystems, and to reduce the number of indicators in need of further definition.

---

* The 2002 report presented 103 indicators, including a Fresh Waters indicator entitled *Changing Stream Flows*. This indicator was dropped in favor of a new core national indicator, *Change in Stream Flows*. Thus, while there are six new indicators, the net increase is only five.

Table B.2   Indicators That Have Been Redesigned Since 2002

INDICATOR	GROUPS/WORKSHOPS INVOLVED WITH INDICATOR DEVELOPMENT	UNDEFINED IN 2002
Core National		
Pattern of "Natural" Landscapes	Landscape Pattern Working Group	■
Farmlands		
Proximity of Cropland to Residences	Landscape Pattern Working Group	
Patches of "Natural" Land in the Farmland Landscape	Landscape Pattern Working Group	
Stream Habitat Quality	Fresh Waters Contact Group	■
Established Non-native Plant Cover in the Farmland Landscape	Non-native Working Group	■
Forests		
Pattern of Forest Landscapes	Landscape Pattern Working Group	
Fresh Waters		
Stream Habitat Quality	Fresh Waters Contact Group	■
Grasslands and Shrublands		
Pattern of Grassland and Shrubland Landscapes	Landscape Pattern Working Group	
Urban and Suburban Landscapes		
Housing Density Changes in Low-Density Suburban and Rural Areas	Landscape Pattern Working Group	■
"Natural" Lands in the Urban and Suburban Landscape	Landscape Pattern Working Group	

Table B.3   Indicators That Have Been Refined Since 2002

INDICATOR	NEW METRIC ADDED	CHANGE IN COMPUTATION OF EXISTING METRIC	NEW REGIONAL PRESENTATION	PROGRESS MADE IN REFINEMENT, BUT INDICATOR REMAINS UNDEFINED
Core National				
Ecosystem Extent	■			
Movement of Nitrogen	■			
Chemical Contamination	■	■		
At-Risk Native Species	■		■	
Species Composition				■
Plant Growth Index		■	■	
Natural Ecosystem Services				■
Coasts and Oceans				
Areas with Depleted Oxygen		■		
Sea Surface Temperature		■		
Established Non-native Species in Major Estuaries				■
Harmful Algal Events				■
Chlorophyll Concentrations		■		
Status of Commercially Important Fish Stocks		■		

Continued

Table B.3   Indicators That Have Been Refined Since 2002, continued

INDICATOR	NEW METRIC ADDED	CHANGE IN COMPUTATION OF EXISTING METRIC	NEW REGIONAL PRESENTATION	PROGRESS MADE IN REFINEMENT, BUT INDICATOR REMAINS UNDEFINED
Farmlands				
Total Cropland		■	■	
The Farmland Landscape		■		
Nitrate in Farmland Streams and Groundwater			■	
Phosphorus in Farmland Streams			■	
Soil Organic Matter	■			
Pesticides in Farmland Streams and Groundwater		■		
Agricultural Inputs and Outputs		■		
Forests				
Forest Area and Ownership			■	
Forest Types			■	
Forest Management Categories			■	
Nitrate in Forest Streams			■	
Carbon Storage			■	
At-Risk Native Forest Species	■		■	
Forest Age			■	
Forest Disturbance: Fire, Insects, and Disease		■		
Timber Harvest			■	
Timber Growth and Harvest			■	
Fresh Waters				
Extent of Freshwater Ecosystems		■		
Altered Freshwater Ecosystems		■		
Phosphorus in Lakes, Reservoirs and Large Rivers		■		
At-Risk Native Freshwater Species	■		■	
Established Non-native Freshwater Species	■	■		
Status of Freshwater Animal Communities		■	■	
At-Risk Freshwater Plant Communities		■	■	
Grasslands and Shrublands				
Area of Grasslands and Shrublands		■		
Number and Duration of Dry Periods in Grassland and Shrubland Streams and Rivers		■		
At-risk Native Grassland and Shrubland Species	■		■	
Established Non-native Grassland and Shrubland Plant Cover		■		
Urban and Suburban Landscapes				
Area and Composition of Urban and Suburban Landscapes	■	■	■	
Nitrate in Urban and Suburban Streams			■	
Phosphorus in Urban and Suburban Streams			■	
Urban and Suburban Air Quality	■			
Chemical Contamination		■		
Natural Ecosystem Services				■

Core National Indicators

The goal for the core national indicators is to stand alone as the most important set of indicators representing the condition and use of the nation's ecosystems as a whole. To make the suite of core national indicators more comprehensive, we have added indicators on *Carbon Storage, Change in Stream Flows,* and *Established Non-native Species.* Other core national indicators were redesigned or refined. The Landscape Pattern Working group designed the *Pattern of "Natural" Landscapes* indicator, filling a placeholder in the 2002 report. The Biological Community Conditions Working Group took steps to redesign the 2002 *Condition of Plant and Animal Communities* indicator. Those steps are not complete; we have refined the concept and renamed the indicator *Native Species Composition,* but this indicator requires additional development. With the help of our Air Quality Working Group we have expanded the scope of the core indicator *Chemical Contamination* to include air quality considerations. We have also added new elements to two of our indicators: the *At-Risk Native Species* indicator now has a metric tracking population trends in at-risk native species, and the *Ecosystem Extent* indicator now includes metrics describing the flux of land between different ecosystem types and a metric describing the overall gain/loss in area of rare community types.

Cross-Ecosystem Consistency

Two major efforts were undertaken to strengthen specific indicator topics across multiple ecosystem types. The Landscape Pattern Working Group assessed the entire suite of pattern indicators to identify potential improvements. This work resulted in creation of two new indicators, *Pattern in Coastal Areas* (with the assistance of the Coastal Pattern Working Group) and *In-Stream Connectivity* (Fresh Waters), definitions for two previously undefined indicators (*Pattern of "Natural" Landscapes,* a core national indicator, and *Housing Density Changes in Low-Density Suburban and Rural Areas,* in the Urban and Suburban Landscapes chapter), and identification of new or improved data for other indicators. These changes provide the foundation for reporting on conversions in landscape types at a national scale and allow for better understanding of how the intermingling of ecosystems and land use types affects the services our ecosystems provide.

The Non-native Species Working Group reviewed and refined the report's non-native species indicators, which included development of a new core national indicator *Established Non-native Species.* The working group examined the non-native indicators from both ecosystem and taxonomic angles, identifying the most appropriate metric for each ecosystem type. Indicator reporting is now limited to non-native species that have become established in the particular ecosystem type.

Additional Refinement Efforts

The suite of indicators was strengthened by incorporating new indicators and metrics to address air pollution, which account for effects on both human health and ecosystem condition. The Air Quality Working Group designed four new metrics: ground-level ozone and fine particulate matter in ambient air and chemical-specific contamination in biota for the core national *Chemical Contamination* indicator and a metric on nitrogen deposition from air to coastal waters for the core national indicator, *Movement of Nitrogen.* The group also designed a new freshwater indicator, *Freshwater Acidity,* which reports on atmospheric nitrogen and sulfate deposition and the acid-neutralizing capacity of streams.

Carbon indicators in the report were also revised with additional data and data more relevant to current policy debates. As noted, a core national indicator (*Carbon Storage*) was added to the report with information on changes in both overall carbon storage and the amount of carbon per unit area for lands and waters (carbon density), as well as changes in atmospheric carbon dioxide and methane concentrations compared with pre-industrial concentrations. The 2008 report includes more detailed regional reporting of carbon storage in forests than the 2002 report.

The Center has also worked with data providers and its Indicator Refinement Subcommittee to provide more explicit regional reporting on a variety of other indicators. More maps are included in the 2008 report, and in many cases reporting regions have been redefined in order to use similar regional breakdowns for multiple indicators, allowing readers to compare data regional data from different indicators (see Appendix D).

Progress on Undefined Indicators

Over the past six years, the Center has convened a number of other workshops and working group sessions to develop indicators that were undefined in the 2002 Report, including *Condition of Plant and Animal Communities* (now titled *Native Species Composition*, Core National), *Natural Ecosystem Services* (Core National), and *Harmful Algal Blooms* (now *Harmful Algal Events*, Coasts and Oceans). These indicators are particularly challenging to develop because they are at the cutting edge of science, and few data exist at a national level to test candidate metrics. While these sessions made enormous headway in defining the critical issues at hand and proposed solutions, further development is required.

Table B.4   Indicator Development Needed
Core National
Species Composition
Natural Ecosystem Services
Coasts and Oceans
Pattern in Coastal Areas
Established Non-native Species in Major Estuaries
Harmful Algal Events
Farmlands
Status of Animal Species in Farmland Areas
Forests
Fire Frequency
Grasslands and Shrublands
Fire Frequency
Riparian Condition
Urban and Suburban Landscapes
Stream Bank Vegetation
Urban Heat Island
Natural Ecosystem Services

Note: Several of these indicators are also listed as "new" or "refined" but nonetheless remain incompletely defined.

Future Needs

More than 40% of the 2008 indicators have not been redesigned or refined since 2002 (those not shown in Tables B.1–B.3). Many of these indicators have full data gaps or were indicators that the Center did not have time or resources to refine; the remainder retain the 2002 design but have been updated with more current data.

Further indicator development work is needed in order to define all indicators fully in future editions of the *State of the Nation's Ecosystems*. In the 2008 report, 12 indicators are classified as needing additional development (see Table B.4). Additional work is needed to ensure that the suite of indicators reflects the most current scientific advances and meets the evolving needs of decision makers and the public.

Key Research Needs

The following topics and issues have arisen in the course of the extensive refinement efforts undertaken in the preparation of this 2008 report. This list identifies a set of "next generation" refinement efforts. In some cases (e.g., Urban Heat Island), we believe these challenges can be solved by focused effort among knowledgeable experts, which the Center would have undertaken but for resource and time constraints. In other cases, such as the sensitivity of various indicators to climate and other ecosystem drivers, we believe more extensive research is required.

- **Identification of Indicator Sensitivity to Climate Change and Other Drivers of Ecosystem Change.** *The State of the Nation's Ecosystems* 2008 includes many indicators relevant to ecological effects of climate change. However, there is a need to investigate the sensitivity of this indicator set to key global change factors in order to identify gaps in our ability to monitor and report on significant regional and national changes.

- **Indicator Development: Urban Heat Island.** The project's Urban and Suburban Landscapes Contact Group identified the need for an urban heat island effect indicator—parameterized as temperature differences between urban areas and less-developed surrounding rural areas—to track interactions of urban land use and climate. To establish a metric and procedures for its calculation, work is required to resolve discrepancies in how warming is measured (ground-level vs. atmospheric measurements) and in how urban and reference areas are identified (population density vs. satellite measurements of night light).

- **Incorporation of Sustainability into Resource Use Indicators: Food, Fiber and Water.** Several indicators in the report touch on whether or not these crucial resources are used in a sustainable manner (e.g., condition of fish stocks; growth compared to harvest in forests). Work is needed to identify and fill gaps in our ability to assess the sustainability of resource use.

- **Review of Contaminants Indicators.** The current treatment of contaminants is complex, in part because of the wide array of contaminants found in diverse environmental media, and in part because both the existence of contaminants and their concentrations with respect to established benchmarks are considered important. Experts on various media (water, air, sediment, biota) should be engaged in discussions to develop an improved reporting strategy for this important suite of indicators.

- **Reconciliation of Data on Nutrients and Groundwater.** Over the past few years, monitoring programs that supply nutrient data have evolved. The USGS National Water Quality Assessment (NAWQA) program, which supplied nutrient data for the 2002 and 2008 reports, has entered a new phase, in which it will sample fewer monitoring sites and will rely more heavily on modeling nutrient concentrations. EPA has recently released nutrient data as part of the Wadeable Streams Assessment. Work is needed to develop a future strategy for reporting that will be both temporally and spatially sensitive and will allow for reporting on specific ecosystem types.

- **Indicator Development: Fire Frequency.** Although the ecological impacts of changing fire regimes on plant community composition, wildlife populations, and soil nutrients have been widely studied, there is no broadly accepted index that reports on national trends in fire frequency, severity, and intensity. A suitable metric needs to be identified not only to report on fire frequency, but also to track fire intensity, extent, and seasonality. Fire frequency indicators are needed for forest and grassland–shrubland ecosystems.

- **Indicator Development: Harmful Algal Events.** The Center has made initial progress on this topic through a scoping workshop; the 2008 report calls for an indicator that reports the number of harmful algal events of low, medium, and high intensity for estuaries and ocean waters within 200 miles of shore and for the Great Lakes. More work is needed to investigate options for classifying event intensity by combining several metrics, measuring different aspects of the intensity of different types of algal events, into an index.

- **Indicator Development: Native Species Composition.** The 2008 report calls for an indicator that will describe native plant and animal species composition as the ratio of the number of observed species in an area to the expected species composition (i.e., had the area been relatively unaffected by disturbance, management, and physical alteration). Work is needed to test a promising candidate metric using a variety of datasets covering different taxonomic groups and regions and then to evaluate the metric's sensitivity.

- **Indicator Development: Native Species in Human-Dominated Systems.** The 2008 report calls for two indicators that would describe the condition of native species in human-dominated systems (farmlands and urban–suburban areas). For farmlands, an indicator is needed that would account for both types of species found on farmland landscapes—those that favor the preagricultural landscape and those that favor (or tolerate) landscapes dominated by agriculture. While perhaps better defined, the urban–suburban indicator faces considerable data limitations, which suggests that some reevaluation of the indicator design may be warranted.

- **Indicator Development: Landscape Pattern in Coastal Areas.** The 2008 report calls for development of a new indicator that describes the intermingling of natural and non-natural landscape (or seascape) features in coastal areas. Work is needed to build upon two workshops that led to the inclusion of this placeholder in *The State of the Nation's Ecosystems 2008*. A number of promising indicator designs have resulted, which require prototype testing by several research groups around the country.

- **Indicator Development: Additional Investigation of Landscape Pattern Indicators.** The 2008 report includes a number of substantially revised or new indicators of landscape pattern. A few additional issues, however, are worthy of additional exploration, including (a) modifying the indicators designed to describe the remaining natural lands in both the farmland and urban–suburban landscapes (the concern is that fine-scale heterogeneity is very important in these settings and is potentially missed), (b) confirming that pattern indicators are sufficiently sensitive to the presence of roads on the landscape, (c) characterizing exurban development, and (d) examining the proximity of open space to urban dwellers.

- **Indicator Development: Riparian Condition.** Currently, there is no adequate and generally accepted single measure of riparian condition, although researchers have developed several approaches that should serve as a starting point for discussions. Work is needed to test and evaluate appropriate metrics that would take into account multiple factors, including hydrology (e.g., relationship to natural flow patterns), geomorphology (e.g., stream sediment transport), and biology (e.g., canopy cover) to provide an overall index of condition.

- **MODIS–LANDSAT Comparison.** Land cover data feature prominently in the 2008 report. To date, the report has relied solely on the National Land Cover Dataset (NLCD) as a data source. The production of this high-resolution (pixels are 30 m on a side) national map is very time-consuming for the agencies involved, and the two time points for which data are currently available (1992 and 2001) are not yet comparable. Land cover data from the MODIS platform are of lower resolution (pixels are 250 m on a side), yet national maps are produced regularly and are intercomparable. A side-by-side comparison of the suite of extent and landscape pattern metrics included in the report is needed to see how the report might rely on MODIS data. Assuming that very different indicator values will result, it would then be appropriate to do a sensitivity analysis to understand how much land cover needs to change for changes to be detectable in the indicators using the different data sources.

Appendix C:
Changes in Data Availability Since 2002 and Remaining Data Gaps

The State of the Nation's Ecosystems was designed as an evolving project, one that explicitly chose not to report only indicators for which data were currently available for national reporting. This appendix compares the status of data availability in this 2008 report to the situation as reported in the 2002 *State of the Nation's Ecosystems*. The criteria for data inclusion in the report are described in Appendix A (p. 252).

Summary of Changes in Data Availability

Of the 108 indicators in the 2008 Report, 68 (63%) have adequate data to report on a national level. This is an increase over the 58 indicators for which adequate data were available for reporting in 2002. In addition, the number of indicators for which multiyear trends are reported rose from 31 in 2002 to 41 in this report, and the number for which an established reference point was include (e.g., comparing concentrations of nitrogen in water to the drinking water standard) rose from 14[*] to 20. (See Table C.1.)

Table C.1 Summary of Changes in Data Availability, 2002 to 2008

DATA AVAILABILITY	2002 %	2002 NUMBER	2008 %	2008 NUMBER
All data	32	33 ⎫ 58	33	36 ⎫ 68
Partial data	24	25 ⎭	30	32 ⎭
Insufficient data	30	31	26	28
Undefined indicator	14	14	11	12
All Indicators	**100**	**103**	**100**	**108**

	2002	2008
Indicators with Trends	31	41
Indicators with Reference Points	14	20
Indicators with Current Data Only	16	27

Of the 68 indicators for which adequate data are available in this report, 36 have all the data required and the remaining 32 have some data gaps (see Table C.2). These gaps may be regional (data are available for part but not all of the country) or they may be topical (data are available on some but not all components of an indicator); they are described in the indicator summary tables in Chapters 2–8.

Three of the six new indicators—*Carbon Storage* (Core National), *Change in Stream Flows* (Core National), and *Freshwater Acidity*—have either all the required data or partial data. For twelve indicators, new data became available since publication of the 2002 report, allowing their data status to be upgraded (i.e., indicators with inadequate data for national reporting may have been upgraded to partial or full data, or indicators with partial data in 2002 may now be categorized as having all required data). In other cases, new data may have become available for indicators but some gaps remain; these remained categorized as "partial data" indicators.

Data were withdrawn from two indicators, *Animal Deaths and Deformities* (Fresh Waters) and *Waterborne Human Disease Outbreaks* (Fresh Waters), because of inconsistent data quality. In both

---

* This figure was reported as 11 in 2002, because three indicators were incorrectly categorized at that time.

cases, we have consulted with the stewards of the relevant data and agree that these data sources, which rely upon incident-based reporting, probably should not have been included in the 2002 report. In four cases, indicators that had been listed as having all required data are now listed as having partial data as a result of redesign of indicators to include new elements, for which some "data gap" exists.

Data newly included in this 2008 report include data from new monitoring efforts, data that existed but had not been sufficiently aggregated or checked for quality to be included in the 2002 report, and data that are included for the first time as a result of indicator development efforts. For example:

- The release of the U.S. Environmental Protection Agency's Wadeable Streams Assessment allowed the inclusion of data for three indicators: *Stream Habitat Quality* (Fresh Waters) (p. 179), *Status of Freshwater Animal Communities* (p. 185), and the new indicator, *Freshwater Acidity* (p. 176).

- The release of the 2001 National Land Cover Data, made it possible to include data for the Urban and Suburban Landscapes indicator *Total Impervious Area* for the first time.

- As a result of recent implementation of a rigorous quality assurance/quality control (QA/QC) process by the NOAA National Status and Trends program, Mussel Watch data meet the report's data quality criteria, allowing inclusion of data for *Selected Contaminants in Fish and Shellfish* (Coasts and Oceans).

- Work by NatureServe identifying riparian communities has made it possible to report on the risk of extirpation of all freshwater plant communities. NatureServe has also provided data for the new population trends metric in *At-Risk Native Species, At-Risk Native Forest Species, At-Risk Native Freshwater Species,* and *At-Risk Native Grassland and Shrubland Species,* which was designed to provide some information on changes in at-risk populations, given the difficulty of reporting changes in rank status over time (see p. 275).

- Indicator development efforts and analysis by USDA Forest Service and the Environmental Protection Agency interagency team has made it possible to use data from the Multi-Resolution Landscape Consortium for many of our landscape pattern indicators.

Increased geographic sampling by federal agencies has allowed the Center to expand its geographic reporting for several of its indicators. For example:

- Between 1998 and 2001, the U.S. Geological Survey's National Water Quality Assessment Program (NAWQA) sampled 15 more major river basins, allowing this report to include data on stream nitrate and phosphorus concentrations and contaminants in 51 major river basins rather than the 36 included in the 2002 report.

- Recent work under the aegis of the interagency* National Coastal Assessment, have allowed the Center to expand its reporting on bottom-dwelling animals and contaminants in sediments to Puerto Rico and the Pacific Coast.

Addressing Data Gaps

Following the publication of the 2002 report, the Heinz Center and its network collaborators assessed the array of data gaps identified in 2002, identified general technical strategies for filling the various gaps, and worked with relevant monitoring programs to develop initial estimates of the cost of doing so. These recommendations were summarized in the 2006 Heinz Center report, *Filling the Gaps.*[†] *Filling the Gaps* identifies the high-priority recommendations for needed investment. Many of these data gaps or clusters of gaps remain in the 2008 report and should continue to be the focus of efforts to improve monitoring programs.

---

* The Environmental Protection Agency is the lead agency for this effort.

† The Heinz Center. 2006. Filling the Gaps: Priority Data Needs and Key Management Challenges for National Reporting on Ecosystem Condition. Washington, DC. http://www.heinzctr.org/publications.shtml.

TABLE C.2 Indicators According to Data Availability

INDICATORS WITH ALL REQUIRED DATA

Core National
- Pattern of "Natural" Landscapes
- Change in Stream Flows
- Production of Food and Fiber and Water Withdrawals

Coasts and Oceans
- Sea Surface Temperature
- Commercial Fish and Shellfish Landings

Farmlands
- Total Cropland
- The Farmland Landscape
- Patches of "Natural" Land in the Farmland Landscape
- Nitrate in Farmland Streams and Groundwater
- Phosphorus in Farmland Streams
- Pesticides in Farmland Streams and Groundwater
- Potential Soil Erosion
- Major Crop Yields
- Agricultural Inputs and Outputs
- Monetary Value of Agricultural Production

Forests
- Forest Area and Ownership
- Forest Types
- Forest Management Categories
- Pattern of Forest Landscapes
- Nitrate in Forest Streams
- Timber Harvest
- Timber Growth and Harvest
- Recreation in Forests

Fresh Waters
- At-Risk Freshwater Plant Communities
- Water Withdrawals

Grasslands and Shrublands
- Area of Grasslands and Shrublands
- Pattern of Grassland and Shrubland Landscapes
- Number and Duration of Dry Periods in Grassland and Shrubland Streams and Rivers
- Population Trends in Invasive and Non-invasive Birds
- Cattle Grazing

Urban and Suburban Areas
- Area and Composition of Urban and Suburban Landscapes
- Total Impervious Area
- Housing Density Changes in Low-Density Suburban and Rural Areas
- "Natural" Lands in the Urban and Suburban Landscape
- Nitrate in Urban and Suburban Streams
- Phosphorus in Urban and Suburban Streams

INDICATORS WITH PARTIAL DATA

Core National
- Ecosystem Extent
- Movement of Nitrogen
- Carbon Storage
- Chemical Contamination
- At-Risk Native Species
- Plant Growth Index
- Outdoor Recreation

Coasts and Oceans
- Coastal Living Habitats
- Shoreline Types
- Areas with Depleted Oxygen
- Contamination in Bottom Sediments
- Unusual Marine Mortalities
- Condition of Bottom-Dwelling Animals
- Chlorophyll Concentrations
- Status of Commercially Important Fish Stocks
- Selected Contaminants in Fish and Shellfish

Forests
- Carbon Storage
- At-Risk Native Forest Species
- Forest Age
- Forest Disturbance: Fire, Insects, and Disease

Fresh Waters
- Extent of Freshwater Ecosystems
- Altered Freshwater Ecosystems
- Phosphorus in Lakes, Reservoirs and Large Rivers
- Freshwater Acidity
- Stream Habitat Quality
- At-Risk Native Freshwater Species
- Established Non-native Freshwater Species
- Status of Freshwater Animal Communities

Grasslands and Shrublands
- Land Use in Grasslands and Shrublands
- At-Risk Native Grassland and Shrubland Species

Urban and Suburban Landscapes
- Urban and Suburban Air Quality
- Chemical Contamination

INDICATORS WITH INADEQUATE DATA FOR NATIONAL REPORTING

Core National
- Established Non-native Species

Coasts and Oceans
- Coastal Erosion
- At-Risk Native Marine Species
- Recreational Water Quality

Farmlands
- Proximity of Cropland to Residences
- Soil Organic Matter
- Soil Salinity
- Stream Habitat Quality
- Established Non-native Plant Cover in the Farmland Landscape
- Soil Biological Condition
- Recreation in Farmland Areas

Forests
- Established Non-native Plant Cover in Forests
- Forest Community Types With Significantly Reduced Area

Fresh Waters
- In-Stream Connectivity
- Water Clarity
- Animal Deaths and Deformities
- Groundwater Levels
- Waterborne Human Disease Outbreaks
- Freshwater Recreational Activities

Grasslands and Shrublands
- Nitrate in Grassland and Shrubland Groundwater
- Carbon Storage
- Depth to Shallow Groundwater
- Established Non-native Grassland and Shrubland Plant Cover
- Recreation on Grasslands and Shrublands

Urban and Suburban Areas
- Species Status
- Disruptive Species
- Status of Animal Communities in Urban and Suburban Streams
- Publicly Accessible Open Space per Resident

INDICATORS NEEDING ADDITIONAL DEVELOPMENT

Core National
- Native Species Composition
- Natural Ecosystem Services

Coasts and Oceans
- Pattern in Coastal Areas
- Established Non-native Species in Major Estuaries
- Harmful Algal Events

Farmlands
- Status of Animal Species in Farmland Areas

Forests
- Fire Frequency

Grasslands and Shrublands
- Fire Frequency
- Riparian Condition

Urban and Suburban Landscapes
- Stream Bank Vegetation
- Urban Heat Island
- Natural Ecosystem Services

Maps of Regions Used throughout the Report

When feasible, indicators in *State of the Nation's Ecosystems 2008* include both national and regional data. Different regional breakouts are used in different indicators, depending both on the data source used and on the type of indicator. Some of the regions used in this report are based on state boundaries, and others use ecoregional data based on land cover, climate, or vegetation.

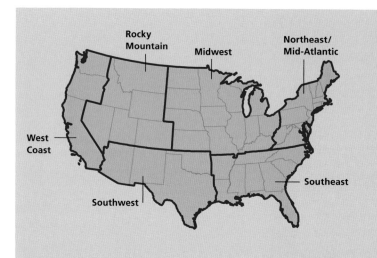

This map applies to the following indicators:

- Core National: Pattern of "Natural" Landscapes (p. 33), Production of Food and Fiber and Water Withdrawals (p. 56)
- Farmlands: The Farmland Landscape (p. 103), Patches of "Natural" Land in the Farmland Landscape (p. 106)
- Grasslands and Shrublands: Pattern of Grassland and Shrubland Landscapes (p. 204)
- Urban and Suburban: Area and Composition of the Urban and Suburban Landscape (p. 230), Total Impervious Area (p. 232), Housing Density Changes in Low-Density Suburban and Rural Areas (p. 234), "Natural" lands in the Urban and Suburban Landcapes (p. 236)

The regional scheme presented here was developed by The Heinz Center based on state boundaries. For the cited indicators, state-level reporting was grouped into the above categories to create these six regions. Data presented in these indicators apply to the lower 48 states only.

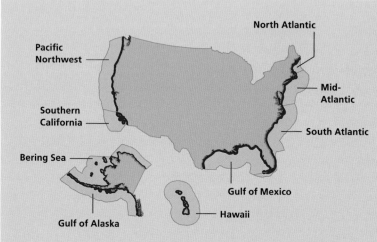

This map applies to the following indicators:

- Coasts and Oceans: Shoreline Types (p. 73), Sea Surface Temperature (p. 79), Condition of Bottom-Dwelling Animals (p. 84), Chlorophyll Concentrations (p. 86), Commercial Fish and Shellfish Landings (p. 87), Status of Commercially Important Fish Stocks (p. 88)

The regions shown here conform to those used by the National Oceanic and Atmospheric Administration and the Environmental Protection Agency in agency reports; they also match the regional structure established for regional marine research under Public Law 101-593. Coverage: all coastal states; some indicators also include Guam, American Samoa, Puerto Rico, and the U.S. Virgin Islands (see each indicator for details). For some indicators, regions are combined, or specific locations are highlighted for reporting purposes.

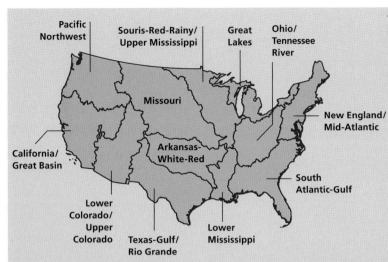

This regional map applies to the following indicator:
- Farmlands: Total Cropland (p. 102)

This map is based on major river basins as defined by the U.S. Department of Agriculture, Natural Resources Conservation Service, National Resources Inventory. Note: Coverage for the Total Croplands indicator is for the lower 48 states only; Hawaii and Alaska are not included.

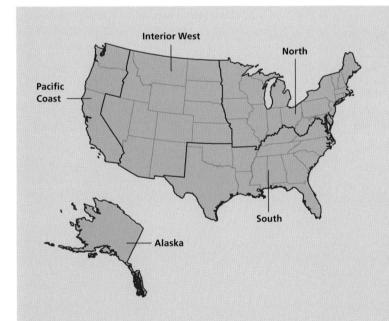

This map applies to the following indicators:
- Forests: Forest Area and Ownership (p.132), Forest Types (p.134), Forest Management Categories (p. 136), Pattern of Forest Landscapes (p. 138), Carbon Storage (p. 142), Forest Age (p. 147), Timber Harvest (p. 154), Timber Growth and Harvest (p. 155)

The regions used in the Forests chapter were defined by the U.S. Department of Agriculture, U.S. Forest Service, Forest Inventory and Analysis program (FIA) for this report.

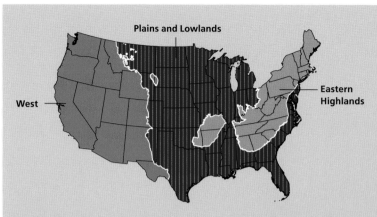

This map applies to the following indicators:
● Freshwater: Freshwater Acidity (p. 176), Status of Freshwater Animal Communities (p. 185)

The regional definitions presented here are based on the Omernik's Level III ecoregions (see http://nationalatlas.gov/mld/ecoomrp.html). These regions are consistent with those used by the U.S. Environmental Protection Agency, Wadeable Streams Assessment.

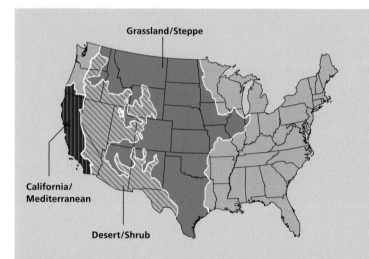

This map applies to the following indicator:
● Grasslands and Shrublands: Number and Duration of Dry Periods in Grassland and Shrubland Streams and Rivers (p. 208)

Regional classification is based on U.S. Department of Agriculture, U.S. Forest Service ecoregional classification scheme (known as Bailey's System). Note: The regional breakdown presented here does not include all grasslands and shrublands in the lower 48 states. For example, grasslands in the East are not shown here and are not covered in the associated indicator. There are also areas on the map covered by these regions that are not grassland or shrubland; however, only grassland and shrubland areas were included in the indicator analysis.

Technical Notes

This section contains technical documentation for the indicators in Chapters 2 through 8. These notes begin with descriptions of major monitoring programs that provided data for multiple indicators, and are followed by sections for each of the indicator chapters (i.e. Chapters 2–8). Within each section, technical notes follow the same order as the indicators are presented in the relevant indicator chapter. More detailed technical notes are provided at http://www.heinzcenter.org/ecosystems.

Program Description for the EPA National Coastal Assessment

Data from this program are presented in the following indicators:

- **Core National:** Chemical Contamination (estuarine sediments, saltwater fish tissue)
- **Coasts/Oceans:** Contaminants in Bottom Sediments; Condition of Bottom-Dwelling Animals

Program Description: The U.S. Environmental Protection Agency's (EPA) National Coastal Assessment (NCA) program provides integrated, comprehensive monitoring of the physical, chemical and biological condition of the nation's coastal resources. In 1990–1997, the Environmental Monitoring and Assessment Program (EMAP)—implemented by EPA, the National Oceanographic and Atmospheric Administration (NOAA), the U.S. Geological Survey (USGS), coastal states, and academia—monitored ecological condition of U.S. estuaries (http://www.epa.gov/emap/). In 2000, EMAP expanded into a series of national surveys (the National Coastal Assessment), including all coastal states and Puerto Rico (USEPA, 2000a).

Data Collection Methodology: Sampling and analysis methods for contaminants in estuarine sediments and fish and shellfish tissue as well as benthic condition are described in http://www.epa.gov/emap/nca/html/docs/c2kfm.

pdf. For the Chesapeake Bay, some data were included from the NOAA National Status and Trends Program's Sediment Triad Studies (EPA-842/B-06-001) and from the Chesapeake Bay Program. (Note that NCA data on chlorophyll and dissolved oxygen did not match the data requirements of the related indicators in this report.) For a complete list of NCA contaminant analytes in estuarine sediment and fish and shellfish tissue, see http://www.epa.gov/emap/nca/html/data/analyte.txt.

Temporal/Geographic Coverage: Sampling was conducted for estuarine sediments from 1998 to 2002 and for fish and shellfish tissue and condition of bottom-dwelling animals from 1999 to 2002. All site selections were based on probabilistic sampling designs that permit the extrapolation of data to 100% of the estuarine resources for the 21 coastal states of the lower 48 states, Hawaii, Puerto Rico and south-central Alaska. The NCA visits new, randomly selected sites each year with the exception of Alabama and Maryland where initially randomly-selected sites (for sediment and benthic sampling) have been re-sampled in subsequent years. Fish tissue contaminant data are not available for the Chesapeake Bay (some tributary data are included), Connecticut, Hawaii or Puerto Rico.

Data Analysis:

Detected Contaminants in Sediments and Fish Tissue: Sediment and fish tissue data were analyzed to determine the percent of estuarine sediment area and fish tissue samples in which contaminants were measured above analytical detection limits. Trace elements were excluded from detection analysis because they can occur naturally in estuarine sediments. All fish tissue analytes were included in detection analysis.

Exceedance of Sediment and Fish Tissue Benchmarks: Measured contaminant concentrations were compared to lower and higher benchmarks for the protection of aquatic life (sediments) and human health (fish tissue) to determine the percentage of estuarine area and tissue samples in which contaminants exceeded benchmarks. Fewer samples will exceed

Table 1.	NCA sampling sites, analytes and benchmarks compared to measured concentrations.		
	Sampling sites	**Analytes**	**Benchmarks**
Estuary sediments	2,146 estuarine sites	81 total analytes—20 pesticide compounds, 24 polynuclear aromatic hydrocarbons (PAHs), 21 polychlorinated biphenyl (PCB) congeners, 15 trace elements (including mercury)	**Aquatic life:** 27 individual or composite benchmarks compared to 6 pesticide compounds, 24 PAHs, 21 PCB congeners, 9 trace elements (Long et al., 1998)
Saltwater fish and shellfish tissue	16 types of fish and 3 types of shellfish at 1,277 estuarine sites		**Human health:** 16 individual or composite benchmarks compared to 19 pesticide compounds, 24 PAHs, 21 PCB congeners, 4 trace elements (including mercury) (EPA-823-B-00-008)
Bottom-dwelling animals	2,150 estuarine sites	—	—

higher benchmark concentration values and, by definition, these samples will also exceed the lower benchmark concentration values. More samples will exceed lower benchmarks so tracking these exceedances can be considered a more stringent approach. Note that many contaminants measured by the NCA do not have established benchmarks (see Table 1) or have a range of benchmark values associated with different types or likelihood of effects. Aquatic life benchmarks for estuarine sediment (also known as sediment quality guidelines) were developed as informal, interpretive tools by NOAA's National Status and Trends Program (for lists of specific benchmark values, see http://response.restoration.noaa.gov/book_shelf/121_sedi_qual_guide.pdf). The lower benchmarks (Effects Range-Low, ERL) identify concentrations below which adverse effects rarely occur and above which adverse effects are considered possible. The higher (Effects Range-Median, ERM) benchmarks identify concentrations above which adverse effects are considered probable. No benchmarks exist for potential human health effects from exposure to contaminated sediments. Lower and higher human health benchmarks for whole-body saltwater fish tissue samples correspond to the range of concentrations associated with non-cancer health endpoint risk for human consumption of four 8-ounce meals per month (for specific benchmark values, see Risk-Based Consumption Limit Tables in http://www.epa.gov/waterscience/fish/advice/volume2/). There is currently no EPA guidance available for evaluating the ecological risk of whole-body contaminant burdens in fish.

Benthic Condition (Bottom-dwelling animals): Benthic condition was analyzed using regional indices that compared the number and kinds of animals found in a sampling site with those that would be expected in an undisturbed area of similar character (a reference site). For further information, see the technical note for coastal indicator Condition of Bottom-Dwelling Animals, p. 292.

Data Quality/Caveats:

Estuarine sediment: It is difficult to evaluate the potential effects of contaminated sediments on estuarine organisms because few applicable state or federal regulatory criteria exist. Also, studies have documented benthic community-level effects at lower concentration levels than those associated with short-term, single-species toxicity—benthic community condition may reflect the sensitivities of multiple species and life stages to persistent exposures under actual field conditions (Hyland et al, 2003). (No data on fish tissue were available for the 2002 report.)

Data Availability: The data presented here were obtained directly from EPA. Data from the National Coastal Assessment are available at http://www.epa.gov/emap/nca/html/data/index.html.

2008 Report Data Update: In the 2002 Report, sediment contamination data for 1992–1998 were reported, however these data are not comparable to the 1998–2002 data presented here due to expansion of the geographic scope of the monitoring program—North Atlantic and Pacific Coast estuaries, Hawaii, and south-central Alaska were added. Sampling and analysis protocols are the same although the pesticide Dieldrin is no longer included in the benchmark exceedance analysis.

Program Description for the EPA Wadeable Streams Assessment

Data from this program are presented in the following indicators:
- **Fresh Waters:** Freshwater Acidity (Sensitivity of Streams to Acidification); Stream Habitat Quality; Status of Freshwater Animal Communities

Program Description: The U.S. Environmental Protection Agency, Office of Water produced the Wadeable Streams Assessment (WSA) in 2006 to report on the ecological condition of wadeable streams in the conterminous US, provide direct measures of aquatic life, identify the relative importance of chemical and physical stressors on stream condition, and increase compatibility of national, regional, state and tribal monitoring efforts. The WSA's statistical design enables EPA to make conclusions about the condition of most wadeable streams in three regions, during the summer index period: 90.5% of Eastern Highland wadeable streams (276,362 stream miles), 98% of Plains and Lowlands wadeable streams (242,264 stream miles) and 98.3% of wadeable streams in the West (152,425 stream miles) (see map, p. 268). Within these three climatic and landform regions, the WSA also reports on nine ecological regions.

Data Collection Methodology: Sediment and habitat features, water chemistry, and macroinvertebrate data were collected by EPA, states, tribes and other federal agencies from over 1,392 wadeable perennial stream locations in the lower 48 states over a five-year period. Sampling sites were randomly located based on the distribution of first order (smallest) to fifth order streams, so that areas with few stream miles had fewer sampling sites than areas with more stream-miles. Multiple sampling transects were taken along each sampled stream segment, or reach.

Data Quality/Caveats: All data were collected during the summer index period (during base-flow conditions). Thus, a single sampling time period may yield a data value that is not representative for parameters that have considerable temporal variation. Fortunately, for most parameters used in this report, such as the index of biotic integrity (IBI) in Status of Freshwater Animal Communities (p. 185), is thought to be integrative, meaning that a sample from a single time point reflects community condition over a reasonably long period of time (e.g., months if not years).

Data Availability: Sampling data are available in the U.S. Environmental Protection Agency's national STORET data warehouse. Links to the warehouse and directions on how to find the WSA data are available at (http://www.epa.gov/owow/streamsurvey/web_data.html).

Program Description for the USDA Forests Inventory and Analysis Program

Data from this program are presented in the following indicators:
- **Core National:** Ecosystem Extent; Carbon Storage; Production of Food and Fiber and Water Withdrawals

- **Forests:** Forest Area and Ownership; Forest Types; Forest Management Categories; Carbon Storage; Forest Age; Timber Harvest; Timber Growth and Harvest

Program Description: The Forest Inventory and Analysis (FIA) program of the USDA Forest Service (USFS) uses a combination of aerial and plot-based data to provide information about all U.S. forested lands, through federal-state partnerships. As mandated under the Forest and Rangeland Renewable Resources Research Act of 1978 (PL 95–307), USFS used a two-phase sample (generally, double sampling for stratification) to collect information on the nation's forests, beginning in the late 1940s. Surveys were conducted on a periodic basis until 1998, when the Agricultural Research, Extension, and Education Reform Act (PL 105-185) required that each state survey 20% of their plots each year to produce a full monitoring cycle every five years. A first step toward achieving this mandate set by USFS requires Eastern states to complete at least 15% of their inventory each year, and Western states to complete 10% of their inventory each year. Alaska, Hawaii, and other island areas are completed on a cycle unique to those areas. Currently, most eastern states contribute funds to leverage the FIA program funding, thereby permitting 20% of plots to be surveyed annually. More information about the FIA program and details about sampling may be found at http://fia.fs.fed.us.

Data Quality/Caveats: Comparisons among individual states are complicated by variability in data collection dates by individual state monitoring programs. Dates of reporting for underlying state-level data are averaged with a weighting factor for individual states, and values between dates are interpolated. Therefore, a reported date of "1997" includes data from each state from 1997 or the most recent year prior to 1997; this varies from state to state. In future years, all states are expected to report a portion of their data to the national FIA office, as described above, and reporting dates should be more consistent with data collection dates (see http://www.fia.fs.fed.us for more information on recent changes to the FIA database). See the 2008 Report website for more detailed information on reporting dates used in this data set by state.

FIA surveys provide forest area data with a reliability of ±3–5% per 1 million acres and volume data with a reliability of ±5-8% per billion cubic feet (both with a 67% confidence limit). This standard applies to all data reported for 1953 and later. Regional totals generally have errors of less than ±2%.

Historical data reported may differ slightly in this report edition compared to earlier editions. This is due to the fact that much of the historical data is still compiled manually from USFS publications each time the data are requested. In future, the USFS plans to enter all historical data into the USFS FIA Database which should eliminate these discrepancies. For the 2008 report, data have been disaggregated into multiple regions (North, South, Interior West, Pacific Coast, and Alaska). The process of reconciling the data into multiple regions may have introduced some differences in the data totals previously reported as the combined East and West regions, due to rounding error.

Data Availability: All data are available from USFS (http://fia.fs.fed.us). Historical area and volume data are available in a variety of USFS publications although data from original publications may be revised due to changes in data

classifications, regional reporting boundaries, or correction of reporting errors.

Program Description for the USDA National Resources Inventory

Data from this program are presented in the following indicators:
- **Core National:** Ecosystem Extent; Carbon Storage
- **Farmlands:** Total Cropland; Potential Soil Erosion
- **Grasslands and Shrublands:** Area of Grasslands and Shrublands

Program Description: The USDA Natural Resources Conservation Service, in cooperation with the Iowa State University's Center for Survey Statistics and Methodology, conducts the National Resources Inventory (NRI) survey to capture data on land cover and use, soil erosion, prime farmland soils, wetlands, habitat diversity, selected conservation practices, and related resource attributes.

Data Collection Methodology: The NRI is a two-stage stratified area sample of the entire country. Stage one is the Primary Sampling Unit (PSU), and it is a sampling of an area/segment of land typically square to rectangular in shape and ranging from 40 to 640 acres but most typically 160 acres in size. Stage two requires the assignment of sampling unit points that are located within the PSU. Data are collected for the NRI using a variety of imagery methods, field office records, historical records and data, ancillary materials, and onsite visits. The data are compiled, verified, and analyzed to provide a comprehensive summary of the state of U.S. non-federal lands. The NRI was conducted on a five-year cycle during the period 1982 to 1997, but is now conducted annually. NRI data were collected every five years for 800,000 sample sites; annual NRI data collection occurs at slightly less than 25 percent of these same sample sites. Current NRI estimates cover the contiguous 48 states. We expect future estimates will also cover Hawaii, Alaska, the Caribbean, and selected Pacific Basin islands.

The land use data come from the NRI data category "Land Cover/Use," which comprises mutually exclusive categories such as cropland, rangeland, forest land, other rural land, developed land, and water. The NRI uses this classification to account for every acre of non-Federal land. Every parcel of land is described by only one of these categories.

Data Quality/Caveats: NRI has used the same sample sites, definitions, and protocols since reporting began in 1982. The inventory accounts for 100 percent of the surface area monitored. NRI estimates are released when they meet statistical standards and are scientifically credible in accordance with NRCS policy, and in accordance with OMB and USDA Quality of Information Guidelines. Margins of error (at the 95 percent confidence level) are presented for all NRI estimates online and in NRI summary publications.

Data Availability: Data are reported at the national and state-level and are available at http://www.nrcs.usda.gov/technical/NRI/. The most recent NRI report is the Summary Report 2003 National Resources Inventory (revised February 2007).

Program Description for the U.S. Fish and Wildlife Service's National Wetlands Inventory

Data from this program are presented or used in the computation of the following indicators:
- **Core National:** Ecosystem Extent
- **Coasts and Oceans:** Coastal Living Habitats; Shoreline Types
- **Fresh Waters:** Extent of Freshwater Ecosystems

Program Description: The National Wetlands Inventory (NWI) Status and Trends program was designed to sample and map wetlands and monitor wetland change. The NWI assessments use a consistent definition of wetlands and standardized protocols for wetland delineation and mapping to facilitate comparisons across regions and over time. The NWI is reported in periodic reports covering three program areas: wetland mapping, trend and change analysis of wetland habitats, and identifying and assessing threats to at-risk aquatic habitats.

Data Collection Methodology: The most recent publication of NWI results, summarized in Dahl et al. (2006), are derived from four separate analyses; one covering the 1950s to the 1970s; one covering the 1970s to 1980s, one covering the 1980s to the 1990s, and one covering 1998 to 2004. NWI counts all wetlands, regardless of land ownership, but recognizes only wetlands that are at least 3 acres in size. The NWI uses a permanent study design, based initially on stratification of the 48 conterminous states by state boundaries and 35 physiographic subdivisions. Within these subdivisions 4375 randomly located 4-square-mile (2560 acres) sample plots are selected. The NWI examines plots with the use of aerial imagery, ranging in scale and type; most were 1:40,000 scale, color infrared, from the National Aerial Photography Program. To ensure adequate coverage of coastal wetlands, the NWI added supplemental sampling along the Atlantic and Gulf coastal fringes.

Data Quality/Caveats: The NWI uses field verifications to address questions on image interpretation, land use coding, attribution of wetland gains or losses, and plot delineations. For example, for the analyses in the 1980s to 1990s, 21% of the sample plots were verified. For all values reported in the NWI, confidence estimates are provided (e.g., the estimate of the total area of freshwater wetlands—102.5 million acres in 2004—has an uncertainty, as measured by a coefficient of variation, of 2.7%).

Data Availability: The Status and Trend of Wetlands in the Conterminous United States 1998–2004 is available on the Web at http://wetlandsfws.er.usgs.gov/status_trends.

Program Description for the USGS National Water Quality Assessment

Data from this program are presented in the following indicators:
- **Core National:** Movement of Nitrogen, Chemical Contamination

- **Farmlands:** Nitrate in Farmland Streams and Groundwater; Phosphorus in Farmland Streams; Pesticides in Farmland Streams and Groundwater
- **Forests:** Nitrate in Forest Streams
- **Fresh Waters:** Phosphorus in Lakes, Reservoirs, and Large Rivers
- **Urban/Suburban:** Nitrate in Urban Streams; Phosphorus in Urban Streams; Chemical Contamination (freshwaters)

Program Description: The U.S. Geological Survey (USGS) National Water Quality Assessment (NAWQA) program provides nationally consistent monitoring of the physical, chemical and biological condition of streams (water, sediments, fish) and groundwater in 51 major hydrologic systems (referred to as study units) in the conterminous U.S., Alaska, and Hawaii, as well as the High Plains Regional Ground Water Study (http://water.usgs.gov/nawqa/). In each study unit, land use and human activities were characterized so that water quality could be compared across different land use and land cover types (Mueller and Spahr, 2006; Koterba, 1998). In 2001–2012, NAWQA monitoring will continue in 42 of the 51 study units completed in the first decade.

Table 2 describes the geographic and temporal coverage of NAWQA's national and land use studies. A comprehensive description of data provided by the NAWQA program is provided by Wilson et al., (2008), available at http://pubs.usgs.gov/of/2008/1110/.

Data Collection Methodology: All water, sediment and tissue samples were collected and analyzed by USGS according to the overall NAWQA design (Gilliom et al. 1995). Analytical methods are described for streams in Shelton (1994), groundwater in Koterba et al. (1995) and nutrients in Fishman (1993) and Patton and Truitt (1992). Typically, streamwater samples were collected using depth and width integrating techniques so that the sample is representative of the water flowing past the sampling point (Shelton 1994). Basic sampling frequency at stream and river sites was monthly with several additional high-flow samples collected during high-intensity sampling years and during time periods when concentrations of certain constituents were expected to be high (Mueller and Spahr, 2006). To compute flow-weighted means, mean-annual loads were estimated by relating individual sample concentrations to the corresponding stream flow for the date and time each sample was collected for each site where samples could be fit to a regression model. The flow-weighted mean concentration was then calculated by dividing the total load by the total flow (Mueller and Spahr, 2005). For pesticides, time-weighted mean concentrations were used. Groundwater samples were collected primarily from monitoring wells and low-capacity domestic wells using procedures that resulted in a sample representative of water in the aquifer (Lapham et al. 1995). Only one sample from each well was analyzed. For streambed sediment the analysis is based on one composite sample per site (Crawford and Luoma, 1993; Shelton and Capel, 1994) and for freshwater fish in streams the analysis is based on one composite sample per site (each sample consisted of 5–8 individual fish belonging to one taxon).

Data Analysis: Table 3 describes the contaminants analyzed in streamwater, streambed sediment, freshwater

Table 2.   NAWQA's national and land use[1] studies.

Study	Coverage	Sampling sites	Timeframe	Indicators
National stream study	51 major hydrologic systems across the nation	186 stream sites	1992–2001	• Core national Chemical Contamination indicator
		957 streambed sediment sites		
		700 freshwater fish sampling sites[2]		
Major Aquifer Studies	92 studies in 54 Principal Aquifers across the nation	2,282 wells (median depth 155 ft)	1993–2001	• Core national Chemical Contamination indicator
Agricultural land use studies	Agricultural watersheds within 51 study units and the High Plains Regional Ground Water Study	130 stream sites for nitrate, 129 for phosphorus, 83 for pesticides	1992–2001	• Nitrate in Farmland Streams and Groundwater • Phosphorus in Farmland Streams • Pesticides in Farmland Streams and Groundwater
		1,412 wells (median depth 34 ft)	1993–2003	
Forested land use studies	Forested watersheds within 51 study units and the High Plains Regional Ground Water Study	117 stream sites	1992–2001	• Nitrate in Forest Streams
		33 wells	1992–2003	• Ecosystem comparison in Nitrate in Farmland Streams and Groundwater
Urban land use studies	Urban/suburban watersheds within 51 major river basins	54 urban streams sampled for nitrate, 53 for phosphorus	1992–2001	• Nitrate in Urban/Suburban Streams • Phosphorus in Urban/Suburban Streams
		861 wells (median depth 30 ft)	1992–2003	• Ecosystem comparison in Nitrate in Farmland Streams and Groundwater
	30 urban/suburban watersheds across the nation	30 stream sites	1992–2001	• Urban/Suburban Chemical Contamination

[1]   Land use classifications were based on an enhanced version of the 1992 National Land Cover Data (NLCD).

[2]   One composite whole-fish sample tested at each stream site.

fish tissue and groundwater and the benchmarks compared to measured concentrations—for lists of specific analytes and benchmarks, see appendices 6, 9, 12 and 16 in Wilson et al. (2006).

Detected Contaminants: For each sampling site, those contaminants measured above the analytical detection limit were summed. Indicator figures present "bins" or groupings of sites based on the number of contaminants detected. Not all measured contaminants are included in detection analyses. Nitrate, ammonia (in streams and groundwater), trace elements (in stream sediments and groundwater), and radon (in groundwater) can occur naturally in the environment so they are included in figures showing exceedances of benchmarks, but not in figures showing detected contaminants.

Exceedance of Benchmarks: For each sampling site, those contaminants measured at concentrations higher than established benchmarks for the protection of aquatic life and human health were summed. Aquatic life benchmarks commonly relate to shorter-term exposure to account for different exposure pathways and generally smaller size of aquatic organisms. Benchmarks for protection of fish-eating wildlife relate to contaminant levels in prey species that can

adversely affect predators (e.g., fish-eating birds). Human health benchmarks relate to chronic exposure to drinking water from streams or groundwater (i.e., consumed daily over a person's lifetime). Note that many contaminants measured by NAWQA do not have established benchmarks or have a range of benchmark values associated with different types or likelihood of effects, affected organisms and exposure duration.

Data Quality/Caveats:

Temporal/Geographic Coverage: The NAWQA study units account for over 60% of the nation's drinking water and irrigation resources and the sites sampled are representative of a wide range of stream sizes, types, and land uses. However, NAWQA sites were not selected to be a statistically representative sample of the nation's aquatic resources. Sampling was not focused on locations where contamination was known or suspected. Each study unit assessment adhered to a nationally consistent sampling and analytical methodology, so that water-quality conditions in a specific locality or watershed can be compared to those in other geographic regions. Because this is a national assessment, the percentage of targeted land use varies across the nation. Water quality is affected by both the percentage of land use in a watershed and the proximity of that land use (as a source of contamination) to streams and rivers.

	Analytes	Benchmarks
Table 3.	**NAWQA analytes and benchmarks compared to measured concentrations.**	
Streamwater	83 pesticide compounds, nitrate[1], ammonia, phosphorus	**Aquatic life:** 63 benchmarks in nine categories for acute and chronic effects on aquatic organisms and communities compared to 62 pesticide compounds and ammonia (Gilliom et al., 2006) **Human health:** 74 individual or composite benchmarks in two categories[2] drinking water compared to 73 pesticide compounds and nitrate
Groundwater	83 pesticide compounds; 87 volatile organic compounds[3] (VOCs), nitrate[1], 22 trace elements[4], radon	**Human health:** 147 benchmarks in two categories[2] for drinking water compared to 73 pesticide compounds, 54 VOCs, nitrate, 18 trace elements, and radon
Streambed sediment	31 pesticide compounds, total polychlorinated biphenyls (PCBs), 63 semi-volatile organic compounds (SVOCs), 9 trace elements (including mercury)	**Aquatic life:** 41 individual or composite benchmarks in three categories for toxic effects on sediment-dwelling organisms compared to 20 pesticide compounds, total PCBs, 24 SVOCs, 9 trace elements (Nowell and Resek, 1994)
Freshwater fish tissue	27 pesticide compounds, total PCBs	**Aquatic life:** 15 individual or composite benchmarks in four categories[5] for toxic effects on fish-eating wildlife compared to 25 pesticide compounds, total PCBs (Gilliom et al., 2006)

[1] *"Nitrate" includes both nitrate and nitrite.*

[2] *USEPA's Maximum Contaminant Levels (EPA-822-R-06-013) and USGS' Health-Based Screening Levels (Toccalino et al. 2006).*

[3] *Censoring level of 0.2 μg/L was applied to achieve a consistent detection limit across the full sampling period.*

[4] *Trace elements include heavy metals and other elements with potential for toxic effects.*

[5] *Whole-body fish tissue concentrations were compared to both lower and higher benchmarks. Fewer samples will exceed higher benchmark concentration values and, by definition, these samples will also exceed the lower benchmark concentration values. More samples will exceed lower benchmarks so tracking these exceedances can be considered a more stringent approach.*

Comparing data from national and land use studies: Most wells sampled for the Major Aquifer Studies are used for drinking water, while the majority of wells sampled for agricultural and urban land use studies were shallow observation wells that are not used for drinking water (some wells sampled in agricultural areas were domestic wells).

Chemical Contaminant Analytes: Pesticide compounds sampled in water account for 78% of currently used agricultural pesticide applications in the U.S. Organochlorine pesticides examined by NAWQA in streambed sediments and fish tissue account for more than 90% of the nation's historical use of these compounds in agriculture. Pesticides tested in water samples include 20 of the 25 most heavily used herbicides and 16 of the 25 most heavily used insecticides. Most of the organochlorine pesticides tested in streambed sediments are no longer used in the United States, but the parent compounds, degradates, or by-products still may persist in the environment (Gilliom et al., 2006).

Benchmarks: Contaminant data on freshwater fish tissue are not compared to any human health benchmarks because such benchmarks apply to edible fish tissue (e.g., fillets), whereas the objective of sampling fish in this assessment was to determine if contaminants are bioaccumulating in any tissues—which is important to both humans and fish-eating wildlife. Thus, entire fish were analyzed for the data reported here.

Data Availability: All data used in this report are summarized at http://pubs.usgs.gov/of/2008/1110/. Additional information on the benchmarks used in this report for pesticides is provided at http://water.usgs.gov/nawqa/pnsp/.

Program Description for the National Land Cover Dataset

Data from this program are presented or used in the computation of the following indicators:

- **Core National:** Ecosystem Extent; Pattern of "Natural" Landscapes
- **Farmlands:** The Farmland Landscape; Patches of "Natural" Land in the Farmland Landscape
- **Forests:** Pattern of Forest Landscapes
- **Freshwaters:** Extent of Freshwater Ecosystems; Altered Freshwater Ecosystems
- **Grasslands and Shrublands:** Area of Grasslands and Shrublands; Pattern of Grassland and Shrubland Landscapes; Number and Donation of Dry Periods in Grassland and Shrubland Steams and Rivers
- **Urban and Suburban:** Area and Composition of the Urban and Suburban Landscape; Total Impervious Area; "Natural" Lands in the Urban and Suburban Landscape

Program Description: The National Land Cover Database (NLCD) is created and funded by the Multi-Resolution Land Characteristics Consortium (MRLC) led by the U.S. Geological Survey (http://www.mrlc.gov). This consortium produces land-cover data for the United States based on nominal 1992 Landsat data (NLCD 1992) and nominal 2001 Landsat data (NLCD 2001). The 1992 data covered the conterminous US, while the 2001 data includes all 50 states and Puerto Rico. Both are 30 meter pixel products, with each square in the grid, or "pixel," approximately 100 ft on a side.

The 2008 edition of this report is based on the updated NLCD 2001, which was generated using protocols outlined in Homer et al. (2004; 2007) for 65 mapping zones of the conterminous United States. These NLCD 2001 products were generated from a standardized set of data layers mosaiced by mapping zone, including multi-season Landsat 5 and Landsat 7 imagery, and Digital Elevation Model based derivatives. The landcover classification was accomplished using decision tree (DT) software applied to zonal layer stacks prepared for each mapping zone. DT is a supervised classification data mining method that relies on large amounts of training data, which were collected from a variety of sources including high-resolution orthoimagery, local and regional datasets, field collected validation points, and Forest Inventory Analysis (FIA) plot data. Data specific to imperviousness and tree canopy were classified using regression tree (RT) software with training data generally derived from 1-m resolution Digital Orthoimagery Quarter Quadrangles (DOQQs). These were classified categorically into canopy/non-canopy, or impervious/non-impervious for each 1-m pixel, and subsequently resampled to 30-m grid proportions. The completed training images were then extrapolated across mapping zones using RT models, to derive continuous canopy and imperviousness estimates.

Data Manipulation: For the various indicators used in this report, NLCD data were aggregated as follows: for *natural* categories: water (data from NLCD classification 11 were used), wetland (90, 95), forest (41, 42, 43), shrubland (52), grassland (71), other (12, 31); for *non-natural* categories: developed (21, 22, 23, 24), cropland (81, 82).

Data Quality/Caveats: Satellite data offer an unprecedented opportunity to classify land cover on a consistent basis over very large areas (i.e., the entire country). The expected accuracy of satellite-derived classifications is related to many factors including amount of input data available, the detail of the land cover legend, and classification methods. Assessments of the NLCD 1992 land-cover accuracy varied by the 10 regions of assessment, but ranged between 70 and 85 percent at the more generalized Anderson level 1 land cover categories (e.g., forest, agriculture, developed; Stehman et al., 2003 and Wickham et al., 2004). Initial cross-validation accuracies for the NLCD 2001 full resolution land cover had accuracy estimates across mapping zones ranging from 70% to 98%, with an overall average accuracy across all mapping zones of 83.9%.

It was necessary to use data on state boundaries (using standard state boundaries available from ESRI) to "trim" the NLCD map in order to be able to report based on states. This resulted in some sand bars, small islands, and other features to be excluded from the analysis.

Data Availability: Data presented in this report were downloaded and analyzed by analysts with the U.S. Forest Service and the U.S. Environmental Protection Agency. The 2001 NLCD data are available from: http://www.mrlc.gov/index.php.

Program Description for the NatureServe Natural Heritage program

Data from this program are presented in the following indicators:

- **Core National:** At-Risk Native Species

- **Coasts and Oceans:** At-Risk Native Marine Species
- **Forests:** At-Risk Native Forest Species
- **Freshwater:** At-Risk Native Freshwater Species; At-Risk Freshwater Plant Communities
- **Grasslands and Shrublands:** At-Risk Native Grasslands and Shrublands Species

Program Description: NatureServe (www.natureserve.org) and its member programs in the network of Natural Heritage programs develop and maintain information on biodiversity. These data are not from a site-based monitoring program, but rather from a census approach that focuses on the location and distribution of at-risk species. For other species, the dataset incorporates information from a wide variety of observations and sources.

On an ongoing basis, NatureServe research biologists gather, review, integrate, and record available information about species taxonomy, status, and use of different habitats or ecological system types. They are assisted in this work by scientists in the network of Natural Heritage programs as well as by contracted experts for different invertebrate taxa. NatureServe staff and collaborators assign a conservation status by using standard Heritage ranking criteria (see http://www.natureserve.org/explorer/ranking.htm) and by using the best information available to them. The Heritage ranking process considers five major status ranks: critically imperiled (G1), imperiled (G2), vulnerable (G3), apparently secure (G4), and demonstrably widespread, abundant, and secure (G5). In addition, separate ranks are assigned for species regarded as presumed extinct (GX) or possibly extinct (GH). These ranks indicate the status for each species across its full range (i.e., its global rank), rather than is status nationally (for species whose range extends beyond the U.S. border) or in any particular region or state. See Stein (2002) for further details on ranks.

Data Manipulation: NatureServe has summarized the actual global ranks into "rounded ranks" for the purposes of presentation and analysis. For example, an actual rank may express the bounds of uncertainty, noting for instance that a given species falls somewhere in the range of "critically imperiled" to "imperiled." In such cases, the rounded rank reflects the more imperiled designation, in this instance, critically imperiled. Such rank rounding applies to between 10-20% of species included here. The analysis of the percent of at-risk species by state is based on all species that are known to occur within that state; a species that is found in multiple states would be included in the statistics for each of those states.

For the at-risk status metric, only species groups for which sufficient information is available on the entire group are reported. Thus, for the core national indicator, mammal status is reported because data are available on the status of all mammals, but the status of mayflies and stoneflies is not included because data on all species in these two groups are not available. For the population trend metric, data are only reported when data are available for at least half of the at-risk group. The percentage of species for which trend data are unavailable is noted.

Population trend data report on short-term changes in populations, specifically changes within 10 years or 3 generations, whichever is longer, with a maximum of 100 years. Nature Serve defines populations as "declining" if changes in population size, range, area occupied and/or number of occurrences affected greater than 10% of the population. Populations are classified as "stable" if they remained unchanged or remained within ± 10 % fluctuation and are classified as "increasing" if the population changed by more than 10 % (Master et al. 2003).

Data Quality/Caveats: Heritage conservation status ranks are updated on an ongoing basis through literature review and feedback from users of the network's databases, and also through periodic review of all statuses. Uncertainty about conservation status of a species is captured in part through the use of range ranks (see "Data Manipulation" above). A species' status may change over time due to several reasons, and not solely due to a species becoming more or less at risk of extinction. For example, more populations may be found than were known to exist, or a species may be split taxonomically into two species, such that the two new species may individually be at greater risk of extinction than their single parent species.

Between 2002 and 2006, there was a 1.3% increase in the number of the at-risk species in the core national indicator; however, this increase was due primarily to the assessment of nearly 300 additional species and re-evaluation of over almost 700 species based on newly available information or changes in knowledge or expert opinion. Of the species for which the reason for rank change is known, less than 4% of species changed rank between 2002 and 2006 due to a genuine change in status. Because status may change for reasons other than an actual change in condition, and because a species may experience a significant increase or decrease in population size without an incremental change in status, trend is itself a particularly useful measure to use in addition to conservation status.

Data Availability: Updated and more detailed information on all species is available at http://www. natureserve.org/explorer/. For more customized data requests, contact NatureServe, Information Products and Services (ProductsandServices@natureserve.org).

Core National

Ecosystem Extent

The Indicator

This indicator reports the area of the various ecosystem types included in this report, both at a broad system level (e.g., forests) and at a sub-system level (e.g., freshwater wetlands). Eventually, data will be presented on net transitions between broad categories of ecosystem types (i.e., "natural" to cropland; "natural" to developed, and cropland to "natural," and cropland to developed). Additionally, when data become available, the change in area of rare ecosystem sub-types will be reported.

Substantial Changes to the Indicator Design: Since the 2002 edition of this report, two elements of this indicator have been added: the net transition of land area between three broad categories of ecosystem types and the change in area of rare ecosystem sub-types.

The Data

Coasts and Oceans: The coastal wetland data came from the U.S. Fish and Wildlife Service's (FWS) National Wetlands Inventory (NWI) and include estuarine vegetated wetlands (see technical note for Coastal Living Habitats, p. 287).

Cropland: Data on total cropland area were obtained from the U.S. Department of Agriculture (USDA) Natural Resources Conservation Service's National Resources Inventory (NRI) program and the USDA Economic Research Service (ERS) (see technical note for Total Cropland, p. 297).

Forests: Data for this indicator were provided by the Forest Inventory and Analysis (FIA) program of the USDA Forest Service (see program description on p. 270, and technical note for Forest Area and Ownership, p. 305).

Fresh Waters: Data on freshwater wetlands are from the U.S. Fish and Wildlife Service's NWI (see technical note for Extent of Freshwater Ecosystems, p. 314)

Grasslands and Shrublands: Data on the extent of grasslands and shrublands (lower 48 states) are from the National Land Cover Dataset (NLCD; see technical note for Area of Grasslands and Shrublands, p. 325, and the NLCD program description, p. 274).

Urban and Suburban Landscapes: Data on the area of urban and suburban landscapes were generated specifically for this report by analysts with the U.S. Environmental Protection Agency and the U.S. Forest Service from primarily land-cover data in the NLCD (see technical note for Urban and Suburban Landscapes, p. 332) Data on the area of urban areas is from the USDA's Economic Research Services (ERS) publication "Major Uses of Land in the United States, 2002" (http://www.ers.usda. gov/publications/EIB14/). The approach adopted by the ERS relies on U.S. Census Bureau data for urban areas is based on different assumptions than the definition of urban and suburban landscapes in this report. The ERS time series is shown to give a sense of the relative change in urban-suburban landscapes since the 1950s. Note that the Census Bureau altered their methods between the 1990 and 2000 censuses, which created a discontinuity in the ERS estimates.

The Land Cover and Ocean Bathymetry Map: The map shown in this indicator was constructed from several datasets by analysts with the U.S. Environmental Protection Agency and the U.S. Forest Service. Land cover data for the conterminous 48 states are from the NLCD (see program description, p. 274). The map also includes NLCD data for Alaska, which was released just before this report went to publication; thus the new data for Alaska are not included in the Area of Grasslands and Shrublands (p. 202). Land-cover data for Hawaii come from NOAA's Coastal Change Analysis Program and are nominally for 2001 (http://www.csc.noaa.gov/crs/lca/hawaii. html). Data on ocean bathymetry and river locations come from ESRI (http://www.esri.com).

Data Quality/Caveats: Data presented here are from multiple sources; in some cases, different land cover definitions or classifications are used by different programs and data may be collected in different years. Every effort has been made here to identify consistent land cover categories and time periods.

Data Availability: Please see references to other technical notes or source links above.

The Data Gap

For additional detail on data for coral reefs and seagrasses and other "submerged aquatic vegetation" as well as vegetated wetlands in other areas please see the technical note for Coastal Living Habitats (p. 287). Further discussion on the absence of national data on lake area is found in the technical note for Extent of Freshwater Ecosystems (p. 314).

The land-cover maps derived from the NLCD could not be compared when data analyses were being completed for this report edition. This was due to intercomparability issues between the two available time points (1992 and 2001). Efforts are underway to make these two time points comparable, which should permit an analysis for small areas how the land cover changed between the two time points.

Data necessary to report on the area of rare community types are likely to become available for a current time point (see discussion in technical note for Forest Community Types with Significantly Reduced Area, p. 311). Such data will need to be periodically updated to permit estimates of changing area of these rare types.

Pattern of "Natural" Landscapes

The Indicator

This indicator describes general patterns of land cover across landscapes that are characterized predominantly by the presence of "natural" land cover (i.e., forest, grassland, shrubland, wetlands, and other water). This is done using two related approaches. The first reports the composition of the surroundings of "natural" pixels on land cover maps using a square observation window that was 1-km on a side or approximately 240 acres in size. Data are reported for several key categories of land-cover composition—ranging from those pixels surrounded by 100% other "natural" pixels (i.e., "core natural") to those pixels having a mix of cropland and development above particular thresholds in the surrounding 240 acres. The second component of the indicator focuses on the resulting "core natural" pixels. "Core natural" pixels that touched were joined together to form polygons across the landscape and the size of these polygons, or patches, is reported.

Substantial Changes to the Indicator Design: This indicator was defined for the 2008 edition of this report by the Landscape Pattern Task Group (see http://www.heinzctr.org/ecosystems for a forthcoming task group report).

The Data

The data for this indicator are derived from two sources. The primary source is the National Land Cover Dataset (NLCD), which is a product of the Multi-Resolution Land Characterization (MRLC) Consortium (see program description on p. 274). In addition, this land-cover map was augmented with data from ESRI on paved roads, which are considered a type of development.

Data Description: The following NLCD categories were treated as "natural" for this indicator: (11) water; (12) perennial ice/snow; (31) barren land (rock/sand/clay); (41) deciduous forest; (42) evergreen forest; (43) mixed forest; (52) shrub/scrub; (71) Grassland/herbaceous; (90) Woody wetlands; and (95) Emergent herbaceous wetlands.

Data Manipulation: Analysts with U.S. Forest Service and the U.S. Environmental Protection Agency performed all steps of this analysis. They started by merging the ESRI street map with the 2001 edition of the NLCD, converting pixels in the NLCD to a new classification of "developed" in cases where a paved road was found to overlap the road. A square analysis tool (window) was centered on every pixel within the map and then the composition of pixels within the window was recorded. A 1-km analysis window was used. Data were reported in the various compositional categories shown. For those pixels that had 100% "natural" surroundings, patches were formed, but only for pixels that shared a common edge (i.e., it was not sufficient if the edge of pixels touched). The area of these patches was reported, by state, and then these data were summarized by region. This procedure caused some patches to be split by state boundaries, meaning that some patches were cut into one or more smaller patches.

Data Quality/Caveats: The barren land category includes features that are decidedly "non-natural" (e.g., it includes strip mines)—it was decided that this category should be included given that "natural" features, such as beaches and bedrock, are also included within the category.

Data Availability: NLCD data are available at http://www.mrlc.gov. The ESRI data come bundled with geographic information system (GIS) software (see http://esri.com); see also ESRI (2005).

Movement of Nitrogen

The Indicator

This indicator reports both how much nitrogen enters major rivers from their watersheds, and how much nitrogen (in the form of nitrate) is delivered by several major rivers to the U.S. coastal ocean. The amount of nitrogen entering rivers from major watersheds is defined as the pounds of nitrogen per square mile of watershed area. The amount of nitrate delivered to the nation's coastal waters is defined as the tons of nitrate carried to the ocean each year and is shown for three of the largest U.S. rivers. When data become available, the indicator will also include atmospheric inputs of nitrogen to coastal areas, in the form of wet and dry deposition.

The Data

Total nitrogen is the preferred form for reporting on the amount of nitrogen delivered from the U.S. landscape to coastal waters, but because the historical record for it for the Mississippi River is short, we chose instead to present nitrate data. Further, nitrate is the largest component of total nitrogen and serves as a strong proxy of total nitrogen. The three major rivers included represent approximately 48% of the freshwater inputs to coastal waters. Note that, because of the upstream location of some of the gauge stations used, key discharges— such as the cities of New Orleans and Baton Rouge—are not captured by these data; we hope that future estimates can resolve this shortcoming. For consistency with other studies (Goolsby et al. 1999), the Mississippi River discharge includes only the portion of the Atchafalaya River that comes through the Old River Diversion.

Data Description: Riverine loads of total nitrogen were estimated using streamflow and water-quality data collected by the U.S. Geological Survey (USGS) as part of the National Stream Quality Accounting Network (NASQAN), the National Water-Quality Assessment (NAWQA) Program, and the Federal–State Cooperative Program. A few of the stream gauges, most notably those at the mouth of the Mississippi River and on the Rio Grande River, are operated by the U.S. Army Corps of Engineers or the International Boundary and Water Commission rather than the USGS.

Data Manipulation: Stream discharge (streamflow) is estimated by frequent measurement of water depth (stage), which is converted to discharge by use of a rating curve. Data are reported as daily averages. Typically water-quality samples are representative of the entire river cross-section (depth- and width-integrated) at the time of collection.

At the sites for which data are included in this report, samples were collected between 1996 and 2005. A minimum of 20 samples collected in at least 3 of the 5 years and in all seasons for both the 1996–2000 and 2001–2005 time periods were required to estimate loads at a site. Data was available for each of the years at most stations. The median number of observations per station for each period was 51 and ranged from 20 to 319.

A regression model relating total nitrogen load to discharge, day-of-year (to capture seasonal effects), and time (to capture any trend over the period) was developed for each station using statistical techniques suitable for data with censored observations (loads derived from concentrations less than the analytical detection limit). These models were then used to make daily estimates of total nitrogen load. Separate models were developed to estimate total nitrogen loads for the 1996–2000 and 2001–2005 time periods.

For the maps, these daily loads were summed for each 5-year period to estimate the load for the entire period and divided by 5 to obtain the average-annual load for each watershed. The standard error of the average-annual load is generally less than 10% of the mean but can be as high as 18%. The incremental load was then calculated as the difference between the output load that flowed from the watershed and the input(s) to the watershed. Outputs include the load at the downstream stations. In the arid western areas, it was assumed that solutes accompanied any water that was lost to irrigation or transfers to other watersheds (i.e., piping water across watershed boundaries). The incremental yield (shown in the maps) is defined as the incremental load divided by the watershed area. The white areas of the map are areas for which insufficient USGS data exist to calculate loads.

For the time-series plots, the daily loads were summed to determine the annual loads shown in the figure. Note that most of the year-to-year variation in the loads is due to differences in runoff, with wet years having higher loads and dry years having lower loads.

Data Availability: Data used in this indicator are summarized by Wilson et al., (2008), available at http://pubs.usgs.gov/of/2008/1110/. All USGS data are available at http://waterdata.usgs.gov/nwis. Further information on NASQAN and the NAWQA program can be found at http://water.usgs.gov/nasqan/ and http://water.usgs.gov/nawqa. The NASQAN Web site contains stream discharge data collected by the U.S. Army Corps of Engineers.

2008 Report Data Update: The new and revised annual nitrogen load data provided by USGS for Update 2005 were revised to account for the increased drainage area in the Columbia and Susquehanna rivers. The USGS Open File report 2006 (http://pubs.usgs.gov/of/2006/1087/) documents the changes made to the nitrogen load data for Update 2005 and in the 2008 report.

The Data Gap

This indicator is intended to include reporting on the percent of U.S. area for which ranges of wet inorganic nitrogen deposition (annual average kg per hectare) have been measured; however, data are inadequate for national level reporting at this time. Further work is needed to assess the relative magnitude of direct atmospheric nitrogen deposition (AD-N) to coastal waters. In the absence of measured or modeled data, direct deposition of atmospheric nitrogen to coastal areas cannot be reported.

Data from the National Atmospheric Deposition Program (NADP) and CASTNet were used by NOAA staff to evaluate the order of magnitude of direct AD-N to estuaries relative to other N sources. While spatial coverage of the NADP (wet deposition) and CASTNet (dry deposition) networks is currently not adequate to produce robust estimates for direct AD-N to coastal areas, rough preliminary calculations for selected estuaries suggested that direct AD-N ranges from negligible to ~17% of total N loading.

The Community Multiscale Air Quality (CMAQ) model is a potential future source of estimates for direct AD-N to coastal areas. The model runs 4-dimensional data assimilation for meteorology and emissions data and produces estimates for wet and dry AD-N; however, it currently does not adequately account for sea salt error or surf zone effects. In addition, current resolution is too coarse (36 km²) for estimating for estuarine surfaces as model grids are likely to overlap both land and sea—better resolution (12 km²) is planned.

Carbon Storage

The Indicator

This indicator reports on changes in carbon density (carbon stored per unit area) and changes in total carbon stored in major ecosystem types, as well as how much recent global carbon dioxide and methane concentrations (chosen for their relevance to ecosystem functions such as photosynthesis and decomposition) deviate from long-term average concentrations. The goal is to provide an overall view of changing carbon levels in U.S. ecosystems and to distinguish the effects of land cover conversion (changes in the extent of ecosystem types) from the effects of management, climate and disturbance on carbon levels. The bins used in the figure "Change in Carbon Density Over Time" were selected in cooperation with the data providers, who advised on the most accurate bin size to describe minimal change in carbon density (±0.04 metric tons acre^{-1} yr^{-1}).

The Data
Data Description:
Forests: Data on forests are derived from the FORCARB model, which uses inputs from the USDA Forest Service Forest Inventory and Analysis (FIA) program (see the FIA Program Description, p. 270, also http://fia.fs.fed.us) to calculate estimates of carbon storage. The field measurements used as the basis for this indicator did not historically include national parks and wilderness areas or slower-growing forests, but expansion to these areas has been implemented. All estimates in the 1990–2005 interval are based on data prepared for the U.S. forest carbon inventory included in the U.S. *EPA's Inventory of U.S. Greenhouse Gas Emissions and Sinks: 1990–2005* (2007c).

Farmlands and Grasslands and Shrublands: Data for farmlands and grasslands and shrublands are derived from the Century Ecosystem Model which integrates base soil carbon measurements and soil properties with change factors including land use data from the USDA National Resources Inventory, the Conservation Technology Information Center, and the USDA Economic Research Service (tillage intensity, soil additions) as well as weather conditions from the PRISM database. Soil organic carbon stock changes have been estimated for the top eight inches for all privately-owned lands classified as farmlands or grasslands and shrublands for the conterminous U.S., which includes the majority of the plow layer in croplands. These estimates include approximately 90% of the private farmland and grasslands amd shrublands. This report focuses on the stock changes during the period 1980–2000 which coincides with the most detailed data on land use and management from the USDA National Resources Inventory. Additional information is provided in the *Inventory of U.S. Greenhouse Gas Emissions 1990–2005* (USEPA 2007c).

Carbon Dioxide and Methane: Data on carbon dioxide and methane mirror those data sets reported by Working Group I of the Intergovernmental Panel on Climate Change in Figure 6.4 of *Climate Change 2007: The Physical Science Basis* (Jansen et al., 2007), with additional data from Etheridge et al. (1996, 1998).

Data Manipulation:
Forests: The FORCARB2 model is used to generate stand-level estimates of carbon stocks for forest ecosystems and regional estimates of carbon in harvested wood based on measurements collected through the FIA program (Smith et al 2006; see also Birdsey 1996). The interval from 1995 to 2005 represents annualized (interpolated per state or substate classification) estimates, most of which originate from the current publicly available inventory data. The tool that is used to calculate these estimates is described further in Smith et al (2007).

Farmlands and Grasslands and Shrublands: The Century Ecosystem Model (Parton et al. 1987, 1988 and 1994) was used to estimate changes in soil organic carbon stocks based

on the input data described above. Simulations of soil organic carbon dynamics were conducted for each National Resources Inventory (NRI) point using a Monte Carlo Analysis with 100 iterations (see also Ogle et al., 2007). Although not provided in this report, an uncertainty value has been derived for each stock change estimate (see USEPA, 2007c).

Carbon Dioxide and Methane: The annual average atmospheric concentrations of carbon dioxide (~313-381 ppm from 1950–2006) and methane (~1.1-1.8 ppm from 1950–2005) in recent decades were divided by average concentrations during the pre-industrial period of 1000 to 1750 AD. The baseline against which current concentrations are compared was chosen to include part of the interglacial period up to the beginning of the pre-industrial era as defined by the Intergovernmental Panel on Climate Change. The data sources used represent a variety of collection schemes (ice core samples, firn samples (that is, samples taken from the layer of ice found between snow and glacial ice), and direct atmospheric measurements). All data from all sources were combined and plotted on the same graph. For any year that had multiple values reported across different data sources, the average concentration was calculated.

Data Quality/Caveats:
Inorganic carbon, while a significant pool of carbon especially in arid and semi-arid ecosystems, is not included in this indicator due to its relatively stable nature, although work is being done to investigate further its carbon storage properties—for example, see Emmerich (2003) and Martens et al. (2005).

Forests: There are two potential sources of uncertainty for these estimates: the FIA plot data collection, and the FORCARB2 model estimates. Sampling error estimates for plot data are provided in the Forest Inventory and Analysis program description (p. 270). Generally, carbon stock and stock changes estimates are based on regional averages, which generally have $\pm2\%$ sampling error. There may also be uncertainty associated with the carbon stock estimates, since the estimates are extrapolated from plot data to represent all forest land (US-EPA, 2007).

Farmlands and Grasslands and Shrublands: For the purposes of carbon storage reporting, carbon stocks for the farmland ecosystem type are reported as carbon in privately-owned cropland soils in the coterminous U.S. only; this approach excludes aboveground carbon in annually cropped soils (considered to be marginal relative to soil organic carbon) as well as carbon in perennial cropping systems and numerous other farmland landcover types.

Grasslands and shrublands as reported in the Century model estimates follow the *rangelands* and *pasturelands* definition used by the National Resources Inventory (NRI), which is categorized as a land cover *and use* description. Therefore, grasslands and shrublands as it is reported in this carbon storage indicator is more inclusive than the definition used elsewhere in the *State of the Nation's Ecosystems* report, which defines grasslands and shrublands only by land cover type. Carbon stock changes reported here for the grasslands and shrublands ecosystem type accounts for about 96% of privately-owned grasslands and shrublands, or 504 million acres; this represents approximately 60% of total grassland

and shrubland area in the lower 48 states (see the Area of Grasslands and Shrublands indicator, p. 202). Note, however, that total acreage estimates are based on remote sensing data, as compared to the plot-based NRI data incorporated into the Century model estimates.

Carbon Dioxide and Methane: It is important to note that data sets which differ in sampling technique as well as sampling location were not treated differently when the data sets were combined. See original data citations for explanation of source-specific caveats.

Data Availability:
Forests: Estimates were processed by Linda Heath and James Smith at the USDA Forest Service (http://www.fs.fed.us/ne/ durham/4104/index.shtml). The base measurements for the carbon estimates are collected through the Forest Inventory and Analysis program (FIA, http://www.fia.fs.fed.us/).

Farmlands and Grasslands and Shrublands: Estimates were processed by Stephen Ogle and Mark Easter at the Natural Resource Ecology Laboratory at Colorado State University (http://www.nrel.colostate.edu/). The base measurements are collected through the National Resources Inventory (NRI, http://www.nrcs.usda.gov/TECHNICAL/NRI/). The Century Ecosystem Model is available on-line at http://www.nrel. colostate.edu/projects/century5/.

Carbon Dioxide and Methane: If not obtained directly from the articles cited below, data sets were downloaded from one of the following: National Climatic Data Center (http:// www.ncdc.noaa.gov/), Carbon Dioxide Information Analysis Center (http://cdiac.ornl.gov/), NOAA Earth System Research Laboratory, Global Monitoring Division (http://www.esrl.noaa. gov/gmd/), Scripps Institution of Oceanography CO_2 Program (http://scrippsco2.ucsd.edu/), and the National Snow and Ice Data Center (http://nsidc.org/). Carbon dioxide concentration values were compiled from the following sources: Etheridge et al. (1996); Monnin et al. (2004); MacFarling Meure et al. (2006); Siegenthaler et al. (2005); Keeling and Whorf (2005); and Tans (2007). Methane concentration values were compiled from the following sources: Blunier et al. (1993, 1995); Chappellaz et al. (1997); Etheridge et al. (1998); Ferretti et al. (2005); Flückiger et al. (2002); and Dlugokencky (2007). Data from Chappellaz et al. (1997) and Ferretti et al. (2005) were obtained directly from Jérôme Chappellaz and James W.C. White, respectively (with thanks).

2008 Report Data Update: This is a new indicator added for this edition of the report.

The Data Gap
This indicator reports change in carbon storage in six major ecosystem types. Total change in the systems for which estimates are reported in this indicator represent less than one percent of the total stocks, although there is still much uncertainty about total stock estimates in ecosystems (see USCCSP, 2007).

Estimates of change in carbon stocks are not available for three of the six major ecosystem types (Coasts and Oceans, Fresh Waters, and Urban and Suburban), as well as wetland

and peatland ecosystems. Estimates are also not available for above- or below-ground biomass in grasslands and shrublands (both public and private lands). There are no estimates available for forest soils, some cropland soils, and public grassland and shrubland soils. Finally, none of the data sets used in this indicator include Alaska or Hawaii. Therefore, a complete picture of carbon storage in U.S. ecosystems is not yet available, even with partial data. Improvements in the estimates reported for forests, grasslands, and shrublands are planned for the near future (see USEPA 2007c).

One program looking at the environmental impacts (including terrestrial carbon storage) of conservation practices on private lands is the Conservation Effects Assessment Project (CEAP, http://www.nrcs.usda.gov/technical/NRI/ceap/index. html). CEAP will estimate effects of conservation practices on private lands. The project consists of three components: national assessments of croplands, wetlands, wildlife and grazing lands; watershed assessment studies for evaluating and improving performance of national assessment models; and bibliographies and literature reviews of current literature on conservation programs for cropland, fish and wildlife, wetlands, and grazing lands.

Another potential future source of data on total carbon content in ecosystems are large-scale carbon budget models for the U.S. that integrate remote sensing, intensive site measurements and ecological process knowledge to generate spatially-explicit carbon sequestration values.

Chemical Contamination

The Indicator
This indicator reports on contamination of streams, streambed sediments, groundwater wells, estuarine sediments, and biotic tissue as well as trends in atmospheric concentrations of ozone and fine particulate matter.

The Data
Data Description
Streams, Groundwater, Sediments and Biotic Tissues: Data for stream water, streambed sediment, freshwater fish and groundwater were collected by the USGS National Water Quality Assessment Program (see NAWQA description on p. 272). Data for estuarine sediments and saltwater fish were collected by the US EPA National Coastal Assessment (see NCA description on p. 269). Contaminant analytes were selected because they occur frequently in ecosystems and/or have a high potential for adverse effects on people or ecosystems. This indicator is intended to report on contaminant levels in a broad suite of plant and animal tissues, but data are available only for freshwater and saltwater fish.

The first five figures report on the percentage of sampling sites, estuarine area or whole-body fish tissue samples in which (1) contaminants are *detected*, and (2) contaminant concentrations *exceed* established benchmarks for the protection of aquatic life and human health. The fifth figure reports on contaminants in fish tissues that most commonly exceed benchmarks. Indicator figures present "bins" or groupings of sites based on the number of contaminants detected or in exceedance of benchmarks. Nitrate, ammonia and trace elements can occur naturally in water and sediment so they are not included in detection analyses for these media. Many contaminants measured by NAWQA and NCA do not have established benchmarks or have a range of benchmark values. For estuarine sediments and freshwater and saltwater fish tissue, exceedances of both 'lower' and 'higher' benchmarks are reported.

Outdoor Air: The sixth figure reports on ozone trends using a calculated index (SUM06) for the cumulative value of ozone concentrations during the growing season. SUM06 is defined as the sum of all hourly average concentrations above 0.06 parts per million (ppm) in a given year. For this national-scale indicator of general exposure to "high" ozone levels, SUM06 is based on 12-hour days (8 a.m. to 8 p.m.) and 3-month growing seasons (June-August). Annual SUM06 values (ppm-hours per year) were calculated for each ozone monitor in EPA's AQS and CASTNet monitoring network for 1994–2005 (the pre-1994 monitoring network was considerably smaller and possibly not comparable to later years). Data from monitors with more than 75% of hourly measurements in a given year were included—for monitors with less than 100% of the relevant values, annual SUM06 calculations were adjusted: (SUM06/hours collected) = (adjusted SUM06/total possible collection hours) – adjusted SUM06 = SUM06 x (total possible collection hours/hours collected). To constrain the influence of individual monitors annual SUM06 maps were constructed using inverse distance squared weighting (IDW) interpolation of the 12 nearest neighbor sites: SUM06 value for a pixel = $\sum$ (squared distance of pixel from monitor x SUM06-monitor) / $\sum$ (squared distance of pixel from monitor). (Interpolation cannot fully account for potential urban or lowland bias in the ozone monitoring network.) Because urban areas have lower nighttime ozone levels relative to rural areas (NO_x production continues overnight and ozone is consumed by reacting with NO), 77 monitors in core urban areas, within ~30 miles of suburban monitors, were excluded to account for NO_x titration effects and resulting urban-rural gradients.

The seventh figure reports on trends in ambient concentrations of fine particulate matter ($PM_{2.5}$). Annual average $PM_{2.5}$ values (micrograms per cubic meter per year) were calculated for each monitor in EPA's Federal Reference Method (FRM) dataset for 2000–2005 (the pre-2000 monitoring network was considerably smaller, with a slightly different regional allocation, and possibly not comparable to later years). Data from monitors with more than 75% of measurements in a given year were included. Eleven or more samples are required for valid $PM_{2.5}$ annual averages greater than 15 micrograms per cubic meter (the concentration associated with EPA's current annual National Ambient Air Quality Standard). Data from EPA's FRM dataset are primarily representative of ambient concentrations in urban areas in the lower 48 states.

Data Quality/Caveats:
Streams, Groundwater, Sediments and Biotic Tissues:
Contamination data are highly aggregated and should be interpreted mainly as an indication of general national patterns. Different agencies and programs are responsible for monitoring freshwater and coastal systems—resulting datasets reflect different site selection protocols, suites of contaminants measured, and collection and analysis procedures. However, within an environmental medium (e.g., sediment, stream

water) consistent methods were used and sampling sites do not represent locations where contamination was particularly likely. Data shown here do not represent assessments of risks posed to people or ecosystems in any specific location since they do not incorporate factors of actual exposure nor do they include all contaminants of possible concern (e.g., endocrine disrupting compounds or brominated flame retardants). The presence of contaminants does not necessarily mean that levels are high enough to cause problems. Also, data include only contaminant concentrations above analytical detection limits—for example, Dieldrin was dropped from NCA sampling because relevant benchmarks were below the analytical detection limit. With technical innovation, contaminants can be measured at lower concentrations, affecting dataset consistency—for example, due to changes in analytical detection limits for VOCs in groundwater over the course of the NAWQA sampling period, a censoring limit had to be applied to the full dataset. While the benchmarks used to help judge the significance of contamination are the best available in use by relevant agencies, they must be interpreted carefully because they are not necessarily standardized or linked to the same level of risk (e.g., aquatic life benchmarks for coastal sediments differ from those for stream sediments), nor do they necessarily account for all aspects of potential toxicity (e.g., chronic and acute exposure; sub-lethal effects; contaminant mixtures; potential effects on the reproductive, nervous, and immune systems).

Outdoor Air: The use of a 12-hour, 3-month SUM06 index is intended to capture ozone exposure conditions when a majority of plant species across the U.S. are engaged in gas exchange and is not optimized for ozone effects on sensitive plant species or those that exhibit night-time gas exchange. While there are no well-established thresholds or benchmarks for ozone concentrations that are harmful to plants and wildlife, 0.06 ppm is used here to approximate ozone levels that are elevated above general background levels and may be associated with adverse effects in vegetation (note that US EPA recently recommended the use of the W126 cumulative ozone index because it cumulates all ozone concentrations, but with substantially smaller weighting on concentrations below 0.04 ppm, US EPA, 2007). The SUM06 and W126 indices are similarly constructed and tend to be highly correlated. Note that reporting ranges for SUM06 are not linked to specific risk levels as organisms differ in their sensitivity to ozone exposure.

Data Availability
NAWQA data for stream water, streambed sediment, groundwater and freshwater fish are summarized at http://pubs.usgs.gov/of/2008/1110/. NCA data for sediments and fish contamination in estuaries are available at http://www.epa.gov/emap/nca/html/data/index.html.

Ozone data are available through EPA's Air Quality System (AQS) http://www.epa.gov/ttn/airs/airsaqs/. Ozone data were obtained from the EPA and analyzed by personnel from the USDA Forest Service. Data for fine particulate matter were obtained directly from US EPA.

2008 Report Data Update:
Streams, groundwater and freshwater fish: In the 2002 Report, monitoring data for 1992–1998 were reported, however these data are not comparable to the 1992–2001 data presented here

due to expansion of the geographic scope of the monitoring program—from 36 to 51 major study units—and a revised set of benchmarks—the 2008 report makes use of Health-Based Screening Levels (HBSLs) in addition to USEPA Maximum Contaminant Levels (MCLs). For details, see http://water.usgs.gov/nawqa/HBSL.

Estuarine sediments and saltwater fish: NCA data has been included on contaminant detection and benchmark exceedance for saltwater fish for 1998–2002 (not previously reported). In the 2002 Report, sediment contamination data for 1992–1998 were reported, however these data are not comparable to the 1998–2002 data presented here due to expansion of the geographic scope of the monitoring program—North Atlantic and Pacific Coast estuaries, Hawaii, and south-central Alaska were added.

Outdoor air: New figures have been included to report on ozone (above 'background') and fine particulate matter ($PM_{2.5}$) in ambient air.

The Data Gap
Data are not adequate for national reporting on:
- *Contaminants in plant tissues and animals other than fish.* No on-going, national-scale monitoring program exists for contamination in mammals, amphibians, birds or plants.
- *Mercury and other metals in freshwater fish.* While many programs measure mercury and other contaminants in freshwater fish, resulting data do not provide a nationally-integrated view of contamination due to variation in sampling designs and analytical methods. In the future, EPA's national freshwater fish contamination survey will provide national-scale data for persistent, bioaccumulative and toxic fish tissue contaminants (http://www.epa.gov/waterscience/fish/study/overview.htm).
- *Combined urban and rural fine particulate matter concentrations.* EPA's FRM dataset primarily represents ambient $PM_{2.5}$ concentrations in urban areas. The Interagency Monitoring of Protected Visual Environments (IMPROVE) program measures $PM_{2.5}$ in Class I areas such as large national parks and wilderness areas (http://vista.cira.colostate.edu/views/). Combined national reporting is not yet possible because of differences in analytical methods.
- Aquatic life benchmarks are not available for saltwater fish and human health benchmarks are not available for freshwater fish.

Chemical contamination reporting would be enhanced if data were available for:
- *Aquatic Contaminants in the Great Lakes.* Data collection for sediment contamination in the Great Lakes is generally focused on areas with highly polluted sediments—resulting datasets do not assess the occurrence of sediment contamination across the range of possible locations and are not comparable to data presented here.
- *Ozone bioinjury:* The USDA Forest Service collects ozone bioinjury data for ozone-sensitive species of trees, woody shrubs, and herb species, but this program does not yet support national reporting.

Change in Stream Flows

The Indicator
This analysis is based on changes in flow characteristics between a 20-year baseline period (1941–60) and 42 rolling 5-year test periods beginning with 1961–65 and ending with 2002–2006. The 1941–60 baseline period for this indicator was chosen to maximize the number of sites included in the analysis. Twenty years was selected as a reasonable baseline period that would allow characterization of hydrologic regimes and reporting for multiple years, while keeping test and reference data independent. A five-year test period was chosen to avoid reporting on annual anomalies and to allow for reporting on trends of sufficient ecological importance.

The indicator assesses changes in the magnitude of low flows and high flows as well as changes in the variability of flow in order to track any changes in flow patterns over time. Three metrics were included in the analysis:
- Annual 7-day low flow rate (% change): assesses the degree of alteration in low-flow magnitude, a parameter of importance to aquatic life.
- Annual 3-day high flow rate (% change): assesses the degree of alteration of the average annual peak flow.
- Annual variability in the one-day flow rate (% change): assesses the change in the variability of almost all flow events.

Analyses are provided for the nation's streams and rivers and a separate set of reference streams that have not been substantially affected by dams and diversions and have had little change in land use over the measurement period. As the geographic distribution of the two sets is fairly similar, comparison of the two can reveal the relative impacts of climate and management.

This indicator is a new core national indicator and a revision of and replacement for the Freshwaters indicator, Changing Stream Flows, from the 2002 edition of this report. The Heinz Center's Stream Flows Working Group (p. viii) redesigned both the content and computation of the indicator. Data manipulations were performed by Heinz Center staff. Summaries of Working Group meetings can be found at (http://www.heinzctr.org/Programs/Reporting/Working%20Groups/Ecosystem%20Services/csf.shtml).

The Data
Data Source: Data reported here are from the U.S. Geological Survey (USGS) stream gage network ("non-reference streams") and from the USGS Hydro-Climatic Data Network ("reference streams") (Slack and Landwehr 1992). USGS has placed stream gages and maintained flow rate records throughout the United States since the late 1800s.

Data Collection Methodology: Stream gauging data are collected using standard USGS protocols (see http://pubs.usgs.gov/fs/2005/3131/).

Data Manipulation: USGS provided the Heinz Center with annual data for each gage. Stream sites were included in the analysis if there were greater than 80 percent data for the baseline period (1941–60) and each of the rolling five-year test periods (1961–1965, 1962–1966...2002–2006), and if the median flow in the baseline period was not zero. For the low and high flow metrics, the median of the annual low/high flow at each site was computed for the baseline period and each of the rolling, five-year test periods. Change in flow (in %) was then computed as 100 x ((median test-median baseline)/median baseline).

The variability of flow was computed using a non-parametric metric. For each site and year (1941–2006), the 1-day 1st, 50th and 99th percentiles of flow were computed. The variability of flow in a year was then computed as (99th percentile—1st percentile)/50th percentile. For each site, the median variability was computed for the baseline period and each of the rolling five-year test periods. Change in the variability of flow (in %) was computed as above: 100x ((median test-median baseline)/median baseline).

Stream Types: The relatively undisturbed sites of the Hydro-Climatic Data Network are referred to as "reference sites" and the USGS stream gage network sites are referred to as "non-reference sites." The following number of streams of each type met the criteria delineated above and were used in the analyses: high flow: 712 reference streams, 1007 non-reference streams; low flow: 673 reference streams, 936 non-reference streams; variability in flow: 733 reference streams, 1021 non-reference streams.

Data Quality/Caveats: Although the sites analyzed here are spread widely throughout the United States, gage placement by the USGS has not been a random process. Gages are generally placed on larger, perennial streams and rivers, and changes seen in these larger systems may differ from those seen in smaller streams and rivers. In addition, the USGS gage network does not represent the full set of operating stream flow gages in the United States. The U.S. Army Corps of Engineers, for example, operates gages, and those data are not available through the USGS; they were not used in this analysis.

Data Access: Stream gage data are available through the USGS Web site at http://waterdata.usgs.gov/nwis/sw.

At-Risk Native Species

The Indicator
This indicator reports on the conservation status of native plant and animal species across their full range (i.e., global ranks) as well as population trends of species that are at-risk of extinction. The species reported here are those in groups (such as mammals, birds, and fish) that are sufficiently well known that their conservation status, habitat, and location (by state) can be assigned with some degree of confidence for all members of the group. The conservation status assessment for each species is an attempt to determine its relative susceptibility to extinction. The assessment process is based on consideration of up to 12 factors that relate to a species' degree of imperilment or risk of extinction throughout its range. Rare species are particularly vulnerable to extinction and so several aspects of rarity are characterized in the assessment process including population size, number of populations, and range extent and area of occupancy. However, trends in population and range size as well as magnitude and immediacy of threats are also important considerations in assessing a species' overall

vulnerability or risk of extinction. Additional information on this ranking process can be found at http://www.natureserve.org/explorer/ranking.htm and in Master (1991).

There is general recognition among experts that both status information (as presented here for animal and plant species) and trend information (as presented here for vertebrate animals) are critical to understanding the condition of species.

The Data
Data Source: NatureServe (http://www.natureserve.org) and its member programs in the network of Natural Heritage programs develop and maintain information on each of the species reported here. For information on the NatureServe program data collection, methodology, data quality/caveats, data availability, and references, see p. 275.

Data Manipulation: All data manipulations were performed by NatureServe. For the core national indicator, only species groups for which sufficient information is available on the entire group are reported. Groups reported for the national measure are mammals; birds; sakes and lizards; crocodilians; turtles; amphibians; freshwater and anadromous fishes; freshwater mussels; freshwater snails; crayfishes; fairy, clam, and tadpole shrimp; butterflies and skippers; giant silkworm and royal moths; sphinx moths; underwing moths; papaipema moths; tiger beetles; grasshoppers; dragonflies and damselflies; ferns and relatives; conifers and relatives; and flowering plants. Combined these groups include over 22,600 species.

2008 Report Data Update: The population trend metric was added to the indicator. Conservation status data from the 2002 report were replaced with 2006 data.

The Data Gap
Population trend data are not included for at-risk native invertebrate animals or plants, because trends are known for only 26% of invertebrate animal species and 12% of plants.

Established Non-native Species

The Indicator
When data become available, this indicator will report:
- The number of new non-native species that become established over time, by decade. In some cases, introduced species will prosper for a while and then disappear from an area; they would be excluded at the point which they are no longer considered to be established.
- The area with different numbers of established non-native species (note that for any given time period, a species would only be included if it is surviving and reproducing during that time period; those species that were formerly—but no longer—established would not be counted)
- The area with different proportions of established non-native species, as a percent of total species.

Note that this indicator was designed based on input from the Heinz Center's Non-native Species Task Group and associated workshops (see http://www.heinzctr.org/ecosystems).

For the purposes of the indicators in this report, non-native species include plants, vertebrates, invertebrates, and plant and animal pathogens, and they are defined as organisms that are not indigenous to the ecosystem or area under consideration and that are capable of surviving and reproducing in that ecosystem or area without human intervention. Established non-native species are those non-native species known to be surviving and reproducing at the present time in the ecosystem or are a under consideration.

The Data Gap

Few consistently reported and nationally comprehensive data sets are currently available on the numbers of non-native species introduced historically or on the current distribution of non-native species established in the U.S. Federal monitoring programs that could provide data to populate this indicator are few, and they have only recently been established. Federal efforts focus almost entirely on exotic pests and weeds, contributing to a lack of monitoring data addressing established non-native species more broadly.

Other than the U.S. Geological Survey (USGS), which collects data on non-native freshwater fish, mollusks and crustaceans for the Nonindigenous Aquatic Species Database Program and records voluntarily reported incidents of wildlife disease at the National Wildlife Health Center (see related Freshwater indicator, p. 182), no other federal agency that collects data on non-native species across the entire U.S. could be identified. NatureServe and the Biota of North America Program (BONAP), two non-government organizations, collect and aggregate data on species distributions for many taxonomic groups nationally. However, the Heinz Center decided, based on comments from reviewers, that additional research would be necessary to understand whether or not these data sets should be included in this national-scale indicator.

Clearly, data have and are being collected on additional species in many locations across the country, but the processing necessary to compile and aggregate many smaller data sets would require resources beyond the scope of the Heinz Center and would still leave major gaps in geographic coverage. When government agencies or other entities are able to combine these data into existing or new national scale databases, however, it will be possible to report on additional species groups within an indicator on the percent of species that are established non-natives.

2008 Report Data Update: This is a new indicator added for this edition of the report.

Native Species Composition

The Indicator

This indicator will likely measure the number of native species observed in an area, compared to that expected if the area were unaffected by disturbance, management, or physical alteration. Such an indicator would report a ratio (observed species composition/expected species composition, O/E) where a value of close to 1 indicates that the community is relatively undegraded, close to reference condition, while a value close to 0 indicates a highly degraded community, with few of the expected native species. The O/E metric would be computed for separate land-use types aggregated to a national level based on the extent of the land-use type.

The indicator will replace the Biological Community Condition indicator, listed as needing development in the 2002 Report. The Working Group assembled to develop the indicator recommended focusing on Native Species Composition as a proxy for biological community condition as it is difficult to capture the many elements of community condition (community structure, function, composition, diversity, age) given the many unknowns about community interactions and the challenges of data collection. The Working Group suggested that additional information on community condition could be attained by stratifying the indicator both geographically (by bioregion and land-use type) and taxonomically. The indicator, for example might report on species composition in clusters of taxa representing different functional or structural groups or age classes. Other candidate indicators—including a population abundance indicator and a multi-metric indicator—were discussed by the Working Group but later eliminated in favor of the Native Species Composition indicator.

Testing is required on multiple ecosystem types before the O/E metric is formally selected. The Working Group has recommended exploring two methods of computing O/E: species-area relationship models (SPARS) and predictive models in which expected species richness is quantified based on the probability that species are present given certain chemical and physical predictor variables. The SPARS approach has been used most frequently in terrestrial ecosystems and is the method recommended in the national native species diversity indicator proposed by the National Research Council (NRC 2000). Predictive O/E models have often been used to assess stream communities (Wright et al. 2000)—they are the foundation of national assessments in Britain and Australia and have recently been used to assess the condition of bottom-dwelling communities in wadeable stream of the US (US EPA 2006b). The method chosen for this report will have to successfully quantify O/E species composition in both aquatic and terrestrial systems.

The Data Gap

If the Native Species Composition indicator is formally accepted, it is likely to have only partial data. Collection of species composition data on a land-use scale is relatively uncommon. Such data are typically collected by academics, state programs, or non-profit organizations (for example, the Illinois Natural History Survey, http://www.inhs.uiuc.edu) and there are currently no regional or national data bases that assemble this information for a broad range of taxa. Moreover, many of the species composition data are not collected in conjunction with species composition data from reference sites unaffected by disturbance, management, or physical alteration. If predictive models are used, indicator models will also require data on population abundance and the chemical or physical parameters of the land-use areas. National species composition data at a land-use scale, currently exist for freshwater macroinvertebrates (US EPA 2006e) see Status of Freshwater Animal Species p. 185. The USDA Forest Service is developing a vegetation indicator to assess the type, abundance, and spatial arrangement of vegetation on its Phase 3 Forest Health FIA plots (http://www.fia.fs.fed.us) (see also the technical note for Established Non-Native Plant Cover in the Forests chapter, p. 309).

Plant Growth Index

The Indicator

This indicator reports on the amount of land area with yearly increases or decreases in plant growth relative to the long-term average, based on the normalized difference vegetation index (NDVI; see below). Data are reported individually by ecosystem type, as well as synoptically for all ecosystem types combined for the full time period (in this case, from 1982–2003).

The plant growth index is based on data collected by the Advanced Very High Radiation Radiometer (AVHRR) aboard the National Oceanographic and Atmospheric Administration's (NOAA) polar-orbiting satellites. The NDVI provides a measure of the density of chlorophyll biomass and is calculated using the equation NDVI = (NIR—VIS)/(NIR + VIS) where NIR is near-infrared light reflected by vegetation and VIS is visible light reflected by vegetation as measured remotely by AVHRR. Low values of NDVI (0.1 and below) correspond to barren areas of rock, sand, or snow. Moderate values represent shrub and grassland (0.2 to 0.3), while high values indicate temperate and tropical rainforests (0.6 to 0.8). For a given type of vegetation (e.g., forest, shrublands, grasslands, croplands), the index can be used as a metric of physiological state. Healthy vegetation (high value) absorbs most of the visible light that hits it, and reflects a large portion of the near-infrared light. Unhealthy or sparse vegetation (low value) reflects more visible light and less near-infrared light.

Because the relationship between NDVI and absorbed photosynthetically active radiation varies by cover type, the growing-season accumulated NDVI was calculated separately for the forest, farmland, and grasslands, and shrubland areas of the conterminous 48 states, for each year between 1982 and 2003.

Substantial Changes to the Indicator Design: New data (see below) were added from a database that has been prepared specifically for time series analyses. Formerly, results were summarized from county-level data; the new results were summarized from 8-km pixels (64 square kilometers).

The Data

Data Description: The raw NOAA-AVHRR sensor data at 8-km spatial and 15-day temporal resolution was reprocessed by the National Aeronautics and Space Administration (NASA) Global Inventory Monitoring and Modeling Studies (GIMMS) group to provide a spatially and temporally consistent representation of global vegetation for climate studies, and to remove effects associated with calibration changes, orbital drift and aerosol contamination of the atmosphere (Tucker et al., 2005).

Data Manipulation: GIMMS data were analyzed by NASA (Terrestrial Observation and Prediction System (TOPS) /Ames Research Center) for this study. A Man-Kendall test was used to estimate trends in annual mean NDVIs over the conterminous U.S from 1982–2003. To summarize NDVI trends and variability for different ecosystems, we used an AVHRR-derived 1km land cover map aggregated to 8km (Hansen et al., 2000).

Data Quality/Caveats: GIMMS data are continuously improved as a part of NASA's efforts at creating long-term climate records. Reducing uncertainties related to atmospheric corrections applied to the NDVI data is part of such on-going efforts.

Data Availability: GIMMS data are available from the Global Land Cover Facility (http://www.landcover.org).

The Data Gap

Similar analyses based on estimates of chlorophyll concentrations have been done for open-ocean waters (see Gregg et al. 2005). In the future this indicator could combine results from those data analyses with the data presented for terrestrial systems.

Production of Food and Fiber and Water Withdrawals

The Data

Forest Products: Data were obtained directly from the USDA Forest Service. The data used in the graph for the entire United States are the same as those used in the Timber Harvest indicator (p. 154).

Marine Fish Landings: Data were obtained directly from the National Oceanographic and Atmospheric Administration (NOAA) and are described in Commercial Fish and Shellfish Landings (p. 87).

Freshwater Withdrawals: Data were derived from the U.S. Geological Survey Circular series *Estimated Use of Water in the United States*, which has been published every 5 years since 1950 (note: consistency issues prevented the use of data prior to 1960). More recent compilations (1985–2000) are available electronically at http://water.usgs.gov/watuse/ (see the technical note for Water Withdrawals, p. 323). Withdrawals for any given year (and region) were divided by the 1980 value.

Agricultural Products: Data are available online from the U.S. Department of Agriculture's Economic Research Service (ERS). State-by-state data are from Table 7 of U.S. Agriculture, 1960–96: A Multilateral Comparison of Total Factor Productivity (Technical Bulletin 1895, available at http://www.ers.usda.gov/Data/AgProductivity/). State data were summed for the entire U.S. graph. The data in Table 7 are normalized such that the output for Alabama in 1996 equals 1. These normalized data were summed, either for the nation as a whole or for each region, and then divided by the 1980 value to produce the index values for all other years. Note that the data series was reanalyzed by ERS, although differences between these new data and those presented in the 2002 Report are slight.

Human Population: Data are available online from the U.S. Census Bureau via the "national" and "state" links at http://www.census.gov/popest/estimates.php. National or summed regional data were divided by the value for 1980 to produce the index values for all other years. Note that data in the 2002 Report for 1991–1999 were based on post-censal estimates. These have been replaced by more accurate inter-censal estimates from the Census Bureau.

2008 Report Data Update: In the 2008 report new and revised data were added for Forest Products (2006), Marine Fish Landings (2005), and human population (2005–2006). Note that slight revisions were made to the entire dataset for Marine Fish Landings. New data were not available for Water Withdrawals.

Outdoor Recreation

The Data

Data Description: Data on recreational activity for the three time points shown (1994–1995, 1999–2001, 2003–2005) in this indicator are from the National Survey on Recreation and the Environment (NSRE). The NSRE is a partnership between the USDA Forest Service Southern Research Station, The National Oceanic and Atmospheric Administration, the University of Georgia, the University of Tennessee and other federal, state or private sponsors. The NSRE gathers data on participation in outdoor recreational activities, (in addition to data on the participants themselves) via phone surveys of households across the United States.

For the 1994–1995 survey, data from a total of 17,216 interviews were collected from January 1994 through May 1995; the 1999–2001 NSRE included 57,868 interviews collected from July 1999 through July 2001; approximately 50,000 interviews were included in the 2003–2005 NSRE survey (complete statistics are not available). The 1994–1995 and 1999–2001 NSRE surveys were composed of two random-digit-dialing (RDD) telephone surveys. During the interviews, which averaged 20 minutes in length, Americans 16 years of age and older were asked, among other questions, about participation in activities and the number of days and trips spent in recreation activities; comparable statistics for the 2003–2005 NSRE survey are not available.

Data Manipulation: The NSRE data are presented as major activity groups (e.g., bicycling, big game hunting, surfing, anadromous fishing). For this indicator, the Heinz Center re-bundled these activity groups, slightly, as can be seen by comparing Table 4.2 in the NSRE report to the reporting categories used here (e.g., walking, motor sports, freshwater fishing). For example, subsumed within our reporting category "snow skiing" are the NSRE data for all forms of skiing and as well as snowboarding and snowshoeing. Note that our reporting categories were adjusted to accommodate differences between the three NSRE reports.

Data Quality/Caveats: The RDD survey approach reaches a random sample of telephone numbers rather than of people. A substantial portion of non-random over- or under-representation of some groups is attributable to the inability to reach selected households and the absence of some households from telephone listings. On the basis of Census data, differences in age, race, and gender were adjusted for over- or under-representation during data analysis.

The number of homes surveyed for the 1999–2001 and 2003–2005 time points were about the same, however the number of homes surveyed increased by 40,652 (17,216 to 57,868) from the 1994–1995 NSRE to the 1999–2001 NSRE. The degree to which this change increased participation for recreational activities reported in this indicator is not known, however it likely had an effect.

Data from other national surveys on outdoor recreation were also examined in the development of this indicator. The U.S. Fish and Wildlife Service (FWS) conducts telephone and in-person surveys of likely participants in wildlife-related outdoor activities. The 2006 FWS Fishing, Hunting, and Wildlife Associated Recreation survey reported declines in the number of residents participating in fishing and hunting activities between 2001 and 2006. Over the same time period, the report found increases in the number of individuals participating in wildlife watching activities. The FWS survey results are available at http://wsfrprograms.fws.gov/Subpages/NationalSurvey/National_Survey.htm. The Outdoor Industry Foundation (OIF) also conducts national surveys on recreation (available at http://outdoorfoundation.org). A survey prepared by RoperASW for The Recreation Roundtable entitled Outdoor Recreation in America 2003: Recreation's Benefits to Society Challenged by Trends 2004 is available at http://www.funoutdoors.com/files/ROPER%20REPORT%202004_0.pdf. The OIF and Roper surveys both observed declines in U.S recreation participation; however, these surveys are not as comprehensive or reproducible as the NSRE surveys. More data points are needed to determine if observed increases in participation in the NSRE survey data are indicative of a long-term upward trend.

Surveys, like the NSRE, are one way of estimating changes over time in recreation participation. Other long-term studies on recreation in the U.S use visitation data from parks or public lands, or hunting and fishing license purchases to monitor trends in outdoor recreation. Pergams and Zaradic (2008) tracked outdoor recreation participation over time using a combination of survey and visitation data. They found significant declines in per capita public land visitation, including declines in camping and fishing participation. The results of the NSRE forest data are not directly comparable to the national visitation data because the NSRE tracks total recreation participation whereas the visitation data is adjusted for changes over time in population. The NSRE data are from surveys, not actual recreation visits, and therefore may not accurately characterize recreation participation. The visitation data are limited in scope in that they only track visits to locations that record visitation records or collect fees. Visitation data do not track recreation on private lands or public lands where visitation is not monitored.

Data Availability: Data from the 1994–1995 NSRE were obtained from the NSRE website at http://www.srs.fs.fed.us/trends/fsoutrec.html. Data from the 1999–2001, and 2003–2005 NSREs were obtained directly from the USDA Forest Service. The 1999–2001 NSRE is available online at http://www.srs.fs.usda.gov/trends/nsre2.html), these data are also published in Cordell (2004).

2008 Report Data Update: Data from the 2003–2005 NSRE were added.

The Data Gap

As mentioned in the text, the list of activities for which recreation days are available is not exhaustive, and further distinctions for some activities (e.g., swimming, hunting, and viewing) such as whether they were conducted in a saltwater or freshwater setting are needed in order to attribute recreation to specific ecosystem types. This data set currently does not report recreation of individuals under the age of 16. Other survey-based reports on recreation participation that have targeted youth have found significant declines in youth recreation participation (Leonard 2007). The NSRE surveys have added a youth module targeting individuals 6 to 15 years of age. When data are available, this indicator will be expanded to include data on youth recreation.

Natural Ecosystem Services

There is no technical note for this indicator.

Coasts and Oceans

Coastal Living Habitats

The Indicator

The coastal living habitats indicator shows the area of "biologically structured habitat" in coast and ocean ecosystems, that is, habitat types that are composed of living organisms or their remnants. Biologically structured coastal living habitats include a range of different habitat types and are typically rich in plant and animal life. Coral reefs and seagrass beds provide habitat for many types of fish, including larvae that are critical to sustaining populations of marine organisms in local and distant waters. Other habitats, such as relict shellfish beds, continue to provide habitat for marine organisms long after the departure of the animals that created them.

This indicator reports only the extent of these biologically structured habitats, not their condition. As a result, this indicator may not sufficiently characterize habitat types such as coral reefs whose function is dependent more on the condition of the habitat than on its extent.

The Data

Data Description: The coastal wetlands data came from the U.S. Fish and Wildlife Service (FWS) National Wetlands Inventory (NWI; Dahl et al. 2006, p. 46). For a description of the NWI program, see p. 272. The data presented here include estuarine vegetated wetlands, which are ~87% of the total coastal wetlands included in the FWS report. Excluded types include estuarine nonvegetated and marine intertidal wetlands, neither of which falls into the category of "biologically structured habitat." This indicator does not include estimates of coastal wetlands before major development along the coastline. Gosselink and Baumann (1980) estimate that 10 million acres of coastal wetlands existed in 1923; using this information, current estimates show a 50% decline in wetland area. The FWS report "Wetland Losses in the United States 1780's to 1980's" (Dahl 1990) also documents long-term trends in wetland extent. Note that data for coastal wetlands extent take into account estimated wetland loss during the 2005 hurricane season.

Data Manipulation: The data presented here, summarized in Dahl et al. (2006), are derived from four separate analyses covering, respectively, the 1950s to the 1970s, the 1970s to 1980s, the 1980s to 1990s, and 1998 to 2004. For this report, decadal estimates are presented as the midpoint of the decade. For example, 1980s data are graphed as 1985. Note that more detailed data are available from the NWI maps and accompanying digital data but that acreage summaries are not compiled for national or regional reporting.

2008 Report Data Update: Data for 1998 and 2004 estimates of vegetated wetland area along the Atlantic and Gulf coasts were added from the updated NWI report. Coastal wetlands loss estimates from the 2005 hurricane season were also added.

Data Availability: "Status and Trends of Wetlands in the Conterminous United States 1998 to 2004" is available on the Web at http://wetlandsfws.er.usgs.gov/status_trends. Estimates of coastal wetland loss during the 2005 hurricane season can be accessed at http://pubs.usgs.gov/of/2006/1274/.

The Data Gap

Vegetated Wetlands: The patchy distribution of Pacific coastal estuarine wetlands precluded gathering statistically valid data on this wetland type. Therefore, consistent with past studies, NWI did not sample Pacific coastal estuarine wetlands such as those in San Francisco Bay, California; Coos Bay, Oregon; or Puget Sound, Washington. Information on several southern California wetlands is available online at http://www.ceres.ca.gov/wetlands/geo_info/so_cal.html.

A 1994 FWS report on the status of Alaska's wetlands is available online (http://www.fws.gov/nwi/Pubs_Reports/Status_of_Alaska_Wetlands.pdf), but trend data are not available. Estimates of coastal vegetated wetlands are unavailable for Hawaii.

Coral Reefs: Most coral reefs in U.S. waters, and particularly those in the Pacific Ocean, have not been accurately mapped with modern techniques and on a scale relevant to emerging conservation issues. In March 2000, a plan of action released by the federal interagency U.S. Coral Reef Task Force (USCRTF; http://www.coralreef.gov) committed agencies to produce comprehensive maps of all coral reefs in the United States and trust territories within five to seven years. The National Oceanic and Atmospheric Administration (NOAA) Coral Reef Conservation Program's "The State of Coral Reef Ecosystems of the United States and Pacific Freely Associated States: 2005" (http://ccma.nos.noaa.gov/ecosystems/coralreef/coral_report_2005) reports on 6 of the planned 14 regions. The report maps coral reef area and estimates biological condition. No repeated mapping or long-term monitoring is planned as part of the NOAA initiative.

Shellfish Beds: The National Shellfish Register of Classified Growing Waters, produced every five years from 1966 to 1998, is available at http://oceanservice.noaa.gov/websites/retiredsites/supp_sotc_retired.html. The Register was a cooperative effort among the nation's shellfish-producing states, federal agencies such as the U.S. Food and Drug Administration and NOAA, and the Interstate Shellfish Sanitation Conference (ISSC).

Submerged Aquatic Vegetation: Although many programs monitor the extent of submerged aquatic vegetation (seagrasses, kelp, and other similar underwater plants), we are aware of no effort to compile and assess national trends. The United Nation Environment Program is actively gathering information on the worldwide distribution of seagrasses which may eventually be a source of data for this indicator (http://unep.org/dewa/assessments/ecosystems/water/vitalwater/marine.htm).

Shoreline Types

The Indicator

The percentage of total miles of U.S. shoreline are shown for the five categories of shoreline type (steep sand, rock, or clay shorelines; mud or sand flats; beach; vegetated; and armored). Additionally, a regional breakdown of shoreline types is shown as a percentage of each region's total shoreline miles. This indicator does not report on the extent (area) of the different categories of shoreline type. Furthermore, it only categorizes the zone of tidal influence and therefore does not capture commercial or housing development along the shoreline or other near-shore inland structures. Coastal living habitats (p. 72) and pattern in coastal areas (p. 74) indicators are designed to describe the pattern and extent of coastal habitats.

The Data

Data Description: Data were provided by the National Oceanic and Atmospheric Administration (NOAA), National Ocean Service, Office of Response and Restoration, Hazardous Materials Response Division. Data on Florida's shoreline were collected by the Florida Marine Institute and processed and interpreted by NOAA. Data were extracted from Environmental Sensitivity Index (ESI) atlases, a product of NOAA's Office of Response and Restoration. The ESI method is a standardized mapping approach for coastal geomorphology as well as biological and human use elements. More information is available at http://response.restoration.noaa.gov/esi/. Data from multiple atlases (1984–2006) were aggregated into the regions used in this report. For most of the regions, digital data were not available for the entire coastline. The currency and the completeness of the coverage affect the quality of the shoreline summary. With regard to these issues, information specific to the nine regions for which data are available is presented in the Data Quality section below. Complete metadata for each atlas, including collection methods and source information, can be viewed at http://response.restoration.noaa.gov/esi/.

Data Manipulation: This indicator presents a simplified summary of shoreline types, by region. It is a summary of the total length of the intertidal zone for the region, as well as the total length of each of the five shoreline types. ESI shoreline types were classified using a combination of overflight information, aerial photography, local habitat maps, National Wetlands Inventory data, and ground truthing. For more detailed information specific to each atlas, see the individual atlas metadata, specifically sections 5.1–Detailed Description: ESI and 2.5.1–Source Information: ESI.

The first step in defining the indicator was to consolidate the shorelines from the various atlases for each region and reconcile older terminology with current ESI shoreline type classifications. The next step was to combine the ESI shoreline type classes into the five more general categories, based on substrate and slope, which are used in this report. The five categories and the ESI types included in each category are as follows:

- *Steep or rocky shoreline.* ESI categories 1 (unvegetated steep banks, cliffs, and seawalls), 1A (exposed rocky shores), 2A (exposed wave-cut platforms in bedrock, mud, or clay), 2B (exposed scarps and steep slopes in clay), 3B (scarps and steep slopes in sand), and 8A (sheltered rocky shores and sheltered scarps in bedrock, mud, or clay)
- *Mud or sand flats.* ESI categories 7 (exposed tidal flats) and 9A (sheltered tidal flats)
- *Beach (sand or gravel).* ESI categories 3AF (fine- to medium-grained sand beaches), 4 (coarse-grained sand

beaches), 5 (mixed sand and gravel beaches), and 6A (gravel beaches)
- *Vegetated wetlands.* Includes grasslands, scrublands/shrublands, and marshes. ESI categories 8D (vegetated, steeply sloping bluffs), 9B (vegetated low banks), 10A (salt- and brackish-water marshes), 10B (freshwater marshes), 10C (swamps), and 10D (scrub–shrub wetlands and mangroves)
- *Armored.* ESI categories 1B (exposed, solid man-made structures), 6B (riprap), 8B (sheltered, solid man-made structures), and 8C (sheltered riprap)

After the regional shoreline was characterized, tables were generated detailing the length of each shoreline segment and its associated ESI type. A series of computer programs summed the shoreline length and the shoreline types. ESI shoreline data are quite complex because a single shoreline segment may contain land identified by up to three ESI classifications. For example, a segment may have a tidal flat on the water side backed by a sand beach, then a marsh on the landward side. If a segment has different shoreline types, that segment may be counted up to three times. However, when the total length of land/water interface is calculated, each shoreline segment is counted only once, regardless of the number of shoreline types it contains. Thus, the sum of the lengths of all the shoreline types will be greater than the total shoreline length.

Data Quality/Caveats: ESI shoreline coverage uses a broader definition of shoreline than other indicators in this chapter because it includes the shoreline of inlets, bays, coastal rivers, and tidal creeks. For example, the Pacific Northwest region includes considerable area along the shore of the Columbia River. Some of the older atlases used for this region were compiled in 1984 for the Mid-Atlantic and Pacific Northwest; some changes to coastline shape or type may have occurred for a small percentage of these regions since then.

Data Availability: The data reported here are from an analysis undertaken specifically for this project; however, some data are available at http://response.restoration.noaa.gov/esi/.

2008 Report Data Update: First-time data were added for the North Atlantic, Mid-Atlantic, Gulf of Mexico, Gulf of Alaska, Bering Sea, and Hawaiian regions. Additional years of data were added to the Pacific Northwest, South Atlantic, and Southern California regions.

Pattern in Coastal Areas

There is no technical note for this indicator.

Areas with Depleted Oxygen

The Indicator

This indicator reports the area of coastal or estuarine waters with dissolved oxygen concentrations that are considered hypoxic (less than 2 ppm dissolved oxygen) for prolonged periods during the summer months. When data are available, the indicator will also report the area of estuarine and coastal waters with dissolved oxygen concentrations that are considered low but not hypoxic (between 2 and 4 ppm).

The Data

Data Source: Data for the Gulf of Mexico are from the annual hypoxia surveys of Nancy Rabalais, Louisiana Universities Marine Consortium (LUMCON), and Eugene Turner, Louisiana State University. Chesapeake Bay data are from the Chesapeake Bay Program (http://www.chesapeakebay.net/)

Data Manipulation: Data for the Gulf of Mexico are from annual midsummer shelf-wide cruises of established monitoring stations. The area of coastal waters with dissolved oxygen below 2 ppm is calculated from interpolating dissolved oxygen measurements at multiple fixed monitoring stations. Metadata and maps of station locations are available at http://www. gulfhypoxia.net. The Chesapeake Bay data are the mean area of Bay waters with dissolved oxygen levels below 2 ppm during the month of July, expressed as a percentage of the total sampled Bay for each time period.

Data Availability: Information and data on Gulf of Mexico hypoxia are available at http://www.gulfhypoxia.net. The Chesapeake Bay Program maintains an online database of dissolved oxygen and water quality data accessible at http://www.chesapeakebay.net/wquality.htm.

2008 Report Data Update: Partial data for the Chesapeake Bay and the Gulf of Mexico were added.

The Data Gap

There are multiple regional dissolved oxygen monitoring programs in coastal bays and estuaries. Currently, however, only the northern Gulf of Mexico and Chesapeake Bay have long-term datasets that allow for comparisons of the extent of hypoxia across multiple years. Further information on state-level dissolved oxygen reporting efforts are available from NOAA at http://www.cop.noaa.gov/stressors/pollution/links. html. NOAA also maintains a link to active regional hypoxia-related research programs, http://www.cop.noaa.gov/#maplink.

More information on regional dissolved oxygen reporting efforts are available online for Long Island Sound (http://www.ct.gov/dep/cwp/view.asp?a=2719&q=325534&depNav_GID=1654), Neuse Estuary (http://www.ncsu.edu/wq/NRMP/index.html), and Narragansett Bay (http://www.dem.ri.gov/bart/netdata.htm).

Contamination in Bottom Sediments

The Indicator

This indicator reports on the area of estuary bottom sediments with contamination levels exceeding established benchmarks. These contaminants can harm fish and other aquatic organisms and can adversely affect human health if tainted fish or shellfish are ingested. In the future, the spatial extent of sediment contamination in the coastal ocean out to 25 miles will also be reported.

The Data

Data Source: Data were collected at 2,146 sites during 1998 to 2002 by the USEPA National Coastal Assessment (for details see the NCA program description on p. 269 and http://www. epa.gov/emap/nca/index.html). Data represent 100% of the total estuarine acreage of the 21 coastal states in the lower 48 states, Hawaii, Puerto Rico, and south-central Alaska. Estuarine sediment surveys for other estuarine areas in Alaska are planned by NCA, but will not be available for another five to ten years.

Concentrations of 20 pesticide compounds, 24 polynuclear aromatic hydrocarbons (PAHs), 21 polychlorinated biphenyl (PCB) congeners and 15 trace elements (including mercury) were measured. Twenty-seven individual or composite benchmarks for the protection of aquatic life were compared to 6 pesticide compounds, 24 PAHs, 21 PCB congeners and 9 trace elements (21 contaminants measured by NCA in estuarine sediments do not have established benchmarks). For each sampling site, the number of contaminants that were measured at concentrations exceeding lower or higher benchmarks was summed. Indicator figures report on "bins" of estuarine area based on the number of contaminants in exceedance.

Data Quality/Caveats: Many contaminants measured by the NCA do not have established benchmarks. Aquatic life benchmarks for estuarine sediment were developed as informal, interpretive tools (see NCA program description on p. 269). No benchmarks exist for potential human health effects from exposure to contaminated sediments.

2008 Report Data Update: In the 2002 Report, sediment contamination data for 1992–1998 were reported, however these data are not comparable to the 1998–2002 data presented here due to expansion of the geographic scope of the monitoring program—North Atlantic and Pacific Coast estuaries, Hawaii, and south-central Alaska were added.

The Data Gap

Data collection has begun for contaminants in ocean bottom sediments (within 25 miles of shore) in the West, Southeast, and Northeast regions and future ocean surveys in other regions will provide one-time "snapshot" information, data are not yet available for reporting on contaminants in ocean bottom sediments.

Coastal Erosion

The Indicator

When data are available, this indicator will report on the condition of the U.S. coastline––whether it is managed or natural, and whether it is eroding, accreting, or stable. Coastal erosion can alter sensitive coastal habitats, change patterns of sediment transport and deposition, and impact water quality. Erosion also threatens coastal settlements.

The Data Gap

As discussed in the indicator text, guidelines will be necessary for classifying stretches of coastline as "accreting" or "eroding." It is thought that the associated change in the horizontal movement of the shoreline will be in the range of one-half to several feet per year. In addition, the coastal management community will need to agree on the impact to the shoreline of groins, which are erosion control structures typically built perpendicular to the shoreline. Further, beach nourishment may be undertaken to control erosion, but it also may be the by-product of harbor or inlet construction or maintenance, when the excavated material is placed on an adjacent beach. Nourishment that occurs as a by-product is typically not well documented.

Most shoreline erosion and beach nourishment data are developed on a short-term, project-specific basis. Few long-term or regional studies have been carried out, and differences in data collection and analysis protocols make it difficult to compare site-specific reports and compile the data for either regional or national reporting. A study by Dolan et al. (1985) contains a compilation of erosion data from the 1960s, 1970s, and 1980s. This one-time study may be a model for future analyses. Regional projects such as the Southwest Washington Coastal Erosion Study (http://www.ecy.wa.gov/programs/sea/swces/index.htm) and Florida's Department of Environmental Protection critical erosion reports (http://www.dep.state.fl.us/beaches/publications/tech-rpt. htm#Critical_Erosion_Reports) are examples of well-documented site-specific coastal erosion reports.

Various methods have been used to determine whether shoreline locations are eroding, accreting, or stable. These include shoreline profiles, the National Oceanic and Atmospheric Administration (NOAA) National Ocean Service topographic survey sheets, and aerial photographs, which can be georeferenced or orthorectified. In addition, light detection and ranging (LIDAR) has been an effective tool for measuring erosion and was used in at least two programs. The Airborne LIDAR Assessment of Coastal Erosion (ALACE) project was a partnership among NOAA, the National Aeronautics and Space Administration (NASA), and the U.S. Geological Survey that utilized aircraft-collected LIDAR to map a good portion of the sandy beaches of the lower 48 states. NOAA continues to utilize LIDAR for site-specific analyses of shorelines rather than broad surveys of the U.S. coastline in its topographic change mapping program. (For further information on ALACE or the topographic change mapping program, see http://www.csc.noaa.gov/crs/tcm/.)

Sea Surface Temperature

The Indicator
This indicator was calculated by determining (A) the yearly seasonal average sea surface temperature (SST) of near-shore water (shoreline out to 200 mi) for the warmest season in each region (termed the "seasonal mean maximum," which typically occurs during summer or fall) and (B) the long-term mean (during the warmest seasons) for the period of observation (1985–2006). The long-term mean was then subtracted from the seasonal mean maximum for each year. Thus, annual values greater than zero are positive "anomalies" (i.e., deviations from the long-term average), and those less than zero are negative anomalies.

Because of the large heat capacity of the ocean, changes in ocean water temperature are less susceptible to daily and seasonal variability than land and air temperatures. The buffering capacity of oceans means that warming trends in sea temperatures lag comparable measurements on the land surface. As a result, significant changes in ocean temperatures over

time are more likely to indicate universal changes in the earth's climate than land or air temperatures. Changes in annual cycles of water temperature and the occurrence of interannual to decadal trends not only will affect the kinds of organisms that will thrive in a region, but also are thought to be associated with the degradation of coral reefs (bleaching), the development of harmful algal blooms, and the growth of invasive species. Over longer time scales (decades to centuries), such changes may be related to decreases in the supply of nutrients to surface waters from the deep sea as well as a cascade of effects from decreases in primary production to declines in fish production.

There is considerable evidence building that the surface waters of the oceans are warming gradually (e.g., Barry et al. 1995 and Levitus et al. 2000). The 2007 Intergovernmental Panel on Climate Change (IPCC) reported that between 1961 and 2003, global ocean temperatures rose by 0.10°C in the deeper ocean (0–700 m; Solomon et al. 2007). The IPCC report also found a correlation between warming trends in the deeper ocean and SST, suggesting that surface trends are also predictive of shifts in whole-ocean temperature budgets (Solomon et al. 2007).

The Data
Data Source: Data from 1985 through 2006 were analyzed for The Heinz Center by the National Ocean Service of the National Oceanic and Atmospheric Administration (NOAA). The NOAA/National Aeronautics and Space Administration (NASA) Oceans Pathfinder SST data were obtained using advanced very-high resolution radiometers onboard several NOAA polar-orbiting environmental satellites.

Data Manipulation: Data were acquired on a grid of square pixels nominally 10 km (~6 mi) on a side. Both the day- and nighttime data were processed to remove clouds (using an "erosion filter") and then averaged to produce monthly means, which were then averaged to produce seasonal means.

Data Quality/Caveats: Systematic errors are rare in such an analysis, and the data are expected to be within 2°F of actual temperatures measured 3.3 ft below the surface.

Data Availability: Data are freely available on the Web from NASA at http://podaac.jpl.nasa.gov/DATA_CATALOG/sst.html/.

2008 Report Data Update: New data from NOAA were added through 2006.

At-Risk Native Marine Species

There is no technical note for this indicator.

Established Non-native Species in Major Estuaries

The Indicator
This indicator is not fully defined. Consistent with many of the other indicators in this report, it is has been proposed that a metric describing the area of major estuaries with different numbers of non-native species (including plants, vertebrates,

invertebrates, and plant and animal pathogens affecting native species) be reported. Such a metric could be broken down by taxonomic group, and numbers of non-native species could be paired with the percentage that these numbers are of total species in the estuary. It is unresolved if such a design would provide spatial resolution across estuaries—especially larger ones that might have areas within them that are more or less affected by non-native species.

This is, admittedly, a simplistic design and may not provide sufficiently useful information on the status of the nation's estuaries. Further, there are similarities to the challenges raised by this indicator and the terrestrial plant cover indicators (e.g., Established Non-native Plant Cover in Forests): both are multilayer systems, and accounting strategies are needed that capture this complexity.

See the technical note for the core indicator (p. 283) for a definition of non-native species.

The Data Gap

Species lists for the five categories of organisms will need to be developed and maintained for each major U.S. estuary through regular data collection and assessment programs. The lists will be based on existing knowledge of the species in the target groupings in each estuary and on ongoing surveys of biological resources that are conducted in these regions for a variety of purposes. These surveys will also furnish the data required to assess the ecological significance of the non-native species found in an estuary.

Species lists, data on ecological significance, and some monitoring data on various species are available from surveys and compilations produced by a variety of sources, including state living-resource and environmental protection agencies, environmental impact statements, and academic research projects. However, such data are not available in any consistent fashion for many of the major estuaries, and there is no nationwide compilation of data. Various programs are working to bring together useful information and data—see The Aquatic Nuisance Species Task Force (http://www.anstaskforce.gov/) and the Smithsonian Environmental Research Center (http://www.serc.si.edu/labs/marine_invasions/).

Reporting the percentages of biomass in estuaries that consist of non-native species is another approach to understanding the impact these species have in aquatic systems. As this indicator develops in the future and data sources are sought, alternate approaches may be considered.

Unusual Marine Mortalities

The Indicator

This indicator focuses on unusual mortalities; deaths from old age, predation, recreational boating accidents, and bycatch are not reported. The reporting of unusual mortality events (UME) by the National Oceanic and Atmospheric Administration (NOAA) National Marine Fisheries Service (NMFS) began in 1991 in response to a major dolphin die-off during 1987–88. NMFS established the Working Group on Unusual Marine Mammal Mortality Events to create criteria for determining when an unusual mortality event occurs and then to direct responses to such events (see http://www.nmfs.noaa.gov/pr/health/mmume/history.htm). This multidisciplinary team determines if a reported

mortality event should be classified as a UME through analysis of (1) number of animals involved; (2) time and location of event; (3) species, age, or sex composition of the animals; (4) identification of any unusual pathological findings or unusual behaviors exhibited by wild populations; and (5) status of the affected species as endangered, threatened, declining, or depleted. For all five criteria, the working group uses prior monitoring and historic data to determine if the characteristic of the mortality event should be considered unusual or represents significant deviations from normal conditions.

The Data

Data Description: NMFS Office of Protected Resources, Marine Mammal Health and Stranding Response Program, provides data on UMEs from 1991 to present.

Data Availability: Data on UMEs were obtained directly from NOAA. Most of these data are available online at www.nmfs.noaa.gov/pr/health/mmume. Data on the multiyear gray whale mortality event were obtained from NOAA Technical Memorandum NMFS-AFS-150, "Eastern North Pacific Gray Whale *(Eschrichtius robustus)* Unusual Mortality Event, 1999–2000," available online at www.afsc.noaa.gov/Publications/AFSC-TM/NOAA-TM-AFSC-150.pdf. Data on the 2002 UME are discussed in Heyning 2003.

2008 Report Data Update: New and revised data on whales, dolphins, porpoises, seals, sea lions, sea otters, and manatees were added.

The Data Gap

Although a stranding and salvage network has been established for sea turtles, there is no program for sea turtles, sea birds, fish, or shellfish similar to that in place for marine mammals. It will be necessary to establish guidelines for what constitutes a UME for these animals, which typically perish in much larger numbers than mammals.

Harmful Algal Events

The Indicator

For the purposes of this analysis, harmful algal events are characterized by (1) an increase in the abundance of species that are known to produce toxins harmful to animals or humans, (2) an increase in levels of shellfish toxin that prohibit their harvest or sales, (3) the occurrence of lesions or mass mortalities of marine or Great Lakes animals caused by harmful algal species, or (4) the occurrence of human pathologies caused by harmful algal species. A single event counts only once toward the relative intensity scale, even if it produces multiple impacts (e.g., an increase in the abundance of a harmful algal species that causes mass mortalities and an increased human health risk will be counted as a single event).

There are approximately 5000 species of microalgae in the world. Of these, about 100 can produce toxins and only a few are nontoxic to humans but can harm fish and invertebrates by damaging or clogging their gills. Harmful algal events involve species representing a broad spectrum of taxa (e.g., dinoflagellates, diatoms, cyanobacteria) and trophic levels (e.g., autotrophic, heterotrophic, mixotrophic). Event frequency, extent, and duration vary by both species and region and can differ significantly from year to year for a given species/toxin within a region. Events may cause problems at low as well as high cell densities—a visible bloom is not necessarily required for a harmful algal event to occur. Current regulatory programs, such as state programs that control harvest of toxin-contaminated shellfish, help minimize the human health consequences of some of these harmful algal events. For examples of harmful algal species, their toxin or mechanism for causing harm, vectors involved, and potential consequences see HARNESS 2005 (p. 14), Hallegraeff et al. 2003 (p. 26), and Moeller et al. 2007.

Another group of problematic algal events is recognized, but not included in this indicator. This group includes macro- and microalgae that by virtue of their biomass impact the surrounding community by depleting oxygen supplies, limiting light penetration, and altering coastal habitat. These issues are addressed to some extent in other indicators.

The Data Gap
Most harmful algal events, such as fish kills, are typically identified after the event has occurred or once it is well under way. Systematic monitoring programs that (1) quantify the abundance of harmful algal species, (2) quantify the concentrations of biotoxins or establish unequivocal causal relations between harmful algal species and mortality events, or (3) quantify increases in human health risks, are rare. Consequently, the data required to calculate this index on a national scale does not exist. Although efforts to monitor and report these events are increasing nationwide, there is no standard measure of harmful algae. This is largely because of the heterogeneous nature of harmful algal species (in terms of taxonomy, nutrition, the conditions under which they become toxic, the kinds of toxins produced, and their effects) and the fact that some species cause problems when they bloom, whereas others cause problems at low cell densities.

State, federal, and academic programs collect most existing data, such as those in the database maintained by the Florida Marine Research Institute, for specific purposes (e.g., research or mitigation) or for specific locations (e.g., the west coast of Florida) where harmful algae have caused problems. Thus, there is little consistency among programs and types of data available. Although there have been efforts to establish regional databases, such as HABSOS, the U.S. Global Ocean Observation System Program's collaborative prototype system in the northern Gulf of Mexico (http://habsos.noaa.gov/), comprehensive regional databases do not exist in many parts of the country. The Harmful Algal Event Database administered through the U.S. National Office for Harmful Algae Blooms, located at Woods Hole Oceanographic Institution, provides basic information on the number, type, and location of events in the United States (see http://www.whoi.edu/redtide/HABdistribution/HABmap.html and http://www.iode.org/haedat). Data are based on reporting from the array of existing monitoring programs, each with its own number of monitoring stations and specific sampling regime. At the current time, data are insufficient to allow reporting on event intensity on a national scale.

In December 2004, the Harmful Algal Bloom and Hypoxia Research and Control Act (1998) was reauthorized (Harmful Algal Bloom and Hypoxia Amendments Act of 2004, PL 108-456).

The reauthorization reestablishes the Federal Interagency Task Force on HABs and Hypoxia and calls for funding for research, education, and monitoring activities related to prevention, reduction, and control of harmful algal blooms and hypoxia. It also mandates that five reports or plans be submitted to Congress, including a scientific assessment of harmful algae and reports on predicting and responding to harmful algae and reducing theirs impacts (http://www.cop.noaa.gov/stressors/extremeevents/hab/habhrca/Predict_Resp_IntRpt_0107.pdf).

A new National Plan for Algal Toxins and Harmful Algal Blooms (HARRNESS 2005) also establishes research foci and a framework for harmful algal initiatives (e.g., federal agency, state, academic, and private) for the next ten years. Among other items, the HARRNESS calls for (1) sustained time series measurements of the biotic, chemical, and physical environments effected by harmful algae; (2) rapid field-based detections of harmful algae and toxins; (3) standard reporting features for HAB toxin incidents; and (4) the development of a common data management and communication structure for harmful algae.

Condition of Bottom-Dwelling Animals

The Indicator
The worms, clams, and crustaceans that inhabit the bottom substrates of estuaries are collectively called benthic macroinvertebrates, or benthos. This indicator reports on the condition of benthos relative to areas that can be considered to be "natural" (i.e., not obviously impacted by human activities, including contamination or more physical disturbances such as trawling for bottom fish and shellfish).

The Data
Data Source: NCA and its precursor program, Environmental Monitoring and Assessment Program for Estuaries (EMAP-E; http://www.epa.gov/emap/nca/index.html) collected these data. See the NCA program description (p. 269) for more information.

Data Collection Methodology: NCA examined benthic samples from over 2,150 estuarine sites from Maine to Texas, from Washington to California, and Puerto Rico. All site selections were based on probabilistic designs that permit the extrapolation of the data to the entire area. Using a Young-modified Van Veen grab, three replicate grabs were collected from each site and forwarded for identification and quantification of species. Using regional indices developed by EMAP-E (Engle and Summers 1999, Engle et al. 1994, Van Dolah et al. 1999, Weisberg et al. 1997), the condition of the benthic community was determined for each replicate sample, each site, and the bottom surface area of U.S. estuaries on the Atlantic and Gulf Coasts. These indices reflect changes in benthic community diversity and the abundance of pollution-tolerant and pollution-sensitive species. A low benthic index rating indicates that the benthic communities are less diverse than expected, are populated by more than expected pollution-tolerant species, and contain fewer than expected pollution-sensitive species. As indices are still being developed for the Pacific Coast and Puerto Rico, surrogate regional indices based on species diversity were used in these regions (USEPA 2004).

The data in this report reflect an assessment of benthic communities as "good" (high index score), "fair" (moderate index score), or "poor" (low index score). For this report, these classes were described using the terms "natural," "moderate," and "degraded." These terms were chosen to ensure a neutral description of the index information.

Data Quality/Caveats: The indices used in the six regions were developed independently and may not be comparable. Each has been demonstrated to be accurate in the region in which it was developed, but there is some question whether they can be combined because of the different procedures used in their development.

The definition of "natural" and "degraded" areas also varied because the levels and types of stress differ from region to region. As a result, the indices in less disturbed areas, such as those in Southern California, are designed to detect smaller levels of perturbation than are indices developed for areas like the Chesapeake Bay, where hypoxia and resulting defaunation are prevalent.

Finally, some indices are closely identified with particular sampling methods, creating challenges for integration of results. For example, Gulf of Mexico and Atlantic coast indices are based on animals held on a 0.5-mm screen, whereas an index used in Southern California is based on samples sieved through a 1.0-mm screen.

Note that in the 2002 Report, data were reported for the "moderate" category for the Mid-Atlantic incorrectly. The data have been revised to reflect the fact that analyses in both the Mid-Atlantic and the North-Atlantic assign either "natural" or "degraded" designations only.

Data Access: The data presented here were obtained directly from EPA.

2008 Report Data Update: The geographic scope has expanded to include Puerto Rico, the North Atlantic, and Pacific coast.

The Data Gap

Benthic infaunal data are available from most areas of the country, but the index tools necessary to conduct regional-scale assessments of benthic condition are not available for estuaries in Alaska or Hawaii. EPA has issued national guidance on index development (EPA 822-B-00-024), which should aid development efforts in the remaining areas. The guidance document is available on the Web at http://www.epa.gov/waterscience/biocriteria/States/estuaries/estuaries1.html. Few data are available on benthic community condition in coastal ocean waters (out to 25 mi).

Chlorophyll Concentrations

The Indicator

Coastal Ocean: For each year, the average chlorophyll-a (referred to here as chlorophyll) concentration (parts per billion, or ppb) for the season with the highest average is reported. This is referred to as the "seasonal mean maximum." Data are reported for each region in a band of coastal water extending 25 mi from the shoreline. This boundary was chosen so that the index would be more sensitive to changes in

nutrients input from terrestrial sources than from influences from the deep sea.

Estuaries: It is proposed to report the percentage of U.S. estuary area that has seasonal mean maximum chlorophyll values below 5 ppb, from 5 to 20 ppb, and above 20 ppb.

The Data

Coastal Ocean: Data from the National Aeronautics and Space Administration's Sea-viewing Wide Field-of-view Sensor (SeaWiFS; see http://seawifs.gsfc.nasa.gov) were analyzed for the nine ocean regions by the National Oceanic and Atmospheric Administration (NOAA) National Ocean Service, based on "water-leaving radiance" data (reflectance, or light reflected from the sea surface).

The data utilized for this analysis are termed "level 3." In all cases, seasonal maxima were determined for strips of water 25 mi wide along the coast. These strips were analyzed using square pixels 6 mi on a side. Note that earlier data from the Coastal Zone Color Scanner are available; they are, however, not directly comparable to the SeaWiFS data.

2008 Report Data Update: New data were added through 2006 and a new index was calculated with this extended timeframe.

The Data Gap

Coastal Ocean: Algorithms used to translate water-leaving radiance into chlorophyll concentration currently provide only rough estimates of concentration in those waters where concentrations of suspended sediments and colored dissolved organic matter are high; for example, near-shore waters influenced by surface and groundwater discharges, coastal erosion, and sediment resuspension. A major research effort is currently under way to improve coastal algorithms. The data presented here are based on a fairly coarse scale (6-mi resolution), but data with 10 times more resolution will soon be available.

To achieve more reliable estimates, satellite data need to be analyzed together with field data (in situ measurements), which typically are not available electronically and, therefore, not easily accessible. In addition, techniques for integrating the two types of data are needed. Currently, data showing relative changes in chlorophyll within a region can be trusted; however, data showing actual concentrations for any given region may be off by a factor of two. Thus, unless differences are large, meaningful comparisons among regions are not yet possible.

Estuaries: As discussed in the text, no regularly reported data are available for this portion of the indicator. Recent data from NOAA (see http://ccma.nos.noaa.gov/publications/eutroupdate/) suggest that in 2004, about half of all monitored estuaries had high levels of chlorophyll, with the Mid-Atlantic region exhibiting the highest concentrations of chlorophyll in estuarine waters (Bricker et al., 2007).

These results are not based on quantitative data analysis, but on the knowledge of scientists familiar with the estuaries in each region. Monitoring data do exist for some estuaries, but need to be assembled into a uniform, national database, and new programs would be required for the remaining estuaries. A combination of aircraft and satellite remote-sensing and in situ measurements will be required to determine the estuarine component of this indicator.

Commercial Fish and Shellfish Landings

The Indicator

This indicator reports changes in the weight of commercial fish and shellfish caught in U.S. waters from 1950 to 2005. Data are presented so that trends in landings over time can be compared among different regions.

The Data

Data Description: Data are from the U.S. Department of Commerce, National Oceanic and Atmospheric Administration (NOAA), National Marine Fisheries Service (NMFS), Office of Science and Technology, Fisheries Statistics and Economics Division. In addition, data on foreign and joint-venture landings for Alaska came from Kinoshita et al. (1993 and 1997) and NMFS "blend data" for June 2000. (For a description of "blend data," see www.fakr.noaa.gov/npfmc/misc_pub/ NorthernEconomics/NorthernEconomics.htm/.) The estimates of foreign catches that occurred before the establishment of the Fisheries Conservation Zone in 1976 (dotted line in the figure, p. 87) came from Wise (1991) and are based on NMFS data.

Fish-landing data for the Pacific Coast were collected by four state fishery agencies, and NMFS reported fish processed at sea by U.S. boats. (Fish processed by foreign boats and then exported are not reported.) On the Atlantic and Gulf coasts, landings data were usually collected cooperatively by the 19 state fishery agencies and NMFS. Some data were also collected by marine fishery commissions.

Atlantic and Gulf commercial fishery data represent a census of landings and were principally reported using seafood dealer weigh-out slips. Data on the Pacific Coast were principally reported using trip ticket reports and observer reports for at-sea processors. Since 1994, an increasing portion of the fishery catch and effort data for federally managed species has been collected using federally mandated logbooks. The use of Vessel Monitoring Systems and other electronic data collection and reporting methods is relatively recent and is limited to a small sector of U.S. fisheries. Note that NMFS has historically included all commercial landings of mollusks in these data, in part because it is not provided with information that will allow it to separate wild-caught from cultured mollusks. In terms of finfish (simply termed "fish" here), those raised by aquaculture are not included—with the exception of Alaska salmon, which are released at smolt size (length 2–4 in) and are caught several years later when they return from the ocean to spawn.

Data Manipulation: All finfish landings have been transformed, when necessary, from landed weight (e.g., dressed, filleted) to round (live) weight equivalents. All mollusks have been standardized from the collected landing report format (e.g., bushels, totes, gallons, counts, and dozens) and reported as meat weight (i.e., without shell) landings. The collecting state and federal agencies transform the landings data.

Data Availability: Nonconfidential commercial fisheries landings data for 1950–2000 are available at no cost from the NMFS Fisheries Statistics and Economics Division Web site (http://www.st.nmfs.noaa.gov/st1/commercial/index.html). The Web site allows users to summarize the data by year, region, state, species, fishing gear, pounds, and dollars. Data on the amount of landings that are fish, shellfish, and others, as well as data on the disposition of U.S. domestic landings for 2004 and 2005, were obtained from the NOAA publication "Fisheries of the United States—2005," available online at www.st.nmfs. noaa.gov/st1/fus/fus05/index.html.

2008 Report Data Update: Data for 2005, and slight revisions to the entire dataset, were obtained from www.st.nmfs.noaa. gov/st1/fus/fus05/index.html.

Status of Commercially Important Fish Stocks

The Indicator

This indicator reports the status of offshore fish stocks with known population trends. Fish stocks refer to a grouping of fish managed as a unit. A stock may include all the individuals of a given species (e.g., ocean pout), individuals of a given species in a specific geographical area (e.g., Gulf of Maine Atlantic cod), or multiple species with similar life histories, distributions, or fisheries grouped together for management (e.g., large coastal shark complex). The trends in stock biomass (weight) regionally are presented over the period 1981 to 2005. Specifically, this indicator presents the percent of stocks (with known status) in each region that are increasing or decreasing in biomass by at least 25%.

The Data

Data Description: Data for this indicator were obtained from The National Oceanic and Atmospheric Administration (NOAA) National Marine Fisheries Service (NMFS).

Data Manipulation: As reported by NMFS, there are 530 stocks and stock complexes within federal jurisdiction. Excluded from these analyses are near-shore stocks, many of which are under state management jurisdiction, and anadromous salmon stocks from the Pacific Northwest.

For 109 of these stocks, at least 10 years of data were available for the period 1981–2005. Our analysis is based on these 109 stocks with known trends. Both spawning stock biomass and total exploitable stock biomass were used to track stock trends. It should be noted that requiring spawning stock biomass or total exploitable stock biomass figures restricted the number of trackable stocks. Other means exist (e.g., catch per unit effort, relative abundance, indices that combine several stocks) to track population trends that were not included in this analysis.

Biomass refers to the weight of fish in a population, which is a function of both the total number of individuals and their size. Stock trends (i.e., "increasing," "decreasing," or "no trend") were determined by linear regression. Trends were determined for six overlapping 10-year periods (1981–1990, 1984–1993, 1987–1996, 1990–1999, 1993–2002, 1996–2005) to reduce the likelihood that normal year-to-year fluctuations would influence the results. (This is analogous to using a running average.) Two conditions were necessary for a trend to be reported: the regression line had to have a correlation coefficient (R) indicating at least 95% confidence that the slope was different from zero, and the regression line had to indicate a minimum 25% change over the 10-year period (increasing or decreasing).

Trends for the following 109 stocks were studied. For each stock, the biomass is reported as (1) B, total exploitable biomass (similar to SB in that it only includes a certain range of age classes); (2) Total B (total biomass), the total weight of fish in a given stock; (3) Sum B (summary biomass), the total weight of fish above a given age in a stock; or (4) SSB (spawning stock biomass), the total weight of the reproductively mature individuals in the stock.

- *North/Mid-Atlantic*. Georges Bank Atlantic cod (SSB), Gulf of Maine Atlantic cod (B), Georges Bank haddock (SSB), Georges Bank yellowtail flounder (SSB), Southern New England/ Mid-Atlantic yellowtail flounder (SSB), Cape Cod/Gulf of Maine yellowtail flounder (SSB), witch flounder (SSB), Gulf of Maine/Georges Bank American plaice (SSB), Gulf of Maine winter flounder (SSB), Southern New England/Mid-Atlantic winter flounder (SSB), Georges Bank winter flounder (Total B), Gulf of Maine Acadian redfish (SSB), summer flounder (SSB), bluefish (B), ocean quahog (B), Delmarva Atlantic surfclam (B), spiny dogfish (B), striped bass (SSB), Gulf of Maine northern shrimp (B), longfin squid (B), Atlantic mackerel (SSB), Atlantic herring (SSB), butterfish (SSB)
- *Alaska*. Eastern Bering Sea walleye pollock (B), Eastern Bering Sea Pacific cod (B), Bering Sea yellowfin sole (B), Bering Sea Greenland halibut (B), Eastern Bering Sea arrowtooth flounder (B), Bering Sea rock sole (B), Bering Sea flathead sole (B), Bering Sea Alaska plaice (B), Eastern Bering Sea/Aleutian Islands Pacific ocean perch (B), Eastern Bering Sea/Aleutian Islands northern rockfish (B), Bering Sea/Aleutian Islands Atka mackerel (B), Alaska sablefish (B), Gulf of Alaska walleye pollock (B), Gulf of Alaska Pacific cod (B), Gulf of Alaska flathead sole (B), Gulf of Alaska arrowtooth flounder (B), Gulf of Alaska Pacific ocean perch (B), Gulf of Alaska northern rockfish (B), Gulf of Alaska rougheye rockfish (B), Gulf of Alaska rex sole (B), Gulf of Alaska Dover sole (B), Gulf of Alaska dusky rockfish (B), Bogoslof walleye pollock (SSB), Bering Sea/Aleutian Islands shortspine thornyhead (B), Bering Sea/Aleutian Islands rougheye rockfish (B), Bering Sea/ Aleutian Islands shortraker rockfish (B), Eastern Gulf of Alaska yelloweye rockfish (B)
- *Southeast*. Gulf of Mexico gray triggerfish (SSB), Gulf of Mexico greater amberjack (B), Gulf of Mexico vermillion snapper (SSB), Gulf of Mexico king mackerel (B), South Atlantic king mackerel (B), Gulf of Mexico Spanish mackerel (B), South Atlantic Spanish mackerel (B), Atlantic snowy grouper (Total B), Atlantic tilefish (Total B), Black sea bass (SSB), South Atlantic red porgy (SSB), South Atlantic menhaden (SSB), Gulf of Mexico red grouper (SSB), Gulf of Mexico little tunny (B), Gulf of Mexico red drum (SSB), Eastern Gulf of Mexico red snapper (SSB), Western Gulf of Mexico red snapper (SSB)
- *Pacific Coast*. California bocaccio (Total B), Southern California bight cowcod (Total B, SSB), Southern California scorpionfish (Total B), California cabezon (Sum B), Pacific Coast Petrale sole (Total B), Pacific Coast English sole (Total B), Pacific Coast starry flounder (Total B), North Pacific Coast yellowtail rockfish (B), Pacific Coast widow rockfish (Sum B), North Pacific Coast Pacific ocean perch (Sum B), Pacific Coast darkblotched rockfish (Total B), Pacific Coast Dover sole (Total B), Pacific Coast

sablefish (Total B), Pacific Coast longspine thornyhead (Total B), Pacific Coast shortspine thornyhead (Total B), Pacific Coast South (most of California) blackgill rockfish (Sum B), Northern California gopher rockfish (Total B), Oregon kelp greenling (Sum B), Pacific Coast lingcod (SSB), Pacific Coast canary rockfish (Total B), Pacific Coast yelloweye rockfish (Sum B), Pacific Hake (Sum B), Oregon/ Northern California black rockfish (Sum B), California chilipepper rockfish (Total B), Northeast Pacific Ocean Pacific mackerel (B), Northern Pacific sardine (B)
- *Highly Migratory*. Western–Central Pacific yellowfin tuna (B), Western–Central Pacific bigeye tuna (B), Western–Central Pacific skipjack tuna (B), South Pacific albacore (B), North Pacific swordfish (B), North Pacific blue shark (B), Pacific blue marlin (B), Atlantic big eye tuna (B), Atlantic bluefin tuna (SSB), North Atlantic swordfish (B), Atlantic white marlin (B), Atlantic blue marlin (B), Atlantic yellowfin tuna (SSB), Atlantic albacore (SSB), Eastern Pacific yellowfin tuna (Total B), Eastern Pacific bigeye tuna (B)

Detailed information on the stock assessment reports for each fish stock included in this analysis are available at:
- Alaska: http://www.fakr.noaa.gov/npfmc/SAFE/SAFE.htm
- Pacific Coast: http://www.pcouncil.org/
- West Pacific: http://www.wpcouncil.org/
- Northeast: http://www.nefsc.noaa.gov/groundfish/
- Southeast: http://www.sefsc.noaa.gov/sedar/ and http:www.iccat.int/Assess.htm

More information on stock assessments is available in the New Hampshire Sea Grant publication, *A Guide to Fisheries Stock Assessment: From Data to Recommendations*, available at www.seagrant.unh.edu/newsstock.html.

Data Quality/Caveats: Note that statistics were included for all stocks for which adequate data are available. Some of the assessments for stocks included in 2002 are not included in the 2008 Report, either because they are considered to be too out of date to be "adequate" for reporting purposes (mostly because of lack of recent years of biomass information) or because acceptable biomass time series could not be produced.

Since the 2002 Report, there has been considerable effort to refine biological demarcation of stock boundaries to improve the accuracy of stock assessments and other scientific advice used to guide management decisions. In some cases, a single stock has been split into multiple stocks; in other cases, one or more stocks have been condensed into a single stock—a result of improved knowledge of the biological characteristics of the stock. Some stocks have been renamed to align naming conventions among different agencies. Additionally, the assessment areas do not always correspond to the management areas (primarily because scientists may not have data to conduct an assessment across the entire stock area).

Most of the stocks examined by this indicator have had updated or new assessments since the 2002 Report, many with improved and more comprehensive input data—including longer time series of previously available types of data to refine estimates of trends and more sophisticated assessment models. Such changes to the input data and assessment models are expected to lead to improved estimates of current and historical stock characteristics such as biomass time series.

Data Availability: Stock biomass data are available by contacting NOAA NMFS research centers.

2008 Report Data Update: New and revised data were included in this indicator for the 2008 Report. These data were obtained directly from NOAA NMFS.

The Data Gap
Currently, we are able to evaluate trends on only about 21% of the commercially important stocks found in U.S. waters. Additionally, this indicator reports only on stocks with known trends since 1981, and therefore excludes stocks that went extinct or suffered significant declines before the mid-1980s.

Selected Contaminants in Fish and Shellfish

The Indicator
This indicator reports on the concentration of PCBs, mercury, and DDT in mussels and oysters. Whole-body and edible tissues are equivalent for mussels and oysters, however, in fish, whole-body analyses can overstate the level of risk to humans as some contaminants concentrate in portions that are not eaten by people (whole-body contamination data are relevant for fish-eating wildlife, as reported in the core national chemical contamination indicator on p. 42). Data are not currently available for contaminants in the edible portion of fish.

The Data
Data Description: Through the Mussel Watch Program, data on contamination in mussels and oysters were collected by the National Oceanic and Atmospheric Administration (NOAA) National Status and Trends Program (NS&T) (http://ccma.nos. noaa.gov/stressors/pollution/nsandt/) from 1986 to the present. Oysters were collected from Delaware Bay to the southern tip of the Texas Gulf Coast; mussels were collected in all other sampling locations. Consistent analyses were conducted for all tissue samples (Kimbrough et al., 2008).

Mussel Watch data collection began in 1986 with 145 sites that were sampled yearly. By 1993, sites were sampled on a biennial basis with approximately half of the sites sampled each year. Currently, 130 sites are monitored annually on average—about 260 unique sites collected on a biennial basis. To account for double sampling of individual sites within biennial time periods in 1987 to 1992, concentration values for twice-sampled sites were averaged for each biennial time period. For example, if a site was sampled in both 1987 and 1988, the two concentration values were averaged to produce a single value for each contaminant for that site for 1987–88. "Bins" of concentration ranges were constructed based approximately on the 15th, 50th, and 85th percentile values in each contaminant's dataset. These reporting bins do not relate to specific benchmarks or health effects.

Benchmarks: Benchmarks for natural and man-made contaminants in edible fish and shellfish tissues are set on a wet-weight basis by the US Food and Drug Administration (FDA) and US EPA (see http://www.cfsan.fda.gov/~comm/haccp4x5.

html), whereas Mussel Watch shellfish contamination data are based on dry weight and need to be increased by a factor of ~7 to be comparable.

- *PCBs (polychlorinated biphenyls):* The FDA wet-weight benchmark for PCBs in edible tissues of "all fish" is equivalent to 2,000 parts per billion (ppb). On a dry-weight basis, the benchmark is ~14,000 ppb—no concentrations above this level were found in the Mussel Watch dataset.
- *Mercury:* FDA's wet-weight benchmark of 1.0 ppm for methyl mercury represents only a fraction of total mercury and cannot be compared to Mussel Watch data on total mercury.
- *DDT (dichloro-diphenyl-trichloroethane):* The FDA wet-weight benchmark for DDT (includes DDT and several breakdown products) in edible tissues of "all fish" is equivalent to 5,000 ppb. On a dry-weight basis, the benchmark is ~35,000 ppb—no concentrations above this level were found in the Mussel Watch dataset.

Data Quality/Caveats: Mussel Watch has characterized contaminant levels at nearly 300 sites nationwide including Alaska, Hawaii and the Great Lakes. In 1992, freshwater sites in the Great Lakes were added to the Mussel Watch Project. In 1994, sites were added on the south shore of the Island of Puerto Rico. Currently efforts are being made to expand Mussel Watch coverage of Alaska.

Data Availability: Mussel Watch data are available from NS&T at http://www8.nos.noaa.gov/cit/nsandt/download/ mw_monitoring.aspx.

2008 Report Data Update: No data were presented in this indicator in previous editions. In this edition, Mussel Watch data for contaminants in mussels and oysters has been included.

The Data Gap
FDA, EPA, and state governments have a variety of monitoring programs in operation; however, there is no ongoing, national-scale monitoring program for contaminants in edible fish tissue. The core national chemical contamination indicator (p. 42) reports data collected by the EPA National Coastal Assessment on whole-body fish tissue contamination in estuaries—in the future, special EPA studies will allow for separation of edible from whole-body tissues.

Fish contamination data collected by individual state programs do not constitute a comprehensive national database because of important variability in sampling strategies and techniques (e.g., sample size, fish size, fish types, composite samples), analytical methods and equipment, and reporting (e.g., wet- vs. dry-weight basis). EPA provides a non-binding national guidance manual (http://www.epa.gov/waterscience/ fish/guidance.html) to states for developing consumption advisories and contaminant monitoring programs, but does not directly conduct such monitoring. EPA maintains a National Listing of Fish Advisories (http://map1.epa.gov/) that houses information provided voluntarily by states and other entities and may not include actual concentration data—advisories may be based on different levels in different states.

FDA works with state regulators when commercial fish, caught and sold locally, are found to contain methyl mercury levels exceeding 1.0 ppm. The agency also checks imported fish at ports, and refuses entry if methyl mercury levels exceed the FDA limit (http://www.cfsan.fda.gov/~lrd/sea-ovr.html). However, there is no FDA reporting program based on these inspections. In its 2003 Total Diet Study (http://www.cfsan.fda.gov/~comm/tds-food.html), FDA determined contaminant intake levels for nine seafood products; this is not, however, a consistent means of tracking contaminant concentrations in fish from U.S. waters.

Recreational Water Quality

The Indicator

The most commonly used indicators of fecal contamination are total coliform bacteria, fecal coliform bacteria, *Escherichia coli*, and *Enterococcus* (the latter two are bacteria, as well). Although indicator bacteria do not necessarily cause illness, they are abundant in human waste where pathogenic organisms, such as viruses and parasites, are also likely to exist. Bacterial indicators are currently measured instead of pathogenic organisms because the indicators occur in much larger numbers and can be measured with faster, less expensive methods than the pathogens of concern. However, with advances in biotechnology, it may soon be feasible to monitor pathogens using genetic tests.

This indicator focuses on *Enterococcus*, which was selected over other measures of bacteria because it has been shown to be the most closely correlated with human health effects. The U.S. Environmental Protection Agency (EPA) recommended the use of *Enterococcus* as the fecal-indicator bacterium for recreational water quality standards in 1986, but it is still not as widely used as the coliform measures. The reporting categories for this indicator correspond to the daily (104 cells per milliliter of water) and monthly (35 cells per milliliter) geometric mean thresholds suggested by EPA as national beach water quality standards. It should be noted that the selection of *Enterococcus* is logical given today's EPA guidelines; however, new recommendations from EPA and other sources may alter the organism(s) reported in this indicator (for a discussion of a multiorganism indicator, see http://www.healthebay.org/brc/).

Because some events are short term but extend over large areas, and others are chronic closures in small areas (near a small local source, for example), the indicator is based on the number of beach-mile-days exceeding thresholds of concern, rather than on the number of exceedances or closures. These different scenarios would be weighted inappropriately if the measure were limited to the number of events or to the mileage of beaches that exceeded thresholds at any time during the year.

The indicator is also based on the underlying microbiological data rather than on the number of beach closures or advisories, as is done in EPA's national report, the EMPACT Beaches Project (http://www.epa.gov/waterscience/beaches/). Differences in procedures used by local governments in making closure decisions make such reporting less informative. Moreover, the amount of beach monitoring varies dramatically among states, and an indicator based on the number of closures may focus undue concern on states or beach areas that are the most vigilant. For more information on national trends in beach closings and advisory days, see the most recent Natural Resources Defense Council "Testing the Waters" report (http://www.nrdc.org/water/oceans/ttw/titinx.asp).

The Data Gap

In 2000, Congress passed the Beaches Environmental Assessment and Coastal Health Act authorizing EPA to award grants to local entities (states, tribes, and territories) to develop and implement monitoring programs at beaches along the coast, including along the Great Lakes. In response to recent legislation, the state of California is moving toward routine reporting of closures in beach-mile-days. Most other states do not summarize their data in this format.

There are several challenges to reporting this indicator at a national level. First, it is necessary for states and municipalities to adopt the use of *Enterococcus* bacteria as an indicator and to use beach-mile-days as the unit of reporting. Second, national reporting will require obtaining the microbiological data from the numerous local governments that collect it. Additionally, an assessment of the extent of beach monitoring is necessary, which will require three additional types of information: an estimate of the number of miles of publicly accessible beach that are available for water-contact recreation, the spatial extent of beach associated with each water quality measurement (e.g., distance to the next measurement location or to the farthest location that would be closed because of results from that sample site), and the time between samples. This can be complex in practice because some programs measure bacteria sporadically, in response to events such as spills or citizen complaints, and defining how much beach is represented by a sample can be difficult. Most monitoring programs use sampling sites a mile or more apart, whereas beach closure decisions typically apply to much smaller areas around any given sampling point.

In addition, many of the agencies and organizations that monitor water quality do not store their data electronically, and even those that do so do not use an agreed-upon storage format. There are also considerable differences in the number, frequency, and degree of coverage of sampling among states—and even among beaches within individual states. More consistency among sampling efforts across the nation would enhance the value of the measure. EPA is working to solve the data management problem by collaborating with coastal states to produce an annual report on the national extent of beach closures. Although this is a start, EPA's reporting effort focuses only on closures, rather than on the underlying water quality. Because the standards used to determine when a beach is unsafe for swimming vary from place to place, this information cannot provide a consistent picture of water quality nationwide.

Farmlands

Total Cropland

The Indicator

This indicator reports the acreage of cropland in the United States. Data from two USDA sources, the National Resources Inventory (NRI) program and the Economic Research Service (ERS), are presented to provide both long-term data and what we believe to be the most relevant current estimates of cropland area. Cultivated and non-cultivated croplands, some haylands and pasturelands, and lands that have been idled in long-term set-aside programs, such as the Conservation Reserve Program

(CRP), are included (see below for definitions of cropland used by both data sources).

The Data

Data Sources: These data were obtained from the U.S. Department of Agriculture (USDA) Natural Resources Conservation Service, National Resources Inventory (NRI) program and the USDA Economic Research Service (ERS). ERS uses Census, public land management and conservation agencies, and other sources to create land use estimates. The NRI is a longitudinal sample survey that estimates land use and land cover using remote sensing and ground surveys. See the NRI program description on p. 271, for more information.

Data Quality/Caveats: The two data sources used to estimate total cropland area differ slightly in their methodology and definitions of cropland. Cropland, as defined by ERS, includes cropland used for crops, cropland used for pasture (including land rotated between crop and pasture use or marginal cropland indefinitely used as pasture), and idle cropland such as lands in the Conservation Reserve Program (CRP; See Krupa and Daugherty 1990, Daugherty 1995, and Vesterby and Krupa 2001). The NRI definition of cropland also includes cultivated and noncultivated lands. Cultivated land comprises land in row crops, close-grown crops, and other cultivated cropland; for example, hayland or pastureland that is in a rotation with row or close-grown crops. Noncultivated cropland includes permanent hayland and horticultural cropland.

2008 Report Data Update: Census of Agriculture and National Land Cover data were dropped and updated data through 2002 (ERS) and 2003 (NRI) were added.

The Farmland Landscape

The Indicator

This indicator is based on a designation of areas that are characterized by the predominance of cropland. Then, an analysis of the land-cover types within these areas is reported.

The Data

The data for this indicator are derived from two sources. The primary source is the National Land Cover Dataset (NLCD). See the NLCD program description (p. 274) for more information. In addition, this land-cover map was augmented with data from ESRI on roads, which are considered a type of development.

Data Manipulation: Analysts from the U.S. Environmental Protection Agency and the USDA Forest Service, using an enhanced land-cover map evaluated the composition surrounding each pixel using a square analysis window that is 3 km on a side (for more on this approach, see the program description for the NLCD, p. 274). For those windows that had at least 10% cropland in them, the center pixel was preliminarily added to one of many farmland landscape polygons. Polygons had a minimum area of at least 9 sq. km. The second step was to report the composition (in terms of land cover) within each polygon designated as part of the farmland landscape. These data were summarized by state and then regionally (see p. 266 for a listing of states that define each region).

Data Quality/Caveats: The analysis approach differed substantially from that used in the 2002 Report; therefore, these results should not be compared to those in the 2002 Report.

This indicator relies on land-cover data, which currently provide limited information about land use.

2008 Report Data Update: The underlying definition of "farmland landscapes" was updated for the 2008 edition of this report to make it more consistent with the other landscape pattern indicators in the report—especially the core national pattern of natural landscapes indicator (p. 33). Data from the 2001 NLCD are presented; comparisons to the 1992 NLCD are not yet possible.

Data Availability: NLCD data can be accessed at http://www.mrlc.gov. The ESRI data come bundled with geographic information system (GIS) software (see http://www.esri.com); see also ESRI (2005).

Proximity of Cropland to Residences

The Indicator

This indicator evaluates the distance between a pixel of cropland land cover and the nearest residence. In general, this metric is a proxy for pressures that are likely to be exerted on the farmer of that cropland, rather than a measure of a direct interplay between the residents and the farmer.

Development patterns in our nation's farmland landscape are no longer characterized by a farmer's house surrounded (or adjacent to) large blocks of land. These homesteads are often occupied by people who do not have a vested interest in agriculture, and therefore, a willingness to accept some level of disruption from agricultural practices. For this reason, it is envisioned that the distance of cropland pixels from all residences would be determined, with no restriction placed on the ownership (e.g., excluding those homes owned by farmers). As multiple time periods of data become available, the indicator values will be most sensitive to newly-added homes—which will generally house residents with no direct ties to agricultural operations.

Substantial Changes to the Indicator Design: This indicator was revised substantially since the 2002 Report. The indicator in the 2002 Report, Fragmentation of Farmland Landscapes by Development, would have relied strictly on land-cover data (data were not prepared for the 2002 Report) and an analysis that evaluated the proportion of developed pixels immediately surrounding a pixel of cropland. The Heinz Center's Landscape Pattern Task Group recommended the revision and stressed that data on the location of individual houses should be sought.

The Data Gap

Data on individual household locations are currently only available on a limited basis. Such data are increasingly available as local property offices digitize their data, although it is unclear if these efforts will yield sufficiently uniform data across the country.

Patches of "Natural" Land in the Farmland Landscape

The Indicator

This indicator describes the size of patches of "natural" land cover in the farmland landscape. The farmland landscape includes many polygons defined from a land-cover map (see p. 29). "Natural" land-cover pixels include forest, grassland, shrubland, wetland, and other aquatic types. The indicator reports the size of patches of touching "natural" pixels within the farmland landscape.

Small patches have little or no "interior" habitat—that is, habitat that is insulated from outside influences by a significant buffer zone. Because some species thrive only in interior habitat—where there is a relatively large and contiguous area of forest, grassland, or other "natural" cover (see the core national pattern indicator, and the forest and grassland-shrubland pattern indicators), small areas may not provide habitat for these species. Beyond simply their area, the shape of "natural" patches will affect the amount of interior habitat available and, therefore, may affect the quality of habitat. Of course, large but narrow strips may tend to have lower habitat value because of the lack of much area that is buffered; however, these same strips of land may provide other ecosystem services such as erosion and sediment control.

Substantial Changes to the Indicator Design: This indicator was revised for the 2008 edition of this report by the Landscape Pattern Task Group.

The Data

The data for this indicator are derived from two sources. The primary source is the National Land Cover Dataset (NLCD; see program description on p. 274). In addition, this land-cover map was augmented with data from ESRI on paved roads (StreetMap data; http://www.esri.com/data/streetmap/), which are considered here as a type of development.

Data Description: See the program description for the NLCD (p. 274) for details.

Data Manipulation: Analysts from the Environmental Protection Agency and the USDA Forest Service, using an enhanced land-cover map (see above), identified those pixels with "natural" land cover (forest, grassland, shrubland, barren, water, or wetland) within the farmland landscape. Those pixels were formed into patches of "natural" pixels that touched along their edges, including at their corners. Data were provided by state, and then summarized by region and nationally. Note that a similar approach was used to describe "natural" patches in the urban and suburban landscape (see p. 236).

Data Quality/Caveats: Because data were summarized by state, some patches of "natural" were split by both farmland landscape boundaries as well as state boundaries. Further analysis would be necessary to understand what impact this had on the reported results.

Data Availability: See the program description for the NLCD (p. 274) for availability of those data, and the ESRI Web site listed above for access to the StreetMap data. Summarized data

from the analyses described here were provided to the Heinz Center by the Center for Landscape Analysis, and are available from the Heinz Center upon request. The Center for Landscape Analysis should be contacted regarding the availability of other data products.

Nitrate in Farmland Streams and Groundwater

The Indicator

This indicator reports the mean-annual discharge-weighted concentrations of dissolved nitrate plus nitrite-nitrogen in farmland streams and the nitrate concentration in farmland groundwater, based on one sampling of each well.

The Data

Data are reported as parts per million (milligrams per liter) nitrate-nitrogen. The data are labeled "mean total nitrate" although the analytical method actually reports nitrate plus nitrite. This reporting convention is reasonable because except in highly polluted waters, nitrite levels are only a very small fraction of the total and can, therefore, be considered insignificant.

Data Source: The data were collected and analyzed by the U.S. Geological Survey (USGS) National Water Quality Assessment (NAWQA) program. See p. 272 for information on the NAWQA program, sampling design, methodology, data availability. Information on the drinking water standard for nitrogen can be found at http://www.epa.gov/safewater/contaminants/index.html#primary.

For information on forest and urban-suburban data used in the ecosystem comparison, see p. 307 and p. 334.

Data Collection Methodology: Stream nitrate data were collected from samples at stream and river sites draining 130 agricultural areas. For groundwater, nitrate data were from samples collected from 1,412 shallow monitoring wells in agricultural settings. The wells were located across the conterminous U.S. and ranged from 7 to 637 ft in depth (mean 74 ft; median 34 ft). Monitoring wells were sampled from 1992 to 2003; one sample from each well was analyzed for nitrate. All wells used to measure nitrate in farmland groundwater were in agricultural land-use studies. These studies were conducted in areas where agriculture was the dominant land use. In general, the land cover upstream from sites in the "Farmlands" category is more than 50 percent agricultural (cropland plus pasture) and less than 5 percent urban. Although Alaska and Hawaii were included in the study, streams and wells were not sampled in these states because land cover within the NAWQA study units was not primarily agricultural.

Data Availability: Data used in this indicator are summarized by Wilson et al., (2008), available at http://pubs.usgs.gov/of/2008/1110/. In addition to NAWQA water quality data, the USGS Economic Research Service (ERS) and USDA National Agricultural Statistics Service (NASS) conducted additional surveys in 12 NAWQA study regions in farmland areas. These study regions were selected on the basis of the presence of agricultural cropland, significance of agrichemical use, the presence of soils that leach, and a significant water quality demand. The results of the ERS and NASS studies on chemical use and farm practice information will be correlated with soil, land use, water quantity and quality, and other hydrologic data to further investigate the impacts of different management practices and land use activities on water quality. When completed, the results of these studies will be available through the National Agricultural Library (http://www.nal.usda.gov/).

Ecoregion criteria for assessing total nitrogen concentrations in all wadeable streams (including farmland streams) during the summer index period can be found in USEPA's Wadeable Streams Assessment (USEPA 2006e).

2008 Report Data Update: The geographic scope of the indicator has increased. The 2008 indicator covers 51 major river basins across 50 states, sampled over the period 1992–2001 (streams) or 1992–2003 (groundwater). Only 36 basins were included in the 2002 Report, sampled over the period 1992–1998. The data presented in the 2008 Report replace data presented in the 2002 edition; they are not comparable.

Phosphorus in Farmland Streams

The Indicator
This indicator reports the mean-annual discharge-weighted concentrations of dissolved phosphorus. Data are reported as parts per million (milligrams per liter) phosphorus, and percentage of streams identified by ranges of phosphorus concentrations (Less than 0.1 ppm, 0.1 to 0.3 ppm, 0.3 to 0.5 ppm, 0.5 ppm or more).

The Data
Data Source: The data were collected and analyzed by the U.S. Geological Survey (USGS) National Water Quality Assessment (NAWQA) program. See page 272 for information on the NAWQA program, sampling design, methodology, data availability. Information on the 1986 phosphorus recommended goal for preventing excess algae growth can be found in EPA 440/5-86-001 (see USEPA 1986). Information on regional nutrient (phosphorus) criteria can be found at http://www.epa.gov/waterscience/criteria/nutrient/ecoregions/. For information on urban data used in the ecosystem comparison, see p. 335.

Data Collection Methodology: Stream phosphorus data were collected from samples at stream and river sites draining 129 agricultural areas. These studies were conducted in areas where agriculture was the dominant land use. In general, the land cover upstream from sites in the "Farmlands" category is more than 50 percent agricultural (cropland plus pasture) and less than 5 percent urban.

Data Availability: Data used in this indicator are summarized by Wilson et al., (2008), available at http://pubs.usgs.gov/of/2008/1110/. In addition to NAWQA water quality data, the USGS Economic Research Service (ERS) and USDA National Agricultural Statistics Service (NASS) conducted additional surveys in 12 NAWQA study regions in farmland areas. These study regions were selected on the basis of the presence of agricultural cropland, significance of agrichemical use, the presence of soils that leach, and a significant water quality demand. The results of the ERS and NASS studies on chemical

use and farm practice information will be correlated with soil, land use, water quantity and quality, and other hydrologic data to further investigate the impacts of different management practices and land use activities on water quality. When completed, the results of these studies will be available through the National Agricultural Library (http://www.nal.usda.gov/).

Ecoregion criteria for assessing phosphorus concentrations in all wadeable streams (including farmland streams) during the summer index period can be found in USEPA's Wadeable Streams Assessment (USEPA 2006e).

2008 Report Data Update: Data presented in the 2008 Report replace data presented in the 2002 edition. New data from the USGS for an extended time period covering 1999–2001 were added. The geographic scope of the indicator has increased. The 2008 indicator covers 51 major river basins across 50 states, sampled over the period 1992–2001. Only 36 basins were included in the 2002 Report, sampled over the period 1992–1998.

Soil Organic Matter

The Indicator
Soil organic matter content in the upper soil profile (top 30 cm) was chosen because human activity, particularly management practices, has its greatest impact here, although it is recognized that some soils (e.g. Histosols and Gelisols) have significant levels of soil organic carbon (SOC) below 30 cm in depth. This indicator as designed and reported in 2002 acknowledged that it may prove difficult to discern trends in organic matter using the coarse ranges chosen (less than 2%, 2 to 4%, and greater than 4%) and that an approach addressing change on the regional or local level may be necessary. This potential impact on the indicator design will be re-assessed in the future as data become available.

A new core national indicator on carbon storage has been developed for the 2008 Report. To facilitate comparison, the soil organic matter indicator design has been amended to include a measure of SOC in addition to SOM.

The Data Gap
U.S. Department of Agriculture soil survey data (contained within the State Soil Geographic Database [STATSGO] and Soil Survey Geographic [SSURGO] datasets) provide an initial county-level estimate of SOM content, but there are no programs in place to monitor and report changes in SOM content on a national basis. Efforts are under way to develop techniques to use satellite data to estimate organic matter in surface soils, whereas others are developing models to provide estimates of soil carbon in croplands.

The Natural Resource Ecology Laboratory (NREL) at Colorado State University has been developing methods, using the Century Ecosystem Model, to estimate stocks of soil organic carbon and organic matter to supplement current estimates of change in stocks of soil carbon using an ecosystem modeling approach. Currently, Century is used to estimate *changes* in SOC stocks on the basis of land use, management, soil properties (e.g., soil texture) and climate data (see Carbon Storage, p. 278, for additional details on the Century model). Limited information about the conditions from the more distant past inhibits precision in estimating total soil organic C stocks. An effort is under way, however, to reduce the uncertainties associated with total stock estimates from Century by including soil series level bulk density values. It is anticipated the resulting estimates for U.S. farmlands will have sufficient certainty to be a useful source of data for this indicator.

Another recent effort is the use of the Environmental Policy Integrated Climate (EPIC) model—formerly Erosion Productivity Impact Calculator—as part of the Conservation Effects Assessment Project (CEAP, http://www.nrcs.usda.gov/technical/NRI/ceap/). The EPIC model was recently updated to model soil carbon using the Century model soil carbon routines. APEX, a variant of EPIC, is being used to estimate effects (including carbon storage) of conservation practices on private lands through CEAP. This effort may yield important information on carbon storage on these lands, and has already generated several interim publications (in particular see Potter et al., 2006).

Another potential modeling tool that predicts the effects of management systems on SOM is the Soil Conditioning Index (SCI) using NRI data. More work is needed to refine its application, especially on irrigated lands, but it has been shown useful and sensitive to trends (Abrahamson et al., 2007). Draft maps are available that show the potential of the SCI tool for comparing cultivated cropland between 1982 to 1997; for more information see http://soils.usda.gov/sqi/concepts/soil_organic_matter/som_sci.html.

Pesticides in Farmlands Streams and Groundwater

The Indicator

This indicator reports on the percentage of monitored streams and groundwater wells in farmland ecosystems in which pesticides and their breakdown products are detected and exceed established benchmarks for the protection of aquatic life and human health.

The Data

Data Description: Data for this indicator come from the USGS National Water Quality Assessment (NAWQA) program and are based on water samples collected from watersheds and aquifer areas across the nation where agriculture was the dominant land use. Streamwater samples were collected from 83 streams over the period 1992–2001. Groundwater samples were collected from 1,423 wells over the period 1993–2003. In general, the land cover upstream from sites in agricultural land use studies was more than 50 percent agricultural (cropland, pasture) and less than 5 percent urban. Most wells sampled for agricultural land use studies were shallow observation wells (median depth 34 ft) that are not used for drinking water, but about 29 percent of wells sampled in agricultural areas were domestic wells. Streamwater samples were analyzed for 83 pesticides and pesticide degradation products. Measured pesticide concentrations were compared to 73 benchmarks for the protection of human health and 62 benchmarks for the protection of aquatic life. Groundwater samples were analyzed for 83 pesticides/pesticide degradation products. Measured concentrations were compared to 73 benchmarks

for the protection of human health. See the NAWQA program description on p. 272 for further details.

For each sampling site, the number of pesticides that were measured (a) above the analytical detection limit and (b) at concentrations higher than established benchmarks for the protection of aquatic life and human health were summed. Indicator figures present "bins" or groupings of sites on the basis of the number of contaminants detected or in exceedance of benchmarks. Many pesticides measured by NAWQA do not have established benchmarks or have a range of benchmark values associated with different types or likelihood of effects, affected organisms and exposure duration.

Data Quality/Caveats: The data are highly aggregated and should be interpreted mainly as an indication of general national patterns. Sampling sites were selected to be representative of specific land use types (rather than locations where contamination was known or suspected). Agricultural land uses can exert a dominant influence on a stream or river, in spite of occupying a small percentage of land cover in the watershed, if these land uses are located near the river or stream—study watersheds had from 10% to 99% cropland and/or pasture land cover. All samples were collected, processed, preserved, and analyzed using the same methods.

The data shown in this indicator do not represent assessments of risks posed to people or ecosystems in any specific location, since they do not incorporate factors such as whether the water tested is actually used as a drinking water source and the time of year when contaminants are found, relative to when animals are most active. The presence of contaminants does not necessarily mean that levels are high enough to cause problems. While the benchmarks used to help judge the significance of contamination are the best available in use by relevant agencies, they must be interpreted carefully because they are not necessarily standardized or linked to the same level of risk, nor do they necessarily account for all aspects of potential toxicity.

Data Availability: All data used in this report are summarized at http://pubs.usgs.gov/of/2008/1110/.

2008 Report Data Update: In the 2002 Report, stream and groundwater monitoring data for 1992–1998 were reported, however these data are not comparable to the data presented here because of expansion in the geographic scope of the monitoring program and a revised set of benchmarks—the 2008 Report makes use of Health-Based Screening Levels (HBSLs) in addition to USEPA Maximum Contaminant Levels (MCLs). For details, see http://water.usgs.gov/nawqa/HBSL.

Potential Soil Erosion

The Indicator

This indicator presents the percentage of U.S. cropland (minus pastures, but including Conservation Reserve Program [CRP] acreage) in each of three categories of land condition (least prone, moderately prone, and most prone to erosion), identified on the basis of both inherent soil properties and management practices, for 1982, 1992, 1997, and 2003 for both wind and water erosion. Also, those lands most prone to wind and water erosion are mapped.

Categories for this indicator were developed using parameters measured for use in the Universal Soil Loss Equation (USLE) and Wind Erosion Equation (WEQ). These equations were developed to predict long-term average erosion based on measurements of the inherent soil and plot features and management and surface treatment factors. For water erosion (USLE), inherent soil and plot factors are R, rainfall and runoff; K, soil erodibility; and L and S, topographic factors related to slope steepness and length of slope. Management and surface treatment factors included C, cover management, which essentially measures whether and how much vegetative cover is left on the soil surface, and P, support practice factor, which measures whether there are features such as terraces. The equation form is A (annual soil erosion per unit area) = $C*P*R*K*L*S$. For wind, the inherent soil and plot factors are I, soil erodibility index, and C, climatic factor. Management and surface treatment factors are K, ridge roughness; L, unsheltered distance along the prevailing wind direction; and V, vegetative cover. Wind erosion, E (annual soil erosion per unit area), is a function of I, K, C, L, and V (see references for more details).

This report uses the underlying principles of these equations to identify cropland area with combinations of inherent soil properties and management practices that are likely to erode most and least. Though inherent soil properties change slowly or not at all, management practices can significantly reduce erosion. Thus, reductions in acreage with high propensity to erode primarily result from application of management practices that reduce erosion, including removal of acreage from cultivation, such as CRP.

Areas with the least susceptibility to both wind and water erosion ("least prone") are generally those with a predicted erosion rate of less than 1 ton per acre per year. Areas with the greatest susceptibility to erosion ("most prone") are those with a predicted erosion rate of three tons per acre or more. Areas with moderate susceptibility to erosion have predicted values between one and three tons per acre per year.

Standard application of both USLE and WEQ uses the equations to predict total erosion, in tons per acre. In this report, we have chosen not to take this last step in the process. We do so because we believe taking this step overstates actual erosion, as the USLE does not account for deposition, only the initiation of soil movement. Some soil particles move only very short distances, and when erosion is reported in units of "tons per acre" there is a strong implication (and sometimes an explicit statement) that these tons of soil are lost from the farm field. The WEQ estimates how much eroding soil leaves the downwind edge of the field, in tons per acre per year.

The Data

Data Source: Acreage estimates for lands in each of the three categories were developed using data provided by USDA's Natural Resources Conservation Service, from the National Resources Inventory (NRI). For information see the NRI monitoring program description on p. 271.

2008 Report Data Update: New data (2003) were provided for the indicator.

Soil Salinity

The Indicator

This indicator would be reported as the percentage of croplands nationally having one of three salinity levels (less than 2 decisiemens per meter [dS/M], 2 to 4 dS/m, and greater than 4 dS/M; see below for discussion/description). In addition, the percentage of croplands with elevated soil salinity (over 4 dS/m) would be mapped on a Major Land Resource Area (MLRA) basis. (MLRAs are aggregations of geographic areas, usually many thousand acres in extent, which are characterized by a particular pattern of soils, climate, water resources, and land use. See http://soils.usda.gov/survey/geography/mlra/ for a discussion and map.)

Soluble salts in soils are measured by determining the electrical conductivity of a saturated paste extract; the units of conductance are reported as dS/m. Few plant species are affected when the extract conductivity is below 2 dS/m, whereas some sensitive plants are affected when values are between 2 and 4 dS/m. Many plants are affected when values are above 4, and few plants can survive at values greater than 16 dS/m. Salts are usually most damaging to young plants, but not necessarily at the time of germination, although high salt concentrations can slow or inhibit seed germination. Most plants are least affected by soil salts when in their mature stages.

Reduced permeability to water is a common problem with salt-affected soil. Soil porosity becomes gradually altered and some soils can become completely impermeable. The mechanisms responsible are swelling of clays, which reduces pore sizes, and dispersion of the soil, so that aggregates break down, and smaller mineral and organic particles move with water and begin to fill smaller pore spaces. Dispersion is the most frequent cause of reduced infiltration. The measurement that most accurately determines whether the soil is affected by soluble salts is the exchangeable sodium percentage, which expresses the portion of the total exchangeable cations that are sodium. An exchangeable sodium percentage value equal to or greater than 15 indicates a sodic soil.

The Data Gap

Soil salinity measurements are needed on dominant soils, on cropping patterns, and particularly on water management practices under both irrigated and nonirrigated conditions in arid and semiarid regions. Salinity measurements are often included in routine soil tests. However, there is no unified effort in place to collect and analyze the results from farmland soils over uniform regions. A program that can monitor changes over time as a function of soils and management practices is vitally needed.

Soil salinity measurements should include data on dominant soils, cropping patterns, and, particularly, water management practices such as irrigation and drainage. Gathering together the existing but fragmented data, collecting new data, and analyzing the results to ensure national coverage require a coordinated effort. Satellite-based technologies, while promising, are able to detect only visible salt deposits. Because visible surface salts are incorporated into the soil by tilling, these approaches may be of use primarily to complement soil testing.

Soil salinity data have been produced by the U.S. Environmental Protection Agency for the western portion of the US (EMAP-West) based on the U.S.D.A. Natural Resource

Conservation Service's (NRCS) State Soil Geographic dataset (STATSGO; http://www.epa.gov/esd/land-sci/emap_west_browser/pages/wemap_mm_sl_table.htm); however the spatial resolution of the data and accompanying models is sufficiently large that at the current time they cannot be paired with farmland landcover. NRCS's Soil Survey Geographic Database (SSURGO) provides salinity data at the soil survey level (1:24K); however, data are not updated on a regular basis and are not cropland-specific.

Stream Habitat Quality

There is no technical note for this indicator.

Status of Animal Species in Farmland Areas

The Indicator

There are multiple approaches to reporting on animal species in farmland areas. One might be to report on the status of species that favor those habitats that existed before farmland was created in an area. Such an approach would, for example, focus on grassland birds in areas of the Great Plains—species that inhabited prairies that have now been converted to farmland. Another approach might be to focus on species that are able to take advantage of farmland landscapes—many game birds and small mammals, for example. Both of these approaches would be useful, but by themselves would be incomplete.

A more appropriate approach, recommended here, would be to focus on the full breadth of species that might inhabit farmlands. To follow the examples above, this would include both grassland birds and game birds and small mammals. Such an approach has been suggested, based on expectations that one might encounter a variety of birds in different regions of the nation. An index could be developed based on comparing this expectation with data on the presence of birds on farmlands in that region—data that may already be available for a significant percentage of farmlands (Breeding Bird Survey, http://www.mbr-pwrc.usgs.gov/bbs/bbs.html; more information on such an approach toward determining an index of bird "integrity" can be found at http://landscape.forest.wisc.edu/LandscapeEcology/Articles/v7i2p137.pdf).

Several reviewers of this report recommended that this indicator focus on domestic animals—their numbers, condition, diversity, and the like. The Farmlands Work Group determined that it was appropriate to focus on the status and trends in wild species as part of this measure (which is intended to describe ecosystem conditions). A measure describing domestic animals would have been appropriate as part of the "human use" set of indicators, but was determined not to be of sufficiently high priority for inclusion.

The Data Gap

There are two major national-scale sources of information on species population status and trends. These include NatureServe's compilation of information from state-based Heritage programs, which provides status information on a global, national, and state basis (http://www.natureserve.org) for a large number of species (see the NatureServe program description on p. 275), and the U.S. Geological Survey's

Breeding Bird Survey (http://www.mbr-pwrc.usgs.gov/bbs/bbs.html), which provides population trend information for a large number of resident birds of North America.

Both programs provide information on a geographic scale that is usually larger than and is not limited to farmlands. Thus, it is likely that it would be necessary to undertake additional work to target these data only to farmlands.

Established Non-native Plant Cover in the Farmland Landscape

There is no technical note for this indicator.

Soil Biological Condition

The Indicator

The Nematode Maturity Index (NMI) is a weighted mean frequency of taxa assigned weights ranging from 1 to 5, with a smaller weight being assigned to taxa with greater tolerance to disturbance and a larger weight to taxa that are more sensitive to disturbance. The index combines both free-living and plant-parasitic nematodes but excludes taxa that simply respond ephemerally to added nutrients. This index can detect differences among fields in a regional survey more reliably than one that measures only free-living nematodes (Neher and Campbell 1996).

The Data Gap

Neher et al. (2005) identified two major impediments to the use of nematode community indices for large-scale environmental monitoring: the lack of empirical tests of the universality of these indices across regions and ecosystems; and the lack of access to taxonomic expertise which is necessary to identify nematodes before indices can be calculated. Research continues on the development and testing of indices and monitoring protocols for soil nematodes. The 2002 edition of this report recommended sampling nematode communities in autumn, following Neher (1999). However, more recent studies have reported conflicting sampling optima, including spring and midsummer (Neher et al 2003; 2005). Neher et al. (2005) conclude that different nematode communities and taxa of interest may have different optimal sampling times.

Following Neher et al. (1998), the 2002 edition of this report suggested that it would be unnecessary to calibrate indices of nematode community structure at a scale finer than the USDA's Land Resource Regions. However, Neher et al. (2005) report regional variation across North Carolina sites for some nematode indices, which suggests that index values may need to be interpreted regionally or even locally (rather than nationally).

Neher et al. (2005) note that taxonomic resolution may affect interpretation of nematode diversity indices. Different genera within a single nematode family may respond differently to disturbance (Fiscus and Neher 2002), suggesting that identification to at least the genus level may be needed for interpretation of ecosystem function (Neher et al. 2005).

Major Crop Yields

The Indicator

This indicator reports the per-acre yield of corn, soybeans, wheat, hay, and cotton over time, with these yields converted to an index for each crop with 1975 as a base year.

The Data

Data Description: Data are from the U.S. Department of Agriculture National Agricultural Statistics Service (NASS). State offices collect and estimate crop yield data from sample surveys of farmers and their business associates (farm service agencies, cotton gins, marketing associates). NASS obtains the yield estimates, which are verified and analyzed on a national level. Survey data are supplemented by information from the Census of Agriculture, which is carried out every five years.

Data Manipulation: Yields, which are generally reported as bushels per acre for corn, soybeans, and wheat, and as tons per acre for hay and cotton, were divided by their respective value for 1975. Thus, values above 1.0 indicate higher yields than in 1975, and values lower than 1.0 indicates lower yields than in 1975.

Data Availability: Data can be downloaded from "Quick Stats" available on the NASS web site (http://www.nass.usda.gov/index.asp). Note that "corn" refers to corn for grain only and does not include corn for silage.

2008 Report Data Update: NASS data were added for 2005 and 2006. All data were downloaded from the NASS Quick Stats link as listed under Data Availability.

Agricultural Inputs and Outputs

The Indicator

This indicator presents the total agricultural inputs and outputs quantified by the U.S. Department of Agriculture (USDA) as well as the ratio of major inputs identified to total agricultural outputs. The intent is to report changes over time in the amount of inputs needed to produce a unit of output.

The Data

Data Description: Data came from Agricultural Productivity in the United States published by USDA's Economic Research Service (ERS).

Data Manipulation: The output data represent all agricultural outputs, including animals and animal products (meat animals, dairy products, poultry, and eggs) and crops (food grains, feed crops, oilseed crops, sugar crops, cotton and cotton seed, vegetables and melons, and fruit and tree nuts). In order to aggregate multiple outputs or inputs into a single index, USDA economists use an approach that involves determining the adjusted price of a given output, which is multiplied by the output quantity, so that all outputs can be added together into the single value. The yearly quantity of each input has been adjusted to some extent by ERS to reflect the changes in quality. For example, similar results can now be achieved with smaller quantities of pesticides. Thus, a larger quantity of less effective pesticide might be treated as equal to a smaller quantity of a more effective pesticide. The same is

true for the other inputs, such as labor, whose quantities have been quality- adjusted over time.

Each input has been divided by the total farm output for that year. The data from ERS are all relative to a given year (1948) and are not reported as actual quantities. Because the focus of this report is on 1950–present, we chose the midpoint (1975) as a more appropriate index year. Because of this, data (inputs and outputs) were divided by the 1975 value. All input data for each category shown here were then divided by the value of the corresponding total outputs for any given year to produce the data shown in the figure.

Data Availability: The data are available at http://www.ers.usda.gov/publications/aib740/; a more detailed version of the data is available at http://www.ers.usda.gov/data/agproductivity/. Data for the 2008 Report were downloaded from the ERS Web site http://www.ers.usda.gov/data/agproductivity.

2008 Report Data Update: Data for 2000–2004 were obtained directly from the ERS Web site listed under Data Access. Data on "chemicals" were replaced with individual categories for pesticides and fertilizers.

Monetary Value of Agricultural Production

The Indicator

The monetary value of agricultural production reports the dollar value of the annual crop output of major crops and livestock. The value is determined by multiplying the physical output of major crops and livestock by the prices (in 2005 dollars) received by producers (adjusted for inflation).

The geographic distribution of agricultural sales is a measure of gross sales by crop and livestock producers per square mile. These data do not reflect payments received by producers through government income support, commodity, or conservation programs, nor do they reflect economic activity associated with food processing and distribution or off-farm service and supply businesses.

The Data

Data Description: Data on the dollar value of agricultural sales are from the U.S. Department of Agriculture (USDA) Economic Research Service (ERS), which reports farm income and farm cash receipts. Data for agricultural sales per square mile are from the U.S. Department of Commerce, Bureau of Economic Analysis (BEA), Regional Economic Information System branch which calculates county cash receipts.

Data Manipulation (Dollar Value of Agricultural Sales): The USDA National Agricultural Statistics Service (NASS) conducts national surveys that measure acres planted and harvested, yields, production, and market prices. The estimates include cash receipts from the marketing of about 150 crop and livestock commodities.

ERS uses NASS-published, calendar-year cash receipts for major livestock and commodity-producing states. ERS develops indexes to indicate direction and magnitude of changes in monthly sales quantities and multiplies them by NASS-published monthly prices. Data for other states are developed in cooperation with the NASS state offices, which use all available sources, including informed opinions, often corroborated by data from state survey programs, producer associations, and the state's extension service. California data come from state-conducted surveys.

ERS adjusts NASS quantity and value of production data for major crop commodities in major producing states to adjust for production of feed used on farms for livestock, for Commodity Credit Corporation sales, and to account for the fact that some sales do not take place in the same year as the crop is harvested. Data from NASS that cannot be released to the public because of confidentiality constraints are included in the overall ERS dataset.

Data were adjusted for inflation using the Gross Domestic Product Implicit Price Deflator (IPD) provided by the Economic Research Service (annual, not quarterly, values used, see NIPA table 1.1.9 at http://www.bea.gov/national/nipaweb/. All data were adjusted to the average level of prices that existed in 2005. The following formula was used to convert each figure in the series from current dollars to constant dollars (available at http://www.bea.gov/bea/an/nipaguid.pdf).

$$\text{Year Z constant dollar value} = \frac{(\text{Year Z current dollar value}) * (\text{Base Year IPD index number})}{\text{Year Z IPD index number}}$$

Data Manipulation (Agricultural Sales per Square Mile): The U.S. Department of Commerce's BEA uses a variety of data sources to develop county-level estimates of farm receipts. For 16 major producing states, NASS-affiliated state offices prepare annual county estimates of farm cash receipts. For other states, state-level cash receipts estimates produced by NASS are allocated by BEA to counties in proportion to the corresponding Census of Agriculture data for the relevant year. These county-level data were used to produce county-level estimates of cash receipts per square mile by dividing total cash receipts by the number of square miles in a county. County area data are from a standard dataset produced by Environmental Systems Research Institute, Inc. (ESRI; http://www.esri.com).

Data Availability: Data on U.S. national farm cash receipts for 1924–2005 are available online at http://www.ers.usda.gov/data/farmincome/finfidmu.htm.

The U.S. county cash receipts data are available online from the BEA, Regional Economic Information System branch (http://www.bea.gov/regional/reis/).

2008 Report Data Update: Data on U.S. national farm county receipts for 2005 were obtained from the ERS Web site listed in Data Availability (Accessed April 9, 2007); county data for 2005 were obtained from the Regional Economic Information System (REIS) Web site also listed in Data Availability (Accessed April 9, 2007).

Recreation in Farmland Areas

There is no technical note for this indicator.

Forests
Forest Area and Ownership

The Indicator
This indicator reports the extent of forested land in the United States, and whether the land is privately or publicly owned. Combined with other information on forest condition, growth and harvest, forest area and ownership are important indicators of the status of our nation's forests.

The Data
Data Description: See the Forest Inventory Analysis program description on p. 270. As defined by the U.S. Forest Service, forest land is any land greater than 1 acre that is at least 10% stocked by forest trees of any size. In order to be reported by the Forest Service, the forest must conform to forest types recognized by the Society of American Foresters (SAF), the tree species must be cited in Elbert Little's Checklist of U.S. Trees (Little 1979) and must meet the definition of a tree. This includes land that formerly had such tree cover and may be naturally or artificially regenerated in the near future. The definition no longer includes certain vegetation types historically treated as forest but not recognized by the SAF (e.g. chaparral). The current definition of "forest" lands also harmonizes with international forest cover definitions. For the forest area and ownership indicator, public forests include those owned by federal, state, and local governments, as well as other public entities such as the Tennessee Valley Authority. Private lands include those owned by individuals, corporations, nongovernmental organizations, and tribes.

Information presented in the text of the forest area and ownership indicator regarding historical trends in forest area (prior to 1953) are derived from data provided by the Forest Service for the 2002 State of the Nation's Ecosystems report. For the 2002 Report, the Forest Service's FIA program derived estimates of historic forest area from a wide variety of sources (e.g. forest clearing data collected during the 1870 and later decennial censuses, limited state and regional surveys, and the expert opinion of resource professionals). No error estimate is provided for data prior to 1953.

Data Quality/Caveats: For 2006, current area and volume data are not available for Mississippi, Oklahoma, New Mexico, Wyoming, interior Alaska, or Hawaii. Also note that the state of Alaska has never had a complete annual inventory covering the entire state. For Alaska, data reported in the area/ownership and forest types indicators, the U.S. Forest Service personnel decided to repeat the values reported for 1987 for 1977, 1963 and 1953 because of lack of reliable data for those earlier years.

Data Availability: Data were acquired from the Forest Service and are available on the Web at http://fia.fs.fed.us.

2008 Report Data Update: Data for 2006 were added in this update, and replace 2002 values reported in the online 2003 Web Site Update. Historical data were adjusted to conform to the current forest definition. The Forest Service no longer separates private ownership into Forest Industry and Other Private categories because of major shifts in industrial ownership patterns. For this report, "Private" is broken out into two categories: corporate (timber holding and forest product firms) and individual (individuals, families, trusts and tribes).

Forest Types

The Indicator

This indicator reports the area occupied by major forest types over time. Both the type of forest and the degree to which the forest is broken into smaller patches and intermingled with nonforest areas (see Pattern of Forest Landscapes, p. 138) are important factors in the survival of many forest species. The types of trees that can be found in a given area can be affected by a variety of factors. Human intervention such as fire suppression, planting and harvesting, development, and grazing can be one type of influence. Natural succession also changes the types and distribution of trees—increases in some forest types may be a result of maturation of second and third growth forests. Ecosystem processes such as wildfires and pest infestation can change the composition of tree species as well. Also, changes in grazing and logging practices may be responsible as well.

The Data

Data Description: see the Forest Inventory and Analysis program description on p. 270.

Data Quality/Caveats: See the Forest Inventory and Analysis program description (p. 270) for a detailed explanation of data caveats.

Data included in this report differ from the data reported in previous reports because of several factors. Because the historical data are compiled manually and are not available in a national database, human error may be introduced as the data are compiled from various Forest Service publications. Changes in the Forest Service definition of "forest" mean that the chaparral cover type is no longer considered a forest type; therefore, those data were removed from the "Western Hardwoods" type. By disaggregating the data into additional geographic regions, some minor differences in the data totals may have been introduced due to rounding error. Finally, there is a lack of reliable survey data for the state of Alaska—for Forest Types in particular, there are no species records; therefore, species data are approximated from remote sensing information.

The categories in this indicator are highly aggregated, which may mask changes in specific tree populations in certain geographical areas.

Data Availability: Data were acquired from the Forest Service and are available on the Web at http://fia.fs.fed.us/.

2008 Report Data Update: Data for 2006 were added in this update and replace 2002 values. A few forest type labels have changed. Previously in the East (North and South), oak-gum-cypress and elm-ash-cottonwood types were combined into the "lowland hardwoods" category—these types have now been split. Also, the "Other forest types" category has been replaced with its main species component, oak-pine. Note that most of the softwoods data are in Alaska, where ground-based survey data are not available to identify specific species.

Also new for 2008, additional regional breakouts of the data have been made available.

Forest Management Categories

The Indicator

This indicator reports the percent of total U.S. forest area that is managed as either reserved forest land, planted timberland, natural/semi-natural forest land, or "other" semi-natural forest land. Interior Alaska forests are reported separately because their unique remoteness makes them similar in management to "reserved lands". Most forest lands in the United States—including those used for timber production—are neither national parks or wilderness areas nor planted forests.

The Data

Data Description: The data for this indicator were collected by the Forest Service's Forest Inventory and Analysis (FIA) program, which is described on p. 270. These data do not include information on private lands that are legally reserved from harvest, such as lands held by private groups like The Nature Conservancy. In addition, many "natural" and "semi-natural" lands are at times reserved from harvest because of administrative or other restrictions.

Note that "interior Alaska" includes all forests except the Southeast Coast area up to and including the Kenai Peninsula. Thus, "interior" includes areas that may not be thought of as part of Alaska's interior, yet they are included because of their remoteness. The acreage shown here for interior Alaska (about 107 million acres) does not include the Tongass National Forest (about 12 million acres).

Data Quality/Caveats: The general quality and caveat statements in the Forest Inventory and Analysis program description (p. 270) also apply to this indicator. In addition, the data reported for 1953 and 1963 in the "Reserved Forest" category did not break out unproductive reserved lands, so those values are interpolated. The "Other Forest" category for those years is therefore the remainder of the forested land minus known timberland areas and calculated reserved forest areas.

Data Availability: Data were acquired from the Forest Service and are available on the web at http://fia.fs.fed.us.

2008 Report Data Update: Data for 2006 were added in this update and replace 2002 values. Note also that there has been an apparent drop in interior Alaska acres since the last report; however, the decrease came about from a reclassification of acreage into the "reserved forest land" from the "other natural/semi-natural forest land" category, not a true loss of forest. As field surveys are conducted in the future, earlier estimates for interior Alaska based primarily on remote sensing will likely include further adjustments.

The Data Gap

We hope that, in future reports, it will be possible to report on the existence of protected or reserved areas on a broader range of land ownerships. One dataset being developed for this purpose will report the acreage of lands according to a system of categorizing management intensity developed by the U.S. Geological Survey Gap Analysis Program (see http://gapanalysis.nbii.gov). This database is currently under development by the Conservation Biology Institute in conjunction with the USDA Forest Service; see http://www.consbio.org/cbi/projects/PAD/index.htm.

Pattern of Forest Landscapes

The Indicator

This indicator reports the size of patches of forest land cover meeting the definition of *core forest*. In general, there is not a single definition of *core forest*, and the term is used here to describe a broad pattern where forest land cover is separated from *nonnatural* land-cover types (e.g., development—including paved roads, and croplands) by a buffer of forest and other *natural* land cover types. Once identified, patches of *core forest* pixels were created and reported in the indicator's graphs, both nationally and regionally.

Substantial Changes to the Indicator Design: This indicator was revised for the 2008 edition of this report by the Landscape Pattern Task Group; a report from this Task Group is forthcoming and will be posted on the Heinz Center Web site (http://www.heinzctr.org/ecosystems).

The Data

The data for this indicator are derived from two sources. The primary source is the 2001 National Land Cover Dataset (NLCD), which is a product of the Multi-Resolution Land Characterization (MRLC) Consortium (see p. 274). In addition, this land-cover map was augmented with data from ESRI on paved roads (StreetMap data; http://www.esri.com/data/streetmap/), which are considered here as a type of development.

Data Description: See the technical note for the NLCD (p. 274) for details.

Data Manipulation: Analysts from the USDA Forest Service and the Environmental Protection Agency performed the analyses described below using a land-cover map that breaks the country up into a grid of pixels each 30-m on a side (~100 ft or about one-quarter acre). The definition of *core forest* is based on the composition of land cover surrounding a given pixel of forest land cover. Specifically, all the pixels in the land-cover map in a 1-km square (3250 ft., or about 240 acres) centered on a given forest pixel were evaluated. In order to be considered as *core forest,* that central forest pixel needs to be surrounded by a specific amount (in this case, 90%) of forest and other *natural* land cover (grasslands, shrublands, wetlands, other fresh waters, and coastal waters). The core forest criteria can be adjusted to provide further insight into the ecological implication of the patterns of forest landscapes. After identifying all pixels of *core forest,* these pixels were merged into patches of pixels touching either on their sides or at their corners. The size of these patches of *core forest* pixels are reported, both regionally and nationally.

Further indicator development could include several analysis combinations (e.g., different window sizes and density thresholds other than 90% *natural*).

Data Quality/Caveats: The size of patches of *core forest* pixels were summarized state-by-state. This procedure undoubtedly caused some patches to be split by state boundaries. Therefore, the patch sizes reported are effectively minimum patch sizes.

Data Availability: See the technical note for the NLCD (p. 274) for availability of those data, and the ESRI Web site listed above for access to the StreetMap data. Summarized data from the analyses described here were provided to the Heinz Center by the Center for Landscape Analysis, and are available from the Heinz Center upon request.

Nitrate in Forest Streams

The Indicator

This indicator reports mean-annual discharge-weighted concentrations of dissolved nitrate plus nitrite-nitrogen in forest streams. Data are reported as parts per million (milligrams per liter) nitrogen. As some proportion of forested watersheds contain non-forested land cover, inputs from farm and domestic fertilizers, discharges from septic systems, and effluents from sewage treatment plants may also add nitrate to forested streams. The data are labeled "mean total nitrate" although the analytical method actually reports nitrate plus nitrite. This reporting convention is reasonable because except in highly polluted waters, nitrite levels are only a very small fraction of the total and can, therefore, be considered insignificant.

The Data

Data Source: The data were collected and analyzed by the U.S. Geological Survey (USGS) National Water Quality Assessment (NAWQA) program. See page 272 for information on the NAWQA program, sampling design, methodology, data availability. Information on the drinking water standard for nitrogen can be found at http://www.epa.gov/safewater/contaminants/index.html#inorganic. For information on farmlands and urban-suburban data used in the ecosystem comparison, see p. 299, and p. 327.

Data Collection Methodology: Stream nitrate data were collected from samples at stream and river sites draining 117 forested areas in the conterminous US. Land cover upstream from sites in the "Forested" category is predominantly undeveloped land (less than 25 percent agricultural and less than 5 percent urban) and where the total area of forested land is greater than that of grassland and shrubland. Whereas Alaska and Hawaii were included in the study, streams and wells were not sampled in these states because land cover within the NAWQA study units was not primarily forested.

Data Availability: Data used in this indicator are summarized by Wilson et al., (2008), available at http://pubs.usgs.gov/of/2008/1110/. Ecoregion criteria for assessing total nitrogen concentrations in all wadeable streams (including forest streams) during the summer index period can be found in USEPA's Wadeable Streams Assessment (USEPA 2006e).

2008 Report Data Update: The geographic scope of the indicator has increased. The 2008 indicator covers 51 major river basins across 50 states, sampled over the period 1992–2001. Only 36 basins were included in the 2002 Report, sampled over the period 1992–98.

Carbon Storage

The Indicator

This indicator reports the trends in the amount of carbon stored in forests, including trees, soil, and plant litter on the forest floor, as well as the amount of carbon stored in carbon pools, by region. Because U.S. forests are most likely responsible for most of the terrestrial carbon sink in North America (Woodbury et al., 2007), understanding trends in carbon storage in the nation's forests is extremely important. Determining the amount of carbon stored in a forest is challenging because it can change dramatically within a few days following a natural event, such as a fire, or timber harvest. Carbon lost during long-term agricultural use of soils can be restored by reforestation. However, this does not take into account the transportation and processing of wood products, burned biowaste, or other ways in which carbon may be lost from forested areas.

The Data

Metric tons of stored carbon are reported for the following forest carbon pools: live trees, standing dead trees, understory vegetation, down dead wood, and the forest floor. As in most international discussions, carbon storage is reported here in metric tons. (Note that there are 1.1 English tons per metric ton.)

Data Description: The estimates for forest carbon storage are based on data from the USDA Forest Service Forest Inventory and Analysis (FIA) program (see FIA program description, p. 270) in particular the field estimates of the size of trees of various species, coupled with statistical models of the relationships between tree stem volume and the other components of carbon storage. Data for Alaska and Hawaii are not included in this data series.

Data Manipulation: All data manipulations described here were performed by the USDA Forest Service. Generally, carbon storage is estimated by applying carbon conversion factors to estimated volumes of live and dead trees, woody debris, understory vegetation and forest floor litter (see Smith et al., 2006 and Smith et al., 2007 for more information).

Estimates of live tree carbon stock from 1953 through 2005 are based on three different sources of forest inventory data (regional summary tables, RPA Assessment, and annualized estimates from the current inventory data), and therefore use three different sets of carbon conversion factors.

Data Quality/Caveats: Estimates of carbon stocks are based on regional averages and reflect the current best available data for developing regional estimates. Overall, regional or national estimates are more precise than local estimates. Variability within region may have a much greater influence on uncertainty than regional values (Smith et al., 2006). See FIA program description, p. 270, for more information on caveats for FIA sampling.

Data Availability: Estimates of carbon in forests used here were obtained directly from the USDA Forest Service. Additional information about carbon storage in forests can be obtained at http://www.fs.fed.us/ne/global/research/carbon/forcarb.html.

2008 Report Data Update: Estimates reported in the 2008 Report represent all forests, not just timberlands as in past reports. In addition, new estimates have been added for carbon stored in the forest floor, down dead wood, understory, and standing dead trees. Note that historical estimates reported may differ slightly from previous reports due to revised carbon conversion coefficients, as well as the addition of non-timberlands to the estimates. The design of this indicator has been adjusted to remove a placeholder for carbon storage estimates in wood products. Wood products may be considered as a future component of the core national Carbon Storage indicator in the Urban and Suburban ecosystem (p. 38) or as a potential future addition to the Urban and Suburban chapter.

The Data Gap

Estimates of carbon storage in standing live trees, including coarse live roots, forest floor, down dead wood, understory, and standing dead trees are presented. Estimates for carbon stored in forest soils are not presented in this report because they were judged not to be adequate for national reporting. More intensive measurements of soil carbon are occurring with the application of FIA's annualized design, and are planned by the Natural Resources Conservation Service (NRCS). Forest soil carbon estimates are calculated by combining base soil organic carbon estimates from the USDA NRCS national STATSGO spatial database with forest type and biomass information from the Forest Service's FIA survey to develop current soil carbon values (for more information see Smith et al. 2006 and Amichev and Galbraith 2004).

At-Risk Native Forest Species

The Indicator

This indicator reports on the conservation status of native forest species across their full range (i.e., global ranks) as well as population trends of species that are at-risk of extinction. The species reported here are those in groups (such as mammals, birds, and amphibians) that are sufficiently well known that their conservation status, habitat, and location (by state) can be assigned with some degree of confidence for all members of the group.

The conservation status assessment for each species is an attempt to determine its relative susceptibility to extinction. The assessment process is based on consideration of up to 12 factors that relate to a species' degree of imperilment or risk of extinction throughout its range. Rare species are particularly vulnerable to extinction and so several aspects of rarity are characterized in the assessment process including population size, number of populations, and range extent and area of occupancy. However, trends in population and range size as well as magnitude and immediacy of threats are also important considerations in assessing a species' overall vulnerability or risk of extinction. Additional information on this ranking process can be found in the technical note describing the NatureServe program (p. 275) and at http://www.natureserve.org/explorer/ranking.htm and in Master (1991).

There is general recognition among experts that both status information (as presented here for animal species) and trend information (as presented here for vertebrate animals are crucial to understanding the condition of species).

The Data

For information on the NatureServe program data collection, methods, data quality/caveats, data availability, and references, see p. 275.

Data Source: NatureServe (http://www.natureserve.org) and its member programs in the network of Natural Heritage programs develop and maintain information on each of the species reported here.

Data Manipulation: Information on NatureServe methods in general can be found on p. 275. All data manipulations were performed by NatureServe. To compute this indicator, NatureServe identified species as "forest species" if they lived in forests during at least part of their life cycle and depended on access to forests for their survival. This was a generally conservative approach—only species that were strongly associated with forest habitat type were included. Groups reported for forests include mammals, birds, reptiles (snakes and lizards), crocodiles, alligators, turtles, amphibians, butterflies and skippers, and grasshoppers. Combined, these groups include over 1700 forest species.

2008 Report Data Update: The population trend metric was added to the indicator. Conservation status data from the 2002 Report were replaced with 2006 data.

The Data Gap

Data are not reported for forest plants because habitat types have not been identified for all plant species. Critically imperiled and imperiled plants (G1 and G2) have been assigned habitat types, and NatureServe is currently working to assign vulnerable (G3) plants to habitats, but the habitat types of plants with more secure status remains unknown. Population trend data are not included for at-risk invertebrate animals, because trends are known for only 15% of invertebrate animal species in forests.

Established Non-native Plant Cover in Forests

The Indicator

This indicator will report total area covered by non-native species. In some cases, the total area covered by any single species may be relatively low, but total area covered by all non-natives may be larger. See the technical note for the core non-native species indicator (p. 283) for a definition of non-native species.

A useful introduction to the issue of non-native species can be found in the Office of Technology Assessment publication Harmful Non-Indigenous Species in the United States (1993; http://eric.ed.gov/ERICWebPortal/custom/portlets/recordDetails/detailmini.jsp?_nfpb=true&_&ERICExtSearch_SearchValue_0=ED368561&ERICExtSearch_SearchType_0=no&accno=ED368561). A more recent, policy-oriented view of non-native species issues can be found in the Congressional Research Service report Harmful Non-Native Species: Issues for Congress (1999; http://cnie.org/NLE/CRSreports/Biodiversity/biodv-26.cfm). Two state-based surveys of the kinds of non-native species and their impacts and controls can be found at http://www.ct.nrcs.usda.gov/plants.html

(Connecticut) and http://www.mdflora.org/publications/invasives.htm (Maryland).

Some common non-native plant species include: kudzu (*Peuraria montana* var. *lobata*), melaleuca (*Melaleuca quinquenervia*), Ailanthus (*Ailanthus altissima*), Medusahead (*Taeniatherum caput-medusae*), salt cedar (*Tamarix* spp), Norway maple (*Acer platanoides*), multiflora rose (*Rosa multiflora*), and Russian olive (*Elaeagnus angustifolia*).

The Data Gap

Monitoring conducted by the Illinois Natural History Survey's Critical Trends Assessment Program (INHS-CTAP, http://ctap.inhs.uiuc.edu/) provides an example, at the state level, of monitoring trends in percentage cover by non-native plants. No comparable data exist for the nation as a whole.

The USDA Forest Service, as part of its Forest Inventory and Analysis (FIA) program, is developing a vegetation indicator to assess the type, abundance, and spatial arrangement of vegetation on its Phase 3 Forest Health plots. Each Phase 3 plot contains four subplots (24.0 ft or 7.32 m radius). In three 1.0m² vegetation quadrats within the subplot, cover is estimated for each vascular plant species present, and the vertical layer where most of the foliage occurs is recorded (Schulz, 2003). There is one Phase 3 plot per 96,000 acres of forest; one-fifth of all plots are measured across most states annually, resulting in a five-year sampling cycle.

Forest Age

The Indicator

This indicator presents data on the average age of trees within a forest stand. It is important to note that the age of a tree does not necessarily convey information about the size of the tree. Fast-growing species attain sizes comparable to much older trees of another species, and trees of the same species and age growing in different locations may be very different in size. In addition, processes such as forest fires and hurricanes can act to limit the age of trees in a region (e.g., hurricanes are more prominent in the eastern United States).

The Data

Data Description: Data for this indicator were collected by the USDA Forest Service Forest Inventory and Analysis (FIA) program (see FIA program description, p. 270). The age of a stand of trees is a classification based on the mean age of trees with dominant or codominant crown positions in the stand. Dominant/codominant crowns are those tree crowns dominating or sharing space in the upper layer of the tree canopy. The age of these trees is generally determined using tree cores from which annual growth increments were counted. More information about stand age calculation may be found in the FIA Field Guide for Phase 2 Measurements (http://fia.fs.fed.us/library/field-guides-methods-proc/).

The data represent a subset of all forests in the United States—those defined by the USDA Forest Service as "timberlands." Timberlands is a designation that covers lands on which harvesting is not prohibited by law and which grow an average of at least 20 cubic feet of wood per acre per year. Note that the use of the "Uneven Aged" category is being phased out of the inventory. This category is a multiage classification that was used in previous inventories. In the past decade, an effort has been made to limit the application of this category by using the dominant or co-dominant tree types to assign stand age, allowing better correlation to remotely sensed data. Therefore, this category will continue to decline over time.

Data Availability: Data were acquired from the Forest Service and are available on the Web at http://fia.fs.fed.us.

2008 Report Data Update: Data for 2006 were added in this update and replace 2002 values. Data for 1987 were also made available for the first time. The data presentation format was changed from a bar graph to an area graph.

The Data Gap

The data presented here do not include national parks and wilderness areas and other natural and semi-natural forestland not classified as timberlands and thus not included in previous inventories. As a result, these data describe nearly all eastern forests, but only about 40% of western forests. Data on slow-growing forests and those in parks and wilderness areas are being collected, but they are not yet available.

Forest Disturbance: Fire, Insects, and Disease

The Indicator

This indicator presents a broad summary of disturbance types in forests, including fire (both wild and prescribed), insects, and disease. It reports the number of acres affected each year by a variety of disturbances. The 2001 peak in insect damage was mainly due to defoliation caused by three species: eastern tent caterpillar (*Malscosoma americanum*), forest tent caterpillar (*Malacosoma disstria*), and locust leafminer (*Odontata dorsalis*).

Substantial Changes to the Indicator Design: Following the 2002 Report, a task group was convened to increase consistency and relevancy across the entire suite of non-native species indicators. Changes to the Forest Disturbance indicator suggested by the committee included altering the presentation to specify the proportion of forest damage caused by non-native insects, diseases and pathogens. Whereas the data are not robust enough to assign causative agents with a high degree of certainty, the design of the indicator has been revised in anticipation that data may become available in the future.

The Data

Data Description: Data reported here for forest damage by insects cover the lower 48 states and portions of Alaska, and are from the USDA Forest Service Forest Health Monitoring (FHM) program (http://fhm.fs.fed.us/). The database is maintained by the Forest Service's Forest Health Technology Enterprise Team (FHTET, http://www.fs.fed.us/foresthealth/technology/). See http://www.fs.fed.us/foresthealth/technology/gis.shtml and http://www.fs.fed.us/foresthealth/publications/id/standards_1099.pdf./ for a description of the program's aerial and ground surveys. For this report, insect damage is defined as defoliation or continuous mortality (although other damage types may impact specific populations significantly). Continuous mortality describes mortality events that are not patchy in distribution, and does not imply that all host species in a given

area are killed. Since trees may recover from defoliation events, defoliation data are reported separately from mortality data.

Information on wildland fires (including acreage but also other fire attributes) are collected by federal, state, local and tribal agencies, but collated and reported by the National Interagency Fire Center.

Data Manipulation: Because multiple damage agents can be assigned to any given polygon, "footprint" totals are calculated to account for any overlap in acreage totals. For both defoliation and continuous mortality, damage for a single year is calculated from distinct polygons for each pest (it does not count areas coded with the same pest more than once). However, there may be multiple counting for damage among pests. The "footprint" total excludes multiple counting among pests.

Data Quality/Caveats: Data for major insect pests (1979–2006) are from three separate data collection and reporting methodologies: the Forest Pest Information System (FPIS) for major pests, FPIS for other pests, and Aerial Insect & Disease Surveys (ADS). Reporting across these different methodologies may have "order of magnitude" differences in the data. From 1979–1996, five major insects are reported: gypsy moth, spruce budworm, southern pine beetle, mountain pine beetle, and western spruce budworm. From 1997–2006, more than 160 insect species categories are reported (including the original five). Any category containing a significant proportion of insect damage (even if mixed with other damage agents) was included as "insect" damage. The data in this report include portions of Alaska (survey area rotated from year to year on an as-needed basis). Therefore, a certain amount of conifer mortality goes unrecorded, particularly when mortality is sparse rather than continuous. Forest fire data are not limited to national forests; also, the data presented here are not able to be separated by land cover type (forest, grassland, and shrubland). Note that data on acreage burned in 2004 does not include state lands for North Carolina. Also note that values from 1960–2006 may have changed slightly since the last reporting due to ongoing efforts at the National Interagency Fire Center to compile and report accurate data from a variety of sources (county, state, and regional/national sources).

Data Availability: Data on insect damage are available from the Forest Health Monitoring program (http://fhm.fs.fed.us/). Data on acres affected by fire were obtained from the USDA Forest Service National Forest System (years 1916–1959; available in GAO (1999) and The Heinz Center (1999)) and the National Interagency Fire Center (years 1960–2006; available online at http://www.nifc.gov).

2008 Report Data Update: The 2002 Report and the 2003 Web-only Update reported damage caused by a select number of insect species. The 2008 Report retained those data, but also added data for additional insect damage agents beginning in 1999. Instead of the line graph previously used, data are presented in a stacked area graph; fire data are separated from insect data since fire data represent both forest and grassland/shrubland areas while the insect data do not. Note that the disease data reported in 2002 and 2003 were dropped from this report, as the data are collected only on an as-needed basis to support local Insect and Disease management programs.

The Data Gap

It is important that data on different types of damage be preserved in the indicator, because focusing on one type of damage could bias the indicator toward effects specific to a limited number of species. One way to aggregate data from multiple sources and across different pathogens and pests is to standardize criteria for degrees of damage (e.g., low, moderate, high). The criteria would have to account for background levels of infestation as well as instances in which most of the trees in an area are affected. As satellite-based remote sensing techniques mature, there may be new data streams for characterizing annual patterns of forest disturbance. Further work is needed to answer questions about separating forest fire from grassland fire and reporting on fire intensity. One future source of fire intensity data may be the Monitoring Trends in Burn Severity (MTBS) project (http://svinetfc4.fs.fed.us/mtbs/). Also, data on the acreage of prescribed fires on forests and grasslands/shrublands is currently available through the National Interagency Fire Center for 1998-present; these data have yet to be assessed and may be included in future reports.

Fire Frequency

Note: This also serves as the technical note for the Grasslands/Shrublands fire frequency indicator.

The Indicator

This indicator was designed to compare current and historic fire frequencies in order to gain an understanding of whether or not forests (or grasslands and shrublands) burn as frequently as they did prior to being influenced substantially by people. The indicator does not incorporate an assessment of fire risk, although risk assessment is an important land management tool.

Fire is an important feature in healthy forest and grassland/shrubland ecosystems. How often, time of year, and with what severity a fire burns in a given area can vary widely by geographic location and within vegetation type—thus it is expected that the developed index would be evaluated at a scale that will capture these wide variations. It is difficult to assess historic fire regimes. Site evidence (tree rings, charcoal, fire scars, pollen) may be used to construct historic fire frequency and severity patterns, but these data are not routinely collected through any national monitoring program. For grasslands and shrubland areas in particular, site evidence is often nonexistent. Current fire regimes can be influenced by a variety of factors, such as land management practices, changes in temperature and precipitation, and changes in vegetation types (including introduction of non-native species). Some scientists advocate prediction of future vegetation types as a more useful measure; others place a heavier emphasis on the incorporation of characteristic fire regimes.

The Data Gap

In the 2002 Report, the technical note for this indicator discussed the Fire Regimes for Fuels Management and Fire Use (Fuelman) project. Estimates through this project were based on expert knowledge and modeling because of a lack of relatively direct measurements of fire return frequency (e.g. tree ring scars and similar site measurements). More recently, the mapping of fire regime condition class (FRCC) replaced Fuelman, incorporating field data from a variety of

contributors, literature reviews, field visits, and communication with regional experts. Mapping FRCC on a national scale was adopted as one tool in the implementation of the National Fire Plan (http://www.forestsandrangelands.gov/NFP/index.shtml), which is coordinated by the Wildland Fire Leadership Council (WFLC). Among other efforts, WFLC sponsored the Landscape Fire and Resource Management Planning Tools Project (LANDFIRE) to map vegetation, fire, and fuel characteristics, including but not limited to mapping FRCC. See http://www.landfire.gov/ for more information.

Another interagency effort sponsored by the WFLC has begun to assess the impacts of large fires. The Monitoring Trends in Burn Severity (MTBS) project will map burn severity and extent of fires occurring between 1984–2010. Data from multiple agencies will be combined and reconciled to create a single database. The data may be a useful starting point for analysis of departure from historical fire regimes. See http://svinetfc4.fs.fed.us/mtbs/ for more information.

Forest Community Types with Significantly Reduced Area

The Indicator

This indicator would be based on identification of forest community types that occupy at least 70% fewer acres than at the time of widespread European settlement (approximately within the years of 1600–1800). Note that the "forest community types" described in this indicator are more specific than the groupings described in the forest types indicator (pp. 134). The "forest types" reported in that indicator are broad classification concepts, each of which would include many "forest community types." Because "forest community types" are not defined or recognized consistently, establishment of a national classification standard is necessary for this indicator. The indicator would report the number of forest community types with significantly reduced area and the present acreage of this suite of community types. It would also report the change in area of these community types from one reporting period to the next, allowing readers to understand whether reductions in the area of these already-reduced types is continuing or has been stopped or reversed.

Note that use of a pre-European settlement baseline is not intended to imply that forest community types were "pristine" or completely unaffected by human activity. The use of a pre-European settlement baseline is also not intended to serve as a goal for action or policy. Rather, it is intended as a relatively long-term reference point, against which to compare, and to better understand, current conditions.

Forest community types for this indicator would use "terrestrial ecological system" concepts developed by NatureServe (NatureServe 2007a). These classification concepts have been described for the United States and Latin America, and form the basis for several U.S. national mapping efforts, such as the inter-agency LANDFIRE effort and the USGS Gap Analysis Program. Terrestrial ecological systems are described in part using hierarchically-organized vegetation concepts derived from the U.S. National Vegetation Classification System (US-NVC; FGDC 1997; Grossman et al. 1998; NatureServe 2007b) and provide a practical mapped expression of the vegetation classification standards. A forest ecological system is a group of US-NVC associations that tend to co-occur in similar environmental settings and are similarly effected by natural dynamic processes. This level of classification is roughly equivalent to "cover type" as defined by the Society of American Foresters.

Ecosystems can decline in area through outright conversion to another land cover or through gradual changes, like those that accompany fire suppression, which allows for changes in forest composition and structure. For this indicator, as long as an area has the characteristics of a specific forest community type, it would be counted as part of that type. If, for example, significant vegetation changes occurred as a result of fire suppression, the forest may eventually be classified as a different type.

The Data Gap

The inter-agency LANDFIRE (also known as the Landscape Fire and Resource Management Planning Tools Project, http://www.landfire.gov/products_national.php) products should aid quantification of forest systems with acreage reduced by greater than 70%. These products are currently available in portions of the country, but complete national data are due in 2009.

NatureServe and the USDA Forest Service Forest Inventory and Analysis (FIA) program are also developing methods that allow estimation of the area of US-NVC concepts from existing FIA data. This also provides a recent historical perspective on changes in vegetation type area, and would allow the area of these community types to be tracked in the future.

Timber Harvest

The Indicator

This indicator reports the volume of timber harvested each year, and six categories of products that are made from it: sawlogs, pulpwood and composites, logging residues/other removals, fuelwood, veneer logs, and other products. Both economic and social changes in our society can influence regional patterns of forest harvest, as well as the types of products which are in demand at a given time.

The Data

The data presented in this indicator are not directly comparable with the data presented in the growth and harvest indicator, p. 155, because that indicator reports only the volume of "growing stock," an inventory category that excludes certain trees (rough, rotten, or dead trees) and parts of trees that do not meet specified standards of size, quality, and merchantability (for example, tree limbs are not considered "growing stock" but may be used for other products such as fuelwood). This indicator includes growing stock as well as other harvested materials.

Data Description: Data on forest products and their source are collected by the USDA Forest Service Forest Inventory and Analysis (FIA) program and the Forest Service Forest Products Laboratory, which also supplements these data with information from U.S. Department of Commerce published reports and industry trade association sources. The FIA program collects data on timber growth through a large-scale field sampling program, described in the FIA program description (p. 270). These FIA plots are used to verify product data collected from periodic Forest Service wood facility

surveys, residential fuelwood surveys, studies of active logging operations, and field inventories of harvested trees. Two types of studies are used to evaluate timber harvest—those targeted at primary industrial wood use (such as pulp mills and sawmills), and those targeted at nonindustrial use (household members and loggers producing residential firewood). FIA conducts these studies in conjunction with each state's forestry agency. Harvest data are collected on different schedules that vary according to the type of study (pulp mill, sawmill, firewood, etc.) as well as location—see May (1998) and Smith (1991) for more information.

Data Manipulation: Mill survey data are used to identify primary products being harvested in forests. Then, FIA field data are used to verify the product data—it is used to estimate harvest distributions by ownership based on trees harvested for products. The Forest Service also conducts utilization studies on active logging operations to estimate wood usage for products and residues left in the woods. These data are merged with log receipt data from wood-using facilities to produce estimates of timber and other material cut to deliver those logs to the facility. Ancillary data from the Department of Commerce on wood use and industry association data are used to validate information on the volume of trees cut annually to produce primary wood products such as sawlogs, pulpwood, veneer logs, fuelwood, and other wood products. Prior to 1992, each study was done independently of studies in other states—see May (1998) for further explanation.

Data Quality/Caveats: Nonfuelwood product totals shown would generally have errors of less than ±10 percent. Data are from FIA wood facility surveys, which are full industry canvasses and are thus assumed to have negligible sampling error. Periodic residential fuelwood studies generally have errors of ±15%. Note that sawlog and veneer log data do not include overseas exports; they only include those logs received and processed by mills in the U.S. or Canada. The Forest Service is developing a process to quantify overseas exports.

Data Availability: All data are available free of charge, except for products that require special processing or shipping fees. Electronic databases are unavailable at the national level before 1987, and most regional data from before 1977 are not available electronically. Forest statistics, online databases, and a map of U.S. forest distributions are on the Web at http://fia.fs.fed.us. Forest Products Laboratory data synthesizing Department of Commerce and industry trade association data are available at http://www.fpl.fs.fed.us/.

2008 Report Data Update: Data for 2005 were added in this update and replace 2001 values. Sawlog and veneer data were corrected for 1952.

Timber Growth and Harvest

The Indicator

This indicator describes how much timber grows each year, compared to how much is cut. Definitions for the terms "growth," "harvest," and "timberlands," as used in this indicator, are those used by the USDA Forest Service. Comparing growth with harvest is a frequently used method of assessing whether wood harvwesting is reducing the volume of tree biomass in a forest. The general principle is that if more material is growing than is being harvested the forest will accrue volume.

The Data

The data presented in this indicator are not directly comparable with the data presented in the timber harvest indicator, because the data presented here report only the volume of "growing stock," an inventory category that excludes certain trees (rough, rotten, or dead trees) and parts of trees that do not meet specified standards of size, quality, and merchantability (these data—defined below—are used for both the growth and harvest categories presented here). The harvest data presented in Timber Harvest (p. 154) encompass a broader suite of timber products, including "growing stock" and other harvested materials.

Data Description: Data for this indicator are collected under the USDA Forest Service Forest Inventory and Analysis (FIA) program. Data on forest growth are collected through a phased plot system (see FIA program description, p. 270). Data on forest harvest are collected through product surveys (see description under Timber Harvest technical note, p. 312).

Data Quality/Caveats: Growth: FIA surveys provide forest volume data with a reliability of ±5-8% per billion cubic feet with a 67% confidence limit. *Harvest:* Nonfuelwood product totals would generally have errors of less than 10 percent. Data are from FIA wood facility surveys, which are full industry canvasses and are thus assumed to have negligible sampling error.

The data for this indicator are limited to "growing stock" trees. Growing stock is a Forest Service inventory category that includes live trees of commercial species meeting specified standards of quality or vigor. When used in calculating volume, this category includes only trees 5.0 in d.b.h. ("diameter at breast height" a common measurement of tree size) and larger, and which have no obvious characteristics that would make them unusable for industrial use (e.g., rot, unusual shape). In addition, volume is computed for the central stem from a 1-foot stump to a minimum 4-in top diameter outside bark, or to the point where the central stem breaks into limbs.

This indicator does not provide data on the species, age, quality, or other attributes of the trees being harvested or of trees whose growth is measured. General trends in growth and harvest in these regions do not reflect some important trends that are occurring at smaller scales.

Because this indicator does not include information on growth in slow-growing forests and those in parks and wilderness, which make up 60% of western forests, it may not reflect significant changes in forest growth in that region.

Data Availability: All data are available free of charge, except for products that require special processing or shipping fees. Electronic databases are unavailable at the national level before 1987, and most regional data from before 1977 are not available electronically. Forest statistics, online databases, and a map of U.S. forest distributions are on the Web at http://fia.fs.fed.us. Forest Products Laboratory data synthesizing Department of Commerce and industry trade association data are available at http://www.fpl.fs.fed.us. Additional data on wood products use may be found at http://www.fpl.fs.fed.us/.

2008 Report Data Update: Data for 2005–2006 were added in this update and replace 2001–2002 values.

Recreation in Forests

The Indicator

This indicator presents the results of surveys designed to track the participation of U.S. residents in various recreational activities in forested ecosystems.

The Data

Data Description: Data for this indicator were obtained directly from the USDA Forest Service, and come from a national survey conducted by phone, which was done as part of the National Survey on Recreation and the Environment (NSRE). See the technical note for the national Outdoor Recreation indicator for more information on the NSRE program design and survey methods, p. 286. The surveys were designed to track participation in recreational activities of noninstitutionalized U.S. residents over the age of 16. The demographic characteristics of survey respondents were compared to national averages based on census data and then weighted accordingly to estimate national recreation participation totals.

Data Manipulation: Data on forest-specific recreation were only collected as part of the two most recent NSRE surveys; therefore data from the 1994–1995 NSRE are not included in this indicator. Data from the 1999–2001 and 2003–2005 NSRE surveys were grouped into the following forest-specific categories:
- Walking
- Viewing Activities: sightseeing, bird-watching, wildlife viewing
- Picnics: picnicking, family gathering
- Motor Sports: off-road driving, snowmobiling
- Snow Skiing: downhill skiing, cross-country skiing, snowboarding, snowshoeing
- Hiking, Climbing, etc.: day hiking, caving, mountain climbing, orienteering, rock climbing, backpacking, horseback riding
- Camping: primitive area camping, developed area camping
- Hunting: big game hunting, small game hunting, migratory bird hunting
- Freshwater Fishing: anadromous fishing, coldwater fishing, warmwater fishing
- Swimming: swimming in lakes, ponds, etc. (nonpool swimming)
- Mountain Biking
- Sailing, Floating, Rowing, etc.: kayaking, floating/rafting, rowing, sailing, sailboating/windsurfing, canoeing

Data Quality/Caveats: Forest recreation data were collected as part of the national survey on recreation designed to monitor total recreation participation, not just recreation in forests. Therefore, forest recreation totals are subject to respondents' interpretation of whether or not a particular activity was conducted in a "forest setting." Respondents were briefed on the expectation for what a forest setting was, however, it is not clear how uniformly this was interpreted by different respondents. For each activity (walking, picnicking, etc.), respondents were asked to first estimate the total number of times they participated in that activity each year. Second, respondents were asked to estimate the number of times they participated in that activity while in a forest setting. This information was used to estimate the proportion of participation in any given activity that occurred in a forest setting. The forest recreation participation values reported here are the product of the proportion of participation occurring in forests and the total amount of participation (calculated by taking the mean survey participation responses and weighting based on census data to obtain a total recreation value scaled to population and demographic characteristics). Data are presented as total recreation participation; data are not adjusted for changes in population over time.

Data Availability: The data reported here were obtained directly from the USDA Forest Service.

2008 Report Data Update: New data on recreation in forests were added for the period 2003–2005; data were revised for the period 1999–2001.

The Data Gap

The NSRE data only reports on recreation participation for adults over the age of 16. The next iteration of NSRE surveys will add a youth module targeting individuals 6 to 15 years of age.

Fresh Waters

Extent of Freshwater Ecosystems

The Indicator

This indicator tracks the extent of freshwater wetlands, lakes, ponds, rivers, and streams. The extent of wetlands, lakes and ponds are reported in acreage covered by each feature. Ponds are reported separately because they are smaller than lakes and ponds are often constructed and therefore should be distinguished from naturally-occurring lakes and wetlands. The extent of rivers and streams will be presented as the length (in stream miles) of small, medium, and large-sized rivers and streams. Additionally, riparian areas are characterized based on the land cover adjacent to the stream or river.

The Data
Wetlands, Lakes, Reservoirs, and Ponds

Data Source: Data for wetlands are from Dahl (2006). Data for lakes, reservoirs, and ponds are from Dahl (2006), Frayer et al. (1983), and unpublished data from the U.S. Fish and Wildlife Service.

Data Collection Methodology/Definitions: The data shown here are derived from the U.S. Fish and Wildlife Service's National Wetlands Inventory (NWI; see p. 272), which produces periodic reports of changes in wetland area. For this indicator, decadal estimates from the NWI are presented as the midpoint of the decade. For example, "1980s" data are graphed as "1985."

The wetland types selected for reporting here were recommended as the most relevant and most reliable for long-term reporting by the NWI (see Dahl 2006). For wetlands, they include forested, shrub, and emergent wetlands. Ponds include the category of open-water ponds and nonvegetated palustrine wetlands (i.e., palustrine unconsolidated shore, which are mudflats and the shorelines of ponds); ponds are generally less than 6 ft (2 m) deep and less than 20 acres. Lakes and reservoirs are generally larger than 20 acres and deeper than 6 ft, although smaller bodies are included if they are deeper than 6 ft or have a wave-formed or bedrock shoreline.

Data Quality/Caveats: Ephemeral wetlands and effectively drained palustrine wetlands observed in farm production are not recognized as a wetland type and are not included. Wetlands that are farmed during dry years but that normally support hydrophytic vegetation were classified as freshwater emergent wetlands.

The U.S. Geological Survey's (USGS) National Hydrography Dataset (NHD) also has information on lake, reservoir, and pond area (at least 6 acres). Considerably higher total acreage (26.8 million acres) is found using this resource. NWI was used because time trends are possible; the cause of the disparity among datasets is not known.

Data Availability: The Status and Trends of Wetlands in the Conterminous United States 1998 to 2004 is available on the Web at http://wetlandsfws.er.usgs.gov/status_trends/index.html.

Riparian Area Land Cover

Data Source: Data are based on the National Land-Cover Dataset (NLCD; see p. 274) and the National Hydrography Dataset (NHD). The NHD is a comprehensive set of digital spatial data that encodes information about naturally occurring and constructed bodies of water (see http://nhd.usgs.gov/). Data on the vegetation cover within 100 ft of streams and rivers were produced by analysts with the U.S. EPA and the U.S. Forest Service.

Data Manipulation: Data from the NHD were combined with land-cover data from the NLCD to identify the dominant land cover along streams and rivers. For each stream reach described in the NHD land cover was characterized in a band ~100 ft wide on either side of the stream. NLCD land cover classes were aggregated to produce four general categories: forested, agricultural, urban, and "other natural vegetation" (grasslands, shrublands, and woody and emergent wetlands). It is important to note that some of these land-cover types may not be the historical (i.e., natural) vegetation for that site, or may have been altered in other ways. This terminology is used to highlight the contrast with the highly altered land covers (urban, agricultural).

Data Quality/Caveats: Based on the underlying data, a distance of roughly 100 ft from the edge of a stream to define "riparian" area. We recognize that no single width is appropriate in all situations. The NLCD and the NHD are currently the most comprehensive datasets available for land cover and freshwater resources, respectively. However, both of these contain inaccuracies that could affect the calculations presented here. Not all hydrographic features are equally well-characterized, and smaller streams are poorly represented in the NHD.

2008 Report Data Update: New data from the 2001 NLCD were added (see above). At the time the analyses, the 2001 NLCD was not comparable to the 1992 NLCD, which had been used in the 2002 edition of this report, only the 2001 data were included.

The Data Gap

Information on the number of small, medium, and large streams and rivers is not available. There may soon be a tool within the NHD-Plus dataset to allow determination of stream order. Flow rate is a much more difficult parameter to determine. In addition, NHD may understate the extent of small streams (see above). Because the rate of conversion and alteration of small streams is believed to be higher than for larger streams, it is important to ensure as great a coverage of small streams as is feasible. For a discussion of the effects of human activities on small streams, see Meyer and Wallace (2001).

Altered Freshwater Ecosystems

The Indicator

This indicator reports the percentage of freshwater ecosystems (rivers and streams, riparian areas, wetlands, and lakes, ponds, and reservoirs) that are classified as "altered". Altered is defined differently for each of the following:

Rivers and streams (all flowing surface waters) are altered if they are leveed, channelized, or impounded behind a dam. Other types of alterations to streams that may be important include changes in sedimentation and temperature, and barriers to movement between stream reaches. Both the stream habitat quality (p. 179) and changing stream flows (p. 47) indicators provide important complementary information on stream conditions.

Riparian areas along rivers and streams are considered altered if they have a predominance of urban or agricultural land use within a zone extending roughly 100 ft from its centerline.

Lakes and ponds are considered altered if the area immediately adjacent to the shoreline has land cover that is predominantly urban or agricultural. This indicator focuses on "natural" waterbodies, that is, those that are not created by impoundment behind a dam (reservoirs).This indicator will be limited to natural waterbodies.

Wetlands are considered altered if they are excavated, impounded, diked, partially drained, or farmed. These categories are used by the U.S. Fish and Wildlife Service's National Wetlands Inventory; they are defined in Cowardin et al. (1979). Wetlands fragmentation (subdivision into smaller and more isolated patches by filling, roads, or other alterations) is also important, but measurement of this change requires detailed site-specific information.

The Data

The methods used to produce the data reported here for altered riparian areas are described in the preceding technical note. The same method could be used to classify the shorelines of ponds and lakes, but the NHD does not distinguish between natural and impounded lakes/reservoirs.

2008 Report Data Update: New data from the 2001 NLCD were prepared for this indicator (see preceding technical note).

The Data Gap

There is no nationally aggregated database of the number of impounded river miles or the number of leveed river miles. There is also no method for calculating the extent of downstream effects of dams, other than by conducting site-specific investigations for each dam.

No nationally aggregated database distinguishes impounded waterbodies from natural ones, or identifies which natural lakes are dammed at their outlets. It is possible that existing databases on dam locations, such as those maintained by the U.S. Army Corps of Engineers, could be merged with other datasets, such as the National Hydrography Dataset, to derive this information.

Data on altered wetlands are available through the U.S. Fish and Wildlife Service's National Wetlands Inventory (see http://www.nwi.fws.gov/). At present, these data are not available in electronic form for the entire United States. The Fish and Wildlife Service is in the process of integrating these data more fully, however, they will be from different time periods in different states, and there is no plan for periodic updating. In addition, there are no plans to produce regional or national reports comparing any updates with past data.

In-Stream Connectivity

The Indicator

This indicator will report on the length of free-flowing stream or river that is below the "pour point" of small watersheds, called subwatersheds, to the nearest downstream dam or diversion. The data would be reported regionally, breaking out those subwatersheds that had unimpeded flow all the way to their natural terminus (e.g., lake or ocean). Changes in connectivity will affect species and processes differently. For example, invertebrates that need to move relatively short distances to complete their life cycles will not necessarily be affected the same way that a far-ranging migratory fish species will. Also, the flow of sediments will not be impeded equally by all dams and diversions.

Higher connectivity within a river system leads to the opportunity for biota to maintain a higher diversity of migratory behaviors, which has been linked—in fish and mussels—to higher probabilities of persistence of individual species and to greater species richness; this presumably holds true for other species as well. In addition, higher connectivity means that more tributary streams are connected to each other, presenting increased opportunities for dispersal, recolonization, and the metapopulation dynamics these can create, permitting broader occupation of historic species ranges, and likely contributing further to increased species persistence and diversity.

A more complex metric might evaluate the length of unobstructed river network both upstream and downstream of a given dam or diversion. As data become available (see below) this may be a simple addition to the current scope of the indicator. Another concept would be to have one metric evaluate the degree of connectivity within a subwatershed and another metric describe the connectivity of that subwatershed to the downstream stream network.

The Data Gap

Briefly, the digital maps of the stream network are of varying quality and detail across the country, and the available data for dams are frequently inaccurate (see http://www.heinzctr.org/ ecosystems for a forthcoming Landscape Pattern Task Group report).Work under way on the National Hydrography Dataset (NHD; http://nhd.usgs.gov) and the NHD-plus (http://www. horizon-systems.com/nhdplus/) should provide data useful for this indicator in the coming years. Note that whereas diversions are nominally considered to be equal to dams in this indicator, minimum characteristics of a diversion will need to be defined (e.g., a diversion causes zero flow events at some point during the year). Data are expected to be less readily available for diversions, and they have not been included in the analyses described here.

Phosphorus in Lakes, Reservoirs and Large Rivers

The Indicator

Total phosphorus (TP) was selected for reporting because it is a comprehensive measure of the many operationally defined and chemical forms of phosphorus, most of which are directly or indirectly available for plant growth. TP includes all forms of phosphorus present in a water sample—dissolved and particulate, inorganic and organic; adsorbed onto suspended clays and hydrous oxides; present in planktonic organisms and in organic detritus; and phosphorus in dissolved natural organic matter. Phosphorus in macrophytes, fish, and bottom sediments generally is not included.

TP levels are a measure of trophic state (Carlson 1977) and general water quality in lakes, reservoirs, and large rivers. (Large rivers typically behave as lakes; water residence times in stretches of large rivers are sufficiently long that substantial phytoplankton growth can occur in them.) The concentrations of TP that contribute to symptoms of eutrophication are poorly understood for flowing waters, but generally they are thought to be higher than the critical levels in lakes. Consequently, TP is reported separately for lakes and rivers. (The effects of phosphorus enrichment are different for lakes and rivers in tropical areas than they are for temperate zones; this discussion relates to temperate zones only.)

TP measurements are straightforward; TP in lakes should be reported as an average over the growing season (e.g., April to September), which will require several samples over the course of the period. Sampling frequency (e.g., Knowlton et al. 1984) and complications of sampling in areas with minimal seasonal influence, such as Florida (Brown et al. 1998) have been studied.

TP measurements in rivers are restricted to those large rivers with flows exceeding 1000 ft^3 per second (cfs). Time-weighted average concentrations were determined for 1996–2000 and 2001–2005. To ensure proper characterization of average values for each river, only sites that had at least 4 samples per year collected during all seasons of the year in at least four of the five years for each period were included in the analysis. Whereas this is a small number of samples per year, Crawford (2004) has shown that for selected pesticides in large rivers 4 samples per year collected seasonally can provide a reasonably accurate time-weighted annual mean concentration.

These findings should hold true for TP concentrations in large rivers as well, as both TP and most pesticides typically have a pronounced seasonal pattern.

Information on the 1986 phosphorus recommended goal for preventing excess algae growth can be found in EPA 440/5-86-001 (see USEPA 1986). Information on regional criteria for TP can be found at http://www.epa.gov/ waterscience/criteria/nutrient/ecoregions.

The Data

Data Source: Data for river phosphorus are from sites operated by the U.S. Geological Survey (USGS). Most are from the National Water Quality Assessment (NAWQA) Program or the National Stream Water Quality Accounting Network (NASQAN). Data were available for 86 sites. The median number of samples at the 86 sites used was 49 for the 1996–2000 and 56 for the 2001–2005 (the range was 16 to over 100).

The NAWQA Program is described elsewhere (see p. 272). While that note describes data collection from streams with relatively homogenous land cover (and often relatively low discharge volumes), the data used in this indicator are from larger rivers, with both larger discharge volumes and watersheds with generally more diverse land uses. Thus, these samples represent the integrating influences of many different land uses.

At present, NASQAN characterizes loads from four major river basins: the Mississippi, the Rio Grande, the Colorado, and the Columbia River. NASQAN stations are located on major tributaries in the four river basins, along the mainstem of rivers where there is a large increase in flow, and upstream and downstream from large reservoirs. The program generally measures both streamflow and a broad range of chemical constituents. An extensive quality-assurance/quality-control program enables constituents present in very low concentrations (micrograms per liter, roughly parts per billion) to be measured with definable accuracy and precision. See http://water.usgs.gov/nasqan/progdocs/index.html.

Because there was concern over the use of STORET data for this indicator (see below) with respect to the possibility that sampling locations might be strongly influenced by virtue of being located near outfalls from wastewater treatment plants, the location of sampling sites was also examined with respect to the NAWQA/NASQAN data. These programs collect data using procedures that ensure that the sample is representative of the entire stream cross-section. So, even if the stream at the point of collection was not well mixed, the samples would still be representative of the entire stream flow. In addition, the measure that is being reported—annual time-weighted average concentrations—addresses the potential concern that samples might be overly representative of summer low flows when wastewater effluent can comprise a large fraction of the flow in some rivers.

Data Access: Data were obtained directly from USGS staff.

2008 Report Data Update: Major river data are included for two time periods in this report, 1991–96 and 2001–2005, compared to only one time period in the 2002 report, 1991–1996. The earlier data were dropped in this report in order to include more sampling sites in the analysis. In this report, sites were included in the analysis if there were at least 4 samples per year collected during all seasons of the year in at least four of the five years for each period (see discussion above); in 2002, sites were included if they has at least 30 samples over the course of 30 years.

The Data Gap

In assessing the availability of data for reporting on phosphorus in large lakes and rivers, we reviewed two major datasets in addition to the one reported here (NAWQA/NASQAN). These were STORET, maintained as a data repository by the Environmental Protection Agency (http://www.epa.gov/storet/), and within STORET, data from the National Water Information System (NWIS), a USGS maintained data system (http://water.usgs.gov/nwis/). See the 2002 edition of this report for details of this analysis that suggested a significant potential for STORET data to be unrepresentative; we thus decided that it would be inappropriate to rely on it until it can be shown to be a suitable data source.

The U.S.EPA is beginning a survey of lakes in the U.S., which will provide data on a variety of parameters, including nutrients. Monitoring data will be compiled at regional and national scales and will include information on the percentage of lakes in good, fair and poor condition. A final report is expected in 2009 (see http://www.epa.gov/owow/lakes/lakessurvey/).

Freshwater Acidity

The Indicator

This indicator reports on the amount of acid deposition in the U.S. and the potential for effects on freshwater ecosystems. Long-term atmospheric deposition of nitrogen and sulfur compounds is associated with acidification of soils and water bodies, mobilization of heavy metals, and impairment of biological condition in lakes and streams, such as change in the number and types of species present and alteration of freshwater food webs. The amount and effect of acidic inputs depend on several factors including variation in regional deposition patterns, acidifying effects of different nitrogen and sulfur species (see Lehmann et al, 2005 and 2006) and soil properties—high levels of base-forming cations (e.g., calcium, magnesium) can offset acidic inputs before soil pH is lowered and acidic water is exported to streams and lakes. Acid Neutralizing Capacity (ANC) is a measure of the abundance of acid-neutralizing ions in water—which is controlled by geophysical factors and acidic inputs—and is commonly used to understand how much more acid can streams and lakes can absorb with minimal changes to pH. When ANC values fall below 0 microequivalents (μEq) per liter, streams are considered acidic and can be directly or indirectly toxic to biota. Streams are considered sensitive to episodic acidification during rainfall events when ANC values fall between 0 and 25 μEq per liter.

The Data

Data Description:
Atmospheric Deposition: Data on annual atmospheric deposition of wet inorganic nitrogen and sulfate were gathered by the National Atmospheric Deposition Program through a national system of monitors (ranging from 192 to 260 monitoring sites over the 1985–2005 reporting period). Wet deposition of inorganic nitrogen (nitrate plus ammonium) and sulfate is measured through chemical analysis of rainwater samples. For each year, data from monitors with less than 75% of valid samples, less than 90% of precipitation amounts available, less than 75% of total measured precipitation associated with samples and less than 75% collection efficiency (sum of sample bucket depths divided by sum of rain gage amounts) were excluded from analysis. For 1985 to 2005, data exclusion rates ranged from 13% to 33%. Data were grouped into reporting ranges based on the distribution of the data over the reporting period (i.e., reporting ranges do not correspond to deposition benchmarks or thresholds).

Acid Neutralizing Capacity (ANC): ANC data were collected through the Wadeable Streams Assessment (WSA)—see the WSA program description for more details (p. 270). In this indicator, stream miles are categorized by ranges of ANC values: greater than 25 μEq per liter (not sensitive), 0 to 25 μEq per liter (sensitive), and below 0 μEq per liter (acidic).

Data Quality/Caveats:
Atmospheric Deposition: To fully characterize atmospheric deposition of nitrogen and sulfate, both wet and dry deposition would be reported—dry deposition constitutes ~20% to ~80% of total deposition depending on location and climate (US EPA, 2007b)—but the NADP network currently measures wet deposition only. Organic nitrogen, which has been estimated to constitute as much as a third of total nitrogen deposition (Neff et al., 2002), is not included in NADP measurements. Also, the NADP network may not fully characterize atmospheric deposition in high elevation areas due to site distribution.

Acid Neutralizing Capacity (ANC): Nationally, 4.1% of the WSA's target streams were not assessed for ANC; 9.5% of Eastern Highlands streams (primarily first order streams) were not assessed even though this region is likely to be significantly affected by acidification. Values for ANC are based on the quantity of inorganic base cations (Ca^{2+}, Mg^{2+}, Na^+, K^+) and inorganic acid anions ($SO4^{2-}$, $NO3^-$, Cl^-), but do not account for naturally-occurring organic acids (Lawrence et al., 2007). Notably, seasonal variation in ANC values is not captured by the WSA program which sampled stream sites during a summer index period. In general, spring high flow is associated with lower ANC values and late summer/fall "base flow" is associated with higher ANC values (i.e., chronic rather than episodic acidification). Summer "base flow" measurements offer interannual consistency in assessing trends over time (i.e., may be more useful for identifying chronic rather than acute acidity). While the WSA sampling program was not designed explicitly for the purpose of characterizing stream acidity (chemical sampling was intended to support a primary focus on biological condition), WSA data are reported here because ANC measurements were collected through a nationally representative stream survey which is scheduled for repetition on a 5-year cycle. The EPA's Temporally Integrated Monitoring of Ecosystems (TIME) and Long-Term Monitoring (LTM) datasets were also considered, however these programs were implemented only in northeastern regions primarily affected by acidification (i.e., sampling was concentrated on waters likely to be at the greatest risk of acidification, but did not include all geographic areas with acid-sensitive lakes and streams). The absence of sampling in the Southeast, West and much of the Midwest made these datasets inappropriate for national-scale reporting. Also, within sampled regions, there was substantial variation in the sampling frames used.

Data Availability:
Atmospheric Deposition: Data are available from the National Atmospheric Deposition Program. Links to tabular and mapped data are available at (http://nadp.sws.uiuc.edu/).

Acid Neutralizing Capacity (ANC): Sampling data are available in the U.S. Environmental Protection Agency's national STORET data warehouse (http://www.epa.gov/storet/). Links to the warehouse and directions on how to find the WSA data are available at (http://www.epa.gov/owow/streamsurvey/web_data.html).

2008 Report Data Update: New indicator.

The Data Gap

Atmospheric Deposition: Currently, dry deposition of nitrogen and sulfate cannot be directly measured due to technical constraints. The Clean Air Status and Trends Network (CASTNet) estimates dry deposition flux based on particle, gas and meteorological measurements and land surface features (http://www.epa.gov/castnet/). These data do not yet support national reporting on dry deposition.

Acid Neutralizing Capacity (ANC): Data for acid neutralizing capacity in lakes and ponds are not available, but will be gathered in future EPA assessments.

Water Clarity

The Indicator

Water clarity is believed to be a good indicator of the trophic status of lakes and reservoirs. Those lakes rich in nutrients (eutrophic) often have abundant algal growth and, therefore, lower water clarity. Lakes with low nutrient concentrations (oligotrophic) typically have high transparency or clarity. Mesotrophic lakes are intermediate between oligotrophic and eutrophic. Lower clarity can be linked with excessive algal growth that can lead to low-oxygen conditions at nighttime that can be harmful to fish and other animals. A lake's clarity can be linked with other aspects of ecological functioning, such as sufficient light for submerged aquatic plants as well as to support feeding activity of fish and other animals. Water clarity affects people's enjoyment of lakes and reservoirs, including swimming and boating, and it influences the quality of drinking water.

Water clarity is primarily affected by the abundance of algae, the concentration of organic matter (humic material), and soil-derived clay and silt particles. Land-use change, especially conversion of forest or wetlands to agriculture or urban development can disturb soil and lead to increased erosion and decreased water clarity. Algal abundance is often related to the nutrient concentration of fresh waters. Nutrients can be added to lakes and reservoirs by the streams and rivers that feed them or directly by runoff from the land surface (see the various nutrient indicators, including Phosphorus in Lakes, Reservoirs, and Large Rivers, p. 174; and Nitrate in Farmland Streams and Groundwater, p. 107). A recent paper by Baker et.

al (2008) found that in Minnesota lakes, phosphorus runoff alone was not a significant predictor of lake water clarity, but rather nutrient runoff, shoreline development, and watershed land use in combination likely influenced water clarity.

This technical note assumes that water clarity will be measured in lakes and reservoirs by the Secchi-disk method. Remote sensing using satellite data may be reported in the future as an alterative method of measuring water clarity at larger scales. Secchi depth measurements of water clarity (or transparency) will be reported in three ranges: low (<3 ft), medium (3–10 ft), and high (>10 ft).

Water clarity values for lakes and reservoirs will be reported in two ways: by lake area falling into the low, medium, and high categories, and as averages for freshwater ecoregions. (Ecoregions are geographic areas having similar climate, geography and ecological conditions (cf. Ricketts et al., 1997)). Measurements should be made annually during an "index" period near the height of the algal growing season, which generally corresponds with the height of the recreational use season. In lakes of the Upper Midwest, for example, the index period is mid-July to mid- September, when Secchi-disk transparency is relatively constant and at annual minimum values. The appropriate length of the index period in other parts of the country needs to be determined, but the mid-July to mid-September period should be suitable for all lakes in temperate climate zones. One measurement during this period should be adequate to define ecoregional growing-season minimum values, although one measurement is not sufficient to define the minimum transparency for an individual lake. Humic-colored lakes and lakes with clay turbidity tend not to have a strong seasonal pattern in water clarity, so a mid-to-late summer sampling period designed to capture the peak influence of algal growth on transparency should also be appropriate for these lakes and reservoirs.

Ponds have been excluded from this indicator, mostly because the hydraulic properties of ponds are quite different from those of lakes. Because of their shallow nature (typically less than 2 m or 6.5 ft), ponds can readily be completely mixed by strong winds. Such mixing can suspend sediments in the water column, which would decrease clarity. Lakes (and reservoirs) typically have a warm layer of water at the surface (epilimnion) that does not easily mix with deeper, colder waters (hypolimnion). Full wind-driven mixing of lakes typically occurs only during the fall and spring when temperatures are fairly uniform across all depths.

The Data Gap

Two approaches for measuring water clarity are measurements of Secchi depth and satellite-based estimates. Since 1994, the U.S. Environmental Protection Agency (EPA) has supported an impressive program that aggregates Secchi disk measurements made by volunteers during July across parts of the United States and Canada (The Great North American Secchi Dip-In; see http://dipin.kent.edu). Because clarity is greatly affected by algal blooms, measurements of clarity should be carried out at the height of the growing season (mid-July to mid-September) in each ecoregion, which may or may not fit with the July observations of the Dip-In program. In addition, scientists are developing ways to measure water clarity from satellite data, which could greatly improve our understanding of how water clarity varies across the country and over time.

Several states (Minnesota and Wisconsin in particular) have extensive volunteer monitoring programs coordinated by state agencies, and some state agencies have extensive collections of historical data.

Using satellite imagery is promising as a way of obtaining essentially complete coverage of lake water clarity. This approach is being tested by a NASA-funded consortium involving the Universities of Minnesota, Wisconsin, and Michigan. The consortium is applying a recently developed protocol using Landsat satellite images from the early 1990s and from 1999 to all lakes over 50 acres in the three-state region (see http://resac.gis.umn.edu/water/regional_water_clarity/regional_water_clarity.htm and Kloiber et al. 2000). For a recent analysis of regional water clarity in lakes of Minnesota using remote sensing see Brezonik et al. 2007.

Stream Habitat Quality

This technical note also serves as the technical note for Stream Habitat Quality in the Farmlands chapter (p. 115).

The Indicator
The indicator reports the percentage of stream miles in the lower 48 states with stream sediments in "natural", moderate and degraded condition as well as the percentage of stream-miles with in-stream fish habitat features in "natural", "moderate" and "degraded condition". When data become available, it will also report on riffles and pools.

Habitat quality is a relative value, meaning that it must be evaluated in relation to the habitat needs of the native flora and fauna in a region. Therefore, this indicator is calibrated using regional references; all metrics of stream habitat quality are measured against the values that would be found in a relatively undisturbed or "natural" reference stream in that region.

The Data
Data Description: Data were provided by the U.S. Environmental Protection Agency, Office of Water and are part of EPA's Wadeable Streams Assessment (2006; http://www.epa.gov/owow/streamsurvey). See the program note on the Wadeable Streams Assessment for more information (p. 270).

Data Manipulation: Sediment and in-stream fish habitat data were collected by EPA, states, tribes and other federal agencies from over 1,392 wadeable perennial stream locations in the lower 48 states over a five-year period. The statistical sampling design allows for representative coverage of wadeable streams in three major climatic and landform regions and nine ecological regions during the summer index period (during base-flow conditions).

Streambed sediments were measured using a relative bed stability index. This metric scales the particle size found in the streambed to that expected, given the stream's scale and hydrology as well as channel characteristics. It is calculated as the mean bed particle diameter, quantified by pebble counts, divided by the diameter of the mobile or "critical" particle size. The critical particle size is computed based on the stream flows at flood stage and the shear force that it takes to mobilize sediment given particular channel conditions (Dingman 1984; Kauffmann et al. 1999). This indicator focuses only on low

relative bed stability, measuring the extent to which streambed sediments are finer and more unstable than sediments in regional, "least-impacted" reference streams (US EPA 2006). Sites with index scores 75 to 95% lower than the reference streams were identified as 'moderate,' whereas sites with index scores lower than 95% of the reference streams were identified as "degraded".

In-stream fish habitat features were measured as using a habitat complexity method (XFC_NAT) that sums the amount of undercut banks, boulders, large pieces of wood, brush and cover from vegetation within a meter of the water surface (Kauffman et al. 1999). Because of the variability of habitat components in different regions, stream sites are scaled against "least-disturbed" reference sites in their region (U.S. EPA 2006). Sites with habitat complexity scores 75 to 95% lower than the reference streams were identified as 'moderate,' whereas sites with habitat complexity scores lower than 95% of the reference streams were identified as "degraded".

Data Quality/Caveats: Data are based on single samples taken once (during the summer index period, during base flow) over a four year period, and therefore do not integrate seasonal changes.

Data Availability: Sampling data are available in the U.S. Environmental Protection Agency's national STORET data warehouse (http://iaspub.epa.gov/storpubl/DW_home). Links to the warehouse and directions on how to find the WSA data are available at (http://www.epa.gov/owow/streamsurvey/web_data.html).

2008 Report Data Update: Partial data are included in the report for the first time; the indicator had inadequate data for national reporting in 2002.

The Data Gap
At the current time there are no national data on riffles and pools. If and when such data become available, it may be prudent to develop a nation stream quality index which combines data on stream bed sediments, in-stream habitat features and riffles and pools. Such an index was recommended in the 2002 State of the Nation's Ecosystems report.

At-Risk Native Freshwater Species

The Indicator
This indicator reports on the conservation status of native freshwater species across their full range (i.e., global ranks) as well as population trends of native species that are at-risk of extinction. The species reported here are those in groups (such as mammals, birds, and fish) that are sufficiently well known that their conservation status, habitat, and location (by state) can be assigned with some degree of confidence for all members of the group.

The conservation status assessment for each species is an attempt to determine its relative susceptibility to extinction. The assessment process is based on consideration of up to 12 factors that relate to a species' degree of imperilment or risk of extinction throughout its range. Rare species are particularly vulnerable to extinction and so several aspects of rarity are characterized in the assessment process including population size, number of populations, and range extent and area of occupancy. However, trends in population and range size as well as magnitude and immediacy of threats are also important considerations in assessing a species' overall vulnerability or risk of extinction. More information on this ranking process can be found in the program note describing NatureServe (p. 275), at http://www.natureserve.org/explorer/ranking.htm and in Master (1991).

There is general recognition among experts that both status information (as presented here for animal species) and trend information (as presented here for vertebrate animals) are critical to understanding the condition of species.

The Data

For information on the NatureServe program data collection, methods, data quality/caveats, data availability, see p. 275.

Data Source: NatureServe (http://www.natureserve.org/) and its member programs in the network of Natural Heritage programs develop and maintain information on each of the species reported here.

Data Manipulation: Information on NatureServe methods in general can be found on p. 275. All data manipulations were performed by NatureServe. For the freshwater indicator, species were first identified as "freshwater species." In this process, species were assigned to fresh waters if they live in fresh water during at least part of their life cycle and depend on fresh water for their survival. This was a generally conservative approach; in preparing these lists, only species that are strongly associated with fresh water were included. This means that some species that make frequent use of fresh water may be excluded, but also that the group of species reported for fresh water is quite representative of species that are dependent upon freshwater habitats for their survival. Groups reported for the freshwater indicator are fresh water and anadromous fish; mammals; birds; reptiles (snakes and lizards); crocodiles and alligators; turtles; amphibians; freshwater mussels; freshwater snails; crayfish; fairy, clam, and tadpole shrimp; butterflies and skippers; and dragonflies and damselflies. Combined, these groups include over 4100 freshwater species.

2008 Report Data Update: The population trend metric was added to the indicator. Conservation status data from the 2002 Report were replaced with 2006 data.

The Data Gap

Data are not reported for native freshwater plants because habitat types have not been identified for all plant species. Critically imperiled and imperiled plants (G1 and G2) have been assigned habitat types, and NatureServe is currently working to assign vulnerable (G3) plants to habitats, but the habitat types of plants with more secure status remains unknown. Population trend data are not included for at-risk invertebrate animals, because trends are known for only 32% of invertebrate animal species in fresh waters.

Established Non-Native Freshwater Species

The Indicator

This indicator reports the percentage of all hydrologic units (a technical term that is often used synonymously with watersheds; see below) having one of several ranges of established non-native species. See the technical note for the core non-native species indicator (p. 283) for a definition of "non-native" used in this report. Ideally, this indicator would track only invasive species (those non-native species that spread aggressively), perhaps by reporting on a selected group of problematic or potentially problematic species, as identified by recognized experts. However, it is not now possible to identify potentially problematic species, and thus we have chosen to report on all established non-native species. It is important to note that hydrologic units, which are represented by hydrologic unit codes (HUCs), can be loosely thought of as watersheds. However, only at the finest resolution is this accurate. Thus, the HUCs shown in the indicator's map may include multiple watersheds in whole or in part, or they may actually represent a single watershed.

The Data

Data Description: Data were derived from the Nonindigenous Aquatic Species Database, Biological Resources Division (BRD), U.S. Geological Survey (USGS). Roughly 82% of the data are derived from the published literature. Data are collected for the most part by federal and state biologists, although the public does contribute by reporting sightings.

Data Manipulation: Data for introduced species are maintained in a database whose units are 6-digit HUCs (there are 356 6-digit HUCs across the lower 48 states). USGS staff spent a considerable amount of effort to distinguish *established* species from all non-native fish species (see data quality/caveats section below).

Data Quality/Caveats: In the 2002 Report, data in this indicator were incorrectly noted as "established" non-native species. The NAS database does not fully distinguish between all introduced species and established non-native species, a subset of introduced species which have successfully-reproducing populations. For the 2008 Report, the USGS has prepared revised data which represent a best effort to report currently *established* populations of introduced fishes nationwide. Future numbers in these regions may increase due to new introductions, new data being entered, or by determining a species is established in an area where the status was not known. Although the BRD database (Web site listed below) is widely known throughout the professional community, in some cases new discoveries are not reported by state and federal biologists. Note that it is often difficult to know the status of a population at a particular location based on literature. Literature often makes reference to the presence of a species or maps it without saying if the species is established or how many were collected.

Because stocked populations are functionally the same as established populations (both have a population of fish present in an area that will use resources), those species were also included. Many of these species (e.g., trout, esocids) are stocked annually on a put and take basis to ensure there are high enough numbers to allow for good angling. Even if not stocked annually, these fish live for many years.

Species that have been extirpated or eradicated have not been included, even if they were formerly reproducing; numbers may decrease if a population becomes extirpated. Collections of single (or small numbers of) individuals are not included where there is no evidence for reproduction.

Note that reported values that appear to have increased between 2002 and 2007 may not be real increases but rather due to publications in that timeframe that reported on introductions not previously in the literature (i.e. new state fish books).

Data Availability: While these types of data are available on BRD's Nonindigenous Aquatic Species (NAS) Web site (http://nas.er.usgs.gov/), the actual data presented here were prepared for this report by USGS.

2008 Report Data Update: In the 2002 Report, data in this indicator were incorrectly noted as "established" non-native species. For the 2008 Report, the USGS has provided revised data which, to the best of their knowledge, represents only *established* non-native fish populations. See *Data Quality/Caveats,* above, for more information.

The Data Gap
NAS includes information on a host of vertebrates, invertebrates, algae, and plants. At this time, however, the database managers do not feel that these data have matured adequately to be presented at the national level.

Animal Deaths and Deformities

The Indicator
This indicator reports both the unusual mortalities in fish, freshwater aquatic mammals (such as otter or beaver) and waterfowl (i.e., ducks, geese, swans), as well as the incidence of deformities in amphibians. An unusual mortality event is defined using multiple criteria; including the number of individuals involved, time period, location, species status (endangered, threatened), cause of death, and credibility of reporting. Most mortality events involve multiple individuals (from three to over 10,000); however, a single death might be considered for inclusion in this indicator if the particular circumstances warranted it—for example, if the bird was part of a flock that was known to have fed at a contaminated site.

This indicator reports mortality events according to the number of individuals involved in each reported event. When data for different species groups become available, it may be necessary to use categories (such as serious, severe and catastrophic) rather than numbers of individuals. This would facilitate comparison of mortality events among different species.

The Data Gap
Waterfowl and wildlife mortalities
Data on animal mortalities are collected by the Department of the Interior, U.S. Geological Survey, Biological Resource Division, National Wildlife Health Center (NWHC). NWHC is a research and diagnostic laboratory, with a primary focus on disease prevention, detection, and control in free-ranging wildlife. NWHC maintains a database of outbreaks of wildlife disease and unusual mortalities, usually affecting multiple animals at the same time. The database covers all 50 states,

Puerto Rico, and the U.S. Virgin Islands, and covers wildlife disease and mortality events over the past 25 years. The database contains information on avian, mammalian, and amphibian mortality events. Information in the database is provided by various sources, such as state and federal personnel, diagnostic laboratories, wildlife refuges, and published reports.

The NWHC database is the most complete and comprehensive resource for documenting wildlife disease over time. However, the data are not adequate for national reporting on trends because the data reported to NWHC may not accurately reflect all causes or cases of mortality, and data are heavily influenced by reporting effort. NWHC is not informed of every mortality event. Smaller events, in particular, may be handled locally and may not be reported to NWHC. The decision whether or not to include a reported event in the database is made by NWHC specialists. In addition, the database was not developed as a tool for reporting on national trends; it was intended for use by NWHC as a tool for tracking epidemiological information over time. The information is generally not from specifically defined surveillance and monitoring systems; rather, information is provided as events are discovered or reported. Furthermore, changes in agency coordination and governance in the mid-1990's likely influenced reporting effort of wildlife mortalities. Prior to the mid-1990's, managers at wildlife refuges were required by law to report wildlife mortalities. After the NWHC became part of the USGS, managers were no longer mandated to report to NWHC and the visibility and compliance with reporting likely declined as a result. As the data presented in this indicator are sensitive to reporting effort they are not indicative of long-term trends in the number of individuals involved in mortality events or the incidence of events over time.

Fish
There is no program in place to collect information about freshwater fish die-offs.

Amphibian Deaths and Deformities
A recent report on the status and trends of amphibian populations worldwide found that amphibians are declining at faster rates than either birds or mammals, with mortalities largely because of habitat loss, overexploitation (harvesting), and fungal disease (Stuart et al. 2004). International efforts, including the recently launched, Amphibian Ark project (see http://www.amphibianark.org/), are aiming to raise awareness and investment in new research on declining amphibian populations.

Additional monitoring of amphibian deformities is through The North American Reporting Center for Amphibian Malformations (NARCAM; see http://frogweb.nbii.gov/narcam/), a project of the U.S. Geological Survey's Northern Prairie Wildlife Research Center. NARCAM is not part of a structured monitoring system, but it cooperates with and receives information from several such monitoring programs, among them NAAMP (North American Amphibian Monitoring Project), Frogwatch USA, ARMI (Amphibian Research and Monitoring Initiative, see http://armi.usgs.gov/), and A Thousand Friends of Frogs. Wildlife refuge personnel, state fish and game agency staff, university students and researchers, and others who have conducted field surveys of amphibians also submit reports, as do members of the general public, who are able to use NARCAM's Web site to submit their reports directly online. As of July 2001, more than 2,000 verified reports, from 47 states and 4 Canadian provinces, had been included in the NARCAM database (see http://www.nbii.gov/portal/community/Communities/Plants,_Animals_&_Other_Organisms/Amphibians/Amphibian_Malformations/). Reports, however, are not evenly distributed among the states; Minnesota, where large numbers of malformed amphibians were first reported, accounts for 22% of all reports, Wisconsin for 12%, and Vermont for 12%. Another nine states account for 26% of all verified reports. According to NARCAM, it is often difficult to find trained volunteers (and funds) for amphibian surveying programs.

2008 Report Data Update: Data on waterfowl mortality events from the USGS, National Wildlife Health Center were reported in the 2002 Report. The data on waterfowl mortalities are no longer reported in this edition of the report because they are influenced by reporting effort and agency changes that prevent the comparisons of mortalities across years.

Status of Freshwater Animal Communities

This technical note also supports the urban and suburban indicator Animal Communities in Urban and Suburban Streams (p. 248).

The Indicator
This indicator measures the condition of fish and benthic macroinvertebrates in wadeable streams. Benthic macroinvertebrates are a heterogeneous assemblage of animal groups that inhabit the sediment or live in or on other bottom substrates in the aquatic environment. Macroinvertebrates are defined as organisms that cannot pass through a No. 30 sieve (0.6-mm, or 0.023-inch openings). The major taxonomic groups of freshwater benthic macroinvertebrates are the insects, annelids (worms), mollusks, flatworms, and crustaceans.

The Data
Data Description: Data are provided by the U.S. Environmental Protection Agency, Office of Water and are part of the EPA's Wadeable Streams Assessment (WSA) (USEPA 2006e; http://www.epa.gov/owow/streamsurvey). See the program description on the WSA for more information (p. 270).

Data Collection Methodology: Macroinvertebrate data were collected by EPA, states, tribes and other federal agencies from over 1,392 wadeable perennial stream locations in the lower 48 states over a five-year period. The statistical sampling design allows for representative coverage of wadeable streams in three major climatic and landform regions and nine ecological regions during the summer index period (during base-flow conditions).

The indicator uses a Macroinvertebrate Index of Biotic Condition to report on benthic animals (USEPA 2006e). The index is based on multiple metrics, which vary slightly by ecoregion, but include such factors as: taxa richness, the evenness of species across taxa, the relative abundance of different taxa, the feeding strategy of taxa, the habitat preference of taxa, and the tolerance of taxa to stressors. "Least-disturbed" reference sites were selected in each region using nine habitat and

water quality variables. To allow for more consistent national thresholds, the macroinvertebrate reference distribution was adjusted in five of the regions to account for the inclusion of somewhat disturbed sites among the reference sites. For each of the nine ecoregions, natural-moderate and moderate-degraded thresholds were set based on the distribution of the macro-invertebrate dataset at reference sites. Sites with index scores 75 to 95% lower than the reference streams were identified as 'moderate,' whereas sites with index scores lower than 95% of the reference streams were identified as degraded. On a scale from 0 to 100, the natural/moderate threshold ranged from an index value of 48 to 63, depending on region; the moderate / degraded threshold ranged from an index value of 34 to 49, depending on region.

Data Quality/Caveats: Data are based on samples taken once (during the summer index period) over a four year period, and therefore do not integrate changes at a site over time

Data Availability: Sampling data are available in the U.S. Environmental Protection Agency's national STORET data warehouse (see http://iaspub.epa.gov/storpubl/DW_home). Links to the warehouse and directions on how to find the WSA data are available at (http://www.epa.gov/owow/streamsurvey/web_data.html). Data used in this indicator were taken directly from the 2006 EPA WSA report.

2008 Report Data Update: Partial data are included in the report for the first time; the indicator had inadequate data for national reporting in 2002.

The Data Gap
Indices of biotic integrity (IBIs) have been developed for fish (see http://www.epa.gov/bioindicators/html/ibi-hist.html) but not at a national scale. IBI methods are also not well developed for major rivers at a national scale. The U.S. Environmental Protection Agency has established criteria for the bioassessment of lakes and reservoirs (US EPA 1998) and is currently monitoring the biological integrity of bottom-dwelling communities in lakes on a regional and national scale; data are expected by 2009 (see http://www.epa.gov/owow/lakes/lakessurvey/).

In order to develop a nationally consistent set of observations, there must be consistency in key aspects of the monitoring in different states or regions. IBI rankings must be based on common reference conditions, scoring methods must be consistent in different places, and the sampling design and intensity must not vary greatly. (regions that are more heavily sampled are more likely to reflect the "true" aggregated condition than areas that are not). A probability-based sampling design, as used in the WSA, can help account for potential regional bias in the selection of sampling sites by weighing such factors as size (e.g. stream order) and spatial distribution across the landscape.

At-Risk Freshwater Plant Communities

The Indicator
This indicator describes the percentage of freshwater plant communities in the U.S. that are at risk of elimination globally. Data are provided on the relative risk of elimination and on the percentage of at-risk freshwater communities in each state.

Risk is assessed based on such factors as the remaining number and condition of occurrences of the community, the remaining acreage, and the severity of threats to the community type. For the purposes of this report, wetlands are defined using the dominant vegetation (including all rooted aquatic species) and hydrologic properties of the National Wetlands Inventory (NWI; for information about the NWI program, see http://www.epa.gov/emap/; for information on the wetlands classification system, see http://www.fws.gov/nwi/Pubs_Reports/Class_Manual/class_titlepg.htm). Riparian areas are the margins of streams or rivers. Riparian areas include a range of plant communities, including both upland vegetation communities (often thriving on the increased moisture available near the stream or river) and wetland plant communities on the floodplain.

Nationally, plant communities are often defined according to the association concept, which is a plant community type of a specific floristic composition resulting from certain environmental conditions and displaying relatively uniform physiognomy. These communities form part of the U.S. National Vegetation Classification System (NVCS), which was adopted as the federal standard for vegetation information by the Federal Geographic Data Committee in 1997. The classification covers uplands as well as wetlands, but does not specifically distinguish all riparian communities.

In order to report on both wetland and riparian communities, this indicator uses NatureServe's terrestrial ecological classification system (Comer et al. 2003; http://www.natureserve.org/explorer/). This classification system identifies groups of plant community types (US-NVCS associations) that are found together in landscape settings with similar ecological processes and gradients (e.g., fire regime, elevation, climate, hydrologic regime), biological dynamics (e.g., succession), and other driving environmental features (e.g., soils, geology). In the conterminous U.S. there are 243 ecological systems types that are classified as wetland or riparian. This classification therefore allows us to specify all US-NVC associations that characterize all wetland and riparian environments.

The conservation status assessment for each community type is called a global rank and is based on the relative rarity and degree of imperilment of the community type across its entire geographic range.

The Data

Data Source: NatureServe and its Natural Heritage member programs develop and maintain information on each ecological system, including information on all component US-NVC associations. See the program note on p. 275 for more information on the NatureServe program.

Data Collection Methodology: NatureServe ecologists gather, review, and integrate available information about vegetation pattern and landscape characteristics from Natural Heritage program databases, published and unpublished literature, and ecology experts in each state. They then assess conservation status using standardized Heritage ranking criteria (see http://www.natureserve.org/explorer/ranking.htm). Heritage ranks range from 1 to 5, with 1 meaning critically imperiled; 2, imperiled; 3, vulnerable to extirpation or extinction; 4, apparently secure; and 5, demonstrably widespread, abundant, and secure.

Data Manipulation: The global ranks are summarized into "rounded ranks." For example, an actual rank may express substantial uncertainty about whether the community is "critically imperiled" or "imperiled." In all such cases, the rank has been rounded to the more imperiled one.

Data Quality/Caveats: Conservation status ranks are continually reviewed and revised by Natural Heritage program biologists. In addition, as development of the system of classifying plant communities evolves, more communities will be recognized in geographic areas that are currently "underclassified." Such revisions could affect the proportion of communities considered at-risk. NatureServe expects to have terrestrial ecological systems mapped and ranked for Alaska and Hawaii by 2012. Future reporting on trends in at-risk plant communities will likely emphasize changes in the extent and condition of ecological systems.

Data Access: Detailed, periodically updated information on each wetland and riparian ecological system and component plant community type, including its status, is available at http://www.natureserve.org/explorer.

2008 Report Data Update: In order to report on both wetland and riparian communities, the 2008 Report uses NatureServe's terrestrial ecological systems classification to identify both wetland and riparian US-NVC associations that form the focus of this indicator. The US-NVC on its own does not facilitate identification of all wetland and riparian associations of interest for this indicator.

Water Withdrawals

The Indicator

Five mutually exclusive categories of water use are reported: "Municipal" supply is water withdrawn by public and private water suppliers and delivered to homes and businesses for drinking, commercial, and industrial uses. "Rural" water use is self-supplied water for domestic use and for livestock. Water used for "Irrigation" includes application to crops, pastures, and recreational lands such as parks and golf courses. "Thermoelectric" is water used for cooling in the generation of electric power. "Industrial" water use includes self-supplied water (i.e., water not drawn from the municipal supply) for fabrication, processing, cooling, and washing. The industrial category includes commercial and mining uses of water.

The Data

Data Description: Using raw data collected by states and other sources, the U.S. Geological Survey (USGS) compiles estimates of water use for each use category and then aggregates the estimates for each state, Puerto Rico, and the U.S. Virgin Islands and for each of the 21 water-resources regions. The data have been published every five years since 1950 in the USGS Circular series *Estimated Use of Water in the United States*. More recent compilations are available electronically at http://water.usgs.gov/watuse/. Some state and federal agencies also publish reports on water use for specific states or categories of use.

Data Manipulation: Sources of information and accuracy of data vary by state and by water-use category (for more information see: http://pubs.er.usgs.gov/usgspubs/tm/tm4A4/). Most public-supply water withdrawals and deliveries are metered. In some states, large irrigation and industrial users are required to have water meters to measure the amount of water withdrawn. For other categories, such as self-supplied domestic ("rural") and small industries (self-supplied commercial), estimates of water use are derived from population or product output. Energy production data obtained from the Department of Energy are used in making water-use estimates for the thermoelectric power category. Information on acres irrigated is obtained from the Department of Agriculture's Census of Agriculture and its Farm and Ranch Irrigation Survey and from state universities. Information on public water supplies is obtained from the Environmental Protection Agency, state agencies, and individual water suppliers.

The steps required to transform the raw data into final form vary with the category of use and with the level of detail of the available raw data. Guidelines used for preparing the most recent estimates are available at http://water.usgs.gov/watuse/. In addition, sources of information and accuracy of data are discussed in the USGS circulars published every five years.

Data Quality/Caveats: The sources of data and the level of detailed information vary for each state, making it difficult to apply an error analysis to the national aggregate water-use estimates. As part of the compilation effort, each USGS compiler is required to provide justification when estimates change by more than 10% from the previous water-use compilation. Once the data are compiled at the state level, they are peer-reviewed by USGS regional water-use specialists and again by USGS national water-use specialists.

Additionally, states are not required to collect or report estimates of water withdrawals for all the categories included in this indicator; the impact this complication may have on the data is not known. Estimates for fresh, ground and surface water withdrawals by county are mandatory for: public-supply, self supplied domestic, industrial, irrigation, and thermoelectric power. "Optional" water use categories are: commercial, hydroelectric, and wastewater treatment, as is "irrigation conveyance loss"—water lost because of leakage or evaporation while in transit through a pipe, canal, conduit, or ditch.

Implementation of more stringent water quality standards (Amendments to the Federal Pollution Control Act of 1972 and 1977) promoted more efficient water use practices; reducing the amount of water used (*Estimated use of Water in the United States in 2000*; see technical note). Employment in the petroleum and coal industries started declining in 1985, likely contributing to the continued decline in water use (*Estimated Use of Water in the United States in 2000*; see technical note).

Data Availability: The data used here are available in the regular USGS Circular series *Estimated Use of Water in the United States* (for historical data) and at http://water.usgs.gov/watuse/ (for more recent data).

2008 Report Data Update: New data were not available for the 2008 Report. Data were lasted updated in the 2005 Web site update when data on water withdrawals for 2000 were obtained from the USGS (Hutson et al. 2004). At this time, the

USGS discontinued monitoring of "self-supplied Commercial" water withdrawals—previously combined with industrial and mining withdrawals in this indicator's "Industrial" category—in the 2000 *Estimated Use of Water in the United States*. Ideally, "Commercial" withdrawals would have been removed from the "industrial" category for all years. However, "Commercial" data could not be excluded from the entire dataset, because separate totals for the "Commercial" freshwater withdrawal component of the "Industrial" category were not available for the years 1960–1980. Note also, 2000 data exclude "Livestock" withdrawals that were not reported for 29 states.

Groundwater Levels

The Indicator

This indicator would describe changes in water levels in major regional aquifers by reporting the fraction of the total area of regional aquifers that declined, increased, or remained stable in comparison to a previous period, and would be reported every 5 years. An example of the kind of data that are available for some major aquifers, and which would be used to develop a national indicator, can be seen in a series of maps depicting changes in the High Plains aquifer, which underlies eight states in the central United States (see McGuire et al. 1999).

The Data Gap

This indicator would require extensive and intensive data on water levels in major regional aquifers (see below). It would also require a scheme for classifying changes in aquifer level as "significant increase," "significant decrease," or "no significant change." Changes in groundwater level have unique levels of significance in different aquifers; a change of a few feet in a shallow coastal aquifer may be quite important in terms of susceptibility to saltwater intrusion, whereas a change of 10 feet on a very large aquifer may not be as significant. Logically, the values for "stable" will be different in different aquifers (e.g., the High Plains case defined –5 feet to +5 feet as "no significant change"). Furthermore, the "significance" of a change in groundwater level can be related to ecosystem impacts as well as simply the availability of water for people. Therefore, definitions of significant increase or decrease (and thus, no significant change) should be determined on an aquifer-by-aquifer basis. Water-level data are available for all or parts of every state, but these data cannot be aggregated to provide national coverage because of limited coverage of most aquifer systems and lack of electronic availability of much of the monitoring data. The High Plains aquifer is one of the few multistate aquifers with systematic and coordinated water-level monitoring. States or areas with good water-level-monitoring programs include parts of Florida, Long Island (NY), Pennsylvania, and Utah. To ensure national coverage, the following points must be addressed:

- Data must be collected from areas that represent the full range of topographic, hydrogeologic, climatic, and land use environments within the major aquifers.
- Data must be collected using standardized methods from monitoring wells or other wells not affected by local pumping. Procedures for well selection and data collection are available in Chapter 2 of the USGS's 1980 National Handbook of Recommended Methods for Water-Data Acquisition.

- There must be agreement on timing of water-level measurements across the country so that the status of major aquifers in a region or in the entire country can be presented as a snapshot in time.
- Plans must be in place to ensure long-term viability of observation-well networks and data collection programs, including plans for a combination of data collection at long-term monitoring wells and periodic synoptic measurements.

There must be agreement among the agencies or other sources of data on electronic data storage, access, and dissemination. The agencies that will be responsible for leadership in compiling and publishing the data must be identified.

Waterborne Human Disease Outbreaks

The Indicator
This indicator will describe the number of human waterborne disease outbreaks attributed to drinking water; and swimming or other recreational contact from lakes, streams, or rivers.

Outbreaks associated with untreated or inadequately treated drinking water count toward the drinking water totals, and outbreaks associated with recreational fresh surface waters will be included in recreational water totals. Outbreaks associated with marine water (see related indicator in Coasts and Oceans chapter, p. 92), spas, whirlpools, hot tubs, and the like will not be reported. This indicator will exclude outbreaks because of problems of unknown origin or contamination of water or ice at the point of use (e.g., a contaminated water faucet).

The Data Gap
Previously, this indicator presented Centers for Disease Control and Prevention (CDC) data (http://www.cdc.gov/mmwr/sursumpv.html) on waterborne human disease outbreaks in drinking and recreational waters. These data are no longer reported in this indicator because they appear to be heavily influenced by reporting effort. This can occur because the state, territorial, and local public health departments that are primarily responsible for detecting and investigating waterborne outbreaks are not required to report them to the CDC. Thus, one county may be responsible for most of the outbreaks occurring in certain time period—even if the actual outbreak is more widespread—if that county was more diligent in investigating, documenting, and reporting outbreaks to CDC.

Additionally, various factors can affect the chances of an individual illness being linked to a water source. These include public awareness, the likelihood that ill people will consult the same health care provider, availability and extent of laboratory testing, local requirements for reporting cases of particular diseases, and the surveillance and investigative activities of state and local health and environmental agencies. Recognition of waterborne disease outbreaks is also dependent on certain outbreak characteristics; large interstate outbreaks and outbreaks involving serious illness are more likely to receive the attention of health authorities. Outbreaks associated with private water systems that serve a small number of residences or farms are the most likely to be underreported because they generally involve only a few people.

Cases of drinking or recreational waterborne human diseases must meet two criteria before the CDC will classify and report them as an outbreak: 1) two or more individuals must have a similar illness following exposure to drinking water or recreational water (exceptions where a single case is an "outbreak": laboratory-confirmed cases of primary amebic meningoencephalitis and chemical poisoning), and 2) epidemiological evidence must identify the drinking or recreational water as the likely cause of illness.

The CDC requests annual reports from state and territorial epidemiologists, or from persons designated as WBDO surveillance coordinators. The U.S. Environmental Protection Agency (EPA) and the Council of State and Territorial Epidemiologists assists with collection and reporting of waterborne disease outbreaks, and collects additional information on water quality and treatment as needed from state drinking water agencies.

The CDC and EPA are currently addressing how to improve the reporting system, and the EPA's National Drinking Water Advisory Council recently held a workshop exploring how to achieve effective reporting on waterborne diseases (http://www.epa.gov/OGWDW/ndwac/sum_wdw1.html)

Freshwater Recreational Activities

There is no technical note for this indicator. The technical note for core national indicator Outdoor Recreation is on page 286 and the technical note for Recreation in Forests is on page 313.

Grasslands and Shrublands
Area of Grasslands and Shrublands

The Indicator
This indicator reports the acreage of grasslands and shrublands—including pastureland and tundra—using land cover data based on satellite measurements. Changes in the extent of grasslands and shrublands over time may be a result of natural drivers such as climate, or human drivers such as changes in land use or management. Extent is also important because it can influence other indicators of grassland and shrubland condition.

The Data
Data Source: The data for the lower 48 states are from the National Land Cover Dataset (NLCD; see the program description on the NLCD, p. 274). Data for Alaska are from a vegetation map of Alaska by Flemming (1996), based on Advanced Very High Resolution Radiometer (AVHRR) remote-sensing images with an approximate resolution of 1 km on a side. The following groupings of classes were used (see http://agdc.usgs.gov/data/projects/fhm/#G [Statewide Vegetation/Land Cover] and the NLCD program description). The following are Flemming's (1996) classes that were included within grasslands and shrublands: alpine tundra & barrens (#3); dwarf shrub tundra (#4); tussock sedge/dwarf shrub tundra (#5); moist herbaceous/ shrub tundra (#6); wet sedge

tundra (#7); low shrub/lichen tundra (#8); low & dwarf shrub (#9); tall shrub (#10); and tall & low shrub (#23).

Presettlement estimates of grass/shrub land cover were derived from data provided by Richard J. Olson, Oak Ridge National Laboratory (personal communication). These data were first published in Klopatek et al. (1979). This dataset provided potential area of Kuchler vegetation types. A set of Kuchler vegetation types provided by the Vegetation/Ecosystem Modeling and Analysis Project (VEMAP) program (http://www.cgd.ucar.edu/vemap/lists/kuchlerTypes.html) was used to select a set of grassland and shrubland vegetation types from Klopatek et al. (1979). Estimates of the percent of the historic extent of tallgrass prairie that remains undisturbed by agriculture were taken from Sampson and Knopf (1994).

Data for recent changes in "nonfederal grasslands and shrublands" are from the U.S. Department of Agriculture Natural Resources Conservation Service National Resources Inventory (NRI) program. NRI uses the term "rangelands," which is consistent with our definition of grasslands and shrublands, except that the NRI data used here do not include pasture or lands enrolled in the Conservation Reserve Program. Data from 1982, 1992, and 2003 are derived from the NRI Summary Report (revised February 2007). See http://www.nrcs.usda.gov/technical/NRI/2003/nri03landuse-mrb.html.

Data Quality/Caveats: Pastures and hay-lands were included in estimates of grassland and shrubland area because many fall within the description of grasslands and shrublands given in the introduction of this chapter, and because it is not clear how well the satellite data distinguish them from less-managed grasslands. Pastures and hay-lands were also included within the farmlands extent indicator and the national extent indicator (under "cropland"). (Note that in the NLCD the classification "pasture/hay" is defined as areas of grasses, legumes, or grass-legume mixtures planted for livestock grazing or the production of seed or hay crops.)

The U.S. Department of Agriculture Economic Research Service (ERS) has carefully tracked changes in different land uses over the past 50 years in its "Major Uses of Land" series (see http://www.ers.usda.gov/data/majorlanduses/); however ERS data were not suitable for use in this indicator. The ERS "grassland, pasture and range" category is inconsistent with the definition used in this report because land is included based on grazing activity rather than on the land-cover classification.

Estimates of the loss of grasslands and shrublands since the time of European settlement may over- or underestimate actual historic grassland and shrubland losses. For example, data on the acreage of pasture do not indicate whether or not the land is heavily managed (i.e., plowed and seeded, and/or subjected to significant grazing). Grasslands converted to pasture could represent a net loss in grassland and shrubland extent. Additionally, some of the land that is now classified as pasture is in the East and was probably originally forest. Hence, to say that grasslands and shrublands declined 40 to 140 million acres since European settlement ignores the fact that more of the original grasslands and shrublands may have been lost but these losses were offset by gains in eastern pastures.

Because at the time the analyses were completed, the 2001 NLCD was not comparable to the 1992 NLCD, which had been used in the 2002 edition of this report, only the 2001 data were included.

Data Access: Please see the NLCD program description (p. 274) for the lower 48 states, and http://agdc.usgs.gov/ for data on Alaska.

2008 Report Data Update: Data from the 2001 NLCD were included for the lower 48 states, and the data for Alaska have not been updated since the 2002 edition of this report.

Land Use in Grasslands and Shrublands

The Indicator
When fully developed, this indicator will present the area devoted to different land uses over time, including: livestock raising, oil/gas/mining, rural residences, "protected areas," and high intensity recreation. Currently, national data are only available to report on the area of grassland and shrubland that is enrolled in the main set-aside program—the Conservation Reserve Program (CRP).

The Data
Data Description: Data on CRP lands are from the USDA Farm Service Agency (FSA), which manages CRP signups and contracts. The data for CRP acreage reported here were provided by FSA and are based on data reported at http://www.fsa.usda.gov/FSA/webapp?area=home&subject=copr&topic=crp-st.

Data Manipulation: Reported here are lands in the following "practice" categories: Introduced Grasses (CP1), Native Grasses (CP2), Wildlife Habitat (CP4), Grass Waterways (CP8), Established Grass (CP10), Wildlife Food Plots (CP12), Vegetative Filter Strips (CP13), Contour Grass (CP15), Snow Fences (CP17), Salt Tolerant Vegetation (CP18), Alternative Perennials (CP20), Filter Strips (CP21), Cross Wind Strips (CP24), Declining Habitat (CP25), and Northern Bobwhite Quail Habitat (CP33). Data from each of these practice categories were summed for all contracts active (that had not expired) at the time the report was prepared.

Data Quality/Caveats: FSA provides information on cover practices for CRP contracts beginning in each program year since the CRP was established (1987). FSA does not verify the implementation of each contract, but rather assumes that the cover practices identified in the contract at the time of signup are implemented for the entire time that contract is in effect (ten years, unless extended). The data provided by the FSA sum the acreage enrolled in each of the 14 cover practices specified above, for all contracts initiated in a given year, and those initiated in previous years that have not expired. Additionally, the FSA uses multiple data sources to estimate acreage enrolled in the CRP, causing some fluctuation in the acreage reported from year to year for each initial contract year.

Data Availability: Data on CRP enrollment were obtained directly from the FSA.

2008 Report Data Update: 2005–2006 CRP enrollment data were added. Data for 2006 included first time data for the new land practice, Northern Bobwhite Quail Habitat (CP33).

The Data Gap

When data are available, this indicator will report on five land use categories—livestock raising, oil/gas/mining, rural residences, "protected areas," and high intensity recreation. These categories need to be defined, and mechanisms developed for the accounting of the acreage in each category and changes in these areas over time.

Pattern of Grassland and Shrubland Landscapes

The Indicator

This indicator reports the size of patches of grassland or shrubland land cover meeting the definition of "core grassland" or "core shrubland", respectively. "Core grassland" or "core shrubland" are used here to describe a pattern where these land-cover types are separated from nonnatural land-cover types (e.g., development—including paved roads, and croplands) by a buffer of natural land cover types.

Substantial Changes to the Indicator Design: The indicator in the 2002 edition of this report had been defined but data were not presented. For this edition, the indicator was revised substantially by the Landscape Pattern Task Group; a report from this Task Group is forthcoming and will be posted on the Heinz Center Web site (http://www.heinzctr.org/ecosystems).

The Data

The data for this indicator are derived from two sources. The primary source is the 2001 National Land Cover Dataset (NLCD), which is a product of the Multi-Resolution Land Characterization (MRLC) Consortium (see p. 274). The NLCD land-cover map was augmented with data from ESRI on paved roads (StreetMap data; http://www.esri.com/data/streetmap), which are considered here as a type of development.

Data Description: See the program description for the NLCD (p. 274) for details.

Data Manipulation: Please see the Forest Pattern indicator (p. 307) technical note for details on the analysis used to calculate patch sizes of "core" lands.

The indicator text reports that 66% of total grassland area and 87% of total shrubland area in the lower 48 states met the definition of "core grassland" or "core shrubland", respectively. These data are not shown because of space constraints, but each percentage was determined by summing the area of all individual pixels that were classified as "core grassland" (or "core shrubland").

In the future, we expect to show several analysis combinations (e.g., different window sizes and density thresholds other than 90% natural) on the report's Web site.

Data Quality/Caveats: The sizes of patches of "core grassland" and "core shrubland" pixels were summarized state-by-state. This procedure undoubtedly caused some patches to be split by state boundaries, therefore the patch sizes reported are effectively minimum patch sizes.

Data Availability: See the program description for the NLCD (p. 274) for availability of those data, and the ESRI Web site

listed above for access to the StreetMap data. Summarized data from the analyses described here were provided to the Heinz Center by analysts from the U.S. Forest Service and the U.S. EPA and are available from the Heinz Center upon request.

2008 Report Data Update: Data were included from the 2001 NLCD.

Nitrate in Grassland and Shrubland Groundwater

The Indicator

When data become available, this indicator will report nitrate-nitrogen concentrations in groundwater. An ecosystem comparison will also be provided, comparing nitrate concentrations in grassland-shrubland groundwater to nitrate concentrations in groundwater in farmlands, forests, and urban and suburban areas. Information on the appropriateness and sensitivity of nitrate as an indicator of ecological condition can be found in Smith et al. 1997.

The Data Gap

Data on nitrate concentration in groundwater need to be collected and reported in a consistent fashion across a broad and representative set of grassland and shrubland areas. Nitrate measurement is simple, straightforward, and largely unchanged since measurements began more than 100 years ago. Because many usable wells already exist, on both public and private lands, the cost of sampling and analysis is the primary factor limiting current efforts.

In addition, careful searching of federal, state, county, municipal, and private records could produce a valuable historical archive that would serve as a baseline against which to compare current conditions. The USGS NAWQA program has nitrate data for 78 wells in areas with land cover greater than 50% grassland or shrubland, less than 25% cropland, and less than 5% urban (2001 National Landcover Data). Further work is required to determine if these wells are representative of grassland-shrubland wells on a national scale.

Data reported in the draft version of this report, and summarized in Wilson et al. 2008, include nitrate data based on grassland-shrubland wells identified using 1992 land cover data. Fewer grassland-shrubland wells were identified when the Center updated the indicator using the 2001 NLCD land cover data. As a result, the Center and NAWQA agreed to leave the indicator as a data gap.

The program note for indicators describing nitrate concentrations in forested, farmland, and urban-suburban landscapes provides information on the U.S. Geological Survey National Water Quality Assessment program, which is a potential future source of data for this indicator.

Carbon Storage

The Indicator

This indicator will track long-term changes in carbon stored in grasslands and shrublands. Total stocks will be reported in this indicator, as opposed to changes in stocks as reported in the national Carbon Storage indicator (p. 38).

White et al. (2000) have estimated that grassland ecosystems worldwide store an amount of carbon that is about half of that stored by the world's forests and roughly equivalent to that stored by agricultural systems. More recently, the First State of the Carbon Cycle Report (USCCSP 2007) has suggested that grassland and shrubland soils (including pasture, rangeland, shrubland, and arid lands) are thought to contain ~33 billion metric tons of carbon (+/- 7.2 billion metric tons C); agricultural soils are thought to contain about half that amount (14 billion metric tons C +/- 3.2 billion metric tons C), whereas total forest carbon (including vegetation and soil) is thought to contain about twice as much carbon as grassland and shrubland soils (67 billion metric tons C +/- 33.5 billion metric tons C).

The Data Gap

Data are not currently available to provide systematic monitoring and reporting of soil and vegetation carbon. There are, of course, many research sites at which such information is collected. Soil carbon can be found at substantial depths, although routine sampling of soils to such depths is uncommon. There is a serious concern about the use of single-point estimates to represent large areas. Some procedures for establishing the representativeness of sites will be required.

There are several ongoing projects which hopefully will provide more information on carbon in grassland and shrubland systems. The Natural Resources Ecology Laboratory (NREL) has been developing methods to estimate total carbon stocks in grassland and shrubland soils using the Century Ecosystem Model (for more information see the technical note for Soil Organic Matter, p. 300). It is anticipated the resulting estimates for U.S. grasslands/shrublands will have sufficient certainty to be a useful source of data for this indicator.

The Conservation Effects Assessment Project (CEAP, http://www.nrcs.usda.gov/technical/NRI/ceap/) will estimate effects (including carbon storage) of conservation practices on private lands (for more information see the technical note for Soil Organic Matter, p. 300). This effort may yield important information about carbon storage in grazing lands.

Number and Duration of Dry Periods in Grassland and Shrubland Streams and Rivers

The Indicator

This indicator has two metrics: (1) the percentage of streams with zero-flow periods (at least one day of zero flow) in a year and (2) for streams with at least one day of zero flow between 1941 and 2006, the maximum duration of zero flow events in a year, averaged over a five-year rolling period, compared to the average maximum duration in a year during the years 1941–1960. Together, these two variables help describe both the frequency and duration of zero-flow events.

The indicator provides information on streams (from the Hydro-Climatic Data Network) that are not substantially regulated by dams and diversions and are in watersheds in which land use has not changed substantially over time (Slack 1992) as well as a separate set of streams that reflect a range of management activities (undisturbed to heavily managed). As the geographic distribution of the two sets is fairly similar, comparison of the two allow readers to identify the relative

impacts of climate and management. Data from the two sets are combined in this indicator.

The 1941–60 baseline period was chosen for this indicator (as well as the national indicator, Change in Stream Flows, pp. 47) to maximize the number of sites included in the analysis. Twenty years was selected as a reasonable baseline period that would allow characterization of hydrologic regimes and reporting for multiple years, while keeping test and reference data independent.

Substantial Changes to the Indicator: The indicator has undergone substantial changes since the 2002 Report, in part to maintain consistency with the new core national indicator, Change in Stream Flows (see pp. 47). The duration metric is now based on the maximum annual duration of a dry period, averaged over five years rather than the total number of zero-flow days in a year averaged over a decade. By focusing on the number of consecutive day of zero flow rather than the total number, the indicator may be more sensitive to potential biological impacts of drought. Substantial change in duration is now based on an increase or decrease in the number of days (± 14) rather than a percentage change in the number of days (> 100% increase; >50% decrease). The baseline used for comparison has also changed from a 50-year average to 1941–60 (see discussion above). In addition, on the enhanced web site, the indicator now reports on the number and duration of dry periods in both reference and non-reference streams in order to identify background climatic trends. All changes were designed by the Project's Stream Flows Working Group (pp. viii).

The Data

Data Source: Data reported here are from the U.S. Geological Survey (USGS) stream gauge network and from the USGS Hydro-Climatic Data Network. USGS has placed stream gauges and maintained flow rate records throughout the United States since the end of the 19th century.

Data Collection Methodology: Stream gauging data are collected using standard USGS protocols.

Data Manipulation: The goal of the initial data manipulation was to identify stream gauges in watersheds where more than 50 percent of the land cover is grassland or shrubland. Each site was referenced to a specific basin in the watershed using a digital elevation model which identifies the land surface draining into the stream segment upstream of the stream gage. Larger drainage basins were delineated using EPA's River-reach File 1 (RF1) stream network linked to a 1-km resolution digital resolution model. Smaller drainage basins were defined using the USGS Elevation Derivatives for National Application (EDNA) streams linked to a 30-m resolution digital elevation model. Grasslands and shrublands were defined using the 2001 National Land Cover Dataset (see http://www.epa.gov/mrlc/nlcd-2001.html) using land cover categories 52 (shrub/scrub) and 71 (grassland/herbaceous) (see http://www.epa.gov/mrlc/definitions.html#2001 and the program description for the NLCD, p. 274). The basins were also paired with their corresponding ecoregions (see below for description of the ecoregions used). Only sites with greater than 50% grassland/shrubland cover and greater than 80% data in each of the five-year rolling reporting periods and in the baseline period were used in the analysis.

The number of streams with at least one no-flow day in a year was determined for each water year (October 1st-September 30th, the designated year being the year it ends) from 1961 to 2006. The corresponding percentage value for that year was also calculated as 100 x (number of sites/total sites). The percentage values for each year were then averaged over a rolling-five year period (i.e., 1961–1965, 1962–1966...2002–2006). This procedure was followed for sites for each ecoregion and the nation as a whole (n=280).

For the analysis of the maximum duration of zero-flow, only sites with at least one no-flow day between 1941 and 2006 were considered. To compute this metric, the average of the maximum annual duration of a zero-flow period was calculated for each five-year test period and the baseline period (1941–60), for each stream site (n=163). At each site and for each five-year test period, the difference in duration was computed between the test period and the reference period (duration test period – duration baseline period). Stream sites were then classified as having a "substantial increase" in the duration of zero-flow periods if the duration of dry periods were more than fourteen days longer during the test period than during the 1941–60 baseline period; sites were classified as having a "substantial decrease" in the duration of zero-flow periods if the duration of dry periods were more than fourteen days shorter during the test period than during the 1941–60 baseline period.

Ecoregions: This indicator is reported using an ecoregional approach developed by the USDA Forest Service (Bailey 1995). We selected three major suites of Bailey's divisions:

- Desert shrub ecoregion, composed of the following Bailey's divisions: 320 (tropical/subtropical desert division), M320 (tropical/subtropical desert division—mountain provinces), 340 (temperate desert division), M340 (temperate desert division—mountain provinces). 70 streams in the analysis fell within this region.
- Grassland/steppe ecoregion, composed of the following Bailey's divisions: 250 (prairie division), 330 (temperate steppe division), M330 (temperate steppe division—mountain provinces), 310 (tropical/subtropical steppe division). 172 streams in the analysis fell within this region.
- California/Mediterranean, composed of the following Bailey's divisions: 260 Mediterranean division, M260 (Mediterranean division, mountain provinces) See http://www.fs.fed.us/colorimagemap/ecoreg1_divisions.html for full definitions and a map showing the individual divisions. 38 streams in the analysis fell within this region.

Stream Types: On the enhanced web site, the relatively undisturbed sites for the Hydro-Climatic Data Network are referred to as "reference sites" and the USGS stream gauge network sites are referred to as "nonreference sites." 90 reference sites and 190 nonreference sites were used report on the percentage of streams with zero-flow periods. 54 reference streams and 109 nonreference streams were used to report on change in the duration of zero-flow periods. In the indicator, "reference sites" and "nonreference sites" are combined.

Data Availability: The data records used in this study are available on the Internet in the form of daily stream flow values

reported as the average volume of water per second over a 24-hour period (http://waterdata.usgs.gov/nwis/sw).

2008 Report Data Update: The computation of the indicator has been refined to reflect changes in the core national indicator, Change in Stream Flows (see above, Substantial Changes to the Indicator).

Depth to Shallow Groundwater

The Indicator
Shallow aquifers, or deeper regional aquifers where shallow aquifers do not exist, are often the water source for the maintenance of riparian and wetland ecosystems (Dawson and Ehleringer 1991, Flanagan et al. 1992). Shallow groundwater is being increasingly withdrawn for agriculture, urban expansion, and mining. Reduction in stream flows, important for maintaining shallow alluvial aquifers, by dams or other activities also reduces the level and availability of this important water source (Shafroth et al. 2000). In addition, deep-rooted plants, such as pinyon-juniper and Western juniper, are capable of lowering shallow aquifers by transpiring large amounts of water. The indicator on grassland and shrubland stream flows (p. 208) discusses the interaction between groundwater, surface water, and land use.

The Data Gap
Although depth to deep groundwater or the regional aquifer is regularly measured in monitoring and withdrawal wells across the country, and the data are reliable and maintained by appropriate agencies, these data have not been integrated either for the grasslands and shrublands regions or nationally (see groundwater indicator in freshwater chapter; p. 189, and USGS 1997).

Data on shallow aquifers are quite limited. Depths for shallow aquifers (e.g., groundwater under riparian communities) and deeper regional aquifers are usually treated separately. The limited shallow aquifer data from the U.S. Geological Survey and many academic and agency research projects dealing with rivers and adjacent floodplains (see citations above) may also be good sources for regional shallow groundwater data.

At-Risk Native Grassland and Shrubland Species

The Indicator
This indicator reports on the conservation status of native grassland and shrubland species across their full range (i.e., global ranks) as well as population trends of native species that are at-risk of extinction. The species reported here are those in groups (such as mammals, birds, and amphibians) that are sufficiently well known that their conservation status, habitat, and location (by state) can be assigned with some degree of confidence for all members of the group. The conservation status assessment for each species is an attempt to determine its relative susceptibility to extinction. The assessment process is based on consideration of up to 12 factors that relate to a species' degree of imperilment or risk of extinction throughout its range. Rare species are particularly vulnerable

to extinction and so several aspects of rarity are characterized in the assessment process including population size, number of populations, and range extent and area of occupancy. However, trends in population and range size as well as magnitude and immediacy of threats are also important considerations in assessing a species' overall vulnerability or risk of extinction. More information on this ranking process can be found in the program description describing NatureServe (p. 275) and at http://www.natureserve.org/explorer/ranking.htm and in Master (1991).

There is general recognition among experts that both status information (as presented here for animal species) and trend information (as presented here for vertebrate animals) are critical to understanding the condition of species.

The Data

For information on the NatureServe program data collection, methods, data quality/caveats, data availability, see p. 275.

Data Source: NatureServe (http://www.natureserve.org/) and its member programs in the network of Natural Heritage programs develop and maintain information on each of the species reported here.

Data Manipulation: All data manipulations were performed by NatureServe. To compute this indicator, NatureServe identified species as "grassland-shrubland species" if they lived in grasslands or shrublands during at least part of their life cycle and depended on access to grasslands or shrublands for their survival. This was a generally conservative approach—only species that were strongly associated with grassland-shrubland habitat type were included. Groups reported for grasslands and shrublands include mammals, birds, reptiles (snakes and lizards), turtles, amphibians, butterflies and skippers, and grasshoppers. Combined, these groups include over 1900 grassland-shrubland species.

2008 Report Data Update: The population trend metric was added to the indicator. Conservation status data from the 2002 Report were replaced with 2006 data.

The Data Gap

Data are not reported for native grassland-shrubland plants because habitat types have not been identified for all plant species. Critically imperiled and imperiled plants (G1 and G2) have been assigned habitat types, and NatureServe is currently working to assign vulnerable (G3) plants to habitats, but the habitat types of plants with more secure status remains unknown. Population trend data are not included for at-risk invertebrate animals, because trends are known for only 11% of invertebrate animal species in grasslands and shrublands.

Established Non-native Grassland and Shrubland Plant Cover

There is no technical note for this indicator.

Population Trends in Invasive and Non-invasive Birds

The Indicator

This indicator reports the change in populations of grassland and shrubland birds, focusing on increasing populations based on the assumption that this single trend would highlight any systemic favoring of invasive species over native species. Birds are divided into two categories: invasive, which includes birds that spread aggressively because of a favorable change in conditions (regardless of whether they are indigenous to the U.S. or not); and native, non-invasive grassland/shrubland birds, which includes only those birds that are indigenous to the U.S. which are known to be dependent upon relatively intact and high-quality native grasslands and shrublands.

Also since 2002, the Heinz Center has invested in significant modifications to the overall presentation of non-native species in this report. See the technical note for the core non-native species indicator (p. 283) for a definition of "non-native" used in this report. It is recognized that some "invasive" bird species may acclimate over time and may therefore no longer share the potential for impacts associated with other non-native species, complicating the original design of this indicator. Significant contributions to the assessment of bird populations in the U.S. and abroad have been made in the interim by the National Audubon Society and the Royal Society for the Protection of Birds (UK), among others. Although this indicator was originally designed to focus on increasing populations, this design element may be revisited in future iterations of this indicator and recent work in this area will be more closely reviewed.

The Data

Data Description: This indicator incorporates population trend estimates for 15 invasive and 35 non-invasive grassland bird species. Estimates are based on data collected for the North American Breeding Bird Survey (BBS), and were estimated by the Patuxent Wildlife Research Center (PWRC), United States Geological Survey and U.S. Department of the Interior. Trends were estimated for grasslands and shrublands in BBS Physiographic Strata (regions) 6–8, 32–56 and 80–91, in eight 5-year intervals from 1966 to 2005 (http://www.mbr-pwrc. usgs.gov/bbs/physio.html).

The following invasive species are included in this indicator: American crow, American robin, black-billed magpie, bronzed cowbird, brown-headed cowbird, cattle egret, common grackle, European starling, gray partridge, great-tailed grackle, house finch, house sparrow, mourning dove, ring-necked pheasant, and rock dove (domestic pigeon). These species are considered invasive for a variety of reasons, including, habitat conversion or fragmentation, and listing as an Old World native.

Native, non-invasive species, which are restricted to those native species known to be dependent upon relatively intact and high-quality native grasslands and shrublands, include the following: Baird's sparrow, black-throated sparrow, bobolink, Brewer's sparrow, burrowing owl, Cassin's sparrow, chestnut-collared longspur, common nighthawk, dickcissel, eastern meadowlark, ferruginous hawk, golden eagle, grasshopper sparrow, greater prairie chicken, Henslow's sparrow, horned lark, lark bunting, lark sparrow, LeConte's sparrow, loggerhead shrike, long-billed curlew, McCown's longspur, mountain plover, northern harrier, prairie falcon, sage grouse, sage sparrow, sage thrasher, savannah sparrow, sharp-tailed grouse, Sprague's pipit, Swainson's hawk, upland sandpiper, vesper sparrow, and western meadowlark.

The BBS is jointly coordinated by the PWRC and the Canadian Wildlife Service, Environment Canada. Summaries of the BBS methodology are provided by Peterjohn and Sauer (1993) and Sauer et al. (2005), and a review of the program is provided by O'Connor, et al (2000).

Data Manipulation: Composite trend estimates (change in population size as a percentage per year) were estimated for each species for the physiographic strata and time interval using an "estimating equations estimator" (described in Link and Sauer 1994). For each group of species (invasive and non-invasive) in each time interval, the percentage of species with increasing populations was calculated using a hierarchical model that accommodates differing precision among estimates for individual species (Sauer and Link 2002). The summary indicator is the percentage of species with positive (increasing) mean estimates. Credible intervals (confidence limits) were used to compare non-invasive with invasive birds. There was some interest in separating the invasive category into native and non-native subcategories, but this would decrease the statistical reliability of the results. Thus, both natives and non-natives were included in the invasive category. John Sauer conducted the statistical analysis for this indicator; Jill Lau summarized the results.

Data Quality/Caveats: Bird species differ in habits, habitat, abundance, and range, all factors that may bias trend estimates for certain species more than for others (see Droege 1990 and http://www.mbr-pwrc.usgs.gov/bbs/introbbs.html). The BBS methods and data have been subjected to peer review, and the results are available at http://www.pwrc.usgs.gov/bbs/bbsreview/. The trend analysis program (Sauer et al. 2005) and hierarchical modeling procedure (Sauer and Link 2002) are based on peer-reviewed methods.

Data Availability: Trend estimates are the output of a publicly-available program (http://www.mbr-pwrc.usgs.gov/bbs/trend/tf05.html) that is part of the BBS Analysis and Summary Web site (Sauer et al. 2005) for which metadata exist (http://www.mbr-pwrc.usgs.gov/bbs/BBS_Results_and_Analysis_2005.html).

2008 Report Data Update: In addition to new data for the current interval, a new method of determining the percent of increasing species was applied to all years of data. For the 2002 Report, the empirical Bayes approach was used to aggregate trends among regions within species. It was determined that conducting this analysis among regions would highlight the trends among geographic strata, rather than presenting a total population estimate for a given species across all strata. Therefore, in the new data methodology, a hierarchical model was used to estimate the proportion of species with increasing populations, thereby highlighting the trends for species across their entire range. The new methodology was applied to all data for all years.

Fire Frequency

The technical note for this indicator is on page 311 (Forests: Fire Frequency).

Riparian Condition

The Indicator

The indicator would report on the ecological integrity of riparian ecosystems, including both physical and biological factors.

The Data Gap

Several measures are being used nationally, but no "simple" index has received general acceptance among the research community. An appropriate "Index of Riparian Integrity" still needs to be fully developed. Several federal agencies use a combined qualitative metric called Proper Functioning Condition (PFC) when evaluating riparian systems (see Bureau of Land Management 1993). However, PFC is primarily hydrogeomorphic and includes little of the biological conditions such as species composition, age classes, understory condition, canopy condition, and successional processes. Another method developed in the past few years is the Hydrogeomorphic Methodology (HGM; Brinson 1996, Smith et al. 1995), which uses a complex of indices for hydrology, geomorphology, land use, biology, and other aspects to create a single index for the riparian system. It is complex, but a simplified version might be developed for broad-scale application. Yet another, simpler method is one that relies on satellite data (Iverson et al. 2001).

Aspects of the riparian condition that can be measured on a regional basis and that should be considered in any multimetric index include hydrology (e.g., relationship to natural flow patterns), geomorphology (e.g., stream sediment transport), and biology (e.g., canopy cover condition; percentage of potential recruitment or successional measures; canopy diversity, or coverage of point bars). Many of these aspects either are being measured now or could be measured as part of a national riparian evaluation system.

Once an index is developed, it would be applied within a sampling design that would allow estimation of the conditions on all streams within a region. Thus, for example, such an approach might provide estimates of the number of miles of stream with "riparian condition index" that is "high," "medium," or "low," each of these being within a selected numerical range of the index.

Cattle Grazing

The Indicator

This indicator reports the July 1st U.S. cattle and calf inventory; excluding cattle in confined feeding operations (feedlots). This indicator assumes that all unconfined cattle graze on grasslands and shrublands (including pasture), however an unknown number of cattle spend time in woodlands or forests.

The Data

Data Description: Data presented here are from the U.S. Department of Agriculture National Agricultural Statistics Service (NASS). NASS conducts annual surveys of livestock herd sizes during January and July of each year. The July reporting date was selected because more cattle are grazing (not on feed) in July than in January.

Data Manipulation: Direct estimates of the number of cattle grazing on grasslands, shrublands, and pastures are not available, thus indicator approximates cattle numbers by subtracting estimates of nongrazing cattle from the estimate of total cattle as of July 1 of every year. Total cattle ("all cattle") numbers include grazing and nongrazing: cows that have calved, bulls, heifers, steers, and calves. (Note that most calves have not weaned by July; however, increased forage consumption by lactating cows compensates for this apparent overestimation of animals). We estimate the number of nongrazing cattle by summing the following categories: cattle on feed ("cattle on feed"), milk cows ("cows that have calved—milk"), and heifers for milk replacement ("heifers 500+ lbs.—milk replacement"). Cattle on feed includes steers, heifers, calves, and some cows, that are generally confined to feedlots where they are fed grain, silage, hay, and/or protein supplements to yield higher grade meat. Estimates for milk cows and heifers for milk cow replacement, include cows and heifers (over 500 pounds) typically—but not universally—confined for the production of milk. Note that our estimate of nongrazing cattle includes some cattle of feed, milk cows, and heifers for milk replacement that may graze on grasslands and shrublands, and pasture; and excludes calves confined for veal production, because estimates of their numbers are not known.

In winter, some cattle are placed on croplands to consume plant products and seeds left behind. More important, the quantity and quality (digestibility and amount of protein) of grassland and shrubland plants decline substantially in winter, so the forage supply on grasslands and shrublands is inadequate. Thus, in many parts of the country, ranchers must feed hay to cattle in winter.

Data Quality/Caveats: Cattle spend some time during the summer months in woodlands and forests which may affect the estimates of grassland and shrubland grazing presented here. The indicator reports the number of cattle rather than the weight of cattle. The average weight of cattle may change over time, so the same herd size may involve more or fewer pounds of livestock. If such changes occur, this indicator may over- or under-represent the production of livestock.

Data Availability: Data are available at http://www.nass.usda. gov/index.asp. U.S. and state data for total cattle ("cattle all"), cattle on feed ("cattle on feed"), milk cows ("cows that have calved—milk") and heifers for milk replacement ("heifers 500+ lbs.—milk replacement") for July 1 are available under "Quick Stats" on this page.

The figure in the text, "88% of beef cattle graze on grasslands and shrublands" is from NASS Annual Agricultural Statistics Reports http://www.usda.gov/nass/pubs/agstats.htm. Data on 10-year cattle cycles were from http://ag.arizona.edu/ arec/wemc/cattlemarket/CatlCycl.pdf and http://usda.mannlib. cornell.edu/reports/nassr/livestock/pct-bb/specat01.pdf. Data pertaining to the historic peak in cattle production during the mid 1970's were provided in the Rocky Mountain Research Station online publication, *Rangeland resource trends in the United States* (Mitchell, 2000). Data on the value of the U.S. cattle inventory are from NASS, 2000 Agricultural Statistics (http://www.usda.gov/nass/pubs/agr00/00_ch7.pdf).

Data from the July 1 inventory were used for this indicator instead of January 1 inventory (also available at the NASS Web site), because January cattle inventories are believed to underestimate grazing cattle (i.e. cattle not on feed). During the winter months, cattle need rations of feed as suitable grazing

land becomes scarce. In the summer, available grazing land is less likely to influence the number of cattle receiving feed rations, thus July cattle inventories provide more accurate estimates of the number of cattle grazing every year.

2008 Report Data Update: Data for 2005 and 2006 were added from the NASS.

Recreation on Grasslands and Shrublands

There is no technical note for this indicator. For information on recreation reporting see the technical notes for core national Outdoor Recreation (p. 286) and Recreation in Forests (p. 313).

Urban and Suburban Landscapes
Area and Composition of the Urban and Suburban Landscape

The Indicator
This indicator reports the area of the urban and suburban landscapes (see below for the definition) based on the predominance of development in a region and nationally. Additionally, the composition of land cover within urban and suburban landscapes is reported.

The Data
The data for this indicator are derived from two sources. The primary source is the National Land Cover Dataset (NLCD), which is a product of the Multi-Resolution Land Characterization (MRLC) Consortium (see the program description for the NLCD on page 274). In addition, this land-cover map was augmented with data from ESRI on roads (StreetMap data; http://www.esri.com/data/streetmap), which are considered a type of development.

Data Manipulation: Analysts with the U.S. Environmental Protection Agency and the USDA Forest Service, using an enhanced land-cover map (see above) evaluated the composition surrounding each pixel using two analysis windows (0.3 km on a side and 1 km on a side). For those windows that had at least 60% developed pixels in them, the center pixel was added to one of many urban-suburban landscape polygons. Polygons had a minimal area of at least 270 acres (one-half square mile).

This indicator also reports the composition (in terms of land cover) within each polygon designated as part of the urban and suburban landscape. These data were summarized by state and then regionally (see program description on the NLCD for a listing of regions). Note that this procedure caused some patches to be split by both urban and suburban landscape boundaries as well as state boundaries.

Data Quality/Caveats: The approach described above to delineate urban and suburban landscapes (formerly called "urban and suburban areas") differed substantially from that used in the 2002 Report. Although preliminary analyses suggest that quantitative differences are small—these results should not be compared to those in the 2002 Report.

Data Availability: Please see the program description for the NLCD (p. 274).

Substantial Changes to the Indicator Design: The underlying definition of "urban-suburban landscapes" was revised in this edition of the report to make it more consistent with the other landscape pattern indicators in the report—especially the core national indicator (p. 33) and the indicator Farmland Landscape (p. 103).

2008 Report Data Update: New data from the 2001 NLCD and a new analysis protocol were used (see above). Data from the 1992 NLCD were previously reported but were excluded because of comparability issues. A new metric was added that reports on undeveloped land as a percentage of the urban-suburban landscape.

Total Impervious Area

The Indicator

The percentage of impervious surfaces such as roads, parking lots, driveways, sidewalks, and rooftops within a watershed is a good indicator of the degree of urbanization and the associated negative ecological impacts (e.g. increased stream temperature, change in stream flows, stream channel modification, increased pollutant loading). Where such data are available, watershed urbanization is most often quantified in terms of the proportion of the basin area covered by impervious surfaces.

Research indicates that when total impervious area (TIA) in a watershed reaches 10%, stream ecosystems begin to show evidence of degradation. Ecological effects become severe as TIA approaches 30% (for more discussion, see Arnold and Gibbons 1996; Booth and Jackson, 1997; Schueler 1994; Schueler and Holland 2000).

The Data

The data for this indicator are derived from two sources. The primary source is the National Land Cover Dataset (NLCD), which is a product of the Multi-Resolution Land Characterization (MRLC) Consortium (see technical note for this program, p. 274). In addition, this land-cover map was augmented with data from ESRI on roads (StreetMap data; http://www.esri.com/data/streetmap), which are considered a type of development.

Data Description: See the program description for the NLCD on page 274. The NLCD map includes a data layer for imperviousness, which has pixel-by-pixel estimates of the percent impervious cover.

Data Manipulation: Analysts with the U.S. Environmental Protection Agency and the USDA Forest Service, using an enhanced land-cover map (see above), reported the average amount of impervious surfaces for each urban and suburban landscape polygon. The amount of urban and suburban area in several ranges of imperviousness (e.g., 10 to 20%) was summed for a state. Data were summarized by state and then regionally (see p. 266 for a description of regions).

Data Quality/Caveats: Estimates of imperviousness (via satellite imagery) are one of the factors used to delineate urban and suburban land-cover classifications in the NLCD. Thus, it is not surprising that urban-suburban landscapes have substantial amounts of impervious surfaces.

Data Availability: See links in the NLCD program description, p. 274.

2008 Report Data Update: Data from the 2001 NLCD were used to report on impervious surfaces. The 1992 NLCD, which was used in the 2002 Edition of this report, did not include estimates of impervious surface cover.

Stream Bank Vegetation

There is no technical note for this indicator.

Housing Density Changes in Low-Density Suburban and Rural Areas

The Indicator

This indicator reports the number of new housing units that are added across the country on land that had various levels of pre-existing development, measured by housing density. Data are reported nationally as well as regionally.

The Data

The data used for this indicator come from the SERGoM dataset created by David M. Theobald, Department of Human Dimensions of Natural Resources and Natural Resource Ecology Lab, Colorado State University, Fort Collins, CO. Further, D. Theobald performed the specific manipulations described below under contract to the Heinz Center.

Data Description: The SERGoM methods used to generate historical and current estimates of housing density (as well as a forecasting model) is described in detail by Theobald (2001, 2005). In short, using census data, the number of housing units built by decade was used to estimate the historical number of housing units in each block. Census data were combined with data on land ownership from the Conservation Biology Institute's PAD v4 database (http://www.consbio.org/cbi/projects/PAD/index.htm), which is largely a consolidation of USGS Gap stewardship maps. The density of major roads (interstates, state highways, county roads) was computed to provide a more accurate allocation of the location of housing units within a block.

Data Manipulation: Data were estimated for each grid cell (100 m x 100 m) across the lower 48 states for two time periods: 1990 and 2000. The number of houses added between the two census points was reported based on the housing density for the grid cell in 1990. Data were then summarized regionally and nationally.

Data Quality/Caveats: As mentioned in the figure legend on the indicator page, the reported data exclude about 25% of the households built on land having a pre-existing (1990) density of 1 house per acre or less. The SERGoM model computes housing densities for all grid cells that have not been excluded (e.g., they have a large water body on them or have a protection status that would prevent home building). Thus, all these grid cells ultimately have a nonzero housing density. Further work is needed to determine whether or not the very low preexisting housing densities are accurate. The SERGoM model had high accuracy overall for 1990 (urban = 93.0%, exurban = 91.2%, and rural = 99.0%) and reasonably high accuracy for 2000 (urban = 84.2%, exurban = 79.4%, and rural = 99.1%)—see Theobald (2005) for more details.

Data Availability: Data were provided by D. Theobald under contract. Contact the Heinz Center or D. Theobald to receive this dataset.

2008 Report Data Update: This is a newly designed indicator with first-time data.

"Natural" Lands in the Urban and Suburban Landscape

The Indicator
This indicator describes the size of patches of "natural" land cover in urban and suburban landscapes. The urban and suburban landscape includes many polygons defined from a land-cover map (see p. 29). "Natural" land-cover pixels include forest, grassland, shrubland, wetland, and other aquatic types. The indicator reports the size of patches of touching "natural" pixels within polygons of the urban and suburban landscape.

Substantial Changes to the Indicator Design: This indicator was revised for the 2008 edition of this report by the Landscape Pattern Task Group (report forthcoming).

The Data
The data for this indicator are derived from two sources. The primary source is the National Land Cover Dataset (NLCD), which is a product of the Multi-Resolution Land Characterization (MRLC) Consortium. In addition, this land-cover map was augmented with data from ESRI on roads (StreetMap data; http://www.esri.com/data/streetmap), which are considered a type of development.

Data Description: See the program description for the NLCD (p. 274) for details.

Data Manipulation: Analysts with the U.S. Environmental Protection Agency and the USDA Forest Service, using a enhanced land-cover map (see above) identified those pixels with "natural" land cover (forest, grassland, shrubland, barren, water, or wetland) within the urban-suburban landscape. Those pixels were formed into patches of "natural" pixels that touched along their edges and not just at their corners. Note that a similar approach was used to describe "natural" patches in the farmland landscape (see p. 106). Data were summarized by state and then regionally (see p. 266 for a description of regions).

Data Quality/Caveats: Because data were summarized by state, some patches of "natural" were split by both farmland landscape boundaries as well as state boundaries. Further analysis would be necessary to understand what impact this had on the reported results.

Data Availability: See the program description for the NLCD (p. 274) for land cover data, and the ESRI Web site listed above for access to the StreetMap data. Summarized data from the analyses described here were provided to the Heinz Center and are available upon request.

2008 Report Data Update: Data from the 2001 NLCD are included in this edition of the report. Data from the 1992 NLCD of the report were included in the 2002 edition of this report; however a different analysis protocol was used (see above).

Nitrate in Urban and Suburban Streams

The Indicator
This indicator reports mean-annual discharge-weighted concentrations of dissolved nitrate plus nitrite-nitrogen in urban and suburban streams. Data are reported as parts per million (milligrams per liter) nitrogen. The data are labeled "mean total nitrate" although the analytical method actually reports nitrate plus nitrite. This reporting convention is reasonable because except in highly polluted waters, nitrite levels are only a very small fraction of the total and can, therefore, be considered insignificant.

The Data
Data Source: The data were collected and analyzed by the U.S. Geological Survey (USGS) National Water Quality Assessment (NAWQA) program. See page 272 for information on the NAWQA program, sampling design, methodology, data availability. Information on the drinking water standard for nitrogen can be found at http://www.epa.gov/safewater/contaminants/index.html#primary. For information on farmlands and forest data used in the ecosystem comparison, see p. 299, and p. 307.

Data Collection Methodology: Stream nitrate data were collected from samples at stream and river sites draining 54 urban/suburban areas across the conterminous US, Alaska and Hawaii. Land cover upstream from sites in the "Urban and Suburban" category usually is more than 25 percent urban and less than 25 percent agricultural. Note that the sites labeled "urban" in this analysis should overlap with the "urban and suburban lands" defined as the subject of this report (see pp. 31), but, because different definitions were used in the two efforts, this might not always be the case.

Data Availability: Data used in this indicator are summarized by Wilson et al., (2008), available at http://pubs.usgs.gov/of/2008/1110/. Ecoregion criteria for assessing total nitrogen concentrations in all wadeable streams (including urban and suburban streams) during the summer index period can be found in USEPA's Wadeable Streams Assessment (USEPA 2006e).

2008 Report Data Update: The geographic scope of the indicator has increased. The 2008 indicator covers 51 major river basins across 50 states, sampled over the period 1992–2001. Only 36 basins were included in the 2002 Report, sampled over the period 1992–98.

Phosphorus in Urban and Suburban Streams

The Indicator

This indicator reports mean-annual discharge-weighted concentrations of dissolved phosphorus in urban and suburban streams. Data are reported as parts per million (milligrams per liter) total phosphorus

The Data

Data Source: The data were collected and analyzed by the U.S. Geological Survey (USGS) National Water Quality Assessment (NAWQA) program. See page 272 for information on the NAWQA program, sampling design, methods, data availability, and references. Information on the 1986 phosphorus recommended goal for preventing excess algae growth can be found in EPA 440/5-86-001 (see USEPA 1986). For information on farmlands data used in the ecosystem comparison, see p. 300.

Data Collection Methodology: Stream phosphorus data were collected from samples at stream and river sites draining 53 urban/suburban areas across the conterminous US, Alaska and Hawaii. Land cover upstream from sites in the "Urban and Suburban" category usually is more than 25 percent urban and less than 25 percent agricultural. Note that the sites labeled "urban" in this analysis should overlap with the "urban and suburban lands" defined as the subject of this report (see pp. 31), but, because different definitions were used in the two efforts, this might not always be the case.

Data Availability: Data used in this indicator are summarized by Wilson et al., (2008), available at http://pubs.usgs.gov/of/2008/1110/. Ecoregion criteria for assessing total phosphorus concentrations in all wadeable streams (including urban and suburban streams) during the summer index period can be found in USEPA's Wadeable Streams Assessment (USEPA 2006e).

2008 Report Data Update: The geographic scope of the indicator has increased. The 2008 indicator covers 51 major river basins across 50 states, sampled over the period 1992–2001. Only 36 basins were included in the 2002 Report, sampled over the period 1992–98.

Urban and Suburban Air Quality

The Indicator

This indicator reports how often (number of days per year) ozone monitoring stations measure peak 8- hour average ozone concentrations greater than 0.08 parts per million (ppm). When data become available, this indicator will also report on the percentage of urban and suburban areas in which ambient air

toxics concentrations are detected above background levels and exceed benchmarks set for the protection of human health.

Of the six 'criteria' air pollutants identified by the Clean Air Act, ground-level (or tropospheric) ozone is responsible for the majority of all days with violations of any air quality standard. In the presence of sunlight, molecular oxygen (O_2), oxides of nitrogen (NO_x) from fossil fuel combustion, and volatile organic compounds (VOCs) from paints, solvents, unburned fuel, and industrial sources generate ozone (O_3) in the atmosphere. Note that stratospheric ozone ("the ozone layer") is considered protective because it absorbs dangerous high-frequency ultraviolet light. Toxic air contaminants include a broad range of synthetic and naturally-occurring chemicals, such as the 188 officially designated Hazardous Air Pollutants. Sources of air toxics can include vehicles, dry cleaning facilities, factories, refineries, power plants, building materials and bedrock. Exposure to toxic air contaminants, most commonly through inhalation, is associated with a range of human health effects including cancer, respiratory irritation, nervous system problems, and birth defects.

The Data

Data Description:

Ozone: Under the Clean Air Act, every state operates a network of air monitoring stations for pollutants, including ozone. Between 1990 and 2005, individual states provided EPA with annual results from 1922 ozone monitors. Data were screened to exclude monitors with: (1) more than 2 consecutive years without annual data; (2) annual data for less than 75% of the 16 years in the time series, 1990–2005; and (3) annual data that had less than 50% of the daily peak concentrations during the ozone season. Of the 624 sites that met screening criteria, the Heinz Center selected the 317 monitors that are in urban and suburban areas (as defined for this report; see Area and Composition of Urban and Suburban Landscapes, p. 230 and the associated technical note on p. 332). Because satellite data were unavailable for Hawaii and Alaska, urban and suburban monitors were identified using Census Bureau Block Groups with at least 1000 people per square mile. Two Hawaiian monitors located in Block Groups with a density of at least 1000 people per square mile were included; however one of these was later excluded due to insufficient data. The single monitor in Alaska was excluded because it was not within a Block Group with at least 1000 people per square mile.

When a monitor exceeds a peak 8- hour average ozone concentration of 0.08 ppm four or more times per year, an area is likely to be out of compliance with the National Ambient Air Quality Standard for ozone (the actual calculation involves a 3-year average of the annual fourth-highest daily maximum 8-hour average concentration). For this reason, maps of monitoring stations with 'less than 4 days' and '4 or more days' of measured concentrations in 2005 exceeding the 8-hour ozone threshold of 0.08 ppm were produced using data from 291 monitors.

Data Quality/Caveats:

Ozone: Variations in weather conditions and other factors can produce interannual variability in ambient ozone levels (see http://www.epa.gov/airtrends/ozone.html). Ozone monitors in EPA's national network conform to criteria for siting, instrumentation, quality assurance and monitoring season.

Since ozone levels decrease significantly in the colder parts of the year in many areas, ozone is required to be monitored only during the "ozone season" as designated on a state-by-state basis. A monitor is considered operational if it reports a measurement for more than half the hours in a year (possible total of 8,760 hourly measurements annually). Data provided by the EPA for 1990 through 2005 were continually revised for the entire time period; differences with previously published data are small. Data that had been flagged for being unreliable (at the state level, with concurrence by the relevant regional EPA office) were excluded.

Data Availability:
Ozone: Ozone data are maintained by EPA in the Aerometric Information Retrieval System (AIRS) and are available at http://www.epa.gov/airs/. EPA provided customized data for this indicator; however, annual summary monitoring data are available at EPA's AIRData Web site (http://www.epa.gov/air/data/index.html).

The Data Gap
Toxic Air Contaminants: The temporal and spatial distribution of toxic air contaminants can vary considerably depending on factors such as the location and amount of emissions and weather conditions. Both the frequency of chemical contamination and the degree to which contaminants exceed benchmarks are important in understanding air quality; however there are many considerations necessary for assessing actual exposure or risk of health effects. To understand how often toxic contaminants are detected in ambient air or exceed human health benchmarks, more robust monitoring and estimation methods for ambient concentrations are needed. Further scientific work is needed to understand 'natural' background levels for air toxics. The U.S. EPA coordinates an air toxics measurement network and uses models to estimate ambient air toxics concentrations; however neither of these data sources currently provides adequate geographic coverage or accuracy to enable national level reporting.

The 23 individual stations of the National Air Toxics Trends Sites (NATTS) network monitor small subsets of the designated Hazardous Air Pollutants—there is considerable variability in geographic coverage and the suite of chemicals monitored (see http://www.epa.gov/ttn/amtic/natts.html). Data are point measures and do not represent actual variability in concentrations across urban and suburban areas. Beyond local uses, NATTS data is primarily used to evaluate and improve models. The small scope of the current NATTS network is due, in part, to methodological challenges in ambient air toxics monitoring. For example, many of these contaminants are difficult to measure accurately at environmental levels (for some, benchmarks that are lower than detection limits) and demonstrate substantial local spatial variability. They require frequent sampling to appropriately characterize temporal variability.

The EPA National Air Toxics Assessment (NATA) estimates ambient air toxics concentrations for 1996 and 1999 using the ASPEN (Assessment System for Population Exposure Nationwide) model which integrates estimated emissions with air transport information (see http://www.epa.gov/ttn/atw/natamain/). Results for a subset of chemicals have been compared to point measures at a limited number of sites, with some evidence of underestimation of ambient concentrations.

While ASPEN-generated concentration estimates provide wide geographic coverage for a large number of air toxics, they do not sufficiently account for the reactivity of toxic chemicals in the atmosphere or other key factors. The EPA Community Multiscale Air Quality (CMAQ) model builds in more realistic terms for atmospheric transport and chemical reactivity and offers promise for producing accurate estimates of ambient air toxics concentration that can be used to populate this indicator. Estimates of 2001 ambient air toxics concentrations have been produced for 36 chemical species and expanded analyses are planned (see http://www.epa.gov/asmdnerl/CMAQ/index.html).

Chemical Contamination

The Indicator
This indicator reports on the percentage of monitored streams in urban and suburban ecosystems in which contaminants (pesticides and their breakdown products, nitrate, ammonia) are detected and exceed established benchmarks for the protection of aquatic life and human health. When data become available, this indicator will report on contaminants found in urban and suburban soils.

The Data
Data Description: Data for this indicator come from the USGS National Water Quality Assessment (NAWQA) program and are based on water samples collected from 30 streams across the nation that drain watersheds where the primary land use is urban or suburban, over the period 1992–2001. Land cover upstream from urban/suburban sites is usually more than 25 percent urban and less than 25 percent agricultural. Streamwater samples were analyzed for 83 pesticides/pesticide degradation products, ammonia and nitrate. Measured concentrations were compared to 73 benchmarks for the protection of human health (72 pesticides, nitrate) and 63 benchmarks for the protection of aquatic life (62 pesticides, ammonia). See the NAWQA program description on p. 272 for further details.

For each sampling site, the number of contaminants that were measured (a) above the analytical detection limit and (b) at concentrations higher than established benchmarks for the protection of aquatic life and human health were summed. Indicator figures present "bins" or groupings of sites based on the number of contaminants detected or in exceedance of benchmarks. Nitrate and ammonia can occur naturally in the environment so they are not included in detection analyses. Many contaminants measured by NAWQA do not have established benchmarks or have a range of benchmark values associated with different types or likelihood of effects, affected organisms and exposure duration.

Data Quality/Caveats: The data are highly aggregated and should be interpreted mainly as an indication of general national patterns. Sampling sites were selected to be representative of specific land use types (rather than locations where contamination was known or suspected).

Urban/suburban land uses can exert a dominant influence on a stream or river, in spite of occupying a small percentage of land cover in the watershed, if these land uses are located near the river or stream—study watersheds had from 6 to

100% urban/suburban land cover. All samples were collected, processed, preserved, and analyzed using the same methods.

The data shown in this indicator do not represent assessments of risks posed to people or ecosystems in any specific location, since they do not incorporate factors such as whether the water tested is actually used as a drinking water source and the time of year when contaminants are found, relative to when animals are most active. The presence of contaminants does not necessarily mean that levels are high enough to cause problems. While the benchmarks used to help judge the significance of contamination are the best available in use by relevant agencies, they must be interpreted carefully because they are not necessarily standardized or linked to the same level of risk, nor do they necessarily account for all aspects of potential toxicity.

Data Availability: All data used in this report are summarized at http://pubs.usgs.gov/of/2008/1110/.

2008 Report Data Update: In the 2002 Report, stream monitoring data for 1992–1998 were reported, however these data are not comparable to the 1992–2001 data presented here due to expansion of the geographic scope of the monitoring program and a revised set of benchmarks—the 2008 report makes use of Health-Based Screening Levels (HBSLs) in addition to USEPA Maximum Contaminant Levels (MCLs). For details, see http://water.usgs.gov/nawqa/HBSL.

The Data Gap

Data are not currently available to report in a consistent manner on chemical contamination in urban and suburban soils.

Urban Heat Island

The Indicator

The "urban heat island" represents the difference between urban and nearby rural air temperatures and is directly related to urban land cover and human energy use. For most cities, this difference often is negligible in the daytime but develops rapidly after sunset. Maximum difference occurs 2–3 hours after sunset and may be as great as 18°F. In general, as the population density of a city increases, the difference in minimum temperature between the urban core and rural site increases nonlinearly. Urban heat island effect for a city is typically calculated by comparing the temperature of a monitoring station in the urban core with a monitoring station from a neighboring rural location. This difference might be reported as the average monthly difference between urban and rural sites. Nationally, the indicator might report the number of cities with various levels of difference between urban and rural sites: 0–6°F, 6 to less than 13°F, or more than 13°F.

As constructed surfaces replace natural vegetation, an area's ability to absorb and store heat increases; the natural cooling effect mediated by trees and other vegetation is reduced. The urban heat island represents a change in the diurnal pattern of ambient temperature. Because many biological processes are temperature dependent, changes in the temperature regime may have profound effects on species and ecological processes.

The Data Gap

National Weather Service temperature data are available for a large number of locations in the United States and could be used to determine urban heat island effect and how this temperature differential has changed over time. Data challenges include obtaining long-term data records for both urban and adjacent rural sites and accounting for changes in monitoring locations or instrumentation and for changes in population densities and human activities around monitoring sites. Remote sensing data have been used to examine temperature differences between urban and rural sites. These measurements record surface temperatures, which may prove to be sufficient predictors of ambient temperatures.

For more information on urban heat islands and guidance on meteorological measurements in urban areas see http://www.urban-climate.org/, the web site of the International Association for Urban Climate.

Species Status

The Indicator

This indicator reports the percentage of "original" vertebrate animals and vascular plants that are at risk of displacement or have been displaced from metropolitan areas (i.e., major cities and their suburbs found within the urban/suburban landscapes defined by this report; small, isolated cities or suburbs would be excluded because it would likely not be feasible to include them in the necessary monitoring program). "Original" is defined as existing before European settlement in the area that is now a metropolitan area. Using the reference point of presettlement is in some sense an arbitrary choice; its use does not necessarily mean that it would be desirable to have all original species present in urban/suburban areas. This indicator includes only vertebrate animals (not insects, worms, and the like) and vascular plants (not mosses, fungi, algae, and so on).

The Data Gap

This indicator should be reported for larger metropolitan regions, where expertise and information are likely to be available. For each of these areas, a list of plant and animal species present before settlement must be compiled. These lists can be derived from reviews of the historical literature, museum records, Natural Heritage program data, and agency files. Information on current status must be obtained through field surveys, which will need to be repeated periodically. If scientists develop standardized protocols for observation and reporting, much of the data could be collected by trained volunteers.

Many organizations collect data about the current distribution and status of species, but few of these provide information on species status or population trends within areas as small as a metropolitan area (Natural Heritage programs are an example; see http://www.natureserve.org/about_nhnoverview.htm).

There are a growing number of city, county, and regional efforts to gather and use biodiversity information, and these efforts could form the basis for reporting this indicator. Two programs that exemplify this trend are the Illinois EcoWatch Network (see http://ecowatch.inhs.uiuc.edu/ecoWatch/ and http://fm2.fieldmuseum.org/urbanwatch/) and Chicago Wilderness (see http://www.chiwild.org). In addition, Robinson et al. (1994), in a study in Staten Island, New York, showed a loss of over 40% of native flora and an increase of over 33% non-native flora during the period 1879 to 1991. DeCandido (2001) found similar results for The Bronx, New York.

Disruptive Species

There is no technical note for this indicator.

Status of Animal Communities in Urban and Suburban Streams

There is no technical note for this indicator.

Publicly Accessible Open Space per Resident

The Indicator
The indicator reports the amount of publicly accessible open space per resident for major urban and suburban areas in the United States. "Natural" lands include areas managed for their natural values as well as areas that are vegetated, but also relatively highly managed, such as playing fields and parks. Minor amounts of pavement or other "hard" surfaces would not preclude an area from being considered "natural."

Definitions: "Open space" means unbuilt land or water areas dominated by naturally pervious surfaces. A grassy park or golf course would qualify as open space; a paved playground would not. Satellite imagery will soon provide 5-meter resolution images, but whether there should be a minimum size to qualify for inclusion––that is, whether open space or parkland loses recreational or aesthetic utility below a threshold parcel size—is a question yet to be answered.

"Publicly accessible" means publicly or privately owned open space to which the general public has legal access, with or without an entry fee. A space is not publicly accessible if access is limited to members of specific groups or organizations. For example, a public or private golf course would be considered publicly accessible unless entry was restricted to club members.

The Data Gap
To calculate the amount of open space that is publicly accessible this indicator could use the self-reported acreage of public parks and open spaces administered by cities, counties, or states inside metropolitan areas. The accuracy of this approach may be limited by inconsistent standards among jurisdictions in the same metropolitan area for defining parks and open spaces. Historical data from cities may be affected by boundary changes associated with annexations. An alternative method is direct measurement using satellite imagery to identify unbuilt open spaces with naturally pervious surfaces. Tax assessment records might be used to locate tax-exempt parcels inside the identified open spaces. The tax records normally identify the basis for each parcel's tax exemption, making it possible to infer which parcels are publicly accessible. More research is needed to determine the suitability of tax assessor records.

Natural Ecosystem Services

There is no technical note for this indicator.

References Cited

Abrahamson, D.A., M.L. Norfleet, H.J. Causarano, J.R. Williams, J.N. Shaw and A.J. Franzluebbers. 2007. Effectiveness of the soil conditioning index as a carbon management tool in the southeastern USA based on comparison with EPIC. Journal of Soil and Water Conservation 62:94-102.

Amichev, B.Y. and J.M. Galbraith. 2004. A revised methodology for estimation of forest soil carbon from spatial soils and forest inventory datasets. Environmental Management 33(Suppl. 1): S74-S86.

Arnold, C.L., and C.J. Gibbons. 1996. Impervious surface coverage: The emergence of a key environmental indicator. Journal of the American Planning Association 62(2):243–258.

Bailey, R.G. 1995. Description of the ecoregions of the United States. 2nd ed. rev. and expanded (1st ed. 1980). Misc. Publ. No. 1391 (rev). Washington, DC: USDA Forest Service.

Baker, L.A., J.E. Schussler, and S.A. Snyder. 2008. Drivers of change for lakewater clarity. Lake and Reservoir Management. In press.

Barras, John A. 2006. Land area changes in coastal Louisiana after the 2005 hurricanes: A series of three maps. U.S. Geological Survey Open-File Report 06-1274. http://pubs.usgs.gov/of/2006/1274/.

Barry, J.P., C.H. Baxter, R.D. Sagarin, and S.E. Gilman. 1995. Climate-related, long-term faunal changes in a California rocky intertidal community. Science 267:672–675.

Berg, N.H., A. Gallegos, T. Dell, J. Frazier, T. Procter, J. Sickman, S. Grant, T. Blett, and M. Arbaugh. 2005. A Screening Procedure for Identifying Acid-Sensitive Lakes from Catchment Characteristics. Environmental Monitoring and Assessment, 105:285-307.

Birdsey, R.A. 1996. Carbon storage for major forest types and regions in the coterminous United States. In: Sampson, N.; Hair, D., eds. Forests and global change. Volume 2: forest management opportunities for mitigating carbon emissions. Washington, DC: American Forests: 1-23, Appendices 2-4.

Blunier T., J. Chappellaz, J. Schwander, J.M. Barnola, T. Desperts, B. Stauffer, and D. Raynaud. 1993. Atmospheric methane, record from a Greenland ice core over the last 1000 years. Journal of Geophysical Research 20:2219–2222. Accessed at http://nsidc.org/data/gisp_grip/tablecon.html.

Blunier, T., J. Chappellaz, J. Schwander, B. Stauffer, and D. Raynaud. 1995. Variations in atmospheric methane concentration during the Holocene epoch. Nature 374:46-49. Accessed at http://nsidc.org/data/gisp_grip/tablecon.html.

Bondy, E., Lyles, L., and Hayes, W.A. 1980. Computing soil erosion by periods using wind energy distribution. Jour. Soil and Water Conserv. 35(4):173–176.

Booth, D.B., and C.R. Jackson. 1997. Urbanization of aquatic systems: Degradation thresholds, stormwater detection, and the limits of mitigation. Journal of the American Water Resources Association 35(5):1077–1090.

Breshears, D.D., N.S. Cobb, P.M. Rich, K.P. Price, C.D. Allen, R.G. Balice, W.H. Romme, J.H. Kastens, M.L. Floyd, J. Belnap, J.J. Anderson, O.B. Myers, and C.W. Meyer. 2005. Regional vegetation die-off in response to global-change-type drought. Proceedings of the National Academy of Sciences 102(42)15144–15148.

Brezonik, P.L., L.G. Olmanson, M.E. Bauer, and S.M. Kloiber. 2007. Measuring Water Clarity and Quality in Minnesota Lakes and Rivers: A Census-Based Approach Using Remote-Sensing Techniques. CURA Reporter. 37:3–13. Available at: http://purl.umn.edu/1939.

Bricker, S., B. Longstaff, W. Dennison, A. Jones, K. Boicourt, C. Wicks, and J. Woerner. 2007. Effects of Nutrient Enrichment in the Nation's Estuaries: A Decade of Change. NOAA Coastal Ocean Program Decision Analysis Series No. 26. National Centers for Coastal Ocean Science, Silver Spring, MD. 328 pp.

Brinson, M.M. 1996. Assessing wetland functions using HGM. National Wetlands Newsletter 18:10–16.

Brown, C.D., D.E. Canfield, Jr., R.W. Bachmann, and M.V. Hoyer. 1998. Seasonal patterns of chlorophyll, nutrient concentrations and Secchi disk transparency in Florida lakes. Lake and Reservoir Management J. 14:60–76.

Bureau of Land Management.1993. Riparian area management: Process for assessing proper functioning condition. Technical Reference 1737-9. USDOI, BLM, Denver, CO. Revised 1995, 1998.

Carlson, R.E. 1977. A trophic state index for lakes. Limnol. Oceanogr. 22:361–369.

Chappellaz, J., T. Blunier, S. Jints, A. Dällenback, J.-M. Barnola, J. Schwander, D. Raynaud, and B. Stauffer. 1997. Changes in the atmospheric CH4 gradient between Greenland and Antarctica during the Holocene. Journal of Geophysical Research 102(D13):15,987-15,997.

Comer, P., D. Faber-Langendoen, R. Evans, S. Gawler, C. Josse, G. Kittel, S. Menard, M. Pyne, M. Reid, K. Schulz, K. Snow, and J. Teague. 2003. Ecological Systems of the United States: A Working Classification of U.S. Terrestrial Systems. NatureServe, Arlington, VA.

Committee on Rangeland Classification. 1994. Rangeland health: New methods to classify, inventory and monitor rangelands. Washington, DC: National Academy Press.

Cordell, K. principal author. 2004. Outdoor Recreation for 21st Century America: a report to the nation, the National Survey on Recreation and the Environment. State College, PA.: Venture Publishing, Inc.

Cowardin, L.M., V. Carter, F.C. Golet, and E.T. LaRoe. 1979. Classification of wetlands and deepwater habitats of the United States, FW/OBS-79/31. Washington, DC: U.S. Fish and Wildlife Service.

Crawford, J.K., and S.N.Luoma.1993. Guidelines for studies of contaminants in biological tissues for the National Water Quality Assessment Program. U.S. Geological Survey Open-File Report 92-494, 69 p.

Crawford, C.G., 2004, Sampling strategies for estimating acute and chronic exposures of pesticides in streams: Journal of the American Water Resources Association 40:485-502.

Dahl, T.E., 1990. Wetlands—Losses in the United States, 1780's to 1980's: Washington, D.C., U.S. Fish and Wildlife Service, Report to Congress.

Dahl, T.E., et al. 2006. Status and trends of wetlands in the conterminous United States 1998–2004. Washington, DC: U.S. Department of the Interior, Fish and Wildlife Service. http://wetlandsfws.er.usgs.gov/status_trends/National_Reports/trends_2005_report.pdf.

Daugherty, A.B. 1995. Major uses of land in the United States, 1992, AER-732, U.S. Department of Agriculture, Economic Research Service.

Dawson, T.E, and J.R. Ehleringer. 1991. Streamside trees that do not use stream water. Nature 350:335–227.

DeCandido, R. 2001. Recent changes in plant species diversity in Pelham Bay Park, Bronx County, New York City, 1947–1998. Ph.D. Dissertation, The City University of New York.

DeWalle, D.R. and T.D. Davies. 1997. Seasonal variations in acid-neutralizing capacity in 13 northeast United States headwater streams. Water Resources Research, 33(4): 801–807.

Dingman, S.L. 1984. Fluvial Hydrology. New York: W.H. Freeman.

Dlugokencky, E.J., Atmospheric Methane Dry Air Mole Fractions from the NOAA GMD Carbon Cycle Cooperative Global Air Sampling Network, 1983–2005. National Oceanic and Atmospheric Administration, Earth System Research Laboratory. Version 2006–08-09.1108. http://www.esrl.noaa.gov/gmd/.

Dolan, R., F. Anders, and S. Kimball. 1985. Coastal erosion and accretion. In National atlas of the United States of America. Washington, DC: U.S. Department of Interior, U.S. Geological Survey.

Droege, S. 1990. The North American Breeding Bird Survey, pp. 1-4. In J.R. Sauer and S. Droege (eds.), Survey designs and statistical methods for the estimation of avian population trends. U.S. Fish and Wildlife Service, Biological Report 90(1).

Emmerich, W.F. 2003. Carbon dioxide fluxes in a semi-arid environment with high carbonate soils. Agricultural and Forest Meteorology 116:91-102.

Engle, V.D., and J.K. Summers. 1999. Refinement, validation, and application of a benthic condition index for northern Gulf of Mexico estuaries. Estuaries 22(3A):624–635.

Engle, V.D., J.K. Summers, and G.R. Gaston. 1994. A benthic index of environmental condition of Gulf of Mexico estuaries. Estuaries 17:372–384.

ESRI. 2005. U.S. Streets. ESRI Data & Maps, 2005 edition, ESRI, Redlands, CA.

Etheridge, D. M., Steele, L. P., Francey, R. J., and Langenfelds, R. L., 1998, Atmospheric methane between 1000 A.D. and present: Evidence of anthropogenic emissions and climatic variability. J. Geophys. Res. 103(D13):15,979 98JD00923). Accessed at: http://www.ncdc.noaa.gov/paleo/icecore/Antarctica/law/law_data.html (Smoothing spline fit with 75 year cut off (Table 2 parts 1 & 2 Etheridge et al., 1998).

Etheridge, D.M., L.P. Steele, R.L. Langenfelds, RlJ. Francey, J.-M. Barnola, and V.I. Morgan. 1996. Natural and anthropogenic changes in atmospheric CO2 over the last 1000 years from air in Antarctic ice and firn. Journal of Geophysical Research—Atmosphere 101:4115–4128. Accessed at: http://www.ncdc.noaa.gov/paleo/icecore/Antarctica/law/law_data.html.

Federal Geographic Data Committee. 1997. Vegetation classification standard, FGDC-STD-005. Available at: http://www.fgdc.gov/standards/projects/FGDC-standards-projects/vegetation/vegclass.pdf.

Ferretti, D.F., et al. 2005. Unexpected changes to the global methane budget over the past 2000 years. Science 309:1714–1717.

Fiscus, D. A. and D. A. Neher. 2002. Distinguishing sensitivity of free-living soil nematode genera to physical and chemical disturbances. Ecological Applications 12(2):565-575.

Fishman, M.J. 1993. Methods of analysis by the U.S. Geological Survey National Water Quality Laboratory—Determination of inorganic and organic constituents in water and fluvial sediments. U.S. Geological Survey Open-File Report 93-125.

Flanagan, L.B., J.R. Ehleringer, and T.E. Dawson. 1992. Water sources of plants growing in woodland, desert, and riparian communities: Evidence from stable isotope analysis. U.S. Forest Service Tech. Report INT-289:43–47.

Flemming, M.D. 1996. A statewide vegetation map of Alaska using a phenological classification of AVHRR data. 1996 Alaska Surveying and Mapping Conference, Anchorage, Alaska.

Flückiger, J., et al. 2002. High resolution Holocene N2O ice core record and its relationship with CH4 and CO2. Global Biogeochemical Cycles 16(1):1010–1017. Accessed at http://www.ncdc.noaa.gov/paleo/icecore/current.html.

Frayer, W.E., T.J. Monahan, D.C. Bowden, and F.A. Graybill. 1983. Status and trends of wetlands and deepwater habitats in the conterminous United States, 1950's to 1970's. Ft. Collins, CO: Dept. of Forest and Wood Sciences, Colorado State University.

FRCC Interagency Working Group. Interagency Fire Regime Condition Class Guidebook, Version 1.2, May 2005. http://www.frcc.gov.

GAO. 1999. Western National Forests: Nearby communities are increasing threatened by catastrophic wildfires. United States General Accounting Office. GAO/T-RCED-99-79.

Gilliom, R.J., W.M. Alley, and M.E. Gurtz. 1995. Design of the National Water-Quality Assessment Program: Occurrence and distribution of water-quality conditions. U.S. Geological Survey Circular 1112.

Gilliom, R.J., and G.P. Thelin. 1997. Classification and mapping of agricultural land for National Water Quality Assessment. U.S. Geological Survey Circular 1131.

Gilliom, R.J., J.E. Barbash, C.G. Crawford, P.A. Hamilton, J.D. Martin, N. Nakagaki, L.H. Nowell, J.C. Scott, P.E. Stackelberg, G.P. Thelin, and D.M. Wolock. 2006. The Quality of Our Nation's Waters—Pesticides in the Nation's Streams and Ground Water, 1992–2001. U.S. Geological Survey Circular 1291, 172 p. http://pubs.usgs.gov/circ/2005/1291/pdf/circ1291_front.pdf.

Goolsby, D.A., Battaglin, W.A., Lawrence, G.B., Artz, R.S., Aulenbach, B.T., Hooper, R.P., Keeney, D.R., and Stensland, G.J., 1999, Flux and sources of nutrients in the Mississippi–Atchafalaya River Basin—topic 3 report for the integrated assessment on hypoxia in the Gulf of Mexico: Silver Spring, Md., NOAA Coastal Ocean Office, NOAA Coastal Ocean Program Decision Analysis Series No. 17, 130 p. Available online at http://www.cop.noaa.gov/pubs/das/das17.pdf.

Gosselink, J.G., and R.H. Baumann. 1980. Wetland inventories: Wetland loss along the United States coast. Z. Geomorph. N.F. Suppl. Bd. 34:173.

Grantz, D.A., J.H. Gamer, and D.W. Johnson. 2003. Ecological effects of particulate matter. Environment International, 29(2-3): 219-239.

Gregg, W.W., Casey, N.W., and McClain, C.R. (2005) Recent trends in global ocean chlorophyll. Geophysical Resarch Letters 32:L03606, doi:10.1029/2004GL021808.

Grossman, D.H., et al. 1998. International classification of ecological communities: Terrestrial vegetation of the United States. Volume I: The national vegetation classification standard. Arlington, VA. The Nature Conservancy. http://www.natureserve.org/library/vol1.pdf.

Hallegraeff, G.M., D.M. Anderson, and A.D. Cembella, eds. 2003. Manual on harmful marine microalgae. Landais, France: UNESCO Publishing.

Hansen, M., R. DeFries, J.R.G. Townshend, and R. Sohlberg (2000), Global land cover classification at 1km resolution using a decision tree classifier, International Journal of Remote Sensing. 21: 1331–1365.

HARRNESS. 2005. Harmful algal research and response: A national environmental science strategy 2005–2015. J.S. Ramsdell, D.M. Anderson, and P.M. Glibert (Eds.). Washington, DC: Ecological Society of America.

Heyning, J.E. 2003. Final report on the multi-species marine mammal unusual mortality event along the Southern California coast. Tech. Memorandum,. Washington, DC: National Marine Fisheries Service.

Homer, C. C. Huang, L. Yang, B. Wylie and M. Coan. 2004. Development of a 2001 National Landcover Database for the United States. Photogrammetric Engineering and Remote Sensing 70(7):829-840.

Homer, C., J. Dewitz, J. Fry, M. Coan, N. Hossain, C. Larson, N. Herold, A. McKerrow, J.N. VanDriel and J. Wickham. 2007. Completion of the 2001 National Land Cover Database for the Conterminous United States, Photogrammetric Engineering and Remote Sensing 73(4):337-341.

Hutson, S.S., N.L. Barber, J.F. Kenny, K.S. Linsey, D.S. Lumia, and M.A. Maupin. 2004 Estimated Use of Water in the United States in 2000. U.S. Geological Survey. USGS Circular 1268. http://pubs.usgs.gov/circ/2004/circ1268/.

Hyland, J.L., W.L. Balthis, V.D. Engle, E.R. Long, J.F. Paul, J.K. Summers, and R.F. Van Dolah. 2003. Incidence of stress in benthic communities along the U.S. Atlantic and Gulf of Mexico coasts within different ranges of sediment contamination from chemical mixtures. Environmental Monitoring & Assessment, 81(1-3): 149-161.

Iverson, L.R., D.L Szafoni, S.E. Baum, and E.A. Cook. 2001. Development of a riparian wildlife habitat evaluation scheme using GIS. Environmental Management 28(5):639–654.

Jansen, E., J. Overpeck, K.R. Briffa, J.-C. Duplessy, F. Joos, V. Masson-Delmotte, D. Olago, B. Otto-Bliesner, W.R. Peltier, S. Rahmstorf, R. Ramesh, D. Raynaud, D. Rind, O. Solomina, R. Villalba and D. Zhang, 2007: Palaeoclimate. In: Climate Change 2007: The Physical Science Basis. Contribution of Working Group I to the Fourth Assessment Report of the Intergovernmental Panel on Climate Change Solomon, S., D. Qin, M. Manning, Z. Chen, M. Marquis, K.B. Averyt, M. Tignor and H.L. Miller (eds.). Cambridge University Press, Cambridge, United Kingdom and New York, NY, USA.

Kaufmann, P.R., P. Levine, E.G. Robison, C. Seeliger, and D. Peck. 1999. Quantifying physical habitat in wadeable streams. U.S. Environmental Protection Agency, Environmental Monitoring and Assesment program (EMAP), Washington, DC EPA-620/R-99/001.

Keeling C.D. and T.P. Whorf. Atmospheric CO2 concentration (ppmv) derived from in situ air samples collected at Mauna Loa Observatory Hawaii. May 2005. Carbon Dioxide Research Group, Scripps Institution of Oceanography, University of California, La Jolla, CA. http://cdiac.ornl.gov/trends/co2/sio-mlo.htm/.

Keeling, R.F., S.C. Piper, A.F. Bollenbacher, and S.J. Walker. Atmospheric CO2 concentrations (ppm) derived from in situ air measurements at Mauna Loa Observatory, Hawaii. Scripps CO2 Program, Scripps Institution of Oceanography, University of California, La Jolla, CA. Data for 2005–2006. http://scrippsco2.ucsd.edu/.

Kimbrough, K.L., W.E. Johnson, G.G. Lauenstein, J.D. Christensen and D.A. Apeti. 2008. An Assessment of Two Decades of Contaminant Monitoring in the Nation's Coastal Zone. Silver Spring, MD. NOAA Technical Memorandum NOS NCCOS 74. 105 pp.

Kinoshita, R.K., A. Greig, D. Colpo, and J.M. Terry. 1993. Economic status of the groundfish fisheries off Alaska, 1991. NOAA Tech. Memo. NMFS-AFSC-15. Washington, DC: U.S. Department of Commerce.

Kinoshita, R.K., A. Greig, D. Colpo, and J.M. Terry. 1997. Economic status of the groundfish fisheries off Alaska, 1995. NOAA Tech. Memo. NMFS-AFSC-72. Washington, DC: U.S. Department of Commerce.

Kloiber, S.M., T. Anderle, P.L. Brezonik, L. Olmanson, M.E. Bauer, and D.A. Brown. 2000. Trophic state assessment of lakes in the Twin Cities (Minnesota, USA) region by satellite imagery. Arch. Hydrobiol. Ergebn. Limnol. 85:1–15

Klopatek, J.M., R.J. Olson, C.J. Emerson, and J.L. Joness. 1979. Land-use conflicts with natural vegetation in the United States. Environmental Conservation 6:191–199.

Knowlton, M.F., M.V. Hoyer, and J.R. Jones. 1984. Sources of variability in phosphorus and chlorophyll and their effects on use of lake survey data. Water Resour. Bull. 20:397–407.

Koterba, M.T. 1998. Ground-water data-collection protocols and procedures for the National Water-Quality AssessmentProgram: Collection, documentation, and compilation of required site, well, subsurface, and landscape data for wells. U.S. Geological Survey Water-Resources Investigations Report 98-4107.

Koterba, M.T., F.D. Wilde, and W.W. Lapham. 1995.Groundwater data-collection protocols and procedures for the National Water-Quality Assessment Program: Collection and documentation of water-quality samples and related data. U.S. Geological Survey Open-File Report 95-399.

Krupa, K.S., and A.B. Daugherty. 1990. Major land uses: 1945–1987, Electronic Data Product #89003, U.S. Department of Agriculture, Economic Research Service.

Lapham, W.W., F.D. Wilde, and M.T. Koterba. 1995. Groundwater data-collection protocols and procedures for the National Water-Quality Assessment Program: Selection, installation, and documentation of wells, and collection of related data. U.S. Geological Survey Open-File Report 95-398.

Lauenstein, G.G., and A.Y. Cantillo. 1993. Sampling and analytical methods of the National Status and Trends Program: National Benthic Surveillance and Mussel Watch Projects, 1984–1992. NOAA Technical Memorandum NOS ORCA 71. Silver Spring, MD: NOAA National Ocean Service.

Lawrence, G.B., J.W. Sutherland, C.W. Boylen, S.W. Nierzwicki-Bauer, B. Momen, B.p. Baldigo, and H.A. Simonin. 2007. Acid rain effects on aluminum mobilization clarified by inclusion of strong organic acids. Environmental Science and Technology, 41:93-98.

Lehmann, C.M.B., V.C. Bowersox, and S.M. Larson. 2005. Spatial and temporal trends of precipitation chemistry in the United States, 1985–2002. Environmental Pollution, 135(3): 347-361.

Lehmann, C.M.B., V.C. Bowersox, R.S. Larson, and S.M. Larson. 2006. Monitoring long-term trends in sulfate and ammonium in U.S. precipitation: Results from the National Atmospheric Deposition Program/National Trends Network. Water, Air, and Soil Pollution:Forum, 7(1-3): 59-66.

Leonard, J. 2007. Fishing and Hunting Recruitment and Retention in the U.S. from 1990 to 2005: Addendum to the 2001 National Survey of Fishing, Hunting, and Wildlife-Associated Recreation. U.S. Fish & Wildlife Service.

Levitus, S., J.I. Antonov, T.P. Boyer, and C. Stephens. 2000. Warming of the world ocean. Science, 287:2225–2229.

Little, E.L. Jr. 1979. Checklist of United States trees (native and naturalized). Agric. Handb. 541. Washington, DC: U.S. Department of Agriculture Forest Service.

Long, E.R., L.J. Field, and D.D. McDonald. 1998. Predicting toxicity in marine sediments with numerical sediment quality guidelines. Environmental Toxicology and Chemistry, 17(4):714–727.

MacFarling Meure, C.M., D. Etheridge, C. Trudinger, P. Steele, R. Langenfelds, T. van Ommen, A. Smith, and J. Elkins. 2006. Law Dome CO2, CH4 and N2O ice core records extended to 2000 years BP. Geophysical Research Letters 33:14810–14813.

Martens, D.A., W. Emmerich, J.E.T. McLain, and T.N. Johnsen. 2005. Atmomspheric carbon mitigation potential of agricultural management in the southwestern USA. Soil and Tillage Research, 83(1):95-119.

Master, L.L. 1991. Assessing threats and setting priorities for conservation. Conservation Biology 5(4): 559-563.

Master, L.L., L.E. Morse, A.S. Weakley, G.A. Hammerson, and D. Faber-Langendoen. 2003. NatureServe Conservation Status Factors. Arlington, VA: NatureServe.

May, D.M. 1998. The North Central Forest Inventory and Analysis timber product output database—a regional composite approach. General Technical Report NC-200. St. Paul, MN: U.S. Dept. of Agriculture, Forest Service, North Central Forest Experiment Station.

McGuire, V.L., C.P. Stanton, and B.C. Fischer. 1999. Water level changes, 1980 to 1997, and saturated thickness, 1996–97, in the High Plains aquifer. U.S. Geological Survey Fact Sheet. FS-124-99. http://ne.water.usgs.gov/highplains/hpfs97.html.

Meyer, J.L. and J.B. Wallace. 2001. Lost linkages and lotic ecology: rediscovering small streams. Pp. 295-317. In: M.C. Press, N. Huntly and S. Levin (eds.) Ecology: Achievement and Challenge. Blackwell Science.

Mitchell, J.E. 2000. Rangeland resource trends in the United States: A technical document supporting the 2000 USDA Forest Service RPA Assessment. Gen. Tech. Rep. RMRS-GTR-68. Fort Collins, CO: U.S. Department of Agriculture, Forest Service, Rocky Mountain Research Station. Accessed at: http://www.fs.fed.us/rm/pubs/rmrs_gtr68.html

Moeller, P.D.R., K.R. Beauchesne, K.M. Huncik, W.C. Davis, S.J. Christopher, P. Riggs-Gelasco, and A.K. Gelasco. 2007. Metal complexes and free radical toxins produced by Pfiesteria piscicida. Environmental Science and Technology 41, 1166–1172.

Monnin, E., E.J. Steig, U. Siegenthaler, K. Kawamura, J. Schwander, B. Stauffer, T.F. Stocker, D.L. Morse, J.-M. Barnola, B. Bellier, D. Raynaud, and H. Fischer. 2004. Evidence for substantial accumulation rate variability in Antarctica during the Holocene, through synchronization of CO2 in the Taylor Dome, Dome C and DML ice cores. Earth and Planetary Science Letters, 224:45-54. Accessed at http://www.ncdc.noaa.gov/paleo/icecore/current.html (Data Contribution Series #2004–055).

Mueller, D.K., and N.E. Spahr. 2005. Water-quality, streamflow, and ancillary data for nutrients in streams and rivers across the Nation, 1992–2001. U.S. Geological Survey Data Series 152. Available online at: http://pubs.usgs.gov/ds/2005/152/.

Mueller, D.K., and N.E. Spahr. 2006. Nutrients in streams and rivers across the Nation—1992–2001. U.S. Geological Survey Scientific Investigations Report 2006–5107. Available online at http://pubs.usgs.gov/sir/2006/5107/.

National Atmospheric Deposition Program. 2006. National Atmospheric Deposition Program 2005 Annual Summary. NADP Data Report 2006–01. Illinois State Water Survey, Champaign, IL.

National Research Council. 2000. Ecological Indicators for the Nation. Washington, DC: National Academies Press.

National Research Council. 2004. Air quality management in the United States. Committee on Air Quality Management in the United States, Board on Environmental Studies and Toxicology, Board on Atmospheric Sciences and Climate, Division on Earth and Life Studies. Washington, D.C.: The National Academies Press.

NatureServe. 2007a. International Ecological Classification Standard: Terrestrial Ecological Systems. NatureServe Central Databases. NatureServe, Arlington, VA. Available at: http://www.natureserve.org/explorer/.

NatureServe. 2007b. International Vegetation Classification: Terrestrial Vegetation. NatureServe Central Databases. NatureServe, Arlington, VA. Available at: http://www.natureserve.org/explorer/.

Neff, J.C., E.A. Holland, F.J. Dentener, W.H. McDowell, and K.M. Russell. 2002. The origin, composition and rates of organic nitrogen deposition: A missing piece of the nitrogen cycle? Biogeochemistry, 57-58: 99-136.

Neher, D. A. 1999. Nematode communities in organically and conventionally managed agricultural soils. Journal of Nematology, 31(2):142-154.

Neher, D. A., J. Wu, M. E. Barbercheck, and O. Anas. 2005. Ecosystem type affects interpretation of soil community measures. Applied Soil Ecology, 30:47-64.

Neher, D.A., M. E. Barbercheck, S. M. El-Allaf, and O. Anas. 2003. Effects of disturbance and ecosystem on decomposition. Applied Soil Ecology 23:165-179.

Neher, D.A., and C. L. Campbell. 1996. Sampling for regional monitoring of nematode communities in agricultural soils. Journal of Nematology 28:196–208.

Neher, D.A., K.N. Easterling, D. Fiscus, and C.L. Campbell. 1998. Comparison of nematode communities in agricultural soils of North Carolina and Nebraska. Ecological Applications 8:213–223.

Neher, D.A., S.L. Peck, J.O. Rawlings, and C.L. Campbell. 1995. Measures of nematode community structure for an agroecosystem monitoring program and sources of variability among and within agricultural fields. Plant and Soil 170:167–181.

Nowell, L.H., and E.A. Resek. 1994. National standards and guidelines for pesticides in water, sediment, and aquatic organisms: Application to water-quality assessments. Rev. Environ. Contam. Toxicol. 140:1–164.

O'Connor, R.J., E. Dunn, D.H. Johnson, S.L. Jones, D. Petit, K. Pollock, C.R. Smith, J.L. Trapp, and E. Welling. 2000. A programmatic review of the North American Breeding Bird Survey: Report of a peer review panel to USGS Patuxent Wildlife Research Center, Laurel, MD. http://www.mp2-pwrc.usgs.gov/bbs/bbsreview/.

O'Connor, T.P., and G.G. Lauenstein. 2006. Trends in chemical concentrations in mussels and oysters collected along the U.S. coast: Update to 2003. Marine Environmental Research, 62(4):261–285.

Ogle, K., T.G. Whitham, and N.S. Cobb. 2000. Tree-ring variation in pinyon predicts likelihood of death following severe drought. Ecology 81(11):3237–3243.

Ogle, S.M., F.J. Breidt, M. Easter, S. Williams and K. Paustian. 2007. Ecological Modeling 205(3-4):453-463.

Parton, W.J., D.S. Ojima, C.V. Cole, and D.S. Schimel. 1994. A General Model for Soil Organic Matter Dynamics: Sensitivity to litter chemistry, texture and management., pp. 147-167 In Quantitative Modeling of Soil Forming Processes, Special Publication 39. Madison, WI: Soil Science Society of America.

Parton, W.J., D.S. Schimel, C.V. Cole, and D.S. Ojima. 1987. Analysis of factors controlling soil organic matter levels in Great Plains grasslands. Soil Science Society of America Journal 51:1173–1179.

Parton, W.J., J.W.B. Stewart, and C.V. Cole. 1988. Dynamics of C, N, P, and S in grassland soils: a model. Biogeochemistry 5:109-131.

Patton, C.J., and E.P. Truitt. 1992. Methods of analysis by the U.S. Geological Survey National Water Quality Laboratory—Determination of total phosphorus by Kjeldahl digestion method and an automated colorimetric finish that includes dialysis. U.S. Geological Survey Open-File Report 92-146.

Pergams, O.R. and P.A. Zaradic. 2008. Evidence for a fundamental and pervasive shift away from nature-based recreation. Proceedings of the National Academy of Sciences. 105:2295–2300.

Peterjohn, B.G., and J.R. Sauer. 1993. North American Breeding Bird Survey annual summary 1990–1991. Bird Populations 1:1–15.

Potter, S.R., S. Andrews, J.D. Atwood, R.L. Kellogg, J. Lemunyon, L. Norfleet, and D. Oman. 2006. Model Simulations of Soil Loss, Nutrient Loss, and Change in Soil Organic Carbon Associated with Crop Production. Washington, DC: U.S. Department of Agriculture, Natural Resources Conservation Service, Conservation Effects Assessment Project (CEAP).

Ricketts, T.H., et al. 1997. A conservation assessment of the terrestrial ecoregions of North America. Volume 1: The United States and Canada. Washington, DC: Island Press.

Robinson, G.R., M.E. Yurlina, and S.N. Handel. 1994. A century of change in the Staten Island flora: Ecological correlates of species losses and invasions. Bull. Torrey Bot. Club 121(2):119–129.

Samson, F. B., and F. L. Knopf. 1994. Prairie conservation in North America. Bioscience 44:418–421.

Sauer, J.R. and W. A. Link. 2002. Hierarchical modeling of population stability and species group attributes from survey data. Ecology 86:1743–1751.

Sauer, J.R., J. E. Hines, and J. Fallon. 2005. The North American Breeding Bird Survey, Results and Analysis 1966–2005. Version 6.2.2006. USGS Patuxent Wildlife Research Center, Laurel, MD. http://www.pwrc.usgs.gov

Schaefer, D.H., and J.R. Harrill. 1995. Simulated effects of proposed ground-water pumping in 17 basins of east-central and southern Nevada. USGS Water-Resources Investigations Report 95-4173.

Schmidt, K.M., J.P. Menakis, C.C. Hardy, D.L. Bunnell, N. Sampson, J. Cohen, and L. Bradshaw. 2002. Development of coarse-scale spatial data for wildland fire and fuel management. General Technical Report RMRS-GTR-87. Ogden, UT: U.S. Department of Agriculture, Forest Service, Rocky Mountain Research Station.

Schueler, T.R. 1994. The importance of imperviousness. Watershed Protection Techniques 1(3):100–111.

Schueler. T.R. and H.K. Holland. eds. 2000. The practice of watershed protection. Ellicott City, MD: Center for Watershed Protection.

Schulz, Beth. 2003. Forest Inventory and Analysis Vegetation Indicator. FIA Fact Sheet Series. http://fia.fs.fed.us.

Scott, M.L., P.B. Shafroth, and G.T. Auble. 1999. Responses of riparian cottonwoods to alluvial water declines. Environmental Management 23:347–358.

Shafroth, P.B., J.C. Stromberg, and D.T. Patten. 2000. Woody riparian vegetation response to different alluvial water table regimes. Western North American Naturalist 60:66–76.

Shelton, L.R. 1994. Field guide for collecting and processing stream-water samples for the National Water-Quality Assessment Program. U.S. Geological Survey Open-File Report 94-455.

Shelton, L.R., and P.D. Capel. 1994. Guidelines for collecting and processing samples of bed sediment for analysis of trace elements and organic contaminants for the National Water Quality Assessment Program. U.S. Geological Survey Open-File Report 94-458, 20 p.

Siegenthaler, U., E. Monnin, K. Kawamura, R. Spahni, J. Schwander, B. Stauffer, T.F. Stocker, J.-M. Barnola, and H. Fischer. 2005. Supporting evidence from the EPICA Dronning Maud Land ice core for atmospheric CO2 changes during the past millennium. Tellus 57B(7):51-57. Accessed at http://www.ncdc.noaa.gov/paleo/icecore/current.html (Data Contribution Series #2005–081).

Skidmore, E.L., and N.P. Woodruff. 1968. Wind erosion forces in the United States and their use in predicting soil loss. Agriculture Handbook No. 346.

Slack, J.R. and J.M. Landwehr. 1992. Hydro-Climatic Data Network (HCDN): A U.S. Geological Survey Streamflow data set for the United States for the study of climate variations. U.S. Geological Survey, Open-File Report 92-129.

Smith, J.E., L.S. Heath, and M.C. Nichols. 2007. U.S. Forest Carbon Calculation Tool: Forest-Land Carbon Stocks and Net Annual Stock Change. USDA Forest Service, Northern Research Station, GTR NRS-13.

Smith, J.E., L.S. Heath, K.E. Skog, and R.A. Birdsey. 2006. Methods for calculating forest ecosystem and harvested carbon with standard estimates for forest types of the United States. GTR-NE-343. Newtown Square, PA: U.S. Department of Agriculture, Forest Service, Northeastern Research Station.

Smith, R.A., G.E. Schwarz, and R.B. Alexander. 1997. Regional interpretation of water quality monitoring data. Water Resources Research 33:2781–2798.

Smith, R.D., A. Ammann, C. Bartoldus, and M.M. Brinson. 1995. An approach for assessing wetland functions using hydrogeomorphic classification, reference wetlands and functional indices. U.S. Army Corps of Engineers, Waterways Experiment Station. Vicksburg, MS. Tech. Rep. TR-WRP-DE-9

Smith, W.B. 1991. Assessing removals for North Central forest inventories. Research Paper NC-299. St. Paul, MN: U.S. Dept. of Agriculture, Forest Service, North Central Forest Experiment Station.

Smith, W.B., J.S. Vissage, D.R. Darr, and R.M. Sheffield. 2001. Forest statistics of the United States, 1997. General Technical Report NC-219. St. Paul, MN: USDA Forest Service, North Central Research Station.

Smith, W.B., P.D. Miles, J.S. Vissage, S.A. Pugh. 2003. Forest Resources of the United States, 2002. General Technical Report NC-241. St. Paul, MN: USDA Forest Service, North Central Research Station.

Solomon, S., D. Qin, M. Manning, Z. Chen, M. Marquis, K.B. Averyt, M. Tignor, and H.L. Miller, eds. Climate change 2007: The physical science basis. Contribution of Working Group I to the Fourth Assessment Report of the Intergovernmental Panel on Climate Change. New York: Cambridge University Press.

Squillace, P.J., and C.V. Price.1996. Urban land-use study plan for the National Water Quality Assessment Program. U.S. Geological Survey Open-File Report 96-217.

Stehman, S.V., J.D. Wickham, J.H. Smith, and L. Yang. 2003. Thematic Accuracy of the 1992 National Land-Cover Data (NLCD) for the Eastern United States: Statistical Methodology and Regional Results. Remote Sensing of Environment 86:500-516.

Stein, B.A. 2002. States of the Union: Ranking America's biodiversity. Arlington, VA: NatureServe.

Stromberg, J.C., J.A. Tress, S.D. Wilkins, and S. Clark. 1992. Response of velvet mesquite to groundwater decline. Journal of Arid Environments 23:45–58.

Stromberg, J.C., R. Tiller, and B. Richter. 1996. Effects of groundwater decline on riparian vegetation of semiarid regions: The San Pedro, Arizona. Ecological Applications 6:113–131.

Stuart, S.N., J.S. Chanson, N.A. Cox, B.E. Young, A.S.L. Rodrigues, D.L. Fischman, R.W. Waller. 2004. Status and trends of amphibian declines and extinctions worldwide. Science. 306:1783–1786.

Tans, P. Global Trends in Atmospheric Carbon Dioxide. National Oceanic and Atmospheric Administration, Earth System Research Laboratory. http://www.esrl.noaa.gov/gmd/ccgg/trends/.

The H. John Heinz III Center for Science, Economics and the Environment. 2002. Dam removal: Science and decision making. Washington, DC: The Heinz Center.

The H. John Heinz III Center for Science, Economics and the Environment. 2000. Evaluation of erosion hazards. Washington, DC: The Heinz Center. (Available at www.heinzctr.org/publications.shtml)

The Heinz Center. 1999. Designing a Report on the State of the Nation's Ecosystems: Selected Measurements for Croplands, Forests, and Coasts & Oceans. The H. John Heinz III Center for Science, Economics and the Environment. Washington, D.C. http://www.heinzctr.org/publications.shtml.

The Heinz Center's Landscape Pattern Task Group Report, forthcoming. See http://www.heinzctr.org/ecosystems

Theobald, D.M. 2001. Land use dynamics beyond the American urban fringe. Geographical Review. 91:544-564.

Theobald, D.M. 2005. Landscape patterns of exurban growth in the USA from 1980 to 2020. Ecology and Society. 10(1):32. (http://www.ecologyandsociety.org/vol10/iss1/art32/)

Toccalino, P.L., J.E. Norman, N.L. Booth, and J.S. Zogorski. 2006. Health-based screening levels: A tool for evaluating what water-quality data may mean to human health. U.S. Geological Survey, National Water-Quality Assessment Program. http://water.usgs.gov/nawqa/HBSL/.

Tucker, C.J., J. E. Pinzon, M. E. Brown, D. Slayback, E. W. Pak, R. Mahoney, E. Vermote and N. El Saleous (2005), An Extended AVHRR 8-km NDVI Data Set Compatible with MODIS and SPOT Vegetation NDVI Data. International Journal of Remote Sensing, Vol 26:20, pp 4485–5598.

U.S. Climate Change Science Program. 2007. The First State of the Carbon Cycle Report SOCCR): The North American Carbon Budget and Implications for the Global Carbon Cycle. A Report by the U.S. Climate Change Science Program and the Subcommittee on Global Change Research [King, A.W., L. Dilling, G.P. Zimmerman, D.M. Fairman, R.A. Houghton, G. Marland, A.Z. Rose, and T.J. Wilbanks (eds.)]. National Oceanic and Atmospheric Administration, National Climatic Data Center, Asheville, NC.

U.S. Environmental Protection Agency. 1986. Quality criteria for water-1986 Report EPA 440/5-86-001.

U.S. Environmental Protection Agency. 1998. Lake and reservoir bioassessment and biocriteria technical guidance document. U.S. Environmental Protection Agency, Office of Water, Washington, DC. EPA-841-B-98-007. http://www.epa.gov/owow/monitoring/tech/lakes.html.

U.S. Environmental Protection Agency. 2000a. Guidance for assessing chemical contaminant data for use in fish advisories, Volume 2: Risk assessment and fish consumption limits–Third Edition. EPA-823-B-00-008. Washington, D.C.: EPA Office of Water.

U.S. Environmental Protection Agency. 2000b. National Coastal Assessment Field Operations Manual. EPA-620-R-01-003. Washington, D.C. EPA Office of Research and Development.

U.S. Environmental Protection Agency. 2004. National coastal condition report II. EPA-620/R-03/002. Washington, DC: EPA Office of Research and Development.

U.S. Environmental Protection Agency. 2006a. 2005 Urban Air Toxics Monitoring Program (UATMP). EPA-454-R-07-001. Prepared by Eastern Research Group for the U.S. EPA Office of Air Quality Planning and Standards, Emissions, Monitoring and Analysis Division, Research Triangle Park, NC.

U.S. Environmental Protection Agency. 2006b. Air Quality Criteria for Ozone and Related Photochemical Oxidants (Final). U.S. Environmental Protection Agency, Washington, DC, EPA/600/R-05/004aF-cF.

U.S. Environmental Protection Agency. 2006c. 2006 Edition of the Drinking Water Standards and Health Advisories. EPA-822-R-06-013.

U.S. Environmental Protection Agency. 2006d. National-Scale Air Toxics Assessment for 1999: Estimated Emissions, Concentrations and Risk, Technical Fact Sheet. Available at (http://www.epa.gov/ttn/atw/nata1999/natafinalfact.html).

U.S. Environmental Protection Agency. 2006e. Wadeable Streams Assessment. U.S. Environmental Protection Agency, Office of Water, Washington, DC. EPA-841-B-06-002.

U.S. Environmental Protection Agency. 2007a. National estuary program coastal condition report. EPA-842/B-06/001. Washington, DC: EPA Office of Research and Development.

U.S. Environmental Protection Agency. 2007b. Clean Air Status and Trends Network (CASTNET) 2006 Annual Report. U.S. Environmental Protection Agency, Office of Air and Radiation, Clean Air Markets Division, Washington, DC.

U.S. Environmental Protection Agency. 2007c. Inventory of U.S. Greenhouse Gas Emissions and Sinks: 1990–2005. USEPA #430-R-07-002. Washington, D.C.

U.S. Environmental Protection Agency. 2007d. Review of the National Ambient Air Quality Standards for Ozone: Policy Assessment of Scientific and Technical Information, OAQPS Staff Paper, EPA-452/R-07-007, U.S. Environmental Protection Agency Office of Air Quality Planning and Standards, Research Triangle Park, NC.

U.S. Geological Survey. National Water Quality Assessment Program. Stream habitat monitoring protocol. http://water.usgs.gov/nawqa/protocols/OFR-93-408/habit1.html

U.S. Geological Survey. 1997. Ground water atlas of the United States—Segment 1 California Nevada. Online data at http://capp.water.usgs.gov/gwa/ and http://water.usgs.gov/ogw/.

U.S.D.A. Economic Research Service. 1997. Cropping Practices Survey Data—1995. Washington, D.C. http://www.ers.usda.gov/data/archive/93018/

U.S.D.A. Forest Service. 1958. Timber resources for America's future. Forest Resource Report No. 14. Washington, D.C.: USDA Forest Service.

U.S.D.A. Forest Service. 1965. Timber trends in the United States. Forest Resource Report No. 17. Washington, D.C.: USDA Forest Service.

U.S.D.A. Forest Service. 1982. An analysis of the timber situation in the United States 1952–2030. Forest Resource Report No. 23. Washington, D.C.: USDA Forest Service.

U.S.D.A. Forest Service. 1989. Forest Statistics of the United States, 1987. Resources Bulletin PNW-RB-168. Portland, OR: USDA Forest Service.

U.S.D.A. Natural Resources Conservation Service. 2000. Summary Report 1997 National Resources Inventory (revised December 2000). Ames, IA: Iowa State University Statistical Laboratory.

Van Dolah, R.F., J.L. Hyland, A.F. Holland, J.S. Rosen, and T.R. Snoots. 1999. A benthic index of biological integrity for assessing habitat quality in estuaries of the southeastern USA. Marine Environmental Research 48(4–5):269–283.

Vesterby, M., and K.S. Krupa. 2001. Major uses of land in the United States, 1997. Resource Economic Division, Economic Research Service, U.S. Department of Agriculture. Statistical Bulletin No. 973.

Vogelmann, J.E., S.M. Howard, L. Yang, C.R. Larson, B.K. Wylie, and N. Van Driel. 2001. Completion of the 1990s National Land Cover Data Set for the conterminous United States from Landsat Thematic Mapper data and ancillary data sources. Photogrammetric Engineering and Remote Sensing, 67:650-662.

Weisberg, S.B., J.A. Ranasinghe, D.D. Dauer, L.C. Schaffner, R.J. Diaz, and J.B. Frithsen. 1997. An estuarine benthic index of biotic integrity (B-IBI) for Chesapeake Bay. Estuaries 20(1):149–158.

White, R.P., S. Hurray, and M. Rohweder. 2000. Pilot analysis of global ecosystems: Grassland ecosystems. Washington, DC: World Resources Institute.

Wickham J.D., SV Stehman, JH Smith, and L. Yang. 2004. Thematic accuracy of MRLC-NLCD Land-Cover for the Western United States. Remote Sensing of Environment 91:452-468.

Wilson, J.T., N.T. Baker, M.J. Moran, C.G. Crawford, L.H. Nowell, P.L. Toccalino, and W.G. Wilber. 2008. Methods and sources of data used to develop selected water-quality indicators for streams and ground water for the 2007 edition of The State of the Nation's Ecosystems report with comparisons to the 2002 edition. U.S. Geological Survey Open-File Report 2008–1110.

Wise, J.P. 1991. Federal conservation and management of marine fisheries in the United States. Washington, DC: Center for Marine Conservation.

Woodbury, P.B., J.E. Smith, and L.S. Heath. 2007. Carbon sequestration in the U.S. forest sector from 1990 to 2010. Forest Ecology and Management 241:14-27.

Woodruff, N.P., and Siddoway, F.H. 1965. A wind erosion equation. Soil Sci. Soc. Amer. Proc. 29(5):602–608.

Wright, J.F., Sutcliffe, D.W. and M.T. Furse, eds. 2000. Assessing the Biological Quality of Freshwaters. Ambleside, Cumbria, UK: Freshwater Biological Association.

Index

Italicized page numbers refer to Summary Tables.

About Island Press

Since 1984, the nonprofit Island Press has been stimulating, shaping, and communicating the ideas that are essential for solving environmental problems worldwide. With more than 800 titles in print and some 40 new releases each year, we are the nation's leading publisher on environmental issues. We identify innovative thinkers and emerging trends in the environmental field. We work with world-renowned experts and authors to develop cross-disciplinary solutions to environmental challenges.

Island Press designs and implements coordinated book publication campaigns in order to communicate our critical messages in print, in person, and online using the latest technologies, programs, and the media. Our goal: to reach targeted audiences—scientists, policymakers, environmental advocates, the media, and concerned citizens—who can and will take action to protect the plants and animals that enrich our world, the ecosystems we need to survive, the water we drink, and the air we breathe.

Island Press gratefully acknowledges the support of its work by the Agua Fund, Inc., Annenberg Foundation, The Christensen Fund, The Nathan Cummings Foundation, The Geraldine R. Dodge Foundation, Doris Duke Charitable Foundation, The Educational Foundation of America, Betsy and Jesse Fink Foundation, The William and Flora Hewlett Foundation, The Kendeda Fund, The Forrest and Frances Lattner Foundation, The Andrew W. Mellon Foundation, The Curtis and Edith Munson Foundation, Oak Foundation, The Overbrook Foundation, the David and Lucile Packard Foundation, The Summit Fund of Washington, Trust for Architectural Easements, Wallace Global Fund, The Winslow Foundation, and other generous donors.

The opinions expressed in this book are those of the author(s) and do not necessarily reflect the views of our donors.